OBAMA

MASTER AND COMMANDER

FREDERICK MONDERSON

SUMON PUBLISHERS

SuMon Publishers
PO Box 160347
Brooklyn, New York 11216

sumonpublishers.com@sumonpublishers.com
blackfolksbooks.com@blackfolksbooks.com
fredsegypt.com@fredsegypt.com   blackegyptbooks.com@blackegyptbooks.com

Copyright Frederick Monderson/ SuMon Publishers, 2013 All Rights Reserved.

No part of this book may be reproduced, stored in a retrieval system, or transmitted by any means without the written permission of the author.

ISBN – 978-1-61023-040-7
LCCN – 2012944212

In the "Tribute to Professor George Simmonds," 'Unsung Hero,' Dr. Fred Monderson sat at the feet of his heroes, Brother X, Michael Carter, Dr. Leonard Jeffries, El Hombre Brath, Dr. Lewis, Prof. George Simmonds, Dr. ben-Jochannan, Sister Camille Yarbrough, Etc.

ABOUT THE AUTHOR

Frederick Monderson is a retired college professor and school teacher who taught African History in the City University of New York and American History and Government in the New York public schools. He has written nearly 1000 articles in the New York Black Press, *Daily Challenge*, *Afro Times* and *New American* newspapers. In this venture, Monderson lends his expertise as a historian,

Egyptologist, journalist and author of several books including *Michael Jackson: The Last Dance, 50 on Point, Black Nationalism: Alive and Well, Barack Obama: Ready, Fit to Lead, Barack Obama: Master of Washington, D.C., Sonny Carson: The Final Triumph,* and on ancient Egypt *Seven Letters to Mike Tyson on Egyptian Temples, 10 Poems Praising Great Blacks for Mike Tyson, Research Essays on Ancient Egypt, Temple of Karnak: The Majestic Architecture of Ancient Kemet, Where are the Kamite Kings?, Abydos and Osiris, Temple of Luxor, Medinet Habu: Mortuary Temple of Rameses III, The Quintessential Book on Ancient Egypt: "Holy Land"* (A Novel on Egypt), *Hatshepsut's Temple at Deir el Bahari, The Majesty of Egyptian Gods and Temples* (a book of Egyptian Poems), *Egypt Essays on Ancient Kemet, The Ramesseum: Mortuary Temple of Rameses II, The Colonnade: Then and Now, Reflections on Ancient Kemet, Grassroots View of Ancient Egypt, Glory of the Ancestors: 19 Letters to O.J. Simpson on Ancient African History* and *Celebrating Dr. Ben-Jochannan.* A student of the esteemed Dr. Yosef ben-Jochannan, Dr. Monderson conducts tours to Egypt.

For Tour information, Please contact Orleane Brooks-Williams at Nostrand Travel, 730 Nostrand Avenue, Brooklyn, New York 11216. Phone Number 718-756-5300. Next Tour of Egypt is July 12-July 26, 2013.

In this the third volume of a **Trilogy on the Obama Presidency**, the author was moved to chronicle some of the efforts of this gifted leader but particularly in response to the words of a faith-based leader who, in exasperation, lamented, **"Do you see what they are doing to our President?"** By that he meant, in addition to Republican obstructionism to the nation's Chief Executive performing his administrative functions, torrential downpouring of *ad hominem* attacks on the man's character, leadership and patriotism ensued forcing the pastor to wonder why no American leader of substance stood up to challenge the scurrilous behavior that was certainly "over the top!" Thus, **Obama: Master and Commander** in addition to chronicling Mr. Obama's legislative, economic and social successes, has become a repository of the negativity directed against a decent family man and leader who happened to be African American. Therefore, readers not familiar with these developments, hopefully, will be able to understand, through this work, some dynamics of how "good ole boys" played their cards as "good ole boys!"

INTRODUCTION
By
Dr. Fred Monderson

Barack Obama's tenure as President can be considered historic because he is the first African American to be elected President of these United States of America, twice; but even more important he must be remembered for the things he accomplished despite the scurrilous invective avalanche arrayed against him. However, because of the nature of causality, as Dr. Leonard James often reiterated, "The higher monkey climbs, the more he exposes himself." Meaning, as the many have flung the filth of disgusting epithets and actions at President Obama as part of their obstructionist strategy, in reality, they revealed the deep-seated inner workings of their true selves and the view is nauseating. Even those black commentators who attacked President Obama for "not doing enough for Black people," have been forced to realize the dynamics at play, if they have; therefore, they must seek to understand the nature of the opposition's obstructionism, their lies and falsification of facts and their unabashed racist rancor that truly characterize the "ugly American" for who he really is!

Still, all in all, President Obama must be numbered among the great presidents of this nation for he has had to heal the severe ills of the nation's domestic and foreign economic policies and practices; repair its relationships with the wider world whose image of America was severely tarnished; and to operationalize effective diplomatic dynamics to successfully conclude American military deployment in Iraq and Afghanistan while challenging Somali Pirates and contending with a ubiquitous global war on terrorism.

Obama - Master and Commander. Barack Hussein and Michelle Robinson Obama, President and First Lady of the United States of America.

To Frederick,
   On behalf of Bo and myself, please accept our gratitude and thanks for your leadership and support at this critical juncture in American history.

Obama - Master and Commander. The President and his dog Bo.

Equally, while the business of nation states never takes a holiday, President Obama has had to deal with issues of nuclear proliferation involving Iran and North Korea, seeking progress on the perennially illusive Middle East peace process and all the other responsibilities of the Presidency in his role as steward of the nation including America's role in global economics, trade, environment, quality of life, and all the dynamic visscitudes of life's existence.

It cannot be understated, Mr. Obama inherited a dire economic situation and in response has demonstrated exemplary leadership in formulating policies and practices that halted the worsening situation despite severe opposition amidst obstructionist behaviors that force right thinking persons to wonder why!

2012 Commemorative Presidential Print
Presented to Frederick Monderson
By President Barack Obama and the Democratic National Committee

Obama - Master and Commander. Portrait of the President's dog in the Rose Garden of the White House presented to Frederick Monderson.

TREASONOUS PLOT TO OVERTHROW A LEGITIMATE AMERICAN GOVERNMENT!

On the day Mr. Obama was Inaugurated as President of the United States a group of influential American leaders met to sabotage his government so as to make his tenure a failure. A form of undermining the leader and inhibiting his governing efforts can be considered **treason** and all perpetrators should be arrested and put on trial! Starting with Senator Mitch McConnell! Equally, treasonous intent and practice have become manifest by the actions of the Republican Party.

1.   The McConnell Mandate - "My job is to make sure Barack Obama is not elected to a second term." Senator Mitch McConnell (R) Kentucky

The **normal definition of treason** is - The crime of betraying one's country.

The **operational definition of treason** is – As America faced the many challenges presented Mr. Obama's tenure, any effort or plan to impede, hinder or undermine the efforts of his legal and legislative leadership is to be considered treason given his is a legitimate government elected by a majority of the people.

I.   Mr. Obama set out to execute the responsibilities of the Office of the President of the United States as Chief Executive Officer of the nation.

Recognizing the grave situation he inherited as President, Mr. Obama took a number of prudent but rapid steps to address some of the nation's problems. The first of these was legislative passage of the:

      a. **Lilly Ledbetter Fair Pay for Equal Work Act** designed to enable women to get compensated for doing the same work men did.

      b. **Auto Industry Rescue** had become necessary for, since America invented the automobile, to have allowed this important engine of the American economy to go bankrupt as Mr. Romney suggested, would have been both an economic and psychological as well as moral let down for the nation.

      c. **Bank Bailout** was essential given banks began to crumble and reverberations would have been far-reaching with potential for global panic.

      d. **Health Care Reform** or **Affordable Care Act** is an idea whose time had come and Mr. Obama in gifted brilliance very early saw the need, formulated a strategy to deal with it, campaigned for this measure during the Primary and Presidential campaigns and upon being elected moved to legislate it into law.

      e. With the nation hemorrhaging jobs at an enormously unhealthy rate, Mr. Obama created a **Jobs Bill** to address problems of domestic infrastructure and put significant segments of the nation back to work. As we have seen, one clear plan of Republican obstruction was to "**Kill the jobs bill**!"

II. As Commander-In-Chief President Obama next turned to address the military engagement in Iraq to stem the loss of American lives, decrease the economic costs of the war and seek a way out of the quagmire, to "bring the boys and girls home" to their families and friends. Ultimately he was able to create an agreement enabling the end of American forces deployment after training Iraqi personnel to assume responsibilities for military defense of their nation. In Afghanistan, Mr. Obama deployed a surge and after ongoing engagements was able to begin to negotiate an agreement that American forces will leave in 2014.

Because Osama bin-Laden, leader of Al Qaeda, and those responsible for the 9/11 catastrophe were still at large, Mr. Obama intensified his efforts to find and eliminate the terror mastermind and his group. After extensive preparation, the commander gave the go ahead to launch the assault on bin-Laden's compound in Pakistan, certainly mindful of the consequences of a failed operation. Not unmindful of the last time American forces had launched an operation of a similarly significant nature to rescue Americans held captive in Iran during the Carter Presidency and with the resulting fallout, Mr. Obama took the chance with full faith in the capabilities of the "Seal Team Six" force. The rest is known! The same leadership daring that brought success with bin-Laden was applied to Somali

Pirates' rampage off the coast of East Africa. Again, when the necessity demanded, Mr. Obama, not simply as Commander-in-Chief but through exemplary leadership, gave the order sending a stern message to these Somali terrorists.

2. EVIDENCE OF TREASONOUS REPUBLICAN BEHAVIOR

In an escapade of non-cooperation, Republican lawmakers with allies in and outside of government began a series of obstructionist behaviors and practices designed to curtail and destroy Mr. Obama's tenure as President in their intent to "Deny Obama a win!" They heaped harrasing verbal scorn on him but really showed their true selves and conversely no one criticized their behaviors! In answer to "Where are the good men?" no one showed-up! Instead, Senator Lindsey Graham's paltry response was: "Criticism by our boys is a little off base."

a. **BUSH TAX CUTS** - The first of these behaviors manifested when President Obama took bold steps not to extend the "Bush Tax Cuts" that primarily benefitted the wealthy "One percent," since as is generally but falsely thought, if the tax cuts are enacted then these people will re-invest in American businesses and other venues to provide jobs for the American people. As this had not worked during the Bush years with unemployment remaining high, Mr. Obama could not envision it working during his term. Therefore, Republicans effected their non-cooperation strategy designed to obstruct proper functioning even threatening to shut down the government. Rather than allow that dire consequence to manifest, Mr. Obama relented but extended the Tax Cuts for a limited time, not indefinitely as Republicans wanted. During negotiations at this time, Senator Mitch McConnell was shown with that broad duplicitous smile as he gave the now-infamous "Thumbs Up" signal many read in code as "I got that NIGGER!" Later he would issue the "**McConnell Mandate**" to "deny Mr. Obama a second term."

b. **DEBT CEILING DEBATE** - By the mid-term election as the insidious treasonous plot thickened, Republicans misrepresented the facts and so gained control of the House of Representatives and John Boehner replaced Nancy Pelosi as Speaker. The next significant agenda item was the Debt Ceiling, where in debate, Mr. Obama again relented for the good of the nation to move the issue forward out of gridlock. At the conclusion of events, Speaker Boehner sarcastically boasted "We got 98 percent of what we wanted!" which is predictable as a pattern of obstruction and benefit to the few rather than many. Even more important, when the President reached out to him, Speaker Boehner refused to return the phone calls of the nation's Chief Executive Officer. This behavior was not only treasonous but contemptuous of the Office of the President and the man as part of the insidious and thickening Republican plot.

Mr. Obama was quite aware of the treasonous actions but his sense of personal dignity and the dignity of the Office would not allow him to respond in kind to the inelegance of the Speaker of the House. This pernicious continuum of disrespect for both the Office of the Presidency and person of the President is identifiable from the day of the President's Inauguration to the present and it is a manifestation of the intent of the political leaders gathered on the day of Inauguration to plot his political demise. To his profound credit, his political sophistication and personal determination, despite the obstructionism, and through exemplary leadership, he has been able to accomplish, as former President Bill Clinton said, "what no other President" including himself "was unable to accomplish;" given the enormous obstacles and dire economic conditions that existed.

So let me identify **3** examples of this elegance of mind and nobility of spirit.

1. **BANK BAILOUT** - The nation was on a trajectory of financial ruin that would most likely engulf the world in a Depression far worse than 1929. Not only was he assailed by people within the Congress but ordinary Americans were quite concerned that the President cared more about Wall Street than Main Street or even Back Street. But, he had the self-confidence and confidence in the nation that once the precipitous fall was avoided, the natural resilience of America's economic capabilities would rectify itself to the benefit of all.

2. **AUTO INDUSTRY RESCUE** - Chrysler and General Motors are two of the most important economic elements of American society. The ancillary impact in supply and employment which support these companies is crucial to the Middle Class and Lower Income Class of the nation. The President was quite aware that these 2 economic sources were absolutely vital to any recovery from the terrifying economic realities of the day. The concerted opposition to his effort to save these companies was most graphically expressed by the President's campaing opponent Mr. Mitt Romney who said, "Let Detroit Go Bankrupt!" Either Mr. Romney and Republican Members of Congress knew the impact of this action or their intent, as reasonable Congressmen, was to sabotage the effort; and thus their actions would lead again to the destruction of the President's term.

3. **HEALTH CARE REFORM** - One of the fundamental principles underlying the Presidency of this Constitutional democracy we call the United States of America, is to protect the interest of all the American people. This is what identifies a nation, this nation, a great nation. Not the military, not the banks, not the economic resources with which it is so blest but the extent to which the life and well-being of each member of this society is recognized and treated with compassion is what truly makes American exceptionalism. It is therefore consistent with his role in his position as leader of this nation but consonant with his philosophy as a Christian.

a. We should love God with all our heart, mind, body and soul and our neighbors as ourselves. That the President would seek to correct a situation in which 45 million people in the United States did not have proper Health Insurance is indicative of his humanity. In human terms this situation was a national shame.

In political terms it was a contradiction between that fact and the pronouncement of this nation that it is "one nation under God, indivisible, with liberty and justice for all." The President thus made the initiation, development and establishment of an Affordable Health Care Plan that would substantially mitigate that deplorable denial of the fundamental right to physical and mental health of all people under the Affordable Health Care Act.

The obstructionists immediately and perniciously named it what they considered it to be, **Obama-Care**. Then there was a concentrated assault not only from within the Congress but from the persuasive mechanisms within the society with few exceptions; pseudo-omniscient pundits, "experts," and other commentators in the print and electronic media assaulted, castigated and vilified the efforts of the President to make Affordable Health Care available to millions of people and their children up to 26-years old. The Health Care Plan was subjected to Judicial Review and to constant derogation and ridicule. They sought to obstruct what the **AHCA** would bestow on millions of their fellow citizens. In the final count the Supreme Court of the United States refused to overturn the Health Care Affordable Care Act to the great dismay of many. This legislation and so many others is an example of the personal and political integrity, courage and leadership qualities of President Barack H. Obama. All have seen, throughout this Presidential Campaign, the President has endured disrespect, insults, vilification, ridicule, and racist attacks. Throughout he has maintained dignity, poise and an internal strength which are true qualities reflective of the highest level of humanity and leadership.

b. All this notwithstanding, and given his Christian background, it is not unreasonable that he has been spiritually nurtured in the 27th and 91st Psalms and they have enabled him to prevail against his adversaries. It is remarkable that Mr. Obama has withstood the assaults and attacks and still maintains his dignity, leadership focus and sense of humanity given his responsibility as President of the United States and leader of "free world" or Western Alliance, particularly.

The 27th Psalm of the King James Version of the Bible
"The LORD Is My Light and My Salvation"

The LORD is my light and my salvation; whom shall I fear? The LORD is the strength of my life; of whom shall I be afraid? 2 When the wicked, even mine enemies and my foes, came upon me to eat up my flesh, they stumbled and fell. 3 Though an host should encamp against me, my heart shall not fear: though war should rise against me, in this will I be confident. 4 One thing have I desired of the LORD, that will I seek after; that I may dwell in the house of the LORD all the days of my life, to behold the beauty of the LORD, and to enquire in his temple. 5 For in the time of trouble he shall hide me in his pavilion: in the secret of his tabernacle shall he hide me; he shall set me up upon a rock. 6 And now shall mine head be lifted up above mine enemies round about me: therefore will I offer in his tabernacle sacrifices of joy; I will sing, yea, I will sing praises unto the LORD.

7 Hear, O LORD, when I cry with my voice: have mercy also upon me, and answer me. 8 When thou saidst, Seek ye my face; my heart said unto thee, Thy face, LORD, will I seek. 9 Hide not thy face far from me; put not thy servant away in anger: thou hast been my help; leave me not, neither forsake me, O God of my salvation. 10 When my father and my mother forsake me, then the LORD will take me up. 11 Teach me thy way, O LORD, and lead me in a plain path, because of mine enemies. 12 Deliver me not over unto the will of mine enemies: for false witnesses are risen up against me, and such as breathe out cruelty. 13 I had fainted, unless I had believed to see the goodness of the LORD in the land of the living. 14 Wait on the LORD: be of good courage, and he shall strengthen thine heart: wait, I say, on the LORD.

The 91st Psalm of the King James Version of the Bible

"Abiding in the Shadow of the Almighty"

He that dwelleth in the secret place of the most High shall abide under the shadow of the Almighty. 2 I will say of the LORD, He is my refuge and my fortress: my God; in him will I trust. 3 Surely he shall deliver thee from the snare of the fowler, and from the noisome pestilence. 4 He shall cover thee with his feathers, and under his wings shalt thou trust: his truth shall be thy shield and buckler. 5 Thou shalt not be afraid for the terror by night; nor for the arrow that flieth by day; 6 Nor for the pestilence that walketh in darkness; nor for the destruction that wasteth at noonday. 7 A thousand shall fall at thy side, and ten thousand at thy right hand; but it shall not come nigh thee. 8 Only with thine eyes shalt thou behold and see the reward of the wicked.

9 Because thou hast made the LORD, which is my refuge, even the most High, thy habitation; 10 There shall no evil befall thee, neither shall any plague come nigh thy dwelling. 11 For he shall give his angels charge over thee, to keep thee in all thy ways. 12 They shall bear thee up in their hands, lest thou dash thy foot against a stone. 13 Thou shalt tread upon the lion and adder, the young lion and the dragon shalt thou trample under feet. 14 Because he hath set his love upon me, therefore will I deliver him: I will set him on high, because he hath known my name. 15 He shall call upon me, and I will answer him: I will be with him in trouble; I will deliver him, and honor him. 16 With long life will I satisfy him, and shew him my salvation.

Thus, with the help and inspiration of divine providence, given that Barack Obama's Mission was divinely inspired, the American people were moved to re-elect Barack Hussein Obama, President of the United States of America in 2012.

OBAMA - MASTER AND COMMANDER

TABLE OF CONTENTS

1. "CUTEST ONE BY FAR!" — 8
2. OBAMA: UNEASY LIES THE HEAD — 22
3. "OBAMA – IN LIBYA – NOW IN AFRICA!" — 32
4. RED – COLOR OF THE GODS — 45
5. WASHINGTON, OBAMA AND CAIN — 58
6. "NIGGERHEAD MOUNTAIN" — 71
7. THE TRUMP CIRCUS — 79
8. MORMON, MORON or WHAT? — 100
9. THE BRILLIANCE OF BARACK OBAMA — 117
10. THANK GOD FOR BARACK OBAMA! — 131
11. OBAMA: ELITIST? NO! — 144
12. CAN WE TRUST REPUBLICANS? — 155
13. OBAMA'S "DIVINE MISSION" — 166
14. MA'AT VERSUS ISFIT IN PRESIDENTIAL POLITICS I. — 174
15. MA'AT VERSUS ISFIT IN — 179

FREDERICK MONDERSON

PRESIDENTIAL POLITICS II.

16. MITT ROMNEY: "RIGHT" and "WRONG" — 188
17. WHERE ARE THE GOOD MEN? — 201
18. ORIGINAL BOYS WEARING HOODS — 209
19. VOTING RIGHTS AND REDISTRICTING — 218
20. LAWMAKERS IN HOODIES — 228
21. OBAMA PRESIDENCY: A FAILURE? HARDLY! — 231
22. REFLECTIONS ON THE NEW OBAMA AGE — 236
23. THE BUCK STOPS WITH BARACK! — 243
24. BARACK OBAMA AND THE POWER OF SYMBOLISM — 246
25. DEBT CEILING: SECOND TIME AROUND — 257
26. OBAMA: DOING A GOOD JOB? — 261
27. OBAMA: "FAITH IN FACE — 262

OBAMA - MASTER AND COMMANDER

     OF DOUBT"
28. MOST DANGEROUS MAN IN AMERICA!   270
29. OBAMA: "COME WITH IT!"   278
30. OBAMA AND THE SUPREME COURT   287
31. THIS ETHNIC THING   293
32. BLACK INFLUENCE ON THE SUPREME COURT I   298
33. BLACK INFLUENCE ON THE SUPREME COURT II   305
34. "IF THE SUPREME COURT OVERTURNS ..."   313
35. JOHN BOEHNER: SPEAKER OR PARTISAN?   320
36. OBAMA "LOOKS LIKE KING TUT"   327
37. "IT'S THE HAIR, STUPID!"   336
38. OBAMA IS NOT GAY!   344
39. OBAMA STYMIED BY FILIBUSTER   353
40. SPIRITUAL VALUES VERSUS SECULAR MATERIALISM   363

41.	CONSPIRACY AGAINST OBAMA?	371
42.	"OBAMA MUST BE DEFEATED!" ARGUMENT FROM AUTHORITY?	378
43.	OBAMA AND EXECUTIVE ORDER	392
44.	PUMMELING THE BLACK MAN	415
45.	OBAMA AND LEADERSHIP	448
46.	THE CONSTITUTION, CHIEF JUSTICE, AND THE PRESIDENT	464
47.	"A WOMAN OF STRAW"	469
48.	CITIZEN DIRECT ACTION	473
49.	OBAMA: "STEADY AS HE GOES"	476
50.	"THE AMERICA WE KNOW!"	482
51.	OBAMA: "SHOULD APOLOGIZE!"	489
52.	AMERICAN LEADERS ABROAD	499
53.	PRESIDENT OBAMA ON DR.	506

OBAMA - MASTER AND COMMANDER

	KING	
54.	SPEAKING FOR GOD!	506
55.	Not 1979	517
56.	HERE AS "Eye Candy"	526
57.	"OBAMA CARES"	528
58.	THREE AMIGOS AND HEALTH CARE	533
59.	"SMOKING JOE BIDEN"	539
60.	"TOO CLOSE TO CALL"	552
61.	ENDORSEMENTS, EDITORIALS AND DEBATES	567
62.	HEAVEN HELP AMERICA!	582
63.	HURRICANE SANDY: ARM OF GOD!	587
64.	GOVERNOR CHRISTIE!	589
65.	VANQUISHING REPUBLICANS	591
66.	APOLOGIES LOWER STANDARDS	596
67.	RUDY GIULIANI WINS: "LITTLE MAN AWARD!"	605
68.	WOMEN!	615
69.	SOME PERSPECTIVES ON	626

FREDERICK MONDERSON

THE OBAMA AGE

70.	ASSESSING THE OBAMA PRESIDENCY	641
71.	BROADSIDE AGAINST OBAMA: Unfair	653
72.	WEST AND RUSHMORE	654
73.	REPUBLICAN SOPHISTRY	657
74.	ROMNEY'S "BELLS AND WHISTLES"	660
75.	AN OPEN LETTER TO MICHAEL GOODWIN	663
76.	CAMPAIGN ROUND-UP	666
77.	ELECTION DAY COMMENTARY	717
78.	CONCLUSIONS I	719
79.	CONCLUSIONS II	735
80.	POST-SCRIPT	741
81.	EPILOGUE	741
82.	INAUGURATION SPEECH	742

The text of this third volume in the **Trilogy of the Obama Saga** was created as events of the last years of Mr. Obama's term unfolded. The articles were generally written and published in New York's *Daily Challenge* newspaper and many of the "Themes" were generated from Media coverage, viz., CNN, *The New York Times*, *New York Post* and *New York Daily News*. As such, much of the repetition is considered natural given the factors but the reality of the repeats have helped reinforce the emphasis to draw attention to Republican methodology in quest of the Presidency at all costs and how they have not simply disparaged Mr.

OBAMA - MASTER AND COMMANDER

Obama but sullied the office he was elected to serve. Republicans have not simply disrespected Mr. Obama but sullied the Presidency, forcing right thinking people the world over to consider whether Conservatives have reverted to a 19th Century mentality!

Obama - Master and Commander 1. Mr. Obama in a reflective mood.

"Given the increasing diversity of America's population, the dangers of sectarianism have never been greater. Whatever we once were, we are no longer just a Christian nation; we are also a Jewish nation, a Muslim nation, a Buddhist nation, a Hindu nation, and a nation of nonbelievers. And even if we did have only Christians in our midst, if we expelled every non-Christian from the United States of America, whose Christianity would we teach in the schools? Would we go with James Dobson's, or Al Sharpton's? Which passages of Scripture should guide our public policy? Should we go with Leviticus, which suggests slavery is ok and that eating shellfish is abomination? How about Deuteronomy, which suggests stoning your child if he strays from the faith? Or should we just stick to the Sermon on the Mount - a passage that is so radical that it's doubtful that our own Defense Department would survive its application? So before we get carried away, let's read our bibles. Folks haven't been reading their bibles." **Barack Obama**, Speech, November 2008

FREDERICK MONDERSON

1. "CUTEST ONE BY FAR!"
By
Dr. Fred Monderson

Poor Speaker John Boehner! Some commentators have remarked he is a captive of young Republican "Tea Party" Congressmen though he wants to help the President be successful in his efforts. Such a view is questionable since his boast of getting "98 percent" of what he wanted in the Debt Ceiling debacle after disrespecting the Office of the Presidency by refusing to return the President's phone calls; not to mention his role in negotiations in renewing the Bush Tax Cuts for the wealthy last December, 2010. Now, where are the jobs promised from those tax cuts? However, beyond all of that, Mr. Boehner's further misstep came in the Chamber of the House of Representatives as he sat beside Vice-President Joe Biden listening to President Obama deliver his "America Jobs Act" speech to the Joint Session of the Congress, on the evening of September 8, 2011. At that time, within earshot of an uncovered microphone, Mr. Biden pointed to the gallery and remarked to Mr. Boehner, "That's my wife up there." Mr. Boehner responded approvingly, "Oh yes, she's the cutest one by far in that whole row." Well, that's your man, guilty of "hoof in mouth" malady, again. Naturally the news media, gorging on tidbits, got some mileage on the notion of being careful of what you say, when all statements are fair game.

Now, to recall, the President's speech to the Joint House of Congress was much heralded in view of the political and economic battles being waged in Washington, the "Tea Party Debate" the night before and the opening game of the football season later that night right after Mr. Obama's speech. Notwithstanding, upon her entry into the chamber, Mrs. Michelle Obama, the First Lady, in that beautiful red attire was given a standing ovation as she made her way to greet neighbors of that row and sit next to Mrs. Biden, as is customary. As a prelude to that event and reflecting on Inauguration Day, Chief Justice Roberts mis-stated the "Oath of the Presidency," some have argued, because he eyed the resplendent Michelle Obama standing beside her husband, attired as a stunning fashionista. Again, following the "Oath" and "Motorcade to the White House," when President Obama exited his limousine to greet bystanders to the consternation of the Secret Service, and the crowd went wild, it was really over Michelle not Mr. Obama, some thought!

OBAMA - MASTER AND COMMANDER

Obama - Master and Commander 2. The White House residence of the President of the United States, Barack Obama.

Obama - Master and Commander 3. View from an upper floor window of art on art on the bridge at the lobby of the Grand Hyatt Washington Hotel.

FREDERICK MONDERSON

Obama - Master and Commander 4. Piano in the Pool at the Grand Hyatt Hotel Lobby.

Later that night, in that beautiful one shoulder strap white ensemble, as Michelle affixed herself to the arm of the President and they danced all night to Etta James' "At Last My Love Has Come Around," attending all the balls, majestic Michelle wowed them all again. That night, America felt proud an intelligent black beauty was the First Lady.

After that, the President went abroad and Michelle again dazzled the Press on board Air Force One before changing and stepping off at Heathrow Airport where she wowed them too. Earning an English press appellate "Mighty Michelle," she bowled over London before having "tea with the Queen." Her Majesty was so taken by Mrs. Obama who chose not to fashionably upstage the monarch; yet, her brilliance caused the great lady to embrace the black beauty, itself an unheard of phenomenon because no one ever touches the Queen. Her Majesty even admonished Michelle "Stay in Touch" to which some speculated Michelle responded, "Your Majesty do come visit, I'm re-doing the White House" to which the Queen probably responded "I'll be there!"

Then it was on to France where Michelle outshined French President Sarkozy's fashion model wife and the beat continued!

OBAMA - MASTER AND COMMANDER

Obama - Master and Commander 5. A beautiful and intriguing piece of glass art in the lobby of the Grand Hyatt Washington Hotel.

FREDERICK MONDERSON

Obama - Master and Commander 6. A. Philip Randolph President of Sleeping Car Porters of America.

OBAMA - MASTER AND COMMANDER

Obama - Master and Commander 7. A family on way to board train at Union Station gave permission to use this pix.

Obama - Master and Commander 8. View of a restaurant by the pool at the Grand Hyatt Washington Hotel.

FREDERICK MONDERSON

The Greek said, "All Greeks are liars!" Now, we don't know if Speaker Boehner was simply "Pulling the Vice-President's chain," when, Mr. Biden spoke to him during preparation for the President's Speech or he was wrong, which he probably was. We have heard Mr. Biden, on past occasions say, "My wife is drop dead gorgeous." That may be rightly so since beauty is in the eyes of the beholder; but for Mr. Boehner, in competition with Obama and Biden to exclaim Biden's wife, sitting in the same row next to Obama's wife and declare her, Mrs. Biden, the "Cutest by far in that row" he might have, and did get it wrong. Not surprising, white men have gotten it wrong about black women from time immemorial.

For example, in the 1970s, the anthropologist Johansson discovered the most complete fossil ever, of a female, dated to several million years old, in the Hadar region of Ethiopia. Listening to a Beatles song "Lucy in the Sky with Diamonds," on the radio, Johansson named his "find" Lucy! The noted Egyptologist, historian and Africanist Dr. Yosef A.A. ben-Jochannan said No! Her indigenous name is *Denk Nesh*!

At the end of the 18th Ancient Egyptian Dynasty, King Dushrata of Syria sent his daughter Thadukippa to marry the aged Amenhotep III, "the magnificent" in a political marriage alliance, a common practice in those days. At that time, Amenhotep III abdicated and his son Amenhotep IV, Akhenaton, assumed the throne as Pharaoh. Well, the marriage occurred but to the younger, not older king.
The ancient Egyptians had some difficulty in pronouncing the name of the Syrian Princess Thadukippa so they changed it to Nefertiti. In the upsurge of 19th and 20th Century archaeological research to reclaim the ancient African, Nile Valley culture, European and American scholars greatly emphasized Queen Nefertiti's name and its meaning, "the beautiful one cometh." Fashion designers got much mileage from Nefertiti's beauty even launching a line of "Nefertiti earrings."

In the confusion everyone overlooked Nefertari, Aahmes-Nefertari, the "coal-black Ethiopian Queen," ancestress of the 18th Dynasty, pictured in the British Museum painting wearing the red, white and blue tricolor; under which Mr. Boehner "fights" today; some 1500 years Before Christ. Interestingly, her name is "the most beautiful one" and she earned the most powerful attributes of wealth, tradition and social position as well as the title "God's wife." As customary, she did not get the "royal treatment" from modern commentators. Equally, at the end of that 18th Dynasty, Nefertiti's mother-in-law Queen Tiy, the power behind the throne for the longest, responded to critics of her son, Amenhotep IV, Akhnaton, Nefertiti's husband, because of the "politics of his Amarna religious revolution." As Prof John H. Clarke told it, Queen Tiy warned his critics, "It is ok if you disagree with my son's policies but if you harm a single hair on his head, I will fight you to the death."

OBAMA - MASTER AND COMMANDER

This is somewhat akin an event on Obama's road to the White House amidst the vitriol of Tea Party initial "terrorism;" Joe the Plumber's "Socialism" rant; Donald Trump's "Birther Movement" buddies' "fools' errand," including Michele Bachmann before she "got respectability;" and the many physical threats and outlandish name calling directed at candidate Barack Obama; Senator De Mint's "Waterloo;" Billy Krystal's "Go for the kill;" Senator Mitch McConnell's "one term President;" Joe "You lie" Wilson's disrespect in the **House**; *New York Post's* "Ape Cartoon;" Governor Palin's "Palling around with terrorists;" Mark Halperin's "Obama acted like a Dick;" and some Republican Congressman exclaiming "The President is an idiot," and another that "Mr. Obama should be ashamed," as well as Joe "the President is a tyrant" Walsh tirade, - all diametrically opposed to the outspoken and more sensible Megan McCain's "I like the President," confession "and I want him to succeed." In this milieu, the *New Yorker* magazine tried to parody Senator Obama on its cover, depicting him in the traditional garb the Elders of Kenya dressed him in on his visit to his father's ancestral homeland; yet, trying to portray him as a Muslim, equating such as terrorist to sully his chances at winning the Presidency. As in all such miscalculations, the magazine placed Michelle Obama behind her husband with rifle and all. Instead of being seen as a moll, Michelle came over as faithful and beautiful spouse who will fight to protect her man, equally winning the respect of her "at ready fighting brigades" across the nation's geographic landscape. This miscalculation instead equated Michelle Obama with Queen Tiy and today she can be proclaimed "Queen of the Black World," succeeding Winnie Mandela whose reign followed Queen Mother Moore's. These people probably visited Lafayette Park, outside the White House, and seen on one of the memorable statues, the woman handing the Frenchman Lafayette the sword to help win the day during the Revolutionary War!

Queen Hatshepsut was criticized and her features ridiculed because she dared to wield power in a male dominated world but today her life and times get special attention because of the avante garde innovations of this great woman ruler, "the first Queen."

FREDERICK MONDERSON

Obama - Master and Commander 9. "Modern Art" in the Lobby of the Grand Hyatt Washington Hotel.

Obama - Master and Commander 10. Church and Rectory on 10th Street and G Street.

OBAMA - MASTER AND COMMANDER

Obama - Master and Commander 11. The sign says it all: Madame Tussauds, Washington, D.C.

King Solomon was considered one of the wisest men of his age and he possessed a harem of several hundred concubines when the beautiful Sheba, Queen of Ethiopia, visited for diplomatic reasons but actually out of curiosity. Solomon was love struck and strategized on how to "win the Queen;" becoming successful and finally having her bear him a son, Menelik I. Interesting, however, while love was a factor, scholars such as Dr. Ivan Van Sertima have argued, Solomon pursued Sheba not because of her beauty, but because her empire was many times greater than his. Even more significant, some years ago, standing in the line for the cashier at a local supermarket, Met Foods, my eye caught one of the customary News *of the World* tabloids with headlines that read "World's Mysteries Solved." Like any enthusiastic of any such esoteric phenomenon, I purchased the paper and took it home. Such topics as a "New discovery of Noah Ark" are recurring historical themes, and "Vatican Confirms the Existence of Angels," were some of the articles in this issue. Turning to the centerfold, my eyes caught the story, "Scientists Discover the Home of the Queen of Sheba" in Nigeria in West Africa. This was a short story, juxtaposed to a large picture of the Queen of Sheba. It was a picture of a beautiful woman, white! What's wrong with this picture? Beauty is only associated with white women!

However, while her empire may have stretched clear across the African continent from Ethiopia to Nigeria, a white woman ruler of an African empire is fictional and false, particularly since much ink has been spilt on who this Queen of Ethiopia really was. As a student of Professor ben-Jochannan, I have often listened to his debates and observed the ink spilled discussing a line in the Bible. Depending on the versions one consults, the question is always did the Queen of Sheba say, 'I am Black and comely.' Or, 'I am Black but comely.' In the first instance she is saying "I'm Black and beautiful," and being proud of it. In the second instance, in

FREDERICK MONDERSON

saying "I'm Black but beautiful;" she is, if you will, denigrating her blackness but affirming her beauty." People on a pejorative bent towards blacks flaunt the latter affirming she was not proud of her Blackness, though they would concede she was beautiful. Nevertheless, she has historically been proven black and any attempt to misrepresent her is false. Did the editor of the tabloid know this or was he simply uncaring and determined to distort in the belief it would go unnoticed. Similarly, in his *Flights Into Antiquity*, the respectable Egyptologist Arthur Weigall offers a chapter on "The Queen of Sheba" where he too presents a photograph of a white woman as the Queen. Of course, if Solomon had married the Queen of Sheba and made "an honest woman" out of her, this matter would probably have been resolved. Don't get me started with President Jefferson and Sally Hemmings who bore him children and upon his death was never freed from slavery.

So, Mr. Boehner was certainly wrong as on so many other occasions in his determining Jill Biden "The cutest one by far in that row," as she sat beside the beautiful First Lady Michelle Obama. Ms. Biden, beautiful in her own right, though never having walked a mile in Michelle's moccasins, and even more modest, would probably have called it a **tie**, but Boehner was "Playing Biden;" though, Joe, an old hand, while he accepted the compliment must have realized he needed to "Beware of Greeks bearing Gifts!"

"A good compromise, a good piece of legislation, is like a good sentence; or a good piece of music. Everybody can recognize it. They say, 'Huh. It works. It makes sense.'" **Barack Obama**

OBAMA - MASTER AND COMMANDER

Obama - Master and Commander 12. Madame Tussauds.' The Presidents Gallery showing Barack Obama with his two recent predecessors George Bush and Bill Clinton as well as Lincoln and some of his predecessors.

FREDERICK MONDERSON

Obama - Master and Commander 13. Entrance to Madame Tussauds.'

Obama - Master and Commander 14. A casual view of cars, buildings and interaction in vicinity of Pennsylvania Avenue at the end intersection.

OBAMA - MASTER AND COMMANDER

Obama - Master and Commander 15. A government building on Pennsylvania Avenue sporting a colonnade of 15 Doric columns.

"It's been funny to watch some of these politicians completely rewrite history now that you're back on your feet. These are the folks who said if we went forward with our plan to rescue Detroit, "You can kiss the American automotive industry goodbye." Now they're saying they were right all along. Or worse, they're saying that the problem is that you, the workers, made out like bandits in all of this; that saving the American auto industry was just about paying back unions. Really? Even by the standards of this town, that's a load of you-know-what. About 700,000 retirees saw a reduction in the health care benefits they had earned. Many of you saw hours reduced, or pay and wages scaled back. You gave up some of your rights as workers. Promises were made to you over the years that you gave up for the sake and survival of this industry, its workers, and their families. You want to talk about values? Hard work - that's a value. Looking out for one another - that's a value. The idea that we're all in it together - that I am my brother's keeper; I am my sister's keeper - that is a value. But they're still talking about you as if you're some greedy special interest that needs to be beaten. Since when are hardworking men and women special interests? Since when is the idea that we look out for each other a bad thing? To borrow a line from our old friend Ted Kennedy: What is it about working men and women they find so offensive?"
Barack Obama, addressing United Auto Workers in Washington DC, February 2012

FREDERICK MONDERSON

2. OBAMA: UNEASY LIES THE HEAD
By
Dr. Fred Monderson

Shakespeare was right on target in saying "Uneasy lies the head that wears the crown," though he referred to physical threats to that head. In other respects, the line may refer to one's job which also depends on performance. In the case of President Obama, all of the above and more could apply to his situation. As such, one thing is certain; the color of his hair has certainly changed as a result of the burdens of the office. Nevertheless, a cursory look at the issues confronting this President can be an indicator of what to expect as the next presidential election approaches and all contenders and their allies make their case to lead the nation at these unfolding and critical times. What is clearly evident, however, political and ideological lines are beginning to solidify. In this respect, an interesting analogy can be applied to this situation. In 1941, after the Japanese attack on Pearl Harbor, one of the significant Japanese naval commanders, though under orders, confessed, "I'm afraid we have awakened a sleeping giant." The rest we know is history! In his case, the astute President Obama, playing it cool, allowed every major Republican player to show the true nature of their inner thoughts as they tried to heap insults and unconscionable demands on his person and office. Even Grover Norquist seems to blatantly wear his bigotry on his sleeve cannot but put the man's title before Obama! This naturally forced onlookers to wonder why the President has not retaliated against trash heapers, but the man is wise not vindictive.

1). From the inception, we applauded President Obama for choosing his team of advisors and support personnel from among the brightest minds America could muster. These people approached their responsibilities with a seriousness of mind, professional intent and began making inroads into the multitudinous problems they were assigned to combat which seem even greater now despite unending effort to create solutions. For example, under Obama's stewardship of Bernanke at the **FEDS** and Geithner at Treasury and the significant input from leading economic experts including former **FED** Chair Paul Volker who advised the President; with rapidity this team began clearing out "Door Number One" through fiscal and financial reform, tackling the loss of jobs, unemployment, housing foreclosure, even rescuing the banking and auto industries and passing meaningful legislation across the board such as Lilly Ledbetter and Credit Card Reform. Some have argued these actions did not make the significant dent that was needed. In jest, having cleaned out "Room Number One," they opened "Room Number Two," not realizing in addition to "Door Number Three" there were also rooms in the basement full of the stuff they had been shoveling in "Room Number One." Notwithstanding, the President remained focused, choosing to make the tough decisions that only extraordinary leaders have the tenacity to make, amidst unrelenting attack by pseudo-patriots.

OBAMA - MASTER AND COMMANDER

Obama - Master and Commander 20. The Ford Theater and Museum housing some interesting features about American history.

FREDERICK MONDERSON

Obama - Master and Commander 21. Ford's Theater: Where Lincoln's Legacy lives. The sign says it all!

OBAMA - MASTER AND COMMANDER

Obama - Master and Commander 22. All kinds of Memorabilia are for sale on the street in Washington, DC.

2). President Obama's foreign policies and relationships bore significant fruit and signaled to the world America had turned onto a different path and now had elected the first African American as its principal spokesman as proof of this new reality. But the President also realized, other major world players as India, China, Japan, Germany, Indonesia, Brazil, and so many others were making significant economic strides as Americans outsourced jobs and bickered over ideological positions. Jennifer Granholm, former governor of Michigan summed up the foreign challenge dilemma by saying, particularly in regard to China, "our passivity is their opportunity." Nevertheless, as the opposition continued to play childish games while strongly defending privileges of the privileged, Obama has stayed the course, taken the long view and to this day continues to say "No to special interest," in his effort to make the economy work for the Middle Class and all other Americans. At the same time, he kept proposing clean energy, industry and educational initiatives to keep America competitive in a fast changing world. By the end of day one, however, "vultures" had begun "circling" his proposed "carcass." He also emphasized infrastructure repair, transportation innovation and new and clean forms of power/energy to reduce dependence on foreign sources.

FREDERICK MONDERSON

Naturally, as steward, Mr. Obama was concerned about the environment, and so, the Environmental Protection Agency became a favorite target of Republicans!

3.   Under a ruse that Obama would abrogate the Constitution and prohibit the "Right of the people to bear arms," right-wing groups in opposition to the Democratic establishment and now purported allies of the Republican opposition began stock-piling arsenals of armaments for the coming "race riots" in the touted but yet realized "Post-racial America." Imagine! However, nearly three years after, the "riots" have not come. Nonetheless, while such "shopping" was good for the economy one important caveat was overlooked. That is, the role of Black Americans in the military, having fought in all of America's wars from the Revolution to the present; and though defending the empire from the perimeter outposts are watching, waiting and wondering.

History has shown, not only was Crispus Attucks the first martyr whose blood fertilized the soil of the American "Tree of Liberty" and Salem Po and his boys backed Washington's play; yet, these unmistaken facts were overlooked for the longest. Equally, while the French under Napoleon, an enemy of the British, were quick to recognize the young American nation and sent Frenchmen to fight; in the "Battle of Savannah," their surrogates were Haitians who performed with commendable excellence. Upon their return to Haiti these veterans were able to launch the Haitian Revolution. However, they did make one confession. "We have learned the ways of the white man!" This meant they had learned how to load and fire the cannon with tremendous accuracy and also how to handle the pistol and rifle with great effect. Distinguished African-American military service in the Revolutionary War continued in the War of 1812; the Mexican War (1845-46); the Civil War (1860-1865); the effectiveness of the Buffalo Soldiers against the Plains Indians (Native Americans) is legendary; the War with Spain (1899-1902); World War I (1914-1918); World War II (1939-1945); the Korean Conflict (1950-1952); the War on Communism (1947-1990); Viet Nam (1954-1975); Grenada (1987); Gulf War I (1991); Gulf War II (2003-Present); Afghanistan (2001-Present); and the ongoing "War on Terrorism." They even fought in the "War on Poverty" and the "War on Drugs." In all this, African-Americans learned every facet of military engagement, strategy and tactics, weaponry, administration, logistics, demolition, aerial flight and even Technological Cyber Warfare. All the while these Blacks who demonstrated exemplary courage and meritorious patriotism were learning, learning, learning and have been watching, waiting, watching, ... if you will, "keeping an eye on the militias," "in case they try something," and they know it!

OBAMA - MASTER AND COMMANDER

Obama - Master and Commander 23. Another government building with detached and attached colonnades.

Obama - Master and Commander 24. J. Edgar Hoover, FBI Building.

FREDERICK MONDERSON

Obama - Master and Commander 25. Department of Justice: Federal Bureau of Investigation (**The FBI**) Building with the institution's "Logo!" of "Fidelity, Bravery, Integrity!"

James Brown sang, "I don't know Karate, but I know Ka-Razor." We are also reminded, in the "Age of Apartheid," when South Africa was accused of pursuing nuclear weaponry, Julius Nyerere, then President of Tanzania, had said, "Let them go ahead, South Africa will be the first Black nuclear nation!" In response to right wing thinking, Black leadership offered, "Have your way, do your thing!" However, using old folks folk-loric advice, they had recounted, a blind white man went to "see a heavyweight fight" between a black and a white contender. He had a companion at ringside who gave blow-by-blow commentary as the fight unfolded. As the action moved into the later rounds and spirits became excited, the blind man asked, "What's happening now?" His companion responded, "The white guy has the black guy down!" The blind man responded in wit and wisdom, "The black man down? Well, keep him down! For when the black man raise, hell raises!" This is excellent wisdom for the arsenaled right-wingers. If their armed over-confidence should precipitate that "race riot" conflict perhaps the blacks who keep killing each other will wise up. Let us not forget the black military veterans, active and retired, whose vigilance is steady, underscores the role they can play and will play. In the tradition of warrior queens, Michelle will also have to step-up to the plate to play her indispensible role.

OBAMA - MASTER AND COMMANDER

4.   President Barack Obama is a genuine, visionary, patriotic American leader; wise, one of the brightest lights, "charged with cleaning out the barn, farming the land and tending the animals with an eye to next season's crops, required to keep an eye on poachers and must negotiate with potential shoppers at home and abroad." Conversely, Mr. Obama has been a victim of perennial criticism and unrelenting obstructionism. Still, the President's "Catch 22" conundrum is to defend the rights of and encourage the progress of the same people mining the fields he must plow, tender and navigate. As such, persons of lesser vision criticize the President's leadership but give a pass to Senator Mitch McConnell whose primary objective from day one has been to "Make Obama a one term President;" Senator Jim DeMint has wanted to create Obama's "Waterloo;" the inelegant Joe Wilson's disrespectful "pearl" is "you lie;" a "Minister of the Cloth" Anderson who prays daily that "Obama dies;" his misguided disciple, the "black protester with guns," who does not realize he is as much a "Nigger" as Obama; not to forget those "circus criers" who shout "Dick;' "ashamed;" "not like us;" "socialism;" "where's your birth certificate?" etc., and any and all such disgusting sound bites that offend. Yet, as Obama listens to those baited distractions he remains steadfast focused on the responsibilities of his job description, viz., leading the nation, reforming the financial and economic system, proposing initiatives for clean energy to make the nation self reliant in this respect, providing for greater oil exploration and drilling, offering benefits to encourage excellence in education teaching and learning, improving conditions of schools and their equipment, passing significant legislation that address the needs and aspirations of the broad masses of the American people, as well as ensuring the safety net is firm, protecting the entitlements of seniors and the most vulnerable, and a whole lot more. Let us not get started on Health Care Reform!

5.   Because Americans were hoodwinked by Republican smoke screen tactics, as a weapon against the Democratic Obama, the 2010 mid-term national elections brought to power the "Teeth (Tea) Party" component of the anti-Obamite Republicans and they have since been manipulating the Congress. These House Legislators particularly, with their "cart before the horse" mentality in the "tail wagging the dog" syndrome, showed their true colors and now as the smoke has cleared onlookers wonder how commentators really missed all this seemingly unpatriotic behavior, all because of the need to sabotage one man's term of office.

With pomposity and arrogance gained from their 2010 election victory, Republicans led by the "Tea Party" minority held hostage the American people's aspirations as President Obama attempted to end the Bush tax cuts for the wealthy. In the "Jobs debate," Obama's performance has been misrepresented to amplify claims he is not producing sufficient jobs, forgetting at the onset of his administration, the nation was hemorrhaging 500,000-800,000 jobs per month and his efforts reversed this, adding low hundred thousands of new jobs. In that same "Jobs debate" as the President wrestled with tax relief for the wealthy the claim has been, these are the same people who create jobs, but despite the years of the

FREDERICK MONDERSON

significant Bush tax cuts, jobs were not created. So, blame the President for not creating jobs even though the Congressional Budget Office gives a figure of some 3 million jobs created or saved by his administration; yet, the rich get credit but Obama demerits.

Again, emboldened with this "win" the unreasonable "Tea Party" leadership of the Republican Party continued making exorbitant demands in their face-off with the President in the Debt Ceiling showdown. In their childish dreams these people could never countenance the significance of the thoughts of John Kennedy in a Speech given January 9, 1961 in the Massachusetts State Legislature where he boldly asserted: "Today, the eye of all people are truly upon us, and our governments, in every branch, at every level, national, state, and local, must be a city upon a hill, constructed and inhabited by men aware of their grave trust and their great responsibilities." Nonetheless, the record shows McConnell played his "mandate card" and John Boehner disrespected the President by not retiring his repeated phone calls. As these minions inflated their situation to be viewed as whales, Obama remained concerned about America's aches and pains and so he invoked that long established tradition of compromise to halt the nation's hurried amble towards the gallows of national and international financial default. In good sense, the President relented and Speaker Boehner effectively boasted his guys "got 98 percent of what they wanted" just after McConnell gave the now famous smiling "I got that Nigger" thumbs up. Reflective of this conundrum, an observed Bumper Sticker read "Liberty means defending someone else's right to do what you don't like." That, then, is Mr. Obama's station!

Obama - Master and Commander 26.   Yes, the Name says it all!

OBAMA - MASTER AND COMMANDER

Obama - Master and Commander 27. Wells Fargo business with its version of the Colonnade.

Obama - Master and Commander 28. US Navy Ad, quoting President Kennedy: "Any man who may be asked, what he did to make his life worthwhile, I think can respond with a good deal of pride and satisfaction: 'I served in the United States Navy!'"

Nevertheless, as Obama continues to take names, is slow to anger and "After a long train of abuses," this "gentleman leader," acting like the adult in the room and in reminiscence of his "If you're listening, lay off my wife" admonition, is justified in spanking "disagreeable children."

"Americans ... still believe in an America where anything's possible - they just don't think their leaders do." **Barack Obama**

FREDERICK MONDERSON

"I reject the idea that asking a hedge fund manager to pay the same tax rate as a teacher or a plumber is class warfare. I think it's just the right thing to do. Both parties agree that we need to reduce the deficit by the same amount, by $4 trillion. So what choices are we going to make to reach that goal? Either we ask the wealthiest Americans to pay their fair share in taxes or we ask seniors to pay more for Medicare. We can't afford to do both. Either we gut education and medical research or we've got to reform the tax code so that most profitable corporations have to give up tax loopholes that other companies don't get. We can't afford to do both. This is not class warfare, its math."   **Barack Obama**, during a speech, September 19, 2011

3. "OBAMA – IN LIBYA – NOW IN AFRICA!"
By
Dr. Fred Monderson

Every great while aspirants to the office of the Executive Branch make statements that are downright false, mistaken fact or so simple one has to wonder about the educational background of these people seeking the highest office in the land. As a youngster, the mnemonic device that instructed our familiarity with some "hard words" dictated "tomat" and potat" have "toes." Yet, Vice President Dan Quayle spelt "potatoe" and we all laughed. In the most recent Western Republican Presidential Debate, Congresswoman Michele Bachmann, never able to say anything good about the President's performance said, "Mr. Obama put us in Libya and now he has put us in Africa." While two principal issues are raised here, there are "more devil in the details." Even more significant, her knowledge of African geography leaves much to be desired. But, Mrs. Bachmann is not alone, because for centuries foreigners particularly from the West have either been mistaken, ignorant or falsely stated "facts" regarding African geography. Remember when early cartographers placed elephants in locations Africans were thought to inhabit?

First and foremost, while single-minded individuals may harp in allegiance to the "Mitch McConnell Mandate" to make Barack Obama "a one-term president;" as America boasts it many virtues and affirms claims to be the only remaining "superpower," it needs be mindful of the "rise of the rest" and the projection of their power to gain influence in volatile areas of the world that compete with American interests.

OBAMA - MASTER AND COMMANDER

Despite what may be said, the multi-faceted nature of American foreign policy dictates not only that we give material support to deserving nations but that human compassion must be an essential part of our relations with other nations. This aid needs be given particularly, to those not as fortunate as we are. However, despite its significant African American population, America has generally ignored Africa focusing first to Europe, then South America and even Asia, giving them prominence in its foreign policy relations. Sure the claim is that Europe colonized Africa at the "Partition" but in the modern world Africa's mineral resource has been instrumental in helping maintain America's and western technological leadership. Nevertheless, in the Hutu-Tutsi genocidal conflict, we stayed silent in face of millions being massacred. In Darfur, we also pursued a hands-off policy and had it not been for the Black Clergy spearheaded by the likes of Rev. Herbert Daughtry, the genocide in that African country would have continued to this day. That does not mean the inhumanity has ceased, only it has subsided. We must remember, Edmund Burke's dictum, "The only thing necessary for evil to triumph is for good men to say nothing!" Thus, since America is good, it must do something and as such, President Obama's decision to send troops to advise and who knows, challenge the genocidal maniacs in Uganda, is the right thing to do! Chinese economic imperialism in Africa and even South America has not gone unrecognized and therein lies another problem in America's relationship with Africa.

In his Keynote Address at the dedication of the Dr. Martin Luther King Jr., Memorial on the historic Sunday October 16, 2011, the 16th anniversary of the Million Man March, President Obama praised the great man for having given his all. In wonderful flourishes the President recounted the challenges Dr. King faced, yet, with his able lieutenants they galvanized a race of downtrodden and abused people who became a powerful force to change the path of America from one of destruction to one on the path of salvation. It is interesting how African Americans have been and continue to play a decisive role in helping America live out the true meaning of its creed. More important, however, Mr. Obama pointed to the vilification heaped on Dr. King by opponents, supporters, even blacks on both side of his movement. So, great men are not immune from criticism which seems par for Mr. Obama's course when the Republicans and now even Mrs. Bachmann criticized him for sending U.S. troops, advisers, to Uganda.

FREDERICK MONDERSON

Obama - Master and Commander 29. The US Navy Building with its version of the Colonnade featuring the Doric model.

Obama - Master and Commander 29a. Companion building of the US Navy with its version of the Colonnade featuring the Doric model.

OBAMA - MASTER AND COMMANDER

Obama - Master and Commander 29b. Both buildings of the US Navy with its version of the Colonnade featuring the Doric model.

Obama - Master and Commander 29c. Celebrating 300 years of German-American Friendship.

FREDERICK MONDERSON

Obama - Master and Commander 30. Memorial to General Banfield Scott HANCOCK.

Two things are evident here. First, it should be restated, as America had neglected to more fully engage African nations, especially because of its large African American population, latecomer nations as China, not to mention the French,

OBAMA - MASTER AND COMMANDER

British, Belgians, Portuguese, who were there for the longest, were making inroads particularly for economic advantage. However, a creeping American interest began by Bill Clinton on humanitarian grounds and somewhat increased under President Bush in his efforts to fight the **AIDS** scourge won praises from several African nations severely affected by this malady. Nevertheless, as the fight against terrorism escalated and Al Qaeda was dislodged from Afghanistan in their dispersal, many settled in Africa prior to Mr. Obama's watch. However, by the time America set up an Africa Command with its sights generally turned to the "Middle East," terrorists had already began to sow their seeds on the continent entrenching themselves in such place as Somalia and later Mali.

Mr. Obama first visited Kenya in East Africa as a Senator then as President he visited Cairo, Egypt in North-East Africa to make a major address to the Islamic world! Next he visited Ghana in West Africa and his wife Michelle and daughters Sasha and Malia visited South Africa to confer with Nelson Mandela among other leaders and to enjoy sights in Southern Africa. Thus, Mr. Obama touched the people and pulse of vast areas of the African continent. This connection seemed in concert with the Africa Command getting its act together to secure a foothold in East and North East Africa focusing Middle East and Persian Gulf terrorist challenges.

Years after independence, many petty African leaders, incapable of subscribing to Nkrumah's idea of a continental African government, allowed the continent to be ravaged by reckless bands under mega-maniacs who raped, maimed and despoiled the land they had hoped to lead. Which brings us to the *Army of the Lord* and its devilish acts and while China and the other European nations did not, President Obama intervened and became the subject of criticism such as those leveled by Congresswoman Michele Bachmann, as she stood "at the bottom of the pile" still aspiring to the Presidency!

However, and again, as the "Arab Spring" unfolded, Mr. Obama was criticized for taking a stand and not taking a stand. Even though, unbeknown to others, he had advisers on the ground even as Republicans challenged his prosecution of the wars in Iraq and Afghanistan, Al Qaeda and even Somali Pirates. Nevertheless, unknown to herself, following Mrs. Bachmann's statement, she has been in distinguished company from time immemorial, albeit among "losers," who flunked African Geography!

If we begin with Hecataeus of Miletus who visited Egypt in Africa at the start of the fifth century B.C., and observing the Nile River, he declared "Egypt is the gift of the Nile." This classic statement was falsely attributed to Herodotus of Halicarnassus who unknowing to modern scholars' knowledge of Hecataeus, as stated in his book *The Histories*, Book II, *Euterpe*, devoted entirely to Egypt, Herodotus was given credit for making the same statement. European designators of things monumental and lasting, viz., the Seven Wonders of the World; the first wonder, the Great Pyramid is the only one "still standing" while the others are in ruins or remembered only in mythology. Even more, Herodotus, the "father of history" held "the Egyptians had thick lips, curly hair and were burnt of skin" but his account is discounted though he observed this but things he was told of such as the process of mummifications are believed, which he probably never observed. In addition, Herodotus claimed the cause of the Nile River's rise during the Inundation was due to melting of snows on the peaks of mountains in Central Africa and this too was also discounted because no one believed snows existed in tropical Africa.

Diodorus Siculus wrote the Ethiopians founded Egypt and gave as evidence the detritus generated by the rainfall in Central Africa, collected in the river and deposited during the Inundation process is what created Egypt from the millennia of build-up of silt deposits. This too was discounted because it made Ethiopian culture anterior to Egypt.

Obama - Master and Commander 31. The Archives of the United States of America fronted by an exceptional colonnade of Corinthian columns.

OBAMA - MASTER AND COMMANDER

Obama - Master and Commander 32. Side view of the National Archives with its 10 composite Corinth columns. "This building holds in trust the records of our national life and symbolizes our faith in the permanency of our National Institutions."

Obama - Master and Commander 33. A close-up view of the make-up of the Corinth capitals of the columns of the National Archives under the equally decorative architrave.

FREDERICK MONDERSON

In the *Histories*, Herodotus recounts that an Egyptian Pharaoh Necho, of the 26th Dynasty, sent Phoenician sailors to circumnavigate Africa in the 6th Century, B.C. Upon their arrival in the Bight of Benin near Cameroons, a volcano atop Mount Cameroons was active, belching fire. This phenomenon the sailors named "Chariots of Fire." Much later, Erik Van Deniken would piggyback on the same name as the title of one of his books. However, on PBS he once denied how a photograph in his book got there because it helped contradict his principal argument that Egyptian civilization was built from the top down by extraterrestrials same as a line of Hollywood's "Battlestar Galactica" fame.

Who would believe, after Rome had defeated Carthage and ravaged then occupied Carthage as a colony, the geography and environment would later contribute to allow many Romans to live past 100 years! Don't let me get started on their role in depopulating the land of its tremendous wildlife including lions killed in the "Games" held in the Roman coliseum. Elsewhere, in the rise of the Sudanic Empires of West Africa, contemporary with the emergence of the Renaissance Movement, as European cartographers were just beginning to get their acts together, having heard of the wealth of this region of Africa; maps showed a huge gold nugget as the domain of Mansa Musa of Mali. In other areas of Africa, not being able to name locations, cartographers placed elephants as markers of habitable regions. Equally, by the time of the Slave Trade, map makers renamed the Ethiopian Ocean, the Atlantic Ocean. African geography suffered in the Slave Trade for besides the demographic catastrophe, physical destruction of the land, equally the land was littered with dead and dying in the horrible march to the coast to be canon-fodder on New World plantation culture. Also, European entrenchment in building and manning forts allowed canon fire to devastate the surrounding areas. These forts then served as holding centers housing persons about to be shipped to the Americas. The Slave Trade was also called African rather than European whose nations were the principal perpetrators.

Amidst the colonial thrust by adventurers, explorers and missionaries in the 19th and early 20th Centuries, European and American writers as James Conrad and Morton Stanley wrote of "Darkest Africa" and the land being inhabited by cannibals. Prof John. Clarke often remarked "Africans invited Europeans to dinner and they became the meal" and "If Africans had eaten the missionaries then the continent would not be in the mess it is today." Still, perhaps cannibalism is a noble practice because civilized Germany recognized such and today boasts hundreds of practicing and registered cannibals.

In contradicting Conrad and Stanley, the *New York Times* of Friday October 14, 2011, p. 14, reported the discovery of a Stone Age paint factory in South Africa dated at more than 107,000 years ago. There were other similar sites dated at 160,000 years. The interesting thing about this find; these "Stone Age Africans" were thinking, expressing cerebral activities predating modern human thinking processes by millennia.

OBAMA - MASTER AND COMMANDER

Obama - Master and Commander 34. The entrance to the Federal Trade Commission depicting men at work.

Let's not forget, *The Times* also reported finding remnants of iron ore mining in South Africa dated at 43,000 B.P. (Before Present) shows the thinking process of locating the mine, mining and collecting the ore and determining how to use the resources. The use of paint and process of mining and collecting iron ore thousands of years before the thinking and blessings of civilization reached Europe shows Africa in the vanguard of humanity's pageantry of deep thinking.

Bauval and Brophy have shown in their book *Black Genesis* (2006), an African people to the west of Southern Egypt can lay claim to being the world's earliest astronomers having created structures oriented to map the drama in the heavens. They left early religious sculptures and provided evidence of Egyptian proto-religious ideas, created a calendar, were agriculturalists and pastoralists, and eventually migrated to the Nile and laid the foundation for pharaonic civilization. Yet, entrenched interests are denying these indisputable factors, geographical and more. In the 19th Century build-up to imperialism and colonialism in Africa and in the attempt to remove Egypt from Africa and Africans from Egypt, European powers created the geographical regions "Africa South of the Sahara" and even

FREDERICK MONDERSON

"The Middle East," placing Egypt in this fictional realm disregarding its geographical location in Africa and confining Africans on their continent to a region classed as "Black Africa." This has held, nonsensically at a time especially when Egypt chaired the Organization of African Unity.

Obama - Master and Commander 35. That great symbol of man in labor, "Taming the Shrew!"

More particularly, because Congresswoman Bachmann is a member of the Anti-Obamite "Party of NO;" she like so many others must challenge every iota of the President's actions and pronouncements but at least she and others could get their facts straight and realize Libya as well as Egypt are both in Africa.

What is interesting, while Mrs. Bachmann criticizes President Obama for sending troops to Uganda, she has had nothing to say about Secretary of State Clinton's visit to Libya in wake of recent developments since this involves political and economic considerations.

"Americans ... still believe in an America where anything's possible - they just don't think their leaders do." **Barack Obama**

OBAMA - MASTER AND COMMANDER

Obama - Master and Commander 36. The Newseum on Pennsylvania Avenue.

Obama - Master and Commander 37. The Canadian Embassy on Pennsylvania Avenue that sits next-door to the Newseum.

FREDERICK MONDERSON

Obama - Master and Commander 38. Visitors file past the National Gallery of Art.

"Change will not come if we wait for some other person or some other time. We are the ones we've been waiting for. We are the change that we seek." **Barack Obama**, speech, February 5, 2008

"Contrary to the claims of some of my critics and some of the editorial pages, I am an ardent believer in the free market." **Barack Obama**, *Business Roundtable*, February 24, 2010

"A good compromise, a good piece of legislation, is like a good sentence; or a good piece of music. Everybody can recognize it. They say, 'Huh. It works. It makes sense.'" **Barack Obama,** The *New Yorker*, May 31, 2004

Obama - Master and Commander 39. Constitution Hall and Daughters of the American Revolution.

OBAMA - MASTER AND COMMANDER

"America and Islam are not exclusive and need not be in competition. Instead, they overlap, and share common principles of justice and progress, tolerance and the dignity of all human beings." **Barack Obama**, Cairo University, June 2009

4. RED – COLOR OF THE GODS
By
Dr. Fred Monderson

More and more, new and dynamic research is blowing away the smoke that clouded interpretation of the ethnological basis of ancient Egypt, grossly misinterpreted to falsely represent Europe, Caucasians, as the creators, originators of a culture steeped in African ethnicity, symbolism, motifs, spirituality and demographic factors. Despite their significant work in archaeology, anthropology, biometric and related fields, it now seems these scholars' efforts in rush to interpret, publish, and propagate through publications, lectures, displays and fund-raising, were fueled by the desire to falsely portray Europeans not Africans as the culture's architects. We know, history is a subject that seeks to include as much credible evidence as possible; to paint a complete picture of any historical phenomenon, but when, upon close examination of information now deemed grossly inaccurate, whether through distortion or omission, fueled by racist notions, it forces future researchers to not simply offer a corrective but question the original motive and intent of such interpretation. This has been the case in Egyptological research over the past two centuries and though currently in vogue, it's being vigorously challenged by new and ground-breaking Afrocentric research.

A recent work entitled *Black Genesis* by Brophy and Bauval argued Black Africans inhabiting a region west of Southern Egypt, Nabta Playa, were likely the forerunners of the pharaohs. These scholars offer archaeoastronomical evidence and sculptured and artistic remains that depict these black people practicing stargazing, calendar creation, mathematically positioning stones to map the heavens and were viewed and seriously considered as laying the foundation of what we today know as science. The area of this early African culture nucleus was also teeming with game and flourishing agricultural practices that benefitted from heavy rainfall in the region, trapped in artificial lakes after torrential down pour. When finally the rains subsided and the area desiccated, not being able to support a thriving agricultural community, the people migrated to the Nile Valley, settling in the region south of the vicinity of Aswan and Elephantine Island. The new research shows the rise, development and decline of this cultural phenomenon has been dated anywhere from 20,000-3500 B.C.

FREDERICK MONDERSON

Evidence has revealed these Africans of that luscious desert region, among other practices were pastoralists. From these endeavors they originated religious worship of the "Cow goddess." We know the "Great Mother" of the universe has been shown as a cow probably because of the nourishment gained from this animal. Interestingly, the Goddess Hathor of Egyptian mythology and religion has been depicted as a cow. It ought not to be forgotten, a popular theme of Egyptian mythology and religion, "the many moods of Hathor," depicts the goddess as a cow, in fact, seven cows in different attitudes assisting the mummy. One such depiction survives in a small room or chapel at Medinet Habu, Mortuary Temple of Rameses III, in the temple proper, the Sanctuary area. We know of the mythological depiction of "Hathor coming out of the hills of Deir el Bahari" and also an image on a wall depicts Hatshepsut in her temple there, drinking at the udders of the goddess Hathor. Equally, it's been clearly stated by E.A. Wallis Budge, noted British Keeper of Egyptian and Assyrian Antiquities of the British Museum and a prolific Egyptological writer who places the "origin of Hathor in the Sudan." His characterization of the goddess as "Sudani" is not in conflict with the time and people of Nabta Playa that Bauval and Brophy have credited with laying the foundations for pharaonic Egypt. "The many moods of Hathor" shows generally the Goddess in her relationship to the mummy on it journey to the next world.

Obama - Master and Commander 40. One of the many roads that lead to the Capital Building.

OBAMA - MASTER AND COMMANDER

Obama - Master and Commander 41. What majestic artistic sculptural decoration crowns the entrance to this church!

Obama - Master and Commander 42. Still another view of the rear of the Capital Building.

FREDERICK MONDERSON

Petrie's pronouncements were driven by racist assumptions of European supremacy, led by the British of course, but under intense scrutiny his views were discounted. Rejecting his findings of a racial supremacy, detractors argued for an indigenous nature of the Egyptians. Amidst several indigenous theories scholars insisted on a North/South dichotomy of two races, one dominating the culture then the other. Still, this originally argued for predominance of the North since this area was nearer the Mediterranean and Sinai Peninsula culture clusters.

By allowing such a view, two peoples were recognized, a black and a white, as occupiers of the land of ancient Egypt, one predominating in the North, one in the South. Naturally, this placed the white element in the North or Lower Egypt and the black element, the South or Upper Egypt. Nevertheless, it is a hallmark of Egyptian scholarship that only when incontrovertible evidence is presented then some consideration is given the argument such articulates. As such, not being able to eliminate the black element from the equation, *ipso facto*, they were placed in Upper Egypt. What is further incontrovertible, for the greatest duration of the cultural development, consolidation, expansion and perpetuation of the Egyptian miracle, Upper Egypt was the driving, creative force of innovation and experimentation as the preponderance of monumental evidence left in the physical geography. Much of this is unequivocally proven in the architecture, art, religion, transport mechanisms and science accomplishments whose remains adorn cultural and academic institutions throughout the world.

In regard the "Boat people" theory, it seems reasonable to argue, people in a riverain culture would more likely be "boat people" than migrating wanderers crossing a desert region to an unknown land. We should be reminded; the black inhabitants of Nabta Playa, west of the Nile in the Upper Egyptian region were on the move by c. 3500 B.C. arriving thereabouts in the vicinity of Aswan, Elephantine Island, the First Cataract region possessing millennia of accumulated scientific knowledge. It is also not coincidental that Bruce Williams of the University of Chicago discovered among that institution's artifactual "holdings," evidence of the world's earliest monarchy resident at Qustol in Nubia/Upper Egypt. Van Sertima frames it as the rise of **Ta-Seti** before Egypt! We must also recognize in those remote times, political boundaries, borders, were not as clearly delineated as we understand such today.

Nevertheless, the outstanding motifs of this discovery involved 3 Nile boats, enthroned pharaoh wearing the White Crown, a serekh atop a palace façade and an incense burner, etc. These features were dated approximately 3400 B.C., some 200 years before we see such pharaonic paraphernalia in Egypt at 3200 B.C. Still, it is more palatable to associate these cultural accomplishments to the early "scientists" of Nabta Playa rather than migrating Caucasians who never arrived in Egypt, if they ever did, any sooner than 2500-2400 B.C., a thousand years later! Notwithstanding, all that has gone before, scientists recently discovered, in a cave in South Africa, evidence that Stone Age man had tools as well as "pottery and

OBAMA - MASTER AND COMMANDER

mixed ocher paint more than 100,000 years ago." This fascinating discovery of an ancient paint factory workshop of the Middle Stone Age raised a number of interesting and intriguing questions relating to then, now and the years-in-between.

It is common knowledge sometime between the Old and New Stone Age man began to transform his habits and his thinking. The only thing is, while Europe was given prominence in researching this area of interest, scholars did not focus much on this transformation unfolding in Africa because the initial research was done in Europe to prove the primacy of Europeans to other peoples on the face of the earth. Let us not forget, as this line of inquiry unfolded in the 19th Century especially, Europe had transitioned from its imperialist practices of "naked imperialism" of the Slave Trade and "New World" conquest to one of "enlightened imperialism" with the ramifications of colonialism and intellectual imperialism that developed there from. As Prof. John H. Clarke pointed out, "the people who preached racism, colonized history" and in so doing, "Europe colonized the world's knowledge." The resulting arrogance of power pitted "European powers" against each other scrambling for colonial territory around the world in general and Africa in particular, and this competition carried them to the precipice of self-annihilation resulting in the First World War and later World War Two.

Obama - Master and Commander 43. A family poses before the statue of his Memorial fronting the E. Barrett Prettyman United States Court House.

Nonetheless, the image we came to associate with Stone Age man is that he was a hunter and gatherer. That is, men hunted and women gathered or foraged for edible

FREDERICK MONDERSON

foods among growing victuals. At that time his food supply was considered 90 percent meats and 10 percent agri-vegetation. In time he developed seed culture and his food changed to 10 percent meats and 90 percent agri-produce. In the division of labor dichotomy, men manufactured tools for the hunt while women tended the family and foraged for edible produce. In disposing of seeds, women accidentally discovered agriculture. As this process unfolded, also through the "Oasis theory" in which animals became domesticated, all parties settled down in change from a nomadic to sedentary existence.

As their social consciousness developed, humans first inhabited natural covers or ravines and caves. Then they later built shelter. Growing culturally, they created sites for various functions. There were butchering sites where game was cut up and workshop sites or floors where tools were crafted and repaired. At ceremonial sites certain rites were celebrated and at burial sites the dead were disposed of. In home bases, having retired for the day and with chores completed, tools of the hunt repaired, man sat by the fireside and began to plan for the next day's hunt, speculate and philosophize. Those with artistic abilities began to paint using the walls of the cave as a canvass. A popular theme was game of the hunt fueled by the belief if such were drawn on the cave walls this may aid in a successful hunt the next day. In North, South and East Africa particularly, evidence remains of Stone Age artists at work. It is interesting that some sites were visited by different generations of artists who used the same "canvass," never erasing but painting over the same surface. It is, however, not certain if particular sites were chosen because of the natural smoothness of the "canvass," the religious or sacred nature of the spot or a superstitious belief painting on that site would bring luck in the hunt. One more important observation can be made of these early artists is that they took liberty in representing their subjects giving them size, legs and loops not actually in their physiogamy. Again, on one particular canvas with giraffe head and horns of wild sheep and other figures, the "expedition discovered 12 superimposed layers painted during a period of perhaps 2,000 years." To this revelation Lhote (1987: 191) reasoned: "It is not known why different artists used the same locations. Some sites may have offered a better painting surface than others or held special religious importance. Perhaps the act of painting filled a ceremonial function more important than the artwork itself."

In the article, "In African Cave, Ancient Paint factory Pushes Human Symbolic thought 'Far Back,'" a science writer, John Noble Wilford, for *The New York Times* dated Friday, October 14, 2011, p. A 14, notes, "These cave artisans had stones for pounding and grinding colorful dirt enriched with a kind of iron oxide to a powder, known as ocher. This was blended with the binding fat of mammal-bone marrow and a dash of charcoal. Traces of ochers were left on the tools, and samples of the reddish compound were collected in large abalone shells, where the paint was liquified, stirred and scooped out with a bone spatula." Even further, the article added, "archaeologists said that in the workshop remains they were seeing the earliest example of how emergent Homo sapiens processed ocher, one of the

OBAMA - MASTER AND COMMANDER

species' first pigments in wide use, its red color rich in symbolic significance. The early humans may have applied the concoction to their skin for protection or simply decoration, experts suggested. Perhaps it was their way of making social and artistic statements or other artifacts."

This is interesting, for we know the ancient Egyptians colored themselves red and this generated a great deal of commentary. Dr. Cheikh Anta Diop, a great proponent of the view that the ancient Egyptians were Black Africans argued the Egyptians painted themselves red so as to be distinguished from other Africans. However, wanting evidence that the Egyptians were Caucasians, proponents of this theory began emphasizing the ancient Egyptians as a race of "Red, white men."

All such designations were intended to remove the discussion from its true nature because Antiquarian Societies in Europe fell in love with Egypt; government, museum and private collections of Egyptian artifacts in Europe and America abounded; academics and lecturers spread the word to a public gullible in accepting unquestioned evidence from "experts" and willing to see their cultural heritage in an ancient setting, accepted the prevailing view; while books, discussions and even movies began to reinforce the view of a white Egypt; and, as no credible and sustained critique of a "Caucasian Egypt" challenged the accepted norm, falsity, distortion and omission reigned! Today, as new evidence begins to chip away at the false notions, this forces us to remember "old ideas die hard" and that people threatened by new information are victims of cognitive dissonance!

Obama - Master and Commander 44. A historic intersection of two historic inter-connections in American political and social history.

FREDERICK MONDERSON

Obama - Master and Commander 44a. Frances Perkin's Department of Labor Building on Constitution Avenue. One thing about Washington D.C. buildings they do not build up but build-out and across.

From the Stone Age to ancient Egypt the color red has had a magnetic attraction, perhaps because of its brightness, also like gold equated with the sun. The color gold was considered god-like. When the poor could not take gold into the afterlife they carried objects painted gold. However, not being able to paint themselves golden, red became the next most logical color considering its history. It is therefore understandable the ancient Egyptians would paint themselves red since they considered themselves special and in addition, their relationship with the gods may also be emphasized. This seems even more reasonable. What is even more significant, they were not the only people to utilize the brightness of red. Dr. Yosef ben-Jochannan pointed out that modern Nubians still paint their young brides red with the henna plant. Equally, if the "modern Egyptians are supposedly no different from the ancient Egyptians" why do they not continue this ancient tradition, yet the modern Nubians do continue such.

Now, continuing the use of red from the South African natives of Kolombo in that early age, we encounter discovered remains in South Africa dated at 43,000 B.P. (Before Present) which means you have to discount 2000 years of the current era (41,000 B.C.), in which residents were mining a form of oxide used for metallurgical purposes but also be part of the paint factory supply. This discovery raised an even more serious issue, that of agriculture. Years ago, when Prof. John H. Clarke of Hunter College of C.U.N.Y. was asked about the significance of this find, his comments were: "If people were mining a form of iron oxide at this time it meant they had to have had a large population. To feed such, they had to begin agriculture" which threw this whole issue into contention since agriculture was thought to have been discovered in South West Asia c. 8000 B.C., spreading throughout Africa after 4500 B.C. Yet, the magazine *Science* reported in 1982 there was evidence of Nile Valley farming of wheat, barley, lentils, beans, fruits, vegetables, etc., at 16,500-14,500 B.P. (14,500-12,500 B.C.). Elsewhere evidence indicated Upper Nile "catch basins" revealed mealing stones for grinding wheat dated at c. 11,000 B.C. This takes us off message, but it certainly fuels questions about entrenched interpretation of issues that point to and question the role of Africans in generating Egyptian civilization.

Louis and Mary Leakey were extraordinary archaeologists who made the world take Africa seriously by first discovering *Zinjanthropus Boisie* dated at 1.75 million years old. Then Mrs. Leakey made discoveries of footprints she dated at a "firm date of 3.25 million" years. However, Mrs. Leakey made another significant contribution by discovering and cataloguing more than a thousand Stone Age sites in East Africa depicting fresh and outstanding Stone Age Art. Much of both members of this team's work were reported in *National Geographic Magazine*. In discussing paints, Mrs. Leakey's "Tanzania' Stone Age Art" (1983: 86) not only mentions the colors Stone Age man used but confessed "Their choice of colors is interesting for: 'the predominant red was made from ocher, which is derived from iron ore. Black probably came from manganese, and bird droppings may have provided the basis for the white.'" In the Sahara the Frenchman Henry Lhote made significant discoveries at Tassili and he too identified these people as black, Negroes, and their art was also predominantly red based. Like so many areas in Africa, the art of Nabta Playa was also red based!

One of the arguments for the origins of the ancient Egyptians put forward by another Frenchman Gaston Maspero is that people from the west, in the Sahara, migrated to the Nile but these were Europeans who may have lived on the North African Mediterranean shore. Two things are clearly evident here. The first is confusing as the European proponents for an external origin of the Egyptians have held they came through the Isthmus of Suez, through the Horn of Africa and even from the Sahara. All this occurred in an age of global white supremacy, colonialism and imperialism when justification for European dominance was the order of the day. Hence, anything African was not considered thinkable.

Second, the new information was not available when the "law" was being laid down, ossifying the falsity in the minds of men. It stands to reason, if red was a "predominant" color in art in South, East, West Central, then why not in North East Africa. It is not farfetched to think they were all connected. To argue otherwise, be careful, the men in white jackets may be lurking!

FREDERICK MONDERSON

Obama - Master and Commander 45. View across the man-made lake at the Ulysses S. Grant Memorial with the Botanic Gardens to the right and government buildings further on.

Obama - Master and Commander 46. Another view of the Capital Building from a slightly different angle.

OBAMA - MASTER AND COMMANDER

Obama - Master and Commander 47. Looking across the Lake at another of those massive government buildings.

Meanwhile, with the ancient Egyptians, symbolism and symbolic logic were the orders of the day in practically every field of expertise and experience. Thus, use of red to symbolically paint or beautify is not a stretch of the imagination; for, when considering the precedent for decoration of the body as a symbolic expression, such practices extended more than 100,000 years in several parts of Africa. To not associate the Nile Valley Africans with this phenomenon but to claim these people were "red Caucasians" not only flies in the face of logic but is downright stupid and racist. This is one example of the falsity African historiographic reconstruction seeks to address.

"And we have done more in the two and a half years that I've been in here than the previous 43 Presidents to uphold that principle, whether it's ending "don't ask, don't tell," making sure that gay and lesbian partners can visit each other in hospitals, making sure that federal benefits can be provided to same-sex couples."
Barack Obama

FREDERICK MONDERSON

Obama - Master and Commander 48. Another look at the massive nature of Washington, DC architecture.

Obama - Master and Commander 49. The Washington Monument stands majestically as a backdrop of the green in these trees (left) and the Original Marker for placement of the Washington Monument which was moved a little to the right.

OBAMA - MASTER AND COMMANDER

Obama - Master and Commander 50. Close-up of the Grant Memorial from across the Lake.

Obama - Master and Commander 51. Another view of the majestic figure who sits "looking out" from the vicinity of the "House of Power" in Washington, DC.

FREDERICK MONDERSON

"We don't begrudge financial success in this country. We admire it. When Americans talk about folks like me paying my fair share of taxes, it's not because they envy the rich. It's because they understand that when I get a tax break I don't need and the country can't afford, it either adds to the deficit, or somebody else has to make up the difference - like a senior on a fixed income, or a student trying to get through school or a family trying to make ends meet. That's not right. Americans know that's not right. They know that this generation's success is only possible because past generations felt a responsibility to each other, and to the future of their country, and they know our way of life will only endure if we feel the same sense of shared responsibility. That's how we'll reduce our deficit. That's an America built to last." **Barack Obama**, State of the Union Address, January 2012

5. WASHINGTON, OBAMA AND CAIN
By
Dr. Fred Monderson

A new idea circulating in some circles attempts to equate Herman Cain with Booker T. Washington. This is particularly in respect to their influence and ideas early in a new century. However, a more fruitful comparison would be to compare Barack Obama with Washington because of the age and temperament in which they both worked. Thus, for argument sake, Washington, Obama and Cain could form a triangle, an isosceles triangle, two lines or angles complementing each other and one diametrically opposed. In this case, the reader's vivid imagination is allowed to speculate on the lines and angles of the triangle based on historical knowledge or personal experience coupled with the legacy by which these three individuals are or will be known. We must be mindful; however, as students of history, comparisons in time are often difficult because conditions differ over time. For example, while Mr. Washington functioned in an age after the Emancipation of Slavery, terrorism was so widespread, national and state governments seemed unconcerned about the plight of the Freedman. Education, jobs, social opportunities, access, and a whole lot more were in effect beyond the reach of these folks. In the "Age of Obama" much has changed and though he was subjected to unrelenting verbal abuse, threats and intimidation, ugly characterizations, freedom of speech in the American system protected such rights of expressions. However, while laws governing behaviors of Washington's time have changed; particularly because he was the President, law enforcement agencies, especially the Secret Service went to great lengths to protect Mr. Obama and even the FBI kept tabs on the more radical elements among Obama's vilifiers, since law enforcement's responsibility was to protect the President. Herman Cain's meteoric rise on the other hand, was not marred by such vilification and one has to wonder why. After all, in the rabid racist mind's eye, he was still as much "Nigger

OBAMA - MASTER AND COMMANDER

as Obama," yet he is considered a "good boy," and this too begs the question, Why?

Obama - Master and Commander 52. Buses line-up for tourists to visit Capital Building.

Obama - Master and Commander 53. Still another view of Grant staying the course!

FREDERICK MONDERSON

Obama - Master and Commander 54. The Capital Building with its Grand Marble Terrace, the green field within its wall and water fountain that does more than just quench thirst.

First, "Booker T." Washington was born a slave on the eve of the Civil War and Emancipation. This was a troublesome period owing to the inhumanity of the slavery system's experience and particularly with its dogged insistence the enslaved African not be allowed to learn to read for therein begins the acquisition of knowledge, a challenge to slavery and the quest for freedom. With Emancipation and the struggle to adjust with the change of status and the vicissitudes of "Jim Crow" practices, the challenge to Reconstruction and southern white backlash in terrorism that aided the systematic effort to deny the Freedman's right to vote, Mr. Washington came of age with a desire to be truly free. He earnestly wished the people of his race be equally free and enjoy the promises of the Constitution and laws designed to aid their social and human dignity.

The story is told and this characterizes the ethical standards' and work ethic of the man in that, after the founding of Historic Negro Colleges "Booker T." sought an education at Hampton Institute. Arriving at the College penniless, reasonable people would wonder how he hoped to pay for an education. However, the Principal or Headmaster took pity on the young man and made him an offer that ultimately defined the man, his moral values and work ethic. He was handed a mop and broom and asked to clean a particularly dusty room in the school. Many a person would probably remark, "Listen Sir, I came to get an education, not become a janitor." Instead, Booker T. Washington scoured the room, and then he cleaned it again. Not satisfied, he cleaned the room a third, perhaps a fourth time.

OBAMA - MASTER AND COMMANDER

Then came the moment of truth! When the Principal came to check his assignment, wearing a white glove, he went straight to the most inconspicuous spots, and ran his hand over window sills and under desks and chairs. Much to his consternation our man had been there, done that, and removed all traces of dust, leaving the duty road spotless. Naturally the Principal was flabbergasted at the speck-less room. Turning to "Booker T.," he promised a free first year of schooling. Working his way through College, our man served as janitor until he graduated, finally becoming a teacher at the school.

Meanwhile, in the concerted southern backlash to regain political and economic control of the South, relaxing of vigilance on part of northern liberals and the national government, terrorism became the order of the day. This gave rise to the emergence of the Ku Klux Klan, Knights of the White Camelia and Red Shirts among other such merchants of misery. Couple this with the humiliation of the "Grandfather Clause," literacy tests, poll taxes, property taxes and other threatening forms of intimidation as lynching, maiming, tar and feather, even murder, all designed to keep blacks away from the polls, this was a time of classical American 19th Century terrorism; a time of hell on earth for the Freedman! Among all this, Mr. Washington was an eye-witness to the plight of the newly freed but socially enslaved African. As Malcolm X would later admonish, Mr. Washington probably looked in the mirror and saw the "redeemer!" Thus, taking into account all that was transpiring and being mindful of how his race was being treated in an era of American emerging industrialization, Mr. Washington decided to set up Tuskegee Institute in Alabama. While the school was probably patterned after the historic Black Colleges, perhaps Hampton Institute, he wanted to concentrate on teaching industrial skills. This was a significant undertaking for an ex-slave in a climate that called into question his and every other African person's humanity, human rights, freed or ex-slave. To accomplish his goal, he had to appeal to white, liberal philanthropists to underwrite his effort. He proved a master in the art of deportment and cultivating goodwill.

On the other hand, Barack Obama was born to an inter-racial couple, a white female from Kansas and a father from Kenya in East Africa. His father died early and he was raised by a single mother with help from his maternal grandparents. Despite having white grandparents, young Obama faced all the challenges a poor child, outwardly black, would encounter. However, there must have been some profound ethical and moral values his grandparents imparted to this young man that encouraged and sustained his quest to get an education and begin to think of playing a positive role in society. This imparted social wisdom led him to Columbia and then Harvard University where he received an excellent education, became a Community Organizer and ultimately a Professor of Constitutional History. Amidst this experience, Mr. Obama entered the political arena to concretize change he had worked to bring about in his sojourn with the masses in Chicago, Illinois. Demonstrably a beautiful mind, possessing an extraordinary work ethic he had an unquenchable desire to bring about social changes in the

American system. Perhaps with a little luck and other people's prayers, this enabled Mr. Obama to become a State Senator and later a federal Senator from Illinois. By this time he had met, been floored by and married to Michelle Robinson and begun to raise a family. However, fate and Fortuna combined, and given the opportunity to address the Democratic National Convention in 2004, Barack made such a remarkable impression on all focused on this phenomenal event. There from, he embarked on a meteoric rise that enabled the young Senator to be considered a serious challenge when he decided to declare for the Democratic Presidential Primary on way to the Presidency of the United States. In many respect, a political operative without a machine apparatus outside of his home state of Illinois, Senator Obama was not given a chance to win the Democratic nomination, much more the Presidency.

Obama - Master and Commander 55. Behind Grant's back looking at the pinnacle of the Washington Memorial.

OBAMA - MASTER AND COMMANDER

Obama - Master and Commander 56. The Capital Building, its Balcony and the Grand Marble Terrace (below) with the green field encased by a wall.

Obama - Master and Commander 57. A "Memorial to the 56 Signers of the Declaration of Independence" : A gift from the American Revolution Bicentennial Administration 1976.

Mr. Obama, visionary that he is, mounted an unbelievable campaign, spoke unendingly in the most passionate and motivating manner, he made extraordinary appeals to the young emphasizing a vision of change. Equally and skillfully he used the Internet to get his message out. In the process he accumulated a tremendous Internet database and raised a lot of money through small donations to fund his campaign. Importantly and conversely, he stayed tremendously positive on message in face of an overwhelming challenge particularly from a well-entrenched and profusely oiled Clinton political machine. However, once beyond this obstacle with the Clinton faction and with the entire Democratic Party behind

FREDERICK MONDERSON

him, Mr. Obama took on his formidable Republican challenger, the military hero John McCain and his firebrand second, Governor Sarah Palin. Well, with a loving and tremendously supportive family providing powerful winds beneath his sails; Mr. Obama continued his unbelievable surge, appealing to a broad segment of disaffected democrats, women, the young, minorities and voila; everyone was sold on his message of "change" and wanted to be part of the historic election of the first African American to the U.S. Presidency. As such, and "winning the day" or election as it was, untold numbers turned out to wish him well at his Inauguration as he set out to tackle the many challenges the nation faced that contributed so much to his election on a platform of change. Stalwarts of the Civil Rights Movement showered tremendous praise on his efforts and the significant realization he had accomplished much they had struggled for.

However, as President Obama set about his task of tackling the nation's economic and financial inadequacies, bank and automobile industry's impending collapse, increasing unemployment and rising home foreclosures, he simultaneously fought two wars in Iraq and Afghanistan. There was a rise in terrorist activities at home and abroad as well as the emergence of Somali Pirates. Even more significant, Mr. Obama faced a world perception of America that became increasingly negative because of perceived past policies and near global condemnation of the invasion of Iraq. Notwithstanding, while proverbial wisdom decries fighting on two fronts; nevertheless, as President Obama confronted the above issues he in turn was confronted, maligned and bombarded by a "Tea Marty Movement" whose activities were "over the top" to say the least. Many viewed the characterization and pummeling he received by these individuals as indeed racist. Adding injury to insult, the highest elected Republican in Congress Senator Mitch McConnell unveiled his "Mandate," a publicly stated policy, "To make Barack Obama a one term President." Thus, from day one McConnell and his Republican Party members must have met, strategized and planned to sabotage the President and in so doing, the American people. One has to wonder why the Patriot Act never ensnarled these "rebels?" Still, this line of assault many believed was unequivocally racist, it certainly looked treasonous.

Nevertheless, not only an astute politician but morally and ethically superior to many of his critic and detractors, Mr. Obama incessantly smiled and took the high road rather than meet his detractors from their perch in the gutter! Their nondescript criticism, notwithstanding, President Obama persevered in his constitutional obligations as Head of State, Commander-in-Chief, and Chief Executive, endeavored to show a new face of America. All the while Republican opponents, dubbed the "Party of No" mined the roadway Mr. Obama has had to function in his many duties. Derailing the "Obama Express" somewhat, and hoodwinking the American people, they became emboldened by their successes in the 2010 election, resulting in Republican control of the House of Representatives which proved a tremendous roadblock, the architecture of gridlock in Congress. In spite of this, Mr. Obama compromised to enact many legislatively constructive

OBAMA - MASTER AND COMMANDER

laws designed to transform the hearts, minds and interests of large segments of the American people. The trouble is Mr. Obama has had a gentleman's approach to dealing with the Republicans, reaching out to them to foster Bipartisanship but this was to no avail, given their subscribing to "McConnell's Mandate."

Herman Cain broken into the Republican campaign and surprisingly his message of 9-9-9 began to resonate and receive unprecedented attention, more so than the messages of seemingly "sacred cows" of the Party. Mr. Cain had been CEO of Godfather Pizza and apparently he was a success in rescuing the chain from the challenges it faced. In a time of American economic troubles Mr. Cain's other experience with Coca Cola, Pillsbury's Burger King Division; his time at Godfather Pizza and as head of the American Restaurant Association has allowed him to tout business experience which also reflects a work ethic that gets the job done. Wow! Was there a conspiracy to get the black businessman out of the way so the white businessman can be the only serious business challenger? However, much can be said about his political experience, his gaffs and certainly his baggage that reveal his early philosophy and activities as it's compared with contemporaries of his early years. Recent allegations of improper behavior towards subordinate female employees threatened to create problems consuming his energies and sidetracking his campaign. Yet he seemed to appear Teflon and raising enormous sums to fund his campaign.

Obama - Master and Commander 58. The United States Botanic Gardens.

FREDERICK MONDERSON

Obama - Master and Commander 59. The decorated wall and entrance enclosing trees before the Capital Building.

Obama - Master and Commander 60. Entrance to the center from which American power emanates within the practice of the Judeo-Christian politico-religious construct, having Tabernacles guarding the portal.

OBAMA - MASTER AND COMMANDER

The comparisons between Mr. Washington and Mr. Obama can clearly be made relative to the climate under which they were forced to function. Mr. Washington had little federal or state protection from the troubles of his times despite laws to the contrary. He appealed to the good will of philanthropists and people of goodwill to fund his efforts. He did not push the envelope of civil rights because he realized the constraints of his time so he argued for gradualism. Importantly, he made a significant contribution in founding the lasting Tuskegee Institute that has trained perhaps millions since his time. Some have argued he did a little "toming" but this was for the greater good. Though he emphasized practical or technical skills, he left a profoundly indelible impression on the intellectual landscape and in the minds of black and white as he unshackled the capabilities of blacks by giving them tools to learn and grow. Mr. Obama too has faced "the hounds of hell" but with an infectious smile he blunted their attacks and was able to enact far-reaching legislation that benefits great segments of the American public. Say what you will, he is the President of the United States and no matter the McConnells, the DeMints, Joe Wilsons; the American people, despite what is said of them, realize this is indeed a hard-working individual doing the best he can, considering the unrelenting nature of the opposition, all in their best interest.

Mr. Cain fits well in the mindset of the "Tea Party Movement" which means he has to genuflect on the "Altar of the McConnell Mandate." He has been praised for being down to earth in his speech but that same mouth can sometimes convict an individual. Mr. Cain first insulted Black Americans by telling them they are "brainwashed for voting Democratic." Imagine! Like so many other issues of which he has very little knowledge, Mr. Cain is very much unaware of the history of Black political expression in this country. Thus, he is very good at "walking things back!" That is, whether it is his own 9-9-9 plan, dynamics of *Roe V. Wade*, foreign policy and even his memory. Consider what would happen today if Blacks instantly left the Democratic Party to follow this "Brother from another Mother," given his and Republican losing streak, this "Pied Piper" would give us nothing to show for it!

Another peculiar characteristic Mr. Cain has demonstrated recently is his "interracial nature." Given the history of debasement enslaved Black women suffered in slavery at the hand of white owners, Mr. Washington may have had mixed ancestors but he clearly recognized his links to the black race. President Obama without a doubt comes from an interracial parentage but he identifies himself as African American. First, Governor Rick Perry of Texas admitted Mr. Cain was his "brother" and Mr. Cain did not disavow this "family relationship!" Recently, Mr. Cain in pandering to Republicans declared he and the "Koch Brothers" were "brothers from another mother." Questions arising from this declaration include, is he declaring he is interracial? Is he pandering to the Koch Brothers money? Some unpleasant things have been said about the Koch Brothers, is Mr. Cain claiming ownership of these assertions made against his "brothers?" Are their "tails wagging his dog" or Vice Versa? Is he becoming so entangled as

FREDERICK MONDERSON

President, if he is that fortunate, will he be able to make independent judgments? Doe he realize "Chickens do come home to roost?"

It is therefore clear, any comparisons to be made between Washington, Obama and Cain can only equate truthfully Mr. Washington and Mr. Obama. This being so, Mr. Cain does not fit anywhere in the equation. Like the triangle earlier mentioned, the two are complimentary while he is opposed. The two seems to have had pride in race but Mr. Cain does not. While Mr. Washington and Mr. Obama could probably boast of being "brothers from another mother," Mr. Cain boasts of his sibling relationship with the "Kock Brothers." Hence, Mr. Cain cannot be compared with Mr. Washington and since "where he sits is where he stands and where he stands is where he sits;" thus, he is diametrically and unalterably opposed to Mr. Obama which means he would also be opposed to Mr. Washington. One thing Mr. Cain ought to be mindful of, Republicans are famous for inviting Blacks to dinner and serving them up as the meal. Case in point! Thanksgiving is coming and as Rahm Emanuel has pointed out these "turkeys" waiting in the winds, beware, Herman the President can only pardon one bird and it has already been chosen!

"But what we can do, as flawed as we are, is still see God in other people, and do our best to help them find their own grace. That's what I strive to do, that's what I pray to do every day." **Barack Obama**

Obama - Master and Commander 61. Headquarters of the American Red Cross: "Saluting Our Troops this Holiday Season."

OBAMA - MASTER AND COMMANDER

Obama - Master and Commander 61a. The National Press Club Building.

Obama - Master and Commander 62. Colonnade on the House wing of the Capital Building as a back-drop to the luscious manicured green lawn.

FREDERICK MONDERSON

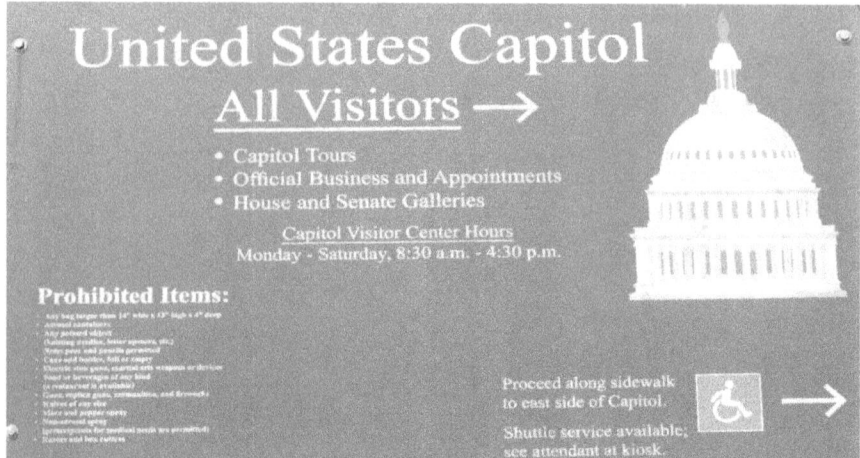

Obama - Master and Commander 63. Sign indicating the Capital Visiting Center as well as listing **Prohibited Items** barred from the building.

"I know my country has not perfected itself. At times, we've struggled to keep the promise of liberty and equality for all of our people. We've made our share of mistakes, and there are times when our actions around the world have not lived up to our best intentions. But I also know how much I love America. I know that for more than two centuries, we have strived - at great cost and great sacrifice - to form a more perfect union; to seek, with other nations, a more hopeful world. Our allegiance has never been to any particular tribe or kingdom - indeed, every language is spoken in our country; every culture has left its imprint on ours; every point of view is expressed in our public squares. What has always united us - what has always driven our people; what drew my father to America's shores - is a set of ideals that speak to aspirations shared by all people: that we can live free from fear and free from want; that we can speak our minds and assemble with whomever we choose and worship as we please." **Barack Obama**, Berlin Speech, July 24, 2008

"This is the moment when we must build on the wealth that open markets have created, and share its benefits more equitably. Trade has been a cornerstone of our growth and global development. But we will not be able to sustain this growth if it favors the few, and not the many." **Barack Obama**, Inaugural Address, January 2009

OBAMA - MASTER AND COMMANDER

6. "NIGGERHEAD MOUNTAIN"
By
Dr. Fred Monderson

An old Washington truism dictates "Where you stand is where you sit and where you sit is where you stand" which means since the "Tea Party Movement" and Republicans are "married," and have progressed as the "Party of No," they can also be characterized as being unpatriotic since they are single-mindedly focused on the economic well-being of the "one" not the "ninety-nine" percent of Americans. As such, their ranks can be perceived as bloated not by visionaries but hypocrites and opportunists. This has become clearly evident as the "winds of change" have begun to sweep across the nation and philosophically speaking "if it ain't tied down" it will be blown away. More correctly, as the winds blow away the smoke obfuscated by the political rhetoric of the last few years, "the King is really naked" except for the one per cent band-aid that covers the American special interest person. But, like old time wisdom has always held, "You can fool some of the people some of the time, but you can't fool all the people all the time." Meanwhile, Barack Obama continues to execute the people's business as the Oath of Office dictated from Day One even though he continues to be pummeled by allies of and proponents of the "McConnell Mandate!"

However, no matter what has been said by whomever, Herman Cain, etc. al. not exempted, American history has been so inextricably intertwined with African Americans, "until justice rolls down like a mighty stream," social relations in this country will have to be viewed from the prism of black and white. Not that white is loyal and black disloyal, for contrary to their percentage in the population, blacks disproportionately serve militarily on the outposts of empire to defend this nation against threats and to defend its general interests. However, all are in agreement that while the general unemployment rate is 9.1 percent, black unemployment is 16 percent, and if we count black youth unemployment at 40-50 percent, it asks the question "Why is this so?" Why despite all the debates this phenomenon never rises to become a front burner issue with all the Presidential candidates who never mention such nor seem to have contemplated a plan to address this issue.

Even more, while some motorists and pedestrians, even shoppers have been stopped and questioned "while driving, walking or shopping black;" no motorist, pedestrian or shopper has been stopped "while being white." That is not to say there are no perpetrators of criminal behavior who are either black and white. But, who could countenance criminal behavior whether from black or white criminals?

Nevertheless, in a recent Republican debate a question was raised about homosexual rights to which, one of the candidates gave an answer and the

FREDERICK MONDERSON

audience responded in a hearty cheer. Another question to Texas Governor Rick Perry was about the several hundred persons executed by that state to which Mr. Perry responded, "The people of Texas know the meaning of justice!" The audience not simply cheered the man and his answer but also the execution of that many people! Are we to believe Texas is such a violent state that it can foster such a preponderance of criminal behavior resulting in that drastic retribution? The world also wants to know, were any of those executed innocent? The *New York Daily News* Sunday October 9, 2011, reported on the death penalty and identified several persons, black and white, who were exonerated thanks to the new science of evidence examination. One person executed was deemed innocent but it was too late to save him. Another inmate, Troy Davis, even as he lay on the executioner's gurney, as a final act of penitence, confessed to the family "I did not kill your loved one!" Thus, many people believe the death penalty should be outlawed because it is not really a deterrent to criminal behavior but simply shows the state demanding "an eye for an eye" justice. In response to Governor Perry's "People of Texas know the meaning of justice," let us not forget an individual languished in a Texas prison for some 30 years even though his initial conviction was overturned right after and the Prosecution did nothing to rectify this way back then!

Obama - Master and Commander 64. How invigorating and beautiful this lovely patch of flowers seem as they greet the visitor. And there is another further on, stationed at entrance to the Capital Building grounds.

OBAMA - MASTER AND COMMANDER

Obama - Master and Commander 65. The curb is always well kept with flowers in a lined arrangement.

Obama - Master and Commander 66. Green, White and Blue. How picturesque!

The great western novelist Louis Lamour painted a wonderful picture of Texas as an upstanding state, its people hardy but just and the Sackets, a Texas family of noble principles. In the old West, when members had gone afar, confronted injustice and caught in a stand-off, word would go out, a Sackett was hold-up against unsightly characters, send help, and those "Noble Texans" would come to the rescue like the cavalry! Naturally, Mr. Lamour was a fiction writer!

FREDERICK MONDERSON

In the movie, *The Great Debaters*, Denzel Washington starred as a Professor in Wiley, Texas teaching young Wiley College students how to debate during the 1930s Depression era. One, actually two, episodes in this movie raise serious concerns relative to this issue of "Texas justice."

In the first of these, the lead actor and three students, two males and a female, were driving home one night from a debate. They came upon a scene, a roast, not a fish fry or marshmellow, but a "Nigger roast." That is, a black man, hung and being roasted on a fire surrounded by a screaming mob from which they were lucky to escape, but that sickening image of "Justice" could not be erased from the young minds!

After a successful debate run, little Wiley College was invited to debate the powerful Harvard University debating team. "In trouble with the law" their coach could not chaperone his charges so the youngsters were on their own in Boston. The entire college and everyone in stores, barbershops and homes back in Wiley listened to the radio as events unfolded debating the question "Whether unjust laws should be obeyed!" In climax, young Farmer brought the House down, when he flourished, "In Texas they lynch Niggers!" Recounting the incident, he continued, "No one was arrested, still we tried to peacefully protest" as a form of civil disobedience as an alternative to violent reaction.

Ida Wells Barnett was an activist in the last decades of the 19th Century who worked tirelessly against lynching. Gilbert Osofsky in *The Burden of Race: A Documentary History of Negro-White Relations in America* provide one example of "Texas justice" when he quotes Ida Wells' description of a "human burning" drawn from her classic work: *A Red Record: Lynchings in the United States, 1892-1893-1894*. In this work, Ms. Barnett identified Bishop Atticus Green Haygood of the Methodist Episcopal Church who used emotively false language to describe a murder. As she puts it: "Nothing is farther from the truth than that statement. It is a cold blooded, deliberate, brutal falsehood which this Christian Bishop used to bolster up the infamous plea that the people of Paris were driven to insanity by learning that the little child had been viciously assaulted, choked to death, and then torn to pieces by a demon in human form. It was a brutal murder, but no more brutal than hundreds of murders which occur in this country, and which have been equaled every year in fiendishness and brutality, and for which the death penalty is prescribed by law and inflicted only after the person has been legally adjudged guilty of the crime." She quoted "a white man's description," not the Bishop's that identified who came out and what impact events of "vigilante justice" has had on those in attendance. The quote states what happened to Henry Smith after he was caught and returned to the town from which he escaped after the murder. After stripping him naked and parading him in the town to the jeers and cheers of a frenzied crowd who collected portion of his ripped clothing as souvenirs, he was then set on a scaffold upon which the crowd piled all kinds of

OBAMA - MASTER AND COMMANDER

combustible stuff around and poured oil on it and set it afire. Here the description gets graphic! "The Negro rolled and tossed out of the mass, only to be pushed back by the people nearest him. He tossed out again, and was roped and pulled back. Hundreds of people turned away, but the vast crowd still looked calmly on. People were here from every part of this section. They came from Dallas, Fort Worth, Sherman, Denison, Bonham, Texarkana, Fort Smith, Ark., and a party of fifteen came from Hempstead County, Arkansas, where he was captured. Every train that came in was loaded to its utmost capacity, and there were demands at many points for special trains to bring the people here to see the unparalleled punishment for an unparalleled crime. When the news of the burning went over the county like wildfire, at every country town anvils boomed forth the announcement."

Even further, in *The Black Book* Harris, Levitt, Furman and Smith (1974), a picture on page 58 depicts a black man roasting on a bed of fire with dozens of well-dressed white men and their sons in great glee over their prize! This is part of the record of racial hatred this nation must try to live down! Also, on page 55 of the same book, four blacks are pictured hanging from a tree with a caption supplied by the African American poet Langston Hughes that read: "I've been a victim, the Belgians cut off my hand in the Congo, they lynched me in Texas."

Additionally, and more contemporary, when the issue surfaced about "Nigger Head Mountain" on Governor Rick Perry's farm, the media was quick to quote him as saying something to the effect, "In 1984 my father painted over the sign." The news reported, however, the sign was there while he was a State Senator, Commissioner of Agriculture and even Governor. A few months ago the news documentary "60 Minutes" did an episode about the murder of a Civil Rights activist in Mississippi. According to the FBI investigator there are more than 100 unsolved Civil Rights murders. The one they were pursuing revealed the killer was alive but no one was talking except the family of the murdered man. Nonetheless, an even more chilling revelation stated in essence by the FBI, in the age of the lynching of blacks and other form of terrorism, anyone who wanted to run for office had to be an active member of one of the terror groups, viz., Ku Klux Klan, Knights of the White Camelia, Red Shirts, etc., or had to espouse their racist views. In essence, if you wanted to hold any office during those times you had to be associated with or in support of the "Lynching Bee" mentality that targeted blacks! Thus, paint is not the issue in this case! The issue is really how many "Nigger heads Rolled" on "Niggerhead Mountain." After all, "Nigger Head Mountain" was not a monument to a Black! To honor someone you need to show some respect. No one said "Mr. Nigger Head Mountain." This begs the question, was it really a killing field, which further asks, how many blacks were lynched there and across Texas in that classic age of American and southern terrorism? To complicate matters, Romney carried Texas as part of his sweep of the "Lynching states!" What does that tell the world about "Texas Justice" and Conservatism? How about Romney's?, Santorums'? Gingrich's? "Extreme Conservatism?"

FREDERICK MONDERSON

At least South Africa sponsored a "Truth Commission" which granted immunity and allowed persons to publicly confess the unspeakable crimes they visited on black Africans. No one ever confessed how many blacks they lynched; how many were tarred and feathered; how many sharecroppers were cheated; how many blacks were purposely and deliberately prevented from voting; and even today, how many blacks are wrongly convicted in the courts, children taken from their parents by judges in Family Courts whose behaviors go unquestioned. Yet America chooses not to discuss race when victims from President Obama, President of the United States, to the lowly black person are subjected to racial discrimination and the economic and social stigma that goes with the territory. They are stopped at whim and frisked for illegal substances or firearms. Who could countenance such behaviors, in view of random violence, but the operative factor primarily is the skin color of those victims. Let us not forget, in "Progressive New York" recently politicians had to protest and have removed a lynched scarecrow. Importantly, the image of lynching is so imbedded in the mentality of Americans it is a symbol that easily sends a message to Blacks that is very sinister. Just before the 2012 election, an individual in New York was observed driving his truck with a noosed effigy of President Obama. It was mentioned on the radio but that's as far as it got!

"Change will not come if we wait for some other person or some other time. We are the ones we've been waiting for. We are the change that we seek."
Barack Obama

Obama - Master and Commander 67. Part of the peaceful scenery that engulfs the Capital Building grounds.

OBAMA - MASTER AND COMMANDER

Obama - Master and Commander 68. More of the wonderful green, white and blue that evokes admiration and pride as visitors mill past.

Obama - Master and Commander 69. Government building sporting a colonnade with Ionic capitals supporting a pediment featuring outstretched wings of the American eagle.

FREDERICK MONDERSON

Obama - Master and Commander 70. One of two seated figures at the entrance to the Rayburn House Office Building.

OBAMA - MASTER AND COMMANDER

Obama - Master and Commander 71. "The Poets who on earth have made us heirs of Truth and Pure Delight by Heavenly Lays."

"I think what you're seeing is a profound recognition on the part of the American people that gays and lesbians and transgender persons are our brothers, our sisters, our children, our cousins, our friends, our co-workers, and that they've got to be treated like every other American. And I think that principle will win out. I think we're moving in a direction of greater equality and - and I think that's a good thing. And we have done more in the two and a half years that I've been in here than the previous 43 Presidents to uphold that principle, whether it's ending "don't ask, don't tell," making sure that gay and lesbian partners can visit each other in hospitals, making sure that federal benefits can be provided to same-sex couples."
Barack Obama, Presidential News Conference, June 2011

7. THE TRUMP CIRCUS
By
Dr. Fred Monderson

Donald Trump continues to dominate the news and forcefully influence developments as Republicans seek to sort out who will be their standard bearer against President Obama in national elections on November 6, 2012. But, as he steadfastly clings to the "Birthers" notion, people are thinking either he's not playing with a full deck or it underscores his master manipulation strategy.

FREDERICK MONDERSON

Coupled with recent and compelling Republican history, this behavior and resulting confusion is really not out of character for the "Party of No" that has refused to tax the rich, many of whose new members, as "Tea Party" candidates took the "Grover Norquist Pledge" and so are vehemently and unalterably opposed to the President, that they will squeeze the country to prevent an "Obama win." More importantly, however, the man, "the Donald," so many are courting is not only rich but an opportunistic showman entertainer with a gigantic ego. In addition, this master manipulator who cannot really be a serious presidential candidate enables a questionable light to be cast on these candidates who truck up to the towering Trump in a way that undermines their credibility.

Many are of the view; Donald Trump is only interested in promoting Donald Trump and will probably exact a price from any political apprentice who hopes to benefit from his supposed "extensive knowledge, leadership and foreign policy experience."

Donald Trump betrayed his un-presidential persona when he challenged Barack Obama over the "Birthers Issue." Adding to this "fool's errand," he threw in questions about the President's academic record. These two huge blunders revealed the shortcomings of Mr. Trump as a political leader and theorist even though he has had some success as a businessman. However, his showman capabilities, his wealth and resultant media calculations have fueled his political prominence in the Republican Party. This shrewd businessman, as a supreme betting man, has donated to both Democratic and Republican causes. Such "hedging his bet" has been a shrewd strategy though he is more welcome in the Republican Party perhaps because of his wealth or that they are more amenable to his machinations.

Some have argued Mr. Trump's interest in presidential politics has been principally to promote publicity for his TV show, *The Apprentice*, and to keep his brand name in public prominence. He, on the other hand, chose to articulate President Obama as an issue because so many Republicans love to hate the man.

Mr. Donald Trump is a late bloomer "Birthers Advocate" who, unfortunately and misguidedly believes the issue was a publicity gravy train for political aspirants. However, in his decision to seek the presidency, Mr. Obama had girded himself with the wherewithal for a successful political campaign, viz., a keen mind grounded in a career of academic excellence; constructive giveback as a Community Organizer; political experience and contacts gained as a state and later federal Senator from the state of Illinois; an impeccable ethical background; and, most important, a wonderful family comprising an intellectually gifted wife and two lovely daughters whose love and support anchored his faith, personality and focus as the winding road of the campaign became long, treacherous and challenging.

OBAMA - MASTER AND COMMANDER

Obama - Master and Commander 72. The Capital Dome behind the flimsy wire fence, that is still secure.

Obama - Master and Commander 72a. Government building across from the Plaza of the Capital Building with its flag flying at half-mast!

FREDERICK MONDERSON

Obama - Master and Commander 73. Ionic columns, this time two rows, adorn a government building behind the bushes.

OBAMA - MASTER AND COMMANDER

Obama - Master and Commander 74. Oh, how the Capital Dome stands majestically behind the bushes and against the blue sky.

Obama - Master and Commander 75. General Grant on guard, even on foggy days, with the Washington Monument in the rear.

FREDERICK MONDERSON

Obama - Master and Commander 76. The massive nature of Washington, DC construction indicate these structures are built for permanence.

Whether intentionally or otherwise, an anti-Obama phalanx coalesced in a "Tea Party Movement;" aligned with right wing groups, blogs, "lone wolves," and a

OBAMA - MASTER AND COMMANDER

recalcitrant cadre of Republican elected officials committed to one goal, that is, to "Stop Obama." In this intensive campaign Mr. Obama was accused of being a "socialist," unpatriotic, inexperienced in foreign, financial and economic policy, his social associations were questioned and his religious beliefs challenged. He was also accused of being a Muslim because, as a youth, following his now deceased mother, he lived in Indonesia for a few years. Equally, when Mr. Obama visited his paternal homeland in Kenya he was dressed in traditional garb by the elders.

This "roots grounding" was misconstrued resulting in him being falsely accused of being a Muslim. In reality, Mr. Obama was sensitive to the role Muslims have played in the evolution of this country and Americas relationships with a global community consisting of more than one billion members. He did recognize there are members of the Muslim religion who are in conflict with America and Americans and are principals in two wars in Iraq and Afghanistan with terrorist members in Africa, the Middle East and Asia. Nevertheless, as opposition mounted against Mr. Obama, his policies and efforts on behalf of the nation, his most potent weapon was being armed with the best advisors as well as an infectious and disarming smile. Nevertheless, having thrown everything at Mr. Obama including the "kitchen sink," which did not stick to his Teflon persona, a "Birthers movement" emerged that several future Republican presidential candidates and other political persons and elected officials began to articulate.

As the world watched unfolding developments and wondered about America's progress, equality, racial prejudice and scorched earth politics, Michele Bachmann became an early "Birthers Advocate" who challenged the nationality of Mr. Obama, claiming he was not born in the United States, but Kenya, per se. Gregory Hollister, a retired United States Air Force Colonel was also an early "Birthers advocate." So too was Lou Dobbs, Sarah Palin, Phil Berg and Orly Taitz, "Queen of the Birthers." However, very early, as this line of attack began to lose its luster, Ms. Bachmann began to back away from such a questionable strategy. Equally, as other branches of the "Birthers Tree" manifested their multi-nefarious behaviors, a state senator from Texas mounted a campaign, ostensively in the "Birthers" vein, but even more sinister, to disqualify Mr. Obama from that state's presidential ballot in the 2012 general elections. This particular individual, when interviewed by Anderson Cooper on CNN's AC 360 stated his case but everyone could see the racial venom in that character, thank goodness the "loser lost!" Even Governor Bobby Jindal of Louisiana sponsored a bill that got nowhere. On the other hand, Arizona's Governor vetoed a "Birthers Bill." Seriously, if Mr. Obama was not a legal, native born citizen, he could not have gotten past Senator McCain and certainly Hillary Clinton, wife of former President Bill Clinton, who turned around and championed his many efforts. Still, as these factors manifested, Mr. Obama remained steadfast committed to addressing problems of economic and fiscal policy and practice, unemployment, housing and auto industries, clean air concerns, the environment, global warming, clean and practical energy, health

FREDERICK MONDERSON

care, equality in the workplace, educational standards with focus on remuneration and the need to provide state of the art infrastructure equipment and instruction, as well as other meaningful issues requiring presidential leadership in such areas as foreign affairs, the global economy, fighting two wars in Iraq and Afghanistan and combating Somali pirates a well as a myriad of issues, foreign and domestic.

In the Republican conspiracy against Democrats, the Presidency and the man Obama, having thrown everything including the kitchen sink to which Mr. Obama simply stepped aside, their "non-card-carrying" allies made an enormous issue of the president's birth certificate. While Donald Trump has harbored strong feelings after running with this issue and remains unrepentant, he also made Rick Perry a disciple and recently a female New England state senator was "slapped down" for trying to make an issue of this misguided belief. How stupid could people be; these members of a lunatic fringe! Unless one can only conclude, there is a sinister motive driving this particular action.

Imagine! In a nation of laws, in Washington, D.C., where you have the United States Supreme Court, the Legislative Body with its enormous powers, even the Secret Service who must protect him; to allow a non-citizen to become president is unthinkable! The President is Commander-In-Chief, commanding some of the world's foremost general officers who follow his orders that put their juniors in harm's way. These people, some of whom may not even like Mr. Obama for whatever reason; to imagine they would blindly follow the orders of an illegal, is preposterous to contemplate.

Obama - Master and Commander 77. The Longworth House Office Building, like so many others, this time with Doric columns, proudly fly the fly!

OBAMA - MASTER AND COMMANDER

Obama - Master and Commander 78. The sign says it all!

FREDERICK MONDERSON

Obama - Master and Commander 79. Visitor examines the Directory of the Cannon House Office Building.

About half a dozen years ago, the "Sniper" terrorized the DC tri-state area. My daughter, resident in Maryland at the time told me, "Daddy, don't come to your grandson's birthday, because a sniper is terrorizing the DC area." I was adamant

OBAMA - MASTER AND COMMANDER

that no sniper would keep me away from my grandson's birthday! However, a not much noticed piece in a local paper indicated, at that time, there were some 42 security agencies that blanketed the Washington, DC area; so every person and inch is scrutinized. We are often told "Justice is blind," but at times she would take a peek from behind the blindfold! Are we to believe none of those security agencies would sneak a peek at Mr. Obama's birth certificate!

So, here we have Mr. Trump and his train of clown followers in their simple minded "fools' errand" insulting the intelligence of the public with the "Birther nonsense." It may very well be this is really a masked pathological hatred for the black man and his family in the White House. Surprise, they're going to be there for another "four more years!"

As Donald Trump manipulated gullible viewers on the airwaves with his "Birthers nonsense" and Michele Bachmann backed away realizing it was counterproductive, the President kept a close eye observing as the "clowns" or more properly Rahm Emanuel's "turkeys," got dressed in their oversized shoes, baggy pants, colorful shirts, painted faces and even red noses and funny hats. As these narcissists enjoyed their colorful appearance in the mirror, Mr. Obama decided to release his birth certificate that a Republican administration in Hawaii had previously authenticated. Still, Mr. Trump claimed a victory for having gotten Mr. Obama to surrender the document. This "winner" who claimed "I was leading in the polls" decided to drop out of the Republican presidential contention. Yet, today though he claims to have "won" he still harbors claims the document is inauthentic.

In one of his songs, "Symptoms," the late Trinidadian Calypsonian Lord Kitchener sang of a lady who offered, "Mr. Kitchener I will predict, either you are sick or a lunatic." Even more, the political cartoonist in the New York *Daily News* Bramhall is an interesting, sometimes, controversial, character who sometimes aggravates and sometimes amuses. Yet, right after Mr. Obama's forces stormed Osama bin-Laden's compound and killed the master terrorist, Bramhall created a cartoon showing Mr. Obama pointing at a display board, addressing uniformed troops at the ready, with a caption that read, "The next compound you will raid is Trump Towers." Of course, Mr. Obama is too nice a guy to order such a move. On Wednesday, December 7, 2011, Bramhall was at it again this time about the GOP Debate. He shows Mr. Trump enthroned high on a pedestal, and, not at their rostrum, Perry, Newt and Santorum are on all fours with face kissing the ground and a caption showing the ringmaster from his throne, asking "First question – Am I a great moderator or what?" Some may argue this genuflecting is the first step in what John Huntsman denied he would do, such as "Kiss Trump's Ring or any other part of his anatomy!" To make matters worse, just as several Republican candidates including Bachmann, Newt Gingrich, Rick Perry and Mitt Romney all have had recent audiences with Mr. Trump and this contrasts with many other Republicans who have shied away from Trump. Even the Republican Chairman

FREDERICK MONDERSON

Priebus has criticized "the Donald" for being a distracting sideshow. While Ron Paul and John Huntsman have spoken out about Donald Trump and the "Trump Debate" as they too declined to attend, Mitt Romney cited a scheduling conflict for his not participating. Seems the smart money is in running away from Donald Trump!

Meanwhile Mr. Trump, in an interview with Wolf Blitzer on CNN's "The Situation Room" has been shooting off his mouth, boasting of his many millions, calling Ron Paul a "fool" who could not get the nomination. He even took a shot at the President denying him credit for ending Osama bin-Laden's reign of terror. When Mr. Blitzer asked Mr. Trump if Mr. Obama has done anything good for the country, he studied long and could not name one good thing Mr. Obama has done for America. He seemed ignorant of the impact the rescue of the auto industry has had for American carmakers; that Wall Street began between 6500-7000 at the start of Mr. Obama's administration and now tops 12,000 points. We cannot underestimate the significance of the Lilly Ledbetter Law, efforts to create Jobs for Veterans, Credit Card Reform, and so on, but Republicans have amnesia about these "Obama wins" for the American people. Either Mr. Trump is getting senile under that fancy hairdo of his, he is a liar or unable to know good from not good. This "cult of denial" is a line from George Bush's and Ron Paul's playbook that is characteristic of Republican "Party of No" membership. Poor Donald Trump, as his circus sludges on, the Ringmaster is more a joke than his circus show itself!

"Contrary to the claims of some of my critics and some of the editorial pages, I am an ardent believer in the free market." **Barack Obama**

OBAMA - MASTER AND COMMANDER

Obama - Master and Commander 80. Entrance to the Cannon House Office Building.

FREDERICK MONDERSON

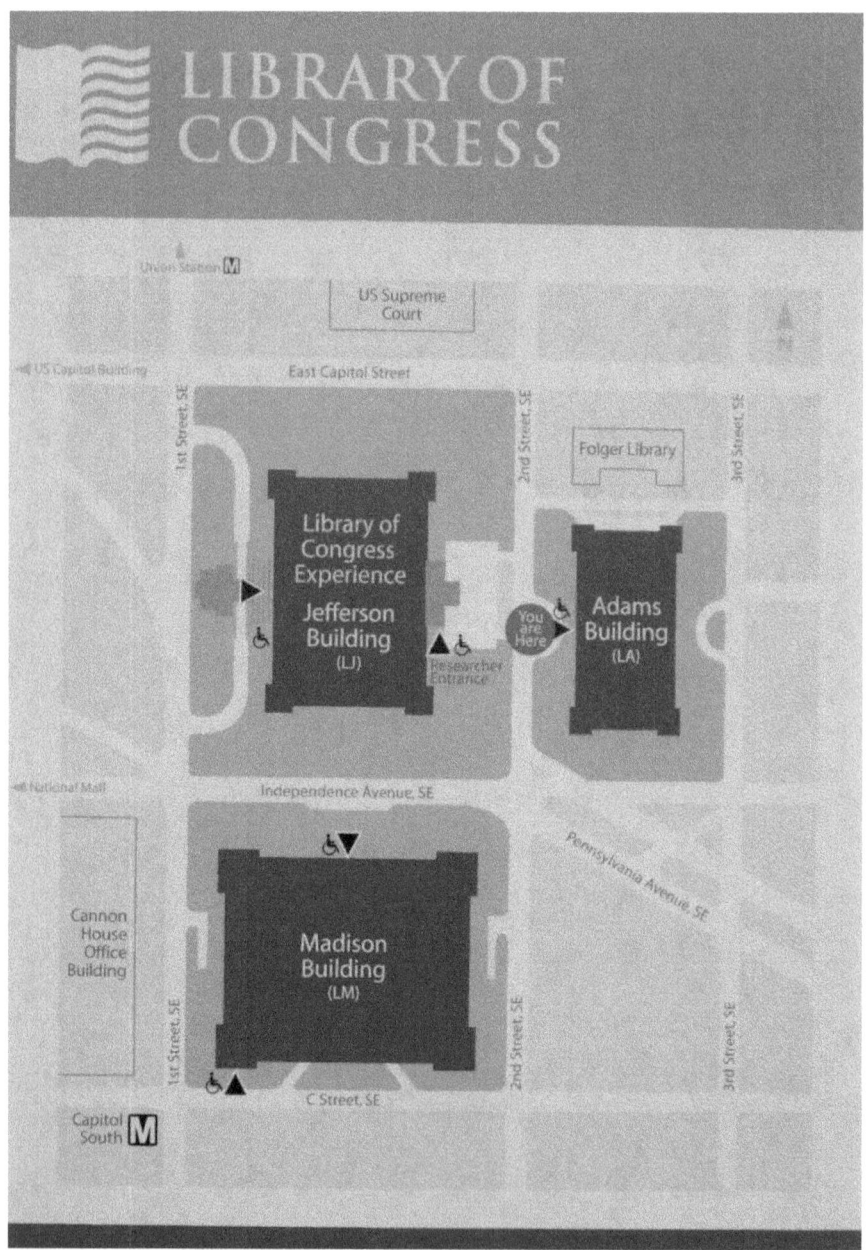

Obama - Master and Commander 81. Sign indicating the three branches of the Library of Congress - Jefferson, Madison and Adams Buildings.

OBAMA - MASTER AND COMMANDER

Obama - Master and Commander 82. The Madison Building of the Library of Congress has on its exterior wall Mr. Madison's first of two famous literary gems which state: "What spectacle can be more edifying than that of liberty and learning. Each leaning on the other for their mutual and surest support."

FREDERICK MONDERSON

Obama - Master and Commander 83. The second of Mr. Madison's two literary gems adorning the Library's outer wall state: "Knowledge will forever govern ignorance and a people who meant to be their governors must arm themselves with the power which knowledge gives." Mr. Madison also said elsewhere, "Education is the true foundation of Civil Liberty."

Obama - Master and Commander 84. Mr. James Madison in a seated and relaxed pose in the lobby of his Library, the Madison Building of the Library of Congress.

OBAMA - MASTER AND COMMANDER

Obama - Master and Commander 85. Front entrance to the James Madison Building of the Library of Congress on Independence Avenue as viewed from the grounds of the Jefferson Building across the street. The architectural décor of Washington construction not only uses columns but also pillars in whatever size and dimension the architect may choose to adorn his structure.

"In the absence of sound oversight, responsible businesses are forced to compete against unscrupulous and underhanded businesses, who are unencumbered by any restrictions on activities that might harm the environment, or take advantage of middle-class families, or threaten to bring down the entire financial system."
Barack Obama, Remarks by the President Announcing the President's Export Council, July 7, 2007

"It was not a religion that attacked us that September day. It was al-Qaeda. We will not sacrifice the liberties we cherish or hunker down behind walls of suspicion and mistrust." **Barack Obama**, commemoration remarks, September 11, 2010

FREDERICK MONDERSON

Obama - Master and Commander 86. South or Independence Avenue entrance of the Adams Building of the Library of Congress.

Obama - Master and Commander 86a. Embassy of Switzerland/Cuban Interests Section.

OBAMA - MASTER AND COMMANDER

Obama - Master and Commander 87. Two of the doors of the Third Street Entrance to the Adams Building of the Library of Congress.

FREDERICK MONDERSON

Obama - Master and Commander 88. The Egyptian god of writing **Thoth** or **Djhuiti** and **Brahma**, the Indian God, among the twelve historical and mythological figures who introduced writing and knowledge to the people of their respective nations.

OBAMA - MASTER AND COMMANDER

Obama - Master and Commander 89. **Ts'ang Chieh**, the Chinese patron of writing and **Cadmus**, the Phoenician prince who brought the alphabet to Greece.

FREDERICK MONDERSON

Obama - Master and Commander 90. Nabu, the Akkadian god and Tahmurath, a hero of ancient Persia.

"On every front there are clear answers out there that can make this country stronger, but we're going to break through the fear and the frustration people are feeling. Our job is to make sure that even as we make progress, that we are also giving people a sense of hope and vision for the future." **Barack Obama**, Remarks at DSCC fundraiser, October 16, 2010

"There is not a liberal America and a conservative America - there is the United States of America. There is not a black America and a white America and a Latino America and an Asian America - there's the United States of America." **Barack Obama**, Democratic National Convention, 2004

8. MORMON, MORON or WHAT?
By
Dr. Fred Monderson

When pastors step over the line in "Endorsing" political candidates they sometimes "step in it" and this brings unwanted attention to them, their political choices and even the religion they seek to uphold as well as the one they deride. Such an event occurred recently which forces us to look at the players, the

OBAMA - MASTER AND COMMANDER

principles and the plight. At a recent Baptist convention, a Bishop, in seeking to endorse the candidacy of Governor Rick Perry of Texas, slammed the Mormon religion of former Massachusetts Governor Mitt Romney by saying his "is not true religion" but a "cult." The dictionary defines cult as "excessive admiration of a person or thing." Former Utah Governor Jon Huntsman in response, himself a Mormon, simply dismissed the Bishop as a "moron" instead who really was pursuing a personal agenda. So the question posed is whether religion should become an issue when it comes to Americans expressing their political views. This is especially so with the Constitution's stated dichotomy between "church and state." Nevertheless, evangelicals continue to push the envelope and since they vote in great numbers, politicians keep courting them. Nonetheless, whether individuals as the Bishop are really "morons" is another matter! But even more important, concomitantly, there are serious questions posed by African people due to their experience in these American States.

Obama - Master and Commander 91. Hermes or **Mercury**, the Greek and Roman messenger of the Gods and **Itzamna**, the Mayan god.

FREDERICK MONDERSON

Obama - Master and Commander 92. **Odin**, the Viking and Germanic creator of their alphabet and **Quetzalcoatl**, god of the Aztecs.

OBAMA - MASTER AND COMMANDER

Obama - Master and Commander 93. **Ogma**, the Irish god who invented the Gaelic alphabet and **Sequoyah**, a Cherokee Native American god.

We know, the Judaea/Christian religion dehumanized Africans and the Mormons excluded them. We know where Christian presidents have stood for centuries on the question of slavery in an independent and "free" society. Another valid question, is, what if Mitt Romney, a Mormon, becomes President of the United States, how will African people be treated? It also asks, if for argument sake, "All is forgiven" then the follow-up becomes, "Why were African Americans excluded from Mormonism, with the attendant ramifications, in the first place?" Even more contemporary, and adding to this controversy, Craig Bergman, Newt Gingrich's Iowa Political Director last week called Mormonism a "cult." then he quit his job! This new development has been so humiliating, hurtful, and totally out of character, Vice President Biden, himself a Catholic and naturally opposed to the Republican choices said he was "angry about the way they're treating Romney, whom I'm not crazy about, but ...." Now, here's a man of substance, of stature, who spoke up about a wrong! Remember, Edmund Burke did say, "The only thing necessary for evil to triumph is for good men to say nothing." Conversely, not a Republican has moved nor has any of them come to the assistance, defense or spoke out when the "Tea Party" and other Republicans attacked President Obama, his family, his faith and even his leadership.

FREDERICK MONDERSON

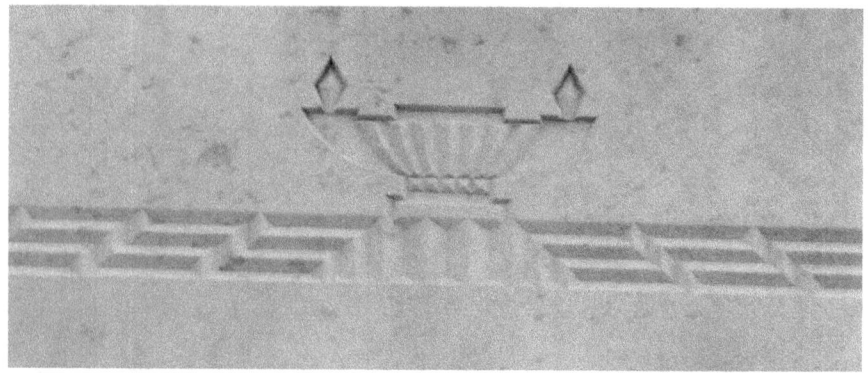

Obama - Master and Commander 94. The Lamp as a symbol of lighting the way to knowledge on the façade of the Adams Building.

Obama - Master and Commander 95. The Open Book or Scroll as a symbol containing knowledge decorates the Adams Building exterior.

OBAMA - MASTER AND COMMANDER

Obama - Master and Commander 96. Third Street Lobby art in the Adams Building.

FREDERICK MONDERSON

Exploring the roots of another but more sinister experience, Patti and Greaves in their *Hebrew Myths* describes "Noah's Curse" that have dehumanized African people for millennia and particularly in an age of "correction" political or otherwise, no one has sought to critique, challenge or even change this view. For centuries biblical scholars have examined the Bible and corrected themes, ideas and verses to bring them current with the literary reality of current times. Still, no one has entertained the thought of eliminating ethnically offensive elements in religious books that stigmatize and degrade African people. Christianity as part of the Judeo-Christian religious tradition accepted the Bible in whole and in part and allowed Noah's racism to remain part of the fundamental belief system that allowed Christian denominations to justify denying the humanity of black people. This carried over in their practicing of Christianity and remains an issue today.

Obama - Master and Commander 97. Close-up of the wall art in the Lobby of the Adams Building, from the Third Street entrance.

OBAMA - MASTER AND COMMANDER

Obama - Master and Commander 98. The floor decoration of the Lobby through the Third Street entrance of the Adams Building.

FREDERICK MONDERSON

Obama - Master and Commander 99. The West entrance and facade of the Adams Building of the Library of Congress on Second Street.

As such, history has shown this nation was principally founded on the principle of providing religious freedom to persons who were primarily persecuted in Europe because they may not have subscribed to Catholicism. This "One True Religion," as preached from the Papacy in Rome, the first Church, was founded on the "Rock of St. Peter." For centuries, the "Doctrine of the Two Swords" dogma has been that Christ gave St. Peter two swords, one temporal, one spiritual; to be wielded by two "Chief Executives." The King was permitted to reign over a temporal realm and the Pope over a spiritual realm of Christian Europe. Recognition of this duality kept Christian rulers in line despite their petty squabbles, wars and indiscretions, for by swearing allegiance to the Pope as religious leader of the Church, their people toed the line, because he held the key to the true other-worldly kingdom. Upon a King's death, the religious leader would administer *Extreme Unction*, the last Christian rite, and he would "Die in the Lord!" On the other hand, if the King appeared to be rebellious against the tenets of Christianity, then the Pope, affirming spiritual over temporal authority, would in turn excommunicate the ruler. This done, his people would then be justified in rebelling against that ruler and the Pope would therefore withhold *Extreme Unction* forcing the King to die a heretic! This state of religious/secular relationship existed from the time the Roman Emperor Constantine recognized Christianity as an official religion and organized the Council of Nicea in 325 A.D. This state of affairs held until Henry VIIIth broke with Rome in 1534 to establish the Anglican Church, and Martin Luther launched his religions revolution, the Reformation, a century later in 1617 by posting his **95 Theses** on the door of the Whitenburg Cathedral in

OBAMA - MASTER AND COMMANDER

Augsburg, Germany. This done, in response to the practicing religious hypocrisy, bigotry and corruption, this religious icon boldly asserted, "Here I stand, and I will not recant!" Apparently, in the Lilliputian world of American religious practice and bigotry, there were and are no giants of such caliber. Nevertheless, from that time onwards various denominations of the Christian Church began to take hold. Even as this was happening, religious persecution was ensuring, forcing the peopling of the "New World" where religious communities began forming along the extent of the colonized eastern Seaboard.

Obama - Master and Commander 100. A close-up view of the driveway of the Second Street entrance to the Adams Building.

Meanwhile the Crusade had been waged from the 12th Century where crusaders wore the Christian cross on their chest as they fought to rescue the "Holy Land" from the Muslim apostate. As this drama played out, the Renaissance exploded and the challenge of "New World" discovery gave rise to Christian conquistadors under an avaricious philosophic mindset of Gold, Glory and Gospel. In this they exterminated great numbers of Native Americans through the harsh reality of conquest and contact! More discoveries followed and this ultimately gave rise to colonization and rise of plantation culture requiring a tremendous labor force throughout the Americas. With the native population decimated under harsh condition and European colonists principally owning not working the land, Africans were chosen by default with the church's blessings.

FREDERICK MONDERSON

First, the Christian nations of Portugal and Spain, then Britain, France, Brandenbergers (Germans), the Dutch, Danish and finally America became involved in Slave Trade trafficking of Africans. This horrendous experience of "Middle Passage" and "Triangular Trade" cost Africa some 100 million souls according to W.E.B. DuBois, the first African American Harvard Ph.D. This is stated in his 1896 thesis entitled The *African Slave Trade to America* 1638-1880. Erik Williams' *Capitalism and Slavery* (1944) later provided much factual intricacies of Slave Trade phenomenon, from the perspective of the British involvement, thereby solidifying a correct interpretation of the unfolding drama.

However, while the secular Christian ruler was prohibited from dabbling in religious matters such as declaring himself *Pontifex Maximus*, the Pope as spiritual leader of the Western Church had embroiled himself in secular matters by dividing the "New World" lands between Portugal and Spain in 1492. This declaration was enshrined in a *Papal Bull* two years later in 1494 entitled the *Treaty of Tordesillas* that moved the *Line of Demarcation* some 200 Leagues to the West, giving Portugal a foothold in Brazil on the South American continent. Meanwhile Africans began to be "procured" and shipped to be enslaved in the "New World" plantation culture that was transforming the newly discovered lands. A primary justification for choosing Africans had been that they were non-Christian, non-Europeans, easily identified if they escaped from bondage, did not know the "New World" terrains and from a tropical environment could work well in "New World" agriculture.

Jim Duffy in the Penguin African Series *Portugal in Africa* pointed to the marble chair on the wharf of Luanda, Angola, in which the Bishop sat as he blest branded Africans being transported to the "New World" to engage in plantation slavery. At a much later time, President Obama visited Ghana, West Africa, where he was taken to Cape Coast Castle to view the slave dungeons. In the Plaza there, he noticed and remarked, "Slave owners who loved their children may have gone to worship in that church." However, as the barbarity of the Slave Trade unfolded, concern began to be expressed by abolitionists and French Philosophes such as Baron Montesquieu author of the *Spirit of the Laws*. In condemnation of the barbarity of the trade, Montesquieu argued "Either we are not Christians or the African are not men." Meanwhile, as this Christian nation enslaved Africans, the founding fathers declared independence from Britain and established the first Republic in the "New World." Founded as a Christian nation, America welcomed any and all persecuted persons for their religious beliefs and allowed them to practice their religion under protection of law though separate from political entanglement, enshrining the church and state dichotomy.

OBAMA - MASTER AND COMMANDER

Obama - Master and Commander 101. The lusciousness of the tree on a green parapet accentuates the rich and fullness of the Jefferson Building of the Library of Congress.

Obama - Master and Commander 102. The "Blashfield Mural Wheel of Knowledge" that depicts the pharaoh, symbolic of ancient Egypt at the foundation of knowledge that educated the world, particularly America.

FREDERICK MONDERSON

Significant in all this, notwithstanding, the new American nation guaranteed freedom of expression, and though Christianity predominated, Catholicism, Judaism, Islam and even Eastern Religions were permitted, "If they did not make much noise." Concomitantly, in this slaving society Africans had early sought an escape from slavery by becoming Christianized but masters soon closed this loophole because they could not reconcile sharing the equality of Christianity embodied in the philosophical principle of the "fatherhood of God and brotherhood of man," with their slaves. Still, without being fully aware of the early role played by fellow Africans in the birth and solidification of Christianity; that is, the great promise of redemption through forgiveness, salvation and resurrection appealed to Africans, while masters now encouraged conversion because the Bible had admonished "Slaves obey your masters!" Even more significant, however, literary Africans, free and enslaved, soon realized the power of the Bible and how influential and instrumental it would be in providing guidance and leadership to their people "Till Jerusalem comes." Hence, the African preacher became a significant force for change where he was permitted to offer religious consul, prove a hub for social connections and even provide the seed germ that plotted to subvert the social system that was oppressing his people

Nonetheless, in a society such as America where inequality existed *de facto* and *de jure* it stands to reason this was the general mindset and belief that inequality would be so in this world and the next. However, while benevolent masters gave their slaves "Sunday off to worship," in fact this meant they were to "repair the mechanism" for the grind of the week ahead. Alas, they did not allow them to sit beside or in the next pew at Sunday worship! Surprisingly, to meet the expanding needs of Christian conversion, churches began to have balconies from where the slave could participate if there was no space in the last pew. Perhaps this idea gave birth to the later "back of the bus" ridership syndrome that has had such challenges for race relations and changes in the social order.

What is even more important, the Declaration of Independence expressed "We hold these truths to be self-evident that all men are created equal, endowed by their creator with the inalienable right of life, liberty and the pursuit of happiness." However, as these sacred words were being uttered Africans were held in a vicious system that denied their very humanity. So much so, in formulation of the United States Constitution in order to leverage political representation for the South in the new order, "Three Africans were elevated to equate with two whites." This has been termed the "Three-fifths Compromise." Fact is; if three Africans were equal to two whites, then the African was considered two-third of a man! However, African Americans laboring in the vineyards of plantation slavery early figured a way to "game the system" and "put on ole Massa" by converting to Christianity that played such a significant role in the lives of people in this country. As this

OBAMA - MASTER AND COMMANDER

avenue was closed with effects on worship rules, African religious leaders as Bishops Allen and Absalom Jones formed their own church denominations such as the African Methodist Episcopal and African Methodist Episcopal Zion among others. What is interesting, as African people have fought for the right to worship and for religious recognition; they have grown sensitive to religious bigotry even if it applies to others.

Obama - Master and Commander 103. A mural that decorates as it encompasses the arch entrance with a caption indicating of the institution, "Founded in 1800, the Library of Congress is America's oldest federal cultural institution."

FREDERICK MONDERSON

Obama - Master and Commander 104. The famous John Flanagan's clock between the columns above the entrance to the Thomas Jefferson Building Reading Rooms.

OBAMA - MASTER AND COMMANDER

Obama - Master and Commander 105. Panoramic entrance to the Jefferson Library Lobby in all its splendor (left) and one of those exceptional Washington trees that double as a Christmas display stage (right).

FREDERICK MONDERSON

Obama - Master and Commander 106. Outside the Jefferson Building, image depicting the "Blashfield Mural Wheel of Knowledge."

The Mormon religion, founded by John Smith denied the humanity of African people and excluded them from membership of this exclusive group. Within the last decade this exclusionary practice has been charged and now an equally valid and revisited question is, "Why are blacks now included and to what extent is their inclusion valid." If so, "Why were they excluded in the first place?" Nevertheless, because of their history and religious experience in America, Blacks or African Americans are concerned about religious prejudice and stand unalterably opposed to such practices. They also remain mindful of the overwhelming pummeling the president received by "Tea Party" members trying to prove Barack Obama was Muslim to disqualify him from the office. Equally, he had to exert great effort to prove he was not and in fact is a practicing Christian. Even more important, the president went to great lengths to prove he was a President of all the people. So much so, he was accused of not showing partiality to Black people and this too is part of the multiplicity of prejudices this nation must rid itself of.

"Cutting the deficit by gutting our investments in innovation and education is like lightening an overloaded airplane by removing its engine. It may make you feel like you're flying high at first, but it won't take long before you feel the impact."
Barack Obama

"This is the moment when we must come together to save this planet. Let us resolve that we will not leave our children a world where the oceans rise and famine spreads and terrible storms devastate our lands." **Barack Obama**, Berlin Speech, July 2008

OBAMA - MASTER AND COMMANDER

"We didn't become the most prosperous country in the world just by rewarding greed and recklessness. We didn't come this far by letting the special interests run wild. We didn't do it just by gambling and chasing paper profits on Wall Street. We built this country by making things, by producing goods we could sell."
Barack Obama, Labor Day Speech, September 2010

"We have an obligation and a responsibility to be investing in our students and our schools. We must make sure that people who have the grades, the desire and the will, but not the money, can still get the best education possible." **Barack Obama**, during a speech, April 2011

"We need somebody who's got the heart, the empathy, to recognize what it's like to be a young teenage mom, the empathy to understand what it's like to be poor or African-American or gay or disabled or old - and that's the criterion by which I'll be selecting my judges." **Barack Obama**, Planned Parenthood Conference, July 2007

9. THE BRILLIANCE OF BARACK OBAMA
By
Dr. Fred Monderson

The brilliance of Barack Obama can be ascertained from a number of perspectives including the dynamics of his campaign strategy, his choices for key positions in his administration and the positively constructive manner in which he tackled the myriad problems facing the nation despite the unrelenting opposition from Republicans. However, if we focus on two examples, Civil Rights enforcement and the Auto Industry Bailout, these can be the exceptions that prove the rule!

It's generally agreed; everyone, critics and supporters alike, applauded President Obama on the choice of his cabinet and advisers and the fact they have fulfilled everyone's expectations with no large scale defections or resignations. Naturally, chided as he was for his selections, as St. Paul believed, "Every man to his own order," and President Obama's choice of both Democrats and Republicans certainly demonstrated his bi-partisanship attempts as a leader but despite such actions, Republicans were bent on making his tenure a failure. Let's not forget he chose Robert Gates as Secretary of Defense, because despite the fact he was a Bush holdover, you don't replace commanders during a war, especially when they are versed in the strategy and tactics of the enemy. Now in the fall of General Petraeus, a Republican, he has focused on chuck Hagel another Republican to replace him as Defense Secretary.

FREDERICK MONDERSON

Secretary of State Hillary Clinton, following in the footsteps of the brilliant Condoleezza Rice, has proved a formidable and knowledgeable replacement who brought a wealth of experience of a multi-faceted nature to the post. Timothy Geithner as Secretary of the Treasury must certainly be among the top 5 bureaucratic administrators of the world with a grasp of not just the American, but also the global economic infrastructure dynamics. The President's retention of Ben Bernanke, a Bush appointee at the **FEDS** is clearly brilliant. Even Eric Shinseki, a retired general officer to head the Department of Veterans Affairs is nothing short of brilliance, for who would understand the plight and concerns of veterans but a veteran himself. And so on down the line.

Again, probably the most important of all his appointments, the one of Eric H. Holder as Attorney General, has certainly helped shape the historical view of his Presidency. It is not inconceivable his wife Michele has had a role in this particular selection, given her roots, as a descendant of former slaves. Equally, the president's appointment of two women to the Supreme Court was consistent with his support for women who feature so prominently in his administration and his un ending efforts to help this important segment of the American population.

Obama - Master and Commander 107. Heads atop arched windows rest below architrave supporting a Corinthian colonnade itself supporting a cornice with top windows decorated with a pediment upper face.

OBAMA - MASTER AND COMMANDER

Obama - Master and Commander 108. Essentially the same features with a different decorated cornice.

FREDERICK MONDERSON

Obama - Master and Commander 109. Even more of the same features with the heads as the only difference going around the Building.

What is more important, however, because of the stellar credentials and his steadfast commitment to perform the functions of the office of Attorney General, Mr. Holder has beat back Republican attempts to impugn his performance but to no avail, showing he will not be constrained and will serve remarkably well in the areas of civil and black rights and their enforcement. Whereas, in the early days of his young administration, African American critics of Mr. Obama, perhaps out of ignorance, chided him for not appointing more African Americans in high visibility roles in his cabinet. They held this view, rather than recognizing the President chose the best people for those positions he thought would more effectively manage the daunting problems, in their assigned areas, that he inherited. That is why, as some have argued, he chose Rahm Emanuel as the "Pit Bull" to guard the White House gates. Conversely, he chose Eric Holder to rectify the Civil Rights issue because of his experience in this area. Even further, Civil Rights application and enforcement, which has not gotten the attention it deserve from previous Attorney Generals, has seen a turnaround in response to the issues.

The Attorney General, a general of law, is the top law enforcement officer in the country. Some have called him the people's lawyer since he represents the government comprising the people's representatives. In this role, the Attorney General prosecutes those who violate federal law and advises the President in legal matters, as well as representing the People in court. He heads the enormous bureaucracy of the Federal Bureau of Investigation; the Drug Enforcement Agency; the United States Marshals Services; Bureau of Alcohol, Tobacco, Firearms and Explosives; the Federal Criminal Division; Civil Rights Division;

OBAMA - MASTER AND COMMANDER

and the Bureau of Prisons. Equally, while he must ensure all facets of the law are effectively and efficiently administered, he has to pay more attention to Civil Rights legislation and enforcement more so than a great many of his predecessors did. Even more significant, in wake of his so called "controversial pronouncements" ranging from the *New York Post* "chimp cartoon," to the "fast and furious" debacle, civil rights violators and even Congressional lawmakers were all put on guard, "the new sheriff is quick on the draw" and takes his responsibilities seriously.

To have an understanding of Civil Rights statues, one must have an equal understanding of the history of Civil Rights legislation and gauge how and if the Attorney General is making any meaningful enforcement in its execution. Again, a glimmer of the brilliance of Barack Obama is reflected in his concern for Civil Rights since past and recent Attorney Generals did not seem to make this a priority; and now, hopefully, with the President's backing and blessing, Holder will.

Civil Rights legislation was first passed after the Civil War by the Radical Republican Congress who engineered the 13th Amendment that freed the slaves (1865); the 14th Amendment (1868), Section 1, accordingly read; "All persons born or naturalized in the United States, and subject to the jurisdiction thereof, are citizens of the United States and of the State wherein they reside. No State shall make or enforce any law which shall abridge the privileges or immunities of citizens of the United States; nor shall any State deprive any person of life, liberty, or property, without due process of law; nor deny to any person within its jurisdiction the equal protection of the laws." The 15th Amendment (1870), Article XV, Section 1 states: "The rights of citizens of the United States to vote shall not be denied or abridged by the United States on account of race, color, or previous condition of servitude."

Now, while the Harlem Renaissance highlighted artistic and intellectual capabilities of blacks, the Depression years took a tremendous toll on black aspirations for economic gains, as it did for so many others, whether in fair housing, quality education, physical safety and other basic human rights expressions. Notwithstanding, when government did not do for black Americans, civic organizations took the lead. One of the first, the Congress of Industrial Organizations, now part of the AFL-CIO, began hiring blacks along with whites during the Depression years. However, while this approach was still in its infancy, by the dawn of World War II, A. Philip Randolph threatened to march on Washington to demand industrial contractors engaged in the war effort hire black workers. This forced the hand of Franklin D. Roosevelt who passed an Executive Order addressing this malady in 1941, and at war's end; in fact, in 1948, President Truman, his successor, integrated the armed forces.

FREDERICK MONDERSON

Obama - Master and Commander 110. Still more of the previous features but this time the decorated cornice is missing.

Obama - Master and Commander 111. The decorated cornice is back.

However, getting there and after was a dusty road of black aspirations, and such, in the 1875 Civil Rights Act, amidst the waning years of Reconstruction, Congress declared it a misdemeanor to deny to anyone: "The full and equal privileges of inns, public conveyances on land or water, theaters, and other places of public amusement; subject only to the conditions and limitations established by law, and applicable alike to citizens of every race and color."

With the withdrawal of federal troops following the election of 1876 that signaled the end of Reconstruction, the Supreme Court rolled back most gains in Civil Rights up to that time. So much so, except for the 13th Amendment, the other Civil War Amendments were severely curtailed, especially during the year 1883, culminating in the "infamous" *Plessey V. Ferguson* decision of 1896 arguing for *separate but equal facilities*. As it has been said, you can lie with statistics; so too, as the Court stringently interpreted Civil Rights legislation claiming they were political not social rights or federal not state obligations and so on. In this, it could be argued; Attorney Generals did not act in the interest of the people! Nevertheless, people of goodwill were working to erode the stingy and innocuous interpretation of the law.

Still, the tide was turning, for since the *Dred Scott* Supreme Court decision of 1857 and culmination of Jim Crow legislation in *Plessey v. Ferguson* 1896, a number of legal activities slowly began to erode the bastions of racial suppression that limited full black participation in the constitutional guarantees. Within this mix, we cannot overlook the roles of Frederick Douglass and W.E.B. DuBois and so many others in emergent Civil Rights struggles; even while Booker T. Washington argued for "Gradualism" and technical rather than civil and political rights. Notwithstanding, as an example of important legal and constitutional decisions having an impact on Civil Rights expressions, the following may be mentioned:

The Civil Rights Act of 1875 gave equal rights to use of inns, theaters, public conveyances, and other facilities as well as including African Americans on juries. As John Newman and John Schmalback in *United States History* (1998: 296) informs: "The law was poorly enforced, however, because by this time, moderate and conservative Republicans had become frustrated with trying to reform an unwilling South - and also were afraid of losing white votes in the North."

Carl Brent Swisher's *Historic Decisions of the Supreme Court* (1958: 92) mentioned black "disillusionment" of prevailing events and surprisingly, in 1883, "the Supreme Court held that the Fourteenth Amendment had not given Congress substantive power to protect civil rights but only to correct abuses by the states. By this decision Congress was relieved of its basic obligation for the protection of civil rights of Negroes. Again the Court showed itself more concerned with the federal balance of power than with substantive rights."

1915 - Repeal of the "Grandfather Clause." The "Grandfather Clause" was part of the enormous and odious effort designed to deny blacks the right to vote aided by

FREDERICK MONDERSON

intimidation and terrorism perpetuated by organized bands including the KKK, White League and Knights of the White Camelia; Literary Tests requiring blacks to read and interpret any section of the Constitution; Poll Taxes; Property Ownership; and "Jim Crow" segregation on railroads, in restaurants, beaches and schools, and the list goes on, were hallmarks of the times some have labeled "The Age of American Terrorism." *The Klansman* by Thomas Dixon Paige and *Rising Tide of Color* by Lothrop Stoddard are excellent sources to study terrorism against blacks in the 19th and early 20th Centuries. The Democratic Party denied blacks membership and so, many, blacks did not vote. Where were the Attorney Generals, in those days of terror and intimidation? Who knows!

1915 - *Guinn v. United* States outlawed the White Primary as unconstitutional
1927 - *Nixon v. Herndon* - argued blacks could participate in Democratic Primaries
1932 - *Nixon v. Condon* - determined the White Primary was unconstitutional
1938 - *Missouri ex Relations Gaines v. Canada*
1944 - *Smith v. Albright* - outlaw *Garvey v. Townsend* (1935), ruling against the White Primary.
1950 - *Sweat v. Painter* - Supreme Court ordered the admission of a Negro to a white college.
1950 - *McLaren v. Oklahoma State Regents* -
1966 - *Harper v. Virginia State Board of Elections* - Outlawed Poll Taxes
1954 - *Brown v. Board of Education of Topeka, Kansas*, ruled that segregation for purposes of education was unconstitutional.
1957- Civil Rights Act – Created the Civil Rights Division in the Justice Department designed to enforce all "federal Civil Rights laws which prohibit discrimination, or national origin in the areas of voting, education, employment, and housing in the use of public facilities and public accommodations, and in the administration of federally assisted programs." This also created the Commission on Civil Rights, as Bone (1977: 253) notes "as an independent agency to investigate complaints of civil rights violation, review of government programs and recommend remedial action to the President and Congress."
1960 - Civil Rights Act - again Bone (1977: 253) writes "increased the penalties against any effort to obstruct either voting or the application of court orders designed to remove impediments to voting." Finally, the Justice Department was given the power to appoint "Referees," to "register potential voters where a court had found a 'pattern or practice' of discrimination. Even more, a new law made it a crime to destroy any voting records for 22 months after an election so that full documentary evidence would be available if any complaints come up."
1964 - Civil Rights Act - Can be considered as landmark as the 1954 *Brown V. Board* Case. Passed by President Lynden B. Johnson, its major provisions, according to Bone (1977: 253) were in the areas of:

OBAMA - MASTER AND COMMANDER

    Voting
    Public Accommodations
    Public Schools
    Private employment

1965 - Voting Rights Act - Provided that: "The Attorney General, with the concurrence of the Civil Service Commission may replace local registers by voting examiners where literacy and other tests are used and fewer than 50 percent of the voting-age individuals participated in the 1964 election." "When evidence indicates that literacy tests are being used as a means of discrimination, the federal registrar may suspend them."

1976 - In *McDonald and Laird v. Santa Fe Transportation Company*, the court ruled, "Whites as well as blacks were entitled to equal protection against discrimination under the 1870 and 1964 civil rights laws."

Obama - Master and Commander 112. Different heads but essentially the same features going around the Building.

FREDERICK MONDERSON

Obama - Master and Commander 113. Different heads, essentially the same features going around the Building, though the decorated cornice is missing.

Obama - Master and Commander 114. More of the same.

The state of Florida held the key in determining who became President in 2000. Clearly, while there was much confusion in the form of ballots used, many voters were disfranchised for one reason or another. This practice certainly continued in 2004 and given the numerous complaints raised in 2008, one could plainly see how Barack Obama, as a lawyer, would appoint Eric Holder, an experienced advocate to the Attorney General position to ensure that each vote gets counted! Again in the 2012 election process Republicans in control of state houses unleashed torrential efforts, whether ID requirements, mis-information, machine

OBAMA - MASTER AND COMMANDER

manipulation, even threats, etc., to dissuade Americans, particularly Blacks, from casting their ballot unrestricted. Clearly the Office of the Attorney General was instrumental in blunting the intended impact and the election results are as recorded.

Obama - Master and Commander 115. A wide colonnade, more heads and the cornice is more expansive.

In the Auto Bailout, Mr. Obama strategically and rightly theorized how important Detroit really was. While many, particularly Republican opposition considered this an improper move, the President saw it as essential to save jobs, strengthen this important industry and in the end, when it counted, as Vice President Biden would boast, "Osama bin-Laden is dead and General Motors is alive! Here we see the wisdom of Mr. Obama in stabilizing this important American economic artery.

Thus, the brilliance of President Obama may be manifest further because he believed Abraham Lincoln may be turning over in his grave when he realizes how descendants of the Radical Republicans have become timid regarding Civil Rights expressions of black people in America. After all, it was the Republican Party's abandonment of guarding the hard won rights of blacks that caused them to switch party in the 1932 election to vote for Democrat Franklin Roosevelt. Perhaps this is why Barack Obama appointed Eric Holder as Attorney General, among other things, but importantly, so that he would vigilantly guard the enforcement of the cherished attainment of Civil Rights enjoyment. Therefore, this appointment can be added to the mountain of evidence extolling the brilliance of Barack Obama. As such, hold fast to cherished ideals for there is more to come in this second term!

FREDERICK MONDERSON

"Focusing your life solely on making a buck shows a certain poverty of ambition. It asks too little of yourself. Because it's only when you hitch your wagon to something larger than yourself that you realize your true potential." **Barack Obama**

Obama - Master and Commander 116. A head above a head that is between a colonnade.

OBAMA - MASTER AND COMMANDER

Obama - Master and Commander 117. Front of the Jefferson Building showing a Pediment feature depicting a different head backed by circular glass window and a baby angelic figure above looking down.

FREDERICK MONDERSON

Obama - Master and Commander 118. Front of the Jefferson Building showing a Pediment feature with a different type of head backed by circular glass window and a baby angelic figure above looking down crowned by Corinth abaci supporting an architrave beneath an intricately decorated cornice.

OBAMA - MASTER AND COMMANDER

"When I heard that BP was not moving fast enough on claims, we told BP to set aside $20 billion in a fund - managed by an independent third party - to help all those whose lives have been turned upside down by the spill." **Barack Obama**, remarks at Xavier University, August 2010

"Where the stakes are the highest, in the war on terror, we cannot possibly succeed without extraordinary international cooperation. Effective international police actions require the highest degree of intelligence sharing, planning and collaborative enforcement." **Barack Obama**, speaking about international cooperation in 2008

"One of the great strengths of the United States is ... we have a very large Christian population - we do not consider ourselves a Christian nation or a Jewish nation or a Muslim nation. We consider ourselves a nation of citizens who are bound by ideals and a set of values." **Barack Obama**, press conference in Turkey, April 2009

10. THANK GOD FOR BARACK OBAMA!

By
Dr. Fred Monderson

In respect to the faith, morals and ethical qualities of Barack Obama as a role model for black men and women, and all people in general, the **Bible** provides excellent example of analogous descriptions and in this respect Proverbs 12: 4 states "A virtuous woman is a crown to her husband;" again, "Who can find a virtuous woman? For her price is far above rubies" and "The heart of her husband doth safely trust in her" (**Proverbs** 31: 10-11). "Her Husband is known in the gates, when he sitteth among the elders of the land" (**Proverbs** 31: 23) and "Strength and honor are her clothing" (**Proverbs** 31: 25). "In her tongue is the law of kindness. She looketh well to the ways of her household, and eateth not the bread of idleness. Her children arise up and call her blessed" (**Proverbs** 31: 26-28). Equally, "Many daughters have done virtuously, but thou excellent them all. Favor is deceitful, and beauty is vain; but a woman that feareth the Lord, she shall be praised. Give her of the fruit of her hands; and let her own works praise her in the gate" (**Proverbs** 31: 29-31). Now the analogy is not about the sex of the individual and as such can be applied to President Barack Obama. However, as an intelligent woman, Michelle Obama is a fine example; an asset to so many and much of this can apply to her as well, being the backbone of a loving family, the "wind behind Barack's sails." However, flip the switch and Michelle Obama could

FREDERICK MONDERSON

be uttering these same sentiments about her beloved. Notwithstanding, here's a profound case for the line of reasoning developed in this argument and why specifically it applies to Barack Obama. For when we examine the moral frailties of man today, Obama stands as a giant in the land of Lilliputian individuals, Republicans and even people of questionable character, tainted morals and bereft of ethical values.

In addition, Mr. Obama has consistently demonstrated qualities of the quintessential leader. As such, one would suppose even his opponents would want to emulate him. However, because they are supposed to be ideologically opposed to him, many probably and secretly affirm, "If only I could, but ...." The reason is quite obvious and has been observable over the last three years, it is clearly evident. Mr. Obama is a leader beaming with confidence, calm and very collected. Not only so but he also engenders confidence in right thinking people. Even more important, while "Tea Party" members, racists and reactionaries bombarded his "cloaking device" Mr. Obama remained unrelenting in pursuit of his objectives, goals and his foes. He never gave up on the American people in whom he placed great confidence, unendingly trying to better their lot.

One of the planks of his campaign was that he would meet with America's enemies and if they would unclench their fists, he would extend a hand! When he met with Venezuela's Hugh Chavez, he was severely excoriated by Republican opponents. Conversely, from day one of his Presidency opposition mounted and Senator Mitch McConnell articulated his "Mandate." Yet, the President met with him. Still, McConnell never changed his intent to make the president a one termer! House Speaker John Boehner disrespected President Obama by not returning his phone calls during the "Debt Ceiling Debate," yet the President met and even played golf with him. Joe Wilson called the President a "Liar" in the House Chamber then wanted to meet with him to apologize, to which the President said No! Send it in the mail! Significantly, Republicans never objected to his still meeting with their members who opposed the President in the most vehement manner.

Demonstrating the seriousness with which he approached his responsibilities, when it came to the pursuit of Somali Pirates he said "Take the shot!" With Osama bin Laden, that famous War Room photo showed the President's "thousand yards stare;" out of leadership concern, as events unfolded in real time. Doing his job as Commander-in-Chief he pursued Al-Awlaki by deploying his drones. Today he is fighting for jobs for Veterans. That is why men in uniform love President Obama, a man not just beaming with confidence; he does not bear malice but chooses the best advisers and remains on task. In that he emphasizes clean energy, better treatment of the environment, "bringing the boys home," infrastructure development, consistent and meaningful research and development in clean and affordable energy, while insisting on revolutionary change in education to return this nation to its top of the line competitive status.

OBAMA - MASTER AND COMMANDER

In the history of this nation, the fate and faith of black men have consistently been issues despite their positive contributions, accomplishments and sacrifices. Now, add to this the childlike and stupid behavior and antics of some black men who have opened themselves to ridicule and we are forced to ask what has happened to the moral and ethical stalwarts of the African pantheon and their role as inspiration to encourage the young to rise to even greater heights. In examination of the roles of these ancestor greats, we can begin with Crispus Attucks who gave his life to spark the American Revolution; Benjamin Banneker, mathematician, scientist, astronomer who created a calendar and helped plan Washington, DC's streetscape; and Salem Po who was among those "Watching George Washington's back." Despite the circumstances of their day, these men demonstrated noble character and exemplary spirit, while rising to extraordinary challenges in the restricted world in which they were forced to live. Also, let us not forget Cinque in the *Amistad* slave ship issue, for together with him was courageous men possessing high ideals and unquestioned integrity despite the hopelessness of their plight. To this lot we could add revolutionaries Gabriel Prosser and Denmark Vesey as well as David Walker who made his "Appeal" in 1826. These latter can very well be equated with Nat Turner who is certainly entitled to claim that revolutionary statement, "I only regret I have one life to give for the freedom of my people." Comedian Dick Gregory recently took to task blacks who painted Bill Clinton "black" but questioned whether Barack Obama was also black! Then if Bill Clinton is black, so too was John Brown who gave his all and William Lloyd Garrison Abolitionist and newspaperman whose organ *The Liberator* championed the cause of African American freedom!

Black abolitionists such as Rev. Henry Highland Garnet, William Wells Brown, Prince Saunders, Lunsford Lane and Charles Lenox Remond, in an "Age of Dred Scott," whose name resounds in American inequality, and Frederick Douglass, "father of the protest movement," who founded the *North Star* newspaper proved a powerful spokesman against slavery and in defense of the humanity of black men and women. These were all men of high morals, tenacious fortitude and unbounded integrity and whose efforts significantly impacted their time and later. Despite the pressing handicaps posed by such groups as the Ku Klux Klan, Jayhawkers, White Brotherhood, Black Cross Cavalry, they still chose to be relevant and history has certainly taken note. Booker T. Washington was a man of great and exemplary resourcefulness, vision and diplomatic suavity who set out to improve black economic capabilities by teaching skills to freedmen to enable them to capitalize on opportunities presented in emerging and expanding American industrialization. Mr. Washington's successes in this venture were seriously dependent on the goodwill of benefactors based on his likability, suaveness and more especially his credibility to make his dream a reality. After all, he had to "con," I mean convince, liberal philanthropists to buy into his idea of "Negro upliftment" through industrial skills in order to fund his enterprise. Naturally, his every thought, word, deed and move was probably scrutinized 24/7 for

FREDERICK MONDERSON

adversaries, which they were certainly many, probably sought to derail his every effort. Yet still, because of his upstandishness he was able to succeed and in process left Tuskegee Institute as an outstanding testimony to his efforts, the legacy which enabled men of unquestioned character and high ideals to soar to even greater heights.

Marcus Garvey was a man of unbounded faith and confidence who believed in the significance of the African heritage that had contributed to the progress of humanity. This was even though he did not fully comprehend nor was privy to the full impact of the African past as explained in the archaeological bonanza of evidence unearthed during the year from 1870-1930. His worldwide following grew and sustained itself because he enmeshed himself in that African cultural heritage which significantly underscored his iconic image as a powerful leader. This was at a time when African people worldwide were socially victimized despite laws that mandated the government provide protections all citizens were entitled to. He also believed that motif, symbolism and substantive actions were powerful antidotes to social ostracism. Hence, as Marcus Garvey would say, "I looked for Africa's men of big affairs and finding none," because of the continent's prostate state, "I created titles as Duke of the Nile and Count of the Congo." He created the Red, Black and Green flag motif as symbolism that still has a life of its own a century later. His organization, the Universal Negro Improvement Association (**UNIA**) and Negroes League created a Black Cross Corps of Nurses and the *Negro World* newspaper became the organ to get the message out undergirded by an economic philosophy that emphasized self-reliance and self-sufficiency. He initiated the concept of black economic internationalism through commerce involving America, the Caribbean and Africa. All this he preached under the mantra of "One God, One Aim, One Destiny!" Equally, to accomplish much of this he created the shipping network Black Star Line. Unfortunately, this particular enterprise was grossly sabotaged and it drained important financial resources from the parent organization allowing others, even law enforcement, to call into question Garvey's management skills and his use of funds collected through the mail from his followers.

OBAMA - MASTER AND COMMANDER

Obama – Master and Commander 119. Front of the Jefferson Building showing another Pediment feature with a different type of head backed by circular glass window and a baby angelic figure above looking down crowned by Corinth abaci supporting an architrave beneath an intricately decorated cornice.

FREDERICK MONDERSON

Obama - Master and Commander Obama 120. Front of the Jefferson Building showing still another Pediment feature with a different type of head backed by circular glass window and a baby angelic figure above looking down crowned by Corinth abaci supporting an architrave beneath an intricately decorated cornice. This time heads of two ladies crown the window decoration of the floor below.

OBAMA - MASTER AND COMMANDER

Obama - Master and Commander 121. Front of the Jefferson Building showing another Pediment feature with a different type of head backed by circular glass window and a baby angelic figure above looking down crowned by Corinth abaci supporting an architrave beneath an intricately decorated cornice. This time the glass door gives access to the veranda of the second floor.

FREDERICK MONDERSON

Obama - Master and Commander 121a. Two females crown an arched doorway to the Jefferson Building with four columns sporting Ionic capitals.

It's been shown, in over three hundred years of slavery there were some 250 slave rebellions and they were all betrayed by blacks who had infiltrated their planning circles and reported this to the authorities. In similar manner, blacks close to Garvey sabotaged his principal ship by destroying parts, using defective parts, and overstating maintenance costs. Blacks also helped the government build a case of mail fraud for which he was convicted and sent to Atlanta's federal prison. On way to do his time, handcuffed, Marcus Garvey raised his manacled arms and boasted,

OBAMA - MASTER AND COMMANDER

"You have caged the lion, but the cubs are running free out there." The cubs he referred to became significant global players such as in the case of Kwame Nkrumah, first President of Ghana in West Africa who, while he studied in America as a young student, was tremendously influenced by Marcus Garvey's writings particularly the book *Philosophy and Opinions of Marcus Garvey*.

Strange that Nkrumah had become so thoroughly Garveyite, W.E.B. DuBois handed over leadership of the "Pan African Movement" at the 5th Pan African Conference at Manchester in 1945. From this mantle he unleashed the onslaught that led to wholesale freedom of the African continent. Other cubs of Garvey were brave American blacks motivated and schooled by Garvey's efforts that kept the UNIA an operational philosophy and movement long after Garvey's deportation and death. Among these may be mentioned Queen Mother Moore, Noble Drew Ali, and especially Elijah Mohammed who schooled and impacted Malcolm X and Louis Farrakhan.

W.E.B. DuBois was a great African American intellectual, by today's standards a revolutionary giant, the father of "Pan Africanism," as well as a prolific writer and founding member of the National Association for the Advancement of Colored People (**NAACP**). However, caught in the vortex of the struggle for black leadership in the early years of the 20th Century, W.E.B. DuBois challenged and attacked Marcus Garvey. Because Garvey was a full-blooded black man from Jamaica, West Indies, he had issues with "mixed blacks" at home and this extended to DuBois in America. However, DuBois also had an issue with Washington, who, in time perspective, had seen the need for and utility of learning industrial skills by the black man. DuBois on the other hand, wanted civil rights and intellectual advancement and opportunities, particularly for his "Talented Tenth" of individuals who would lead the race. However, despite its good intentions, this was an elitist aspiration that could not appeal to the broad masses that Washington's approach was seeking to include. However, years later, after the dust had settled, DuBois saw and praised the wisdom and work of Marcus Garvey who by that time had risen to remembrance in iconic proportions. All this notwithstanding, in the minds and hearts of the people, these men possessed tremendous moral resourcefulness and a century later their names and significance are still powerful reservoirs of inspiration and topics of discussion because such men were single-mindedly devoted to upliftment of the black man in America and to the extent that it did, worldwide.

In the struggle to uplift a race of people the next generation of men of honor saw Paul Robeson, a man of high aspirations and noble character pursuing high ideals, withstand assaults on his very humanity. Still, he held firm to pass on the spirit of nobleness embodied in the work of A. Philip Randolph and Rev. Fred Shuttlesworth who laid the foundation for Martin Luther King, Rev. Joseph Lowery and John Lewis, men of distinction and unblemished character. These

FREDERICK MONDERSON

tillers of the vineyard paved the way for a bright young Obama to move the ball nearer the goal post of the "dream" Dr. King envisioned.

In Barack Obama America was blest to have a leader of extraordinary moral qualities, possessing a keen mind, an intellectual visionary with futuristic insights as well as a tremendous work ethic and we could never overstate the power of his infectious smile and wonderfully supportive family structure.

Obama - Master and Commander 122. Two more females crown an arched doorway to the Jefferson Building with four columns sporting Ionic capitals.

OBAMA - MASTER AND COMMANDER

Obama - Master and Commander 123. View of the Capital Building's Dome as seen from the balcony of the Plaza of the Jefferson Building.

Obama - Master and Commander 123a. A mural depicting a beauty beside "Hail thou goddess sage and holy, Hail divine and melancholy."

Coming into national prominence and upon his announcement to make a run for the Presidency Barack faced significant challenges from people of all persuasions. That is, particularly from within the Democratic Party, many of whose members

FREDERICK MONDERSON

had, whether through perceived abilities of the other principal candidate or owed prior commitments to the Clinton machine made their choice for the position. The organizational dynamics and logistical challenges inherent in the audacity of this declaration notwithstanding, the opposition attacked Mr. Obama with a viciousness unparalleled. However, having secured the Democratic nomination in a united party, racial opposition emerged and coalesced in the "Tea Party Movement" that attacked young Obama with a vehemence in-clandestine calling into question his very humanity, not to mention his patriotism, citizenship, leadership experience, etc. Everyone is familiar how these opportunists used Mr. Obama's race as a rallying cry demonstrating vituperative racial venom, ludicrous characterization, pressuring him more than any other aspirant to the office of president. This assault continued well into his assumption of the mantle of leadership of the American nation. In a sustained effort to derail his presidency Republicans threw everything at President Obama, including the "kitchen sink," by blocking his legislative agenda while catering to the interests of a rich minority. Nevertheless, the most significant realization in all of this has been Mr. Obama's character as he withstood the best they could muster and smiled. Like Booker T. Washington's room after it was cleaned, they could find no dirt on Obama! Strange, a black man without skeletons in his closet simply armed with good intentions and an honest desire to rescue his nation from the perdition it did not deserve, is not only a rarity but invidious minds see him as a threat because he could and would expose them!

As his detractors bombarded Mr. Obama with all manner of accusations, hideous characterizations, even attempting to impugn his patriotism and that of his wife, the one thing they could not sully was his moral character. After all, Mr. Obama never "hiked the Appalachian Trail;" Michelle would never permit it! He was too busy working as a Community Organizer bringing about social change to send racy pictures in the mail; and he certainly would never think of misbehaving in public restrooms. Meanwhile he remained overwhelmingly committed to doing the people's business of rescuing his beloved nation, countering Republican obstructionism and meeting all the challenges his office was dedicated to tackling. Abroad he was the epitome of "Presidential timber" and this won respect for America on the world stage. When we consider how racial characterization has attacked the flaws in any black man's character blocking any and all aspirations of high ideals, we have to thank God Barack Obama, Colin Powell's "transformational figure" full of "spark," fire, was wise, careful and circumspect enough to prepare for that eventuality and "best the best of their bad lot." In all this, an unmistaken fact has been the profound religious conviction that armor plated all included here. In fact, many have been more Christ-like that most American Christians for they manifested that godlike fire from being baptized in the revolutionary consciousness that had spurred Jesus on his way to speak truth to power. These black men of boundless faith manifested the highest aspiration of the human spirit for, having risen from the depths of the cauldron of American hypocrisy they could still look back pitifully and affirm as members of the human

OBAMA - MASTER AND COMMANDER

family, we must co-exist under the philosophic tenet of the "fatherhood of god and the brotherhood of man!" Thank God Barack Obama was a member of this Choir!

"Even when folks are hitting you over the head, you can't stop marching. Even when they're turning the hoses on you, you can't stop." **Barack Obama**

"With patient and firm determination, I am going to press on for jobs. I'm going to press on for equality. I'm going to press on for the sake of our children. I'm going to press on for the sake of all those families who are struggling right now. I don't have time to feel sorry for myself. I don't have time to complain. I am going to press on." **Barack Obama**, speech to Congressional Black Caucus, September 2011

Obama - Master and Commander 124. Above a doorway to the Jefferson Building, an enthroned figure is sandwiched by two angelic infants while seated are historical figures of Greece with Music; a religious figure with a Christian Cross; a Mosaic personality; and an Egyptian pharaoh.

"That is the true genius of America, a faith in the simple dreams of its people, the insistence on small miracles. That we can say what we think, write what we think, without hearing a sudden knock on the door. That we can have an idea and start our own business without paying a bribe or hiring somebody's son. That we can participate in the political process without fear of retribution, and that our votes will be counted - or at least, most of the time." **Barack Obama**, speech at Democratic National Convention, 2004

FREDERICK MONDERSON

11. OBAMA: ELITIST? NO!
By
Dr. Fred Monderson

Governor Rick Perry of Texas recently accused President Obama of being "elitist" and that he came from a privileged background and didn't understand ordinary people's problems. Mr. Perry claimed Mr. Obama "never had to really work for anything. He never had to go through what Americans are going through." Perry said further, "We need a president who has been through their ups and downs in life and understands what it's like to have to deal with the issues of our economy that we have today in America." In fact, it is Mr. Perry who should be accused of being elitist having had the most significant form of support, a two parent family, to enjoy this privilege. We know Mr. Obama loves basketball but there was no father to cheer as he shot his many jumpers. In Middle and High school there was no "Basketball Mom" to not only cheer, but to pull him out of the Principal's Office. Mr. Obama attended Columbia and Harvard Universities, but there was no mom to be proud at graduation and to enjoy the luncheon and laughter that followed. Mr. Obama was not elitist; he was hardy and full of ambition. Very early he realized hard work is the American way and pulled himself up by his own, not his parents', bootstraps! Much later, Mitt Romney would state "students should borrow money from their parents." There was no money for Obama to borrow nor parents who possessed such resources.

Mr. Perry's campaign has been declining in the polls after his macho image suffered from a number of factors fueled by mis-steps on his part. Backed by an image of never losing an election, Governor Perry rolled out and challenged Governor Romney for front-runner status, but to no avail! Giving a speech in New England he was accused of being intoxicated! At a recent Republican debate he could not remember the name of a government department he wants to abolish! His cliché "Oops" became a household word! Widening the scope of his focus, he challenged Nancy Pelosi to debate. The former Speaker of the House, now minority leader, offered three reasons why she could not debate Mr. Perry. The first two were prior out of state commitments and taking a jab at Mr. Perry, simply stated she could not remember the third reason for not debating him. Now, in a mad dash to still appear relevant, he launched a broadside on the President in the claim he was "elitist." Mr. Perry may have opened a mischievous "can of worms" with this new challenge. Perhaps it was because he is running out of ideas to rescue his fledging campaign. Nevertheless, he has unintentionally given Mr. Obama an issue that can tremendously aid his re-election campaign. Follow me on this as I frame this particular line of argument.

First, when the ramifications of "Nigger Mountain" surfaced regarding a sign on his family farm, Governor Perry responded that "In 1984 my father painted over the sign" despite claims the offensive epithet was still visible over the years when

OBAMA - MASTER AND COMMANDER

Mr. Perry became a Texas State Senator, Minister of Agriculture and Governor. However, "Nigger Mountain" aside, the governor's answer itself betrays the validity of his criticism of President Obama. Governor Perry's excuse unintentionally cloaked in his father's actions inadvertently counterpoises the man he is criticizing. Governor Perry came from a functionally intact family and perhaps still enjoys benefits from the luxury of having a father who must have certainly been influential in his rise to prominence as a politician and as an American of substance and equally the joys of a mother's comforting words and encouragement.

On Mr. Obama's part, perhaps it's because he had "nuts" the size of "watermelons," intellectual fortitude, vision and a terrific work ethic to support his declaration for the US Presidency. Most important he cultivated a closet devoid of skeletons! Thus, in this venture Barack Obama was both troubling and attractive to large segments of the American electorate. Those to whom he was attractive donated to his campaign, volunteered to get the word out and voted in unprecedented numbers to effectuate the possibility Mr. Obama could have been elected President. Those to whom this possibility appeared troubling coalesced in the "Tea Party Movement" and other anti-Obamite efforts who launched unrelenting attacks on the person, integrity and capability of the probability of an Obama Presidency.

Obama - Master and Commander 125. Entrancing the Jefferson Building, images of two angelic youths crown engaged stone pillars with curved Ionic capitals

FREDERICK MONDERSON

Obama - Master and Commander 126. More of the same two angelic figures at the entrance to the Jefferson Building, who crown engaged stone pillars with curved Ionic capitals.

One of the early drum majors of this phalanx of negativity was "Joe the Plumber" who exploited his "15 minutes" before the *New York Post* depicted Mr. Obama, in a political cartoon, flushing "Joe the Plumber" down the bowl! In his rise to fame, Joe accused Mr. Obama of being a "socialist" because, perhaps ahead of his time Obama perceived and may have precipitated recognition of the conditions that spawned "Occupy Wall Street," that has extended across local, national and international landscapes. Joe, who incidentally was not a registered plumber, purportedly got a singing contract, and now has reappeared from oblivion to run for political office seeking to become a Congressman. Fast, fast forward to the 2012 national election, he was endorsed by Allen West. As faith would have it; they both lost!

In addition, the attack on Mr. Obama questioned his patriotism, birthright, his judgment, memory, foreign policy experience and even his religious affiliation and association. However, one thing they could not do was produce any women, especially "blondes," to contend, either Mr. Obama had "fondled them" or, "they had a relationship." Of course, there was one woman of whom the *New York Post* published a photo, doctored to falsely show Mr. Obama looking at her backside! This is particularly significant because he has been a man of extraordinary faithfulness to his married partner and equally shown great respect for his children. The irony here is that while not having had the growing childhood security of love

OBAMA - MASTER AND COMMANDER

and experience of a two-parent family, Mr. Obama was still the epitome of what the truest Americans, and all people, wanted in a practicing family relationship. Nevertheless, the criticisms, like that of Governor Perry have kept coming.

Some years ago, my eldest daughter was visited by a friend named Yvette, as I was on my knees cleaning the kitchen floor. My daughter remarked, "See my father on his knees cleaning the floor." To this Yvette responded. "I did not have the privilege of having a father!" The same can be said for Mr. Obama!

Barack Obama's parents separated early and his father later died in an automobile accident. Here we have a young African from Kenya who met a young white female from Kansas. They fell in love, conceived, got married and separated. Happy to have her child, despite whatever perceived stigma, his mother chose to raise young Barack. That famous photo of the two of them together says a great deal. He tells how a single mother raised him, would help with homework, and even got food stamps and welfare assistance from the government. When his mother passed and "Grandmother Toots" stepped up to Barack's plate, she lived in a modest apartment in Honolulu, Hawaii. From here she showered him with love, philosophic insights and cultivated his work ethic and respect for the human spirit.

As a student, in "Black Community Problems" class, I'm reminded of college Professor Leonard James' analogy of the bird feeding in a black urban environment compared to one in an affluent white neighborhood. In the former, the bird would swoop down to drink from pools of water caught by the curb from some recent downpour. On the other hand, in the latter case, however, a stone or marble fountain or bird bath greeted our feathered friend. Interestingly however, these diametrically opposed scenarios contrast the life stations of the growing Perry and Obama youths. The reality of a single mother raising a child, that is a white mother raising a black boy, is an experience that can fill many *Encyclopedia American* or *Britannica* volumes and undermines any purported claims Governor Rick Perry could raise regarding the growing experiences of a Barack Obama. Even more, while Mr. Perry had both father and mother who provided family nurture, comfort, guidance and support, Mr. Obama had no father, then no mother, then no grandparents. Even more importantly, only recently Governor Perry was still able to enjoy the wonderful benefits of a loving mother who publicly proclaimed, "He was a good boy" as he grew. All this despite former President Bill Clinton professing Governor Perry is "a good looking rascal!"

It's arguable the memory of his mother's plight as a single parent raising a child has influenced Mr. Obama's efforts as president forcing him to recognize, assist and showcase the role of women in his administration and across the American social and political landscape. Contemporary records portray the plight of single female households in this country.

FREDERICK MONDERSON

The putative record shows non-Hispanic white single female-headed households at 24 percent of the population; Black or African 67; American Indian 53; Asian and Pacific Islander 16; Hispanic or Latino 40; and overall 34 percent of American families are headed by single parents. Even in Texas, Governor Perry's state, non-Hispanic whites are 23 percent of the population headed by single parents; Black or African American 62; Asian and Pacific Islander 12; Hispanic or Latino 39; and total are 35 percent.

Without a doubt, women played an important role in galvanizing support for Mr. Obama's victory in 2008. Perhaps this support was instrumental in passage of President Obama's first substantial legislative accomplishment, the Lilly Ledbetter Fair Play Restoration Act granting women equal pay for equal work. But it is not simply that women should get equal pay because of low wages. It is also an attempt to address the financial strain of being single women who are victims of high rates of poverty, whose young experience rates of poverty, in this vicious cycle that Governor Perry could never imagine. These factors contribute to problems as domestic violence against women and other debilitating experiences that act against the best interests of women and child in society. Couple this with the demands of childcare, health care, school concerns of the young and even insurance which affects the health and well being of women and their family. Still, more women than men, then and now, support Obama.

Obama - Master and Commander 127. Above a doorway to the Jefferson Building, an enthroned and beautifully dressed female figure holds a book and is assisted by two angelic youthful figures who also manage books.

OBAMA - MASTER AND COMMANDER

Obama - Master and Commander 128. Still more of the images of two angelic youths crown engaged stone pillars with curved Ionic capitals at the entrance to the Jefferson Building.

Obama - Master and Commander 129 Beneath an arch crowning a doorway of the Jefferson Building, an enthroned female seemingly comforting a youth and holding an instrument confers with seated Native Americans.

FREDERICK MONDERSON

Beyond "Lilly" and the significant roles women were assigned in his administration, President Obama signed an Executive Order creating a White House Council for Women and Girls. Accordingly, "The purpose of this council is to ensure that American women and girls are treated fairly in all matters of public policy," the President said in a statement. "My administration has already made important progress toward that goal. I am proud that the first bill I signed into law was the Lilly Ledbetter Fair Pay Restoration Act. But I want to be clear that issues like equal pay, family leave, child care and others are not just women's issues, they are family issues and economic issues. Our progress in these areas is an important measure of whether we are truly fulfilling the promise of our democracy for all our people. I am confident that Valerie Jarrett and Tina Chen will guide the Council wisely as its members address these important issues."

The council, the White House says, "will provide a coordinated federal response to the challenges confronted by women and girls and to ensure that all Cabinet and Cabinet-level agencies consider how their policies and programs impact women and families."

Mr. Obama's adviser and friend Valerie Jarrett heads the Council and in clear contradiction of Governor Perry's contention, Mr. Obama had said: "I sign this order not just as president, but also as a son, a grandson, a husband and a father, because growing up, I saw my mother put herself through school to follow her passion for helping others." He also said. "But I also saw how she struggled to raise me and my sister on her own, worrying about how she would pay the bills, educate herself and provide for us." Thus, this initiative is designed to include support by providing (1) college grants for single mothers; (2) comprise a global health initiative; (3) offer scholarships for mothers willing to return to school to further their education; (4) and it will also address obesity concerns, job training programs, and naturally all the benefits that come with Health Care Reform.

The most recent initiative of Mr. Obama concern for women particularly as well as his re-election strategy is to further involve women in unfolding events of the exciting year ahead. The following memo from his wife Michelle puts the concerns and states the case best.

From: Michelle Obama
Sent: Monday, November 14, 2011
Subject: Women for Obama

Friends,

As I have traveled across the country, I have had the privilege of meeting incredible women from all walks of life. From young women paying their own

OBAMA - MASTER AND COMMANDER

way through college, to moms working the extra shift to keep food on the table, to women struggling to make ends meet during retirement.

We talk about their bills, their children - how they're constantly striving to strike that balance between work and family. And no matter what kind of challenges they're facing, they don't complain. They just work harder.

This is what we do as women. We persevere. Because no matter our ages, backgrounds, or stations in life, we are determined to leave a better world for our children and give them opportunities we never even dreamed of.

Women have always been the heart of the Obama organization. We make up nearly half of the American workforce and are the majority of students in America's colleges and universities. We're the primary caregivers for our children and seniors. We're the heads of households and workplaces across the country.

And right now, it's time for us all to dig deep, step up, and keep building this campaign together: person by person, discussion by discussion.

Today, we are officially launching Women for Obama - and I am incredibly honored to be serving as its chair. This is a special group dedicated to growing this campaign from the ground up. Because we know better than anyone that movements for real and lasting change have got to start at the grassroots - and they're sustained by the relationships we develop with one another. Together, that's what we're going to do - build relationships with supporters, new and old, and grow this campaign - one woman at a time.

I wanted to ask you myself if you'll sign on to join us.

The stories of the incredible women I meet serve as a constant reminder of why we're all here: because American families all around the country are facing very real problems. They're balancing mortgage payments and utilities bills with full-time jobs and raising children. They're struggling to make ends meet while still trying to put money aside to send their kids to college one day.

Barack understands these issues because he's lived them. He was raised by a single mother who struggled to put herself through school and pay the bills. When she needed help, Barack's grandmother stepped in, waking up every morning before dawn to take a bus to her job at a bank. And even though she worked hard and was good at what she did, she ultimately hit a glass ceiling and was passed over for promotions time and again because she was a woman.

So Barack knows what it means when a family struggles. He knows what it means when someone doesn't have a chance to fulfill their potential. And today, as a

FREDERICK MONDERSON

father, he knows what it means to want your daughters to grow up with no limits on their dreams.

That's why, since taking office, he's worked tirelessly to make sure every child and every family gets a fair shake.

The historic health reform he passed is making sure every American family gets the quality and affordable care they need to stay healthy. The crucial investments he's made in our students and workers - raising the standards in our public schools and building out job-training programs at community colleges - are investments in our country's economic future. And the very first bill he signed into law - the Lilly Ledbetter Fair Pay Act - will help make it easier for women to get equal pay for equal work, because he knows that women's success in this economy is the key to families' success in this economy.

But we have so much more to do. And, as women and supporters of this campaign, we need to keep showing up - and we need to keep fighting the good fight.

So I'm asking you to join me, and women all across the country who support this movement. I'm asking you to say you're ready to work.

Join Women for Obama, and help us grow this organization:

http://my.barackobama.com/Women-for-Obama

Thank you for being a part of this,

Michelle

These factors contradict Mr. Perry's criticism of President Obama being elitist and not being able to understand the plight of the ordinary person, particularly women. All this is evident in President Obama's efforts to help women, the burden bearer of single, female headed and poor households. In fact, Mr. Perry's charges should be directed at himself for he certainly seems to reflect such. Nevertheless, this one like so many of the challenges Republican have posed for Mr. Obama will fail because he has the greatest concern for the American people in his many and constant efforts. President Obama is not elitist; he is a man of the people, all the people, the American people!

OBAMA - MASTER AND COMMANDER

Obama - Master and Commander 130. Architectural nicety at building joint depicting the decorated features surrounding an Ionic capital.

Obama - Master and Commander 130a. More architectural nicety at building joint depicting the decorated features surrounding an Ionic capital.

FREDERICK MONDERSON

Obama - Master and Commander 131. Still more architectural nicety at building jointing depicting the decorated features surrounding Corinth capitals.

Obama - Master and Commander 132. Not as intricately defined but just as delicately designed, this outside cornice of the Jefferson Building completes examination of the wonderful work done here.

OBAMA - MASTER AND COMMANDER

Obama - Master and Commander 133. This Jefferson Building Cornerstone was dated as indicated, August 28, 1890.

"I believe in American exceptionalism, just as I suspect that the Brits believe in British exceptionalism and the Greeks believe in Greek exceptionalism."
Barack Obama

"Hope is what led a band of colonists to rise up against an empire; what led the greatest of generations to free a continent and heal a nation; what led young women and young men to sit at lunch counters and brave fire hoses and march through Selma and Montgomery for freedom's cause. Hope is what led me here today–with a father from Kenya, a mother from Kansas; and a story that could only happen in the United States of America. Hope is the bedrock of this nation; the belief that our destiny will not be written for us, but by us; by all those men and women who are not content to settle for the world as it is; who have courage to remake the world as it should be." **Barack Obama**, speech, January 3, 2008

"The success of our economy has always depended not just on the size of our gross domestic product, but on the reach of our prosperity, on the ability to extend opportunity to every willing heart - not out of charity, but because it is the surest route to our common good." **Barack Obama**, Inaugural Address, January 2009

FREDERICK MONDERSON

12. CAN WE TRUST REPUBLICANS?
By
Dr. Fred Monderson

"Our want of trust justify the deceit of others." La Rochefoucauld!

In a recently concluded New Hampshire Republican presidential debate, the contenders certainly looked impressive, on paper, as the pundits debated who did well. While the candidates made their case as to whom, a year from today, will be their party's standard bearer, one weak link in their chain may have been evident from an answer given to a question by the Moderator John King. Mr. King asked Congressman Ron Paul, one of the eight hopefuls, "Can you think of one good thing President Obama has done for the economy?" Mr. Ron Paul either did not want to appear a lover of President Obama, soft among his colleagues, or he has faulty memory; perhaps this malady comes with age! Mr. Paul thought long and hard, and finally he admitted he could not identify anything good President Obama had done for the economy. Perhaps he never knew the Mr. Obama rescued the auto industry! As fate would have it, on election eve, November 2012, autoworkers printed T-shirts that read: "He saved our jobs. Now we must save his!" Perhaps Mr. King should purchase one T-shirt and mail it to Mr. Paul.

Some years ago, President Number 43, George Bush, was asked "Can you think of one bad thing you have done in your Presidency?" The President thought long and hard, racking his brains for an iota, then he replied in the negative. "I cannot remember anything I have done wrong in my Presidency." Not that "Mission was Accomplished;" or even one day choosing the wrong tie or cuff links with the right shirt can be considered. It's generally believed, Mr. Bush is a piece of work! The same line of reasoning characterized Congressman Paul, both in question and answer. This makes him so "Bushesque!" But, does this mean if elected President, despite what he says, there will be no more wars; foreclosures will not rise; unemployment rates will not quadruple; Wall Street will not tank; and the world will not again have a negative view of the United States?

Since history has a tendency to repeat itself, maybe Barack Obama will comeback, again rescue the nation from its economic ditch and Sarah Palin, "Joe the Plumber," Senator DeMint, even Joe Wilson will ask for an encore! Even more important, perhaps, Donald Trump will insist on prolonging the "Birthers" issue.

Congressman Ron Paul could have responded, if he remembered, after thinking for a while; the December 2010 bill he voted for, where the wealthy Republican base got a hefty tax break, could have been a good thing for the economy. But it was not; it was simply a "money grab for the Republican base," the rich, that is! To Mr. King's question, and holding the President's feet over the fire; to get that concession in the Bill which Republicans voted overwhelmingly for was either

OBAMA - MASTER AND COMMANDER

good for the economy or Republican would appear hypocrites voting adamantly for a measure that did not help the nation's economic situation but only benefitted the "One Percent."

Equally, the "Debt Ceiling Debate," where Republicans held the President and the American people hostage, is another example of Mr. Obama making concessions and taking heat for appearing bipartisan in a seemingly hopeless situation. In many respects, after Speaker John Boehner had disrespected President Obama by not returning his phone calls and had been in contact with the Media, he was ultimately able to boast "We've gotten 98 percent of what we wanted." Right after the negotiations, Senator Mitch McConnell of publicly stated "I intend to make Barack Obama a one-term President" fame, who gave his now famous thumbs-up, a veiled communicated boast, "I got that Nigger" in the White House code had won for his base in congruence also with Speaker Boehner's boast of besting the President. As these events unfolded, it would be naïve for anyone to believe what may seem disparate elements of the Republican Party and its associates, that they do not coordinate various avenues of their strategy in attacks on President Obama. So, you need to use the Hubble Telescope to see the difference between Paul, McConnell, Boehner, Gingrich, Cain, Santorum, Bachmann, Romney, Sununu, Joe Wilson, DeMint, Krystal, "black protester with guns," his pastor Anderson, Donald Trump, Sarah Palin, Michael Steele, Allen West, etc. The problem of how to identify the "best of a bad lot" has been solved! It is Mitt Romney!

For example, a number of early Ads against the President have been not simply negative but also false. *Americans for Prosperity* financed by David H. and Charles G. Koch (Coke) have been behind criticism of the President because of his support for a tax increase on those making high incomes. Equally, the Conservative Advocacy group *Crossroads* of Carl Rove recently spent some $2.6 million in a negative Ad charging "President Obama, it's time to attack problems, not people." This is because he had been speaking out about Republican behavior towards him. No one in recent memory has been more attacked, *ad hominem* and performance wise, than Mr. Obama. Yet, Republicans want "blood out of their stone!" Thus, without a doubt, every "victory" of the Republicans against President Obama is also a victory over the American people. It's like the one percent and more against the ninety nine percent and less. We know who is winning!

Let us remember, on his assumption of the Presidency Mr. Obama, as the nation's Chief Executive, inherited an America losing more than 500,000 jobs per month. The **Housing Industry** experienced severe hemorrhage with new construction at a standstill and foreclosures on the rise. The **Auto Industry** experienced severe challenges from foreign competitors whose autos promised greater performance, better fuel efficiency and labor costs that were below American standards. As a result, the industry needed significant government assistance to avoid bankruptcy. In rescuing the Auto Industry, Mr. Obama not just saved many

FREDERICK MONDERSON

more than a million jobs of an industry America pioneered but he insisted on reorganization, better efficiency in performance, management and operation. This resulted in these companies becoming much more productive and competitive. In this, they have not simply held their own of market share but have also been increasing sales, particularly due to Japan's nuclear troubles.

Obama - Master and Commander 134. What an architectural contrast with the Doric capital of the Lincoln Memorial with the Jefferson Building. Here, the capitals are more "masculine" as compared with the "feminine" Ionic and the more decorative "composite" Corinthian.

With the fall of **AIG** (American Investment Group) and **Bears Stearns**, the nation's financial and economic sectors were greatly in need of regulation, reform and resuscitation. So much so, the government bailout Mr. Obama's advisors recommended, not simply rescued the banking industry and Wall Street financial sectors but allowed them to be put on a more firm footing. For example, by the time of Mr. Obama's first day in office, the **DOW** industrial numbers had plummeted to 6500-7000! Today it stands at approximately 11,500 [13,000]! This particular rescue was so significant; Wall Street, to the consternation of many, began issuing tremendous bonuses to its traders. Since the CEOs and traders were making big bonuses and corporations were also reporting gains, then industry, investors of these firms, corporations, and such entities were benefitting. By extension, these rich, Mr. Bush's "base" were making lots! For example, if we were to possibly accept the Republican Romney's contention that "Corporations are people too;" then Barack Obama benefitted the economy by way of enabling Corporations and the American investors to be profitable. Thus, in this way, through his initial policies of bailout, coupled with financial and economic reform and regulation; unquestionably, President Obama brought the American economy back from the precipice of collapse with even greater global impact.

Seems *Psalms* 2:12 had Barack Obama's efforts in mind in the saying: "Blessed are all they that put their trust in him!"

OBAMA - MASTER AND COMMANDER

However, one has to wonder if people like Mitch McConnell, John Boehner, Senator DeMint and others who often parrot the "I like the President" hypocritical party line; if they had "truly shown the man love from day one," the American economy and social situation would have been far better today.

Without question, every commentator at home and abroad has recognized and given the President credit for bringing the nation's economy back from the brink of economic collapse. Now, for the Republicans; either they were "out to lunch," grabbing "98 percent" for their special interest base, and the likes of Ron Paul, either have "clouded vision," bad memory or "play fast and furious" with the numbers, if they cannot think of any one thing good that Mr. Obama has done for the economy! Then again, the "Party of No" could never ever say "Yes!"

That same "Party of No" whose affiliates as the "Tea Party Movement," militias and other right wing groups hammered Barack Obama on way to and in the White House; and together with their allies in Congress littered the path of Mr. Obama creating a minefield to sabotage his every legislative initiative. Still, he persevered in passing Lilly Ledbetter Equal Pay Law, Health Care Reform, Credit Card Reform, Student Loan Aid Reform, and a slew of social programs to benefit broad segments of the American populace.

Recognizing that along every journey an imprint is made, Republicans and their allies have said some of the darnest things about Mr. Obama. We know "Joe the Plumber" called Mr. Obama a "socialist" which stuck. Significantly, this became a campaign issue and in the debate between John McCain and candidate Obama, Joe's name was mentioned more than twenty times. Still Obama persevered! Today, Governor Rick Perry released an Ad parroting this ancient line of socialism. Next Sarah Palin charged "Obama is not like us" and "We must take our country back." Among her other nonsensical mis-statements, Ms. Palin also said, "I can see Russia from my front porch." However, many commentators expressed even this statement was incorrect.

Senator Mitch McConnell, Republican Minority leader, seemed to have let slip an intent now called the "McConnell Mandate" of his commitment to make Barack Obama a "one term President." What is significant about this statement, with his "McConnell's Mandate," the Senator may have honed this strategy with any number of individuals and groups of like minds with the same objective to thwart and stop Obama! While this was probably a "day one" strategy, it could have also been a contingency plan from the time he announced his candidacy for the Presidency.

When the President proposed his Health Care Reform Agenda, this legislative action generated a great deal of animosity among Republicans whose efforts on the street painted the President in the most malicious manner imaginable through characterization that appeared without question, racist! In Congress South

FREDERICK MONDERSON

Carolina's Senator DeMint exhorted, "If we could stop and derail Obama's Health Care Reform Agenda, this would be his Waterloo!" Then he added more malicious fuel saying he "likes the President" but that Mr. Obama gives "false numbers." Chirping in, Billy Krystal admonished, "Go for the kill!" Birds of a feather, when the President addressed a Joint House of Congress to some given data, Carolina Congressman Joe Wilson retorted disrespectfully "You lie!"

Seems like not only are the Republicans not to be trusted but they are also tremendously disrespectful of the Presidency and this latter is especially so because of President Obama's race. One scholar likes to say, "Blacks may be crazy, but they are not dumb." Blacks are observing all these developments particularly how these people are treating their hero, a man of high moral integrity and unquestioned patriotism, all because he is Black!

Obama - Master and Commander 135. Window arched and Pediment with floral decoration beneath at the Jefferson Building.

OBAMA - MASTER AND COMMANDER

Obama - Master and Commander 136. A somewhat different window crown but still intricate workmanship.

Obama - Master and Commander 137. What a contrast, subtle but still significant.

FREDERICK MONDERSON

Even though the economy got better but not great, the attacks against Obama continued unabated. That is, while the nation is not losing 500,000 jobs per month it is only adding low 100,000 jobs. Still, the Republican wealthy base that got tax cuts for the last 10 years have not helped in creating jobs but everyone blames the President who must contend with Republicans at war with him. Are we to believe the Republicans are terrorists? We must not forget, as the tax cuts are still in effect, even during the last Bush years, they have not produced jobs! Imagine, noble men and a woman attacking each other to be first to challenge an even greater noble! Yet, these Republican presidential debate attacks make seriously false statements that have exposed a sinister side of these contenders as they wade into Mr. Obama. Earlier Speaker Boehner remarked "I like the President," still he seems unalterably committed to the "McConnell Mandate." On the other hand and conversely, Megan McCain, daughter of John McCain opined, "I like the President and am praying for him to succeed." Meanwhile, from the bottom of the pile, Rick Santorum has charged, "President Obama is dividing the country." Why, because Blacks had to wait until after 43 presidents had presided before one like theirs was afforded the opportunity. Whereas, President Obama was attacked before he got to the White House, while he resides there and perhaps even after he leaves! A more sinister charge of Rick Santorum is that President Obama has "poisoned the well!" Can honest men, in this modern world, accuse the President of the United States, a lawyer and constitutional professor, of using "poison" against the nation he took an oath to defend and administer even as he has spent the last three years eliminating some of its most feared enemies, has rescued its economic slide and improved its image abroad! This is a serious charge! However, either the former Senator does not understand the potency of his language or such language is truly reflective of the nature of the man with no control over his orifice. Maybe Republican voters truly understand this issue more than any other and that is why Mr. Santorum gets low marks. More correctly, as Sean Penn explained: "Rick Santorum represents narrow-minded leadership!"

"The man that hath no music in himself,
Nor is not mov'd with concord of sweet sounds,
Is fit for treasons, stratagems, and spoils;
The motions of his spirit are dull as night,
And his affectations hard as Erebus

Let no such man be trusted" says Shakespeare in *The Merchant of Venice* V, i, 83

Former Speaker Newt Gingrich has been described as highly intellectual, yet, unintentionally he has betrayed the true nature of the opposition to President Obama in the statement, "The day after Obama's defeat jobs will return to America!" A good question is whether this statement is accidental or a design? This is the loser, I mean man, who boasted, "I will be the nominee!"

OBAMA - MASTER AND COMMANDER

Even Governor Rick Perry of Texas made a charge that President Obama is elitist being raised in a "privileged" background. From a man who has enjoyed both parents accusing a person with no parents, such talk is disingenuous. Former Massachusetts Governor Mitt Romney recently released an Ad criticizing the President, deemed to be based on falsity; but Michele Bachmann takes the cake. Imagine, Congresswoman Michele Bachmann accused President Obama of "running a gangster government in Washington, DC." In the heart of a nation of laws, with such great power and oversight it should be criminal to utter that the leader is a "gangster." That he heads a "gangster government." Imagine Vice President Joe Biden, who spent more than three decades in service to the nation, would countenance to serving second to a "gangster" which makes him a "gangster" also!

"They that put their trust in him shall understand the truth." *The Wisdom of Solomon* 3: 9

Now this cursory sketch is just a fraction of insidious Republican behavior towards President Obama. Republicans seems to be playing to win by whatever means necessary, even if false and disrespectful claims are made in process. As President Obama has said, "Republicans drove the car into a ditch and now they want the keys again." But, the American people can see through this deception and will deny them leadership of the country because, perhaps, Republicans cannot be trusted with the true welfare of the nation; that is, well-being of all of the American people!

Obama - Master and Commander 137a. Entrance U.S. House of Representatives between the columns.

"I don't care whether you're driving a hybrid or an SUV. If you're headed for a cliff, you have to change direction. That's what the American people called for in November, and that's what we intend to deliver." **Barack Obama**

FREDERICK MONDERSON

Obama - Master and Commander 138. Flowers and trees decorate this end of the Jefferson Building.

Obama - Master and Commander 139. Two travelers repose before the mythological figures adorning the front entrance to the Jefferson Building of the Library of Congress.

OBAMA - MASTER AND COMMANDER

Obama - Master and Commander 140. Eagles on guard and scholars reading characterize the Library of Congress on this arched doorway.

Obama - Master and Commander 141. A family of mother, daughter and son rest during a visit to the Jefferson Building.

FREDERICK MONDERSON

"In a global economy where the most valuable skill you can sell is your knowledge, a good education is no longer just a pathway to opportunity - it is a pre-requisite." **Barack Obama**, Address to Joint Session of Congress, February 24, 2009

"The best judge of whether or not a country is going to develop is how it treats its women. If it's educating its girls, if women have equal rights, that country is going to move forward. But if women are oppressed and abused and illiterate, then they're going to fall behind." **Barack Obama**, Ladies Home Journal, September 2008

13. OBAMA'S "DIVINE MISSION"
By
Dr. Fred Monderson

That Barack Obama's mission is divinely inspired and guided by a higher power should be evident to all even those purposely wearing blindfolds. In so many ways, this has been demonstrated as, first, in the rescue of the American Auto Industry saving untold numbers of jobs; yet, so many have decried this action because of their short-sidedness. If this truly indigenous American enterprise with ancillary suppliers employing millions of workers failed, it would have signaled the beginning of America's precipitous decline. What a laughing stock the nation would have become. Even our fighting forces abroad would have begun questioning their own defense of the nation from distant shores. Let's be serious, if Jerry Falwell, Tammy Fay Baker and husband as well as Pat Robertson all could "talk to God" and more modern Michele Bachmann could claim "God told her to run for President;" it is not farfetched to see the significance of Barack Obama's meteoric rise, his impact on the world and particularly his defense of America, as divinely inspired! Perhaps it was written in destiny as foretold in 1922 by Caseley Hayford of Ghana, West Africa, who decried the mechanical, calculating and inhuman relations of modern man. He predicted only the humane nature of the African can save humanity from its impending destruction. Thus, the African can come in many forms and sizes, but the divine mission remains undoubted!

The interesting thing about Michele Bachmann's claim "God told me to run for the Presidency" was purely a political ploy playing to a particular base. If god wanted her to run for the Presidency, all that was missing was the actual handing over of the keys! He would have provided the wherewithal and resources, a plan of what to say and do, to distance her from Republican contenders and then she would have mopped up Obama. There is a failure in there somewhere! Obama on the other hand, continues to successfully "do god's work," does well in the name of humanity, gets good grades and seems to be riding on an express elevator to

OBAMA - MASTER AND COMMANDER

heaven! Thus, I ask you, parroting Patton, "Whose side is God on?" The Democrats are lucky to have Barack Obama as their leader.

Within the construct of the dynamics of such an undertaking we look to the ancient for wisdom. The *Ancient Egyptian Book of Coming Forth By Day* or *Book of the Dead* speaks of the challenge of *Ma'at*, viz., - goodness, right, truth, balance, against *Isfet* - evil, wrong, disequilibrium. As such, many contemporary Republican presidential contenders question Mr. Obama's leadership but unfortunately their cataract clouded vision preclude their understanding of true leadership as the president struggles to move the nation from the mist and morass of recent moral, social and economic failures of which Republicans bear great responsibility. A typical example of questioned leadership can be seen in the withdrawing of American forces from Iraq where Obama's critics saw weaknesses in this strategy. History teaches, George Washington crossed the Delaware to "winter his forces" before successfully attacking the British. Napoleon invaded Egypt also to "winter" and "lick his wounds" following a British defeat; and though he later lost the "Battle of the Nile" he did unleash the wonders of ancient Egyptian discovery. Again, Osama bin Laden was evil and in President Obama's quick dispatch of the Mephistophelian mastermind, many Republican contenders wanted to see the body; like Barnabas they wanted to "See the wounds and put their fingers therein." Well, they could dispatch divers to the deep to recover what's left! Teddy Roosevelt once said, "I walk softly and carry a big stick." Barack Obama could also say, "I too walk softly, but I send in the Navy Seals!"

Obama - Master and Commander 142. What a magnificent view of intricate Corinthian colonnades topped by and buttressed by arched decorated artistic nicety in stone and colorful paint.

FREDERICK MONDERSON

Obama - Master and Commander 143. More but a different and magnificent view of intricate Corinthian colonnades topped by arched decorated artistic nicety in stone and colorful paint.

Obama - Master and Commander 144. One of two stairway entrances to the magnificent decorative features on the second floor that pays tribute not simply to a great nation but equally to the minds that could conceive and execute this wonderama of American art and architecture represented here.

OBAMA - MASTER AND COMMANDER

Obama - Master and Commander 145. Busts of George Washington (left) and Thomas Jefferson (right).

Obama - Master and Commander 146. Intricate mastery in stone and paint creating an unforgettable experience for the untold numbers of visitors who come for the remarkable view.

FREDERICK MONDERSON

Perception of the loss of the U.S. Drone in Iran is another example of vision diametrically opposed to sound leadership. Remember Kosovo or whatever; John McCain said "Let's go in!" Obama, on the other hand, said. "I consulted with my advisers. Let's proceed with caution." The Joint Chiefs and other advisers at the President's disposal are the best in the world! Many of these brilliant minds, military and otherwise, are the same personnel who will advise any Republican presidential winner in the upcoming 2012 election. Many critics proffered that Mr. Obama bomb the drone or send in a team to recover it. Mr. Obama cautioned No! This was a violation of that nation's sovereignty. Bombing was an act of war! Hurried rescue of a minuscule objective is risky; remember President Carter's Iran rescue. So, President Obama politely asked Iran to return the drone to which they said No! He knew this would be their reply! Meanwhile the sanctions are working!

Demonstrating his studied leadership, Mr. Obama realized loss of the drone is a casualty of war! In Iran's position, we have to at least assume they photographed and possibly dismantled it and not-inconceivable they shopped it around to interested parties. Fact is, upon the request which Iran refused, therein lies a major error on their part. Like Ra's defeat of the evil Apepi monster; St. Michael vanquishing the Devil; and even Blade telling the Vampire, "I'll Catch You Later;" President Obama knows Ahmenijhdad and his cohorts are evil and is planning to "Catch them later." The problem is that he won't tell the Republican blowhards what his plans are for those "bad boys!"

In his *The Book of Coming Forth By Day: The Declaration of Innocence* Maulana Karenga elucidates on "The Essentiality of Moral Social Practice." While Obama is concerned with the many, Republicans are only interested in protecting the few, their base, the rich one percent! In essence, in this respect, we could see President Obama practicing Ma'at and Republicans, in vigorous opposition, practicing its opposite, Isfit! This philosophic concept of "Ma'at" Karenga writes, "Is the essentiality of moral social practice in human development." He defines Ma'at (1990: 31) as "that which endures and raises a person and people up, but Isfit leads to destruction. Ma'at, as social practice, serves several functions in human development. First, it is the basic means by which the affinity of God and humans is expressed. Ma'at is the essential substance and sustenance of God and humans as expressed in earlier Kemetic anthropology which equated God and King .... Ma'at then is both the nourishment and essence of God and to practice it is to share in his essence and be in harmony with his desire for the world. Therefore, Ma'at is the grounds for ontological unity and affinity of God and humans and again the grounds of human potential for perfectibility, i.e., moral and spiritual development which leads to assimilation with God."

When Congresswoman Michele Bachmann in her misguided innocence said President Obama has changed history she was probably right in a wrong but really right sense of the thought. Perhaps, unknowingly, she is referring to, championing,

OBAMA - MASTER AND COMMANDER

Mr. Obama's divine task of maintaining Ma'at in the world. This, in turn, means "maintaining the creation and righteousness of the order this implies and necessitates." For as leader or ruler, he must remain "committed" to "restoring, establishing and expanding Ma'at." As the *Book of Rising and Transformation* affirms, in his divine mission Obama seeks to set "Heaven ... at peace and earth ... in joy, for they have heard that [he] will set Ma'at in the place of Isfet, i.e., right in the place of wrong, order in the place of disorder." Mid-course correction is useful in any journey for the long duration and America can certainly benefit from such a course of action, if as it's claimed to be the last hope for humanity.

Obama - Master and Commander 147. The second stairway with its classic view of the colonnades accentuating the colorful paintings that help to make a visit to the Thomas Jefferson Library Building such an exhilarating experience.

FREDERICK MONDERSON

Obama - Master and Commander 148. Is it vertical? Is it horizontal? No. Its two beautiful and expansive parts of a ceiling in this stupendous building.

OBAMA - MASTER AND COMMANDER

Obama - Master and Commander 149. More of the same that speaks to the conception and completion of this masterpiece as part of the greater grand construction.

As the biggest stumbling block to President Obama's success, the economy has begun to cast more light in the tunnels; we equally begin to see the wisdom and results of his efforts in fiscal and economic policy. Having brought the nation a long way, he must continue the journey!

Obama - Master and Commander 150. *Exploring the Early Americas* is an exhibition currently running in November and December 2012.

"For we know that our patchwork heritage is strength, not a weakness. We are a nation of Christians and Muslims, Jews and Hindus, and non-believers. We are shaped by every language and culture, drawn from every end of this Earth; and because we have tasted the bitter swill of civil war and segregation, and emerged from that dark chapter stronger and more united, we cannot help but believe that the old hatreds shall someday pass; that the lines of tribe shall soon dissolve; that as the world grows smaller, our common humanity shall reveal itself; and that America must play its role in ushering in a new era of peace."
Barack Obama, Inaugural Address, January 2009

"With the magnitude of the challenges we face right now, what we need in Washington are not more political tactics - we need more good ideas. We don't need more point-scoring - we need more problem-solving." **Barack Obama**, press conference, March 17, 2009

14. MA'AT VERSUS ISFIT IN PRESIDENTIAL POLITICS I.
By
Dr. Fred Monderson

History has shown any movement for the better is always first met with opposition and skepticism. Take the case of all great reformers, Osiris, Buddha, Jesus, Joan of Arc, even George Washington with all his faults, not excluding Martin Luther King, Malcolm X and Medgar Evers. In that mountain of a man, Barack Obama, we see no difference as he has struggled to defend what is right, doing *Ma'at* even to his opponents while ignoring the stone throwers. Subscribing to the higher mission, President Obama realizes, as Maulana Karenga (1990: 32) says, "Creation, then, is constantly threatened by chaos, disorder or Isfet, and humans are morally compelled to share the responsibility with God of defending the boundaries of good, right and order, and expanding them. In this activity humans become like God."

"The Ma'atian stress on moral social practice is rooted in the assumption that self-actualization of humans is best achieved in morally grounded relations with others." "The operative principle here is self-realization and grounding in moral relations with others. It is at this point that the ethic of care and responsibility or rather of love in the most human sense [*merut*] and service [*wenut*] are evident and required in Ma'at. To serve is to benefit not only others but also oneself."

OBAMA - MASTER AND COMMANDER

Oh, what great wisdom the ancient possessed! For example, the *Book of Ankhsheshonqi* teaches "Service is righteous action towards and for God, humans and by extension, nature which in some meaningful and moral way returns a reciprocal benefit." This moral responsibility to respect and protect the earth is what Karenga preached in his *Kwanza Message* at Boys and Girls High school in Brooklyn, New York, on December 27, 2011. Now, contrary to past deregulation, as per his mission, the president insists the Environmental Protection Agency must enforce strict regulation to play its part in saving the earth from becoming another mars. Therefore, when Republican contenders tout "Abolish the EPA" they are acting as agents of Isfet.

Again, Ankhsheshonqi cautions, "The only real good deed is the one done for one who needs it." Perhaps that proponent of ancient African deep thought foresaw and foretold of the conflict of the one and the ninety-nine percent. Within this same prophetic construct can be placed the "Millionaires Tax Cut" for those who do not need it; and to this we may add the Health Care Reform Act that benefits the fifty million Americans who need its protection. Can we thrown in the Lilly Ledbetter Act for women certainly need to earn the same as men? Last but not least, President Obama's insistence on and support for educational initiatives, upgrade of school facilities, repair of roads, ports, airports, tunnels, rail lines and even high speed rail service will not only improves performance and infrastructure of the American landscape but also put Americans back to work, helping to improve their economic and social positions.

Now to contrast the "highly intellectual," "smartest guy in the room," "I'm going to be the nominee" arrogance of Newt Gingrich with the deep thinking Barack Obama, the vision is like night and day and too the thanklessness of a well-done job. Nevertheless, Ankhsheshonqi admonishes as Karenga has pointed out, "One should not be disappointed for not being recognized or thanked by everyone for whom one does good." Antedating the wisdom of the *Book of Ecclesiastes* which urges, as we all sometimes do, "Cast your bread upon the waters and after many days it will return to you;" Ankhsheshonqi admonishes, "If you do good by a hundred persons and just one of them acknowledges it, no part of it is lost." His optimism is reflected in the law of reciprocity in that, "Do a good deed and throw it in the water and when the water dries up, you will find it." Again, we see in the ancient Egyptian/African reservoir of deep thought wisdom many paraphrased modern wise sayings such as "It's better to give than to receive." In Ankhsheshonqi's original thought, "Sweeter is the water of one who has given than the wine of one who has received."

FREDERICK MONDERSON

Obama - Master and Commander 151. Ladies at the ready, "Fortitude" and "Justice."

Today we recognize Republican claims to have borrowed Jesse Jackson's "Big Tent" idea that should shelter great diversity among its presidential candidates and supporters. This, however, is not the case for recently a young Black Republican on CNN decried the rhetoric of the recent CPAP convention's racism in modern dress, not considering the realities of 21st Century politics. Did Congressman Allen West from Florida hear the same message? After all, in addition to Jim Crow, Jr., Esquire, the Republican tent includes the "Black protester with guns;" his "praying for Obama's death" Pastor Anderson; the "Koran burning Florida pastor" declaring his intention to run for the Presidency as a Republican; Ringmaster Donald Trump with his magnetic attraction for clowns; illegal immigrant chasing Sheriff Arapaio; "Waterloo" DeMint; "You lie" Wilson; "Poisoning the well" Santorum; "Gangster government" Bachmann; "Corporations are people" Romney; "I'll be the nominee" Newt Gingrich; "I can't remember which Department I will abolish" Perry; "Blacks are brainwashed for voting Democratic"

OBAMA - MASTER AND COMMANDER

Herman Cain; and hopefully, Ron "I can't remember anything good President Obama did for the economy" Paul. All these, to again borrow a phrase from Rahm Emanuel, "turkeys" have been chosen to play a key role in effectuating the divine mission of Barack Obama. As such, they mirrors the antithesis of *Ma'at*; or put in Christian historical parlance, they exhibit the "Petrine Syndrome" of denial, viz., Bachmann, Trump, Santorum; and Judas "Escariot Syndrome," Cain, Allen, "Black Protester With Guns," as well as Cornell West, Tavis Smiley and so many other pessimists.

Obama - Master and Commander 152. More Ladies at the ready, this time "Concordia" and "Industry."

FREDERICK MONDERSON

Now, as many of these players fade into oblivion and President Obama pursues his platform of better educational opportunities and practices, particularly with greater emphasis on the role of Community Colleges in retraining especially in the industrial arts; emphasizing the need for research and development of clean energy sources, and a more vigorous enforcement of environmental use, paying greater attention to overhauling the nation's physical infrastructure and as the economy continues to improve, the American people will see the wisdom of Obama's leadership and play their part in his re-election and in fulfilling his divine mission designed for their betterment.

Obama - Master and Commander 153. Image of early man in the architectural creative process.

"After a century of striving, after a year of debate, after a historic vote, health care reform is no longer an unmet promise. It is the law of the land." **Barack Obama**

"There's something about the American spirit - inherent in the American spirit - we don't hang on to the past. We always move forward .... We are going to leave something better for our children - not just here in the United States, but all around the world." **Barack Obama**, speech during DNC fundraiser, October 2009

OBAMA - MASTER AND COMMANDER

"You know, there's a lot of talk in this country about the federal deficit. But I think we should talk more about our empathy deficit - the ability to put ourselves in someone else's shoes; to see the world through the eyes of those who are different from us - the child who's hungry, the steelworker who's been laid-off, the family who lost the entire life they built together when the storm came to town. When you think like this - when you choose to broaden your ambit of concern and empathize with the plight of others, whether they are close friends or distant strangers - it becomes harder not to act; harder not to help." **Barack Obama**, speech, August 2006

15. MA'AT VERSUS ISFIT IN PRESIDENTIAL POLITICS II.
By
Dr. Fred Monderson

As the Republican candidates battle to be chosen as their party's standard bearer to oppose President Obama in the 2012 national elections, besides beating up on each other, they collectively stand unalterably opposed to the man whose job they are seeking, not in principle but on political expediency. For example, if the President favors an issue the Republicans oppose it in a manner that all Republicans are so disposed and this is purely ideological opposition. In this respect, the President's every action falls short of Republican expectations. No matter how much a policy or practice benefits the nation, more than 9 out of 10 times such action falls below Republican expectations primarily because they generally play to their base in opportunistic politics of denial. Thus, something seems wrong with that math wherein a culture of division is fostered. Many have interpreted all the flack directed towards President Barack Obama as racial hatred while others, even Mr. Obama himself, has chosen to see it as Republicans "playing hard." Nevertheless and perhaps, if an adversary executed some vile act against the nation, Republicans will still demonstrate solidarity in support of a response but even then they would criticize the manner in which the President handled the matter.

On rare occasions as when Mr. Obama extended the millionaires tax cut, despite Republican insistence on fiscal austerity and that the measure would add to the deficit, Republicans were delighted in the results even though they were branded hypocritical. Or, in the Debt Ceiling debacle, in what was tantamount to an old adage, "I robbed Obama blind" Speaker John Boehner boasted "We got 98 percent of what we wanted" forcing some to believe Mr. Obama had capitulated to his opponents. Yet, as a realist with a global view from the Oval Office, the President executed the best possible strategy at the time in a strategic compromise in the nation's best interest. However, some observers still considered Republicans in lipstick at the trough were still pigs no matter the squeal! Nonetheless, if one side could boast of getting such a high percentage of what they sought in a bargaining trade off, then something is wrong with that math!

Obama - Master and Commander 154. "Knowledge comes but Wisdom lingers."

Obama - Master and Commander 155. "Wisdom is the principal thing. Therefore get Wisdom and with all thy getting get Understanding."

OBAMA - MASTER AND COMMANDER

Obama - Master and Commander 156. "Ignorance is the curse of God. Knowledge the wing wherewith we fly to Heaven."

Obama - Master and Commander 157. "It is the Mind that makes the man and our Vigor is in our Immortal Soul."

FREDERICK MONDERSON

Now, despite this negativist view, Barack Obama has achieved a great deal as President. Or, as a current political commercial reminds, "The Presidency is a management position" and Mr. Obama has exemplified the highest form of management, given no support from Republicans probably subscribing in totality to the McConnell "One term" mandate. That is, current Republican criticism, playing to its base, notwithstanding, when we consider the depths to which the American state had succumbed, internationally and domestically, at the start of his administration, the rescue, recovery and revamping or resuscitation of the nation's economics, moral fiber, foreign policy transformation, its insistence on and re-cultivation of America's creative spirit of giving, imbuing the nation with a greater force to slingshot into a brighter and even more successful future, few presidents faced similar challenges and performed as well. Thus, when all things are considered, the current round of Republican contenders pales in significance when compared with President Barack Obama in terms of his executing strategy to confront issues, challenging conflict, making the most of his resources, work ethic and intellectual abilities.

Whereas, in the 2008 election the significant attraction was the election of the first African American President; in contrast, this election of 2012 is important but also a referendum on a man of great moral stature, possessing and employing a tremendous work ethic, choice of competent assistants, not only unparalleled but one that strives to advance the cause of all Americans in many facets of this social and legal existence. All this is buttressed by some of the most capable advisers, viz., military, economic, family, political and moral and spiritual whose efforts, while not given significant credit have been successful in many undertakings involving assisting and shaping Barack's vision for America. As such, Mr. Obama continues to dumfound his critics in practically every conceivable way, so much so, the *Newsweek* magazine ran a cover feature entitled "Why are Mr. Obama's critics so Dumb!" Perhaps there is something in this exasperated question! Well, let's take a look at the Obama record as President because in answer to "What has President Obama accomplished in the last three years?", the following will show he has done a great deal for this nation and having sailed the ship of state out of the perilous waters of international scorn, two active wars, terrorist confrontation, Somali Pirates, an economy tremendously hemorrhaging jobs and a depressing housing market, with Wall Street and the Auto Industry in turmoil, instituting policies and plans to "out educate" and "out produce" the world, America is blest in having this visionary as its leader, at this critical time in its history. Therefore, under the President's continued leadership, with the policies he has instituted, America will be able to boast its greatest days lie yonder in the calm waters, under the blue skies and among even greener pastures of the future.

The putative record shows, one of the first significant acts of the Obama Presidency was the passage into law of the *Lilly Ledbetter Fair Pay Act* designed to ensure women get paid the same as men for doing the same type of work. Beginning this year, new health insurance plans will be required to cover women's

OBAMA - MASTER AND COMMANDER

preventative services such as mammograms, domestic violence screenings and contraception without charge. As Republicans tried to roll back a woman's right to choose and defund Planned Parenthood, the President showed some grit standing up to them and even reversed the Global Gag Rule which banned government from providing aid to international family planning groups.

Everyone is familiar with the contentious nature of the environment surrounding discussion and passage of the landmark Affordable Care Act designed to restore health care as a basic cornerstone particularly of middle class security in America. This Health Care Reform Act was not only historic because many previous administrations had tried to get it passed but Mr. Obama was the first to get as far and succeed; so, it also brought out the worst in Republicans! Let us not forget "Waterloo DeMint," "Go for the Kill" Billy Krystal, the coalescing of the "Tea Party" movement who had some vicious things to say about Mr. Obama and so demonstrated the most vile and disrespectful caricature of the man. Yet still, he prevailed because the Democrats were in the majority in Congress and that new reality emboldened them to be part of this historic legislation. Some of the provisions of the Health Care Reform or Affordable Care Act were designed to help the nearly fifty million Americans who have had no health insurance has so aggravated Republicans, repeal of the measure has become a hallmark platform issue for them. Still, such a strategy is a big gamble because the many people benefitting from this legislation will vote to maintain rather than repeal this important measure.

Additionally, in this Affordable Care Act Mr. Obama's strategy has been to end insurance company abuses by prohibiting insurers from denying coverage to people with pre-existing conditions and cancelling coverage when someone gets sick. As an effort to keep premiums low, the Act has insisted insurance companies must justify rate hikes; they must provide rebates if they don't spend at least 80% of consumers' premiums on care instead of overhead, marketing and profits. This issue is so significant, it boasts of providing first time affordable insurance to more than 32 million Americans and equally nearly all Americans - 95% of those under the age of 65 will have health insurance. In closing the Medicare Prescription Drug "Donut Hole" more than 2.6 million seniors have purportedly saved an average of over $550.00 each annually on their prescription drugs and by 2020 the Medicare "Donut hole" will be completely closed. Again, repeal of this measure is like swimming against the tide.

FREDERICK MONDERSON

Obama - Master and Commander 158. "How charming is Divine Philosophy."

Obama - Master and Commander 159. "They are never alone that are Accompanied with Noble Thoughts."

In the election year of 2008 the nation's job loss was somewhere around 800,000 per month and by February of 2009 when Mr. Obama took office the nation had lost some 5.1 million jobs over a five year period. The president thus took immediate action to address the crisis particularly as it affected the middle class, hurting not simply from job loss but also from home foreclosures and declining home value. Addressing this issue, Mr. Obama initiated an economic recovery program that supported as many as 3.6 million jobs by cutting taxes, investing in

OBAMA - MASTER AND COMMANDER

clean energy, repairing roads and bridges, tunnels and ports, keeping teachers in the classrooms and protecting unemployment benefits. Significantly, bailing out the auto industry prevented the loss of more than 1.4 million jobs, recently fighting for passage of the American Jobs Act and encouraging private sector job creation resulted in some 3.5 million jobs created between February 2010 and February 2012. In fact, as of today March 10, 2012, the latest labor report shows job growth for the third month in a row.

From day one of his administration the President has concentrated on strengthening the economy so that Americans are able to raise a family, send their kids to school, own a home and also put enough away to retire. In order to do this, the President emphasized Education Reform through restructuring to "out-educate" the world and by innovating new teaching strategies and replacing outmoded textbooks and equipment with state of the art technology assisted by innovative instructional methodology. In this he further emphasized strengthening Community Colleges and thus making college education accessible to hundreds of thousands more students by ending billions of dollars in subsides to banks and using savings to double funding for Pell Grants. This will buttress the technological level of a new and transformed work force. Mr. Obama insisted on, encouraged and made substantial investments in clean energy manufacturing standards to create jobs of the future in America and to reduce the nation's dependence on foreign oil. He has also pursued a policy of protecting the environment and that is why he has insisted on studying the pipeline issue further. Addressing the Wall Street mess, he insisted on fiscal and financial reform to protect American families from unfair lending practices, rein in excesses on Wall Street and prevent future financial crises. When Mr. Obama took office the **DOW** stood at approximately 6500 and today it has rebounded and stands above 13,000. He addressed Credit Card inequities and also called for closing tax loopholes to ensure millionaires and billionaires don't pay less in taxes than the middle class.

In his campaign for the Presidency Mr. Obama pledged to end the war in Iraq in a responsible manner and he kept his word by bringing these troops home. However, in transitioning full responsibility to the Iraqi people the US remains committed to Iraq's long-term security and will continue to develop a strong and enduring partnership with that nation. During this current presidential campaign Republican contenders, in playing to their base, accused Mr. Obama of "appeasement to terrorists" and other "bad boys." The President's response in the White House Briefing Room was simply "Ask Osama bin-Laden and the 22 of 30 top Al Qaeda leadership removed from the battlefield if I'm an appeaser!" In this, he remains committed to dismantling and defeating Al-Qaeda and its affiliates. To honor his commitment to the great American warriors of Iraq, Afghanistan, those who captured Osama bin-Laden and all servicemen in general, the President proposed tax credits to encourage businesses to hire unemployed and disabled veterans, provide for medical assistance for returning veterans and strengthening the GI Bill.

FREDERICK MONDERSON

These then are just some achievement of the Obama administration and the current sophistry of Republican contenders will prove the President is a formidable opponent in the 2012 elections.

"America and Islam are not exclusive and need not be in competition. Instead, they overlap, and share common principles of justice and progress, tolerance and the dignity of all human beings." **Barack Obama**

Obama – Master and Commander 160. "Man is one World and hath Another to Attend Him."

Obama - Master and Commander 161. "Tongues in Trees, Books in the Running Brooks, Sermons in Stones and Good in Everything."

OBAMA - MASTER AND COMMANDER

Obama - Master and Commander 162. "Such as hang on Hebe's Cheek and Love to Live in Dimple Sleek" and "Come thou Goddess fair and free, In heaven Yelep'd Euphrosyne, and by men hearth easing mirth."

Obama - Master and Commander 163. "Haste thee nymph and bring with thee Jest and youthful jollity" and "Quips and cranks and wanton wiles, Nods and becks and wretched smiles."

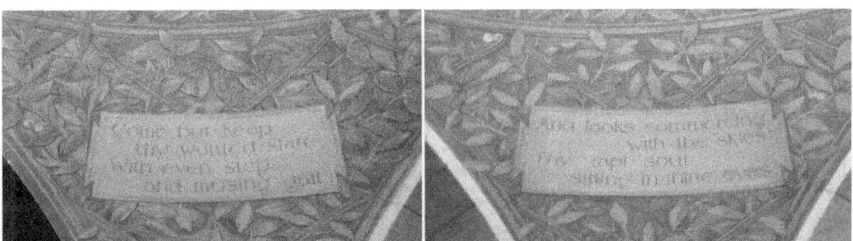

Obama - Master and Commander 164. "Come but keep thy wonted state, with even step and musing gait" and "And looks commercing with the skies, thy rapt soul sitting in thine eyes."

FREDERICK MONDERSON

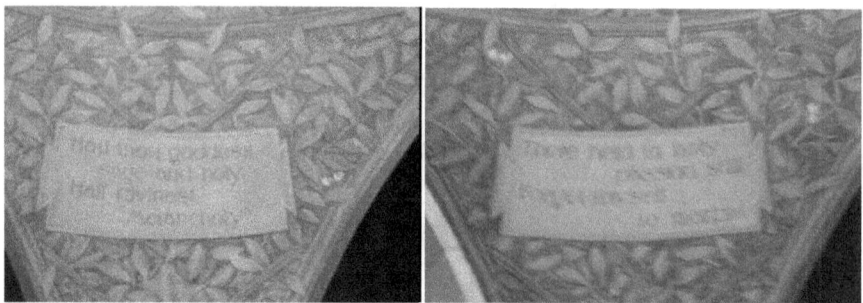

Obama - Master and Commander 165. "Hail thou goddess, Sage and Holy, Hail divinest Melancholy" and "There held in holy passion still, Forget thy self to marble."

"When we send our young men and women into harm's way, we have a solemn obligation not to fudge the numbers or shade the truth about why they're going, to care for their families while they're gone, to tend to the soldiers upon their return, and to never ever go to war without enough troops to win the war, secure the peace, and earn the respect of the world." **Barack Obama**, speech at Democratic National Convention, 2004

"I trust the American people to realize that while we don't need big government, we do need a government that stands up for families who are being tricked out of their homes by Wall Street predators; a government that stands up for the middle-class by giving them a tax break; a government that ensures that no American will ever lose their life savings just because their child gets sick. Security and opportunity; compassion and prosperity aren't liberal values or conservative values - they're American values." **Barack Obama**, speech, May 2008

16. MITT ROMNEY: "RIGHT" and "WRONG"
BY
Dr. Fred Monderson

Recently, former Massachusetts Governor Mitt Romney, the Republican front-runner, has said "Republicans are doomed in the 2012 elections if they do not speedily choose a nominee" as the party's standard bearer to oppose President Obama. In this Mr. Romney is "right" and "wrong." He is "right" that Republicans are doomed, and "wrong" for the reasons he gives. He is "right" Republicans are doomed, because despite Republican non-cooperation Mr. Obama's exemplary, non-scandalous, leadership has forthrightly addressed the significant issues confronting the nation, whether domestic or in foreign policy. He is "wrong" as to

OBAMA - MASTER AND COMMANDER

why they are doomed in that he wants the coronation before the ceremony! Now, having spent twice as much in his campaign as Rick Santorum, Newt Gingrich and Ron Paul combined, the front-runner, Romney has not been able to outdistance his competitors nor blunt their challenge. Yet, Mitt Romney wants to be the "nominee" before the Republican Convention so as to avoid a brokered convention experience. However, on Candy Crowley's State of the Union program Sunday March 18, 2012, Rick Santorum questioned Romney's support among the Republican base, pointing out "He is not the strongest candidate in the field." Again, Romney is "right" that the Republicans are doomed in the election but he is "wrong" as to the cause having discounted the formidable challenge President Obama will present. This is significantly so because Mr. Obama will or has probably blocked or neutralized traditional Republican issues of campaign significance such as the "Willie Horton" type leniency, John Kerry's "Swift Boat" war controversy, and even the "soft on terror" claim often made against Democrats. Thus, they have to contend with the President's record on foreign and domestic issues coupled with his terrific campaign mode of operation; his charisma; and the power of incumbency.

When it comes to the question of the "nominee" we must remember Newt Gingrich once boldly proclaimed "I'll be the nominee!" as he has so blatantly also said, "The day after I am elected jobs will return" to America and "Health Care Reform will be repealed." At this stage of the game he is more a candidate for the "club of losers" as Herbert Cain, Michele Bachmann, Rick Perry, Tim Pawlenty, the "Koran Burning pastor" and the immigrant chasing Sheriff, among others. Still, his dismal showing, notwithstanding, in arrogance Gingrich believes he is the only candidate who can beat President Obama! If that is the case, and he is doing so bad, then the ultimate choice whether Santorum or Romney falls well within the "Doomed Republican" prediction for the national election. Notwithstanding, in his stumbling Mitt may arrive at the Florida Republican National Convention in a crawl because while Rick Santorum is mounting a sustained challenge and Newt Gingrich remains falsely confident he is still the conservative alternative to Mitt Romney, there thus is confusion in the Republican camp. Nevertheless, while we know Ron Paul will not bow out then these three contenders' narrow viewpoint fuel their false aspirations each will be the "nominee."

A credible assertion is as we approach the election homestretch a critically credible question is always who will bell the cat? While conservative votes thus far notwithstanding, former Senator Bob Dole questioned Rick Santorum's presidential leadership "timber;" David Axelrod remarked Mitt Romney "got his facts wrong;" and somehow, many people do not see Newt Gingrich at the G-8 Summit, addressing the United Nations or anywhere in the world standing as the United States representative and leader. As such, this brings us to that important juncture where the weak underbelly of the Republican Party is exposed and in their confused state must throw up "Holy Mary's" in hopes of fulfilling "McConnell's Mandate." Therefore, whether Mitt is "wrong" or "right' this brings us to the stark

FREDERICK MONDERSON

reality of President Obama's record and his having "not yet begun to fight" mantra for as wise men predict, his re-election is the best possible outcome, all things considered.

Speculators, pundits, nationalists, racists, all express some take on Mr. Obama, but most seem to wrongly assess the man's divine mission, his performance in office and his capabilities to wage a credible campaign creating the positive outcome. First, Mr. Obama admitted he ran for President to make America a better place and within the constraints he has been forced to operate under, the President confessed to not selling his vision short even if it means he serve only one term! That candid revelation stated; he has nothing to lose. In such a case, voters can respect such a frank confession.

Second, the record of Mr. Obama's performance has been stellar for the things he has achieved such as the Lilly Ledbetter Act, Health Care Reform, Auto Industry Rescue, focus on and reform of Wall Street enabling the Dow to jump from 6500 when he took office to more than 13,000 recently, to which we can add a shift in job performance numbers from minus 500,000 - 800,000 per month before he came into office to plus some 200,000 today. Added to this, Mr. Obama initiated credit card and student aid reform, insisted on a cleaner environment, encouraged experimentation to produce clean energy resources and permitted production of more oil through drilling than within the last decade. In his "Race to the Top" initiative and other such educational programs, the President vowed to reform education methodology and mechanics, emphasizing the means to improve transportation, whether through upgrading roads, bridges, tunnels, ports, airport infrastructure or building new corridors for high speed trains, and through it all Mr. Obama has singlehandedly navigated Republican minefields designed to stymie his domestic performance. On the foreign relations front he has genuinely changed the world's perception of America, opened new markets for America's products, offered incentives and encouraged some businesses to return home, taken a stand on nuclear proliferation and while he has failed to make a breakthrough in the Israeli-Palestinian issue even though he has been accused of being more pro-Palestinian, the highest echelons of Israeli administration have confessed the President has been a staunch ally of Israel. Even more important, whether we accept this or not, the "Arab Spring" has happened on Mr. Obama's watch and it may be due to seeds planted in his two addresses to the Muslim world made in Egypt and Turkey.

OBAMA - MASTER AND COMMANDER

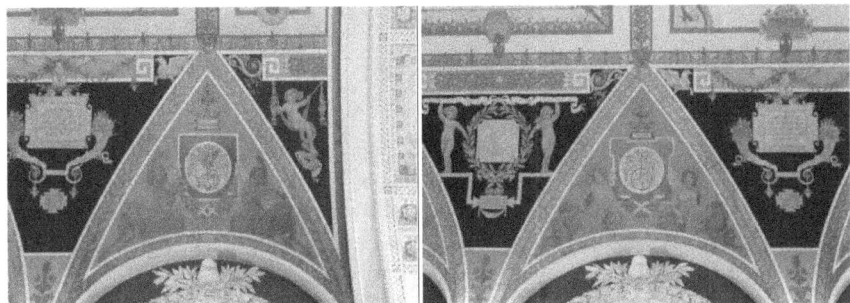

Obama - Master and Commander 166. Gryphe and Morin.

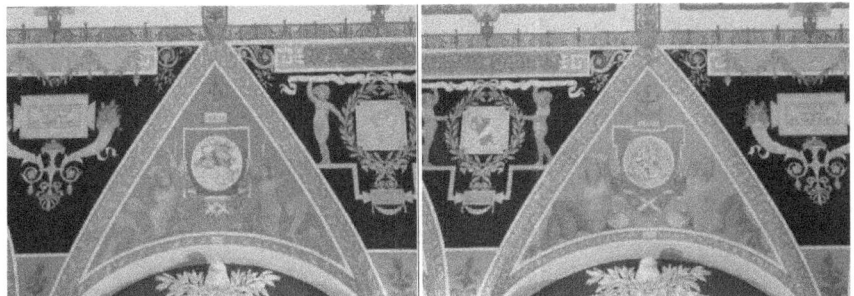

Obama - Master and Commander 167. Nivelle and Vostre.

While heavy vigilance and some luck has thwarted any terrorist successes on American soil, Mr. Obama has broken the back of Al Qaeda resistance with the killing of Osama bin-Laden and some 22 high profile members of the organization, disrupted their financial network and severely curtailed their abilities. He has taken on Somali Pirates, satisfactorily concluded the war in Iraq, is moving towards transitioning from Afghanistan and fought for new and improved benefits for the military and veterans and their families.

Certainly the economy is getting better even as Mitt Romney confessed; housing foreclosures have stabilized and new building starts are on the rise. Granted, the cost of oil rising to four dollars per gallon has become a campaign issue that Mitt Romney has seized upon. In trolling for votes, he has floated "Two something a gallon gas" as did Michele Bachmann's losing proposition. This naive view is totally unmindful of global factors such as tensions with Iran and other emerging great nations' incessant demands to fuel their economic growth. However, while Mitt feels in this climate such "oil talk" is credible and legitimate, the President's adviser Axelrod believes Mr. Romney's brand is actually "snake oil talk!"

Another important point to be considered, Mitt Romney recently won the Illinois Republican Primary trouncing Rick Santorum, Ron Paul and Newt Gingrich. For example, it is generally believed candidates tend to win their home state, a la

FREDERICK MONDERSON

Gingrich in Georgia. That makes Illinois a win for the incumbent because of the pride and benefits it brings. Given such, in Obama's stronghold Mrs. Ann Romney, in introducing her husband's victory speech, spoke of "taking back our country." Who is she referring to? The British, Germans, French, Italians, Japanese, Al Qaeda who have all killed Americans. No, she means taking it back from the black man and his family now in the White House and we know the despicable code words and their meanings. Let us not forget the Mormon question for that faith initially denied the humanity of the Black man! That was a questionable statement by a woman vying to be First Lady. Perhaps we need a more suave and sophisticated, intelligent First Lady such as Michelle Obama who will win congratulatory accolades for America at home and abroad rather than generate racial questions and sultry responses.

These factors being the case, when Mitt and his team are ready for the final push voters should ask 'Can you match Mr. Obama's performance record?' 'Do you have a magic formula that is fundamentally different than the President's efforts?' and 'Can you bring about a speedy transformation of the economy?' 'How have you helped the economy, the environment, the social climate over the last three years other than just saying "No" in a non-cooperative deconstructive campaign fueled by racial hatred?' 'When Speaker John Boehner boasted "We got 98% of what we wanted" in the Debt Ceiling debacle, coupled with the largess of the Bush Tax Cuts, and Republicans continue to threaten Health Care Reform, as well as fostering a climate of hostility without denouncing all such behaviors, all creating an ominous cloud on the nation's future, where did you stand?' Therefore, the Republican choice is, "wrong" and the "right" choice for a promising future is to continue along the Obama path of the promise of a brighter future.

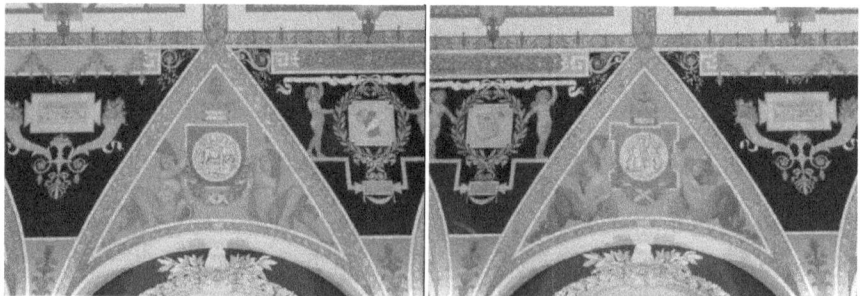

Obama - Master and Commander 168. Regnault and Colines.

OBAMA - MASTER AND COMMANDER

Obama - Master and Commander 169. Estienne and Velpius.

Obama - Master and Commander 170. Tory and Wechel.

"And I will do everything that I can as long as I am President of the United States to remind the American people that we are one nation under God, and we may call that God different names but we remain one nation." **Barack Obama**

"Acts of sacrifice and decency without regard to what's in it for you create ripple effects. Ones that lift up families and communities that spread opportunity and boost our economy." **Barack Obama**, Arizona State Commencement Speech, 2009

FREDERICK MONDERSON

Obama - Master and Commander 171. O, Minerva Champion of Enlightenment, thy list is indeed long! "Agriculture, education, mechanics, commerce, government, history, astronomy, geography, statistics, economics, painting, sculpture, architecture, music, poetry, photography, geology, botany, medicine, philosophy, law, politics, arbitration, treaties, army-navy, finance, art of war," and more!

OBAMA - MASTER AND COMMANDER

Obama - Master and Commander 172. "Theology" and Brooks, Edwards, Mather, Channing and Beecher.

Obama - Master and Commander 173. "Medicine" and Pinckney, Kent, Hamilton, Webster and Curtis.

FREDERICK MONDERSON

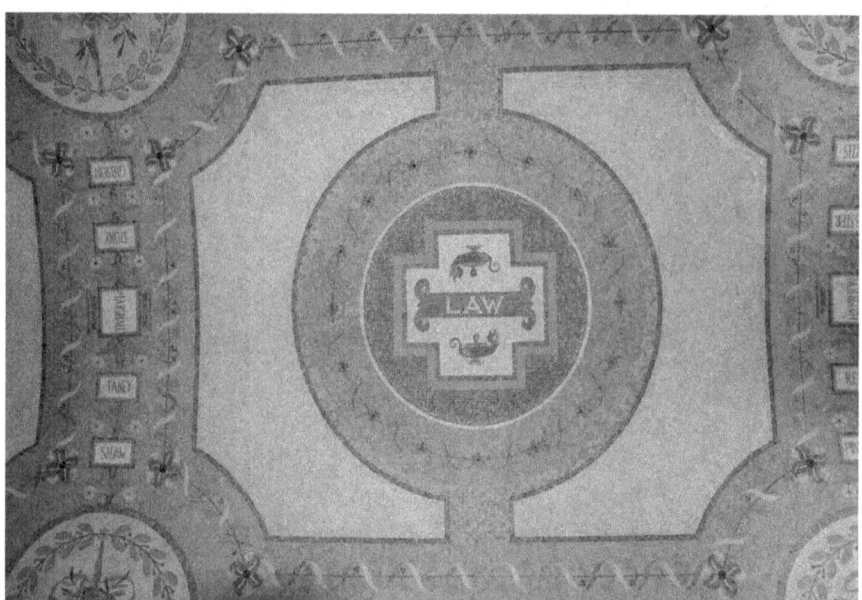

Obama - Master and Commander 174. "Law" and Shaw, Taney, Marshall, Story, Gibson.

Obama - Master and Commander 175. Artistic connections with a protractor and book and Brooks.

OBAMA - MASTER AND COMMANDER

Obama - Master and Commander 176. Artistic connections with writing and scientific instruments.

Obama - Master and Commander 177. Artistic connections at an Ionic column's capital with hammer and chisel.

FREDERICK MONDERSON

Obama - Master and Commander 178. Artistic connections and musical instrumets between Gross and Mason.

Obama - Master and Commander 179. Artistic connections and a globe signifying universality below Shaw.

OBAMA - MASTER AND COMMANDER

Obama - Master and Commander 180. Artistic connections, a palette and painter's supplies below Curtis.

Obama - Master and Commander 181. Artistic connections and an anchor and protractor to balance and steady things below Pinckney.

FREDERICK MONDERSON

Obama - Master and Commander 181a. Concave images encasing "Good and Bad," or "Aged and youth!"

Obama - Master and Commander 181b. "Memory is the Treasurer and Guarding of All Things."

"There's new energy to harness, new jobs to be created, new schools to build, and threats to meet, alliances to repair. The road ahead will be long. Our climb will be steep. We may not get there in one year or even in one term. But, America, I have never been more hopeful than I am tonight that we will get there. I promise you, we as a people will get there. There will be setbacks and false starts. There are many who won't agree with every decision or policy I make as president. And we know the government can't solve every problem. But I will always be honest with you about the challenges we face. I will listen to you, especially when we disagree. And, above all, I will ask you to join in the work of remaking this nation, the only way it's been done in America for 221 years - block by block, brick by brick, calloused hand by calloused hand." **Barack Obama**, Election Night Speech in Chicago, November 4, 2008

17. WHERE ARE THE GOOD MEN?
By
Dr. Fred Monderson

Are they scurrying for, or resting comfortably under, their rock of respectability, when they should be vigorously defending the integrity of America's most important institutions and their leaders. In this respect, they should surely know, at the height of the French Revolution and its bitter aftermath, the Englishman Edmund Burke in his treatise *Reflections on the Revolution in France 1791, 1792* wrote: "The only thing necessary for evil to triumph is for good men to say nothing!" I submit today, "Evil has triumphed in America this day" when an unrepentant racist monickered "Grand Pappy" could pen "Don't Re-Nig" - "Don't Re-elect Barack Obama." At this moment 8 such racist gems of similar sinister creativity, as they say, "have gone viral" on the Internet; not only to disparage Mr. Obama its purportedly intended victim but also to demean and debase the U.S. Presidency, the American nation, black Americans and the American people in general which is crass, arrogant, stupid, and is symptomatic of the white supremacy putrificatory sickness that is a subliminal sore constantly oozing puss like a raging storm in the intellectual, political, religious and social consciousness of this nation! As the world and Internet watch and wonder how such rotten apples can spoil the American barrel!

Conventional wisdom dictates the racist rant be ignored because it's designed to generate a response. However, as a current Advertisement on buses and trains in New York City reminds all, "If you see something, say something!" Particularly important, while conscious black people know what the code words, catch phrases, hand signals, Ads and even placards are saying; other blacks should have no illusions of the mental and spiritual putrefication that lies at the structural core of this nation and we must expose these cowardly racists for their insidious venom emanating from the core of the very apple they purportedly love and are seeking to defend in their disguised but distorted political attempts to defeat President

FREDERICK MONDERSON

Obama. Thus, we must never forget this malignant mindset at the root consciousness of a great part of this nation is a continuum of the mentality of the "white days of this nation" when the institution of slavery bred a viciousness and false sense of superiority aided by guns and Bible that committed and justified the most horrendous treatment of human beings in a nation founded on Christian principles. Much of this found justification in "Holy Writ" where either slavery is justified or pseudo-science in defense of slavery ingrained in the consciousness of the mind of the "Christian South" that the African was sub-human and any and all forms of savagery against him was justified. At this point, the savagery is not really directed at the savage but that savagery is directed by and reflective of the savage! After all, the white supremacist ideology ingrained in the founding philosophy of this nation that falsely believed the African was inferior in the natural order and therefore he should be inferior in the social order. Therefore, any other interpretation becomes illogical and "going against the will of God." Equality for Africans in this system not only opposes logic but also opposes God. As such, electing Barack Obama goes against the will of God as these pseudo-theorists affirm. Thus, as these twisted minds so argue, and given that view, from the highest echelons, whether political candidates or even committees in government, individuals create a climate of hatred that, as they say, some "nut" will seek to effectuate, as in the case of the Congresswoman Gifford.

Obama - Master and Commander 181c. Six patterns of stain glass surrounded by wonderful murals adorn the ceiling of the Jefferson Building of the Library of Congress.

OBAMA - MASTER AND COMMANDER

Obama - Master and Commander 182. Homer (left) and Milton (right).

Obama - Master and Commander 183. Dante (left) and Bacon (right).

Obama - Master and Commander 184. Aristotle (let) and Goethe (right).

Obama - Master and Commander 185. Shakespeare (left) and Moliere (right).

FREDERICK MONDERSON

To understand some aspects of the process of conditioning we look to Kenneth Stampp's book *The Peculiar Institution* Chapter IV entitled "To Make Them stand in Fear," where he outlines practical efforts the nefarious slave system utilized to mentally and physically shackle the African being subdued in the horrendous institution often decried as a "crime to humanity" and the methods they used to justify such brutality. On page 146 Mr. Stampp, recounts a discussion between Mary W. Bryan to Ebenezer Pettigrew contained in the Pettigrew Family Papers where he mentions a "North Carolina mistress, after subduing a troublesome domestic, realized that it was essential to 'make them stand in fear!'" Or, whether through the actions of any white person no matter how large or small, such can instill "Fear, awe, and obedience ... [and these] are interwoven into the very nature of the slave." Complementing the physical intimidation was the mental onslaught of the "Willie Lynch syndrome" pitting the black female against the black male in a "divide and conquer" offensive resulting in today's disrespect of blacks for blacks further contributing to "black on black crime." We therefore ask, when Newt Gingrich speaks of returning this nation to its core values is this what he means by returning this nation to that troubled past? Or, are we to aspire to the more creatively constructive vision articulated by Barack Obama of an America with equality for all creating an undergirding strength that allows the nation to soar and outdistance global competitors to live out its true creed that all men are created equal with the ability to propel this great land even forward. Fast, forward, and the "lynching states" all voted for Romney meaning they are buying what Republicans are shoveling. Old ideas die hard!

It is not surprising that Christian Ministers have led the charge in attempts to dehumanize the African in America to effectuate his exploitation and project a false sense of white superiority. As such, one has to wonder how many Christian ministers and their Bible reading flock will rush to denounce "Grand Pappy's" racist rant this Sunday morning March 18, 2012, because of its sinister nature easily in tandem with Republican aspirations to unseat President Obama in the 2012 general elections.

Even more significant, among the great Congressional leaders, viz., "Waterloo" DeMint who said "I like the President but his numbers are wrong;" we look for him to denounce this racism. As for, "I got that Nigger" thumbs up, "I intend to make Barack Obama a one term President" Mitch McConnell, he should introduce a measure in the Senate, not necessarily in defense of President Obama but to show the world the caring and respectable side of himself and such men of substance. Even "Poisoning the well" Rick Santorum who called Mitt Romney to wish him a happy 65th birthday should have been informed by his people of "Grand Pappy's" release as he "sun bathe shirtless" in Puerto Rico, photographed and have that image put on the Internet but equally pay no attention to disgracing the Presidency and disrespecting President Obama. This silenced is consistent with the different lanes but with the same objective of winning the Presidency at all

OBAMA - MASTER AND COMMANDER

costs. Will these leaders take a stand as decent individuals who will denounce "Grand Pappy's" racist gutter mentality? Hardly!

Let us never forget that great Republican Abraham Lincoln reminded all "To be silent in the face of wrong doing is to share culpability in that wrong." This development is equally a stark reminder to those deluded and "walking wounded individuals as Herbert Cain and Allen West" that if the President of the United States, the leader of the free world, a Black man, an African American, can be labeled with such disgusting appellation as "Nigger" then what are you!? One has to also wonder whether these latter as well as Republican icons Michael Steele and J.C. Watts will have table tennis or watermelon **balls,** if any, to say enough of that "Nigger talk!" And, that is the conundrum they face, for speaking out may get them "fired," but acquiescing in silence questions their manhood meaning they have compromised their souls and will perhaps never fight the omnipresent racist white supremacy sickness manifested by that minority who have hijacked the future of this nation tying it to a malignant past.

"And so our goal on health care is, if we can get, instead of health care costs going up 6 percent a year, its going up at the level of inflation, maybe just slightly above inflation, we've made huge progress. And by the way, that is the single most important thing we could do in terms of reducing our deficit. That's why we did it." **Barack Obama**

Obama - Master and Commander 186. Two of the four corners on the ceiling.

FREDERICK MONDERSON

Obama - Master and Commander 187. Two additional of the four corners of the ceiling.

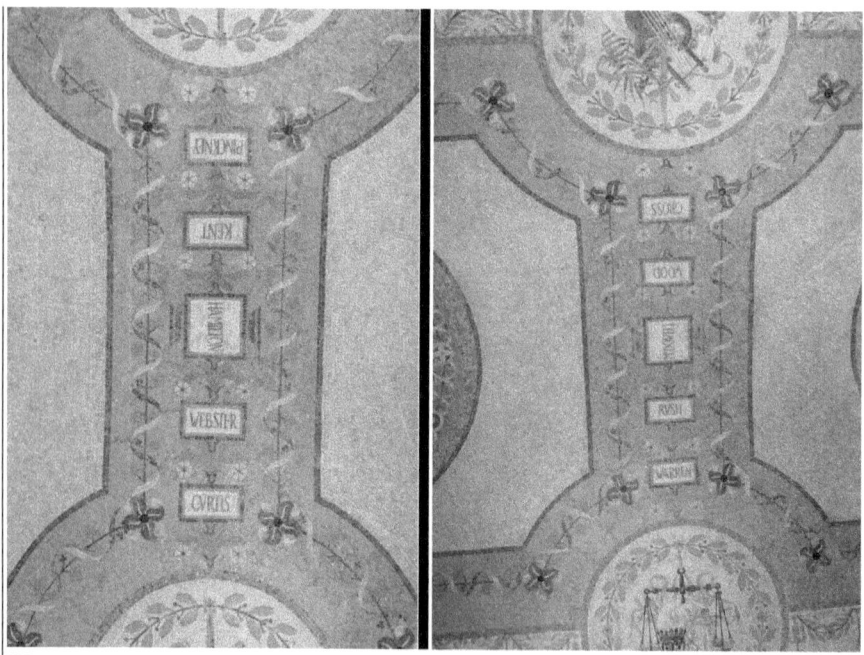

Obama - Master and Commander 188. Curtis, Webster, Hamilton, Kent and Pinckney(left) and Warren, Rush, McDowell, Wood, and Gross (right).

OBAMA - MASTER AND COMMANDER

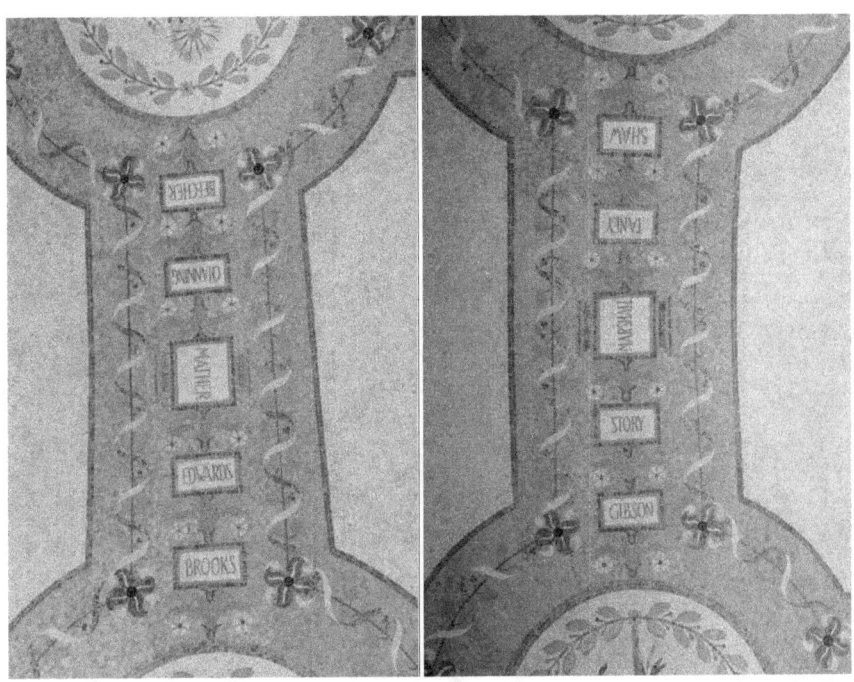

Obama - Master and Commander 189. Brooks, Edwards, Mather, Channing, Beecher (left) and Gibson, Story, Marshall, Taney and Shaw (right).

Obama - Master and Commander 190. Dodd Mead and Co. (left) and J.B. Lippincott Co. (right).

FREDERICK MONDERSON

Obama - Master and Commander 191. The Century Company (left) and The Riverside Press (right).

Obama - Master and Commander 192. Harper and Brothers (left) and The Devinne Press.

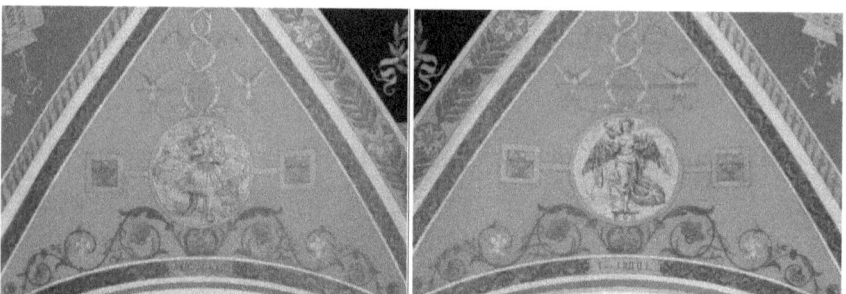

Obama - Master and Commander 193. Wolfgang Kopfel (left) and T. and J. Rihel (right).

"Everyone here knows that we have badly decaying roads and bridges all over this country. Our highways are clogged with traffic. Our skies are the most congested in the world. This is inexcusable. Building a world-class transportation system is part of what made us an economic superpower. And now we're going to sit back and watch China build newer airports and faster railroads? At a time when millions of unemployed construction workers could build them right here in America?" Barack Obama, speaking about infrastructure during jobs plan speech to Joint Session of Congress, September 2011

OBAMA - MASTER AND COMMANDER

18. ORIGINAL BOYS WEARING HOODS

By
Dr. Fred Monderson

Make no mistake the "Original Boys Wearing Hoods" were members of the Ku Klux Klan and many have argued they metamorphosed into elements of the "Tea Party" Movement's conservatism as a new assertion of the Klan, born of a hatred that never seems to end! Suppressed by the federal government's use of marshals and troops authorized under the Force Acts of 1870 and 1871, the Klan's terrorism was halted during Reconstruction though it was replaced by Jim Crowism and similar sinister strategies in alliance with the southern white power structure who influenced poor whites through the notion of white supremacy against political action by the newly freed African-American. However, by 1915, the year the "Grandfather Clause" was repealed, the Klan rose again to fight, as Unger states, "for native born, white, gentile Americans" against Negroes, Jews, Catholics and foreigners. By the end of World War I Klan members were incensed by black soldiers returning from Europe, as Lerone Bennett, Jr. says in *Confrontation: Black and White* (1966: 121) because Blacks had been "killing white men and sleeping with white women." In the post-war years they gained attention by distributing literature and selling Klan paraphernalia; so much so, membership increased to more than five million members in the 1920s. But, as Unger (1971: 120) again writes, "By 1927, however, the Klan had begun to overreach itself and its excesses of violence and vigilante tactics, as well as the corrupt and immoral behavior of some of its leaders, repelled many Americans. By the end of the decade, it had declined leaving behind an ugly legacy of hatred and violence endorsed in the name of one hundred percent Americanism." One commentator noted they metamorphosed into James Crow, Jr., Esquire and so functions today.

Notwithstanding, this terror group continued to function somewhat openly, somewhat under cover, though somewhat checked by strategies of black assertiveness and many believe the election of Barack Obama galvanized that brotherhood of sinister behavior; only at this later time the hoods were replaced by casuals and business suits, still in the name of conservatism. However, while the Civil War Amendments were designed to free and empower the ex-slave, southern conservatism engaged a number of devious strategies to regain power and limit black new found effectiveness. In one instance, Irwin Unger's *American History II: Reconstruction to Present*, New York: Monarch Press (1971: 7) ties southern Conservatives to the Ku Klux Klan in the following statement: "Some of these Southern Conservatives were happy to use the regular political process to achieve their ends. Others were willing to use violence and intimidation against Scalawags, Carpetbaggers, and Negroes. The more violent conservatives organized groups like the Ku Klux Klan, a secret society founded in 1866 to help 'redeem' the South

FREDERICK MONDERSON

from Radicals, black and white. The Klan was most active between 1868 and 1870 when its members, dressed in white sheets and hoods, threatened, beat and even killed supporters of the Radical state governments."

This was generally in response to events of 1867 in which, as Lerone Bennett in *Before the Mayflower* (1964) (1978: 196) wrote: "During the summer and fall of 1867, the Negro masses were stirred by an unparalleled ferment of political activity. Negroes flocked to huge open-air meetings, registered and organized political groups. Leaders emerged from the masses and demanded political and civil equality. The white South was stunned. It was believed at first that 'Sambo' would fall flat on his face. But the freedmen disappointed their late masters: They demonstrated a real genius for what one writer called 'the lower political arts.'" Explaining Klan origins and intent, Bennett (1978: 196-197) continued further that the first national meeting of the Klan occurred in April 1867, Room 10 at the Maxwell House in Nashville where in attendance were: "Confederate generals, colonels, substantial men of church and state, from Georgia, from Alabama, from all over. The leader: Nathan Bedford Forest, the strong man of the Fort Pillow Massacre. The plan: reduce Negroes to political impotence. How? By the boldest and most ruthless political operation in American history. By stealth and murder, by economic intimidation and political assassination, by whippings and maiming, cuttings and shootings, by the knife, by the rope, by the whip. By the political use of terror, by the braining of the baby in its mother's arms, the slaying of the husband at his wife's feet, the raping of the wife before the husband's eyes. By *fear*. Soon the South was honeycombed with secret organizations: the Knights of the White Camelia, the Red Shirts, the White League, Mother's Little Helpers and the Baseball Club of the First Baptist Church."

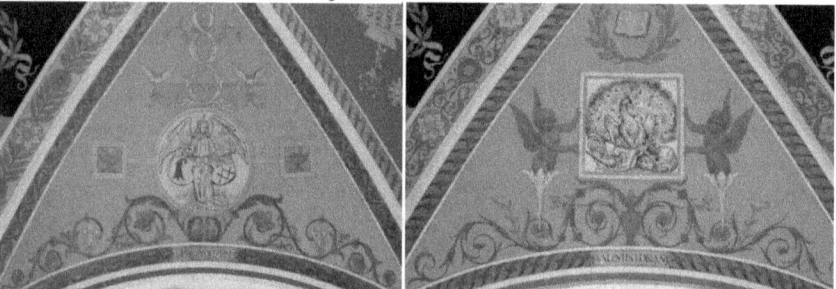

Obama - Master and Commander 194. Jacob Pfortzem (left) and Valentin Kobian (right).

OBAMA - MASTER AND COMMANDER

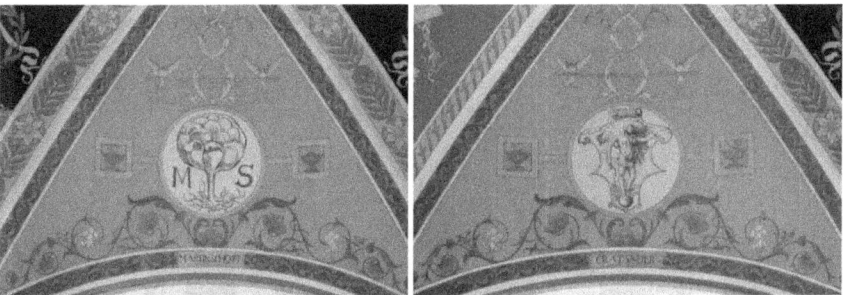

Obama - Master and Commander 195. Martin Schott (left) and Cratander (right).

Obama - Master and Commander 196. Fust and Schoffer (left) and Melchor Lotter (right).

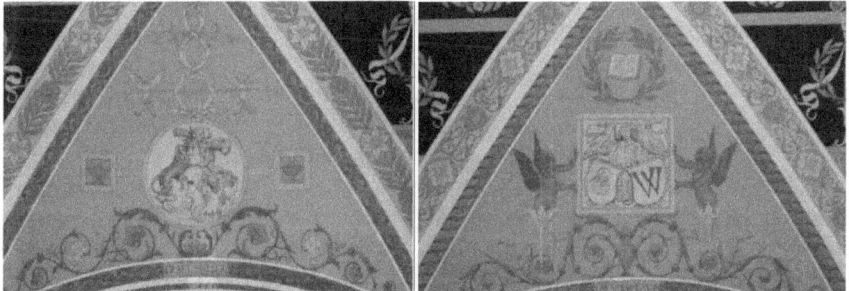

Obama - Master and Commander 197. Craft Muller (left) and Conrad Baumgakien (right).

In a somewhat prejudiced analysis attempting to explain the above dynamics, William Dunning of the "Dunning School" at Columbia University, according to Norman Hodges's *Black History* New York: Monarch Press (1974: 113) theorized an interpretation on influential events in the South following the Civil War, of which the last of five states now: "driven to desperation by misrule, the long

FREDERICK MONDERSON

suffering Southerners formed vigilante groups like the Ku Klux Klan to rescue the region from the carpetbagger regime." Hodges (1974: 113) continued his insight by stating further: "Morison has summed up the imagery of the Dunning interpretation in these words: 'The accepted fable represents Reconstruction as the ruthless attempt of Northern politicians to subject the white South, starving and helpless, to an abominable rule by ex-slaves ... and from which it was rescued by white-hooded knights on horseback who put the Negro 'back where he belonged.'" However, in *The Afro-American in United States History* (1972: 211-212) Da Silva, Finkelstein and Loshin remind us in this new advantage: "The men who gained power in Southern local and state governments could do much as they pleased. The power of the Federal government was not used to protect rights. That left each town, county or state its own master. The KKK and groups like it could attack a black person without fear of real punishment. The men who owned newspapers in the south began to work with the political leaders and KKK groups. They filled the minds with Jim Crow ideas. Terror silenced all men, white and black, who could not agree with them. They forced the entire south to accept Jim Crow." In this, "White men in the south built a wall between themselves and all blacks. They did this by laws and customs that pushed black people lower and lower. Rich and poor whites worked together to make this wall higher and higher. Rich men did it so they could keep their wealth and power. Poor whites did it to feel better than someone - in his case the Afro-American." Today we ask, 'Is that where we're heading' as we listen to the rhetoric of the conservative right wing?

Thus, as "forward to the Past" Newt Gingrich and "Poison the well" Rick Santorum vie to be considered the most conservative one has to wonder if this is where they want to take the Negro and the nation? After all, and we must never forget, as Hodges (1974: 117) writes: "The historical record strongly supports the view that the former rebel White South was unrepentant and vengeful in its treatment of Blacks during the two years of home rule that followed in the wake of war (1865-1867). A Black doctor, Daniel Norton, of Williamsburg, Virginia, described the situation to a Congressional Subcommittee, in 1866 [where he states] : '... the spirit of the whites against the blacks is much worse than it was before the war ..." In addition, he declared Klan behavior was such that blacks 'would be in danger of being hunted and killed.' In many respects, a century and a half later this attitude has continued though the law has more vigorously prosecuted such practitioners. Attorney General Eric Holder has remained ever vigilant!

If we explore this some more, we recognize it's a fact, "Newspapers tell the story of a nation" and that "One picture can tell a thousand words" but equally one movie can graphically implant images in the mind that, on the one hand, paints a picture of events but also sends a message of past issues or a reminder to others of returning to behaviors of the past. Take for example, the movie *Ten Commandments*, perhaps the most shown of all produced films; about ancient Egypt but purportedly shot in Arizona and seen thousands of times around the world; it is a great distortion, yet considered "gospel" in the minds of many.

OBAMA - MASTER AND COMMANDER

Additionally, Dr. Yosef ben-Jochannan always railed about social upheaval events in this nation that preceded the return showing of *Gone With the Wind*, while the book *The Clansman* by Thomas Dixon is another example of a moving tale, depicted in the movie *Birth of a Nation* portraying Klan misdeeds. In *Race: The History of An Idea in America* (1963) (1968: 339-340) Thomas F. Gossett writes *Birth of a Nation's* "version of history is frankly and crudely racist. The last half of the movie deals with the horrors of carpetbagger and Negro rule in South Carolina during the Reconstruction. Negroes are shown wildly reveling at elections, voting with both hands, and keeping the white man from the polls by force. As members of the state legislature, Negroes sit with their hats on and their bare feet on the desks as they drink liquor from flasks and pass an intermarriage law. The leading white Radical Reconstructionist in the North is shown with his Negro mistress. In the climax of the film, a renegade Negro pursues a young white girl through the woods. In order to avoid rape, she leaps to her death from a high rock. Her brother leads a mob to lynch the Negro and then organize a unit of the Ku Klux Klan to regain control of society by white men. He breaks up a crowd of rioting Negroes just in time to save another white girl from forced marriage with the mulatto lieutenant-governor. The film was one of the great box-office successes of all time; millions of Americans flocked to see it and to absorb its 'message'"

Even Gene Hackman's *Mississippi Burning* painted a grim reality of events that is a powerful reminder of behaviors still not extricated from the history or current practicing mindset of some in this nation. The movie, *In the Heat of the Night*, showed the Mayor telling top cop Gillespie if the black cop failed to produce the killer then he would get blame for the failure, not the town! Recently, within the last week, the movie *Oh Brother, Where Art Thou* was shown on a local channel. While the general theme said one thing, thousands of words of a photograph and one million of a movie enabled people with vision to see the subliminal messages extrapolated from imaged realities past and present.

Obama - Master and Commander 198. Gryphe (left) and Morin (right).

FREDERICK MONDERSON

Obama - Master and Commander 199. Nievelle (left) and Vostre (right).

Obama - Master and Commander 200. Regnault (left) and De Colines (right).

Obama - Master and Commander 201. Estienne (left) and Velpis (right).

One particular scene in *Oh Brother*, while it never got to that horrifying scene of a "hung and burning black man" as in The *Great Debaters*, or as in *The Black Book* showing "a roasting black man" surrounded by jeering white men, the movie scene depicts the Ku Klux Klan in full panoply, battledress, white uniforms, in measured formation in white headgear as the "Original Boys Wearing Hoods." While a seeming glimpse of a colorful spectacle, the scene is actually a microcosm of longstanding terrorism against the African enslaved in America, dehumanized and

OBAMA - MASTER AND COMMANDER

debased in a system practicing lynchings, tar and feathers, intimidation, denial of human and civil rights, Blacks discriminated against at the ballot box and even killed. So much so, commentators have labeled the decades following the Civil War that destroyed the system perpetuating the "Crime against humanity" within the Institution of Slavery as the "Classic Age of American domestic terrorism." This is because institutions of men on horsebacks and in hoods, particularly in collaboration with the white southern elite spewed carnage against black men, women and children in this nation as they sought to instill and reinforce a false notion of white supremacy. What was not apparent at the time, contrary to some of America's greatest theorists, the African or Negro in America was never inferior mentally but got inferior treatment in a land that boasted of freedom and equality.

Another interesting thing about *Oh Brother*, it reinforced the view of Ku Klux Klan as an organized and regimented racist system. However, like all organisms in nature, these do not terminate themselves but evolve in strategy, tactics, make-up, all forcefully albeit, designed to perpetuate their founding philosophy. In this manner they attract new converts to their way of thinking despite new generations' attempts to distance themselves from that disdainful past.

Obama - Master and Commander 202. Erotica (left) and Tradition (right).

FREDERICK MONDERSON

Obama - Master and Commander 203. History (left) and Comedy (right).

The CBS public affairs program **60 Minutes** ran an episode of the FBI investigating one of more than one hundred unsolved Civil Rights murder cases in Mississippi and elsewhere in the South. The subject of one case in particular was still alive but no one was talking except the victim's family members. The FBI's lead detective did say, in the climate of the time anyone who wanted to run for any office had to be a member or espouse the philosophy of the hooded terrorist groups as the KKK, Knights of the White Camellia, White Citizens Council and so on. None of these groups truly disbanded, revoked their philosophy or left their area of operation. They may have gone underground, changed their tactics and their attire from hoods to business suits, studied the law to more effectively get around it and been elected to government as conservatives serving as clogs in the system or patronage mills for people of similar minds, yet still continuing to recruit members. Thus, thinking people must wonder, particularly when presidential candidates, seeking to unseat President Obama tell how conservative they are, one has to wonder, is there a connection with past terrorism? We must not forget, Mitt Romney won all the "lynching states!"

OBAMA - MASTER AND COMMANDER

"But if you - if what - the reports are true, what they're saying is, is that as a consequence of us getting 30 million additional people health care, at the margins that's going to increase our costs, we knew that." **Barack Obama**

Obama - Master and Commander 204. Tragedy (left) and Lyrica (right).

FREDERICK MONDERSON

Obama - Master and Commander 205. Romance (left) and Fancy (right).

"I trust the American people to realize that while we don't need big government, we do need a government that stands up for families who are being tricked out of their homes by Wall Street predators; a government that stands up for the middle-class by giving them a tax break; a government that ensures that no American will ever lose their life savings just because their child gets sick. Security and opportunity; compassion and prosperity aren't liberal values or conservative values - they're American values." **Barack Obama**, speech, May 2008

19. VOTING RIGHTS AND REDISTRICTING
By
Dr. Fred Monderson

Attorney General Eric Holder gave an interesting speech on Tuesday December 13, 2011 at the Lyndon B. Johnson library in which he took on the issue of redistricting that has been causing some concern across the South as the nation gears up for the 2012 national elections. President Johnson, who signed the 1965

OBAMA - MASTER AND COMMANDER

Voting Rights Act would have been proud of Mr. Holder whose Justice Department promises to move aggressively in reviewing, according to *New York Times* Wednesday December 14, 2011 in which Charlie Savage's "Holder signals Tough Review of State Laws on Voting Rights," "Voting laws that civil rights advocates say will dampen minority participation in next year's election. Pulling no punches and promising to use the full weight of his department to ensure that new electoral laws are not discriminatory, the Attorney General held protecting ballot access for all eligible voters must be viewed not only as a legal issue but as a moral imperative.'" Thereupon he called on all Americans to urge their "political parties to resist the temptation to suppress certain votes in the hope of attaining electoral success and, instead achieve success by appealing to more voters."

Obama - Master and Commander 206. Archaeology (left) and Astronomy (right).

FREDERICK MONDERSON

Obama - Master and Commander 207. Botany and Chemistry.

Obama - Master and Commander 208. Geology and Mathematics.

OBAMA - MASTER AND COMMANDER

Obama - Master and Commander 209. Physics (left) and Zoology (right).

For some time now attention has been focusing on voting rights as it has been affected through redistricting which occurs every ten years after the census count. The argument has been made that the dominant political party in state legislatures has a tendency to redraw the lines in a manner that benefits that party's incumbent members and the new candidates they intend to field. This method of manipulating the political boundaries has been called gerrymandering after an original theorist called Jerry. Apparently, such an individual had been assigned to draw up a particular voting district and he skewed the configuration to such an extent, one observer remarked the new district lines looked very much like a salamander. The author then responded, "This is not a salamander, it is a gerrymander!" The name stuck and so any attempt to carve unusual district voting lines that include certain groups or exclude or hinder others, is considered "Gerrymandering." However, while this "pre-carving" may not be considered illegal, it certainly is unethical and immoral in that it seeks to diffuse, limit or diminish the voting strength of one or more groups to aid or advance the cause of another to give that group an edge at upcoming elections.

FREDERICK MONDERSON

Obama - Master and Commander 210. Hugo (left) and Musset (right).

Obama - Master and Commander 211. Byron (left) and Shelley (right).

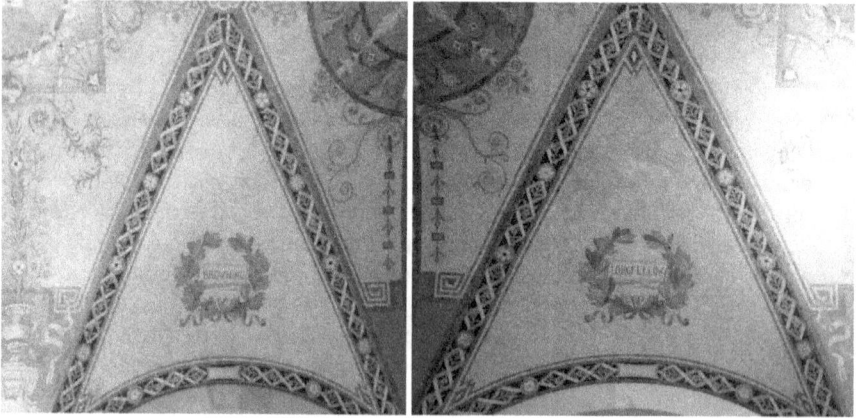

Obama - Master and Commander 212. Browning (left) and Longfellow (right).

OBAMA - MASTER AND COMMANDER

Obama - Master and Commander 213. Lowell (left) and Whittier (right).

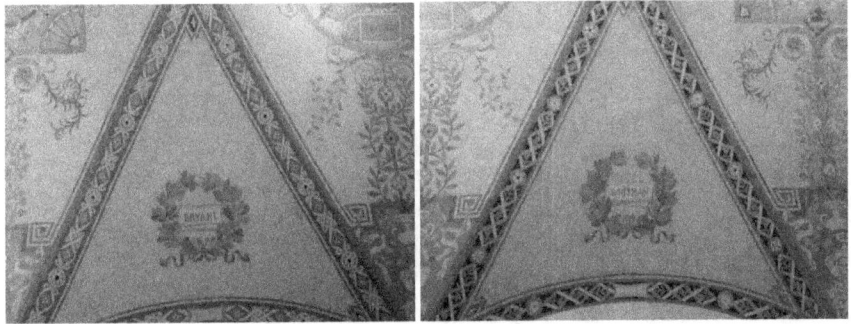

Obama - Master and Commander 214. Bryant (left) and Whitman (right).

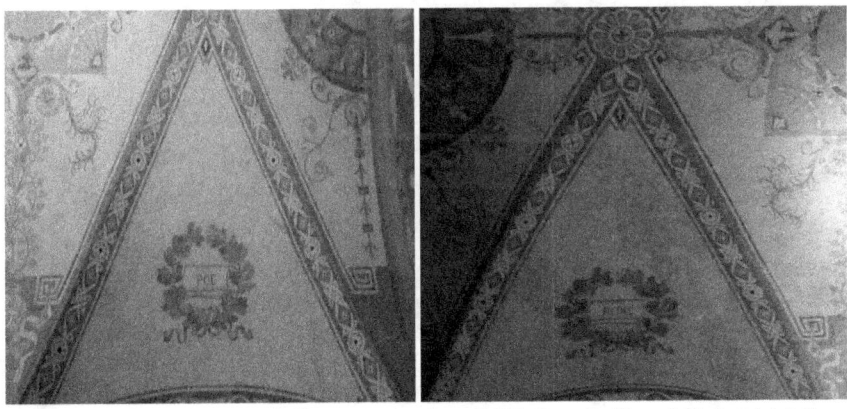

Obama - Master and Commander 215. Poe (left) and Heine (right).

FREDERICK MONDERSON

Gerrymandering is not the only way in which the voting strength and *ipso facto* voting power of different, albeit minority groups are targeted as part of a general strategy of disfranchisement. In various regions of the country people convicted of a felony are deprived of their voting rights. Some have argued in several southern states the criminal justice system is used as a mechanism to disfranchise minorities who disproportionately comprise prison populations. In this, the argument has been made that misdemeanor criminal behavior is oftentimes elevated to felony standard and as such these individuals are removed from the voting rolls. Advocates for these dispossessed persons have argued once a person has paid the debt to society then all of the individual's natural and civil as well as political rights should be reinstated.

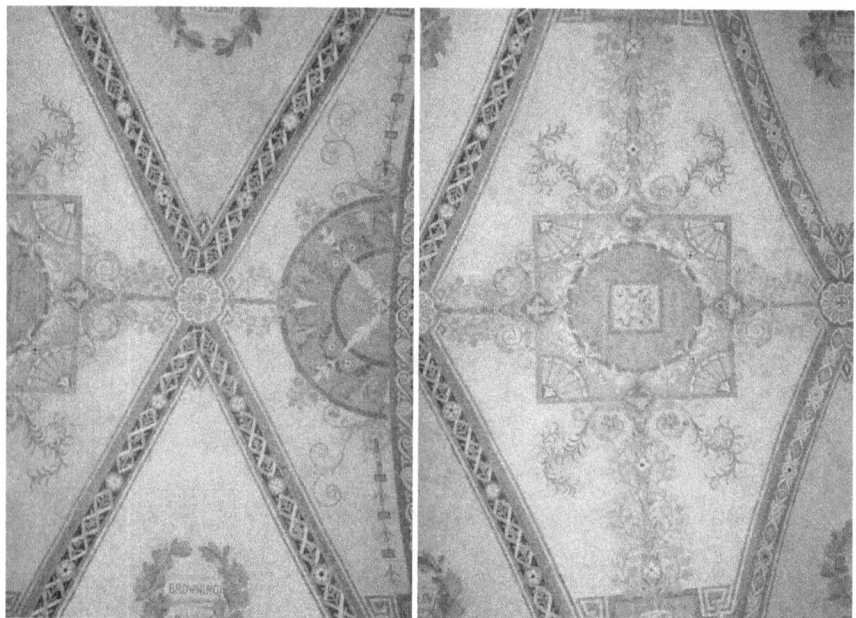

Obama - Master and Commander 216. Criss-cross squares (left) and circle (right).

Another method used to purge the voting rolls is to insist people who have not voted in recent elections be deemed ineligible. However, while this may create a gray area, nefarious individuals with a party agenda often take the initiative and remove persons in unscrupulous moves. This form of behavior is a throwback to the post civil war era when southern voting and polling individuals went to great lengths to deny and invalidate the intent of the 13th, 14th, and 15th Amendments that followed the conflict. To recall, southern polling officials required of freedmen

OBAMA - MASTER AND COMMANDER

that they take literacy tests, show proof of property qualification, evidence of paid poll taxes and they even invented a "grandfather clause" which held, if one's grandfather had voted, then regardless of one's literacy, intellectual or other qualifying factors they were entitled to vote. Naturally, Blacks *en masse* who had been enslaved and denied the ballot previously were automatically disqualified. For more than four decades the "Grandfather clause" held sway and helped and hurt voters until it was declared unconstitutional by the Supreme Court in 1915. Matching these "legal machinations" of voting denial, threats and intimidation in face of a national government turning a deaf ear, black voting rights had been effectively nullified and a manipulated "White Primary" further alienated those hardy enough to attempt to exercise the franchise.

There is evidence of white men with guns at polling stations and this was designed to intimidate black voters. The secret nature of the ballot was betrayed and an individual's voting preference was reported to his employer the next day almost certainly to get him fired from a hard won job. In addition, signs indicating polling sites were often turned around sending voters in the wrong direction to be often waylaid by highwaymen as all part of the conspiracy to nullify black and other minorities' votes. These sinister deeds do not exhaust efforts to block legitimate black ballot expression. What is interesting, as later as the 2008 national election Republicans engaged in similar dishonest practices generating paperwork insisting on "Day One" Republicans vote and on "Day Two" Democrats vote. This was designed to confuse persons not really astute about the process. People were informed if they had outstanding warrants or parking tickets the police would be there to arrest them if they tried to vote. People's jobs were threatened if they tried to vote and a whole lot more strategies were used to dissuade would-be voters who tended to vote democratic. In addition to the above, disqualification methods may be mentioned "mental incompetents, election law violator and vagrants."

While the 13th Amendment freed the slaves, the 14th gave citizenship to persons born in the United States and the 15th Amendment, adopted in 1870, forbade any state from denying persons the right to vote because of race, color, or previous condition of servitude. Jack C. Plano and Milton Greenberg in *The American Political Dictionary* (1962) (1989: 71) summed up the significance of the Fifteenth Amendment. To explain this they wrote: "Although the Fifteenth Amendment does not give anyone an absolute right to vote, it does prohibit any discrimination because of race or color. Not until recent years have blacks made significant advances in realizing the goals established by the amendment. In 1960, for example, the Supreme Court ruled that the racial gerrymandering of Tuskegee, Alabama, so as to exclude all Black voters from city elections violated the Fifteenth Amendment (*Gomillion v. Lightfoot*, 364 U.S. 339). The Civil Rights Acts of 1957, 1960, 1964 and the Voting Rights Act of 1965, 1970, and 1975 was passed by Congress and the Twenty-Fourth Amendment prohibiting poll taxes was adopted to aid blacks in overcoming the various devices used by some southern states to frustrate the purposes of the Fifteenth Amendment." It may well be that

FREDERICK MONDERSON

history has repeated itself as gerrymandering is being driven in the rush to redistrict in the several states and as such Attorney General Eric Holder's intervention is not only timely but necessary.

We recognize time is now for the process of redrawing political boundaries based on the newest census data and this is necessary to determine how recourses and representation in local school board, city council, county commission and state legislatures can be allocated. However, what led to the Attorney general's intervention is the manner several state legislatures under Republican control seem to rush to target black areas that potentially vote democratic.

"I can make a firm pledge, under my plan, no family making less than $250,000 a year will see any form of tax increase. Not your income tax, not your payroll tax, not your capital gains taxes, not any of your taxes." **Barack Obama**

Obama - Master and Commander 217. Longfellow.

OBAMA - MASTER AND COMMANDER

Obama - Master and Commander 218. Browning!

Obama - Master and Commander 219. Circles in square.

FREDERICK MONDERSON

"We have a huge opportunity, at this moment, to bring manufacturing back. But we have to seize it. Tonight, my message to business leaders is simple: Ask yourselves what you can do to bring jobs back to your country and your country will do everything we can to help you succeed." **Barack Obama**, State of the Union Address, January 2012

20. LAWMAKERS IN HOODIES
By
Dr. Fred Monderson

Taking the law into their own hands, several lawmakers have made a clear and unmistakable statement by wearing a "Hoodie" on the floor of their legislature. First, the *New York Post* of Tuesday March 27, 2012 featured a photograph of New York State Senators Kevin Parker, Bill Perkins and Eric Adams wearing Hoodies "in Albany yesterday in tribute to Trayvon" which said "The demonstration of minorities by policies was born here in New York City!" Now, Congressman Bobby Rush (D. Illinois) has been removed from the U.S. House of Representatives chamber for wearing a "Hoodie" on the floor of that legislative body while giving a speech on Trayvon Martin, the young man shot to death by Neighborhood-Watch Volunteer George Zimmerman. The significance of such social protest within a legislative body seems designed to call attention for government to more closely view this case, examine existing laws that actually undercut citizens' rights and equality by even more serious undercurrents taking Black Americans more seriously.

Every American takes pride in their ethnic heritage and so does the African American. When Barack Obama declared his candidacy for the Presidency of the United States, having declared his ethnicity, African Americans took great pride in seeing a Black man with a black wife and two lovely black daughters representing the best of an American family. They turned out in droves to vote for Mr. Obama for President to be part of the historic moment when the nation would elect its first African to the nation's highest office. After all, we have experienced the first Black Governor, Senator, Congressman, Police Captain, Corrections Officer, General, Admiral, Cabinet member and so much more. Therefore, many argued, the nation was ready for a Black President, Commander-In-Chief and a Black First Lady and a Black First Family. Many people hailed this as the beginning of a "post-racial America." However, subsequent events proved this was wishful thinking because of the many "fifth wheels to the coach" and the numerous individuals setting backfires that did nothing but agonize the soul of this nation.

Many people argued the birth of the "Tea Party" movement was an outgrowth of the Ku Klux Klan with the same racist outlook as they evolved from white hoods to business suits. As they caricatured the President, observers noticed the racial

OBAMA - MASTER AND COMMANDER

animosity in the attacks. Yet, Mr. Obama, smart as he is and more American than most of the critics of his birthright and patriotism dismissed those roasting simply as "youthful temper tantrums." However, others saw a more sinister side to it. African Americans complained, "Look at how they are treating the President, our hero!" The "Tea Party" attacked the president! They questioned his birthright, his religion, his patriotism, his leadership skills, his right to be Commander-In-Chief, his sincerity, his numbers and his judgment. No one said anything to challenge this venomous behavior from in and outside of government. Race baiters accused the President of going to change the constitutional right to bear arms and in response they stocked up on armaments in preparation for a race war they thought would come but didn't.

Obama - Master and Commander 220. "A little learning is a dangerous thing. Drink deep or taste not of the Pierian Spring" (left) and "Vain, very vain the weary search to find that bliss which only centers in the mind" (right)

Obama - Master and Commander 221. "Learning is but an adjunct to ourself" (left) and "Creation's heir - The World. The world is mine" (right).

FREDERICK MONDERSON

Obama - Master and Commander 222. "Studies perfect nature and are perfected by experience" (left) and "The universal cause acts to one end. But acts by various laws" (right).

Obama - Master and Commander 223. "Dreams books are each a world. Books we know are a substantial world both pure and good" (left) and "The fault is not in our stars but in ourselves that we are underlings" (right).

When Mr. Obama set about tackling the many challenges facing the American nation such as profuse job loss, home foreclosures, Wall Street in rapid retreat, the auto industry failing miserably, deterioration of social and physical infrastructure, education in decline, while two wars waged in Iraq and Afghanistan, Al Qaeda terrorists threatening, Somali Pirates abducting on the high seas and the world angry at the image of America, he got no cooperation from Republicans. Despite the trumping of every conceivable anti-Obama sentiment the President was proved successful in tackling nearly ninety percent of those listed maladies despite "I got that Nigger" thumbs up Senator Mitch McConnell's mandate to make Mr. Obama "a one term president;" Jim DeMint wanted to create his "Waterloo;" and every Republican stood in total opposition to the president and his policies.

"I know my country has not perfected itself. At times, we've struggled to keep the promise of liberty and equality for all of our people. We've made our share of mistakes, and there are times when our actions around the world have not lived up to our best intentions." **Barack Obama**

OBAMA - MASTER AND COMMANDER

"I reject the view that says our problems will simply take care of themselves; that says government has no role in laying the foundation for our common prosperity. For history tells a different story. History reminds us that at every moment of economic upheaval and transformation, this nation has responded with bold action and big ideas. In the midst of civil war, we laid railroad tracks from one coast to another that spurred commerce and industry. From the turmoil of the Industrial Revolution came a system of public high schools that prepared our citizens for a new age. In the wake of war and depression, the GI Bill sent a generation to college and created the largest middle-class in history. And a twilight struggle for freedom led to a nation of highways, an American on the moon, and an explosion of technology that still shapes our world. In each case, government didn't supplant private enterprise; it catalyzed private enterprise. It created the conditions for thousands of entrepreneurs and new businesses to adapt and to thrive."
Barack Obama, Address to Joint Session of Congress, February 2009

21. OBAMA PRESIDENCY: A FAILURE? HARDLY!
By
Dr. Fred Monderson

Recently, former Massachusetts Governor Mitt Romney boldly proclaimed the Obama Presidency a failure which forces serious minded individuals to ask whether his sophistry is well earned or his pronouncement is grounded in uncontroverted facts. First, let us not forget, Senior Obama Adviser David Axelrod had previously pointed out, "Mr. Romney got his facts wrong" and also accused him of spewing "Snake oil talk" in his efforts to convince Republican voters he is their "nominee" at a time when he can't "put away" his principal rivals "poison the well" Rick Santorum and "I'll be the Nominee" Newt Gingrich. We must also remember, Santorum in his frustrated state said essentially "a bad Obama is still better than a best Romney." That is, before he was called out and recounted this particular statement.

Notwithstanding, while the pundits trumpet the inevitability of a Romney nominee and despite high level Republican operatives' call for Santorum to drop out of the race, he keeps winning as he did in Louisiana in his "fool's errand." All this forces us to conclude far from the Obama Presidency being a failure, the failure is with Romney, a man with more flip-flop slippers than Imelda Marcos has shoes and it is no wonder Republicans are distrustful of their "frontrunner."

FREDERICK MONDERSON

Thus, right thinking individuals recognize the rhetoric in the Republican presidential primary's "age of sophistry" and the fact Mr. Obama has not yet begun to fight. When Mr. Obama does enter the fray in a head-to-head contest, he is sure to point to Mr. Romney's weaknesses, his flip flops, mis-statements as "corporations are people too" because of his Wall Street largesse, his less than stellar record as Governor of Massachusetts and the even greater muddle Republicans bequeathed Mr. Obama. However, a look at Mr. Obama's record clearly demonstrates leadership, empathy and concern for all Americans.

"I miss Saturday morning, rolling out of bed, not shaving, getting into my car with my girls, driving to the supermarket, squeezing the fruit, getting my car washed, taking walks." **Barack Obama**

Obama - Master and Commander 224. Method in the Madness as these artistic lights in the constellation certainly impress in variety of composition, dynamics of color and variety in display.

OBAMA - MASTER AND COMMANDER

Obama - Master and Commander 225. The decorative marble-like arrangement of squares, circles, semi-circles and crosses and hearts is truly masterpiece in composition.

Obama - Master and Commander 226. "No musician but be sure he heard and strove to render feeble echoes of celestial strains" (left) and "No true painter ever set on canvas all the glorious visions he conceived" (right).

Obama - Master and Commander 227. "Dwells within the soul of every artist more than all his effort can express" and "No great thinker ever lived and taught you all the wonder that his soul received."

FREDERICK MONDERSON

Obama - Master and Commander 228. Praise for "The poets who on earth have made us heirs of truth and pure delight by Heavenly lays."

"What I've tried to do since I started running for President and since I was sworn in as President, is to communicate the notion that America is a critical actor and leader on the world stage, and that we shouldn't be embarrassed about that, but that we exercise our leadership best when we are listening; when we recognize that the world is a complicated place and that we are going to have to act in partnership with other countries; when we lead by example; when we show some element of humility and recognize that we may not always have the best answer, but we can always encourage the best answer and support the best answer." **Barack Obama**, press conference, April 2009

OBAMA - MASTER AND COMMANDER

Obama - Master and Commander 229. Sciences: Astronomy, Geology, Physics, Chemistry and Mathematics.

Obama - Master and Commander 230. Rosettes in squares against embroidery edges.

FREDERICK MONDERSON

22. REFLECTIONS ON THE NEW OBAMA AGE
By
Dr. Fred Monderson

President Obama has been villainized by so many persons who lay claim to being "analysts" one has to wonder how we could trust such persons who have now shown their biased, even bigoted underbelly. One thing that can be said for Mr. Obama, he takes these insults in stride allowing others to see how ridiculously insulting, to the President of the United States, the most powerful man in the world, these individuals could demonstrate their disrespect.

In aftermath of the Navy Seals' raid on Osama bin-Laden's compound, at the height of his "birther charade," in the *New York Post* a political cartoon appeared showing President Obama instructing his forces "the next compound you will raid will be Trump Towers." Unfortunately, this never materialized for Donald Trump soon self-destruct and reclused himself as a Presidential contender. The brilliance of Obama is seen in his brushing the nuisance from his shoulder, allowing his disrespectful clients to bake and eat their own baked "crow pie."

It is interesting how Republicans, unable to tarnish Obama's brilliance in their never ending critique of his social policies constantly revert to their last line of armament, *ad hominem*.

Obama - Master and Commander 231. Circles in circles.

OBAMA - MASTER AND COMMANDER

Obama - Master and Commander 232. "This is the state of man today. He puts forth the tender leaves of hope" (left) and "For a web begun, God sends the thread" (right).

Obama - Master and Commander 233. "Tomorrow blossoms and bears his blessing honors thick upon him" (left) and "The web of life is of a mingled yarn, good and ill together" (left).

Obama - Master and Commander 234. "Comes the blind fury with the abhorred shears and slits the thin spun life" (left) and "The third day comes a frost and nips his root and then he falls" (right).

One has to wonder at Republican "big guns" McCain, Palin, McConnell, Boehner, Graham, DeMint, etc., after a "busy day at the office," when they get home, flop down on the couch, unfold the newspaper or turn on the TV, only to be greeted by

FREDERICK MONDERSON

the fallout of "One of our guys," "our allies" has called President Obama a "dick" or as Rep. Wilson did in the Chamber of the House, tell the President "you lie" etc., "stupid" Grassley, "stupid" Sununu. Do these guys high-five themselves, get on the phone to congratulate each other for another notch of insult in their belt or squirm in the seats or hide under the sofa, having unlocked Pandora's, I mean, the Republican's "box" ofstupid and scurrilous negativity.

The newest shoot from the lip attack on the character of the President was made by Mark Halperin, a commentator on MSNBC who thought he was on "delayed feed," called Mr. Obama a "D" word that was not Democrat. Naturally, CNN's ticker has reported "MSNBC panelist suspended after Obama insult." In this case, while Republicans may be able to claim Mr. Halperin is not a "card carrying member" of their club, independent critics opposed to Mr. Obama are on their side of the line and therefore are unwilling and as such, perhaps, unintentional allies.

On CNN's "In the Arena" with Elliot Spitzer, former Governor of New York, a commentator Abrams seems one of the first and honest voices, in commenting on MSNBC's action in response to the President's press conference and Mr. Halperin's remarks, said "This is not something you say about the President of the United States."

Obama - Master and Commander 235. Agra, Rome, Athens, Gizeh.

OBAMA - MASTER AND COMMANDER

Even more! In the run-up to the Supreme Court ruling on Health Care Reform, Senator Charles Grassley thought President Obama "stupid" if he believed the Court would uphold the law. Well, Grassley turned out to be the stupid one. Bet he did not apologize for his foot in mouth. Still more! Former Governor John Sununu also thought the President "stupid. " You have to wonder how these individuals got to the top in their career. Perhaps we need to enquire how many persons they shortchanged in rise to their emptiness. All this may teach us, even "nice looking" supposedly "normal" people can drop "bombs" and one has to wonder what about President Obama that really motivates people to speak so loosely and disrespectfully about this man. We also had a Republican Senator say on the floor "The President should be ashamed ...." For what? He did not reach to grab some person's ankle in a public restroom! He has never been "hiking the Appalachian Trail." President Obama has not fathered any illegitimate children and been unfaithful to his wife!

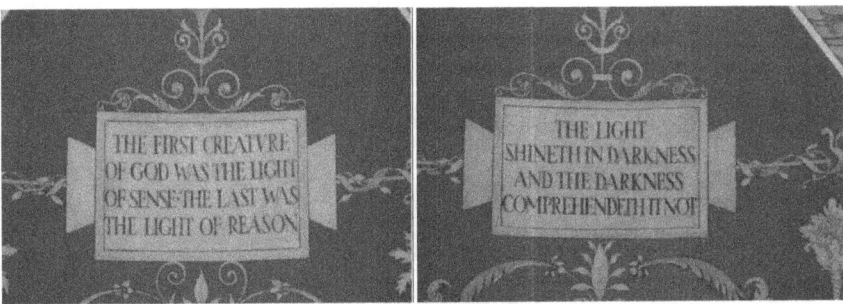

Obama - Master and Commander 236. "The First Creature of God was the Light of Sense. The last was the Light of Reason" (left) and "The Light shineth in Darkness and the Darkness comprehendeth it Not" (right).

Obama - Master and Commander 237. "All are but parts of one stupendous whole whose body Nature is and God the soul" (left) and "In Nature all is useful, all is Beautiful" (right).

FREDERICK MONDERSON

Now, in the smoke and mirrors euphoria that clouded "Arnold's" rise to become Governor of California, many Republicans began championing the notion of changing the constitutional requirement that a presidential candidate not necessarily be native born so Arnold Schwarzenegger could run for and become President of the United States. How beautiful the music of that Pied Piper sounded! Unfortunately he had pooped on the party but bottled it up in a closet that was finally opened. Meanwhile, other wings of the Republican Party were incessantly, vehemently and inclandestinely denying Barack Obama's citizenship and right to be President. As betting men, these Republicans, in their tunnel vision, chose the potential long shot as a safe bet, while ignoring the safe bet as a long shot. In other words, they were willing to choose a man who cheated on his wife, sleep with the help, fathered an illegitimate child over a respectable married man with a beautiful wife and two lovely children who are ideals of what even Republicans themselves want in a family and leader.

Obama - Master and Commander 238. Majesty and strength in sculptural creation.

OBAMA - MASTER AND COMMANDER

Obama - Master and Commander 239. Beauty and strength in delightful sculptural creation.

For argument sake, let us suppose the covered farce was successful and Arnold elected President of the United States. So here we have him attending a G-8 meeting and there he is on the platform with leaders of the other great nations and the customary anarchists are outside picketing. Now, **Wikileaks** leader Assange releases the ethically damaging information about his philandering, can you imagine how much mileage this nation's enemies would get in criticizing America. Here again, on that Spitzer program, another Republican Congressman had boasted and took credit for saying the President should be ashamed, for whatever. Now, here we have an intelligent, professionally and academically qualified Mr. Obama, whose stamina and strategies and tactics awarded him the US Presidency. The people, whether in government or not, who have disparaged Mr. Obama constantly, do not have the intellectual fortitude or academic accreditation of a man genuinely committed to improving the condition of his nation from these changing times. Word has it, in the academic age of the 1970s, when young Adjuncts and Professors applied for teaching positions, particularly in the Community Colleges, the people in control of P and B (Personnel and Budget) would demand some of the highest qualifications from these new people. They, on the other hand, had "slipped in" with degrees in "Basket-making" and "Pottery" and were now in those powerful committees.

Perhaps if these people had the educational qualifications of Mr. Obama then they would not be so outlandish. With a sound educational background, you see the world and people differently.

Again, that Congressman added the president launched his re-election campaign nearly two years before election date. What he did not include, President Obama has been attacked before he became President, while he is president, on his way to

FREDERICK MONDERSON

re-election, and will be even after he is re-elected and perhaps after he leaves office in 2017. Well, let the American people do the math!

"I said that America's role would be limited; that we would not put ground troops into Libya; that we would focus our unique capabilities on the front end of the operation, and that we would transfer responsibility to our allies and partners."
Barack Obama

Obama - Master and Commander 240. Man in "The State of Nature!"

OBAMA - MASTER AND COMMANDER

Obama - Master and Commander 241. Circles make a wonderful decorated pattern.

"The only way to fully restore America's economic strength is to make the long-term investments that will lead to new jobs, new industries, and a renewed ability to compete with the rest of the world. The only way this century will be another American century is if we confront at last the price of our dependence on oil and the high cost of health care; the schools that aren't preparing our children and the mountain of debt they stand to inherit." **Barack Obama**, Address to Joint Session of Congress, February 2009

23. THE BUCK STOPS WITH BARACK!
By
Dr. Fred Monderson

Every once in a great while along comes an equally, great individual who not only levels the playing field but also moves the ball towards the goal line to score. History will show Barack Obama as a leader genuinely concerned with the future of this nation and has done everything possible in his first term to remedy the situation he inherited, despite the odds of succeeding, particularly and in spite of the tremendous efforts of the stone throwers. Sure the buck stops with the top guy and even Barack Obama is sufficient of a pragmatist to recognize, to be in the left lane you must speed but also look out for Smokey!

FREDERICK MONDERSON

Not only has Mr. Obama recognized his "shovel ready" projects were not always "shovel ready," but he has made significant efforts to address those crucial sectors of the economic and social sectors of the America landscape that would aid progress in moving the nation forward. It's interesting no matter how much he employs the tremendous brain power of the American intellectual genius, he comes up short in affecting meaningful change in those critical areas of economics that it forces right thinking commentators to re-examine the starting point of the journey which should show unrevealed data that will show the pile to be shoveled was greater than thought because at the inception it was so very well-camouflaged. Without question, Obama stands ready to take responsibility for the condition of the ship of state he was elected to sail. That is because 'The buck stops with Obama!'

Still, the opposition never gives credit for the good things done, they only focus on what is negative and so because President Obama has not dramatically reduced unemployment, a significant barometer of the nation's lifeblood, people want his head, in some respects, literally. Though he has initiated the most comprehensive approach to health care reform that economically is a significant player in the nation's lifeblood, the opposition complains about this positive development.

Coming to power with two wars being waged in Iraq and Afghanistan, though he campaigned to end the nation's involvement significantly, once in the seat of responsibility and decision making, it became difficult to easily cut and run. The President is Commander-in-Chief, but he is no battlefield command strategist and must rely on his officers who understand ground conditions. As such, he has to make mid-course corrections along the way so as save some credibility for the men and women who waged the struggle, died on the field of battle or were significantly impaired. Now critics challenge the President on every aspect of his actions in these theaters. Still, instead of these "tail try to wag the dog" they should stop being defective "fifth wheels" and instead put their shoulders to the wheel so as to insure we still have some credibility as the time goes by. Notwithstanding, while "uneasy lies the head" that wears the crown, still the "Buck stops with Obama!"

Obama - Master and Commander 242. Dolet (left) and Brenville (right).

OBAMA - MASTER AND COMMANDER

Obama – Master and Commander 243. Giam (left) Rizzardi and Wechel (right).

Obama – Master and Commander 244. Le Rouge (left) and Chaudiere (right).

"I opposed the Defense of Marriage Act in 1996. It should be repealed and I will vote for its repeal on the Senate floor. I will also oppose any proposal to amend the U.S. Constitution to ban gays and lesbians from marrying." **Barack Obama**

"Hostility and hatred are no match for justice; they offer no pathway to peace."
Barack Obama, speech, February 2009

FREDERICK MONDERSON

Obama - Master and Commander 245. P. and A. Meietos (left) and G. Legagno (right).

"If we neglect or abandon those who are suffering in poverty ... not only are we depriving ourselves of potential opportunities for markets and economic growth, but ultimately that despair may turn to violence that turns on us."
Barack Obama, press conference, April 2009

24. BARACK OBAMA AND THE POWER OF SYMBOLISM
BY
Dr. Fred Monderson

Imagine a Black student standing among graduates at Notre Dame University's Commencement, watching President Barack Obama receive a resounding applause as he walked to stand on the platform, then to the podium to give his Address. The significance of the President's visit, that of being a black President of the United States, the audacity of accepting the invitation despite all the controversy surrounding the choice of speaker, to be present at that historic moment in time, witnessing a prestigious academic institution giving an honorary degree to a constitutional scholar and the prospect of a Commencement Address that praises young graduates to engage the world and constructively build the future in the interest of humanity, is phenomenal. However, the symbolism of being a part of all this is a tremendously powerful stimulus and motivator to a young mind setting out on a constructive path of who knows where into the future, and as such, this is an experience that comes once in a lifetime.

OBAMA - MASTER AND COMMANDER

Obama - Master and Commander 246. Corrupt legislation affected the administration of justice.

Obama - Master and Commander 247. From that corruption, anarchy and chaos resulted.

FREDERICK MONDERSON

From the vantage point of being among the graduates, that young Black student would experience any number of emotional, philosophical and spiritual reverberating highs to last a lifetime. As to the true meaning of a day as this; when a black person would be awarded a college degree as an alumnus of the President and also be privileged to witness the President of the United States give the address that begins the new journey of the rest of his or her life, is truly an unforgettable experience. The significance of the day is even more meaningful for the student because of the historic nature of the 2009 Commencement. For here is a Catholic University, celebrating 163 years dating back to 1846, a time when it was illegal for enslaved Africans in America to learn to read, much more be able to attend such an institution, to graduate and to see the President of the United States, an African American, receive an honorary degree and have the honor of addressing its 2900 graduates, of which that student is a member.

There was much press coverage and controversy in the days leading up to Sunday, May 17, 2009 and numerous questions as to why a Catholic University, guided by strict religious principles, particularly strongly anti-abortion, would not only invite to speak but also bestow an honorary Doctor of *Noris Causa* degree on someone, the President of the United States, who strongly believed in a woman's right to choose, as upheld by *Roe v. Wade*. Yet, in the aftermath of the pre-graduation publicity, protests, and arrests and even heckling drowned out by a rousing "Yes We Can," President Obama chose to speak, and delivered his message, because in his view, many of those in attendance welcomed his appearance.

Father John Jenkins, President of Notre Dame University, in introducing President Obama, recounted a litany of accomplishments; while not spanning a great number of years, contradicted Arizona State University's contention that Obama had not achieved sufficient; which reflected the human side and simplicity of the man despite the powerful nature of the office he now held.

In his Introduction, Father Jenkins identified a sign on the East Bay of Notre Dame's Basilica that reads "God, Country and Notre Dame." In his message, he recognized the President's trait of appealing to reason and his efforts to dialogue based on ethical principles, healing not being hateful, and engaging in responsible and respectful dialogue. He is endowed with tremendous human reason and emboldened to serve mankind, seek god and serve humanity, Father boasted, which he continued is consistent with the mission of Notre Dame. His is a human reason, tempered by faith seeking common good in life. Notre Dame is a primary and privileged place for dialogue between gospel and culture. The President listens carefully and speaks honestly. For that, a great deal of attention surrounded his visit to Notre Dame. He is one who does not stop talking with those who differ with him, and this is a quality the American people admired whey they elected him. For that, his appeals transcends race and he is a healer, Father Jenkins concluded.

OBAMA - MASTER AND COMMANDER

Before issuing the first among the eight honorary degrees on Sunday, Father Jenkins praised President Obama for his "enormous potential to impact the world for others." This ability culminated his rise from being the child of a single mother whose family was on food stamps; yet, he engaged in a struggle for a quality education. He chose to serve the people of Chicago as a Community Organizer and worked alongside a diverse group of people. Significantly, from "relative obscurity" Obama triumphed in a political world; demonstrated a tremendous ability to build consensus and bring world leaders and opposing sides together, which demonstrates his desire to ease hateful divisions among mankind. Even more important, Father Jenkins pointed out, President Obama, while realizing all the controversy awaiting him at Notre Dame, did not decline the invitation but chose to come and give his address. For this, it was not so much that the University in South Bend, Indiana was honoring President Obama but that Dr. Obama, a constitutional scholar in his own right, was honoring the University by coming to speak at that glorious occasion of its Commencement.

For his part, President Obama, like so many great orators, punctuated his presentation with anecdotes of humor; began by being "honored to be here," "grateful to be part of your graduation" and reminded the audience, "Honorary Degrees are hard to come by;" in that he is "one for two," referring to his denial by Arizona State University. Recognizing his motivation to speak has "not been without controversy," he insisted no one should "shy away from things that are uncomfortable." He informed the graduates, they have "come of age at a time of great challenge in the world," but they were "privileged and have a responsibility to be constructively meaningful." He faulted the "global economic crisis caused by greed and short term thinking that was rewarded over hard work." Yet he admonished his audience, "We must find a way to live as one human family." This way, we must strive for "greater cooperation and great understanding among many people."

Quoting Dr. Martin Luther King, the President reminded those in attendance, "our fate is tied up in a single garment of destiny" and that "no one person or religion can meet world challenges alone." Therefore, "we must work together for humanity," even though "finding common ground is not easy." Continuing, he pointed out, "We too often seek advantage over others" and "bringing together people of goodwill can be difficult." Yet, he asked, "How do we work through these conflicts?" He insisted, we "remain firm in our principles without demonizing others on the other size" or making "caricatures" of them.

When he ventured into the abortion debate, he spoke of a doctor who wrote him insisting he use, "fair minded words" to find the "possibility of common ground." Rightly pointing out, "Abortion is a heart-wrenching decision for a woman." Therefore, he offered alternatives of reducing abortion, and the need to help that mother carry her child to full term. He suggested that adoption be made easier; that

FREDERICK MONDERSON

there be "support for women who give birth and honor the conscience of those who disagree with our views."

Recognizing that everyone is entitled to passion and conviction in their beliefs, President Obama insisted opposing views on abortion may be "irreconcilable" but we ought not to mock people to "caricature." He praised Notre Dame as a "lighthouse" that stands at the "crossroads" of religion, culture and love. Then he praised the graduates for the "maturity and commendable responsibility" they demonstrated in their approach to the issue of abortion and the controversy surrounding his coming to the University. Showing his respect for Catholic beliefs, he confessed how Cardinal Bernadine of Chicago and the Catholic Church helped him learn cooperation and understanding, and the importance of "finding common ground." He quoted Cardinal Bernadine who taught "you can't get on teaching the gospel until you touch hearts and minds." Then he told the graduates "you will be drawn to public service or to be an active citizen. You will be called to restore a free market that is also fair. You must stand as a light-house. Remember, you can also be a cross-road." He insisted the graduates "have confidence in the values with which you've been raised;" and that they "hold firm to your faith and allow it to guide you on your journey."

President Obama called on everyone in attendance to live by the "Golden Rule," to "Love One Another as you have others love you." He then issued a "call to love; call to serve. Call to share this law of love on your brief sojourn here on this planet." Praising Father Hessberg who President Eisenhower appointed to the Civil Rights Commission in 1957 to work on behalf of humanity and who also walked with Dr. Martin Luther King, Barack Obama believed those in attendance should "make the tradition of love a part of life." He reminded them "community service breaks down walls, fosters cooperation." Ending his speech, he reminded all, "life is never easy" and that "somehow we are all fishermen," expressing the view of Jesus when he admonished St. Peter to propagate the faith and be the rock on which the Church was built.

Father Jenkins, who described the President as someone who never stops talking with anyone who disagrees with him, also informed Mr. Obama, "you bring honor to this University by being our commencement speaker. You also felt honored at the crossroad and lighthouse. We thank you."

To be part of that tremendous experience, to bear witness to such history is an extraordinary motivator for that young Black graduate and many students across the nation who can gain inspiration from the symbolism that President Obama represents.

OBAMA - MASTER AND COMMANDER

Obama - Master and Commander 248. Through the institution of order with safeguards, good government returned to prosecute the will of the people.

Obama - Master and Commander 249. With order and justice re-established, good administration was instituted and equality and learneing returned.

FREDERICK MONDERSON

Obama - Master and Commander 250. Once good administration reterund, peace and prosperity became the order of the day.

Obama - Master and Commander 251. J. Rosembach (left) and A. Torresano (right).

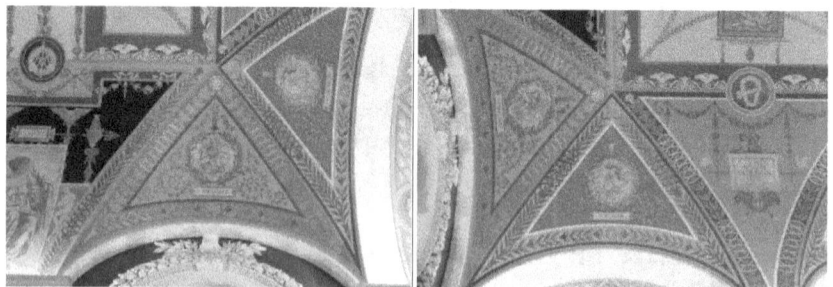

Obama - Master and Commander 252. V. Fernandez (left) and C. Plantin (right).

OBAMA - MASTER AND COMMANDER

Obama - Master and Commander 253. Green, Daye, Franklin, Thomas and Bradford.

Obama - Master and Commander 254. Cuvier, Linnaeus, Schliemann and Copernicus.

FREDERICK MONDERSON

Obama - Master and Commander 255. The artist at work!

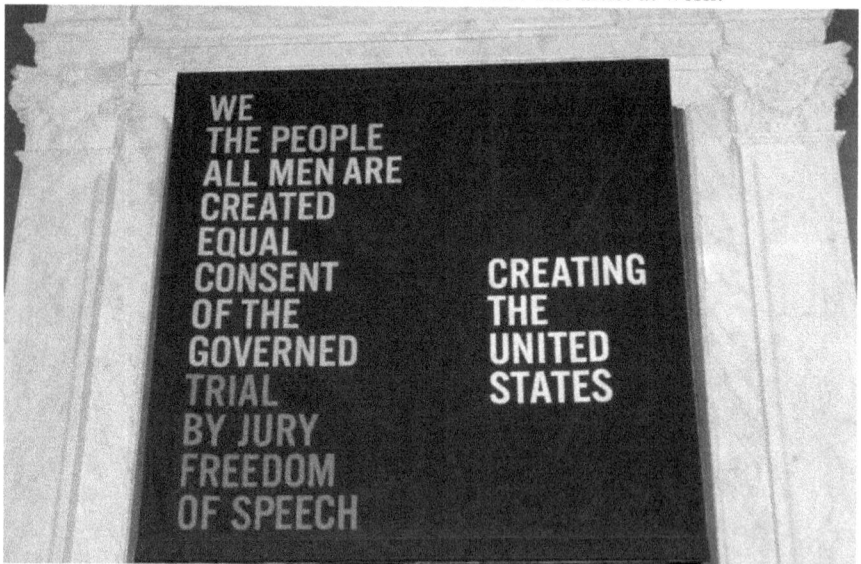

Obama - Master and Commander 256. The sign identifies the "Pillars of American government" that have made the United States, in its practice of democracy, a political success.

OBAMA - MASTER AND COMMANDER

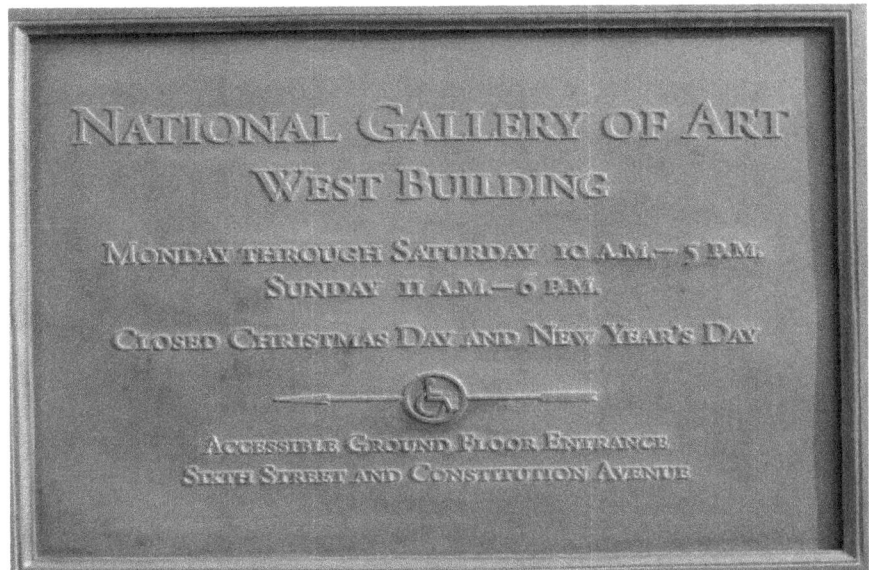

Obama - Master and Commander 256a. National Gallery of Art, West Building.

Obama - Master and Commander 257. This mural with its many features is reflective of the United States and its great diversity that makes it strong in so many ways.

FREDERICK MONDERSON

Obama - Master and Commander 258. Well, "Old Glory" - the American flag - in all its glory!

OBAMA - MASTER AND COMMANDER

"I know that there are some on Wall Street and in Washington who've said that we should only focus on the banking crisis and one problem at a time. Well, we're spending a lot of time focusing on this banking crisis, and we will continue to do so because until we get liquidity flowing again, we will not fully recover. But the American people don't have the luxury of just focusing on Wall Street. They don't have the luxury of choosing to pay either their mortgage or their medical bills. They don't get to pick between paying for their kids' college tuition and saving enough money for retirement. They have to do all these things. They have to confront all these problems. And as a consequence, so do we!" **Barack Obama**, press conference, March 2009

25. DEBT CEILING: SECOND TIME AROUND
By
Dr. Fred Monderson

The nation's debt ceiling is once again an issue subject to political posturing and a threat of government shutdown looms if this matter is not resolved quickly. In fact is is now called "fiscal Cliff." It should not be forgotten, the shenanigans surrounding the first time Debt Ceiling standoff resulted in America losing its "AAA" financial rating. However, like every experience in life, a trail is left, a history is made and a record is kept of events that have unfolded over the road traveled. Interestingly enough, there is a famous American cultural photograph showing five dogs at a table playing poker and the players each seem bent on winning by concealing high cards, aces, on some part of their anatomy. In this current debt ceiling negotiations President Obama has invited all the significant players in Congress. These include Senator Harry Reid, Majority Leader; Senator Mitch McConnell, Minority Leader; Representative John Boehner, House Speaker; and Nancy Pelosi, House Minority Leader. It is clear, Harry Reid and Nancy Pelosi, Democrats, are "on the President's side;" while Mitch McConnell, Republicans, "are disposed to act in the people's interest" but seem unalterably opposed to Mr. Obama and his policies. If we could envision a scenario in which Nancy Pelosi, the only female at the table, decides to deal the cards, giving each two and placing three in the "Community Pool."

As the Chief, Obama receives two aces while John Boehner gets two queens. Mitch McConnell is dealt two jacks and Harry Reid gets two kings. Nancy deals herself five and seven of spades. The Community cards are an ace, queen and jack. Now begins the difficult part of determining what each player has. As James Bond once said, "You don't play the cards; you play the man opposite you!"

FREDERICK MONDERSON

President Obama surveys the faces of all the players. He feels confident Harry Reid has his back. He wonders if Nancy Pelosi will deal him the best hand. As he looks to the other two players, he surveys their grim faces, never betraying any emotion, just sitting there with Mitch McConnell thumping the table with his fingers as John Boehner lights another cigarette in his chain-smoking mantra. Even though he is thumping, the President is suspicious of Senator McConnell who is fidgeting and seems to be reaching under the table. The President begins to think, 'What does Senator McConnell have?' He remembers Senator McConnell's mantra of "I intend to make Barack Obama a one-term President!" He muses, an Editorial entitled "Mr. Boehner and the Debt" on Wednesday, May 16, 2012, the *New York Times*, p. A 24 stated: "It does not bother Speaker John Boehner that he pushed the United States to the brink of default last year. It does not matter that the deep spending cuts in the resolution he demanded to end that crisis will hurt economic growth. It does not even matter that the House he leads is determined now to break that agreement with even deeper cuts in vital programs." Meanwhile Nancy Pelosi deals on as the game continues!

Obama - Master and Commander 259. **LIBERTY**, encapsulated in a semi-circle (left) and artwork above a pot of flowers (right).

Obama - Master and Commander 260. No, it's not the same pattern for in the center is a face with a bird flying overhead (left) while (right) the message is clear, "**Knowledge is power!**"

OBAMA - MASTER AND COMMANDER

"An official who actually wanted to help the country rather than appeasing the Tea Party might have remembered what happened a year ago, after Mr. Boehner first made that extortionate demand. The bond rating agencies said the country's credit and reputation had been seriously damaged, and the government lost its "AAA" credit rating. (Mr. Boehner shamelessly blamed Mr. Obama for that on Tuesday.) The Federal Reserve warned of 'catastrophic' and 'calamitous' effects if Republicans carried through on their threat to default. The stock market sank and Congress's approval rating has never recovered."

"Mr. Boehner said on Tuesday that his party would again refuse to raise any taxes, relying on spending cuts to offset the debt increase. He also announced that the House would vote before the November election to continue all the Bush tax cuts, set to expire on Jan. 1, depriving the Treasury over a decade of more than $3.5 trillion that could be used for deficit reduction."

In "G.O.P. Pledges New Standoff On Debt Limit" in *New York Times* Wednesday May 16, 2012, p. 1, 16, Jonathan Weisman writes: "Democrats accused Mr. Boehner of once again holding the nation's full faith and credit hostage to his conservative political agenda, even as Republicans cut corners on the deal struck last summer to end the last debt-ceiling crisis."

Treasury Secretary Tim Geithner explained: "Our objective should be to replace that very large set of expiring tax provisions and broad-based automatic, pretty crude spending cuts with a more responsible, balanced glide path to fiscal sustainability," he said.

"The main objective of the Republicans is to embarrass the president by forcing the Senate to vote on his budget, which may not get a single vote. That is not because no one supports his plan, but because a presidential budget - which finances the government line by line, agency by agency - is much more detailed than a Congressional budget, which creates a broad outline for spending and taxes to be filled in later by the committees of jurisdiction. Accepting a presidential budget in its totality would be tantamount to ceding Congress's constitutional power of the purse."

"But Republicans have not been able to unify around an alternative. Instead, they will bring forward four different budgets for the 2013 fiscal year, which begins Oct. 1 – with a budget passed by House Republicans viewed as the most liberal of the lot. One by Senator Rand Paul of Kentucky would eliminate the Departments of Education, Commerce and Energy; cut the National Park Service by 30 percent and NASA by a quarter; and end Medicare in 2014. Senator Mike Lee of Utah proposes a budget that would raise the retirement age to 68, cut the size of government in half over 25 years, and end the payroll tax as well as all taxes on savings and investment and replace them with a 25 percent flat tax."

FREDERICK MONDERSON

"I found this national debt, doubled, wrapped in a big bow waiting for me as I stepped into the Oval Office." **Barack Obama**

Obama - Master and Commander 261. The arts that make life so interesting, including architecture, sculpture, painting, music and poetry.

"I know some have argued that brutal methods like water-boarding were necessary to keep us safe. I could not disagree more. As Commander-in-Chief, I see the intelligence, I bear responsibility for keeping this country safe, and I reject the assertion that these are the most effective means of interrogation. What's more, they undermine the rule of law. They alienate us in the world. They serve as a recruitment tool for terrorists, and increase the will of our enemies to fight us, while decreasing the will of others to work with America. They risk the lives of our troops by making it less likely that others will surrender to them in battle, and more likely that Americans will be mistreated if they are captured. In short, they did not advance our war and counter-terrorism efforts - they undermined them, and that is why I ended them once and for all." **Barack Obama**, speech, May 2009

OBAMA - MASTER AND COMMANDER

26. OBAMA: DOING A GOOD JOB?
By
Dr. Fred Monderson

Emboldened by his wins in Wisconsin, Maryland and Washington, DC, and still trying to quash the formidable challenge of Rick Santorum, Newt Gingrich and Ron Paul, front-runner Mitt Romney mocked President Obama saying he was "not doing a good job." Just as "beauty is in the eyes of the beholder," the Republican challenger cannot see the trees in President Obama's forest of a successful Presidency. In presidential primaries or national elections winners boast "a win is a win" no matter how narrow the margin of victory. In an up-and-down vote, 51-49 is considered a win. When the federal senate is deadlocked on a measure 50-50, the Vice President casts the deciding vote making a tally of 51-50. All this means, since 51 percent is a majority, the same can be applied to good as opposed to not good. Even more, baseball hitters who hit the ball 3 out of 10 times for a 300 lifetime batting average go to the Hall of Fame. Therefore, based on his questionable boast Mitt Romney wouldn't recognize a good job, if as E.F. Hutton used to say, it "Sneaked up, slapped you on the bottom and said I'm here!"

Early in the Obama Administration, Secretary of State Hillary Clinton remarked in an Interview, "If President Obama walked on water," former United Nations Ambassador under President Bush, No. 43, "Mr. Bolton would say he couldn't swim." Thus, from behind their foggy spectacles, for Romney and the Republican "Party of No" Obama's "good is bad" but Bush's "bad is good."

"I just miss - I miss being anonymous." **Barack Obama**

Obama - Master and Commander 261a. View from the National Gallery of Art Sculpture Garden, two sides of the same building, the Archives of the United States, showing to the right, on the cornice, "The ties that bind ...."

FREDERICK MONDERSON

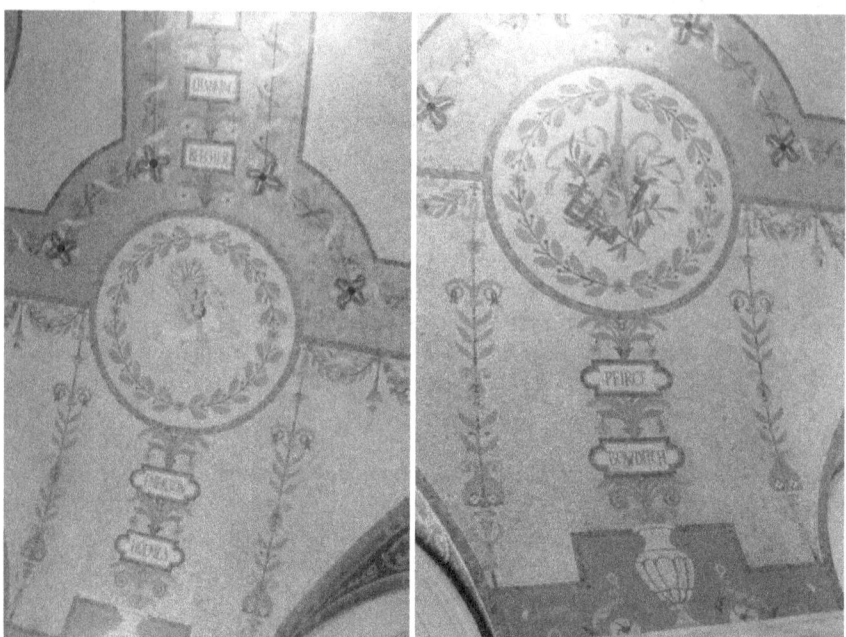

Obama - Master and Commander 262. Not one but two treats, depicting (left) Channing, Beecher, Emerson and Holmes and (right) Pierce and Bowditch.

"Discrimination cannot stand - not on account of color or gender; how you worship or who you love. Prejudice has no place in the United States of America."
Barack Obama, speech, July 2009

27. OBAMA: "FAITH IN FACE OF DOUBT"
By
Dr. Fred Monderson

President Barack Obama is a man of unbounded faith in America in face of doubt demonstrated by the many who contend for his job, those who hate and malign him and those waiting in the wings to return the nation to bygone days when its image was tarnished and its capacity severely tested. But, again, Mr. Obama's religious conviction and his unmatched faith in the goodness the nation is capable of will not allow him to surrender in face of the untold numbers marshaled against

OBAMA - MASTER AND COMMANDER

him and his vision for his beloved nation. As *Corinthians* 5: 7 holds, "He walks by faith, not by sight" and so he came "fresh and full of faith" knowing that as Moliere (1622-1673) noted, "Doubts are more cruel than the worst of truth" and that is why the nation must be rescued. That is why, in some people's view, the struggle, particularly from a political power perspective as waged in Washington is a contest between good and evil and Mr. Obama stands firmly on the side of good for evil has had its day but its agents are still busy at work. As such, Obama believes as Franklin Delano Roosevelt has informed "the only limit to our realization of tomorrow will be our doubts of today. Let us move on with strong and active faith."

As for example, strip away all the spurious claims Republicans and their allies have made and continue to make against President Obama and the only credible deduction left is the color or race of the man. These factors aside, the intellect of Mr. Obama is also an issue of contention because he has to "stay ahead of the pack" in terms of demonstrating fortitude, defending himself against the unrelenting attacks on his character, actions even against his family and still he has to initiate policies indicative of superb leadership that characterize the position he holds as Head of State, Commander-In-Chief of American forces and leader of the Western Alliance confronting challenges of a military, economic, foreign policy and terrorist nature. Then against there is the political challenge Mr. Obama faces waged by Republicans and their allies whether conservatives or other radical elements who find issue with a Black President! Notwithstanding, the "black magic" of Black Women Praying (BWP) for his success that serves as halo or a "Staff of faith to walk upon;" the love of his family; and the man's unbounded religious faith all keep propelling Mr. Obama into the future he envisioned. Yet, he has realized "the dream" is still far from being accomplished and only unrelenting perseverance, commitment and hard work of keeping his "Eyes on the Prize" will save this nation and bring about the equality of legality and opportunity that will encourage the creativity to keep America competitive rather than allow "the little people to overcome Gulliver."

All this can be accomplished only through unflinching "Faith in Face of Doubt" as the President sketched in his prayer meeting with Christian ministers during this "Holy Week" preceding the climax of the Christian experience that promises so much to human religious beliefs as this nation does to the future of the social welfare of humanity. Nevertheless, in his address to the Christian ministers at that Prayer Breakfast during this "Holy Week," Mr. Obama reiterated his Christian conviction and even posited the view suffering was a natural redemptive elixir. He even saw goodness in the suffering of Jesus and tried to equate such with attacks on his person and character. More important, he emphasized his faith in the meaning and significance of the American creed particularly in view of the doubt and animosity directed to and at him by a wide range of negativists who, as "people of little faith" question his patriotism, intellect and vision because of his race!

FREDERICK MONDERSON

Obama - Master and Commander 263. Sculptured masterpiece depicting females in different attitudes and the book and light for reading are significant hallmarks of civilization.

OBAMA - MASTER AND COMMANDER

Obama - Master and Commander 264. What more can be said for this wonderfully sculptured masterpiece that forces us to rethink originality.

A number of spurious challenges directed against Mr. Obama can be seen particularly from a religious perspective for in deconstructing the contradiction it becomes very apparent. A recent book reports Mr. Obama complained Fox News has perpetuated a falsity that he is a Muslim though he has insisted he is in fact a Christian. On Easter Sunday, April 8, 2012, Mr. Obama was photographed walking with his wife Michelle, and daughters Sasha and Malia accompanied by Secret Service personnel on his way to church across the street from the White House. A credible argument for the myth of his Muslim faith is fueled by his Kenyan father's Muslim background and after his death Barack's mother's marriage and sojourn in Indonesia. We hear so much of "conversion" and even "born again" yet one in five Americans have consumed the falsity Mr. Obama is a Muslim. Other than his reception of and interaction with Muslim world leaders, besides his visit to his father's homeland, perhaps the closest Mr. Obama has come

FREDERICK MONDERSON

to Muslims was when he delivered two important speeches to the Muslim World in Turkey and Cairo. Still, these were masterpieces of foreign policy steeped in superb oration because as a tactician Mr. Obama realized strategically it was in the best interest of the nation to make such deliveries.

The conundrum in this situation is confounded in Mr. Obama's position as an adult having declared he is a Blackman, African American and a practicing Christian. In the remarkable confrontation with the radical African American preacher Jeremiah Wright it was reported Mr. Obama had attended his church for 20 years. Now, this lengthy attendance certainly challenges the contention that he is Muslim for it seems unreal that he could attend a church publicly for so long yet, privately practice Muslim tenets. Equally, events feeding this false claim of being Muslim, continued when Mr. Obama visited his paternal homeland Kenya, where elders enthused by the visit of a sitting US Senator with roots to their country dressed him in the traditional garb to show their appreciation, anoint him with their blessings and declare to the world his ancestral connection as shown in photograph. The then "Tea Party" and other miscreants who challenged his candidacy and Presidency extracted much mileage from the event. The reception and fanfare Mr. Obama received was not unusual. Any successful American with foreign roots returning to his or her ancestral homeland generally receive this same type of treatment but therefore, in the concoction against Mr. Obama, those who wanted to malign or criticize him used the photograph along with other elements of their pernicious arsenal with great effect.

To understand the dynamics of the above doubt in challenge to his faith, one has to view the experience in three parts, viz., (1) the decade preceding Mr. Obama's election; (2) the events of his Presidency; and (3) Mr. Obama's faith grounded in his view of the future of an America in which he has a vested family interest and as a constitutional scholar he must be mindful of how history will treat his legacy. George Walker Bush was elected President under questionable circumstances in 2000. The false confidence of the nation created in the prize of victory and the "big payback to the Republican base" emboldened enemies as Al Qaeda to set in motion, blindsided America and accomplish the events of 9/11 with resulting great mortality at the World Trade Center. Equally, the involvement in two wars in Afghanistan and Iraq and on the domestic front the severe economic problems; Wall Street mismanagement; prolific hemorrhaging of jobs losing some 500,000-800,000 per month; melt down of the housing market in home value and foreclosures; the significance of the auto industry loss of market share; and deterioration of the social infrastructure as well as the negative perception propagated by elements of the nation and the equally negative image the world had cultivated about America created great challenges for the new administration. In that Chaotic climate, one of the worst recessions since the great depression that brought the nation to the cusp of a failed state, together with an assertive and effective campaign enabled Mr. Obama to win the Democratic primary and ultimately the Presidency. After all, British Prime Minister Benjamin Disraeli in

OBAMA - MASTER AND COMMANDER

his March 17, 1845 *Speech on Agricultural Interests* reminded all, "A conservative government is an organized hypocrisy." And no one wanted to return there!

Mr. Obama's tenacious faith in the need to rescue his nation coupled with his vision of a bright future and assisted by the prayers and well-wishes of so many set sail his administrative ship of state. Mr. Obama's brilliant team of economic, environmental and infrastructure experts put in place plans that halted the decline, removed the "car from the ditch" and repaired and set it in motion. He even began to change national and international views of the nation. Just then, conservative Republicanism happened by and his sailing vessel was hit by an iceberg of targeted racial doubt fed by a Republican "Party of No" whose stated mission was to do everything in its power to see the first Black President of the United States fail in his mission to rescue his and their nation from the ditch its previous guardians, these individuals, had driven it into. Yet, because of his faith, religious and secular, he ignored the criticisms of the "doubting Thomases" and persevered in his objective quest of providing for all Americans not just the wealthy few who could bankroll the election of men with conservative interests. Still, in this Mr. Obama could have said to such individuals as Rudolf Raspe (1737-1794) in *Travels of Baron Munchhausen* (1785) reminded, "If any of the company entertains a doubt of my veracity, I shall only say to such, I pity their want of faith."

Obama - Master and Commander 265. Breville (left) and Chaudière (right).

Obama - Master and Commander 266. Rouge (left) and Tory (right).

FREDERICK MONDERSON

Obama - Master and Commander 267. Wechel.

However, let us also not forget, in his *First Inaugural Address* on March 4, 1801, Thomas Jefferson spoke of "Equal and exact justice to all men, of whatever state or persuasion, religious or political; peace, commerce, and honest friendship with all nations, entangling alliances with none .... Freedom of religion; freedom of the press, and freedom of persons under the protection of the *habeas corpus*, and trial by juries impartially selected. These principles form the bright constellation which has gone before and guided our steps through an age of revolution and reformation. The wisdom of our sages and the blood of our heroes have been devoted to their attainment. They should be the creed of our political faith, the text of civil instruction, the touchstone by which we try the services of those we trust; and should we wander from them in moments in error or alarm, let us hasten to retrace our steps and to regain the road which alone leads to peace, liberty and safety." Still, it seems the Republicans have crossed the Rubicon and cannot walk back their behavior.

Thus, Mr. Obama continues to be driven by his faith and as fate has it, many of his policies have begun to bear fruit; whether it is stock market gains, new housing starts, gradual but steady increases in job creation, extrication from foreign wars, greater market share of the automobile industry, insistence on greater efforts to improve education and more experimentation to produce clean and renewable energy resources. All this is because President Obama has not succumbed to the pounding assaults and consistent non-cooperation as he maintained a "strong faith in face of doubt!" Nevertheless, however things turn out, in the end Barack Obama

OBAMA - MASTER AND COMMANDER

can boast as the *Second Epistle of Paul to Apostle Timothy* 1: 7 states: "I have fought a good fight, I have finished my course, I have kept the faith."

"I would put our legislative and foreign policy accomplishments in our first two years against any president - with the possible exceptions of Johnson, FDR, and Lincoln - just in terms of what we've gotten done in modern history. But, you know, but when it comes to the economy, we've got a lot more work to do. And were gonna keep on at it." **Barack Obama**

Obama - Master and Commander 268. No! It is not fair to say the artist "went overboard" for the same magnificence follows below.

"We should all want a smarter, more effective government. And while we may not be able to bridge our biggest philosophical differences this year, we can make real progress. With or without this Congress, I will keep taking actions that help the economy grow. But I can do a whole lot more with your help. Because when we act together, there is nothing the United States of America can't achieve."
Barack Obama, State of the Union Address, January 2012

FREDERICK MONDERSON

28. MOST DANGEROUS MAN IN AMERICA!
By
Dr. Fred Monderson

Recently, a big Republican donor described President Obama as "the most dangerous man in America" though the FBI are not pursuing him; but in fact, such rhetoric is in keeping with the "Party of No" position in opposing Mr. Obama. The problem with the designation is that it is directed toward the wrong individual and should more aptly describe Congressman Allen West (R. Florida). Mr. West seems a man who takes himself seriously, is "quick out of the gates" and this is a sure sign of a short lived political career. He is the kind of person Malcolm X spoke so eloquently about; that is, if there is "no back door," he will make one!

Mr. West may very well be ignorant of history which dictates "those who forget the past are bound to repeat its mistakes" and be victims of its process. A few recent examples may suffice to make a point about Blacks in the Republican Party particularly where there is great emphasis on being a conservative. We also know, back in the past conservatives were very influential members of the Ku Klux Klan, and other terror groups as the Red Shirts, Knights of the White Camellia and White Citizens Council, many of whom wore white sheets and did dreadful things! For example, Herman Cain declared as a candidate in the Republican presidential primary. He had a 9-9-9 Plan that was promising, so we were told. Somewhere I read passingly, the number 9, the highest single number is so powerful, when Jesus performed one of his greatest feats, he shouted nines, perhaps a hundred times in a single breath. Nevertheless, one of Mr. Cain's shortcomings is that as he came out swinging, he claimed Blacks who voted Democratic were brainwashed and that thirty-five percent of Blacks were ready to vote for him. He also boldly proclaimed the Koch brothers were his "brothers by another mother." Well, we know his fate! Yes, he now resides in the forgotten piles of potentially promising Black Republicans!

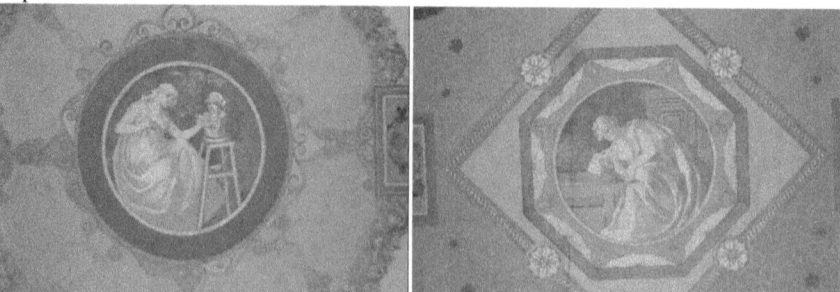

Obama - Master and Commander 269. Mallet and chisel, tools of the sculptor (left) and "Bending to admire or contemplating in sorrow."

OBAMA - MASTER AND COMMANDER

Obama - Master and Commander 270. This is what is meant in the above statement!

When the Republican Party could not settle on a leader after several rounds of voting, they elected Michael Steele as Chairman of the Republican National Committee. Many have argued the strategy was to pit him against President Obama, for what better way to bring down the Black man from the lofty position of leadership than to set another Black man against him. Mr. Steele came out swinging saying "I will engage the Black Community" but his attacks on the President were scathing yet ineffective, and this raised eyebrows that Blacks needed to be careful of this one. Even when some of the most vile criticisms and racist animus characterizations were leveled against Mr. Obama, Mr. Steele, as a Black man, did not have the guts to say, "Wait a minute, that is out of bounds!" The end result, Mr. Steele "could not touch Barack Obama" and so he was

FREDERICK MONDERSON

demoted and replaced as Chairman of the RNC! It's as Malcolm often said, "Blacks are not attacked because they are Democrat or Republican, Masons or Elks, but because they are Black!" Now, Mr. Steele as a Black American leading the Republican Party, in their rowdiness rank and file referred to the Democratic President of the United States as a "Nigger" and he had "no comment" means it's ok with him; or, "He may be a Nigger but I'm not, I'm Republican." Well, Mr. Steele seems to have lost more than his job. Now he is merely a meaningless has been who is no longer a news item!

Obama - Master and Commander 271. The Capital Building stands resplendently as seen from the Jefferson Building of the Library of Congress.

During the Reagan Administration, Clarence Thomas was nominated to the Supreme Court replacing the only Black man to sit on the Court. As a Republican, many people believed Thomas was not really a replacement of the Liberal Thurgood Marshall who was instrumental in the historic *Brown v. Board of Education of Topeka, Kansas* in which the Supreme Court ruled segregation was illegal and unconstitutional. In the pushback against Thomas during the Congressional hearings, to vet his candidacy, Mr. Thomas described the hearing as a "high tech lynching of a Nigger." Nevertheless, while he was approved and appointed to the Supreme Court, the sugar to make the medicine go down was, Mr. Thomas is young, he will outlast the older members of the Court and one day he will become Chief Justice. Well, Justice Thomas went to work; he issued some of the most Conservative rulings imaginable. Some said he was "Clarencized!" Notwithstanding, his judicial record, President George W. Bush happened and Voila! Justice Roberts was appointed to the Court and made Chief Justice. Some commentators have remarked, choosing a Chief Justice from outside the Court was

OBAMA - MASTER AND COMMANDER

unprecedented. Nevertheless, this act sealed Mr. Thomas' chance to become Chief Justice, and it became a sort of disappointment.

J.C. Watts is another case! He was young, articulate and good looking and presumably with a good future in the Republican Party. Who knows why he was soon "retired" and only trucked out now and then to make a comment about some insignificant issue? This brings us to Congressman Allen West, military veteran of Afghanistan, still enthused with the "Gung Ho" spirit who has come home to fight the Republican battles. The only problem is he wants to fight anyone who is not Republican or more specifically Democrats whose ranks comprise Blacks, Whites, Latinos, Asians, Gays, Lesbians, Handicapped, women and especially immigrants.

Spouting the "right type of rhetoric" Mr. West became "a darling of the Tea Party Movement" and was elected to Congress from Florida. To recall, Herman Cain disparage Blacks for voting Democratic; yet, there are some 42 elected Democratic members of Congress who are members of the Black Caucus. Prior to Mr. West's election there was one, no more than two elected Black Republicans in the House. Hence, it is reasonable to argue, the "Tea Party Movement," born in the cauldron spewing racial venom toward Mr. Obama, needed to attract Black members. They needed a sort of "Spook who sat by the Door!" They got Mr. West because he spoke their language and so they bankrolled his candidacy. The burning question is whether Mr. West did a "Faust" in order to acquire political elevation? Still, Herman Cain recommended Mr. West for the Vice President position. Fast forward and both men lost in the 2012 election.

Obama - Master and Commander 272. Lagrange, Lavoisier, Rumford and Lyell (left) and A. Hester and R. Pynson (right).

FREDERICK MONDERSON

Obama - Master and Commander 273. Clymer, Adams, Gordon, Hoe and Bruce (left) and Cervantes (right).

Recently, top rated Republicans have dropped Mr. West's name as a potential Vice Presidential candidate on the Romney ticket. This honorary mention certainly got to Mr. West's head, so much so, at a recent fundraiser with his rhetoric ratcheted up and with his chest out, Mr. West informed the audience "There are 78-81 Democratic House members in Congress who are card carrying members of the Communist Party." It's as if he was reading from the list of membership in the Communist Party! However, while much of this has inflated Mr. West's ego, the reality is he has a minus-40 percent chance of getting the nomination particularly his having bad talked everyone; the Republicans will not be able to defeat Mr. Obama. Besides what does Mr. West bring to the ticket other than empty rhetoric? He certainly cannot deliver the Black vote because many blacks see Mr. West as anathema. Before Mr. West's name was dropped, Senator Marco Rubio of Florida was the "Tea Party Darling" and was considered a viable candidate because as conventional wisdom holds, he could attract Hispanic voters. There is also Senator Robert Portman (R. Ohio) and the "firebrand" Sarah Palin, former Vice Presidential candidate on John McCain's ticket. To make Sarah a two-time loser is not a viable strategy. In addition, such heavyweights as Condoleezza Rice, Paul Ryan, Rick Santorum and Governor Christie have also been mentioned.

The Republican commentator Bay Buchannan made an interesting comment which is, the Vice Presidential choice should be someone who "Can do no harm" and is "absolutely ready to be President" in the event the top guy falters. On the question of whether Mr. West is ready to be president, the answer is very probably not. However, on the more important issue of "Do no harm" a cursory look at some firebrand statements by Mr. West automatically disqualifies him. On CNN's morning program with Soledad O'Brien, Allen West argued, "In this new century, communists, progressives, Marxists and socialists renamed themselves the Progressive Caucus." Mr. West seems to view himself as some kind of 'Super, Super patriot!' Such is a fragile and dangerous mindset. After all, Former Vice President Dan Quayle gave the following advice: "Remember, you are number two, do not act like number one. Do not go out there campaigning."

OBAMA - MASTER AND COMMANDER

A cursory look at Internet statements made by Mr. West certainly fails the "Do no harm" test. For example,

Obama - Master and Commander 274. Columns, arches and beautiful art.

Obama - Master and Commander 275. How picturesque! A forest of columns!

FREDERICK MONDERSON

On October 21, 2009, Mr. West was well on way to show his colors with the following tirade as he tried to engage supporters.

"If you're here to shrink away from the duties, there's the door. Get out. But if you're here to stand up, to get your musket, to fix your bayonet, and to charge into the ranks, you are my brother and sister in this fight. You need to leave here understanding one simple word. That word is 'bayonets.' And charge this enemy for your freedom, for your liberty, for the future and the legacy of that young lady right here ... you leave here today charge!" If this a terrorist flapping? This veteran of Afghanistan, seeing the Commander-In-Chief as the enemy? Does he smoke? If yes, then what?

On April 21, 2009, Mr. West stated: "We must take our country back!" Here he is parroting a questionable "Tea Party" rallying cry! Does he mean back to the time of Malcolm X's "House Negro" - "We sick boss!" Back to the time of Chattel Slavery. Remember what Disraeli believed about a conservative government!

On April 5, 2012, Mr. West advising "Tea Party" activists on what to do to become "major players" stated: "Let me tell you what you've got to do. You've got to make the fellow scared to come out of his house. That's the only way you're going to win. That's the only way you're going to get these people's attention." Scared? Sounds like terrorist jargon! When General Honore was assigned to Katrina ravaged Louisiana and the men in his command advanced with rifles and bayonets at the ready, the wise warrior commanded his men: "Turn those weapons down, you're in America not Afghanistan." Mr. West did not get that memo!

On January 30, 2012, Mr. West told liberals to "Get the hell out of the United States." This seems like a 1920s KKK mantra!

In regard to President Obama's recent visit to Florida, Mr. West had this to say: "Obama Visit Shows 'Divide and Rule' has replaced 'Hope and Change'"

"Palm Beach County, FL - Today Congressman Allen West released the following statement in response to President Obama's visit to South Florida: "Four years ago our President's campaign of hope and change inspired and united millions of Americans. Listening to President Obama's speech at Florida Atlantic University today, it is clear that 'hope and change' has been replaced with 'divide and rule.' President Obama's only hope for re-election seems to be that Americans will overlook his failed economic policies if he can successfully divide people along the lines of income and wealth. But the unfortunate reality is, even if the electoral fortunes of President Obama and Democrat congressional candidates improve by demonizing people and turning the American people against each other, cynical and divisive political strategy does nothing to create jobs for the 14 million unemployed Americans, it does nothing to alleviate soaring gas prices that pinch

OBAMA - MASTER AND COMMANDER

family budgets and prevent small businesses from hiring, and it does nothing to increase opportunity for all Americans, regardless of skin color, gender, age or income. I will continue to present a different vision for America. I believe the greatness of America lies in the goodness of Americans and their individual pursuit of their hopes and dreams. History has shown that economic freedom improves the condition of all. Economic dependency only ensures mediocrity and suffering for all. The best way we can create a bright future for all Americans is to get Washington politicians out of the way and out of the pockets of hardworking taxpayers, get our debt under control to provide long-term economic certainty, and ensure we enact energy and national security policies that allow Americans to work, invest, innovate and prosper."

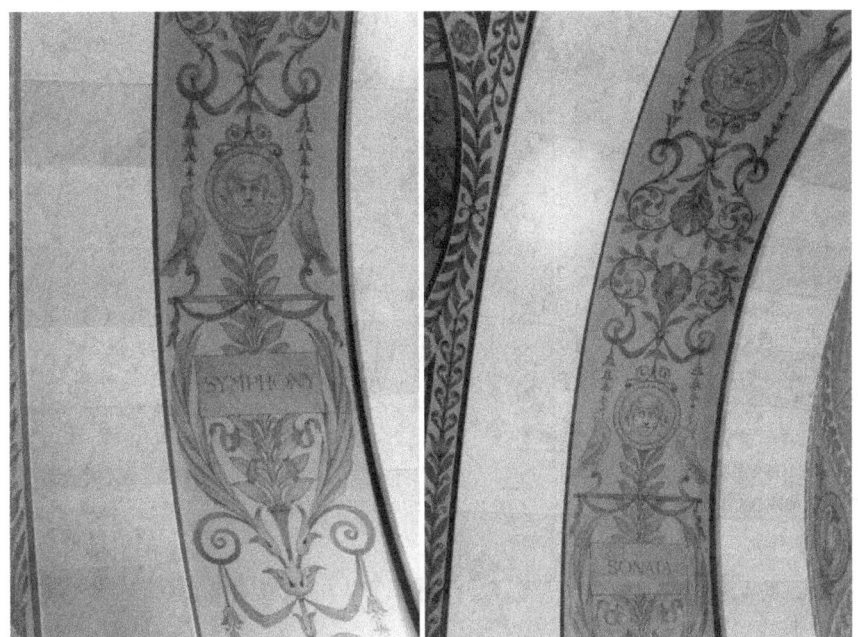

Obama - Master and Commander 276. Symphony and Sonata.

Here is even more evidence of non-presidential material. "While serving in Taji, Iraq, West received information from an intelligence specialist about a reported plot to ambush him and his men. Yahya Jhodri Hamoodi, a civilian Iraqi police officer, was implicated in the plot. Hamoodi was detain and beaten when he allegedly reached for his weapon. West then fired his pistol near Hamoodi's head, after which Hamoodi provided West with names and information, which Hamoodi later described as 'meaningless information induced by fear and pain.' One of these suspects was arrested as a result, but no plans for attacks or weapons were found. West was charged with violating articles 128 (assault) and 134 (general article) of the Uniform Code of Military Justice. West later stated, 'I know the method I used was not right, but I wanted to take care of my soldiers.' West was fined $5,000. LTC West accepted the judgment and retired with full benefits in the summer of 2004.

Mr. West's e-mail to Democratic National Committee Chairwoman Debbie Wasserman Schultz, calling her "vile, unprofessional, and despicable," "a coward," "characterless," and "not a Lady," and demanding that she "shut the heck up." This seems a man without any class, what a pity! If this is a "Tea Party" darling, heaven help them, much more us!

Hopefully, and even more important, fate may allow the experience of the ghosts of Clarence Thomas, Michael Steele and J.C. Watts to give Mr. West his just rewards.

"I've said very clearly, including in a State of the Union address, that I'm against 'don't ask, don't tell' and that we're going to end this policy." **Barack Obama**

"I don't believe that the American people want us to focus on our job security. They want us to focus on their job security. I don't think they want more gridlock. I don't think they want more partisanship. I don't think they want more obstruction. They didn't send us to Washington to fight each other in some sort of political steel-cage match to see who comes out alive. That's not what they want. They sent us to Washington to work together, to get things done, and to solve the problems that they're grappling with every single day." **Barack Obama**, remarks to GOP House Issues Conference, January 2010

29. OBAMA: "COME WITH IT!"
By
Dr. Fred Monderson

Now that Mitt Romney is no longer the "presumptive" but "actual nominee" for the Republican "party," the real contest to unseat President Barack Obama can really begin well before that party's convention in August. However, even though some months remain before the Republicans party, as the ducks begin to line up behind the leader, some Republican power players still have reservations about their leader. Even more important, while President Obama's record will be an issue in debates and final voter choice, issues raised regarding Mitt Romney by his Republican challengers in the primary contest will also be fair game as Democratic strategy unfolds. While the primary cycle is a natural part of the process of choosing the best candidate as the party's standard bearer, the critique of

OBAMA - MASTER AND COMMANDER

contenders is not only fair game of opponents but can also pinpoint weaknesses in the armor of the eventual nominee. In the case of the Republican primary contest, despite Rick Santorum caustic challenges there may be some credibility in his criticism of Mitt Romney that Democrats will seek to exploit as weaknesses if Mr. Romney becomes President. All this notwithstanding, President Obama stands ready to defend the accomplishments of his tenure while pointing out, despite the grave state of affairs he inherited, Republicans prolifically planted landmines in his path fueled by their "Party of No" philosophy of non-cooperation as the publicly stated effort to make Barack Obama's Presidency a failure!

Now, as the two main contenders, Republican and Democrat, line up to contest the Presidential election, the question of record becomes a major factor. In the case of President Obama, his record has been on public display, commented on by pundits, criticized by challengers and defended by his supporters, advisers and members of the Administration, who seem to know more than most. Mr. Romney's record on the other hand is of a different sort. As a successful businessman and former governor of Massachusetts those years of his involvement in private and public practice provide meaningful evidence of how he will perform as Chief Executive of the United States. Still, there are other factors that can and will shape the totality of the man who wishes to succeed as the 45th President of the United States. Principal among those factors are the actions and intent of the 43-47 percent of voters who voted for Senator John McCain and against Mr. Obama in the 2008 election.

Obama - Master and Commander 277. These beauties are holding up their end.

FREDERICK MONDERSON

Obama - Master and Commander 278. Marble edges of an exquisite flavor.

It is reasonable to conclude a significant portion of that McCain constituency who voted against Mr. Obama were influenced by the characterization of the Democrat by people, who had, as they say, "An axe to grind." An unmistakable fact is Mr. Obama was first viewed as a young upstart, a "Whipper Snapper" who came out of nowhere, on a meteoric rise, to contest the Presidential election. As an African American, many thought him presumptuous but this was a bold move by a young bright, likeable and courageous leader. As such, elements such as right wingers, conservatives, nuts, activists fueled by money, who attacked Mr. Obama's race, religious affiliation, birth-right, leadership skills, patriotism, judgment, economic philosophy, social relations, and decision making capabilities, have all miscalculated as to the sustainability and visionary nature of the President and his unconquerable spirit.

First his opponents underestimated the man's wherewithal to wage a long, drawn-out and successful, against all odds, campaign to become President. In their inability to estimate Mr. Obama's potential as a leader, that anti-Obama block was even more ignorant of or chose to ignore the economic, infrastructural, social and foreign policy mess their side had created and bequeathed the 44th President. That is, they had not been able to grasp the near failed state quagmire Mr. Obama inherited from Republican control of the Presidency and Congress. As such, they could not see "Mr. Obama's forest for the trees."

OBAMA - MASTER AND COMMANDER

In this continuing state of big picture denial, Republican ducks lined up behind a mantra of No! To wit, every measure Mr. Obama proposed to rescue his beloved country, the Republicans answered "No!" Meanwhile, from within the elected representation of Republicandom, the theme and color of the opposition to Mr. Obama became evident in battle after battle. From the inception, Mitch McConnell publicly stated "My intent is to make Barack Obama a one-term President" and in an extremely important decision making process he signaled his sides' win by giving that now famous coded "I got that Nigger" thumbs up! Speaker John Boehner disrespected the President by not returning his phone calls, meeting with the media before he spoke to him and in that important Debt Ceiling standoff, he boasted "We got 98 percent of what we wanted" which was at the expense of the American people. In the heated Health Care Reform debate, South Carolina Senator DeMint uttered "If we stop Obama it will be his Waterloo!" and Billy Krystal of the *Weekly Standard* offered "Go for the Kill!"

In the House of Representatives gathering for the State of the Union Address, in response to Mr. Obama's statements, South Carolina's Representative Joe Wilson told the President "You lie!" One has to wonder whether people in South Carolina gave "thumbs Up" to these two dinosaurs. After all, they represent the state Jesse Jackson once pointed out had 36 state prisons and 1 state college. He question is, 'Where do they stand on state prisons, versus state colleges?'Imagine, these "super patriots" rather than work to help rescue the nation from the ditch it had sunk into attacked Obama because of his race and party! Now, added to this addled mentality, in the Republican primary Rick Santorum thought the nominee Mitt Romney "a leader worse than Obama." Though he later said, "All sorts of things are said in the heat of the campaign." Still, no one has recanted any of the obnoxious claims made about President Obama. Yet, Republicans have patched up their straw man and sent him forward to do battle with Barack Obama for the Presidency. What then are the credentials Mr. Romney brings to the contest and if successful to the Presidency of the United States and as leader of the Western Alliance, how will he fare?

FREDERICK MONDERSON

Obama - Master and Commander 279. Cooper! What a tribute!

OBAMA - MASTER AND COMMANDER

Obama - Master and Commander 280. Sir Walter Scott.

FREDERICK MONDERSON

Obama - Master and Commander 281. Victor Hugo.

OBAMA - MASTER AND COMMANDER

Obama - Master and Commander 282. Bancroft.

On Tuesday, April 24, 1012, Ben Labolt, the 2012 Obama Press Secretary appearing on Erin Burnett's *Out Front*, just after CNN projected Romney win in 4 state Primaries reminded viewers, though the Republican in his victory speech proclaimed "A Better America Begins Tonight" in fact, Mr. Romney's vision is "Back to the future." He pointed out, during the Governor's tenure Massachusetts experienced more taxes and the much touted job creation mantra was a farce because the state stood at 47 out of 50 in job creation. Mr. Labolt strongly believes that Mr. Romney and Republicans, "Stack the deck against the Middle Class and seniors." They promise more tax cuts for the wealthy, allows Wall Street to set its own rules, and the prospects for grown and job creation are dismal.

Mr. Labolt went on to reiterate that Mr. Obama rescued the economy from the brink of collapse, he infused new energy into the auto industry and now they're making great strides. In his strategy of out-innovating and out-educating the world, Mr. Obama is "building an economy that lasts, where everybody plays by the same rules." We have seen a rise in exports and small business is doing more business. Mr. Obama is certainly more charismatic than Mr. Romney. He is a normal guy; more in touch with the pulse of the nation and doing the best he can despite Republican efforts to sabotage his every move. While Mr. Romney made a big splash that Mr. Obama should "start packing," the President's message is simply "Come with it!"

"If the people cannot trust their government to do the job for which it exists - to protect them and to promote their common welfare - all else is lost." **Barack Obama**

"I know that there are those who disagree with the overwhelming scientific evidence on climate change. But here's the thing - even if you doubt the evidence, providing incentives for energy-efficiency and clean energy are the right thing to do for our future - because the nation that leads the clean energy economy will be the nation that leads the global economy. And America must be that nation."
Barack Obama, State of the Union Address, January 2010

Obama - Master and Commander 282a. Image of a two-headed eagle on the facade of the House of the Temple on 16th Street.

OBAMA - MASTER AND COMMANDER

30. OBAMA AND THE SUPREME COURT
By
Dr. Fred Monderson

Quite frankly, because President Obama is a straight shooter, any measure of his that Republicans oppose is good for America! Let us not forget, a recent *Newsweek* magazine cover story entitled "Why is Obama's Critics So Dumb" summed up the flaw in Republicans' methodology and any challenge to President Obama's statement regarding the Supreme Court's review of his Health Care Reform legislation, amidst unimaginable rancorous discussion, is in keeping with their consistent obnoxious behavior. So much so, Republican Senator Charles Grassley of Ohio said, President Obama, as an ex "constitutional professor" was "stupid" to think the Supreme Court would uphold his legislation. It is a stretch to say a scholar, particularly of the United States Constitution is "stupid." Perhaps "stupid" Grassley did not understand the comment and intent, for after all, if you're on the fourth floor speaking it can be difficult for someone in the basement to grasp fully your meaning on an issue. That is, the issue of Health Care Reform, its meaning and means are unprecedented, the President's considered opinion is in itself equally unprecedented and the Supreme Court's role in this particular issue is also in itself unprecedented and that is why they will uphold Health Care Reform. But first, let us look at some of the facts that have led to President Obama's statement.

In order to balance the distribution of power in the national government, "founding fathers" created three branches of government that is Legislature, Executive and Judicial in what is considered "Separation of Powers." In this unique concept, created when it was, the Legislature, meaning both Houses, makes the laws; the Executive signs and executes the laws; and the Judicial Branch acts as a sort of people's referee to see the laws are fair and do not infringe on the rights of the people guaranteed by the Constitution. Fact is, government's grab for power has been a source of contention from the beginning and that is why this system was created. Nevertheless, the first to extend its reach or powers was the Judicial Branch.

FREDERICK MONDERSON

Obama - Master and Commander 283. Gibbon.

The Judiciary was created under the Judicial Branch of government and John Marshall presided as the first Chief Justice. The first real constitutional test in that fiery age in the long way forward, came in the form of the case of *Marbury v.*

OBAMA - MASTER AND COMMANDER

Madison which has remained a significant constitutional benchmark. The issue, as Irving L. Gordon in *American Studies* ((1975) (1984: 222) puts it reads: "*William Marbury*, a Federalist, was appointed justice of the peace for Washington, D.C. by outgoing President John Adams in 1801, but was denied his official papers, or commission, by James Madison, the incoming Democratic-Republican Secretary of State. In accordance with the Judiciary Act of 1789, Marbury went *directly* to the Supreme Court for an order, called a *writ of mandamus*, to compel Madison to deliver the commission." In the competing political drama of the nation this case threatened the stability of the young republic and only the wisdom of Mr. Marshall was able to navigate through the minefield the issue presented.

In the Chief Justice's decision of the case, Gordon (1984: 222) writes, "Speaking for a unanimous Court, Marshall declared that, although Madison was wrong in withholding the commission, the Court could not grant Marbury the requested writ. Marshall explained that the section of the 1789 Judiciary Act expanding the Supreme Court's original jurisdiction to include the issuing of writs of mandamus violated the Constitution. Marshall reasoned that (1) the Constitution is the supreme law of the land, (2) the Supreme Court is the final interpreter of the Constitution, and therefore (3) the Supreme Court may declare unconstitutional and inoperative any law contrary to the Constitution. Acting boldly and confidently, Marshall thus established the precedent of judicial review." Even more, Jack C. Plano and Milton Greenberg in *The American Political Dictionary* 8th Edition (1989: 259) further explained the significance of the decision: "Few cases have had the impact upon American governmental development as has *Marbury v. Madison*, in which Chief Justice Marshall struck a decisive blow for judicial supremacy. The case was essentially a political controversy between the defeated Federalist Party and the incoming Jeffersonian party over last-minute Federalist Party appointments to the federal courts. Marshall used the occasion to write a strong, logical defense of the role of the judiciary under the separation of powers doctrine, which is generally assumed to reflect the views of the framers of the Constitution. Although the Constitution fails to mention judicial review, the American people have accepted its exercise by the courts as an integral part of the American constitutional system. In 1974, in rejecting President Richard M. Nixon's claim that the separation of powers doctrine precluded judicial review of his claim of executive privilege, the Supreme Court relied heavily on the statement from *Marbury v. Madison* that 'it is emphatically the province and duty of the judicial department to say what the law is'" (*United States v. Nixon*, 418 U.S. 683) Of course, Nixon's case was about an individual's behavior shielded by the pejorative of Executive Privilege while Health Care Reform is a medical-economic issue about the whole nation proposed from a grassroots groundswell.

FREDERICK MONDERSON

Obama - Master and Commander 284. Longfellow.

OBAMA - MASTER AND COMMANDER

Plano and Greenberg (1984: 259) state further, "A portrait of the Judiciary Act of 1789 was declared unconstitutional in the famous case of *Marbury v. Madison*, 1 Cranch 137 (1803), because in it, the Congress had unconstitutionally added to the original jurisdiction of the Supreme Court. Changes of significance include the Act of 1891, which ended 'circuit riding' by Supreme Court justices and established the courts of appeals, the Act of 1925, which gave the Supreme Court discretionary authority to issue writs of certiorari, and the Act of 1988, which gave the Supreme Court virtually complete control over its docket by eliminating most mandatory review requirements. In 1982, Congress established the Court of Appeals for the Federal circuit, the first court of appeals to have specialized subject matter jurisdiction from all over the nation on specified matters of business, international trade, and civil service." Notwithstanding the expanded powers of the Constitution, Health Care Reform is in a different category, to be explained later, which allows the constitutional scholar to declare the Court's actions unprecedented.

Additionally, a Bill is a law that emanates in the House. Plano and Greenberg (1984: 114) describes a Bill as a proposed law in which: "members of the House officially 'introduce' bills by dropping them into a 'hopper;' in the Senate, bills are introduced by verbal announcement. All bills introduced during a two-year congressional term are designated 'HR' and 'S' in the Senate, with consecutive numbers assigned in the order in which they are introduced in each chamber. After introduction, bills are sent to a standing committee where, typically, they receive their most thorough airing and consideration. Committees and subcommittees often revise bills in a process called a 'markup session' in which the bill is approved or revised on a section-by-section basis. On occasion, the committee will completely rewrite a bill during a markup session, with the new version called a 'clean bill.' Each bill must have three readings in each house, be approved by a majority vote in each house, and, normally, be signed by the President to become law. A bill passed in one house is called an 'engrossed bill' and the final authoritative copy of a bill passed by both houses and signed by their president offices is called an 'engrossed bill.' Public bills deal with matters of general concern and may become public laws. Private bills are concerned with individual matters and become private laws if approved."

Now, having reviewed Judicial Review and how a Bill become law, we turn to Mr. Obama's Health Care Reform issue and the reason why he took that position. In the case of Mr. Obama, here we have a private citizen who decides to run for President. He formulates an idea of Health Care Reform and makes this a Plank of his campaign. He campaigns on this issue in which the electorate votes to elect him President which means they support his Health Care Reform proposal by a majority. As such, with a majority in Congress he introduces his Health Care Reform measure and it was approved. As President, he signs the historic measure into law. Now, with Republicans marshaled against him, a judicial challenge against Health Care Reform is mounted and the measure makes its way to the

FREDERICK MONDERSON

Supreme Court. Mr. Obama's statement that it's unprecedented that the Court would overturn his legislation is simply because it is not like a Bill that originates in the House and voted into law after deliberation. There is a big difference in the two types of measures and as such, the Supreme Court, as in the case of *Marbury v. Madison* will do well to reinforce its right to judicial review but maintain that the president was right in creating the law and in his statement. Let us not forget, as a principal item in his campaign the people were told of Health Care Reform and in essence, in electing him President voted to approve the measure. After all, as a constitutional scholar he must have a basis for thinking this particular measure creates the particular unprecedented nature that prohibits overturn. We now know, after all, Mr. Obama was not "stupid" as Mr. Grassley exhorted. It is a pity Mr. Obama's critics cannot see past the race of the man and see the brilliance that keeps him light years ahead of the clowns arrayed against him in their circus costumes.

"If we choose to keep those tax breaks for millionaires and billionaires, if we choose to keep a tax break for corporate jet owners, if we choose to keep tax breaks for oil and gas companies that are making hundreds of billions of dollars, then that means we've got to cut some kids off from getting a college scholarship."
Barack Obama

Obama - Master and Commander 285. Moliere (left) and William Shakespeare (right).

OBAMA - MASTER AND COMMANDER

Obama - Master and Commander 286. Goethe (left) and Moses (right).

"People raise capital and get loans and invest their savings. That's part of what has made America what it is. But a free market was never meant to be a free license to take whatever you can get, however you can get it. That's what happened too often in the years leading up to this crisis. Some - and let me be clear, not all - but some on Wall Street forgot that behind every dollar traded or leveraged there's a family looking to buy a house, or pay for an education, open a business, save for retirement. What happens on Wall Street has real consequences across the country, across our economy." **Barack Obama**, speech, April 2010

31. THIS ETHNIC THING
By
Dr. Fred Monderson

When Barack Obama, as a United States Senator visited Kenya, his paternal homeland, elders were flabbergasted at the thought, presence and actuality of his coming. In appreciation of being blest by such a phenomenon, these elders prepared, welcomed, blessed and dressed Mr. Obama in traditional garb and sent him home to America. Perhaps this spiritual, philosophic and ethnic undergirding generated the fire unleashed in his assertion to challenge for the presidency. As a result, Mr. Obama, in traditional or ethnic garb generated a firestorm in the general onslaught against the candidate as unscrupulous individuals sought to paint him as "Muslim." At the "Rally on the Mall" last year, one sign carried by a young female read: "I don't care if the President is Muslim." Naturally, Mr. Obama had professed his Christian faith but in the broad-brush attacks on his person, patriotism, socialism, inexperience, blackness, throw in Muslim, etc., our man Barack weathered the unrelenting attacks.

FREDERICK MONDERSON

An important observation can be interjected to highlight fallout for personal acrimony. As Republicans launched their 2012 presidential campaign primary through debates and under the spotlight of media inquiry, the wife of Texas Governor Rick Perry complained of the strain of the scrutiny on her and his family. Imagine the impact a two month journey has had on a family beginning a lengthy process and contrast this with the perennial assaults and how this has affected Michelle Obama and her daughters as Mr. Obama stood on a "dart board." Yet, Mr. Obama weathered all such assaults with that tremendous smile while he also employed his studious mind to press forward with his agenda defending these same people's rights to criticize him but also rescue his beloved nation from the quagmire they placed it in.

All this notwithstanding, African American people, after centuries of no ethnic connection with presidential leadership were tremendously motivated, appreciated and turned out to play a significant role in the effort to get Barack Obama elected. As this process unfolded, they looked in great dismay as their champion swelted under the strain of attack on his person, family and performance.

Obama - Master and Commander 287. Herodotus (left) and Milton (right).

Naturally, people may question the significance and relevance of ethnicity as expressed by African Americans as they identify and support President Obama but this is not altogether different from the admiration expressed by other groups. If we begin, not with ethnicity per se, but with the "local hero theory." We know presidential politics is an important affair and so much so, great pride and recognition is given to an individual from a particular area. Let say, for example, a candidate for president is given a tremendous boost from and is expected to win his "home state." We tend to believe, because of the prestige gained for the state in

OBAMA - MASTER AND COMMANDER

media recognition, perhaps the many times its featured in reporting, times the president return home, deep pockets may contribute to his campaign and even re-election bid and a whole lot more. Perhaps, in return he would steer dollars their way in the form of grants, job creation for pet projects and may even underwrite local industry if they create a product he may be touting in his overall strategy.

Beyond state affiliation and support for one's *Alma Mata*, favorite home team and even religious affiliation, in a country of immigrants comes the most important appreciation for the hero achieving the determined goal. In this country especially, even though tradition has shied away for royal identification, because the core immigrant group of the early population was of English, British, extraction, many leading politicians, businessmen and even sacerdotal individuals have sought to connect with their ancient heritage. Many presidents, perhaps Ronald Reagan and Jimmy Carter especially have sought to trace their lineage back into "British Royalty." Certainly the Kennedys were all when all "Irish eyes are singing" and Italians are certainly proud of their ancient connection. In fact, upon the nation's founding and architectural layout of Washington, DC, the goal was to create "ancient Rome in America." This notwithstanding that famed city of columns has more symbolism, motifs of ancient Africa, Egypt, than the average person realizes.

Herein then is the conundrum, despite what may falsely be said about "Who were the ancient Egyptians," at a time when the nation was enslaving Africans it was engendering the cultural ethos of the Nile Valley into architecture, body politic, psyche of the new nation while simultaneously denying Africans in America any connection with their heritage. The universal, but falsely believed, notion of a "Caucasian Egypt" may certainly have been seed-germed in this era, particularly since Hegel and other German nationalists masterminded the idea in their day.

Nevertheless, Martin Luther King has preached, "truth crushed to earth shall rise" and today thanks to the work of credible African, African and African Caribbean scholars, Africa's place in Egypt, the Nile Valley and the historical record is firmly being reaffirmed.

"We should be working on comprehensive immigration reform right now. But if election-year politics keeps Congress from acting on a comprehensive plan, let's at least agree to stop expelling responsible young people who want to staff our labs, start new businesses, and defend this country. Send me a law that gives them the chance to earn their citizenship. I will sign it right away." **Barack Obama**, State of the Union Address, January 2012

FREDERICK MONDERSON

Obama - Master and Commander 288. Homer.

Obama - Master and Commander 289. Dante.

OBAMA - MASTER AND COMMANDER

Obama - Master and Commander 290. P. and A. Meietos.

Obama - Master and Commander 291. Aldus Manutius.

FREDERICK MONDERSON

32. BLACK INFLUENCE ON THE SUPREME COURT I
By
Dr. Fred Monderson

No ethnic group has had more of an impact on the United States Supreme Court than African Americans, for the Court has ruled against Black interest and has even had to reverse itself, before making its most significant rulings in favor of Blacks. However, huge as this influence has been, it has been excluded from the narrative of history. Thus, we must follow its most important cases and even measure how blacks have wielded their influence whether as attorneys before the bar or as in the extraordinary work of Jurist Thurgood Marshall who rose from the law ranks to be one of the most influential voices on the bench. Now, the African American President Barack Obama has appointed two women to the Court. In the history of the Republic, Presidents Washington, Jackson, Lincoln, Grant, Harrison, Taft, Harding, Franklin Roosevelt, Truman, Eisenhower and Nixon have appointed four or more members of the Court. In the event of his being re-elected, President Obama will have the opportunity to impact the Court even more with one, possibly two additional appointments and join this exclusive group. This latter reality is especially troubling for many people who are disposed to see him defeated in the up-coming 2012 election. As such, this election will be truly historic to determine whether the nation moves forward or return to its tattered conservative past.

Thus, to understand the Black influence and how it has shaped the Constitution through the Court one has to even antedate the Supreme Court sitting for the "Three Fifths Clause" of the Constitution. This **Compromise** had to do with apportioning enslaved Africans for Southern representation initially in the political and taxation dispensation to create the National instrument of government. Make no mistake; the **Compromise of 1820** defined the condition of Blacks! Even with the **Compromise of 1850** the Court remained silent on the condition of Blacks as chattel, meaning property! However, within less than a decade the Court could no longer hide behind the *fait accompli* of silence and was forced to show its true colors in the 1857 case of Dred Scott. After Dred Scott, while there were others of a lesser import, the 1896 *Plessey v. Ferguson* case affirming "separate but equal," and the culmination of "Jim Crow," is another milestone in landmark Supreme Court rulings. Again, while the "Grandfather Clause" reversal of 1915 is also of minor import among others whittling away at the second class Black condition, cases such as *Smith v. Albright* outlawing the "white primary" in 1944, and the more landmark 1954 *Brown v. Board of Education of Topeka, Kansas* affirming "segregation is illegal" represented the next and most significant Black

OBAMA - MASTER AND COMMANDER

impact on the Court. Thurgood Marshall, the man who led that fight would ultimately wield untold influence on the Court and at his death praised for his efforts, even by his adversaries on the bench. To his efforts we could add the various *Civil Rights* and *Voting Rights Acts* passed to strengthen previous legislation and to protect Black gains that also benefitted all Americans. Now, President Obama is poised to add even more Black influence regarding the direction of the Court.

Obama - Master and Commander 292. Green, Daye. Franklin, Thomas and Bradford

Historically speaking, the "Three-Fifths Compromise" of 1787 was instrumental in moving forward with acceptance of the Constitution. However, as Chief Justice Roger Taney later pointed out in the Dred Scott decision of 1857, Africans then enslaved were not considered citizens! In fact, they were not considered as fully human at the time of the formation of the Constitution, but only "Three-fifths" of persons. Equally, that year of 1787, the Compromise also outlawed the importation of slaves after 1808 but this practice continued unabated surreptitiously until the Civil War. To get their way, the South played hardball because their economy depended on slavery. This is made clear by Mary Frances Berry (1971: 7) who point out: "The Fugitive Slave Clause was scarcely noticed by northern delegates to the ratifying conventions, but in the South, it was used as a definitive selling point. James Madison particularly emphasized its usefulness in Virginia, as did some of the Federalists in the North Carolina convention. These debates lend credence to the view that the southern states would not have ratified the Constitution without the proslavery compromises." The Compromise required two thirds of the Senate to approve treaties and prohibited the national government

FREDERICK MONDERSON

from taxing exports or interfering with the slave trade until 1808, the year after the British outlawed their involvement in the trade.

Obama - Master and Commander 293. G. De Legnano

Obama - Master and Commander 294. J. Rosembach

OBAMA - MASTER AND COMMANDER

Obama - Master and Commander 295. A. Torresano

In the *American Political Dictionary* (1989: 29-30) Plano and Greenberg make reference to the significance of this agreement. They state, Southern delegates, "feared that northern majorities might cut off the slave trade and discriminate against the profitable cotton trade …. It was believed that a sufficient number of slaves would be available by 1808, although illegal slave trade continued until the Civil War of 1860. The treaty and foreign commerce provisions continued to influence the making of American foreign policy." To this we may also add the "Internal Slave Trade" with its tremendously depraved practices on Southern "Slave Farms." Yet, the Supreme Court chose not to be "activist" in this respect and in its silence upheld the institution of slavery that denied Africans any rights and in turn supported the falsely construed sub-human status. To be sure, in a *Brief Review of United States History and Government* (2001: 94) Briggs and Peters write: "Until the Civil War, the Constitution had recognized and protected slavery in three ways: the Three-Fifths Compromise, the provision that Congress could not end the importing of slaves before 1808, and the fugitive slave clause. These compromises had been made in order to encourage southern states to ratify the Constitution. With the expansion of American territory in the West, controversy brewed over whether these new territories should allow slavery or not."

After the Louisiana Purchase by Thomas Jefferson, the status of the states, free and slave became a Sectionalism issue regarding division of the new territory. The

FREDERICK MONDERSON

North wanted more Free States; the South wanted more Slave States. To settle this matter, Irving L. Gordon's *American Studies* (1984: 106-107) point out: "The North and South agreed to the Missouri Compromise of 1820 admitting Maine as a free state and Missouri as a slave state and prohibiting slavery in most of the Louisiana Territory." Thus, Sectional balance was maintained.

The Industrial Revolution in America was spurred by Eli Whitney's Cotton Gin of 1793 among other inventions that ultimately saw "Cotton become king!" And, in 1815 at the end of the War of 1812, Internal Improvements opened the way. As labor demands of the agrarian South expanded with plantation culture of tobacco, rice, sugarcane, and cotton, Encyclopedia Britannica's *The U.S. Government: How and Why it Works* (1978: 210) explained: "By 1850 there were 3,204,000 slaves in the area, and it has been estimated that 1,815,000 were connected with the cultivation of cotton. Perhaps this is why the Court cast a blind eye to abolition and reform until the Compromise of 1850 tried to settle the significant issue of expanding states. Three key provisions were agreed to in this measure, include:

"California entered the Union as a free state."

"The Fugitive Slave Law required that escaped slaves be returned to their owners, providing Slave Catchers with unchecked power."

"Through a vote, people living there would determine whether a territory in the Mexican Cession chose to be slave or free."

"In December, I agreed to extend the tax cuts for the wealthiest Americans because it was the only way I could prevent a tax hike on middle-class Americans. But we cannot afford $1 trillion worth of tax cuts for every millionaire and billionaire in our society. We can't afford it. And I refuse to renew them again."
Barack Obama

OBAMA - MASTER AND COMMANDER

Obama - Master and Commander 296. V. Fernandez.

Obama - Master and Commander 297. Circles and arches.

FREDERICK MONDERSON

If the floor looks this good, no wonder the walls and ceiling are exquisite.

"We need to give consumers more protection and more power in our financial system. This is not about stifling competition, stifling innovation; it's just the opposite. With a dedicated agency setting ground rules and looking out for ordinary people in our financial system, we will empower consumers with clear and concise information when they're making financial decisions. So instead of competing to offer confusing products, companies will compete the old-fashioned way, by offering better products. And that will mean more choices for consumers, more opportunities for businesses, and more stability in our financial system. And unless your business model depends on bilking people, there is little to fear from these new rules." **Barack Obama**, speech, April 2010

OBAMA - MASTER AND COMMANDER

Obama - Master and Commander 298a. Sculptured floral decoration from the Capital Building vicinity.

33. BLACK INFLUENCE ON THE SUPREME COURT II

By
Dr. Fred Monderson

Mary Frances Berry's *Black Resistance, White Law* (1971:7) pointed out: "The Fugitive Slave Clause and the commitment of the national government to protect slavery, but not interfere with it, were indispensible parts of the Constitution." However, this band aid solution as part of denial of black rights was short lived in the abolitionist and reform era, forcing the 1957 *Dred Scott v. Sandford* landmark decision which clearly defined the status of the African in America.

According to the evidence, Dred Scott was an enslaved African whose master took him into a Free State in 1834 and back into a Slave State. Upon his return in 1846, Mr. Scott sued for his freedom on grounds of having set foot on free soil; he therefore claimed he was entitled to be free. In 1857, Chief Justice Roger Taney (1836-1864) ruled in this historic case. In *American Historical Documents*, Edited

FREDERICK MONDERSON

and with an Introduction by Harold C. Syrett (New York: 1965, 250), we are told: "The Court considered the following points: whether Scott was a citizen of Missouri (if he was not, he could not sue in a federal court); whether residence in a free area gave Scott his freedom following his return to Missouri; and whether the Missouri Compromise (under the terms of which slavery was prohibited in the Wisconsin territory) was constitutional."

In answer, Bonnie-Anne Briggs and Catherine Fish Petersen in *Brief Review in United States History and Government* (2001: 95-96) have argued: "The ruling held that no African Americans, slave or free, were citizens, and therefore, they were not entitled to constitutional protection. The ruling also held that the Missouri Compromise was unconstitutional because Congress could not deprive people of their right to property - slaves - by banning slavery in any territory." Still, we know of Lincoln's "House divided" speech and its subsequent implications in the Civil War.

Soon, however, despite Taney's decision on Dred Scott, John S. Rock of Massachusetts was the first Black invited to practice at the Supreme Court under the new Chief Justice Salmon P. Chase (1864-1873). Entering the bar and wearing 'Buck Wheat,' to plead his case he stood defiantly, as Page Smith in *The Constitution: A Documentary and Narrative History* (1978: 440) stated, "[I]n the monarchial power of recognized American manhood and American Citizenship, within the bar of the Court which had solemnly pronounced that Black men have no rights which white men were bound to respect .... By Jupiter the sight was grand!" Even further, Smith (1978: 441) noted: "The Court in the case of *Ex parte Milligan* ruled that Lincoln had acted unconstitutionally when he ordered military courts in places where civil courts were functioning." Lincoln saw this action as necessary, notwithstanding Chief Justice Chase's contention: "The Constitution of the United States is a law for rulers and people, equally in war and peace, and covers with the shield of its protection all classes of men, at all times, and under all circumstances."

This was a powerful statement for the War settled two questions as *Encyclopedia Britannica* (1978: 215) states: "First, it killed the idea of state sovereignty and the right of secession. Second, it ended the institution of slavery." It did, however, little to change the agrarian basis of the South's economy, since slavery was an economic system of slave ownership and racial control. Still, *Britannica* (1978: 215) continued: [T]he institution of slavery was replaced by three others. The economic system of sharecropping, the political system of one-party politics, and the social system of segregation supported both by law and by custom." Clearly then, despite the Civil War Amendments, Reconstruction was betrayed and white southern backlash gave birth to "Jim Crow." Aided by Black Codes, this new state of affairs began to curb the newly secured rights of African Americans. As part of the grand strategy to gain political power in the South, while some whites sought legal means, some conservative southerners employed terror groups as the Ku

OBAMA - MASTER AND COMMANDER

Klux Klan, Red Shirts and Knights of the White Camellia to intimidate and terrorize Blacks from going to the polls. Now successfully in control, southern legislators imposed poll taxes and literacy tests on the Freedmen and used the "Grandfather Clause" to empower poor whites who could not pass the literary tests. Thus, "Jim Crow" laws created segregation of African Americans and whites in schools, parks, public buildings and public transportation. In challenges to these practices, in the 1883 Civil Rights Cases, the Court ruled the "Thirteenth Amendment abolished slavery but did not prohibit discrimination and that the Fourteenth Amendment prohibited discrimination by government but not by individuals."

Obama - Master and Commander 299. Floor extraordinary.

FREDERICK MONDERSON

Obama - Master and Commander 300. Floor, floor and more floor!

Obama - Master and Commander 301. Still more floor!

In this period of "The Nadir," the mood of the country fueled by "Jim Crow" practices forced the Supreme Court to consider the case of *Plessey v. Ferguson* in 1896. The Court upheld "Jim Crow" by ruling in favor of "equal but separate" or

OBAMA - MASTER AND COMMANDER

"separate but equal" facilities which in fact was actually "separate and unequal." Plano and Greenberg (1989: 296) pointed out: "Under this doctrine, a wide pattern of segregation developed in schools, transportation, recreation and housing." As such, the ruling encouraged the highest forms of social depravity visited upon Blacks until the conscience of the Supreme Court really began to stir. First it outlawed the "Grandfather Clause" in 1915 and several minor racist rulings until the 1940s when even the armed forces became desegregated.

In the 1954 *Brown v. Board of Education of Topeka, Kansas* the Supreme Court ruled "separate but equal" inherently unequal and therefore unconstitutional. In *United States History and Government* Paul Stich, Susan Pingel and John Farrell (1989: 241) recognize the roles of the Truman and Eisenhower administrations in facilitating integration despite southern senators' use of the "filibuster" to stymie legislation. However, the Supreme Court was not hamstrung by these tactics. They write: "After World War II, in a series of civil cases brought by the National Association for the Advancement of Colored People (NAACP), the court began applying 14th Amendment's 'equal protection of the laws' phrases against various state segregation laws. In 1954, the Court issued its decision in *Brown v. the Board of Education of Topeka*, which reversed the doctrine of 'separate but equal' put forth in the 1896 Plessey case. At the time of Brown, racially segregated schools was the norm in nearly 20 states. In Brown, the Court used a procedure called 'orbiter dictum' to 'speak beyond' the Topeka situation and announced that racial segregation of schools were inherently wrong and must cease throughout the nation." This they moved expeditiously to correct!

Often times the work of a single person is overlooked but that of Thurgood Marshall, first as a lawyer influencing the Court, and then as jurist influencing the Court's direction is unparalleled among American men of law. This enormous capability is best reflected in the laudatory commentary by the trustees of Howard University after Marshall, ten years out of law school, successfully argued *Smith v. Allwright* overthrowing the "white primary" in 1944. According to Michael Davis and Hunter R. Clark in *Thurgood Marshall: Warrior at the Bar, Rebel on the Bench* (1994: 11) the University's citation read: "You are winning significant and enduring victories for a disadvantaged people. Your increasing labors are opening the way for the achievement of an even greater measure of justice and equality under the law. Your star still rises, and though it is not yet at its zenith the brilliance of your accomplishments and the value of your service to your fellow man already marked you as an advocate, a legal scholar and humanitarian of the highest magnitude."

Equally, the Eulogy at his death summed up the work and influence of this extraordinary man of law. Davis and Clarke (1994: 385) additionally say: "[I]nscribed above the front entrance to the Supreme Court building are the words 'Equal justice under law.' Surely no one individual did more to make these words a reality than Thurgood Marshall." Thus, with the all-inclusive phrase 'no one,'

FREDERICK MONDERSON

Rehnquist ranked Marshall alongside Washington, Jefferson, and Lincoln. This statement was from the same man who, as a law clerk some thirty years earlier, had urged that *Plessey's* separate-but-equal doctrine be upheld." William T. Coleman, former transportation secretary who also worked on *Brown*, observed, "History will ultimately record that Mr. Justice Marshall gave the cloth and linen to the work that Lincoln's death left undone." And Vernon E. Jordan of the National Urban League and advisor to President Clinton said Marshall's mission, according to Davis and Clarke (1994: 388) had been "to cleanse our tattered Constitution and our besmirched legal system of the filth of oppressive racism and to restore to all Americans a Constitution and a legal system newly alive to the requirement of justice."

Clarence Thomas replaced Thurgood Marshall as the only Black on the bench. However, his policies and writings were utterly opposed to those of Marshall. Davis and Clarke (1994: 376) write, in 1990 President Bush No. 41 appointed Thomas to the U.S. Court of Appeals and in 1992 he was appointed to the Supreme Court. "At first, Thomas's nomination appeared to be a shrewd political move on the part of the president. By making effective, if cynical use of the skin color of a nominee opposed to racial preferences, Bush threatened the Democratic coalition of liberals, women's groups, and blacks. Liberal feminists were aligned against Thomas because of his conservatism and outspoken opposition to abortion. At the same time these groups risked antagonizing blacks whose paramount goal was to have an African American succeed Marshall. The white liberal leadership of the Democratic party knew that by opposing Thomas, they also risked further alienating white middle-class voters - the so-called Reagan Democrats - who regarded racial preferences as reverse discrimination." Even further, Davis and Clarke (1994: 378) continued: "During the 1991-92 term, his first as an associate justice, Thomas demonstrated himself to be exactly what his conservative proponents had hoped and his liberal opponents had dreaded. Most often, he aligned himself with the Court's two most conservative members, Rehnquist and Scalia. He has voted to restrict constitutional protection accorded prison inmates; he has called for softening the wall that has traditionally separated church and state; and, dissenting from the Court's ruling in *Planned Parenthood of Southeastern Pennsylvania v. Casey*, decided on June 29, 1992, he has called for *Roe v. Wade* to be overturned outright." Still, Justice Thomas characterized Thurgood Marshall as "a great lawyer, a great jurist and a great man."

OBAMA - MASTER AND COMMANDER

Obama - Master and Commander 302. The floor at entrance to the Jefferson Library.

Obama - Master and Commander 303. Floor and stair to the second floor of the Jefferson Building.

FREDERICK MONDERSON

Obama - Master and Commander 304. Crab (left) and flower (right).

Nevertheless, so much has transpired once the Court assumed an "activist" posture recognizing and safeguarding the rights of African Americans. Given the vote, educational and other social and economic opportunities, and flexing new won power, Blacks began making strides in electing representatives and finally became an election force owing to the backing of the Court. Now, an African American President is poised to move this historic legal institution even further in recognizing and securing a more just future for all America's people. Without question, rights gained by Blacks have benefitted all segments of the American populace whether black or white, Jew, Gentile, Catholic, Protestant, Asian and Latino, Gays and Lesbians, handicapped and especially women and the work of the Supreme Court has been instrumentally prodded by Black influence.

"In fact, the best thing we could do on taxes for all Americans is to simplify the individual tax code. This will be a tough job, but members of both parties have expressed an interest in doing this, and I am prepared to join them." Barack Obama

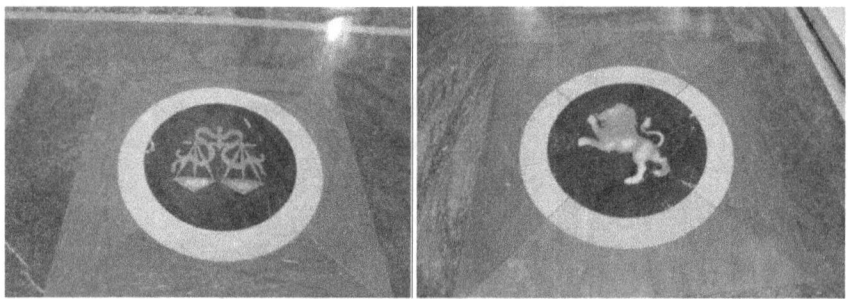

Obama - Master and Commander 305. Scales (left) and lion (right).

OBAMA - MASTER AND COMMANDER

Obama - Master and Commander 306. Virgin (left) and Scary figure (right).

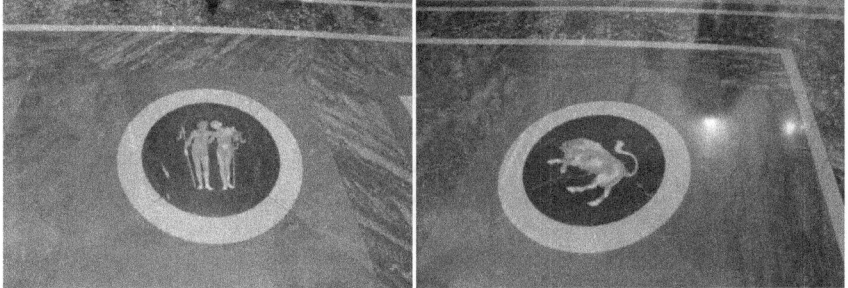

Obama - Master and Commander 307. Twins (left) and bull (right)!

"We've been fighting about the proper size and role of government since the day the Framers gathered in Philadelphia .... But what troubles me is when I hear people say that all of government is inherently bad .... When our government is spoken of as some menacing, threatening foreign entity, it ignores the fact that in our democracy, government is us. We, the people - we, the people, hold in our hands the power to choose our leaders and change our laws, and shape our own destiny. Government is the police officers who are protecting our communities and the servicemen and women who are defending us abroad. Government is the roads you drove in on and the speed limits that kept you safe. Government is what ensures that mines adhere to safety standards and that oil spills are cleaned up by the companies that caused them." **Barack Obama**, speech at University of Michigan, May 1, 2010

FREDERICK MONDERSON

34. "IF THE SUPREME COURT OVERTURNS ..."
By
Dr. Fred Monderson

On CNN's **The Cafferty File** of April 26, 2012, a respondent noted "If the Supreme Court overturns Health Care Reform and rules in favor of the State of Arizona's immigration bill, it would be a major blow against President Obama, particularly because he is a lawyer and should know better." Well, that ruling may happen, but at times ideology does influence judges' rulings and that is why laws are overturned by subsequent interpretations. Then again, Presidents have faced significant threats particularly when the nation faced important and crippling events especially in times of serious economic challenges. President Franklin D. Roosevelt is a good and interesting example following the Great Depression as he tried to implement a New Deal Program and the Court seemed ideologically opposed to his ideas. As such, the President threatened to "Pack the Court" by appointing extra judges beyond the present nine members. That is, before the Court began to see the world and the dangers from the President's point of view. In many respects, practically the same situation faces the nation currently as President Obama continues his work of rescuing and moving the nation forward. However, to try and speculate on how the Supreme Court will rule in these two important cases, one has to examine the body's record of overturning laws and even reversing its position on previous rulings. Keep in mind, in his "Bibliographical Essay" chapter, Robert McCloskey in *The American Supreme Court* (1971: 240) reminds all: James B. Thayer, "The Origin and Scope of the American Doctrine of Constitutional Law," 7 *Harvard Law Review* 129 (1893) is dedicated to the proposition that the Court should only overturn legislative acts when they are invalid beyond 'rational question,' and this view has undoubtedly influenced generations of judges and critics." McCloskey goes on to add (1971: 241) in his view, "Another judge-anchored book of interest is Charles E. Hughes, *The Supreme Court of the United States* (1928). Hughes was to serve, of course, as Chief Justice of the Court during one of its stormiest periods, and the volume is thus significant as a document as well as a description. Although the author does concede that the Court has sometimes erred, his sentiments are heavily and sometimes uncritically pro-judicial."

The right and power to even consider a law made by Congress gets its precedent from the famous case *Marbury v. Madison* (1803) where Chief Justice John Marshall established the Court's right of Judicial Review, even when a matter may not have a decision, one way or the other. Hence, in the case particularly in the Health Care Reform law now being examined before the Court, the Supremes' action particularly as in the case of Madison may surprise onlookers. After all, Chief Justice Roberts, the leading Conservative on the Court may be the deciding

OBAMA - MASTER AND COMMANDER

voice. This point is underscored by Robert G. McCloskey in *The American Supreme Court* (1971: 40) when he wrote, "Marshall did establish almost at one the custom of letting one justice's opinion usually his own, stand for the whole court, and this gave the judicial pronouncements a forceful unity they had formerly lacked." Thus, it is not surprising one of the more significant Supreme Court rulings by Roger Taney, Dred Scott of 1857, that not simply denied Scott's right to sue, emphasized his not being a citizen, the Chief Justice wrote the decision ruling the *Missouri Comprise of 1820* unconstitutional and overturned it.

In *Ex Parte Mulligan* (1866) the Court invalidated wartime military trial of civilians and in 1870 in *Hepburn v. Griswold* the Court invalidated the Legal Tender Act in certain respects and a year later, 1871, the Court upheld the Legal Tender Act in all respects. In 1890, the Court ruled state rate regulation without judicial review denies due process. Six years later in *Plessy v. Ferguson* the Court upheld Jim Crow ruling "the state may require separate facilities for different races providing that the facilities are equal - the 'separate but equal doctrine.' In 1915 the Court ruled against the "Grandfather clause" enacted in the southern backlash to Reconstruction that enabled whites who could not pass literacy tests to still be able to vote. Equally, in *Schenck v. United States*, "the clear and present danger rule" of 1919, the Court ruled against unrestricted freedom of speech. Equally, in *Schecter Poultry Corp v. United States* of 1935, the Court held the National Industrial Recovery act unconstitutional. Another of the *New Deal* rulings, *United States v. Butler* of 1936, the Court held the Agricultural Adjustment Act unconstitutional. That same year, in *Carter v. Carter Coal Co.*, the Bituminous Coal Act and in *Morehead v. Tipaldo*, the New York Minimum Wage law was held to be unconstitutional. The next year, 1937, President Roosevelt threatened to "pack the court" before that body fell in line with his view to rescue the nation.

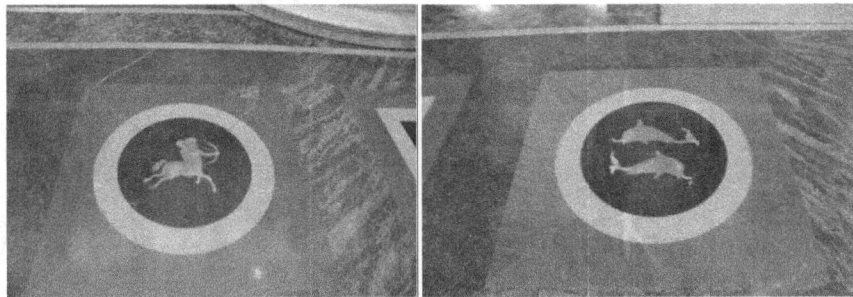

Obama - Master and Commander 308. Archer (left) and fishes (right).

FREDERICK MONDERSON

Obama - Master and Commander 309. The Ram.

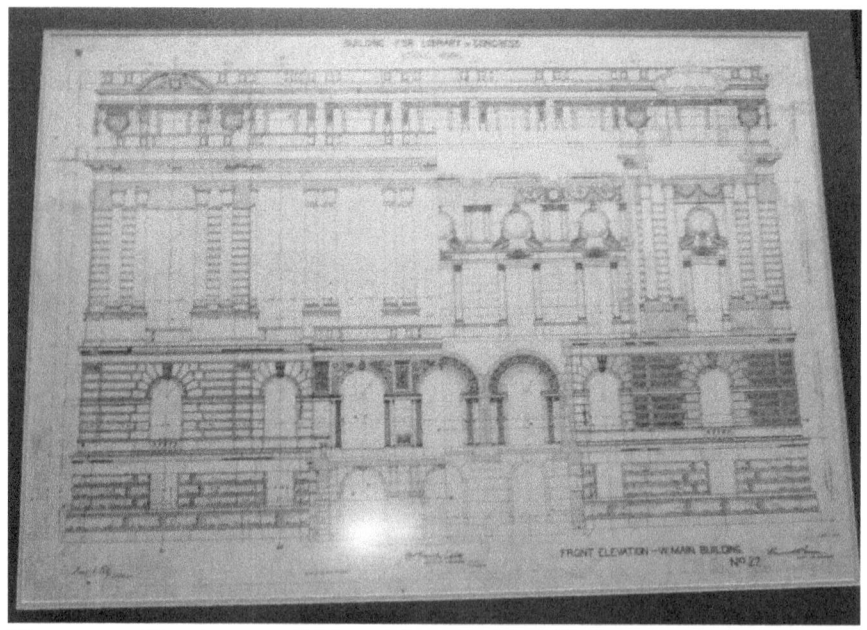

Obama - Master and Commander 310. Plan of the Building for Library of Congress.

OBAMA - MASTER AND COMMANDER

Obama - Master and Commander 311. Langrange, Lavoisier, Rumform, Lyell

FREDERICK MONDERSON

Obama - Master and Commander 312. C. Plantin

Within six weeks in *West Coast Hotel v. Parrish*, the Court upheld the Minimum Wage Law of the state of Washington. In *Smith v. Allwright*, future Jurist Thurgood Marshall pleaded the case that overturned the racist "White Primary." A decade later Mr. Marshall pleaded *Brown v. Board of Education* (1954) in which the Court overturned the "separate but equal" ruling of *Plessey v. Ferguson*. The next year it issued an enforcement decision desegregating public school education. Also, in *Pennsylvania v. Nelson* (1956) the Court invalidated State Sedition Laws.

In a recent article in the *New York Times* by Pam Belluck entitled "Health Care After the Supreme Court Ruling" in seeking to determine which side of the issue the decision will favor, the author writes: "No matter the decision, the political ramifications in this election year will be big. After all, the presidential contenders are President Obama, the top-ranking promoter of the law, and Mitt Romney, the architect of a 2006 health care overhaul in Massachusetts that was, in pivotal ways, the model for the national law." Continuing she writes, "But experts on health care policy say the practical effect of the court's decision will probably be less earth-shattering than some people think. If the court takes what many observers believe will be the most likely route and strikes down the individual mandate – the requirement that virtually everyone purchase insurance - many more currently uninsured people are still likely to receive health coverage, they say."

Nevertheless, the record has shown the Court does overturn laws, even reverses itself at times. That notwithstanding, President Obama showed true grit in first advocating this law, campaigning on it and once elected legislated it amidst great

OBAMA - MASTER AND COMMANDER

rancor, doing what none of his predecessors have done. So now we await the Supreme Court's decision but still, many parts of the law have begun to be applied and expectations for coverage of health issues will make President Obama seem a champion of the poor, downtrodden, voiceless and those who can least afford the high cost of medical care.

"In the absence of sound oversight, responsible businesses are forced to compete against unscrupulous and underhanded businesses, who are unencumbered by any restrictions on activities that might harm the environment, or take advantage of middle-class families, or threaten to bring down the entire financial system."
Barack Obama

Dr. Fred Monderson could be reached at fredsegypt.com@fredsegypt.com

Obama - Master and Commander 313. Clymer, Adams, Gordon, Hoe and Bruce.

"There's no reason why Congress shouldn't at least set a clean energy standard that creates a market for innovation. So far, you haven't acted. Well tonight, I will. I'm directing my administration to allow the development of clean energy on enough public land to power 3 million homes." **Barack Obama**, State of the Union Address, January 2012

FREDERICK MONDERSON

35. JOHN BOEHNER: SPEAKER OR PARTISAN?

By
Dr. Fred Monderson

On April 29, 2012, House of Representative Speaker John Boehner (R) appeared on CNN's Candy Crowley's program State of the Union and expressed ideas emanating from his "best view in the House." However, while he had some interesting things to say as to his position as Speaker for the nation, some of his views about President Obama are questionable, particularly because he is a significant leader of the "Party of No!" After all, Republicans have been against Mr. Obama "before day one" and sometimes Mr. Boehner seems to be riding a bucking bronco because he cannot get all his Republican ducks in line. Nevertheless, in that case, he would bang his gravel, duck, and move on to the next issue knowing; even the Speaker can win some and lose some.

First, Mr. Boehner pointed out he is interested in creating "a new way forward" and as Speaker, he is trying to "rebuild" and "strengthen the institution of the House of Representatives." He indicated he is "making progress" and making "positive steps in the right direction." He proudly proclaimed that there were "no earmarks" in his basket and that he has maintained "an open process" as a Representative of the entire nation. Still, he believes Republicans will retain the House in the 2012 elections and defeat Mr. Obama. Without a doubt, these final projected results are questionable.

Next, Ms. Crowley asked Speaker Boehner to compare the Republican contender with President Obama whose office he is seeking. He thought Mr. Romney a "very likeable" person who has had a "successful career." He admitted both he and Mr. Romney were "Striving for the same thing." That is, "to make sure our kids and grandchildren have a secure future." Finally, in his view as to why Mr. Romney will defeat President Obama, Mr. Boehner expressed, "Americans don't like to vote for a loser. They will vote for a successful person." Naturally the Speaker, notwithstanding, is entitled to his own opinion.

All this nevertheless, Speaker Boehner's comments about President Obama is both questionable and disturbing despite the fact he stated, "The President and I have a good relationship." As such, "I avoid making personal attacks on the President." Still, he believes, "The President is getting bad advice." While this statement is questionable, the disturbing utterance that Mr. Obama "has lost his courage" and even more hurtful that "he is diminishing the Presidency" dictates that conscientious Americans should say, "Hold it there Mr. Speaker, you have not only contradicted yourself but you have falsely characterized Mr. Obama. Still, at least you are smart enough to admit he is the President of the United States."

OBAMA - MASTER AND COMMANDER

Now, if we concede his efforts to reform the Institution of the House and focus on his *ad hominem* arguments then we have to conclude Mr. Boehner, as Speaker, is very partisan! After all, he is a major player in the Republican Party, unquestionably and seemingly unalterably opposed to President Obama, and this is based on the party's actions over the last there years.

First of all, if we examine the statement that "the President has lost his courage" then a number of things can be gleamed from this utterance. This line is very consistent with earlier Republican bait that, "The President is an appeaser in Chief." To this falsity, Mr. Obama personally responded in the Press Room, "You should ask the 22 top Al Qaeda leaders taken off the battlefield if I am an appeaser." Certainly, despite what is said, giving the order to assault bin Laden's compound was courageous, for, in a failure he would have been blamed. Equally, we may add his decision to the Navy seals to "take the shot" at the Somali Pirates who were holding captive the Captain of the Maersk Alabama. Now that Mr. Obama's people have come out with a new TV Ad extolling the raid on Osama bin-Laden's compound, Senator McCain has responded it was "shameful self-congratulation." McCain himself should be ashamed! Unlike many veterans wounded, maimed or captured, none exploited shamefully the hero-congratulation as he did for fifty years!

Obama - Master and Commander 313a. R. Pynson

FREDERICK MONDERSON

Obama - Master and Commander 314. I. Elzevir

Their seniority in Congress places both the Speaker and Senator McCain contemporary with President George Bush's term in office. None of these people complained when Mr. Bush's people posted the "Mission Accomplished" banner aboard a navy ship. The Admiral's son stayed silent! What would his father have said? Thus, while Mr. Obama's mission was accomplished and a success, that of George Bush was not accomplished and a failure! Even more, these two gentlemen's Congressional longevity places them; perhaps, contemporary with that era when Republicans touted Democrats were "soft on terror," a la Dukakis and the "Swift Boat" move against John Kerry. Now that Obama's bold and courageous actions have removed foreign policy and "soft on terror" from the Republican arsenal, they are trying a back door, seeming more humane approach. Still, you still can't trust Republicans do the right thing!

Another of Mr. Boehner's utterances that "Mr. Obama is diminishing the Presidency" because he is contesting all issues in the interest of the American people, no matter how small, is very troubling and incorrect. Memory serves very well, even before he was elected President, Mr. Obama was a victim of the most vicious characterization, inundated with racist under and overtones. Boehner and McCain said very little, if anything about these scurrilous and personal attacks on an upstanding gentleman!

Even as events unfolded around the Debt Ceiling Debate, Mr. Obama tried to phone the Speaker. Anyone in this country who receives a phone call from the President responds instantly. Mr. Boehner ignored the President's attempts to

OBAMA - MASTER AND COMMANDER

reach him. He went to the Press before getting in touch with Mr. Obama. Playing hardball as he did, as events unfolded, Mr. Boehner finally and gleefully announced "We got 98 percent of what we wanted!" Without a doubt, in a plurality, any group that gets 98 percent of anything did not play by fair rules, particularly if they do not constitute that percentage of the population. In that House where Mr. Boehner presides, Joe Wilson told the President "You lie!" As an "elder statesman," did he call in Joe? This act certainly diminishes the Presidency but who knows what Mr. Boehner told "old Joe!" if any? When his Republican colleague McConnell gave that famous "Thumbs up" with the big smile that many read as "I got that Nigger" boast, Mr. Boehner, who knows, probably congratulated Mr. McConnell or he probably just remained silent; which is accent by silence! When Senator DeMint on CNN boasted, "I like the President, but he uses bogus numbers," and in the Health Care Reform drama, that "If we stop Obama, it will be his Waterloo," Speaker Boehner never published his response. Perhaps he was out on a cigarette break! Certainly these things diminished the Presidency, but by Republican doings not Mr. Obama's doing!

"Joe the Plumber" and the "Tea Party Movement" attacked Mr. Obama in the most unconscionable manner but we did not hear from Mr. Boehner. While Mr. Boehner acknowledges Mr. Obama is the President, when Michele Bachmann and Donald Trump trumpeted the "Birther Line" the Speaker's silence seemed to say, "You guys run with it!" When the Arizona preacher started praying for the death of the President and his lackey, the "the black protester with guns" took a stand against President Obama, the Speaker was silent. Accent by silence is what we call it! Let us not forget, Edmund Burke reminded the world, "The only thing necessary for evil to triumph is for good men to say nothing." When these evil doers were spewing their evilness, diminishing the Presidency, where was Representative Boehner?

FREDERICK MONDERSON

Obama - Master and Commander 315. A. Hester

Obama - Master and Commander 316. Arbuthnot

OBAMA - MASTER AND COMMANDER

Obama - Master and Commander 317. R. Grafton

Obama - Master and Commander 318. Fratres de Sabio

Speaker Boehner is right that "Americans don't like to vote for a loser" and he should be careful, people are watching and weighing the actions of the Speaker of the House. Who knows, he could lose his job in November! Then again, who can accurately predict the actions of the electorate?

"In the end, that's what this election is about. Do we participate in a politics of cynicism or a politics of hope?" **Barack Obama**

FREDERICK MONDERSON

Obama - Master and Commander 319. W. Jaggard.
"Tonight, I can report to the American people and to the world that the United States has conducted an operation that killed Osama bin Laden, the leader of Al Qaeda, and a terrorist who's responsible for the murder of thousands of innocent men, women, and children. It was nearly 10 years ago that a bright September day was darkened by the worst attack on the American people in our history. The images of 9/11 are seared into our national memory - hijacked planes cutting through a cloudless September sky; the Twin Towers collapsing to the ground; black smoke billowing up from the Pentagon; the wreckage of Flight 93 in Shanksville, Pennsylvania, where the actions of heroic citizens saved even more heartbreak and destruction. And yet we know that the worst images are those that were unseen to the world. The empty seat at the dinner table. Children who were forced to grow up without their mother or their father. Parents who would never know the feeling of their child's embrace. Nearly 3,000 citizens taken from us, leaving a gaping hole in our hearts .... For over two decades, bin-Laden has been Al Qaeda's leader and symbol, and has continued to plot attacks against our country and our friends and allies. The death of bin-Laden marks the most significant achievement to date in our nation's effort to defeat Al Qaeda. Yet his death does not mark the end of our effort. There's no doubt that Al Qaeda will continue to pursue attacks against us. We must - and we will - remain vigilant at home and abroad. As we do, we must also reaffirm that the United States is not - and never will be - at war with Islam. I've made clear, just as President Bush did shortly after 9/11 that our war is not against Islam. Osama bin-Laden was not a Muslim leader; he was a mass murderer of Muslims. Indeed, Al Qaeda has slaughtered scores of Muslims in many countries, including our own. So his demise should be welcomed by all who believe in peace and human dignity .... Americans understand the costs of war. Yet as a country, we will never tolerate our security being threatened, nor stand idly by when our people have been killed. We will be relentless in defense of our citizens and our friends and allies. We will be true to the values that make us who we are. And on nights like this one, we can say to those families who have lost loved ones to Al Qaeda's terror: Justice has been done. **Barack Obama**, announcement of the death of Osama bin-Laden, May 1, 2011

OBAMA - MASTER AND COMMANDER

36. OBAMA "LOOKS LIKE KING TUT"
By
Dr. Fred Monderson

When President Obama visited Egypt to make his address to the Muslim world at Cairo University, he took time out to visit the Pyramids on the Ghizeh Plateau. His official guide and one of his biggest supporters was Dr. Zahi Hawass, Chairman of the Egyptian Antiquities Council. To say the least, Mr. Hawass was very impressed by Mr. Obama's intelligence gauged by the questions he asked and by the fact he thought Mr. Obama looked very much like King Tut. In a tour of the Great Pyramid, Mr. Hawass recounted the President was moved by the dimensions and engineering dynamics of this first and greatest of the Seven Wonders of the World. Outside the great structure he enquired of the much smaller nearby pyramids and told these were where the king's queens and female relatives were buried, Mr. Obama remarked, "I guess Michelle and I won't be buried together."

In a nearby tomb, Mr. Obama saw a much heralded image of a male figure to which the President quickly remarked, "That figure with the big ears looks a lot like me! " The more important likeness, however, is Mr. Hawass' comparison of Mr. Obama with King Tutankhamon of the 18th Dynasty of the New Kingdom. It's interesting, nevertheless, that though the likenesses of the two leaders is a subject for "barbershop discussion" and late night comedy talk, there are in fact some serious comparisons that can be made, no matter how outlandish they seem.

While inheritance is not an American leadership trait, Mr. Obama succeeded to the Presidency at a most difficult time in the Republic's history. In fact, despite all we know, the experts are still puzzled by the gravity of the nation's economic condition with Wall Street in a mess, the Dow Jones Average down to some 6500; job loss remarkably high reaching some 500,000 to 800,000 per month; housing foreclosures escalating; the national debt and foreign trade deficit ballooning; the nation's physical infrastructure seriously challenged in wake of neglect; educational methodology, equipment, facilities and graduation rates in a dismal state. With two wars being waged in Iraq and Afghanistan, terrorists running amok at home and abroad, Somali Pirates feeling invincible and the world frowning at America, the new kid on the block at home took his turn at bat. Moving rapidly, Mr. Obama targeted financial and economic institutions, Wall Street regulation, convinced the Congress of the need to spend the TARP and Stimulus Funds, insisted teachers and first responders as firemen and police now be exempt from any layoffs and began doling out assistance to state and local governments challenged by shortfalls in revenue owing to rising unemployment and scarcity of tax revenue. However, rather than assuming an isolationist posture to lick American wounds, Mr. Obama went abroad, to Canada, Europe and the

FREDERICK MONDERSON

Caribbean signaling "We may be taking a licking but were still ticking." He delivered important messages in Cairo, Turkey and Ghana as well as Trinidad and was hosted by the British, French and Germans. Meanwhile, Mr. Obama deployed his not so secret weapon, Michelle Obama, who floored everyone from Queen to rook!

Obama - Master and Commander 320. W. Jaggard

Obama - Master and Commander 321. John Day

OBAMA - MASTER AND COMMANDER

Obama - Master and Commander 322. Vau Trollier

Obama - Master and Commander 323. Melchior Sessa

King Tut came to power following the downfall of Amenhotep IV, Ikhnaton, the "Heretic Pharaoh" who led the Amarna Revolution at the end of the glorious 18th

FREDERICK MONDERSON

Dynasty. Amenhotep IV was the son of Amenhotep III and Queen Tiy and he inherited a kingdom from his father who had ruled Egypt during "a golden age." He has been called the first monotheist because he proclaimed the Aten, the Sun Disk, the one true god and set about abolishing the ideas and instrumentation of the New Kingdom deity, Amon-Ra, who ruled from his sacred mound at the Temple of Karnak. Akhnaton, or Ikhnaton set about writing poetry in praise of the Aten, introduced new forms of artistic representation and decreed that the name Amon-Ra should be sought out and eradicated. In this he built a temple at the east end of Karnak and set about worshipping his new deity while his men went about in their violent acts to eradicate Amon's memory.

The ancient Egyptians believed every town had its own god who had founded its beginnings and to eradicate the god meant the soul and memory of the town and its people would be forever lost. Akhnaton became uncomfortable every time he had to trek along the central axis of Karnak to reach his temple for, despite deleting the name of Amon from the monuments, his memory still remained. As such, Amenhotep abandoned Thebes, the nation's capital and the temple of Karnak and founded a new city called Tell el Amarna where he moved with his royal retinue and national administration. Within two decades he was overthrown and Tutankhamon succeeded him. Prior to his ascension, the young king's name was Tutankhaten but with the restoration and move back to Thebes and Karnak, he changed his name to Tutankhamon. Healing the schism in the nation, he ruled for a dozen or so years before he deceased. Prof. John H. Clarke expressed: "King Tut was a minor king who got a major funeral." We know much about his tomb's discovery and its untold wealth. However he was succeeded by two weak kings, Smenkhare and Aye, before they themselves were succeeded by Horemhab who rescued the nation and ended the glorious 18th Dynasty.

If it is possible, we could compare the "Golden Age" of Amenhotep III with the economic successes of the American President Bill Clinton and the budget surplus he left to President No. 43. Then, the chaos of the Amarna Heresy, despite its positive historical contributions, can, even though somewhat of a stretch, be compared to the near failed state ending George W. Bush's tenure. As such, Tutankhamon "Restoration" or rescue that set the nation back into the orbit of normalcy could, again through a stretch, be compared with Barack Obama's rescue of the nation when he succeeded as President No. 44. Republican mayhem as the "Party of No" during Mr. Obama's first term can, perhaps, be compared to the backbiting that undermined King Tut's rule. Removed from the scene, he was succeeded by the two weaklings, Smenkare and Aye.

OBAMA - MASTER AND COMMANDER

Obama - Master and Commander 324. William Caxton

Obama - Master and Commander 325. A. Hester

FREDERICK MONDERSON

Obama - Master and Commander 326. F De Giunta

Obama - Master and Commander 327. O. Scotto "Civis Modetiesis"

Is it possible Dr. Hawass, in making the comparison of Barack Obama with King Tut not only sees a likeness in physiological structure but can portend the future that Mr. Obama's tenure will be sabotaged and he succeeded by Republican weaklings? Let us hope Mr. Hawass is only half right and President Obama will

OBAMA - MASTER AND COMMANDER

beat back the forces of weakness until another time when Republicans can really marshal a Presidential timber who can really challenge the Democratic juggernaut.

"It was not a religion that attacked us that September day. It was Al-Qaeda. We will not sacrifice the liberties we cherish or hunker down behind walls of suspicion and mistrust." **Barack Obama**

Obama - Master and Commander 328. W. Jaggard

Obama - Master and Commander 328a. In the National Gallery of Art Sculpture Garden, Louise Bourgeois, American, born France, 1911-2010 **Spider**. 1996 (cast 1997) bronze with silver nitrate patina, Gift of the Morris and Gwendolyn Cafritz Foundation 1997.136.1 (left) and Roy Lichtenstein, American, 1923-1997 **House I**, 1996/1998. Fabricated and painted aluminum. Gift of the Morris and Gwendolyn Cafritz Foundation 1998 1470 (right).

FREDERICK MONDERSON

Obama - Master and Commander 329. Giam. Rizzardi

Obama - Master and Commander 330. The Folger Shakespeare Library where so much literary history and tresure is housed.

OBAMA - MASTER AND COMMANDER

"At a time when our discourse has become so sharply polarized, at a time when we are far too eager to lay the blame for all that ails the world at the feet of those who think differently than we do, it's important for us to pause for a moment and make sure that we are talking with each other in a way that heals, not a way that wounds." **Barack Obama**

"If poverty is a disease that infects an entire community in the form of unemployment and violence, failing schools and broken homes, then we can't just treat those symptoms in isolation. We have to heal that entire community. And we have to focus on what actually works" **Barack Obama**

Obama - Master and Commander 331. The sign says it all!

FREDERICK MONDERSON

Obama - Master and Commander 332. Be not mistaken, these are the steps leading to the Folger Shakespeare Library.

37. "IT'S THE HAIR, STUPID!"
By
Dr. Fred Monderson

Recently, President Obama made the day of a youngster by bending over and allowing him to pat his hair which was of the same texture as that of the young man. Since symbolism is so significant and that human side of President Obama beams in remarkable splendor, the message of the act is tremendous in its ripple effect around the world. Here, little black boys and little black girls will see the great and the humble being united by hair but even more important, it intriguingly motivates them to aspire to attain the realm of power and prestige the President of the United States acquired despite his hair and African heritage. They will get to realize that hard work, education, perseverance, nobility of spirit and good character opens the door to all possibilities of human endeavor, and as Kunta Kinte said to his son, holding him skyward, "There is nothing greater than you!" Add to this, you can achieve anything if you try hard enough; the image of the powerful, and the meek, men of color, bound together by black hair is a powerful statement and aspiration as we move forward in this twenty-first century.

This symbolism of the two men, young and old, in the White House, united by skin color and hair texture, for when compared with another significant

OBAMA - MASTER AND COMMANDER

occurrence, the impact spoken to in the above example was lost. For example, right after bicentennial, an exhibit of the boy king Tutankhamon's jewelry toured the United States. The mascot or face of the exhibit was an alabaster bust of the boy king. Since alabaster is a white stone material, black boys and black girls the world over, in fact, all boys and girls, were deluded into thinking King Tut was white. Now, if sponsors of the exhibit had chosen one of the two replica black statues of the king, black boys and girls worldwide would know the young King Tut looked like them.

Interestingly enough, while African American groups protested the distortion, until recently the controversy raged forcing a reappraisal as to who he actually was. In the 2011 return of the king's jewels, this time the emblem was a brown skinned head. So much for this example!

Obama - Master and Commander 333. A recurring theme of Washington, DC, architecture is the use of "Heads" to decorate and showcase its construction genius.

FREDERICK MONDERSON

Obama - Master and Commander 334. The winged steed so famously reflect good tidings.

Obama - Master and Commander 335. "The First Part of Henry the Fourth."

OBAMA - MASTER AND COMMANDER

It is pretty well recognized, the teaching and representation of the history and culture of ancient Egypt is greatly distorted, projecting a white, European, oftentimes Nordic type, a "blond beast" as the originators, rulers and upper classes of this ancient African nation of Egypt. Yet, Herodotus, the "father of history" in his *Histories*, Book II *Euterpe* on Egypt stated, "the Colchians, Egyptians an Ethiopians have thick lips, broad nose, wooly hair and they are burnt of skin." Count Volney, one of the savants who visited Egypt with Napoleon in his book *Ruins of Empire* p. 17 wrote, "There a people now forgotten discovered while others were yet Barbarians, the elements of the arts and sciences. A race of men now rejected for their sable skin and frizzled hair, founded on the study of the laws of nature those civil and religious systems which still govern the universe."

Thus, hair is particularly interesting a topic in ancient Egypt. It is not often discussed in writing but whenever it's shown, it's easily construed as "black hair." However, because priests, a significant element in the population, and often associated with the surviving evidence, are generally shown with shaven heads. These particular individuals, because of their association in the ritual and worship of the gods, practiced a regimen of cleanliness that required them to wear cotton clothes, wash their bodies three times per day and shave body hair no less than every other day. Notwithstanding, members of the upper class, the nobility who left images of art in their tombs show them wearing "black hair." This is clearly opposite to the images in Greek and Roman art, even Western art, that shows the long flowing type of hair.

This feature of "black hair" is replete in Old Kingdom art particularly at Sakkara where the great mastabas are housed. As we approach the Middle and New Kingdoms, the art form persists, though the king is often shown wearing a crown or the Nemes headdress. In the Cairo Museum of Egyptian Antiquities, in a single gallery on the second floor, there is a display housing a set of hair in the "big Afro" mode. It is off the "beaten path" and only the most resolute visitors to the Museum would find it. Of course, if you had the right Guide he would point it out. That is, if he or she knew of it or its significance! This unique surviving example was found in the Deir el Bahari "cache" discovered in 1881 when mummies of the great eighteenth dynasty monarchs were unearthed. The following quotation from Frederick Monderson's *Hatshepsut's Temple at Deir el Bahari* (2011: 172-173) puts the find's hair in perspective. "Fifteen enormous wigs for ceremonial occasions form a striking feature of the Deir el-Bahari collection. These wigs are nearly 2 ft. high, and are composed of frizzled and curled hair. There are many marked points of resemblance between the legal institutions of ancient Egypt and of England. For instance, pleading must be 'traversed,' 'confessed and avoided,' or demurred to. Marriage settlements and the doctrines of uses and trusts prevailed in ancient Egypt, but the wearing of these wigs was not extended to the members of the legal professions, but was reserved exclusively for the princes of the blood and ladies of very high rank."

FREDERICK MONDERSON

Obama - Master and Commander 336. "The Life and Death of Richard the Third."

Obama - Master and Commander 337. "The Tragedie of King Lear."

OBAMA - MASTER AND COMMANDER

Obama - Master and Commander 338. "The Tragedie of Julius Caesar."

Te bottom line is; picturing of "black hair" in ancient and modern times is a hall mark of humanity, cultural attainment and leadership. It is remarkable how President Obama features so prominently not just as a leader but in association with ancient Egypt, that is, with the "big ears" individual in the Sakkara tomb; Zahi Hawass' belief that "Obama looks like King Tut;" the hair of leadership; for after all, when he visited Egypt a local tabloid in this country ran an article entitled "Return of the Pharaoh."

"It was the labor movement that helped secure so much of what we take for granted today. The 40-hour work week, the minimum wage, family leave, health insurance, Social Security, Medicare, retirement plans. The cornerstones of the middle-class security all bear the union label."

"It's time to fundamentally change the way that we do business in Washington. To help build a new foundation for the 21st century, we need to reform our government so that it is more efficient, more transparent, and more creative. That will demand new thinking and a new sense of responsibility for every dollar that is spent." **Barack Obama**

FREDERICK MONDERSON

"There are a whole lot of religious people in America, including the majority of Democrats. When we abandon the field of religious discourse - when we ignore the debate about what it means to be a good Christian or Muslim or Jew; when we discuss religion only in the negative sense of where or how it should not be practiced, rather than in the positive sense of what it tells us about our obligations toward one another; when we shy away from religious venues and religious broadcasts because we assume that we will be unwelcome - others will fill the vacuum. And those who do are likely to be those with the most insular views of faith, or who cynically use religion to justify partisan ends."

Barack Obama, *The Audacity of Hope: Thoughts on Reclaiming the American Dream*

Obama - Master and Commander 339. "The Tragedie of Macbeth!"

OBAMA - MASTER AND COMMANDER

Obama - Master and Commander 340. "The Merchant of Venice."

Obama - Master and Commander 341. "The Tragedie of Romeo and Juliet."

FREDERICK MONDERSON

38. OBAMA IS NOT GAY!
By
Dr. Fred Monderson

Now that *Newsweek* magazine has dubbed Mr. Obama as "The First Gay President" some examination of the issue is only appropriate since this man has been smeared in the most unimaginable ways. From the time Mr. Obama publicly stated "Gays should be permitted to marry" all manner of takes have been advanced from questionable moral conduct on his part to his re-election chances. However, while it must be reiterated the President's position reflects his personal belief rather than official policy, he feels the rights of Gay people to marry means they will be accorded the equality all Americans are entitled to. Nevertheless, groundbreaking as it is, he has attracted the enmity of persons from a wide variety of spectrums but the redeeming factor is; gays love the fact the President recognizes their right to happiness and equality! The troubling development is, however, conservatives who never liked Mr. Obama is now seeking to win converts among blacks, particularly the Clergy, who seem to be leaning towards withdrawing their support for the President because of his new position on gay marriage.

Mr. Obama's statement about the status of gays is a natural response from a prominent personality about an increasingly important issue fast gaining acceptance among a new generation of Americans. The problem with the President's statement, no matter what he says, his comments become an issue, most often misconstrued. For example, when Prof. Henry "Skip" Gates was arrested while trying to enter his own house and President Obama commented on his friend's arrest, Mr. Obama was castigated for his comments on what appeared a racial matter. In the Trayvon Martin killing, the President expressed a practical fact, that is, "If I had a son he would look like Trayvon!" Newt Gingrich and many others, at the time candidates for the Presidency, accused him of exploiting the situation and creating a racial divide in the country. This is not necessarily so. If we remember when Mr. Obama was attacked particularly by the nascent "Tea Party" Movement, first as a Senator and then as President, many people thought the outlandish accusations had crossed the line, were racist in intent. Mr. Obama said, 'No," these were just Americans expressing a respected right to protest and demonstrate! Here is a man, then, trying not to infuse or see racial behavior even in such questionable expressions consistently attacking his patriotism, moral character, leadership, vision, even his family! However, he did take a stand when he looked into the camera that day and said: "If you're listening, lay off my wife!" You see, Mr. Obama does know his strengths and he knows a great many of the American people are with him.

Nevertheless, the subtle but powerful attack on Mr. Obama's candidacy in the appeal to the Black Clergy is on the grounds that support for homosexual behavior

OBAMA - MASTER AND COMMANDER

by the President was immoral and against Biblical dogma. The question really is, can these pastors who exert influence from their pulpits distinguish between the social drama and the political ramifications of unfolding events as we approach the November elections. The President's position on the right of gay and lesbian Americans to get married and enjoy the benefits of matrimonial protection was based on one man's conviction of the need for fairness. Yet, it involves a great many Americans, declared or not! After all, civil unions do not go far enough to protect the rights and visitation privileges of homosexuals in committed relationships that sometimes, outlast even heterosexual marriages, where by last count, the rate of divorce has been spiraling. Its been shown, homosexuals earn more and owe less than most Americans!

Obama - Master and Commander 342. "A Mid-Summer Night's Dream."

FREDERICK MONDERSON

Obama - Master and Commander 343. Exhibition on View. Open City: London, 1500-1700, June 5, September 30, 2012.

OBAMA - MASTER AND COMMANDER

Obama - Master and Commander 344. Side of the Folger Shakespeare Library with inscriptions on the Cornice, metal bars on the windows, raised sculpture in alabaster.

Obama - Master and Commander 345. "This therefore is the praise of Shakespeare, that his plays be the drama of life." Samuel Johnson.

FREDERICK MONDERSON

Obama - Master and Commander 346. "Wit can no more lie hid. then it could be lost. Reade him. Therefore: and againe. and againe." John Heminge. Henrie Condell.

Obama - Master and Commander 347. "Thou art a moniment without a tombe. and art alive still. While thy booke doth live. And we have wits to read. And praise to give." Ben Johnson.

Many men of the cloth have expressed disagreement with some things said in the Bible, as unalterabe Gospel. In the period when America practiced the institution of slavery, defenders of that horrible experience often sought Biblical justification for their actions. Recently, Rev. Joseph Lowery, that venerable civil rights icon was on CNN with Don Lemon and expressed the view "I find problems with a fellow named Paul saying 'slaves obey your masters.'" Naturally, to quote J.E. Harris in *Africans and Their History* (1972: 14) quoting Robert Graves and Raphael Patai, *Hebrew Myths* (New York: 1964: 221) description of this issue wrote: "... it must be Canaan, your firstborn, whom they enslave .... Canaan's children shall be born ugly and black! Your grandchildren's hair shall be twisted

OBAMA - MASTER AND COMMANDER

into kinks, [their lips] shall swell; ..." Men of this race are called Negroes; their forefather Canaan commanded them to love theft and fornication, to be banded together in hatred of their masters and never to tell the truth." In this age of political correction no one has chosen to remove this disgusting description from the Gospel. As Malcolm said: Perhaps the "House Negro" will accept being a slave but the "Field Negro" will always reject such outright. Harris (1972: 14)-15) continued his explanation, that the "passage includes not only a pretty clear description of the color and physical type of the 'cursed' people, it also presents the principal stereotypes associated with blacks - thieves, fornicators, and liars. The translation of a Hebrew manuscript of Benjamin ben Jonah, a twelfth-century merchant and traveler from Spanish Navarre, not only supports the same theme but also suggests that it was fairly widespread" for that commentator had written: "There is a people ... who, like the animals, eat of the herbs that grow on the banks of the Nile and in the fields. They go about naked and have not the intelligence of ordinary men. They cohabit with their sisters and anyone they find .... These sons of Ham are black slaves."

Even Christian missionaries, ministers and others "explained that an African was better off a slave in a Christian society than free in African savagery." Imagine! Hence, it is obvious, the mindset of these people who seek to undermine the efforts of Barack Obama. Thus, we can see the connection of Republican political theoretical strategists appealing to the Black Clergy to denounce the President for his stand on Gay Marriage. Therefore, if blacks, in accepting the religious argument, decide to oppose the President on the Gay issue and stay home from the voting booth on Election Day, they give Republicans two votes. That is, the one they will cast against the Republican candidate and the one they did not cast for the President.

FREDERICK MONDERSON

Obama - Master and Commander 348. The Lutheran Church of the Reformation: The Nativity of St. John the Baptist - Sunday Worship 8:30 and 10:00 am.

Obama - Master and Commander 349. Across from Folger Shakespeare Library, the rear of the Jefferson Building of the Library of Congress.

OBAMA - MASTER AND COMMANDER

Obama - Master and Commander 350. On the Cornice of the rear entrance to the Supreme Court: "**Justice - The Guardian of Liberty**."

Obama - Master and Commander 351. Male and female images adorn these vessels of stone on the entranceway to the rear of the Supreme Court.

FREDERICK MONDERSON

Now that Julian bond, icon of the Civil Rights Movement has made the distinction on the gay right issue and the NAACP board has recognized and supports it as a social and "civil right" then we see the wisdom of Barack Obama in further leveling the field for all Americans. Gays cans serve in the military, judicial system, schools, in all walks of society but it is ok to continue to discriminate against their right to marry? One commentator noted if an American marries a woman from a foreign country she is entitled to immigrate and join her husband. This right does not belong to a gay American who marries a non-American male abroad. There is even more to this. As such, only the visionless can see the wisdom of President Obama's continuing efforts to level the playing field in all facets of American existence and create a better, more just and competitive society, as we challenge the world armed with the power of the principles that govern our lives in this country.

"Let me be absolutely clear. He United States is a strong friend of Israel's. It will be a strong friend of Israel's under a McCain administration. It will be a strong friend of Israel's under an Obama administration. So that policy is not going to change." **Barack Obama**

Obama - Master and Commander 352. Along the way, Florida House.

OBAMA - MASTER AND COMMANDER

Obama - Master and Commander 353. Great Seal of the State of Florida: In God We Trust and the Screaming Eagle with symbols of peace and war, olive branch and arrows, beneath the sign of the original 13 colonies.

39. OBAMA STYMIED BY FILIBUSTER
By
Dr. Fred Monderson

Recently Illinois Democratic Senator Richard Durbin on CNN's Candy Crowley's State of the Union program Sunday morning May 13, 2012, pointed out there were "more filibusters in the history of this nation" during the Obama administration, than ever before. He attributes this reality, particularly and in conjunction with Kentucky Republican Senator Mitch McConnell's publicly pronounced statement that he intended and there being no change, still intends "to make Barack Obama a one term president." In all likelihood, this position was first formulated against the candidacy of Senator Barack Obama and as the reality of his election manifested, the "long knives" coalesced. The end result was Senator Mitch McConnell's classic statement, conservative, and some say racist! Thus, with this "Pied Piper" up front, legislative Republicans and their allies fell in line, began dancing to this tune being played and threw up every conceivable roadblock possible in Congress in opposition to President Obama's policies. As several measures in the Senate needed more than a simple 51-49 majority vote, Senate Republicans, though in the minority, effectively used the filibuster to frustrate, delay and ultimately challenge

FREDERICK MONDERSON

if not defeat practically every important legislative initiative the President proposed. As such, without the needed number of Senate votes, cloture on any filibuster issue could not be gained and many measures were "talked to death."

Conceivably, an examination of the origin and role of the filibuster can shed some light on its use in this case and how the Obama Administration has been able to manage despite its crippling effect. In a rare recent development the Senate defeated a filibuster measure.

In order that every legislative measure is given the fullest consideration or unanimous consent, unlimited debate is permitted in the U.S. Senate. Thus, pending legislation is oftentimes subjected to the filibuster treatment that is considered "a unique senatorial parliamentary technique." As such, any party in the Senate can use this measure to delay legislation and in some respects cripple it. Some of the more legendary senators in the national government gained their reputation through the filibuster.

Obama - Master and Commander 354. Claes Oldenburg and Coosje Van Bruggen, American, born Sweden, 1929, American, 1942-2009 **Typewriter Eraser, Scale X** 1998 (fabricated 1999) painted stainless steel and fiberglass. Gift of The Morris and Gwendolyn Cafritz Foundation 1998.1.50.1 (left) and Joan Miro, Spanish, 1893-1983 **Personnage Gothque**, Oiseau-Eclair (Gothic Personage, Bird-Flash), 1974, cast 1977 bronze. Gift of The Morris and Gwendolyn Cafritz Foundation 1992.53.1 (right).

OBAMA - MASTER AND COMMANDER

Obama - Master and Commander 355. A panaramic street view of the Capital Building.

FREDERICK MONDERSON

Obama - Master and Commander 356. Street scape. Colorful floral decoration that pleasantly greets the visitor.

In their *The American Political Dictionary*, Plano and Greenberg (1962) (1989: 128) define the filibuster as: "A parliamentary device used in the United States senate by which a minority of senators seeks to frustrate the will of the majority by literally 'talking a bill to death.' Senators are proud of their chamber's reputation for being the world's greatest forum for free discussion. Custom and Senate Rule 22 provide for unlimited debate on a motion before it can be brought to a vote. A filibuster is a misrule of this freedom of debate, since full exploration of the merits and demerits of the pending measure is not objective. Rather, the minority of senators seeks to gain concessions or the withdrawal of the bill by delaying tactics. These include prolonged debate and speeches on relevant and irrelevant topics, parliamentary maneuvers, dilatory motions, and other tricks of the legislative game. The objective of the minority is to delay action on the measure interminably, until the majority is forced by the press of other business to withdraw it from consideration." The authors (1989: 128) further explain the significance of the filibuster. They state: "Over the years, many important bills have been filibustered to death. Many more have been killed by using the threat of a filibuster to force withdrawal of a bill. Until the enactment of the Civil Rights Act of 1957, for example, the filibuster or threat of it had been used successfully for many years by southern senators to forestall civil rights legislation. Senator Strom Thurmond of South Carolina holds the record for the longest individual filibuster, speaking for more than twenty-four hours against enactment of civil rights legislation in 1957. In 1975, the use of the filibuster to kill legislation was

OBAMA - MASTER AND COMMANDER

weakened in the senate by making it easier to invoke cloture on debate under Rule 22. Filibusters may also be defeated by extending the legislative day and holding round-the-clock sessions of the Senate."

Despite what may have been said, when President Obama assumed the Presidency in January of 2009, Democrats in the Senate enjoyed a majority with a Republican or two that tantalized the magical number of 60 votes but maintaining that number was difficult and within no time it evaporated. As such, as the President sought to pursue his legislative agenda, the McConnell "mandate" began to materialize and though he won some he lost others or was stymied by Republicans. So much so, Republicans made so much progress in "stopping Obama," in the election of 2010, the "Tea Party Movement" held court and the American people fell hook, line and sinker for their line of argument. However, as their austerity measures began to show its true meaning and having sworn and signed a "No Tax" oath to Mr. Grover Norquist, and as such blocking every measure to raise revenue in these trying times were stalled. So the Tea Party Republican Movement began to cause people to wonder, are their draconian methods really worth it. The interesting thing about Barack Obama is that under attack unendingly, he has maintained his cool, flashing that ubiquitous smile as if to say, "I will not let those actors from Washingclown un-nerve or derail my agenda!"

Obama - Master and Commander 357. Decorative features on the cornice of the Library of Congress, Jefferson Building, where faces act as drainage holes, and the different levels of architrave are undergirded by engaged pillars capped by Ionic Capitals and other features signalling this is a place of great wisdom and knowledge.

FREDERICK MONDERSON

Obama - Master and Commander 358. The elevated colonnade at this end of the Jefferson Building of the Library of Congress is further accentuated in contrast of the polished and well manicured lawn with floral decoration.

Obama - Master and Commander 359. Another view of the colonnade feature of the Library of Congress, Jefferson Building.

OBAMA - MASTER AND COMMANDER

Obama - Master and Commander 360. Panoramic view of the front entrance to the Capital Building, after its upgrade done in 2005.

Nevertheless, the filibuster seems to have been used not necessarily as a political party rivalry but more as a conservative, anti-social reform mechanism. In their work, *United States History and Government*, Paul Stich, Susan Pingel and John Farrell (1989: 121) point to two particular periods, the 19th Century Jim Crow's Reconstruction backlash and efforts to forestall John Kennedy's initiatives to address the civil rights challenges presented in the 1960s. In the section entitled "The Search for Racial justice" they write: "The movement for racial equality and equity of treatment was divided over the policies and programs of Booker T. Washington and W.E.B. DuBois. Lynching reached its peak during the Jim Crow era in the South. A number of pieces of anti-lynching legislation were introduced in Congress, but were blocked in the Senate when Southern Senators filibustered (endless debate used to postpone a vote)."

Again, after John Kennedy was elected he tried to inject new ideas into the American way of thinking with a bold new program entitled the "New Frontier." In this regard, Stich, Pengel and Farrell (1989: 248) write: "The youth-oriented Kennedy promised to lead a new generation of Americans to a 'New Frontier' with energetic proposals for the space program, civil rights, urban renewal, social welfare, and a new image in foreign policy. To achieve his ambitions, Kennedy convinced the Democratic Congress to pass legislation which lowered tariffs, increased the minimum wage and Social Security benefits, and helped the

FREDERICK MONDERSON

beleaguered cities. Most of his suggestions ran into opposition from conservative Republicans and Southern Democrats opposed to expanding federal influence, especially in civil rights. Federal aid to education, subsidized medical care for the poor and elderly, tax cuts, and civil rights reforms met with defeat, often through the use of Senate filibusters. Many of these programs did eventually become law, but not until after the young President's tragic assassination." Kennedy's social agenda was not dissimilar to that of Barack Obama who seems more concerned especially about Americans without health insurance and equal pay for women, better educational opportunities to improve science and math performance and technical skills in schools, innovative clean energy sources with concern for the environment, among other efforts. Fortunately, the filibuster failed to derail the first two signature successes of the Obama Administration, that is, Health Care Reform and the Lilly Ledbetter law of equal pay for equal work. Respect for the treatment of women and equality for all Americans regardless of their race, religious affiliation, ethnic origin, physical capacity or even sexual orientation is also of concern to President Obama.

In their book, Plano and Greenberg (1989: 118) explain the method of circumventing the filibuster is the technique of "Cloture." They write: "Cloture safeguards majority rule by limiting the power of the senate minority to kill bills by parliamentary maneuvers. Since Rule 22 was amended in 1917, there have been over 100 cloture votes, of which only 20 percent have succeeded, including the following notable votes: Versailles Treaty, 1919; World Court, 1926; Branch Banking, 1927; Prohibition Reorganization, 1927; Communications Satellite, 1962; Civil Rights, 1964; Voting Rights, 1965; Open Housing, 1968; Draft Extension [twice] 1971; Equal Job Opportunity, 1972; and Public Campaign Financing, 1974. The reluctance of senators to vote cloture stems from pride in the Senate's tradition of freedom to debate, as well as from the practical fear of jeopardizing the minority weapon of filibuster, which each senator may someday want to use. Attempts to invoke cloture have occurred with increased frequency since 1960. In 1975, after many unsuccessful attempts since 1917 to make it easier to limit debate, the Senate changed Rule 22 to make it possible to invoke cloture of debate by three-fifths of the entire Senate rather than by the traditional two thirds of senators present and voting. The two-thirds, however, still applies to debate on Senate rule changes."

As part of their arsenal to defeat President Obama Republicans have used every measure including their majority in the House of Representative, PAC and Super PAC capabilities and all forms of surrogates including rich donors who can and do make lucrative donations or contributions to their cause. Nevertheless, the filibuster in the Senate has been an effective weapon particularly because of its usefulness to the Republican minority leader Senator Mitch McConnell. This is understandable since his principal agenda has been to "make Barack Obama a one term president!

OBAMA - MASTER AND COMMANDER

"My family, frankly, they weren't folks who went to church every week. My mother was one of the most spiritual people I knew but she didn't raise me in the church, so I came to my Christian faith later in life and it was because the precepts of Jesus Christ spoke to me in terms of the kind of life that I would want to lead."
Barack Obama

Obama - Master and Commander 361. Sign providing information to visitors to the U.S. Capital.

FREDERICK MONDERSON

Obama - Master and Commander 362. At the National Gallery of Art Sculpture Garden Roxy Paine American, born 1996 **Graft**, 2008-2009 Stainless steel and concrete, (top left); David Smith, American, 1906-1965 (top right); and Alexander Calder, American 1888-1976 **Cheval Rouge** (Red Horse) 1974 (bottom). **Cubi XXVI**, 1965 steel.

OBAMA - MASTER AND COMMANDER

Obama - Master and Commander 363. What more can be said of this magnificent structure, the United States Supreme Court, except to be reminded of its motto - "**Equal Justice Under Law**."

40. SPIRITUAL VALUES VERSUS SECULAR MATERIALISM
By
Dr. Fred Monderson

The Media has flashed information of various Anti-Obama groups such as Carl Rove's Super-Pac that has spent some $10m in Advertisement against the President with another $15m more waiting to be spent and Rickets of TD Bank fame donating another $10m in essentially the same cause. To this we could add the efforts of the Koch Brothers and combined Obama adversaries plan to inject some One Billion Dollars in the campaign to defeat him. It is a valid question to ask "Why?" Quite frankly, there is too much effort and rapidity to defeat President Obama and in this money becomes a primary God! After all, the motto of this nation is "One Nation under God, with liberty and justice for all." When oligarchic whites invest to gain profit from their investment, under the Judea-Christian religious and philosophic principle, the answer is privilege, profit and power! Since secular materialism buys the God, buys the government, the question becomes "Is it one nation under god or under material mammoth?" Equally, one has to ask, "What is the return and who gets it for such lucrative investments?"

Nevertheless, in the movie "Rocky" when confronted by the challenger who said, "I'm going to bust you up," Rocky said "Go for it!" It will ultimately be proven; these large sums spent to negatively paint Barack Obama will prove futile even though the forces arrayed against President Obama are wealthy, powerful, unrelenting and formidable representations of materialism. Thus, despite his

FREDERICK MONDERSON

position, in those respects, President Obama becomes an underdog and America loves an underdog. It's been said one man can become a majority if he believes in himself and his truths are immutable. Thus, as this situation reflects his state of preparedness, honest integrity and bold vision, Mr. Obama will win the election going away! This is equally a view expressed by Bill Clinton on CNN's Piers Morgan on Thursday, May 31, 2012.

We believe the win is predictable because, among other efforts at grassroots organizing, President Obama is collecting vast but small sums of American money to wage his campaign and this is being undergirded by his trump suit of "Spiritual Currency" with its potential miraculous effect. This secret weapon, enshrined and encapsulated in the Sunday morning prayers by the grandmothers, grandfathers, uncles, aunts, brothers and sisters as well as cousins across this land; people invigorated by the good works of the ancestors who have seen and weighed in the balance the heart of the man Obama and they have seen the illuminating beacon of his vision of the future. This is the idea and advantage Obama has over his adversaries and competitors. As such, if we follow some of the old aphorisms we're told, "Money is the root of all evil;" though Rev. Ike often proclaimed "The lack of money is the root of all evil!" Yet, in the movie *Green Berets* starring John Wayne and Raymond St. Jacques, when the soldiers tried to solicit assistance and offer protection to a nearby village of Mountainards, they promised "We'll give you money." The Chief then asked "What is money?" Even these days, amidst much glaring Media fanfare Mr. Zuckerberg launched his **Face Book IPO** with shares set relatively high. Word has it, so many billion dollars were made and days after he was being raked over a bed of flaming coals for some form of stock impropriety. Thus, money is not always everything. For one thing, money can't buy health and it cannot thwart the will of the people determined and united in a cause they deem correct and inclusive.

Obama - Master and Commander 364. Barry Flanagan, British, born 1941. **Thinker on a Rock**, 1997 cast bronze. Gift of John and Mary Pappajohn 1999.30.1 (left) and Mark Di Suvero, American born 1933 **Aurora**, 1992-1993 steel. Gift of The Morris and Gwendolyn Cafritz Founation 1996.72.1 (right).

OBAMA - MASTER AND COMMANDER

Obama - Master and Commander 365. Signage that shows ownership, United States Capital Police.

Obama - Master and Commander 366. Property of U.S. Capital Police, even the fence has some majesty to it.

FREDERICK MONDERSON

Obama supporters should take heart, there is a "spiritual force" at work in Mr. Obama's campaign, an unseen power; the obstinate and arrogant cannot comprehend its prevalence, for it undergirds the divine mission of Mr. Obama. Interesting, he does not flaunt his spiritual values; he lets it permeate his being in doing god's work. He upholds the nation's and universal Christian philosophic admonitions to "love god, love yourself and love your neighbor." After all, the souls of the righteous are immortal and divine! Thus, in his humanity and social policy, Mr. Obama manifests the beatitudes Jesus admonished. These, according to *Matthew* 5: 3-10 are:

Blessed are the poor in spirit, for theirs is the kingdom of heaven.

Blessed are the meek for they will inherit the earth.

Blessed are those who hunger and thirst for righteousness, for they will be filled.

Blessed are the merciful, for they will be shown mercy.

Blessed are the pure in heart for they will see God.

Blessed are those who are persecuted because of righteousness, for theirs is the kingdom of heaven.

I could add, "Blessed are those who have no health insurance for they will have it under Health Care Reform." Thus, Mr. Obama adheres to the basic philosophic and moral tenets of this Christian nation. This, the giddy multitude of anti-Obamites could never envision nor comprehend!

However, while I cannot equate Mr. Obama with Jesus, his philosophy of leveling the playing field, giving everyone a fair shot, insisting everyone pay their fair share, even his concern for the millions with no health insurance is consistent with the aspirations inveighed in *Matthew* 5, which is also, the 'Meek shall inherit the earth ....'

As he gives hope to the masses, the spirit of god is upon Barack Obama! He becomes the salt of the American earth! This light of the world is a beacon, a light that shines from the City on a Hill making manifest the American mission as the last hope for humanity. Compare the President's compassionate concern with the secular materialism's privilege, profit and power; we notice the nation has moved off its moral foundation; its moral compass, as Dr. Martin Luther King would say! This contradicts every spiritual value of one nation under god. His concern for the millions without health care, believing everybody is entitled to medical care forces us to ask, "Which stance or campaign worships secular materialism, which supports spiritual values?"

OBAMA - MASTER AND COMMANDER

Therefore, as the forces of history teach us; Christian belief holds Jesus and the Saints have amassed an enormous amount of good will through their good works. This is stored in a container in the Vatican which the Pope can draw upon to carry through his mission of mercy and salvation in the world. Equally, the African American ancestors who have toiled unpaid in the fields of the institution of slavery, suffered the indignity of the emasculating experience, been victims of racial discrimination and terror, created and experienced the joys of Negro Spirituals to ease their suffering while caring for the young, old and infirm, all the while still looking toward emancipation and salvation, have amassed the spiritual currency that will undergird Mr. Obama's efforts. These are the people who, with faith in the future, could only bank "spiritual capital," "spiritual currency." Believe it or not, besides Mr. Obama, their good works keeps America buoyed and "still standing!" The prayers, dreams, aspirations and expectations of these martyred visionaries, for all we know, probably foresaw the rise and elevation of Barack Obama. This long vision has also recognized the challenges to Mr. Obama as he seeks to complete his mission and contribute to the elevation of their progeny through educational advancement, economic empowerment and political practicalities. That is why the ancestors bequeathed the potency of a "spiritual currency bank" for Mr. Obama to draw on to contend and conquer the forces of materialism committed to derail his divine mission. Thus, the people's champion will prevail because through god "Spiritual capital" will win out against the financial prodigiousness of mammoth designed to thwart the will of destiny and the divine!

FREDERICK MONDERSON

Obama - Master and Commander 367. A resplendent view of the Capital Building's entrance and close-up of the magnificent dome.

OBAMA - MASTER AND COMMANDER

Obama - Master and Commander 368. Colonnade of the House section of the Capital Building.

Obama - Master and Commander 369. Colonnade of the Senate section of the Capital Building, just beyond the fountain with its floral decoration.

FREDERICK MONDERSON

Obama - Master and Commander 370. Another view of the fountain, its surrounding ambience and a government building peeping out in the rear.

Obama - Master and Commander 371. Close-up of the decorated surroundings of the fountain.

"My parents shared not only an improbable love, they shared an abiding faith in the possibilities of this nation. They would give me an African name, Barack, or blessed, believing that in a tolerant America your name is no barrier to success."

Dr. Fred Monderson could be reached at fredsegypt.com@fredsegypt.com

OBAMA - MASTER AND COMMANDER

"The boarded-up homes, the decaying storefronts, the aging church rolls, kids from unknown families who swaggered down the streets - loud congregations of teenage boys, teenage girls feeding potato chips to crying toddlers, the discarded wrappers tumbling down the block - all of it whispered painful truths."
Barack Obama, *Dreams from My Father: A Story of Race and Inheritance*

41. CONSPIRACY AGAINST OBAMA?
By
Dr. Fred Monderson

Now that most of the dust has settled after nearly four years, in view of all that has happened to the President it's time to ask whether there is a conspiracy against the Presidency of Barack Hussein Obama, the first African American to hold the office of President. When, as we approach the next general election and President Obama is attacked for his record as the Executive President of the United States, it is appropriate that we evaluate the people, events and sayings seemingly waged against Mr. Obama by Republicans, allies, supporters and donors. We can also question whether race has anything to do with it. However, when all is said and done, the putative record depicts a super abundance of negatively pernicious behavior directed against Mr. Obama at a time when he has full-fledged devoted tremendous intellectual, moral and spiritual leadership to combat the enormous economic, financial and social quagmire he inherited in a nation at war while having equally to contend with pernicious Americans practically at war with him! Given the situation he inherited, the effort he expended to address such and nevertheless, has had to contend with such animus directed towards him, one has to conclude, all things being equal, racist behaviors undergirded the attacks on Mr. Obama's integrity, nativity, patriotism, judgment, even leadership skills. So, reasonable people can only conclude Mr. Obama's racial heritage, African American, is at the root of his many problems despite claims, party politics, to the contrary. This is problematic because many people felt his election signaled a post-racial America was underway. Nevertheless, remaining tremendously optimistic and even more strategically astute, Mr. Obama chose to dismiss these actions attributing all such behaviors as "Good ole boys" being "Good ole boys!"

FREDERICK MONDERSON

Obama - Master and Commander 372. Another one of the red granite decorations fronting the entrance to the Capital Building.

OBAMA - MASTER AND COMMANDER

Obama - Master and Commander 373. One of the red granite decorations fronting the entrance to the Capital Building.

Obama - Master and Commander 374. Still another one of the red granite decorations fronting the entrance to the Capital Building.

There is "hard campaigning" and then there is "hard campaigning," but from the inception Barack Obama's very humanity was challenged, fueled particularly by right wing media. In the Presidential Primary against Hillary Clinton, his experience and leadership skills were an issue as to what he would do "when the

FREDERICK MONDERSON

Three AM call came in." He weathered that storm! Having overcome that hurdle as the first African American nominated by a major party, Mr. Obama turned to face his Republican challenger, John McCain. Just then, the "Birther" issue surfaced giving rise, perhaps by whomsoever initiated the "Tea Party Movement," to an unrelenting denial of his nativity and resultant patriotism and right to the Office of President. Strange that concurrently, Republicans were proposing changing the Constitution to allow a foreigner, Arnold Schwartznegge, then Governor of California, to be eligible for the Presidency. Even more, in their nascent stage, then Senator Barack Obama was caricatured in the most ridiculous fashion; who could forget the "Witch Doctor" and "Hitler" associations as well as the hanging effigy! At their rallies some supporters, whipped up by the likes of the Sarah Palin's "He's not like us," "Cross hairs" invective, elements within shouted "Kill the Nigger!" No Republican of substance disavowed this! As the "Birther" propaganda fermented people would inject such questions in a racial tone. In one incident, during the presidential campaign, McCain was man enough to extol a female member of an audience, "No madam, he is a citizen, we only have differences on the issues." Nevertheless, as President Obama would later confess, Fox News was behind the "Birther" viral. The "Birther Mama" ran with it. Michele Bachmann took it up conveniently then dropped the issue before Donald Trump embraced "Birthism" and been running with it ever since. In view of the power of American law and enforcement mechanisms, at the last round of Trump's "Birther malady," Wolf Blitzer of CNN's Situation Room, though he was being ridiculous and another commentator labelled him a "jackass!"

Given America's racist past, many believed the election of Barack Obama would herald a new post-Racial America but old ideas die hard. Threats against the new President's life increased, rising beyond what George Bush or any other president faced. One "Christian Hypocrite," I mean pastor, began praying for the President's death! How do you square this with a beneficent god or are we now subscribing to radical terrorist posturing? One of his young "stool parishioners," earned the title "black protester with guns" as he came out to greet the President to show his right to bear arms. We know the President is not losing sleep over the Reverend and his praying pigeon, I mean parishioner. Question is, 'Are they still praying, every day, once a week?' Are they getting tired? Have they looked like jackasses? How effete these idiots look! It makes one wonder does god answer prayers?

The "circus criers" notwithstanding, Republicans running blocks of every legislative move the President initiated forces one to question their motivation and who gave them their marching orders. Not content with waging *ad hominem* war on Mr. Obama, every legislative action he initiated, Republicans said "No to this," and "No to that." His most significant measures, viz., Lilly Ledbetter, Health Care Reform, Repeal of "Don't Ask," "Don't Tell," Credit Card Reform, the TARP Funds, Stimulus Package, etc., were all successes when the Democrats held a majority in Congress. When that fragile majority dissipated, Republicans held him at a standstill. Yet still, as Republicans full-court press of negativity escalated, they

OBAMA - MASTER AND COMMANDER

eroded the edges by donting everything they could. Whilst, unbeknown to everyone a field of young "Tea Party" Republicans did a "Faust" and sold the American people a package of goods, got lucky and ended up in control of Congress.

Obama - Master and Commander 375. Two red granite decorations of a bird (left) and floral centerings fronting the entrance to the Capital Building (right).

Obama - Master and Commander 376. Two more red granite decorations of birds (left) and floral pattern fronting the entrance to the Capital Building (right).

The little men of tunnel vision from, viz., Republican leadership in and out of Congress especially the Tea Party cabal in the House and right wing commentators and talk show hosts, choose to put politics before the American economy. They refused to acknowledge the gravity of the nation's economic plight that Mr. Obama inherited, but simple-mindedly choose to focus all their attention and effort to make his tenure a failure. Rather than put their shoulder to the American wheel to move the coach forward, they sought to remove the wheel! In a jet age, their pedestrian understanding of the impact of Europe's debt and China's growing economic influence on the American system signaled they could not comprehend or refused to recognize the sincerity of the President's efforts to clean the stables inundated with Republican manure! So much so, they dismissed the positive 4.3

FREDERICK MONDERSON

million jobs created during Obama's administration when, upon his assumption of leadership, the nation was losing some 500,000 to 800,000 jobs per month.

Adding injury to insult, among the things the Republican controlled House refused is to pass the President's "Jobs Bill" now in Congress. Equally they downplay the Auto Industry rescue that saved more than one million jobs, his economic renewal effort and the infrastructure refurbish program, his program of tax cuts for small businesses, tax cuts for businesses that hire Veterans, as well as not giving the administration credit for increases in exports of American made products. All this Republicans have done to deny Obama "a win" in his vision for the country. They're doing a "Nero" I mean Congress, "fiddling while Rome" or "America "is burning" act. Blindsided by the need and effort to "make Obama a one term President," Republicans have demonstrated insensitivity to the American people's economic plight of unemployment, home distress, etc., while proffering worn out policies and promises of tax cuts for the wealthy which do not produce jobs as history has shown. If the tax cuts do work, why as they are still in effect, have been for more than a decade, and there are no jobs produced? Even if Mr. Obama is running in his lane, why are no jobs being produced in their lane from the tax cuts?

Given all this and more, a legitimate question is whether there is a 'Conspiracy against President Obama?' The answer seems to be Yes! Yes! Yes!

"My task over the last two years hasn't just been to stop the bleeding. My task has also been to try to figure out how do we address some of the structural problems in the economy that have prevented more Googles from being created."
Barack Obama

Dr. Fred Monderson can be reached at fredsegypt.com@fredsegypt.com

Obama - Master and Commander 377. Still more red granite decorations with birds in center fronting the entrance to the Capital Building.

OBAMA - MASTER AND COMMANDER

"The study of law can be disappointing at times, a matter of applying narrow rules and arcane procedure to an uncooperative reality; a sort of glorified accounting that serves to regulate the affairs of those who have power - and that all too often seeks to explain, to those who do not, the ultimate wisdom and justness of their condition. But that's not all the law is. The law is also memory; the law also records a long-running conversation, a nation arguing with its conscience."
Barack Obama, *Dreams from My Father: A Story of Race and Inheritance*

Obama - Master and Commander 378. Tony Smith American, 1912-1980 **Moondog**, 1964/1998-1999 painted aluminum. Gift of the Morris and Gwendolyn Cafritz Foundation 1997.137.1 (left) and Scott Burton American, 1939-1989 **Six-Part Seating**, 1985-1998 polished granite Gift of the Collectors Committee 1998.146.1 (right).

Obama - Master and Commander 379. Alexander Calder, American, 1898-1976 **Tom's**, 1974 painted sheet metal Courtesy Calder Fooundation, New York (left) and Ellsworth kelly American, born 1923 **Stele II**, 1973 one-inch weathering steel Gift of the Morris and Gwendolyn Cafritz Foundation 1999.15.2 (right).

FREDERICK MONDERSON

Obama - Master and Commander 380. Sol Lewitt American, 1928-2007 **Four-sided Pyramid**, first installation 1997, fabricated 1999 concrete blocks and mortar. Gift of the Donald Fisher Family 1998.149.1

42. "OBAMA MUST BE DEFEATED!" ARGUMENT FROM AUTHORITY? BY DR. FRED MONDERSON

From his magisterial throne of "absolute wisdom," Obama's former Professor Robert Unger propounded a new, bold and somewhat questionable mantra, that the President "must be defeated." Such a direct shibolleth seems a shameful display of "*Alma Mata* envy" manifesting the fingerprint of "Tea Party" Republican critical and shameless assault on Mr. Obama's integrity and leadership. "Where you sit is where you stand and where you stand is where you sit!" This forces us to see Professor Unger's chant as similar to the Roman Senator Cicero's admonition that "Carthage must be destroyed," because the North African state posed a threat to Rome's Mediterranean mercantile economic interest. Because he is a professor and because he taught Barack Obama, Professor Unger's criticism of his former student lets many people will wonder whether he has "legitimacy because he is an authority." In days of youe, in the age of Mark Rudd, students at Columbia

OBAMA - MASTER AND COMMANDER

University would hAve demanded Professor Unger be fired for his remarkably poor visionof the future and his remarkably partisan position in a losing campaign. The shameless professor should "fall on his sword!" Afterall, who would today trust his judgment or knowledge? Notwithstanding, however, there are probably twice as many professors at Harvard University who taught Obama and may offer a diametrically opposed view!

Nevertheless, the caustic nature of this criticism dictates that the Professor himself come under some scrutiny for the timing of his announcement that coincides with the Republican nominee's mobilization of his political challenge to the President. That a "Harvard man" in Massachusetts attacks an alumnus whose opponent is from the state of the institution's residence allows one to can ask the legitimate question, 'Which master is this academic "Authority" serving' and whether it is conceivable he may have been 'contacted?' If stern faced body language is any indication as he made his case, added to the content of his commentary, all questions whether this is a legitimate and credibly neutral critique or an axe-man on a mission! That he is a Professor there is no doubt. That Barack Obama may have taken a course or two since they were both at the same academic institution is not in dispute. Given the right to be critical, even the right to comment, one can still question the justification for the magisterial condemnation expressed in a professor's shameless and caustic critique of a student not as a corrective but as a negative admonition since the student is engaged in a political contest. This critique and its timing is a stealth endorsement of the student's opponent.

Not to diverge but a case in point can add some clarity to this assessment! As a student this writer tried to get into a particular University's Ph.D program. No names! The professor, Chairman of the Department suggested I take a course or two. One year later having taken two of his courses, received As, he refused to let me into the Department's program that he headed! Years later, in a public forum this professor confessed "It was a case of the student knowing more than the professor!" The greatest aspiration of a professor is to see his student excel beyond the limitations of his station. Mr. Obama exceeded expectations. More than three years into the President's term, Professor Unger had not expressed any condemnation of the tremendous forces at work, the unrelenting attacks, Republicans "mining of his pathway," threats of physical harm and criticisms against Mr. Obama's integrity, his academic record, his leadership skills, patriotism, birthright, social associations, religious affiliation, obstructionism, you name it! What Professor Unger fails to recognize, the student has learned well and is more astute in innovating creative stratgegies to thwart insidious verbal attacks disguised as legitimate political criticisms of the issues.

FREDERICK MONDERSON

Obama - Master and Commander 381. Two red granite decorated pillars fronting the entrance to the Capital Building.

OBAMA - MASTER AND COMMANDER

Obama - Master and Commander 382. An etched decorated bowl with flowers as part of the red granite decoration fronting the entrance to the Capital Building.

FREDERICK MONDERSON

Obama - Master and Commander 383. Decorated stone atop an attached pillar as part of the red granite decoration fronting the entrance to the Capital Building.

The Professor remained shamelessly silent when Senator Mitch McConnell boldly and publicly stated his mission "to make Barack Obama a one term president!" In President Obama's tremendous effort against all the opposition to pass Health Care Reform, the pushback generated, and given Senator DeMint's "If we stop Obama, it will be his Waterloo" directive, the professor remained silent. As a man of conscience the professor remained silent when the President of the United States was called a "Nigger," told "You lie" in the House of Representatives amidst a State of the Union Address and his life often threatened because of his race. He stood on the sidelines as the "Birther" controversy manifested, even when Donald Trump assininely questioned Barack Obama academic record and his citizenship, Professor Unger remained silent as a voice of conscience. Now with the Republican nominee virtually declared as we head into the final leg of the campaign towards the election, with the lights now on, Professor Unger has come out of the fabric of the nation's woodwork and expressed his shamelessly considered, perhaps racially cloaked, views as an authority.

Given all we know, all that President Obama sees from the Oval Office, does this student know more than the Professor? Is this exhortation a vendetta, warranted criticism or a hatchet job? Is his coming out a work for hire?

OBAMA - MASTER AND COMMANDER

Now let's look at the Professor's criticisms:

Roberto Unger, Obama's Former Harvard Law School Professor, Says the President 'Must Be Defeated!' One of President Barack Obama's former professors appears to have turned against him, according to a recent YouTube video.

"President Obama must be defeated in the coming election," Roberto Unger argued in a Post on May 22. "He has failed to advance the progressive cause in the United States." Unger said that Obama must lose the election in order for "the voice of democratic prophecy to speak once again in American life."

He acknowledged that if a Republican wins the presidency, "there will be a cost ... in judicial and administrative appointments." But he said that "the risk of military adventurism" would be no worse under a Republican than under Obama, and that "the Democratic Party proposes no new direction." He fails to recognize Republican policy created the economic quagmire we are still battling and their administration never achieved what Obama did in the 'War on terror!'

Obama - Master and Commander 384. Another one of the flowered bowls etched as part of red granite decorations fronting the entrance to the Capital Building.

FREDERICK MONDERSON

Obama - Master and Commander 385. Another one of the flowered bowls etched as part of red granite decorations fronting the entrance to the Capital Building.

Obama - Master and Commander 386. Bird in flowered flight as part of red granite decorations fronting the entrance to the Capital Building.

OBAMA - MASTER AND COMMANDER

Obama - Master and Commander 387. Another one of the flowered bowls etched as part of red granite decorations fronting the entrance to the Capital Building.

"Give the bond markets what they want, bail out the reckless so long as they are also rich, use fiscal and monetary stimulus to make up for the absence of any consequential broadening of economic and educational opportunity, sweeten the pill of disempowerment with a touch of tax fairness, even though the effect of any such tax reform is sure to be modest," he said. "This is less a project than it is an abdication." If this is so, 'why is Wall Street turning against Obama in favor of Romney?'

The professor went on to list his complaints:

- "His policy is financial confidence and food stamps."

Food stamps is a part of the safety net for Americans below the poverty line while the "Republican base" with its millionaires and billionaires are getting more of the American pie.

FREDERICK MONDERSON

- "He has spent trillions of dollars to rescue the moneyed interests and left workers and homeowners to their own devices."

Much of this resource has gone to fill the great void created by Mr. Obama's predecessor and rescuing the nation and before you know it, 'Republican obstructinist' boldly challenged the President's efforts. We could list the President's Jobs Bill and aid to home owners.

- "He has delivered the politics of democracy to the rule of money."

Given the enormous sums committed to defeat President Obama as he fights against Republican obstructionism, the contributions he elicits are of a paltry sum. How much did the professor donate to either Republican or Democratic contender?

- "He has disguised his surrender with an empty appeal to tax justice."

If Republican Tea Party members can make a **NO TAX** pledge to get elected to Congress then to criticize President Obama for insisting on repeal of Bush Tax cuts and tax increases on people making over $250,000.00, then the professor's claim is very disenginous.

- "He has reduced justice to charity."

Obama - Master and Commander 388. Another one of the flowered red granite decorations fronting the entrance to the Capital Building.

OBAMA - MASTER AND COMMANDER

Obama - Master and Commander 389. A slinging monkey as part of red granite decorations fronting the entrance to the Capital Building.

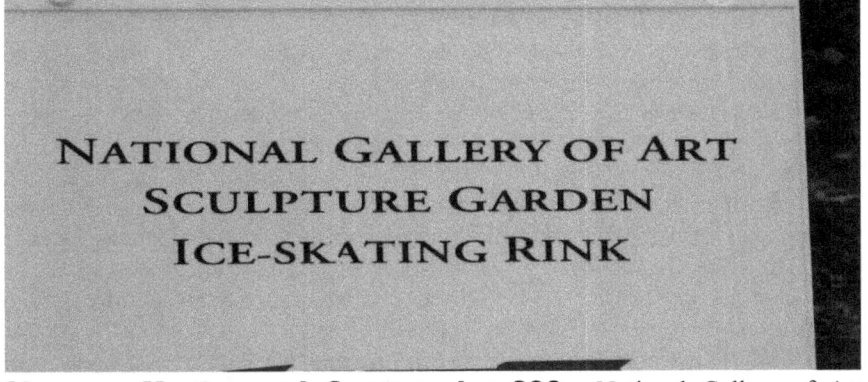

Obama - Master and Commander 390. National Gallery of Art Sculpture Garden Ice-Skating Rink.

The President has proposed trying terrorist detainees in civil courts and spoke out for the arrested Harvard Professor and on behalf of Travon Martin.

- "He has subordinated the broadening of economic and educational opportunity to the important but secondary issue of access to health care in the mistaken belief that he would be spared a fight."

He has sought to broaden economic opportunity through the Jobs Act and lowering student loan rates, emphasizing "Race to the Top" and favoring educational overhaul and state of the art equipment as well as supporting job training through support for communty colleges.

- "He has evoked a politics of handholding, but no one changes the world without a struggle."

FREDERICK MONDERSON

On the contrary, Mr. Obama has struggled from the time of his delcaration to run for the Presidency to the day of the professor's critique.

The beauty of the American system is that it allows for free expression and therefore as a rebuttal and corrective, this writer asks the reader to constructively view the facts. As the first African American citizen to marshal the wherewithal to sustain and win the democratic primary and be nominated by a major political party, then wage a successful campaign against an American hero, John McCain and the enormous resources of the Republican Party fueled in hatred and assaults by many Americans bent on holding back the dawn of racial discrimination, is this a major accomplishment?

Mr. Obama emerged as one of the greatest modern humanitarians to occupy the American Presidency and as such enraged the enmity and reaction of so many. Depending on where one sits, the professor's critique as disguised may very well be an attempt to soft pedal the continuing assault on Mr. Obama. Nevertheless, when one weighs President Obama's accomplishments on the foreign relations/foreign policy fronts, viz., the decimation of the Al Qaeda threat and killing Osama bin-Laden, curtailing Somali Pirates' rampage, expressed support for Israel, put Iran, North Korea and other threatening regimes on notice, "Behave or else," unrelenting in his efforts to stem nuclear proliferation, recognizing and engaging China, India, Japan, Brazil and Indonesia as significant global economic players, increased foreign trade and blunted foreign animosity towards America stemming from George Bush's "Go it alone" policy on Iraq. The President has concluded the war in Iraq and negotiated a reduction of forces and exit strategy form Afghanistan. How about them apples Professor? He has curtailed efforts of Somali Pirates and with vigilance and some luck has forestalled terrorist attacks on the homeland and these are indeed significant accomplishments. He has not followed through on his pledge to close Guantanamo Bay terrorist prison but he may know something many are not aware of! Similar administrations pale in significance.

On the domestic front, despite unrelenting obstructionist opposition and expressed hatred towards this first African American President, Mr. Obama passed Health Care Reform, Lilly Ledbetter "equal pay for equal work" legislation, repealed "Don't Ask, Don't Tell" in the military and insists, personally, gays should be permitted to marry. Inheriting an economy buried in quagmire and hemorrhaging some 500,000 to 800,000 jobs per month, the President has presided over some 27 months of consistent job growth, added 4.3 million jobs, rescued Wall Street from c. 6500 to now 12,500 on the Dow, rescued the auto industry saving 1.5 million jobs and stood up for women's issues since his mother-in-law, wife and daughters Sasha and Malia as well as women in his administration have a stake in the nation's future. He has sponsored Credit Card Reform, created environmental, financial and economic reforms, made significant efforts to aid homeowners affected by foreclosures and decline in property value and proposed tax incentives

OBAMA - MASTER AND COMMANDER

for small businesses to hire workers and also for businesses who hire veterans. While business boasts of sitting on trillions of dollars waiting on more opportune times to invest, much of this, invested in Wall Street is making more trillions while purporting Mr. Obama is being unfair to business. We could add Obama's brighter view of the future by investing in new and clean energy, the environment, with emphasis on educational methods and materials and infrastructure and transportation upgrades and initiatives.

Obama - Master and Commander 391. Another one of an etched bird (left) and floral patter in a circle (right) as part of red granite decorations fronting the entrance to the Capital Building.

Obama - Master and Commander 392. Tony Smith, American, 1912-1980. **Wanderign Rocks**, 1967 painted steel. Gift of the Collectors Committee 1981.53.1 (left) and David Smith American, 1906-1965 **Cubi XI**, 1963 stainless steel The Moris and Gwendolyn Cafritz Foundation (right).

FREDERICK MONDERSON

Obama - Master and Commander 393. Another one of the etched bird (left) and floral pattern in a circle (right) as part of red granite decoration fronting the entrance to the Capital Building.

Thus, the reader is asked to compare what Mr. Obama has accomplished despite "McConnell's Mandate," the "Tea Party" members of Congress holding the nation hostage, John Boehner working to achieve "98 percent of what we wanted," DeMint and his likes setting backfires to sabotage the Obama presidency while Republican surrogates *a la* "*Birther*" *Trump*, the "Koran Burning Pastor," "Pastor Anderson praying for the President's death" and many more odious forms of despicable behaviors are designed to make his presidency a failure. Because the student has risen above the professor and the American people are wise they will see beyond the professor's shrill, then support Obama's view of a promising future rather than the dismal future sitting and pessimistic charlatans wish to paint.

"Now, anybody who thinks that we can move this economy forward with just a few folks at the top doing well, hoping that it's going to trickle down to working people who are running faster and faster just to keep up, you'll never see it."
Barack Obama

Dr. Fred Monderson can be reached at fredsegypt.com@fredsegypt.com

"And as John F. Kennedy described the ideals behind what would become the Peace Corps, he issued a challenge to the students who had assembled in Ann Arbor on that October night: 'on your willingness to contribute part of your life to this country,' he said, 'will depend the answer whether a free society can compete. I think it can,' he said." **Barack Obama**

"On every front there are clear answers out there that can make this country stronger, but we're going to break through the fear and the frustration people are feeling. Our job is to make sure that even as we make progress, that we are also giving people a sense of hope and vision for the future."
Barack Obama

OBAMA - MASTER AND COMMANDER

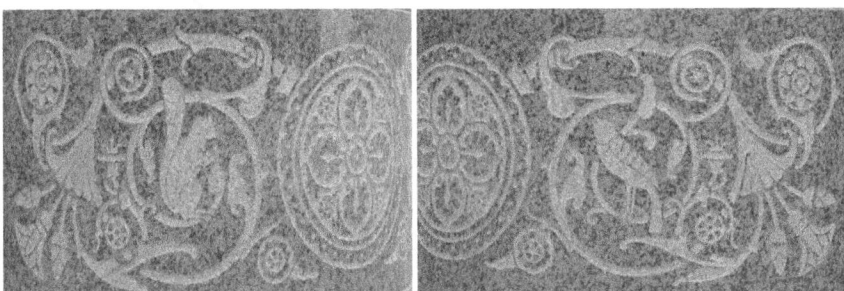

Obama - Master and Commander 394. This time its a squirrel (left) and an etched bird (right) in the red granite decoration fronting the entrance to the Capital Building.

"We have been told we cannot do this by a coarse of sentence: it will only grow louder and more dissident. We have been asked to pause for a reality check, we have been warned about offering this nation false hope, but in the unlikely story that is America there has never been anything false about hope."

"Nothing can stand in the way of millions of voices calling for change the hopes of a little girl who goes to a public school in Dillon are the same as the dreams of a little boy who learns on the streets of L.A. We will remember that there is something happening in America; that we are not as divided as our politics suggest, that we are one people, we are one nation and together we will begin the next great chapter in the American story with three words that will ring from coast to coast, from sea to shining sea: **YES WE CAN**! Yes we can to justice and equality, yes we can to opportunity and prosperity" **Barack Obama**

Obama - Master and Commander 395. More of the decorations as part of red granite decoration fronting the entrance to the Capital Building.

FREDERICK MONDERSON

Obama - Master and Commander 396. This time it's etched birds as part of red granite decoration fronting the entrance to the Capital Building.

43. OBAMA AND EXECUTIVE ORDER
By
Dr. Fred Monderson

When President Obama issued his Executive Order regarding the immigration status of young immigrants brought to this country illegally by their parents, this act engendered great enmity by Republicans who never liked him to begin with. As such, a cliché spoken by Secretary of State Hillary Clinton is a good barometer of his opponents' behaviors. Mrs. Clinton, in an interview once said, "If President Obama walked on water," former U.S. Ambassador to the U.N. under President Bush, "Bolton would say it's because he could not swim!" To examine this statement further reveals a lot about Mr. Obama's opponents. To "walk on water" is an extraordinary feat. Only one man in history has been able to execute this phenomenon, and he certainly had divine connection. For Mr. Obama to accomplish far reaching legislation means he is exceptional, possibly possessing a tincture of divine essence himself. Given the above, his actions, activities, accomplishments must be of a higher standard; yet, in every iota it never matches up to Republican expectations, whether this is purposeful or not! Even the killing of Osama bin-Laden and dismantling of his terror network could not garner much praise from Republicans who only clapped once and blinked momentarily then closed their eyes. The "blink" was necessary otherwise people would see Republicans for the real hypocrites they truly are.

Now, that there was precedence in the issuing of an Executive Order and that this was Mr. Obama's first did not matter! Recently, some "What's his face" lawmaker, I mean Senator Charles Grassley said Mr. Obama was "stupid!" Imagine! A Doctor of Law, Constitutional scholar, graduate from two of the nation's finest Ivy League Universities of Columbia and Harvard, President of the Harvard Law Review and an individual possessing all the temerity and wherewithal to campaign successfully to become President of the United States, accomplish legislative and policy gains as he has, is "stupid." Equally, that he is a

OBAMA - MASTER AND COMMANDER

"tyrant" for leading not following seems more reflective of the person making the statement. Now, after the Supreme Court's ruling, this writer asks, "Who's stupid now Grassley?"

This *ad hominem* attack is in keeping with Republican pernicious "bloopers." Remember "You lie" Wilson; "Waterloo" and "faulty numbers" DeMint; "the President should be ashamed of himself" Congressman; and the McConnell Mantra, "I intend to make Barack Obama a one term President!" What Republicans need to do is borrow the Hubble Telescope to see they are dealing with a very intelligent, astute, strategically savvy mind not only at the pinnacle of power but at the top of his game! Add to this the top notch advisers who surround him and you have a formidable opponent amking mincemeat of little minds!

Much has been said about President Lincoln and the issue of slavery and Secession but at a time when the nation's fabric was torn asunder, Mr. Lincoln issued the Emancipation Proclamation which was itself an Executive Order and his Order insisting Confederates should be tried in federal courts ecen though this latter was eventually overturned. These actions showed a leader not afraid to take action in face of legislative sloth and inaction. Faced with the calamity of the Great Depression and stymied by the "9 old men," President Franklin D. Roosevelt issued Executive Orders to inaugurate many programs to get the nation moving forward. In modern times, Presidents Nixon, Reagan, Clinton and George W. Bush issued Executive Orders. Some issued multiple such orders, but this was Mr. Obama's first Executive Order and in keeping with the "Party of No" objection to the President's every action, Republican opposition to the Order granting reprieve to immigrants who fit the discussed category is not surprising. However, an explanation of what constitutes an Executive Order is in order. From the Republicans' playbook its best if the President never issued any executive orders.

Obama - Master and Commander 397. A bird (left) and floral pattern (right) as part of red granite decorations fronting the entrance to the Capital Building.

FREDERICK MONDERSON

Obama - Master and Commander 398. Continuing the pattern as part of red granite decorations fronting the entrance to the Capital Building.

Obama - Master and Commander 399. Another one of the etched birds, an owl, as part of red granite decoration fronting the entrance to the Capital Building.

In *The American Political Dictionary* Jack Plano and Milton Greenberg (8th Edition, 1989: 169) define an Executive Order as, "A rule or regulation, issued by the President, a governor, or some administrative authority, that has the effect of law. Executive orders are used to implement and give administrative effect to provisions of the Constitution, to treaties, and to statutes. They may be used to create or modify the organization or procedures of administrative agencies or may have general applicability as law. Under the national Administrative Procedure Act of 1946, all executive orders must be published in the *Federal Register*." They further state its significance (1989: 169) as, "The use of executive orders has

OBAMA - MASTER AND COMMANDER

greatly increased in recent years as a result of the growing tendency of legislative bodies to leave many legislative details to be filled in by the executive branch. The President's power to issue executive orders stems from precedents, custom, and constitutional interpretation, as well from discretionary powers given to the President by Congress when enacting legislation. This trend will likely continue as government involves itself further with higher complex and technical matters."
On Jack Cafferty's CNN program, in answer to a question, someone noted, "The 2012 election began on November 4th, 2008." Thus, given the methodology of Republican strategy towards Mr. Obama's administration, the "McConnell Mandate" and "lone wolf" legislators' attacks on the very being of the president; these people cannot yet comprehend the superior nature of the mind they are in contention with who continues to stay ahead of their pack. For example, for some three and a half years Mr. Obama has tried to govern effectively in the interest of the American people, reached out to create bipartisanship legislation but to no avail. Yet, he was still able to accomplish significant legislative successes in the interest of the American people. Many of his followers wondered, after the manner Republicans treated Mr. Obama, in Spike Lee's words, "When is he going to take off the gloves?" Now, as Republicans boast of the one billion dollars they will raise to defeat Mr. Obama, the President finally began to deploy his strategy, emphasize the power of incumbency and build coalitions among significant voting blocks, viz., women, gays, Catholics, immigrants, Blacks, Hispanics, Muslims, labor, etc. As such, Republicans have accused him of playing "dirty pool!" Well, look under Republican fingernails and you will see the pool chalk accumulated over their years of "dirty pool!"

To recall, after the "Debt Ceiling" debacle, Senator Mitch McConnell was shown smiling giving his now famous "I got that Nigger Thumbs up;" Speaker John Boehner refused to return Mr. Obama's phone calls but met with the Press and later, smoking, boasted "We got 98 percent of what we wanted" as people wondered why is the President allowing "minions to think they're whales!" Then a *New York Post* political cartoon featured President Obama looking through the White House window as the New York Yankees relief pitcher Rivera approached asking himself, "I wonder why he sent for me!" Thereafter, "Gentleman Jim" Obama invited "Smoking Boehner" to a game of golf. As these gentlemen teed off in their golfing shorts, the President looked at the Speaker and thought, "Don't worry, I've got a gift for you, Mr. Speaker!"

After the bin Laden compound raid by Seal Team Six, the *Post* again featured a political cartoon showing Mr. Obama instructing the team, "The next compound you will raid will be Trump Towers!" After the "Gang" of Karl Rove, the Koch Brothers, the TD bank official and other Super PACs boasted, "We will raise one billion dollars to defeat Obama" the President said, "Oh yes, well employers must pay for Women's Contraceptives." From the "Bully Pulpit" he preached, "Gays should be allowed to marry to protect the rights of people in long term relationships" in what the NAACP termed "a Civil Rights Issue." As Chief

FREDERICK MONDERSON

Executive he challenged the Supreme Justices to rule on his challenge to the many features of Arizona's immigration law and his own Health Care Reform measure. To protect his Attorney General Eric Holder from a Republican "witch hunt" over "Fast and Furious" the President exerted "Executive Privilege" that Plano and Greenberg (1989: 169) defined as, "The right of executive officials to refuse to appear before or to withhold information from a legislative community or a court."

"Executive Privilege is enjoyed by the President and those executive officials accorded the right by the President. No legal means by which executive privilege could be denied to executive officials existed for many years, but in 1974 the Supreme Court established a landmark precedent (*United States v. Nixon*, 418) U.S. 683 [1974] by unanimously ordering President Richard M. Nixon to release recorded tape with allegedly criminal information on them that eventually led to his resignation." The significance of this action is explained further by Plano and Greenberg (1989: 169) that, "Executive privilege in the American system is claimed as an inherent executive power under the constitutional separation of powers and on time-honored tradition. Although the right of the President to refuse to appear before congressional committees is generally unchallenged, the issue remains as to whether his major advisers should enjoy the same privilege. The right of Congress to obtain information for the lawmaking process and to investigate for possible impeachment actions, and the right of the courts to hear and decide cases involving executive officials, clash with the President's right to function as the head of a coordinated branch of the national government. Critics charge that executive privilege is often invoked to deny the American people information critical of executive policies."

Obama - Master and Commander 399a. Another view of the National Archives building from the National Gallery of Art Sculpture Garden.

OBAMA - MASTER AND COMMANDER

Obama - Master and Commander 400. Another one of the etched bowls as part of red granite decorations fronting the entrance to the Capital Building.

FREDERICK MONDERSON

Obama - Master and Commander 401. Another one of the etched flowered bowls as part of red granite decorations fronting the entrance to the Capital Building.

OBAMA - MASTER AND COMMANDER

Obama - Master and Commander 402. Still, another one of the etched flowered bowls as part of red granite decorations fronting the entrance to the Capital Building.

Obama - Master and Commander 402a. Memorial to Dr. Hahnemann.

FREDERICK MONDERSON

Obama - Master and Commander 402b. The young man studiously engaged in his reading and studies and the dynamics of science experiments in the laboratory.

Obama - Master and Commander 402c. Theory and practice go hand in hand in the medical profession so that the sick can be healed but importantlyo scholars can also learn to further their practice.

Ronald Reagan had said of Walter Mondale, "I will not, for political purposes, exploit my opponent's youthful age and inexperience." Now, as the Junior Senator from Florida, Marco Rubio, became intoxicated with hearing his name mentioned as a possible Romney Vice-President nominee, he started "pussyfooting" over an immigration bill Romney had decried in his "immigrants should self-deport" insult during the Primaries. The President, as Commander-In-Chief, soared like the American Eagle, legal and otherwise; fired on the "Rebels' Camp" by issuing his new Immigration Executive Order, forcing Senator Rubio to abandon his idea. Thereafter, his name seemed to drop from the short list because he could no longer deliver significant numbers of Latino votes. Instead, Mr. Romney argued Congress should offer a permanent solution but given his past stance and the House objection to Mr. Obama this may not happen soon. Thus, Mr. Obama's discretion ahead of Republican stall, at least temporarily eased the agony of the young immigrants.

OBAMA - MASTER AND COMMANDER

Instantly in their confused state of shock, Republicans cried "foul," the President is "playing dirty pool!" Imagine, after their nearly four years of unrelenting assaults on every legislative initiative, attacks on his integrity, leadership and judgment, these people forget they're dealing with the most powerful man in the world, the President of the United States and leader of the Western Alliance. Somehow Mr. Obama seemed to remind his opponents, "The circus may be in town, but I'm the ringmaster of Washington, DC."

All this notwithstanding, Ralph C. Chandler and Jack C. Plano in *The Public Administration Dictionary* (1982: 249-50) provide further insights into the history of the Executive Order and its historic use that states: "The earliest executive orders were neither numbered nor issued in any standard format, and there was no requirement for official notices or publication. As the mechanism became more formalized, however, a chronological numbering system came into use in 1907, and all earlier orders were assigned numbers. The Federal Register Act of 1935 required all executive orders of general interest to be published in the Federal Register, with a later act requiring publication of all executive orders. Executive Order Number 1 was issued by President Abraham Lincoln in 1862. It concerned the establishment of military courts in Louisiana. Since that time, executive orders have been used in a wide range of policy areas, depending on the president's personal values and his perception of his constitutional responsibilities. Beginning in the 1960s, executive orders were used more and more in controversial social and political policy areas. They were frequently issued as a result of recommendations made by task forces and special committees, which were first introduced by the Kennedy administration as new policy-making groups. Once a president has decided to make an authoritative policy statement, there are a number of factors involved in the decision to use an executive order, as opposed to some other means of proclamation. First, there must be a strong public demand for solution to a given problem. For example, Executive Order Number 11491 was issued in 1969 by President Richard M. Nixon in response to growing federal employee discontent over the limited provisions for public sector labor relations contained in Executive Order Number 10988, which had been issued in 1962.

Second, the president must consider whether there will be funding for, and enforcement of, the directive. Both factors are crucial to the success of an executive order. Third, the president must consider whether Congress or the courts will effectively address the policy needs he has in mind. If they will act, perhaps he does not need to act. Neither Congress nor the courts seemed inclined to deal with discrimination in public housing in the early 1960s. Executive Order Number 11063 was therefore issued by President John F. Kennedy in 1962, setting the official national policy of nondiscrimination in federally assisted housing. Executive orders are subordinate to statuary law, to decisional law by the Supreme Court, and even to the legislative intent of Congress. An executive order can be declared invalid by the courts if it conflicts with any of these 'laws of higher authority.'" Thus, despite what has been said by his Republican opponents, the Supreme Court has not rushed to declare invalid Mr. Obama's immigration Executive Order.

Obama - Master and Commander 403. United States Botanic Garden lit at night and its Conservatory sign.

OBAMA - MASTER AND COMMANDER

Obama - Master and Commander 404. Department of the Treasury Buiding.

To the above, Plano and Greenberg add (1982: 250-510) the significance of the measure. "The executive order is an important policy-making tool which is more flexible and adaptive than statuary law. It allows an opportunity to experiment with programs at the federal level without full-scale congressional involvement. The availability of the executive order serves a safety-valve function as part of the overall system of checks and balances. If a critical issue gets bogged down in congress, the executive order is a mechanism available to fill a policy void until a statuary decision can be made. Some critics object to a president's use of the executive order, considering it a usurpation of legislative power."

Now, after Mr. Romney told the President to "start packing" and the Republican camp has been writing his Obituary, flexing his muscle of incumbency, Mr. Obama, like John Paul Jones reminded everyone, "'Surrender, I have not yet begun to fight' for the interest of all the American people, my considered vision for this great nation and that my children and grand-children will have a better and brighter future resulting from the environmental, educational, immigration, clean-energy and humanitarian policies I enact. If I have to I will bring Congress along, reluctantly or otherwise, into a clearer understanding of our combined responsibilities to all the American people because our system is 'of the people, by the people and for the people' that is the one hundred percent not just the one percent." Dr. Fred Monderson, a retired NYC educator who taught American history and government can be reached at fredsegypt.com@fredsegypt.com

FREDERICK MONDERSON

"One of the great strengths of the United States is... we have a very large Christian population - we do not consider ourselves a Christian nation or a Jewish nation or a Muslim nation. We consider ourselves a nation of citizens who are bound by ideals and a set of values." **Barack Obama**

Obama - Master and Commander 405. Replica and description of an Olmec Head at the Smithsonian Museum (left) and the "Scales of Justice" hanging in the balance (right).

OBAMA - MASTER AND COMMANDER

Obama - Master and Commander 406. Close-up of the Capital Building showing the Pediment crowning the colonnade at its entrance as well as circular decorations of the dome in its resplendent majesty. Evidently, some work of restoration is being done here.

FREDERICK MONDERSON

Obama - Master and Commander 407. View of the front entrance of the Capital Building from down the street showing the colonnade, architrave, pediment, "Old Glory," and the colonnade of the rotunda in all its majesty.

OBAMA - MASTER AND COMMANDER

Obama - Master and Commander 408. The Capital Building lit at night!

Obama - Master and Commander 409. The manicured lawn gives greater impetus to green, white and blue!

FREDERICK MONDERSON

Obama - Master and Commander 410. Now, there's the flag between the trees!

Barack Obama - Master and Commander 411. The Capital Building Christmas Tree, lit at night.

OBAMA - MASTER AND COMMANDER

Obama - Master and Commander 412. Mat at the National Archives and Records Administration.

FREDERICK MONDERSON

Obama - Master and Commander 413. The National Bird on the facade at Constitutional Hall.

OBAMA - MASTER AND COMMANDER

Obama - Master and Commander 414. George Washington, his sword and horse with colleagues on the outer wall of Constitutional Hall.

Obama - Master and Commander 415. Justice (left) and Agriculture (right).

FREDERICK MONDERSON

Obama - Master and Commander 416. "Words like Sapphires" (left) and "The Civil War in America" (right) are two exhibits now playing at the Jefferson Building of the Library of Congress.

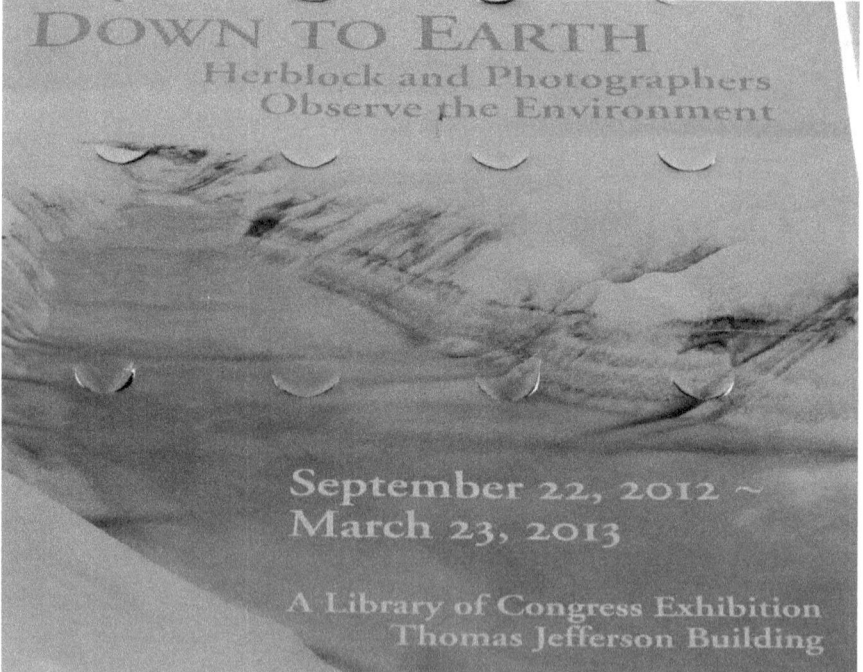

Obama - Master and Commander 417.   Down to Earth: Herblock and Photographers Observe the Environment.

OBAMA - MASTER AND COMMANDER

Barack Obama - Master and Commander 418. Ho, Ho, Ho and a Merry Christmas to you too!

Barack Obama - Master and Commander 419. The National Christmas Tree lit and being viewed by many enthusiastic citizens.

FREDERICK MONDERSON

Barack Obama - Master and Commander 420. The Civil War Memorial with the Treasury as a backdrop, at night.

Barack Obama - Master and Commander 421. Forward to Victory!

OBAMA - MASTER AND COMMANDER

"Change will not come if we wait for some other person or some other time. We are the ones we've been waiting for. We are the change that we seek." **Barack Obama**

"If the people cannot trust their government to do the job for which it exists - to protect them and to promote their common welfare - all else is lost." **Barack Obama**

"I think when you spread the wealth around it's good for everybody." **Barack Obama**

44. PUMMELING THE BLACK MAN
By
Dr. Fred Monderson

Once in every extraordinary occasion, people of disperate ideological persuasions tend to agree on an issue especially if it sounds questionable. Then they find themselves alligned with the likes of Rush Limbaugh and his "ilks" in defense of a Herman Cain which goes against much of what most people believe and stand for; but sometimes one has to take a stand and say "Damn the torpodoes, full speed ahead." As such, and in light of this fourth accuser against Republican presidential contender Herman Cain, this is probably one of those times when "one and one is not three." In explanation, the story is told of an incident in the "old country" where a youngter was caught misbehaving by an elder who promised to "tell his parents." Amidst gushes of eye-water, he begged "No, No, Please don't," to which the elder responded, "Ok. How much is one and one?" The youngster replied, "Three, Mr. Pete!" The older man was aghast!

In all apects of human experience, history is considered significant except when it comes to the history of African people in America. The respected scholar Cheikh Anta Diop in reminding African researchers why they must connect ancient Egypt with the history of continental Africa noted, "Imagine a western historian writing about European experience without including Greece and Rome and passing that off as history." This would be a laughable exercise. A such, we cannot explain the African American experience outside the historical context which includes the moral and mental legacy it visited upon these people. Case in point. The fear and trepidation visited upon the black man by blaming him for all manner of acts as done in America, particularly after he had been subjected to the intolerable acts of the institution of slavery and its legacy.

FREDERICK MONDERSON

What has been bothersome, however, is people like the "blond-headed woman," hopefully in the minority, at one of Senator McCain's rallies, who described Senator Barak Obama as "an unaccomplished black man," who aspires to be President of the United States of America. Clearly such an ignoramus would not know "an accomplished black man," if, as the E.F. Hutton's spokesman used to say, "He showed up, slap you on the bottom, and said I'm here." Opponents rolled out a "Blonde haired woman" who accused Senatorial candidate Harold Ford and ended the commercial gesturing to her ear and saying "Harold, call me." Now, whether or not there is any credibility to this round of accusation, two "blonde haired women" have accused Herman Cain of sexual harassment. Whether factual or not they fall into the same categorization of "totting out" the "bogeyman" or "bogeywoman" used in accusing black men of wrongdoing. What ever happened to the brunettes? Then again, so many brunettes are blondes we are not sure whether we are dealing with circus performers, mannequins or real people.

> **Welcome to the Hirshhorn Museum's Sculpture Garden**
>
> First opened in 1974, this garden displays sculptures from Europe and North America dating from the 1880s to the present. More than 400,000 people visit this garden each year. **So while we invite you to look, relax, study, stroll, sketch, and take photographs, we ask that you please do not touch the sculptures.**
>
> Sculptures are more fragile than most people realize. Steel and other metal works are made from several pieces welded together. These connections can weaken and break when weight is applied. Bronze sculptures are actually hollow casts with thin surfaces that are easily dented or scratched. In addition, all outdoor sculptures suffer from urban air pollution, so we protect them with a delicate coating of clear wax. But this invisible protectant erodes when touched, even lightly, leaving that part of the piece exposed to the elements. Also, fingernails and jewelry may cause tiny scratches that can never be fixed. **For these reasons, climbing, sitting on, or leaning against any sculpture is not permitted.**
>
> Please help preserve these remarkable artworks for future generations.

Obama – Master and Commander 421a. Sign of welcome to the Hirshhorn Museum Sculpture Garden.

OBAMA - MASTER AND COMMANDER

Obama – Master and Commander 422. The Hirshhorn Museum, home of the Hirshhorn Sculpture Garden.

> OUT OF OUR MEMORY... OF THE HOLOCAUST WE MUST FORGE AN UNSHAKABLE OATH WITH ALL CIVILIZED PEOPLE THAT NEVER AGAIN WILL THE WORLD STAND SILENT, NEVER AGAIN WILL THE WORLD... FAIL TO ACT IN TIME TO PREVENT THIS TERRIBLE CRIME OF GENOCIDE... WE MUST HARNESS THE OUTRAGE OF OUR OWN MEMORIES TO STAMP OUT OPPRESSION WHEREVER IT EXISTS. WE MUST UNDERSTAND THAT HUMAN RIGHTS AND HUMAN DIGNITY ARE INDIVISIBLE.

Obama – Master and Commander 422a. Declaration on the Holocaust signed by President Jimmy Carter.

FREDERICK MONDERSON

Obama – Master and Commander 423. Jeff Koons. American, b. York Pennsylvania, 1955. **Kiepenkerl**, 1987. Stainless Steel. Joseph H. Hirshhorn Purchase Fund and Smithsonian Collections Acquisition Program, 1998 (98.21)

OBAMA - MASTER AND COMMANDER

Obama - Master and Commander 424. Henry Moore. British, b. Castleford, England, 1898-1986 - **Two-piece Reclining Figure Points**. Gift of Hirshorn Museum.

Obama - Master and Commander 425. Henry Moore. British, b. Castleford, England, 1898-1986. **Stone Sclpture**.

FREDERICK MONDERSON

Obama - Master and Commander 426. Alberto Giacometti (Swiss b. Borgonova, 1901-1966. "**Monumental Head**." 1960. Bronze. Gift of Joseph H. Hirshhorn 1966 (66-2042)

OBAMA - MASTER AND COMMANDER

Obama - Master and Commander 427. Aristide Maillol. (French, b. Banyulus-sur-Mer, 1861-1944). "**Nymph (Central Figure for *The Three Nymphs*)**" 1930, Cast b7 1953. Bronze. Gift of Joseph H. Hirshhorn, 1966 (66.3203)

FREDERICK MONDERSON

Obama - Master and Commander 428. Auguste Rodin French, b. Paris, 1840-1917. "**Crouching Woman**." 1880-1882, enlarged 1907-1911, Cast 1962. Bronze. Gift of Joseph H. Hirshhorn, 1966 (66.4342)

OBAMA - MASTER AND COMMANDER

While Voltaire once said, "Crush the Accursed thing," regarding Friday the 13[th;] but such an admonition ought to be applied to the notion of the "Bradley Effect" that "white people will say but not vote for a black man." In case of Barack Obama, he has worked tremendously untiring, in a unifying campaign with a powerful message of progress but still, others try to make this an issue of the past! His aura and its attraction to diverse people, as evident from his recent political rallies makes one feel confident "Bradley," is no more! What worries some people is the questionable intent of such a person like the "blond-headed woman," hopefully in the minority, at one of Senator McCain's rallies who described Senator Barak Obama as "an unaccomplished black man," who aspires to be President of the United States of America. Barak Obama is a Columbia University graduate; a Harvard University law graduate; and he was President of the Harvard University Law Review. Everyone knows he was a Community Organizer in Chicago. Subsequently he became an Illinois State Senator and later became a Federal Senator from Illinois. He authored two books! As the son of a single mother who died early, whose father abandoned him, he was raised by his grandmother, and where he is today is clearly a significant accomplishment for a black man in America! For Obama to be competing with John McCain for the Presidency, against a man born with "a gold spoon" in his mouth, Obama's "silver spoon" sure looks polished today! His eloquence, intellectual fortitude, cool demeanor, social adjustment and attractiveness outdistanced his opponent, the "Admiral's son" and "war hero." These issues, while they applied to the 2008 campaign very much equally apply to the 2012 campaign as seen in the manner he has been pilloried over the last four years and especially recently.

Some commentators believe the "black man" is an endangered species, but an even more daunting specter surrounds the "black man," for whether he is Senator Barack Obama or the man in the street, it can equally apply. Interesting, if a United States Senator, a distinguished individual, could be subject to such invidious name calling, threats, innuendos, false accusations, disrespect, code words, etc., imagine what type of victimization the average "black man" is susceptible to. Nevertheless, lest we forget, Philip Forde, a "black man," some say Native American, stands atop the Capital Dome in D.C. However, without question, blacks built that structure with free labor! Therefore, to understand this racial phenomenal predicament across the American historical and political landscape, one has to look at the history of how Americans have treated the "black man" for much of his time in this country. However, today, the world is now looking on as this 2012 election unfolds, and it's even more important the wrong impression is not conveyed through the actions of those who exhibit racist behaviors. This notwithstanding, it's important that we provide a sketch of the "evolution of the black man" to civil tendencies and financial and social accomplishment, despite the many hurdles he has had to scale on his way to the top!

FREDERICK MONDERSON

Obama - Master and Commander 429. Henry Moore. British, b. Castleford, England, 1898-1986. "**King and Queen**" 1952-53. Bronze. Gift of Josheph H. Hirshhorn, 1966. (66.3635)

OBAMA - MASTER AND COMMANDER

Obama - Master and Commander 430. Giacomo Manzu. Italian, b. Bergamo, 1908-1991 "**Self Portrait with Modelat Bergamo**" 1942. Bronze. Gift of Joseph H. Hirshhorn, 1966 (66-3293)

FREDERICK MONDERSON

Obama - Master and Commander 431. Emile-Antoine Bourdelle. French, b. Montaugan, 1861-1929. "**The Great Warrior of Montaugan**." 1898-1900, cast 1956. Bronze - Gift of Joseph H. Hirshhorn, 1966 (66-593)

First of all, as Malcolm X has pointed out, all peoples who came to America, viz., Chinese, Japanese, Indian, French, Italian, German, Swede, Englishman, Irish, etc., upon their arrival here remained Chinese, Japanese, Indian, Italian, German, Swede, Englishman, Irish, etc. All, except the African who was kidnapped, brought across the Atlantic Ocean, chained in the most dreadful manner, subjected to unspeakable trans-Atlantic horrors, denied his manhood, dehumanized and disrespected over the centuries of slavery, until he was finally freed by Abraham Lincoln. This magnanimous act still had to became legal under the Civil War Amendments, wherein the thirteenth legalized his freedom, the fourteenth make him a citizen and the fifteenth gave him the right to vote. Malcolm often said, "The blackman is not discriminated against because he is a mason or elk; Protestant or Catholic; certainly not Muslim. He is discriminated against because he is black!" Thus, after Emancipation, the freedman had to struggle to regain his manhood; to acquire a sense of human decency; and to reflect and demonstrate social civility and citizenship within the strictures accorded him in the society he helped to build, generation after generation, laboring for free; all the while "conservatives" acting as "terrorists" made his life miserable in all manner of "socially acceptable behaviors" of a criminal, terrorist intent, perpetrated in a civilized society. The methods may have changed somewhat, in this enlightened age, but this is what happened to Barack Obama, even as President of the Unted

OBAMA - MASTER AND COMMANDER

States, despite his appeal to broad masses whose goodness were shamed by perpetrators of evil intent whose racism is appalling.

As all of this transpired physically and psychologically in a manner, as Kenneth Stampp has written about slavery, in *The Peculiar Institution*, a chapter entitled: "To Make Them Stand in Fear;" while amazingly, the freedman metamorphosed through being an African, then slave, freedman, ex-slave, Negro, colored, black and today African American, with a whole host of disgusting epithets also applied to him along the way and in the most demeaning manner. Complementing this state of affairs, the "black man" remained black in the minds and actions of many persons who sought to demean and accuse him, to cover their misgivings, or to further their own sinister aims. At the end of all this, he was asked to forgive his merciless slave master and his descendants, and to overlook the wealth they accumulated as they perpetrated, at his expense, unspeakable horrors through the duration of the slavery experience and after, and the ensuing psychological, social and economic lacertaion they inflicted, then they denied his promised "40 acres and a mule."

Obama - Master and Commander 432. Auguste Rodin. French, b. Paris, 1840-1917. "**The Burghers of Calais**." 1884-89, cast 1953-59. Bronze - Gift of Joseph H. Hirshhorn, 1966 (66-4340)

FREDERICK MONDERSON

Obama - Master and Commander 433. Auguste Rodin. French, b. Paris, 1840-1917. **"The Burghers of Calais."** 1884-89, cast 1953-59. Bronze - Gift of Joseph H. Hirshhorn, 1966 (66-4340)

OBAMA - MASTER AND COMMANDER

Obama - Master and Commander 434. Auguste Rodin French, b. 1840-1917. "**Walking Man**." 1900, enlarged 1905, cast 1962. Bronze - Gift of Joseph H. Hirshhorn, 1966 (66-4343)

FREDERICK MONDERSON

Obama - Master and Commander 435. With permission. "Lady and Child" in the Hirshhorn Garden beside Francisco Zuniga Mexican, b. San Jose, Costa Rica 1913 "**Seated Yucatan Woman**" 1973 Bronze - Gift of Joseph H. Hirshhorn, 1976 (76.93).

While Chief Justice Taney's *Dred Scott Decision* of 1857 and *Plessey v. Ferguson* of 1896 represented *de jure* definition of the status and position of the "black man;" during the period of Reconstruction and in the age of "Jim Crow," terror groups as the Ku Klux Klan (KKK), Knights of the White Camellia, as well as several stratagems were employed to terrorize, intimidate and keep the "black man" "in his place." In the South, to keep the "black man" from expressing his right to vote under the Fifteenth Amendment, literacy tests, poll tax, property tax, "grandfather clause" and particularly election site shenanigans were effectively employed to nullify the "black man's" vote. Whippings, tar and feather, killings, lynchings, burnings, destruction of house and homes, and all forms of odious behaviors were resorted to in order to halt the "back man's" forward progress in those dark days of the "Birth of the Nation."

While only a dozen cases need suffice, Ralph Ginsburg's *100 Years of Lynching*, Baltimore, MD., Black Classics Press (1962) 1988, chronicles untold numbers of the most hideous forms of "white behavior" towards the "black man." Most, particularly those chosen were committed against innocent "black men,' and importantly it shows the uncontrollable rage of the mob fueled by the belief in

OBAMA - MASTER AND COMMANDER

white supremacy. All this as the society progressed, stampeding upon the physical and moral fiber of the black man.

"New York Truth Seeker. April 17, 1880. "First Negro at West Point Knifed by Fellow Cadets." West Point, N.Y. Apr. 15. – James Webster Smith, the first colored cadet in the history of West Point, was recently taken from his bed, gagged, bound, and severely beaten, and then his ears were slit. He says that he cannot identify his assailants. The other cadets claim that he did it himself." (p. 9) This is difficult to understand how he could raise himself from his bed, gag and bound himself, then severely whip himself and finally cut his own ear. One has to wonder, Who was the Commanding Officer who believed this story?

Chicago Tribune. November 22, 1895. "Texans Lynch Wrong Negro." Madisonville, Tex, Nov. 21 – News has been received here of the lynching of a Negro in this part of Madison County on Tuesday night. He was accused of riding his horse over a little white girl and injuring her. On Wednesday it was discovered that the wrong Negro had been gotten hold of by the mob. The guilty one made his escape." (p. 21) Question is, how many Negroes had horses to ride around, that such a mistake could be made.

Obama – Master and Commander 436. Close-up of Pediment on the cornice of the Archives of the United States of America.

FREDERICK MONDERSON

Obama - Master and Commander 436a.   Willem de Kooning. American, b. Rotterdam, the Netherlands, 1904-1997. "**Clamdigger**" 1972, cast 1976 Bronze - Gift of Joseph H. Hirshhorn Bequest, 1981 (86. 1363)

OBAMA - MASTER AND COMMANDER

New York Times. June 11, 1900. "An Innocent Man Lynched." New Orleans, June 10 – A mob willfully and knowingly handled and burned an innocent man, as well as another who was probably innocent, near Mississippi City, Miss., between midnight and 1 o'clock this morning. The lynching was the result of impatience on the part of the people of Biloxi, a nearby town, over the failure of the officers of the law to produce the man who a week ago murdered Christina Winterstein, a schoolgirl who was returning to her home near Biloxi after attending the commencement exercises at her school." (p. 31) So they go about grabbing whoever they find. The gall of these people!

Houston Post. June 11, 1900. "Two Blacks Strung Up; Grave Doubt of Their Guilt." Biloxi, Miss., June 10 – Lynch law ran rampant in this section last night. Two Negro men were lynched, possibly for one man's crime, early this morning at Mississippi City, and it is not absolutely certain that either victim of mob law was guilty. Henry Askew and Ed Russ, held as suspects, were taken out and strung up to a tree in a thicket, just behind the railway station at Mississippi City." (p. 32) Where was the Governor, Mayor, Police Commissioner, Sheriff or Marshal when the mob ruled?

Chicago Record-Herald may 12, 1901. "Believes Wrong Man Lynched." Birmingham, Ala., May 11 - A Negro supposed to be James Brown, accused of assaulting Miss Della Garrett of Springsville, was shot and killed by a number of white men near Leeds, near here, to-day. The coroner is of the opinion that the wrong man has been killed." (p. 39) Who investigated this incident and what action was taken? For an assault you kill a man as if his life had no value!

Chicago Record-Herald, July 27, 1903. "Wrong Man Lynched as Rapist." Savannah, Ga., July 26 - Several days ago a Negro supposed to be Ed Claus, was lynched near Eastman, Ga., for assaulting Miss Susie Johnson, a young school teacher. The Negro protested he was not Claus and asked for time to prove his statement. But the mob was merciless. It now transpires that the Negro was not Claus and had never seen Miss Johnson. Claus, who assaulted the girl, has been located near Narien, Ga., and officers passed through here tonight to secure him. It is believed Claus will be taken from the officers and lynched." (p. 60) They never gave him a chance to present his ID. One has to wonder what these people felt and did when it was realized they had killed an innocent man. Not satisfied with one life for an assault, they took another!

New York Press. March 26, 1904. "9 Lynchings in One Week." Little Rock, Ark., March 25 - A special from Dewitt says five Negroes have been taken from the guards at St. Charles, this county, and shot to death by a mob. This makes nine negroes who have been killed in the last week in the vicinity of St. Charles on account of race troubles." (p. 69) What does history say of these men? The victims and those who perpetrated this heinous crime.

Obama - Master and Commander 437. Giacomo Manzu Italian, b. Bergamo, 1908-1991. **"Young Girl on a Chair**." 1955 Bronze - Gift of Joseph H. Hirshhorn, 1966 (66.3290)

OBAMA - MASTER AND COMMANDER

Obama - Master and Commander 438. Willem de Kooning. American, b. Rotterdam, the Netherlands, 1904-1997. "**Seated Woman on a Bench**." 1972, cast 1976 Bronze - Gift of Joseph H. Hirshhorn Bequest, 1981. (86-1364)

Obama - Master and Commander 438a. "The Common Law is the Will of Mankind" (top) and "Issuing from the Life of the People" (bottom).

FREDERICK MONDERSON

Obama - Master and Commander 439. Marino Marini. Italian, b. Pistoia, 1901-1980. "**Horse and Rider**." 1952-53 Bronze - Gift of Joseph H. Hirshhorn, 1966 (66-345)

OBAMA - MASTER AND COMMANDER

Montgomery Advertiser. September 12, 1912. "Lynched 'For Being Black.'" United States District Attorney O.D. Street, of Birmingham, today made public a letter which he is forwarding to Governor O'Neil. The letter is from C.P. Lunsford of Hackleburg, and reads as follows: "On last Wednesday there was a Negro man chased and hounded down and murdered while going peacefully along the railroad. There was not anything against him, but a party of men got after him because his skin was black and murdered him. The grand jury was in session at the time, and has not paid any attention to the murder, not even so much as to put the parties under arrest. The Negro who was murdered was Willie Perkins of Sheffield, and I am reliably informed that he was of an excellent character." (p. 77) So, "walking while black" is an old act of racial vindictiveness. One thing is certain; some men have no respect for the law!

Harrisburg (Pennsylvania) Advocate Verdict. September 13, 1912. "Wrong Man Believed Lynched." Princeton, W.VA., Sept. 7 – That a mistake was made in lynching Walter Johnston, a colored man last night, is now believed by the authorities. A statement was issued by Mayor Bennington, Sheriff Ellison, Judge Maynard and Prosecuting Attorney J.O. Pendleton stating that there is plenty of evidence that Walter Johnson did not commit the crime for which he was lynched. A mob lynched Johnson last night, allegedly for attacking Nite White, 14-year old daughter of a railroad man. Today's statement said that Johnson fell far short in dress and physical appearance of the man described by the girl." (p. 78) Question is, what did these public officials do to and for the victim's family?

Chicago Tribune. December 31, 1914. "1914 Lynchings Show Rise." The number of lynchings in 1914 shows a small increase over that of 1913, being 54, as compared with 48 in 1913 and 64 in 1912. The following table showing the annual number during the last thirty years may be of general interest.

Year	Count	Year	Count
1865	184	1900	115
1866	138	1901	130
1887	122	1902	96
1888	142	1903	104
1899	176	1904	87
1890	127	1905	60
1891	193	1906	60
1892	205	1907	65
1893	200	1908	100
1894	170	1909	87
1895	171	1910	74
1896	181	1911	71
1897	106	1912	64

FREDERICK MONDERSON

| 1898 | 127 | 1913 | 48 |
| 1899 | 107 | 1914 | 54 (p. 94) |

These numbers are mind-boggling and one has to wonder, How many were not recorded and also how many people were arrested, charged, convicted, and executed for their lawless terrorism?

Atlanta Constitution. February 23, 1916. "All Five Lynched Negroes Were Guiltless, Says Keith." Tefton, Ga., Feb. 22 - Jim Keith, sentenced to a life term in prison for complicity in the killing of Sheriff Moreland of Lee county, talked freely of the crime today as he was carried to Richmond County to begin serving his term. He declared that Rodius Seamore and old man Lake and his three sons, who were lynched last month for Sheriff Moreland's death, were entirely guiltless. The fact is now generally believed." (pp. 99-100)

New York Times. May 27, 1961. "Attorney General Foresees a Negro as U.S. President." Washington, May 26 - Attorney General Robert F. Kennedy, in a broadcast to the world over the Voice of America, today acknowledged the United States' imperfections in the areas of equal rights for Negroes. He said, however, that progress was being made in that area so rapidly that "There's no question that in the next thirty or forty years a Negro can achieve the position ... of President of the United States. " (pp. 251-252)

Obama - Master and Commander 440. Henry Moore, British, b. Castleford, England, 1898-1986. "**Working Model for 'Three Way Piece No. 3: Vertebrae'**" 1968, cast 2969 Bronze - Joseph H. Hirshhorn Bequest. 1961 (86. 3278)

OBAMA - MASTER AND COMMANDER

Obama - Master and Commander 441. From within, entrance to the Hirshhorn Museum.

Obama - Master and Commander 442. Judith Shea. American. b. Philadelphia, Pennsylvania. **Post-Balzac**. 1991. Bronze. Museum Purchase, 1991 (91.20) (left) and David Smith. American, b. Decatur, Indiana, 1906-1965. **Voltri XV**, 1962 Steel. Gift of Hoseph H. Hirshhorn, 1966 (66. 443) (right).

FREDERICK MONDERSON

Obama - Master and Commander 443. Joan Miro. Spanish, b. Barcelona, 1893-1983. "**Lunar Bird**." 1944-46, enlarged and cast 1966-67 Bronze - Gift of Joseph H. Hirshhorn, 1972 (72-20)

We are all told Audie Murphy was the most decorated World War II veteran. Not so as Harry Belafonte told it. The most decorated World War II veteran was a "black man," who, returning to the South, in full uniform with his medals, rode in the front of a segregated bus. When the driver asked him to sit in the back, he refused. The driver called the police to remove the "black man" in uniform. The brutes disable him on the spot. Harry says this is what led him to become an activist. In more modern times, Massachusetts Governor Michael Dukakis was the 1988 Democratic standard-bearer and in that election for President, the Republicans waded into him, using the sinister "black man" smear and fear tactic.

Apparently, as Governor, Dukakis issued some form of release to a convict named Willie Horton, who, upon gaining his freedom, attacked and killed a woman. The Republican candidate, the first George Bush, pounced on this and made a fuss about the weakness or softness of Dukakis on crime, while playing up the notion of the sinister "black man." Naturally, Dukakis lost the election as his opponents proclaimed the brilliance of their strategy. In fact, what they had done is, reinforce the specter that the "black man" is bad and this rationalizes the attacks, charges, claims, insinuations, etc. that generates fear in the minds of whites. This fear is probably even more widespread, as it even allows law enforcement officers to stop the "black man," in "stop and frisk" and most often particularly when "driving while black!"

OBAMA - MASTER AND COMMANDER

Obama - Master and Commander 444. Jacques Lipchitz. American, B. Druskieniki, Lithuania 1891-1073. "**Figure**" 1926-30, cast 1958-61 Bronze - Gift of Joseph H. Hirshhorn, 1966 (66.3101)

FREDERICK MONDERSON

Obama - Master and Commander 445. Auguste Rodin. French, b. Paris, 1840-1917. "**Monument to Balzac.**" 1891-98, cast 1965-66. Bronze - Gift of Joseph H. Hirshhorn, 1966 (66.434)

Not so long ago, the "Smith woman," involved in a love affair of some sort, rolled her car into a pond while her two children sat in the back seat. Then she confused

OBAMA - MASTER AND COMMANDER

the investigation by claiming a "black man" attacked her, high-jacked her car, and kidnapped her two children. In time, the lie was bared, and as she broke down, she confessed her story was a hoax; and then showed where she had disposed of the car and kids. She was considered mentally disturbed and that was that.

In Jasper, Texas, within recent memory, a "black man," I think, Brandon McClelland, who was chained to a pick-up truck and dragged to his death. The more things change, the more they remain the same.

A man in Massachusetts killed his wife and children then claimed a "black man" invaded their home and did the beastly act. This gristly crime helped fan the hysteria against the "black man." Naturally he confessed to the wrongdoing, for which he blamed the "black man."

During the 2008 election campaign, a deranged woman Ashley claimed a "black man" robbed her at an ATM, and noticing she had a McCain/Palin sticker on her car's bumper, carved a "B" on her cheek. The bank's cameras did not even pick up her presence there nor did it record any assault nearby. Turns out the story was false, but the nut was later admitted to a program.

Obama - Master and Commander 446. Ellsworth Kelly. American, b. Newburgh, New York 1923 Untitled 1986, **Stainless Steel** Museum Purchase, 1986 (86. 5897). An extension of the Garden with a globe in the rear.

FREDERICK MONDERSON

The above are only a sample of instances where the "black man" was innocently harassed, victimized, killed and falsely accused, and all because of his race. Today we profess the sanctity of a single American life, even the birth of the unborn child, but we know many do not consider black life on par with white. But this notion of white is nonsense. Those Americans who lay great store in ancestral heritage, when they return to those ancient lands, they are not considered white but English, French, German, and so on.

Notwithstanding, sometimes symbolism means more than substance, and for the descendants of those who traversed the incendiary strewn, social minefield, of American society, the Obama candidacy, while substantive, is also more symbolic for the millions of African Americans in this country, and so many "black men" worldwide. The significance of the Obama candidacy is, internally it demonstrates a coming of age of America particularly in view of its emerging multi-ethnicity; and externally to the world it signaled a radical change in America's personality and image, for which its true nature as the world leader will manifest.

Well Mr. Kennedy, having said all of that, it actually took 47 years in a long and arduous walk to the White House. But, most important, "the Black man" did it, despite the distractions, odds, and it shows while this significant milestone has been reached, there is still more work to be done to achieve Dr. King's color-blind society, where a person based on intellect and integrity rather than rage and race.

This brings us to the revelations of the recent and fourth Herman Cain's sexual harrassment accuser. Like all human interactions, questions of why and how are the most important of the "5-W." Here is a woman, blond, blue eyed, white, who comes forward with a powerful "money Mill" attorney, who represented several high profile clients securing lucrative settlements for them. She takes center stage and emotively confesses, some 14 years ago, a black man who had gained her confidence put his hand on her leg and in her crutch touchng the most sensitive and personal part of her human anatomy. She never slapped his face but simply asked to be driven home, which he readily complied. Accordingly, she got home and told her boy-friend and another person and simply forgot the episode without being sworn to secrecy, all parties allowed this incident to go unreported. As it turned out, Mr. Cain's "9-9-9 plan" was beginning to gain some traction but his past with extra-marital associations allowed his foes to produce more career destroying evidence forcing him to withdraw from the Republican Presidential Primary.

OBAMA - MASTER AND COMMANDER

Obama - Master and Commander 447. Henry Moore. British, b. Castleford, England, 1898-1966. "**Draped Reclining Figure**.' 1952-53, cast 1956. Bronze - Gift of Joseph H. Hirshhorn, 1966 (66.3634)

FREDERICK MONDERSON

Obama - Master and Commander 448. "Child reflected in the Glass" Hirshhorn Garden.

OBAMA - MASTER AND COMMANDER

Obama - Master and Commander 449. Henry Moore. British, b. Castleford, England, 1898-1966 "**Seated Woman**" 1956-57, cast 1962. Bronze - Joseph H. Hirshhorn bequest, 1986 (86.3277)

All this goes to show, Mr. Obama being black, has remained in the "crosshairs" of individuals such as Senator Mitch McConnell and his allies bent on making Mr. Obama a "one term president!" It would be difficult to deny that his race had anything to do with this endeavor and the ancillary insults and obstruction the President of the United States has been subjected to!

"The best way to not feel hopeless is to get up and do something. Don't wait for good things to happen to you. If you go out and make some good things happen, you will fill the world with hope, you will fill yourself with hope." **Barack Obama**

FREDERICK MONDERSON

"In the face of impossible odds, people who love this country can change it."
Barack Obama

"A change is brought about because ordinary people do extraordinary things."
Barack Obama

"Good morning. In less than an hour, aircraft from here will join others from around the world, and you will be launching the largest aerial battle in the history of mankind. Mankind. That word should have new meaning for all of us today. We can't be consumed by our petty differences anymore. We will be united in our common interests. Perhaps it's fate that today is the Fourth of July, and you will once again be fighting for our freedom. Not from tyranny, oppression, or persecution ... but from annihilation. We're fighting for our right to live. To exist. And should we win the day, the Fourth of July will no longer be known as an American holiday, but as the day when the world declared in one voice: We will not go quietly into the night! We will not vanish without a fight! We're going to live on! We're going to survive! Today we celebrate our Independence Day!"
Barack Obama

45. OBAMA AND LEADERSHIP
By
Dr. Fred Monderson

Of all American presidents demonstrating outstanding leadership in challenging times, perhaps none has faced more difficulties than Barack Obama. Granted each president faced their own challenges, for example, George Washington and foundation of the nation; Thomas Jefferson and the Louisiana Purchase and Barbary Pirates; James Monroe and his "Doctrine;" Abraham Lincoln and Secession and Civil War; Franklin D. Roosevelt and the "New Deal" and World War II; Dwight Eisenhower and the Korean War and Communism; Ronald Reagan and the Cold War; and George W. Bush and September 11, 2001; but none, in time perspective, has faced the challenges meted out to President Obama. Thus, contrary to misguided belief fed by insidious propaganda whether legislative, political, religious or lay, Mr. Obama had demonstrated exemplary leadership though some people need a Hubble Telescopic vision to understand then to appreciate his accomplishments and this is what makes his tenure as the 44th President, so exceptional.

OBAMA - MASTER AND COMMANDER

Obama - Master and Commander 450. David Smith. American, b. Decatur, Indiana, 1906-1965. "**Cibi XII**." Stainless steel - Gift of the Jacob H. Hirshhorn Foundation, 1972 (72. 268)

FREDERICK MONDERSON

Obama - Master and Commander 451. Henry Moore. British, b. Castleford, England, 1898-1986. "**Three-Piece Reclining Figure No. 2: Bridge Prop**." 1963, cast 1964. Bronze - Gift of Joseph H. Hirshhorn, 1966 (66.3656)

OBAMA - MASTER AND COMMANDER

Obama - Master and Commander 452. Alexander Calder. American, b. Lawnton, Pennsylvania 1898-1976. "**Sky Hooks**." C. 1962 Painted Sheet Metal - Gift of Jerome L. Greene, 2001 (01.12).

FREDERICK MONDERSON

Following cessation of hostilities in Europe ending the aftermath of the French Revolution and Napoleonic Wars; and in America, the War of 1812, the "Second War for Independence" against Britain that ended in 1815; James Monroe faced the horde of European imperialists seeking to regain their New World empires through re-colonization. His issuing the "Monroe Doctrine" was a bold move that created a lucrative economic market for the US in Latin America and was hailed as a great leadership strategy. Since there are "no permanent enemies only permanent interests," co-opting the recent British enemy into providing the naval Men-O-War power to enforce a doctrine that would stand for centuries, was a stroke of genius.

With a nation divided culturally, economically and politically, and with the beating of potential drums of war, talk of Secession and actual Civil War, the loyalists supported Mr. Lincoln and hailed his leadership at a time of great distress for the nation. Winning the day, or war, outlining a plan to bind the wounds of conflict and heal the nation; then deploying a plan towards a path of economic recovery and development demonstrated his brilliance in word and deed. As such, Mr. Lincoln was seen as a genius. Losing his life as he did, his greatness was amplified and the dynamics and aura of his memorial demonstrate his profound influence in rescuing and shaping the course of the nation's history.

Franklin D. Roosevelt was elected in 1932 on a "New Deal" promise as the nation swelted under the trials and tribulations of the Great Depression. In a "damn the torpedoes, full speed ahead" attitude, Mr. Roosevelt challenged the nation from "Captain to Cook," to rescue his beloved land by initiating untold numbers of programs, in a "If one does not a work, try another" mindset frame of reference. Ahead of his time in recognizing the aspirations of all Americans, viz., labor, immigrants, power companies, industrialists, blacks, women, he pressed ahead with his "alphabet programs" until finally challenged by the "9 old men" of the Supreme Court. Men of vision and tenacity such as Franklin Delano Roosevelt are seldom stopped in their tracks but either walk around or through obstacles. In time, even the Supreme Court came around to his point of view and with lots of help from this country's involvement in World War II, Mr. Roosevelt pulled the nation out of the Depression placing it on a path of economic prosperity providing untold economic and scientific leadership with other safeguards in place.

The size of the Roosevelt Memorial in Washington, DC is indicative of the expansiveness of the man's thinking and actions. His panoramic horizontal vision seemed to indicate "all people lent their shoulders to his wheel" as he rescued his nation from the clutches of its most catastrophic challenge initiated in the laxity of economic and commercial oversight that led to the Great Depression.

Dwight Eisenhower, a general in World War II became President from 1952-1960 and had to contend with the Korean War and also the "Cold War" spread of communism under the Soviet Union. He was well-liked and Americans rallied to his efforts to readjust the nation in the post-World War II and Korean conflict eras.

OBAMA - MASTER AND COMMANDER

Obama - Master and Commander 453. Jean Arp. French, b. Strasbourg, 1887-1966. **Evocation of a Form: Human, Lunar, Spectral 1950**, enlarged and cast 1957 Bronze. Gift of Joseph H. Hirshhorn, 1966 (66.107) Mystery? Let the visitor guess!

FREDERICK MONDERSON

Obama - Master and Commander 454. Arman. American, b. Nice, France, 1928-2005. "**Eros, Inside Eros**" 1986. Bronze - Joseph H. Hirshhorn Bequest by exchange, 1987 (87.10).

OBAMA - MASTER AND COMMANDER

Obama - Master and Commander 455. Ellsworth Kelly. American, b. Newburgh, New York 1923. "**Untitled**" 1988. Stainless Steel - Museum Purchase, 1986 (86.5897).

Ronald Reagan, the actor and governor of California, certainly in radio and in movies endeared himself in the minds and hearts of the American people through a career that spanned several decades. As President, his publicly flaunted political capital proved favorable in acceptance of his social and economic policies aided by his military build-up that resulted in collapse of the Soviet Union as they tried to match his level of military preparedness. So much so, no modern President received the posthumous recognition accorded Ronald Reagan in his extensive funeral and memorials in naming of airports and public buildings in his honor. His 11th Commandment mantra "Thou shall not criticize a fellow Republican" became enshrined in American and Republican political lore. His aura continues to radiate from the shrine of his memory as Republican "wanna-bes" continue to exploit mileage of his blessings through contracts with Mrs. Nancy Reagan, identification with the Reagan Library or curry-favoring to Reagan's lieutenants, even exploiting the notion "I was in the room with Ronald Reagan!"

FREDERICK MONDERSON

Obama - Master and Commander 456. Arnaldo Prododogo. Italian, b. Morciano, 1926. **Sphere No. 6** 1963-65. Bronze Gift of Joseph H. Hirshhorn, 1966 (66.4094).

Pulling all the strings that got him into the White House, George Washington Bush lulled the nation into a false sense of security that Al Qaeda exploited in effectuating their 9/11 plan of an unprecedented attack on the homeland killing thousands. It was foolish that conspiracy theorists blamed Mr. Bush for concocting the attack! Notwithstanding, his cherishing respect for history given his being named after the first George Washington and his oath to uphold the office should allay fears he was conspiratorial. That he made some faulty decisions, as a human being, is understandable, owing to poor advice and faulty intelligence. On the other hand, some have argued Sadam Hussein's attempt on the life of the Senior Bush prompted George to invade Iraq after the Afghanistan "Shock and Awe" blitz. Nevertheless, the reality of two wars, the "Bush Tax Cuts" for his "base," an unpaid for Prescription Drug Plan as well as skull-duggery speculation in banking, unregulated Wall Street running amok, and the housing market collapse as a result of lax regulation and oversight brought America to the brink of economic disaster and failed state status. Now, having laid low at the end of his tenure, Mr. Bush is being rehabilitated through exploitation of his good side and the good things he did such as fight the scourge of AIDS in Africa. Notwithstanding, the goodwill endeared to these great twice elected, presidents, did not include endowing such benefits upon Barack Obama.

With Mr. Obama, we have "a horse of a different color!" He broke the mold of 43 only male white presidents. However, none of the former presidents had risen from the humble beginnings of Barack Obama, struggled to acquire that "Million Dollar White man's education" from Columbia and Harvard, "done business white

OBAMA - MASTER AND COMMANDER

but married black" and possessing the tenacity and wherewithal to challenge for, campaign and create history by winning the Presidency of the United States. As such, a credible argument can be made; losers wanted to shift the responsibility for the nation's calamity and so acquiesced in Mr. Obama's victory in hopes to benefit from his cleaning out the "messy stables." However, in a nation of contingency planning from day one if not earlier, elements probably hatched the plan to create his demise as he first tackled the problems, created constructive solutions and moved the nation from the brink. Then, Mitch McConnell and his "Mandate" happened!

Obama - Master and Commander 457. Arnaldo Prododogo. Italian, b. Morciano, 1926. **Sphere No. 6** 1963-65. Bronze Gift of Joseph H. Hirshhorn, 1966 (66.4094).

FREDERICK MONDERSON

Obama - Master and Commander 458. "Presented by the Docents of the Hirshhorn Museum and Sculpture Garden, May 10, 2005.

Obama - Master and Commander 459. David Smith. American, b. Decatur, Indiana. 1906-1965. Pittsburgh Landscape 1954. Painted Steel. Gift of Joseph H. Hirshhorn, 1972 (72.20)

OBAMA - MASTER AND COMMANDER

Obama - Master and Commander 460. Joan Miro. Spanish, b. Barcelona, 1893-1963 Lunar Bird 1944-46, enlarged and cast 1966-67 Bronze. Gift of Joseph H. Hirshhorn, 1972 (72.04).

Obama - Master and Commander 460a. Smithsonian Institution National Museum of Natural History and National Museum of Man.

FREDERICK MONDERSON

Obama - Master and Commander 461. Silver figure at entrance to the Hirshhorn Garden Museum.

OBAMA - MASTER AND COMMANDER

Obama - Master and Commander 462. Mark di Suvero. American, b. Shanghai, C hina, 1933. "**Are Years What**?" (For Marianne Moor) 1967 Painted steel and cables. Joseph H. Hirshhorn Purchase Fund and Gift of the Institute of Scrap Recycling Industries, by Exchange, 1999 (99.19).

Despite his years in Congress, Mitch McConnell does not seem capable of single-mindedly originating his "I intend to make Barack Obama a one-term President" vocation. He must have had input, followed orders to hatch such a seemingly brilliant yet flawed, outwardly racist, statement and assignment! "Original as it may seem, one has to wonder if he is actually capable of writing his own material even though he seems to be doing a good job, so far executing it" and getting others to buy in! Still, this is a sinister pursuit and it is bound to fail because of its un-American nature.

From that day-one seedling planted in the nucleus of the anti-Obamite temple, a forest of ill-will germinated as countless off-shoots vied with each other to disrespect, threaten his life and block Mr. Obama's every legislative initiative designed to aid the broad masses of the American people. Ignoring his leadership, not assisting in the nation's rescue, Republicans removed their focus from effectively doing all the people's business to insuring Mr. Obama's tenure as President is a failure. However, untold numbers of Americans see Republicans as they truly are, beholden to the one percent at the expense of the ninety-nine percent! Equally, connecting the dots, it is evident racial animus has been a catalyst for all such behaviors. The interesting thing about Barack Obama, he continues to demonstrate exemplary leadership, while strategically choosing to see

FREDERICK MONDERSON

the "boys will be boys" nuisance as just that as he continues to execute the requirements of the office, to rescue the American economy despite the work of purposeful "front and back fires" scorching his path and keeping the! "wolves at bay." This unending sabotage is not by "angels with dirty faces" but "devils with clean faces.

"If you're walking down the right path and you're willing to keep walking, eventually you'll make progress." **Barack Obama**

Obama - Master and Commander 463. The Carousel on the Mall.

OBAMA - MASTER AND COMMANDER

Obama - Master and Commander 464. Statue of Mr. James Henry at the Mall entrance to the Smithsonian Castle.

FREDERICK MONDERSON

"I'm inspired by the people I meet in my travels - hearing their stories, seeing the hardships they overcome, their fundamental optimism and decency. I'm inspired by the love people have for their children. And I'm inspired by my own children, how full they make my heart. They make me want to work to make the world a little bit better. And they make me want to be a better man." **Barack Obama**

"Nothing can stand in the way of the power of millions of voices calling for change." **Barack Obama**

"One voice can change a room, and if one voice can change a room, then it can change a city, and if it can change a city, it can change a state, and if it change a state, it can change a nation, and if it can change a nation, it can change the world. Your voice can change the world." **Barack Obama**

46. THE CONSTITUTION, CHIEF JUSTICE, AND THE PRESIDENT
By
Dr. Fred Monderson

The recent Chief Justice ruling that President Obama's Health Care Reform or the Affordable Care Act is constitutional generated a great deal of animus commentary regarding the Chief Justice's ruling, the Constitution and the President's mandate. Republicans grinding their axe, notwithstanding, the Chief Justice has always played a key role in swaying the Court to deliver far-reaching rulings with long lasting implications. Nevertheless, though most rulings stand, the occasional one is overturned owing to its biased nature or mass-mobilization of the American people in opposition to the law forcing Congress to repeal the act with a replacement more amenable to the conscience and rights of the great masses of the people. Again, because of the inherent checks and balances of the Constitutional system, the judicial branch beaded by the Chief Justice must rule on the law's constitutionality in its role as a watch-dog of the people's interest. In all this, the "Commerce Clause" and the "power to Tax," two of the most important of Congress' powers to effectively legislate always raise questions about the constitutionality of control mechanisms and revenue measures.

The President's lawyers argued in the Supreme Court's Brief that the Health Care Reform Act or the Affordable Care Act (**ACA**) was presented under the Commerce Clause. The Court of Chief Justice Roberts ruled the bill is constitutional and while not permitted under the Commerce Clause is permitted under the power to tax measures.

OBAMA - MASTER AND COMMANDER

Accordingly, under the Constitution, Article 1, Section 8, sub-section 4 states, "Congress shall have power to regulate commerce with foreign nations, and among the several states, and with the Indian tribes;" while, in addition, the body is empowered, "To lay and collect taxes, duties, imposts, and excises, to pay the debts and provide for the common defense and general welfare of the United States; but all duties, imposts, and excises shall be uniform throughout the United States."

Jack Plano and Milton Greenberg in *The American Political Dictionary* (Eight Edition) (1989: 30) explain the meaning of this important constitutional power enabling the government to exercise great discretion in extending its provisions. That is: "The term 'commerce' has been interpreted to include the production and buying and selling of goods as well as the transportation of persons or commodities. Any of these functions are subject to national regulation and control if they affect more than one state or the free flow of commerce among states." The significance of this is further explained as, "The commerce power is one of the major constitutional provisions used by Congress to expand national power. A broad interpretation of what constitutes interstate commerce has enabled Congress to regulate such matters as manufacturing, child labor, farm production, wages and hours, labor unions, civil rights, and criminal conduct. Any activity that in any way 'affects' interstate commerce is subject to national rather than state control. So many functions are interstate in character that the role of the states in the federal system has been considerably altered or diminished."

There were several factors that made this law different. As a federal senator Barack Obama confronted with the rising cost of health care and the increasing number of Americans who had no coverage, the fact of insurance companies discriminating particularly against the most vulnerable Americans; in fact as the unemployment numbers rose more and more people began to lose what medical protections they had; the legislator felt he had to act to alleviate the problem. Even more important, all the numbers pointed upwards except protections. As such, in his strategy to get elected to the Presidency Mr. Obama formulated a platform to champion Health Care Reform, campaigned of this promise and having won the election and with a majority in Congress passed the Affordable Care Act. This was a significant achievement since administrations, Republican and Democratic, for more than half a century had tried to pass the measure but with little success. Modern Republicans with little concern for the "Grassroots" cried "foul," their favorite word after "No!"

FREDERICK MONDERSON

Obama - Master and Commander 465. The Castle of the Smithsonian Museum.

OBAMA - MASTER AND COMMANDER

Obama - Master and Commander 466. Freer Gallery of Art.

Obama - Master and Commander 467. "Musician on the Mall."

FREDERICK MONDERSON

Hoodwinking the American people in alliance with the anti-Obamite forces and with the albatross of the "McConnell mandate" as their guidepost in sabotaging the president's legislative agenda, Republicans gained control of the House of Representatives in 2010. Fact is, if Mr. Obama held a news conference and said, for instance, "Good morning, today is Monday" ... Republicans would say it's not! This therefore has been the environment under which Mr. Obama's administration has had to function. Thus, instead of running for and alongside for a touchdown for the American people, tunnel vision Republicans remained committed to one goal, viz., "Stop Obama," ensure his tenure is a failure, like a recurring decimal use every available legislative minute to repeal the Act they labeled "Obamacare." Recently using their majority in the House they passed a repeal measure for the 33rd time knowing the Democratic controlled Senate will not pass it and that the President would veto the measure if it got to his desk! Americans want to know, why have they not voted to approve the President's "Jobs Bill" even though they have consistently criticized the high rate of unemployment.

"What I've realized is that life doesn't count for much unless you're willing to do your small part to leave our children - all of our children - a better world. Any fool can have a child. That doesn't make you a father. It's the courage to raise a child that makes you a father." **Barack Obama**, *The Audacity of Hope: thoughts on Reclaiming the American Dream*

"Our stories may be singular, but our destination is shared." **Barack Obama**

"While we breathe, we will hope." **Barack Obama**

"If there is anyone out there who still doubts that America is a place where all things are possible; who still wonders if the dream of our founders is alive in our time; who still questions the power of our Democracy; Tonight is your answer."
Barack Obama

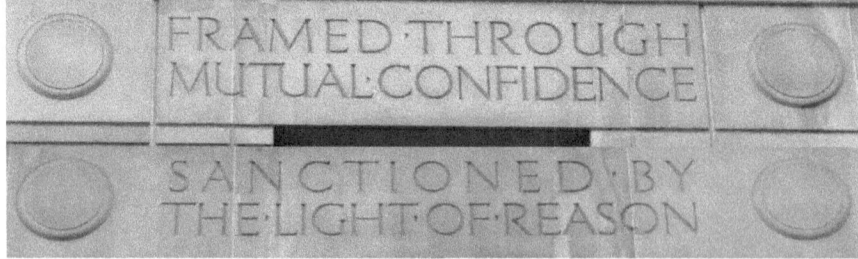

Obama - Master and Commander 468. Justice is "Framed through mutual confidence" (top) and "Sanctioned by the light of Reason" (bottom).

OBAMA - MASTER AND COMMANDER

Obama - Master and Commander 469. Vendors on the Mall in preparation for the Smithsonian Folklife Festival Program.

47. "A WOMAN OF STRAW"
By
Dr. Fred Monderson

Michele Bachmannn is very much like the character "Gunboat Johnson," in a *Three Stooges* movie, who had 50 fights, lost 49 and spent 6 weeks in hospital after fighting to a draw in the 50th. Yet, he still wanted to be considered a legitimate contender! As in his case, Michele Bachmannn has consistently exhibited shades of Mr. Johnson and by being in the Supreme Court Chamber when Chief Justice Roberts issued his ruling in Health Care Reform or Affordable Care Act, her disappointment showed greatly. As such, despite what she says publicly, "It's easy to set fire to such a woman of straw" whose aspirations to be president have revealed questionable positions. First and foremost, she told the world "God told me to run," but he did not give her the running shoes!

FREDERICK MONDERSON

From the bottom of the Republican contenders' pile in the presidential primary, Michele Bachmannn, has again "put foot in her mouth" by issuing another silly statement. To recall, Congresswoman Bachmannn first echoed the lunatic fringe's "Birther Mantra" by questioning President Obama's birthright and when this issue did not garner traction she backed away from the nonsensical position. Gaining respectability and still with attacks on Mr. Obama, Ms. Bachmannn won the Iowa straw poll, which in that legend's mind was a great achievement. However, rather than being catapulted into the stratosphere of Republican first choices, the candidate began stumbling and ended up back of the line of contenders. So much so, very early a credible Republican voice called on Ms. Bachmannn to quit the race for Republican nomination for president in the 2012 national elections. Yet, undeterred by her low percentages she persisted and stumbled every step of the way.

In a recent book Michele Bachmannn accused President Barack Obama of running a "gangster government" in Washington. Understandable, the economy is far from where it should be because of a number of factors germane to and external to Washington, D.C., including European economics; and thus, the ecoomy is indeed a credible line of attack against Mr. Obama, but to accuse him of "running a gangster government" is more than a stretch, its beyond dishonest. After all, the FBI does not see it that way! Thus, such ludicrous statements are not simply disrespectful, dishonest and disheartening to foreign observers of American political and social dynamics but it certainly upsets a great deal of the electorate, particularly Mr. Obama's grassroots base.

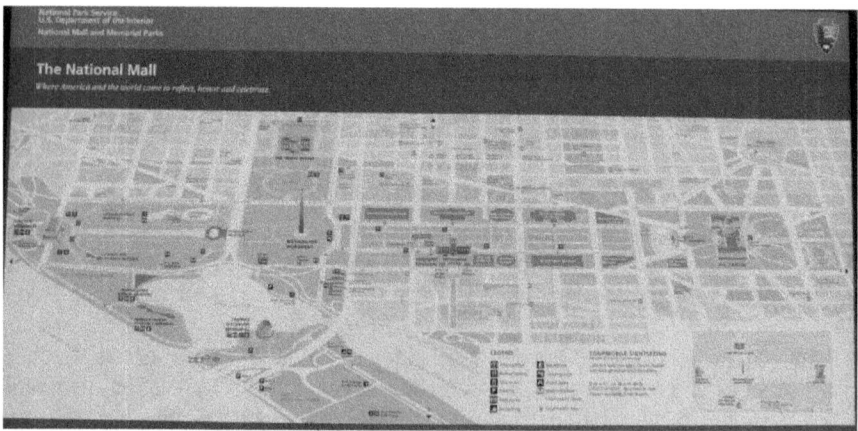

Obama - Master and Commander 470. Another view of the plan of the National Mall.

OBAMA - MASTER AND COMMANDER

Obama - Master and Commander 471. Vendors on the Mall in preparation for the Smithsonian Folklife Festival Program.

The *Oxford Dictionary* defines "Gangster" as "a member of a gang of violent criminals." *Webster's New World Dictionary* defines gangster as "a member of a gang of criminals." *Roget's College Thesaurus* offers the following synonyms for gangster as "hoodlum, thug, racketeer, tough, syndicate man, mobster, goon, hood, thief, illegality, evil." Now, are we to believe, President Obama with the members of his administration characterized as Ms. Bachmann has done, operates a "gangster government," in Washington under the sights of the FBI, Congress, the Judiciary and *ipso facto* commands the generals who lead the might of America's military and these people willingly follow.

What Ms. Bachmannn has done is defame President Obama at all costs but every claim, every criticism is either false or underscores the inherent shallow mindset or lack of knowledge on the part of this claimant. Additionally, Ms. Bachmannn has insisted it is "time for a mother to be in the White House." Fact is, there is a mother in White House, or for that matter two mothers! The problem with the Michele Bachmannn types, whom Rahm Emanuel called "turkeys" when not putting foot in mouth, mis-stating or feigning ignorance of a subject, they're either insulting the likes of Barack and Michelle, or ignoring their existence, accomplishments or capabilities and with all due respect to the Congresswoman, she is grossly naive!

FREDERICK MONDERSON

As part of the Republican culture of Obama denial, Bachmannn again misspoke in the statement "the President put us in Libya and now he has put us in Africa!" Not realizing Libya is in Africa, she meant to criticize Mr. Obama for putting troops in Uganda. Despite what may be said, with the considered judgment of his advisers and generals, in view of two wars being fought in Iraq and Afghanistan, the President decided to let Europe play a bigger role in Libya in the intent of removing the brutal and intransigent Ghadafi regime.

Yes, "Money talks and BS walks" and Ms. Bachmann like many who talk Pan-Africanism and criticize America's role in Africa remain ignorant and silent on China's colonialism cloaked in imperial economic investment expansion in Africa, the Caribbean and Latin America. However, Ms. Bachmannn's ignorance of Geography notwithstanding, she remains another of those contenders, vanquished and left lying in the dust as the Obama Express moves Forward!

"Our challenges may be new. The instruments with which we meet them may be new. But those values upon which our success depends - honesty and hard work, courage and fair play, tolerance and curiosity, loyalty and patriotism - these things are old. These things are true. They have been the quiet force of progress throughout our history. What is demanded then is a return to these truths. What is required of us now is a new era of responsibility - a recognition, on the part of every American, that we have duties to ourselves, our nation, and the world, duties that we do not grudgingly accept but rather seize gladly, firm in the knowledge that there is nothing so satisfying to the spirit, so defining of our character, than giving our all to a difficult task." **Barack Obama**

"To the Muslim world, we seek a new way forward, based on mutual interest and mutual respect. To those leaders around the globe who seek to sow conflict, or blame their society's ills on the West - know that your people will judge you on what you can build, not what you destroy. To those who cling to power through corruption and deceit and the silencing of dissent, know that you are on the wrong side of history; but that we will extend a hand if you are willing to unclench your fist." **Barack Obama**

"Making your mark on the world is hard. If it were easy, everybody would do it. But it's not. It takes patience, it takes commitment, and it comes with plenty of failure along the way. The real test is not whether you avoid this failure, because you won't. It's whether you let it harden or shame you into inaction, or whether you learn from it; whether you choose to persevere." **Barack Obama**

OBAMA - MASTER AND COMMANDER

48. CITIZEN DIRECT ACTION
By
Dr. Fred Monderson

While Wisconsin Governor Scott won out against the challenge to his term in office, as well as union issues, budgets and big money from outside and inside the state, with purported implications for the national elections later this year, the more important issue was the mechanism at play. That is, the Recall as a means of terminating the term of service of an elected official or reforming government which was part of the Populist Progressive Movement of the late 1890s. Interestingly enough, the state of Wisconsin under Governor Robert M. La Follette was the Model for Progressive reform by citizens appalled by corruption in government and unrestrained control by monopolies. How interesting and in retrospect, Ms. Bachmannn's "Gangster Government" comment notwithstanding, Wisconsisn voted for Obama while all the "Lynching southern states," mentioned above voted for Romney! This is something to remember!

As part of the greater reform movement enabling Direct Democracy, challenging monopoly practices and corruption at the state and local government levels, the secret ballot, initiative, referendum and the direct primary allowed the average citizen to be part of the political process and not allow political bosses to run amok. The **Direct Primary** is thus an important part of modern election in which candidates are chosen from a field with party winners meeting in the November general election. That is, the party primary is held in September and the general election in November as part of Gubertorial or local elections. At the national level, in the spring, the party **out of** the White House holds a presidential primary to choose a standard bearer to challenge the President in the November elections. Oftentimes a popular president, who is also the leader of his political party, is not generally challenged to oppose the opposition. However, if the President is considered weak, upstarts in his party may challenge him in the party's primary. If there is no challenger, then there is no primary for him which means he does not have to spend monies from his "war chest" to check his challengers. However, in 1980, Senator Ted Kennedy challenged President Jimmy Carter. Kennedy was so relentless, he softened up Carter and Ronald Reagan, the Republican, took advantage of this to defeat Carter, the Democrat.

FREDERICK MONDERSON

Obama - Master and Commander 472. Preparation for the Smithsonian Folklife Festival Program.

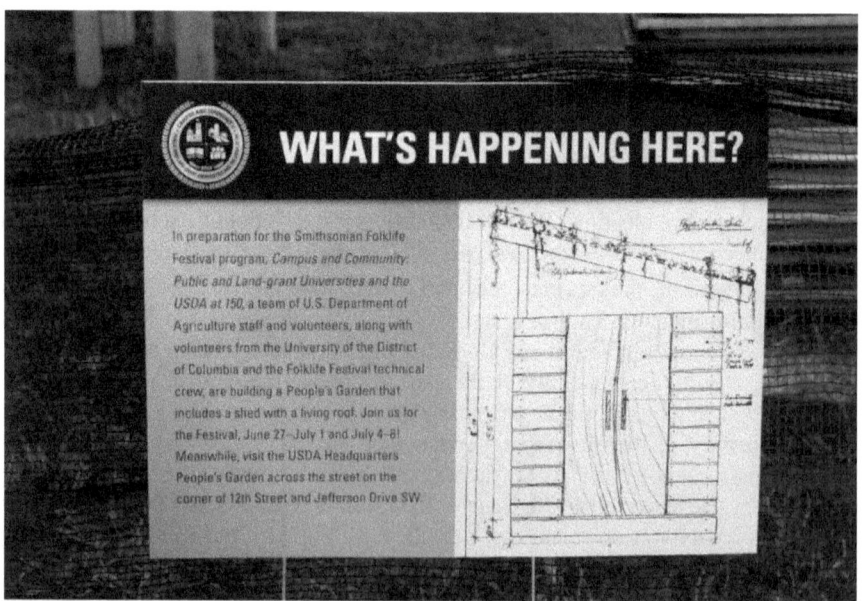

Obama - Master and Commander 473. Preparation for the Smithsonian Folklife Festival Program.

OBAMA - MASTER AND COMMANDER

Obama - Master and Commander 473a. Classic scene of two youths for the forthcoming National Museum of African American History and Culture.

In the Populist Reform Age, even though the political bosses such as "Tweed" actively operated, people were more concerned with "bread and butter" issues such as bill paying. In Bonnie-Anne Briggs and Catherine Fish Petersen's *Brief Review in United States History and Government* (2001: 166) they point out: "One significant urban reform was the regulation of utilities such as water, gas and electricity. In many cities, utilities were controlled by monopolies. Beginning in the 1890s, cities began to extend control over utilities, and by 1915, two out of every three cities had some form of city-controlled utilities. This provided residents with more affordable services." These successes led to more concentrated efforts to regulate other services such as transportation systems, sanitation, etc. These efforts "also tried to improve the appearance of cities by constructing large, elaborate libraries, museums and other public buildings."

"Yes, we can heal this nation. Yes, we can seize our future. And as we leave this great state with a new wind at our backs and we take this journey across this great country, a country we love, with the message we carry from the plains of Iowa to the hills of New Hampshire, from the Nevada desert to the South Carolina coast, the same message we had when we were up and when we were down, that out of many, we are one; that while we breathe, we will hope." **Barack Obama**

FREDERICK MONDERSON

"More than a building that houses books and data, the library has always been a window to a larger world - a place where we've always come to discover big ideas and profound concepts that help move the American story forward. . . . "

"Libraries remind us that truth isn't about who yells the loudest, but who has the right information. Because even as we're the most religious of people, America's innovative genius has always been preserved because we also have a deep faith in facts. And so the moment we persuade a child, any child, to cross that threshold into a library, we've changed their lives forever, and for the better. This is an enormous force for good." **Barack Obama**

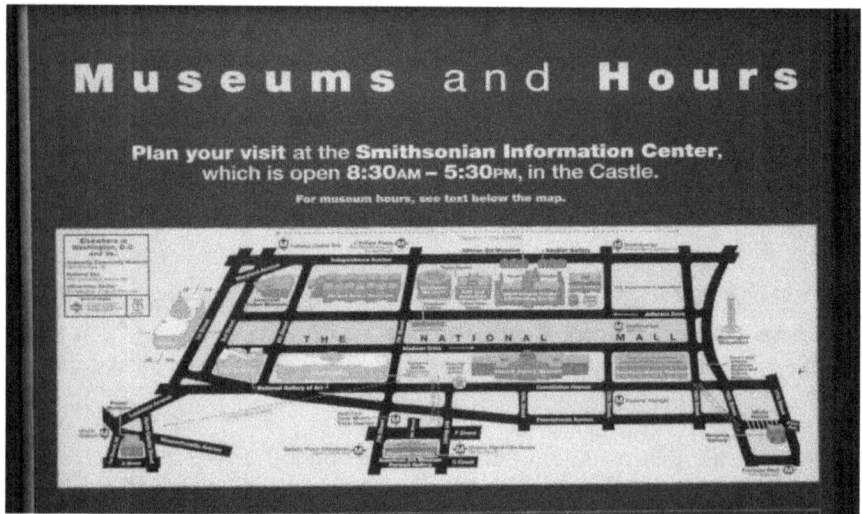

Obama - Master and Commander 473b. Museums and Hours of the Smithsonian Institution on the National Mall.

"Where you are right now doesn't have to determine where you'll end up" **Barack Obama**

49. OBAMA: "STEADY AS HE GOES"
By
Dr. Fred Monderson

Many people were amazed by Barack Obama's organizational ability, positive persistence at challenging times and unrelenting efforts to make his election victory possible. His cool demeanor was also impressive. But, as Condoleezza Rice has pointed out, the view is different from the Oval Office and many people,

OBAMA - MASTER AND COMMANDER

viz., experts, commentators; even casual observers expected he would come apart with the challenges and pressures posed to the President of the United States. But this was not to be. A particular case in point can be referenced. We know it's been said one photo can speak a thousand words and the one from the Situation Room as the assault on Osama bin-Laden's compound speaks volumes. A more pertinent photo is the one with him on the tarmac with Arizona's Governor Jan Brewer carrying on and gesturing with her finger while Mr. Obama just stood there as the world has come to see.

The picture of Governor Jan Brewer on the airport tarmac wagging her finger and presumably speaking harsh words to President Obama, arguably the most powerful man in the world, speaks volumes about America. The President's demeanor equally says a great deal, not simply because he did not shout "Security," but that he let her have her say while his cool demeanor provided a glimpse at the man who faces innumerable issues on a daily basis, whether its domestic or foreign. Perhaps in half of the countries of the world, the next picture frame would be a Mack Truck swinging by and sweeping off the governor.

Obama - Master and Commander 474. The sign says it all!

That President Obama is a "Cool Cat" as Sammy Davis Jr. used to say was perhaps evident in the Presidential Campaign when the DeMints, Joe Wilsons, Bachmannns, Joes the Plumbers, and Tea Partiers and their surrogates pounded Mr. Obama. He stood there, took it all and probably wondered, "Is that all you got?" Such a posture is being exceptionally smart, but that is the nature of the man.

FREDERICK MONDERSON

Obama - Master and Commander 474a. National Museum of History.

Obama - Master and Commander 475. Signs say so much!

He thinks before putting his mouth in gear, unlike opponents such as Senator "Stupid" Grasley and his cohort Governor "Stupid" Sununu.

To recall, during the Presidential Campaign in 2008, an issue in Eastern Europe, Kosovo or elsewhere and John Mc Cain said, "Let's go in!" Mr. Obama, on the other hand, said "I consulted with my advisers, so let's proceed with caution!" And so it has been.

OBAMA - MASTER AND COMMANDER

Obama - Master and Commander 476. Smithsonian Folklife Festival sign for Campus and Community.

FREDERICK MONDERSON

Obama - Master and Commander 477. Just plain folks milling around and heading towards the Washington Memorial.

After the insult and "You Lie" Wilson wanted to meet the President to apologize, Mr. Obama replied, "Send it in the mail!" Speaker John Boehner boasted, after the Debt Ceiling stalemate, that he had essentially robbed Obama blind in his statement, "We got 98% of what we wanted," but the President responded "Let's play golf!" More importantly, when Senator Mitch McConnell gave his now famous thumbs up and "I got that Nigger" smirk, Obama probably thought "I got a few tricks for this trickster out to make me a One Term President." That much and

OBAMA - MASTER AND COMMANDER

more characterized his domestic front demeanor and strategy while on the foreign policy front he was just as smooth!

Not discounting the suavity and effectiveness that Mr. Obama's has shown on the road in Canada, then England, France and Germany, and on to Turkey, Egypt and Ghana; in Trinidad Hugh Chavez tried to upstage Obama for a photo Op designed to play in Venezuela but Obama didn't bite the bait!

Some months ago, President Obama appeared in the White House Briefing Room and reported, "We conducted operations against Al Qaeda and killed Osama bin-Laden." While George Bush issued the "Wanted Dead or Alive" poster it was the Marshall Barack Obama who found, killed, washed, wrapped and disposed of bin-Laden. Months later, Mitt Romney, trying to play to the Republican base that have consistently accused Democrats of being soft on national security and terror tried to make the same argument against Barack Obama saying he appeased "global bad boys." Again, the President calmly responded, "Ask Osama Bin Laden and some of the 22 of 30 top Al Qaeda leaders removed from the battlefield, if I'm an appeaser!" Thus, he removed fighting terror from among the premier litany of issues Republicans like to exploit in their campaign challenges.

The President came into power with a plan to engage Asia, recognizing that China, India and Japan as well as Indonesia are significant economic and political players in that region. He dispatched Secretary of State Hillary Clinton to the region to establish this view and he made a couple of Presidential visits to reiterate and reinforce this new policy of his administration. On a visit to Australia he reminded the world America is a Pacific Power and that "We're here to stay!" Then began the quiet yet effective diplomacy to woo the small states and reassure the large ones of the good faith in the approach while cultivating constructive relationships with all these states. For someone touted as being inexperienced in foreign policy during the campaign, Mr. Obama has come a long way, demonstratively achieved much in negotiations and been blest with knowledgeable and effective advisers.

On the nuclear front, Mr. Obama said he would talk to Iran. If they unclenched their fists, he would extend a hand and in view of their boastful intransigence he imposed more and more sanctions on that nation, reaffirming his stated position, "No Nukes for Iran!" To achieve such he had placed all options on the table, diplomatic, economic, and even military! An effective carrot and stick approach has also put all nuclear aspirants even "kindergarten nuclear powers" like North Korea, "the U.S. will keep a close eye on how you behave!" In the wider world "Grassroots analysts" with a bone to pick with the U.S. insist Iran has a right to nuclear power! That may be so; but, Iran has consistently stated an objective of obliterating Israel, a member of the United Nations community. This must not happen! The United Nations has recognized Israel as a member. To destroy Israel, a member, means you challenge to will and might of the United Nations. What will happen next? Will Iran leave the United Nations? Will it still want to pursue relations with other members of the United Nations, or will the country just pick up and relocate in space? What about the consequences of their actions? How stupid that their theorists and equally followers believe their nuclear actions will go unpunished! Equally, a further belief is that "rogue nations" pursuing nuclear power tend to destabilize their region forcing neighboring nations to defend themselves through acquisition of nuclear power. The end result is more nations will generate an arms race and a greater destabilizing effect will result. Hence, No "Nukes for Iran!"

"The American story has never been about things coming easy. It has been about rising to the moment when the moment is hard. About rejecting panicked division for purposeful unity. About seeing a mountaintop from the deepest valley. That is why we remember that some of the most famous words ever spoken by an American came from a president who took office in a time of turmoil: 'The only thing we have to fear is fear itself.'" **Barack Obama**

"Teachers matter. So instead of bashing them, or defending the status quo, let's offer schools a deal. Give them the resources to keep good teachers on the job, and reward the best ones. In return, grant schools flexibility: To teach with creativity and passion; to stop teaching to the test; and to replace teachers who just aren't helping kids learn." **Barack Obama**

"As president, I believe that robotics can inspire young people to pursue science and engineering. And I also want to keep an eye on those robots in case they try anything." **Barack Obama**

50. "THE AMERICA WE KNOW!"
By
Dr. Fred Monderson

Appearing on **John King's America** on CNN, May 22, 2012, Reince Priebus spoke of defeating President Obama and "returning to the America we know and love." While the Chairman of the Republican National Committee may be speaking to a particular segment of the American electorate, thinking Blacks certainly query his meaning and see more than the average person does. These days, key words or code words have replaced the more blatant, some say racist Republican rallying cry. Whether it is Sarah Palin's "He's not like us;" Joe the Plumber's "Sounds like socialism to me;" "We must stop Obama," this will be his "Waterloo," Senator DeMint (R. SC); "I intend to make Barack Obama a one term

OBAMA - MASTER AND COMMANDER

President" Mitch McConnell (R. Kentucky); Senator Charles "stupid" Grassley; and let us not forget John "stupid" Sununu. These are experts in some of the blatant and code words used to disparage in effort to derail the President's agenda. But what Mr. Obama has done other than being the first Black President is having succeeded forty-three white Presidents of the Republic who in turn succeeded President Henson, a Black man who headed the nation as President under the Articles of Confederation and whose blessings and spirit may have been instrumental in guiding the successes of the new nation under the Constitution.

While astute Blacks may understand Republican code words, people in general may not reasonably decipher Reince Priebus' "The America we know!" Depending on where you stand or sit, the America we know may be different from the narrow Republican view and the historical America molded in the caldron of its experiences. That is, an America for centuries enslaved people like Michele Obama's ancestors in an institution of slavery considered "a crime against humanity;" exterminated native Americans; fought a Civil War to defend an oppressive system; denied the humanity of black men through *Dred Scott v. Sandford* and instituted "Separate but equal," really, "Separate and unequal;" created fugitive slave laws and Black Codes, formed the Ku Klux Klan, enabled "Jim Crow" and the "Grandfather Clause," all pure mechanisms of terror; sanctioned untold lynchings, segregation and incarceration, while allowing Black unemployment to soar, mis-education to fester and health and nutrition maladies to grow in their communities and still recruit Blacks and other minorities to defend the "American way of life" as we know it, at home and abroad.

Unmistakably, had it not been for men of great conscience as William Lloyd Garrison, John Brown, Charles Sumner, John Kennedy, Lyndon Johnson, Teddy Kennedy aiding the efforts of Frederick Douglass, Mary McLeod-Bethune, A. Philip Randolph, Martin Luther King, Malcolm X, Randall Robinson and Colin Powell; we would not be where Barack Obama could be in a position to be elected, empowered to rescue America from the abyss of two concurrent wars, escalating unemployment, skyrocketing home foreclosures, bank and investment firm failures, crumbling social infrastructure, escalating medical costs and a whole lot more, while the wealth of the top one percent, the "Republican base," increased tremendously at the expense of the ninety-nine percent.

FREDERICK MONDERSON

Obama - Master and Commander 478. The site of the future African-American Museum.

Obama - Master and Commander 479. Harry Belafonte (far left) and Harriet Tubman (right).

Obama - Master and Commander 480. Frederick Douglas (left) and James Baldwin (right).

OBAMA - MASTER AND COMMANDER

Obama - Master and Commander 481. An image of the African Museum Plaza and the expected date of Opening, 2015.

That "America we know" was clearly enunciated during the challenges of the Republican presidential primary under the banner of conservatism where people like Newt Gingrich wanted to take the nation into that storied past as he and Rick Santorum vied to be more conservative. Or who would take us further back! In that contest, these straw men rather than set the nation afire were themselves burnt in the process because even using the Hubble Telescope they failed to observe the brilliance of Barack Obama who rescued the nation's economy despite, at his every step, act, leadership feat, obstructionism and sabotage by the "Party of No" guided by "Mitch McConnell's Mandate" was the order of the day. Mr. Obama brought equality and dignity to the value of woman labor by passing the "Lilly Ledbetter Law." He alleviated the stigma against gays by renouncing "Don't Ask, Don't tell" practice and rightly affirming the right of gays to be married, what the NAACP called a civil rights issue. Mr. Obama changed the world's view of America, got bin-Laden, ended the war in Iraq and negotiated an Afghanistan exit strategy. With some luck and due diligence, terrorist plots have been foiled; the nation has enjoyed some 26 months of consistent job growth in the private sector, foreclosures have slowed, housing sales and starts are on the rise, Wall Street is booming so much, they're giving out big bonuses and the wealthy "Republican base" is still getting richer. Still, the ingrates want to crucify Mr. Obama foregoing all that he has done to return the nation to normalcy and pointed in the right direction.

His clean energy program is designed to reduce the nation's dependence on foreign oil; his encouragement of more drilling and oil exploration is designed to further reduce the nation's dependence on foreign oil sources. His environmental concerns about industry and particularly in upgrading the automobile systems are designed to save the nation from industrial pollution and to get increased mileage for a gallon of gas; and his educational initiatives are designed to reclaim America's leading role in industrial and scientific innovation. Now, with these priorities set, thinking Americans do not want to return the nation to the arrogance we know and despite the millions being spent by Carl Rove's group and other

FREDERICK MONDERSON

Super PACs, the President should be re-elected because his vision is of the future not the past.

"... faith doesn't mean that you don't have doubts ... [you] still experience the same greed, resentment, lust, and anger that everyone else experienced ... the lines between sinner and saved [are] more fluid; the sins of those who come to church are not so different from the sins of those who don't ... You [need] to come to church precisely because you [are] of this world, not apart from it; rich, poor, sinner, saved you [need] to embrace Christ precisely because you had sins to wash away ... that religious commitment did not require me to suspend critical thinking, disengage from the battle for economic and social justice, or otherwise retreat from the world ..." **Barack Obama**, *The Audacity of Hope: Thoughts on Reclaiming the American Dream*

"You know, sometimes I'll go to an 8th-grade graduation and there's all that pomp and circumstance and gowns and flowers. And I think to myself, it's just 8th grade ... An 8th-grade education doesn't cut it today. Let's give them a handshake and tell them to get their butts back in the library!" **Barack Obama**

Obama - Master and Commander 482. The Washington Monument, Memorial as seen from the grounds (Notice the flags in tribute to the states - left) and across the Lake from the Jefferson Memorial.

OBAMA - MASTER AND COMMANDER

Obama - Master and Commander 483. The Inscription read: "This cornerstone was laid by Franklin Delano Roosevelt, President of the United States of America 1939."

Obama - Master and Commander 484. The Jefferson Memorial with its magnificent dome and colonnade of columns with Ionic capitals.

FREDERICK MONDERSON

Obama - Master and Commander 485. The monumental Thomas Jefferson in his Rotunda while he looks steadfastedly forward past the Washington Monument and towards the White House, some say keeping an eye on both these iconic structures and what they represent.

"You can't let your failures define you. You have to let your failures teach you."
Barack Obama

OBAMA - MASTER AND COMMANDER

"I confess to wincing every so often at a poorly chosen word, a mangled sentence, an expression of emotion that seems indulgent or overly practiced. I have the urge to cut the book by fifty pages or so, possessed as I am with a keener appreciation for brevity." **Barack Obama**

51. OBAMA: "SHOULD APOLOGIZE!"
By
Dr. Fred Monderson

A new controversy brewing today, July 12, 2012, in which the Romney camp made a statement that the President "should apologize" for saying Mitt Romney understated his tenure at Bain Capital, the investment firm he founded and became a financial success. Mr. Romney camp, on the other hand, fielding a presidential challenger, accused a sitting president of being a "liar." As the American public listens to the charges and counter-charges being made, it becomes clearer that the campaign for President has descended to a vicious and low state. Some may say "Mr. Romney, Welcome!" However, in his recent TV interview, Mr. Romney clearly demonstrated a new public relations campaign about his role at Bain Capital though he further raised many questions as to his true involvement with the company and the nature of his wealth.

After the Rodney King beating caught on tape, a new T-Shirt slogan emerged: "Do you believe me or your lying eyes!" People are asking, are we to believe the documents with his signature or his new Public Relations position. Let's not forget, after the cat had eaten the rat, even with juices on his mouth he proclaimed his innocence; the Mighty Sparrow sang, "Me and the woman didn't do nothing!" Bill Clinton said, "I did not have sex with that woman." Anna Nicole smith said she married for love! It was said there were WMDs in Iraq. Even Jerry Sandusky affirmed his innocence when arrested and that the truth would come out. Well it did! Perhaps Mr. Romney will release additional documents that may clear up his present situation that has people wondering.

FREDERICK MONDERSON

ALMIGHTY GOD HATH CREATED THE MIND FREE. ALL ATTEMPTS TO INFLUENCE IT BY TEMPORAL PUNISHMENTS OR BURTHENS···ARE A DEPARTURE FROM THE PLAN OF THE HOLY AUTHOR OF OUR RELIGION···NO MAN SHALL BE COMPELLED TO FREQUENT OR SUPPORT ANY RELIGIOUS WORSHIP OR MINISTRY OR SHALL OTHERWISE SUFFER ON ACCOUNT OF HIS RELIGIOUS OPINIONS OR BELIEF, BUT ALL MEN SHALL BE FREE TO PROFESS AND BY ARGUMENT TO MAINTAIN, THEIR OPINIONS IN MATTERS OF RELIGION. I KNOW BUT ONE CODE OF MORALITY FOR MEN WHETHER ACTING SINGLY OR COLLECTIVELY.

Obama - Master and Commander 486. "Almighty God hath created the mind free. All attempts to influence it by temporal punishments or burthens ... are a departure from the plan of the Holy Author of our religion ... No man shall be compelled to frequent or support any religious worship or ministry or shall otherwise suffer on account of his religious opinions or belief. But all men shall be free to profess and by argument to maintain, their opinion in matters of religion. I know but one code of morality for men whether acting singly or collectively."

OBAMA - MASTER AND COMMANDER

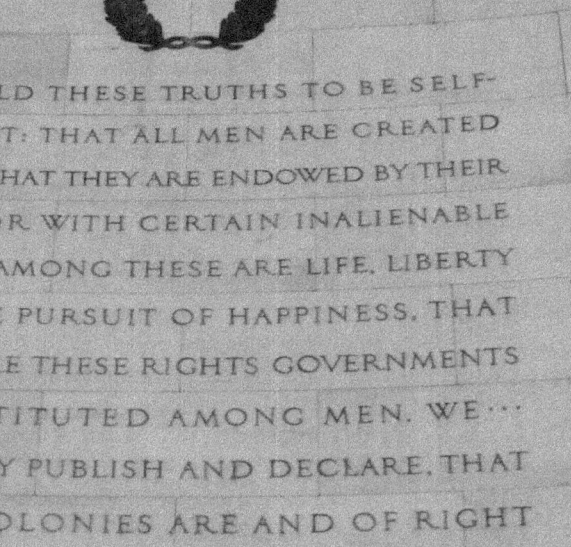

Obama - Master and Commander 487. "We hold these truths to be self evident: That all men are created equal, that they are endowed by their creator with certain inalienable rights among these are life, liberty and the pursuit of happiness. That to secure these right governments are instituted among men. We … solemnly Publish and declare that, these colonies are and of right ought to be free and independent states … and for the support of this Declaration, with a firm reliance on the protection of divine providence, we mutually pledge our lives, our fortunes and our sacred honor."

FREDERICK MONDERSON

During the Republican presidential primary campaign, all the contenders took shots at Mr. Romney's leadership, business acumen, and his successes and even, through surrogates attacked his Mormon religion calling it a cult. Newt Gingrich, Rick Perry and Rick Santorum all called on Mr. Romney to release his tax returns but he has only released 2010 and promises to release one additional, no more! Naturally, these people broke Ronald Reagan's 11th Commandment, "Thou shall not speak ill of a fellow Republican." Appearing on CNN's Piers Morgan, Rich Santorum, "a good loser," a loser nevertheless, responded to a particular question now that he had made up with Romney, stating - "Lots of things get said in a political campaign." Any of these candidates who attacked Mitt Romney were subsequently welcomed into his camp once they recognized his "presumptive" and "actual" nominee status and offered to campaign and fundraise for his campaign. He never, certainly publicly, asked any of them to retract any statement much more "apologize" as his camp has insisted the President of the United States do for "lying" about Mr. Romney. Fact is, Mr. Romney's signature on documents contradict each other which seems to indicate either he is lying or misleading. No other person is listed as CEO of Bain Capital in the time at issue, nor is any other shown as sole Owner, Share Holder or Sole Director. Now all this has to do with the issue of outsourcing during these years Mr. Romney has said he was not administering his company though he was making money and probably being paid. He did not object to any "improper practice" the company engaged in such as outsourcing, call centers, and its moves against GST Steel Company where many people lost their jobs, pensions and health coverage. Naturally Mr. Romney's critics also call attention to his Swiss Bank Account and financial dealings with Bahamas and such "Tax shelter" havens.

Mr. Obama launched a TV Ad and even made public statements about Mr. Romney's tenure with Bain Capital, the time he claims to have actually left the company yet, the fact, his name appeared on legal documents as CEO, Sole Owner, etc. Mr. Obama's position was based on articles published in *The Washington Post* and *The Boston Globe*, which showed despite Mr. Romney's claims he left Bain in 1999 to undertake management of the Winter Olympics in Salt Lake City; but security and Exchange Commission documents for 1999-2001 show he was listed as CEO and Sole owner. The claim is that as he was listed in this position more people lost their jobs and more jobs were sent overseas in "outsourcing." The important thing seems to be Mr. Romney stayed at Bain Capital 3 years more than he stated.

However, the question of "apologize" is what Mr. Obama's supporters have issue with!

OBAMA - MASTER AND COMMANDER

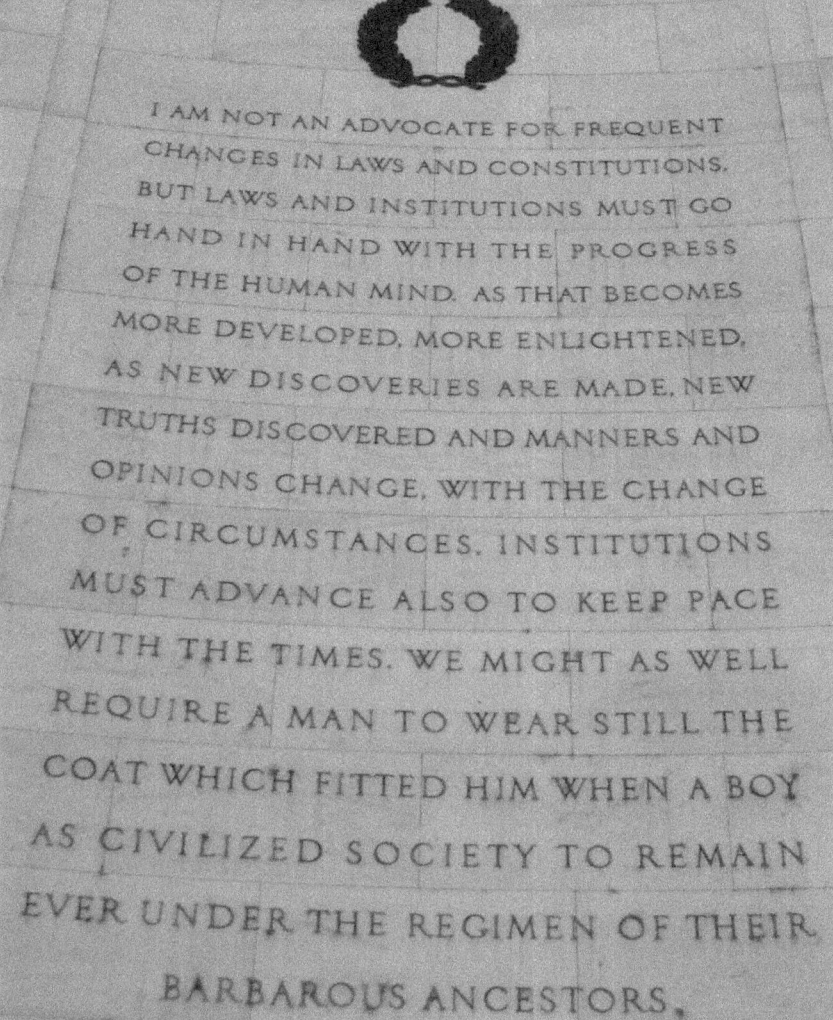

Obama - Master and Commander 488. "I am not an advocate for frequent changes in laws and constitutions. But laws and institutions must go hand in hand with the progress of the human mind. As that becomes more developed, more enlightened, as new discoveries are made, new truths discovered and manners and opinions change, with the change of circumstances, institutions must advance also to keep pace with the times. We might as well require a man to wear still the suit which fitted him when a boy as civilized society to remain ever under the regimen of their barbarous ancestors."

FREDERICK MONDERSON

> GOD WHO GAVE US LIFE GAVE US LIBERTY. CAN THE LIBERTIES OF A NATION BE SECURE WHEN WE HAVE REMOVED A CONVICTION THAT THESE LIBERTIES ARE THE GIFT OF GOD? INDEED I TREMBLE FOR MY COUNTRY WHEN I REFLECT THAT GOD IS JUST, THAT HIS JUSTICE CANNOT SLEEP FOREVER. COMMERCE BETWEEN MASTER AND SLAVE IS DESPOTISM. NOTHING IS MORE CERTAINLY WRITTEN IN THE BOOK OF FATE THAN THAT THESE PEOPLE ARE TO BE FREE. ESTABLISH THE LAW FOR EDUCATING THE COMMON PEOPLE. THIS IT IS THE BUSINESS OF THE STATE TO EFFECT AND ON A GENERAL PLAN.

Obama - Master and Commander 489. "God who gave us life gave us liberty. Can the liberties of a nation be secure when we have removed a conviction, that these liberties are the gift of God? Indeed I tremble for my country when I reflect that God is just, that his justice cannot sleep forever. Commerce between master and slave is despotism. Nothing is more certainly written in the book of fate than that these people are to be free. Establish the law for educating the common people. This it is the business of the state to effect and on a general plan."

OBAMA - MASTER AND COMMANDER

First, as a Senator from Illinois contending for the Democratic nomination, Mr. Obama's leadership abilities were challenged by Senator Hillary Clinton, whose offerings were consistent with Rick Santorum's contention "All kinds of things are said in a campaign!" However, like the Republicans, Mrs. Clinton closed ranks, endorsed, supported Mr. Obama's candidacy and ended up as his Secretary of State. As Mr. Obama turned to combat John McCain for the Presidency a whole slew of negatives greeted him, viz., the "Tea Party's" birth in the anti-Obama cauldron; "Joe the Plumber's" socialism characterization; the "Birther" controversy; right wing threats; the Donald trumping; the "black protester with guns" and his pastor praying for Mr. Obama's death; and much more. Then, with Mr. Obama elected as President, Senator Mitch McConnell threw down his gauntlet; Senator DeMint wanted to create Obama's "Waterloo;" Representative Joe Wilson, in the hallowed halls of Congress shouted to Mr. Obama, "You lie;" Billy Krystal advised in the Health Care Debate "Go for the Kill;" in the Bush Tax Cut debacle McConnell gave the now infamous "I got that Nigger" finger and smirk; and Speaker John Boehner in the Debt Ceiling stand-off boasted, after disrespecting the President by not returning his phone calls, "We got 98% of what we wanted." Throughout these litanies of disrespectful acts against the President of the United States, some have argued, perhaps it's because he is black; yet, not one of these honorable, respectable individuals apologized for their actions. That is, perhaps, only Joe Wilson, but he wanted to personally meet the President to offer his apology. Mr. Obama simply said, "Send it in the mail!"

Things got so bad as these people disrespected the President and the Presidency, people began to accuse Mr. Obama of being soft, being an "appeaser" and wondering when he would "take off the gloves." That is, at a time when he was busy "removing some 22 of 30 top Al Qaeda operatives from the field of battle," killing Osama bin-Laden, taking out Al Awlaki, contending with the Taliban in Afghanistan after drawing down from Iraq and moving against Somali Pirates while holding the Korean and Iranian leadership in a stalemate. All this after Mr. Obama had rescued the nation from falling over the fiscal cliff, stopped the nation from shedding several hundred thousand jobs per month, and had to rescue the banking industry, fix Wall Street through economic and fiscal regulation, infuse tremendous capital into the auto industry and preside over the addition of some 4 million jobs. Still the attacks came!

Some guy got fired from his job for saying "Money talks, and BS walks." Yet, in that vein, Karl Rove's group outlaid $25 million to defeat Mr. Obama. The fellow with T.D. Bank pledged $10 million and more millionaires and big money people, as *The Distinguished Gentleman* was told, "are lining up to take a ticket to throw money" into the effort to defeat Mr. Obama.

However, very much like Rameses III of the 20th ancient Egyptian dynasty who fought only when he was ready, Mr. Obama, finally, like John Paul Jones uttered,

FREDERICK MONDERSON

"Surrender, I have not yet begun to fight." After taking all the opposition could muster and finally taking off the gloves, the CNN commentator and presidential adviser David Gergen finally uttered: "The Obama campaign is now playing a rough form of politics."

The problem with "bullies" and the reason they lose is because they take advantage but when the victim finally strikes back, they cry foul. But, seriously, to accuse Mr. Obama of a failure of leadership, and blame him as Cornell West has held, "truth, justice and compassion is dying in America" under his watch is essentially one sided for as West's buddy Tavis Smiley also pointed out, "Campaigning and governing are two different things." The conservative nature of the nation is such that, people only fight for the rich as the Republicans are doing while they equ ally block every measure for the poor and middle classes.

"What Washington Needs is Adult Supervision." **Barack Obama**

Obama - Master and Commander 490. Ionic capitals crown columns in the Jefferson Memorial.

OBAMA - MASTER AND COMMANDER

Obama - Master and Commander 491. Base of columns in the Jefferson Memorial.

Obama - Master and Commander 492. Ionic capitals of columns that support the simple yet picturesque ceiling of the Jefferson Memorial.

FREDERICK MONDERSON

Obama - Master and Commander 493. Another view of column, capital, architrave and ceiling of the Thomas Jefferson Memorial.

Obama - Master and Commander 494. Sportsmen and others on the grounds of the Jefferson Memorial.

OBAMA - MASTER AND COMMANDER

Obama - Master and Commander 495. A truly panoramic view of the majestic Washington Monument as seen from across the Lake at the Jefferson Memorial.

"And where we are met with cynicism and doubt and fear and those who tell us that we can't, we will respond with that timeless creed that sums up the spirit of the American people in three simple words - yes, we can." **Barack Obama**

52. AMERICAN LEADERS ABROAD
By
Dr. Fred Monderson

The mettle of an American leader is generally tested on his first trip abroad which gives notice to allies as well as adversaries what type of individual they are dealing with, particularly if he or she aspires to the highest office of the land such as President of the United States. The former among such leaders of nation states would welcome a personable American leader who is intelligent, knowledgeable about events they may agree on or disagree about; for the perceived perception questions whether this individual can be strong, decisive and if need be, can cooperate on important issues of mutual interest. Adversaries equally assesses such a leader to determine how experienced he is, and whether they can challenge his authority to determine how much they can get away with. However, while self-assured and decisive leaders on that first trip abroad may wow their audience and put adversaries on notice; weak and indecisive, irresolute and flip-flopping leaders often put their foot in mouth, embarrass or insult allies, or potentially offer a long

FREDERICK MONDERSON

leash to adversaries who are emboldened by their amateurish behavior. The classic case sketched above features Barack Obama and Mitt Romney, the former first as United States Senator, and now President on the one hand, and the latter as former Governor and now aspirant for the Presidency.

In time perspective, when both leaders made their first trip abroad, America faced many challenges but each of a different nature. One thing is certain, their first trip sets the bar, high or low, of future expectations.

Barack Obama's first venture on the world stage, as all aspirants to the U.S Presidency would normally do, met with resounding success. Here was a black man, a leader, senator of a great nation who was cool in demeanor; articulate in thought and speech; well-liked by his constituency; and possessed an ability to flourish convincingly in any argument or situation and proved attractive to great masses of people. In Europe he was an instant hit and received "rock-star" reception. The Germans wanted to elect him President of their country. In Kenya, the elders were flabbergasted and welcomed a "returning son." Those elders of his paternal heritage gave him the royal treatment, dressed him in traditional gear and reconnected his heritage endowed with the power of the spirits of creation first manifested in the land where "the gods first dwelt." Then they sent him forth. Perhaps the essence of this endowment made the difference in his election victory.

Obama - Master and Commander 496. Abraham Lincoln Memorial with its 36 Doric Columns on four sides, (12 each at front and back and 6 at each side) one each for every state in the Union when the President was assassinated.

OBAMA - MASTER AND COMMANDER

Obama - Master and Commander 497. Abraham Lincoln, in that majestic and powerful seated position gazing into the great beyond.

FREDERICK MONDERSON

Obama - Master and Commander 498. An indelible imprint at the Lincoln Memorial where Martin Luther King, Jr. made his historic "**I have a Dream**" Speech as part of the "March on Washington for Jobs and Freedom," August 28, 1963.

As President, Mr. Obama visited friendly Canada, then with his beautifully fashionable wife had tea with the Queen in England, having wowed and bowled over the British; fresh from a tumultuous welcome by the Germans he then fascinated the French, disarmed the Muslim world and had time to surprise the troops in Iraq he led as their Commander-In-Chief. Moving on to Trinidad he stood up to Hugo Chavez of Venezuela and told Ahmenidjad of Iran to behave or else! Now, having assuaged the world and changed its image of America, President Obama returned home to the wrath of Republicans, viz., McConnell, DeMint, Joe Wilson and all subscribers consistent with the "McConnell Mandate!"

First, Governor Mitt Romney at the time of the 2012 Olympics in London visited that country. Having greatly exploited the "Romney saved the Olympics" slogan, he arrived amidst the hustle and bustle of Olympics preparations. We should not forget, for any nation to host the Olympics its an honor and source of national pride and so, not a single American would cast a vote against any attempt to "Save the Olympics." That is to say, 101 percent of Americans cast their support behind Governor Romney's attempts. Yet, misconstruing this reality, Mr. Romney arrogantly believed and parleyed "he built that" single-handedly. It is an arrogance and bloated ego Mr. Romney took on his trip to London.

Perhaps it was Jet Lag that caused Mr. Romney, upon landing in London, to begin insulting the British by telling them how to prepare for the Olympics and whether they were doing a good job. We must keep in mind, the Winter Olympics in America, Governor Romney "Saved" was smaller in scope than the Summer Olympics in London where more nations participated. Despite anarchists, activists and terrorists active in the free British society, there were no incidents to report and events went on peacefully. From London, Governor Romney moved on to

OBAMA - MASTER AND COMMANDER

Poland where his "people" verbally "roughed up" reporters seeking answers to questions he would not answer. Whereas, on his part Mr. Obama was generating "rock star" status crowds, people in London were hoping Mr. Romney move on quickly. Next the traveling politician visited Israel, visiting the significant and historic religious sites to be "seen "really, in an effort to "pander to Jewish voters" in America. It is interesting, in the Third Presidential Debate, as he continued to falsely portray that Mr. Obama's "Muslim Tour" constantly "apologized" for America" and that the President "did not visit Israel while he was in the Middle East!"

Obama - Master and Commander 499. The same Ionic capital columns in the Lincoln Memorial as the Thomas Jefferson Memorial but not as ostentatious.

FREDERICK MONDERSON

Obama - Master and Commander 500. Mural on the wall of the Lincoln Memorial praising Native Americans.

Obama - Master and Commander 501. Mural of enthroned female figure with female assistants at the Lincoln Memorial.

Obama - Master and Commander 502. Mural of a winged Native American figure at the Lincoln Memorial.

OBAMA - MASTER AND COMMANDER

Obama - Master and Commander 503. Tribute to Abraham Lincoln in his Memorial that reads: "In this Temple as in the hearts of the people for whom he saved the Union the memory of Abraham Lincoln is enshrined Forever."

Obama - Master and Commander 504. Majesty and power among Native Americans.

Rightfully, Mr. Obama indicated you can't visit every country on a single visit. It is equally wise to not visit opposing countries and contradict what one says in each for political expediency sake. Mr. Obama did make it clear when he visited Israel, he did not visit the "Tourist spots" but the more significant venues commemorating the suffering of the Jewish people so as to better understand the inhumanity of man to man. More importantly, in the devastating punch line, Mr. Obama slammed, "When I visited Israel, I did not take donors and hold fundraisers!" So, we must constantly ask about the proper behavior of American leaders abroad and whether they embarrass America or come away with people such as Queen Elizabeth telling Barack and Michelle, "Come back soon" or hoping "Mitt and Ann" would not come back!

FREDERICK MONDERSON

53. PRESIDENT OBAMA ON DR. KING
By
Dr. Fred Monderson

Unveiling of the Martin Luther King Memorial on the Great Lawn of Washington, D.C., marked a milestone of epic proportions in recognizing the genius, profoundly philosophic, spiritual and resolute creativity of the man, the Civil Rights icon, whose words changed America. It also recognizes the organizational abilities of the Organizing Committee who put such a venture together that not simply praises Dr. King, his remarkable leadership but also recognizes the inner strengths, vision, determination of the man and how he galvanized a movement, empowered a generation of men and women to assume roles of leadership that benefitted a race, neutralized the horrific onslaught of "dye in the wool racists" in and outside of public life, by his insistence of simple slogans resulting in effectuating profound changes in the American body political and social institutions across this great land.

Obama - Master and Commander 505. Close-up of the female winged figure holding hands and uniting two Native American people.

54. SPEAKING FOR GOD!
By
Dr. Fred Monderson

From time memorial a certain genre of men and women have professed to "Speak for God" in revealing his thoughts, commandments and covenants. Within recent memory, however, people have revealed or have their followers believe "they are god," "sent by god," or have even "spoken to god." However, even more recently, some have even claimed to "speak for god" and not being "men of the cloth" this has seemed to trivialize the experience leading to skepticism in divine-human

OBAMA - MASTER AND COMMANDER

interaction, questioning whether god exists or whether people are really playing politics with god or exploiting politics in god's name. Despite misguided teachings, the general consensus is that god does exist and first appeared to Africans along the Nile at a time some 300,000 years ago. As one of the earliest organized societies with a record of religious belief and practice, the ancient Egyptians pinpointed god's earliest earthly home and the place of their origins. Accordingly, a 19th Dynasty nobleman's funeral book, the *Papyrus of Hunefer* states as to the origins of the ancient Egyptians, "We came from the headwaters of the Nile River at the foothills of the Mountains of the Moon where the God Hapi dwells." This area has been identified as the East African plains beside Mounts Kenya, Kilimanjaro and Ruwenzori. It's generally believed the ancient Egyptian society experienced millennia of evolutionary development before the first dynasty's Unification given c. 3100 B.C. though some scholars date this happening of Unification at least a thousand years earlier at 4241 B.C. when the calendar was generally believed invented. However, the people of Nabta Playa, a region to the south-east of Egypt who were unquestionably the first astronomers may have in fact invented the calendar sometime after 20,000 B.C. Equally, we know the Egyptians possessed a precession time cycle of some 26,000 years that some scholars have argued, to dat one required two, three, possibly a fourth such cycles for measurement, extending for a period of first 26,000; then 52,000; 78,000; and possibly 104,000 years of African star-gazing; still less than the period of the 300,000 year intellectual of consciousness of divinely inspired recognition because this phenomenon of divine/human interaction was first taking place in the Central African region. Interesting, thousands of years later, we can trace Barack Obama's heritage to this area! Thus, we can ask the reader to determine whether Barack Hussein Obama's lineage is divine!

The ancient "Egyptian Bible," the New Kingdom *Book of the Dead* by way of the Middle Kingdom *Coffin Text* that evolved from the thousand of years in the making Old Kingdom *Pyramid Texts*, show evidence of their religious beliefs dating back millennia before Unification. One important early Egyptologist has argued, the earliest architects were priests, who, in contact with divinity was instructed as to what type of dwelling to build to house the God's corporal form on earth. Priestly functions grew into a powerful priestly body, the Priesthood. As the king was considered the Son of God, his earthly representative and a god on earth; he had to officiate in the temples in ritual straddling the spiritual and temporal realms, between the divine and human forms. Since he could not perform all the rituals in all the temples at the same time, his stand-in became the priest. Each temple had a chief priest and the Priesthood, as a national religious body had a chief or high priest. In fact, there was a chief priest for each of the four principal religious centers where the four principal deities resided and were worshipped, viz., Ra at Heliopolis; Ptah at Memphis; Amun at Karnak; and Osiris at Abydos. Even at Assuit where Thoth, the intellect, chronographer and legal eagle of the gods resided as head of the Ogdoad, these centers each had a priesthood that ritualized their god, interpreted his commands and spoke for him as did all the chief priests of the respective temples.

The king was recognized as the legitimate successor to the first God King Horus and strong pharaohs exploited this fact. They became imperial conquerors who won booty and tribute and endowed the priesthood by supplying food and bulls for sacrifice at the festivals as well as building temples for the worship of the gods. The kings also built temples to worship themselves, for upon death they joined the realm of the divine beings. Weak kings, on the other hand, were unsure of their own divinity and unsure how much the priests knew relative to their connection with divinity, and thus they trembled in the presence of priests who spoke for God and knew what god meant and wanted!

The reverence of these divine voices continued down through the ages though charlatans have exploited the position of author even giving bad decisions and advice. Some have become involved in the more mundane acquisition of wealth and social power. Dr. Martin Luther King railed against hippocritical religious worship and secular materialism critiquing the classic admonition "Praise God but pass the ammunition!"

America proved an animal of a different breed even though the state was founded on the principles of a Christian nation under the separation of church and state notion. At the time of independence, practitioners of the institution of slavery denied the humanity of blacks, the mono-genesis theory and that "these Africans were not children of god." This position was enshrined in the mentality of founding fathers who were themselves slaveholders under the practicing institution of slavery. In fact, the "inferiority of the Negro" genetically, physically and socially, permenated all facets of the society. As such, Dr. ben-Jochannan has always pointed out, racism and religious bigotry is at the foundation of western and Christian religious practice. Such practice was instrumental in forcing the creation of the African Methodist Episcopal Church in the early 19th Century.

In recent times, Reverends claimed to have spoken to and "spoke for god." While both are "men of the cloth," Jerry Falwell prognosticated on political matters but Pat Robinson practiced the political craft, even seeking the U.S. Presidency. There have also been cases where Republican politicians, in trouble with the electorate, "trot out" Pat Robinson as part of their apologetic strategy spin. Now, the newest generation of aspirants to this highest office added refinement, to the "speaking for god" spin.

OBAMA - MASTER AND COMMANDER

Obama - Master and Commander 506. The names of states as part of the decoration on the cornice of the Lincoln Memorial.

Obama - Master and Commander 507. The names of states as part of the decoration on the cornice of the Lincoln Memorial.

FREDERICK MONDERSON

Obama - Master and Commander 508. The names of states as part of the decoration on the cornice of the Lincoln Memorial.

Obama - Master and Commander 509. The names of states as part of the decoration on the cornice of the Lincoln Memorial.

OBAMA - MASTER AND COMMANDER

Obama - Master and Commander 510. Two winged horses line the bridge towards Arlington Cemetery.

Michele Bachmann was one of the first out of the gates in the 2012 political primary season. Embolden by her Iowa Caucus win, she emphatically announced, "God told me to run" for the United States Presidency. This revelation may force listeners to believe God's direct intervention into human affairs as he became busy picking candidates for national leadership across the many nations of the globe. This being the case, he must have certainly expressed interest at the state and local level in America also. However, finding no traction as her campaign began to falter in the Republican Presidential Primary, critics pounced, enquiring as to why god did not give Ms. Bachmannn the wherewithal, viz., money, gifted advisers, stamina, volunteers in significant numbers, strategists, and all that was necessary for a god ordained victory! When god want you to win or do somehting he provides the resources. After all, he told Abraham to "look in the bushes" for the sacrificial lamb. As such, some observers could argue "God lost this one" as Ms. Bachmann exited the contest, yet struggled to remain visible and viable in events and issues surrounding the 2012 presidential election.

Ann Romney was another "spokesperson for god" when she proclaimed "God told" her husband, "Mitt Romney to run for the Presidency." Unlike Ms. Bachmannn, in as much as Mr. Romney, viz., won the Republican contest, in a field of weak candidates, his track record in a previous run for the Presidency created a national campaign structure. However, possessing great wealth with an ability to attract supporters and donors from the wealthy class, disarming many who questioned the legitimacy of his Mormon religion and in turn galvanizing the religious right and possessing only one ticket to the big dance; Republicans had no choice than to stand behind Mitt, being the "best of a bad lot!" Then the Romney campaign machinery took off.

That is not to say Mr. Romney's Primary opponents had not sought the god connection, for Texas Governor Rick Perry was endorsed by a Bishop at a Baptist Convention while simultaneously disparaging Mr. Romney's religion as a cult. So much so, the other Mormon in the race dismissed the Bishop as being a "moron" for criticizing Mormonism. Much later, Evangelist Billy Graham, who for eons advertised the Mormon religion as a "Cult," recently removed the sign. After his Richard Nixon endorsement, Mr. Graham vowed to stay out of politics. Now, well up in age, Mr. Graham is purportedly making politico-religious statements and endorsements forcing thinking Americans to wonder if its the man or are surrogates using his name to essentially support Mr. Obama's rivals. Nevertheless, religion has always played a crucial role in American politics, for besides, kissing babies, candidates visit churches seeing pastoral endorsement and the visibility their presence portray with the congregation and potential voters. Equally, if the candidate is a member of a large church or a national religious body and any such affiliation this may have, it generally proves beneficial to the candidacy of the particular politician. However, while association may have positive benefits, there is a down-side as well.

Obama - Master and Commander 511. The names of states as part of the decoration on the cornice of the Lincoln Memorial.

OBAMA - MASTER AND COMMANDER

Obama - Master and Commander 512. The names of states as part of the decoration on the cornice of the Lincoln Memorial.

Obama - Master and Commander 513. The names of states as part of the decoration on the cornice of the Lincoln Memorial.

FREDERICK MONDERSON

Obama - Master and Commander 514. The names of states as part of the decoration on the cornice of the Lincoln Memorial.

In the 2008 Presidential Campaign, then Senator Barack Obama had been a member of a Chicago based religious institution headed by Reverend Jeremiah Wright. The media exposed excerpts from taped sermons of the Reverend which in inflammatory flourishes Mr. Wright castigated America for past and present wrongs especially towards African people. Opponents quickly characterized these utterances as anti-American; never mind the context; and sought to tie the two individuals in an effort to derail Mr. Obama's candidacy. The rest is known. Fast-forward to 2012, both President Obama and Mr. Romney have pledged to keep religion out of politics. However, while not slinging religion, these individuals attend church services, for a great theorist once said, "Politicians must be seen attending church on Sunday!"

However, while the "church angle" is good politics, ridiculously exploiting this connection smacks of nothing but ludicrous charlatanism. Case in point! At the 2012 Democratic Political Convention their platform plank seems to have unintentionally omitted the word "God" and even "Israel." Republicans and other commentators pounced on what was called an "oversight" that was subsequently corrected. The propagated implication is that Obama was "declaring war on God" and by extension, failure to mention Israel meant that he was throwing America's strongest ally in the Middle East, "under the bus." To recall, President Obama's paternal heritage is linked to where God dwelt and thus, to accuse Mr. Obama of "declaring war on God" is more than a stretch, its "dirty pool," I mean "dirty politics!" Yet still, President Obama has consistently declared his religious affiliation as Christian while trumpeting America's tolerance for all forms of

OBAMA - MASTER AND COMMANDER

religious worship. This is significant, particularly in view of the most recent catastrophe having to do with falsely characterizing the Muslim prophet Mohammed. Notwithstanding, Mr. Obama has consistently reaffirmed his faith, tolerance and belief in God. the conundrum her is that while elements accused mr. Obama of being a longstanding member of Reverend Jeremiah Wright's church. they still accuse him of being a Muslim!

Governor Romney stood with Pat Robinson to castigate President Obama in a shameless attempt to use religion for political gain because of the Democratic platform plank. Since Pat Robinson speaks to and for God, Mr. Romney should have first enquired of him whether God had any opinion on the matter. Another line of spurious attack on Mr. Obama is that he has essentially abandoned Israel, because he has expressed some disagreement with the Israeli Prime Minister. Though Ehud Barak speaks glowingly about President Obama's continued support for his nation, more so than any other American leader. Even family members sometimes disagree and perhaps Mr. Romney has had some disagreement with the Prime Minister. However, this line of political pandering is below the pale since the former Prime Minister Ehud Barak has consistently offered the view, "Mr. Obama has been one of the most ardent supporters of Israel."

Obama - Master and Commander 515. Close-up of the two winged horses lining the bridge towards Arlington Cemetery.

FREDERICK MONDERSON

Obama - Master and Commander 516. The sign directs to Arlington Cemetery and the George Washington Memorial Parkway.

Republicans unleashed a new "War on God" line of attack. Perhaps the "War on God" attack line was a continuation of the President's insistence religious affiliated organizations must provide birth control support for their employees. Let us not forget, in the beginning, Mr. Obama was accused of being a Muslim not against god and religion. In the Jeremiah Wright attack he was not accused of being against religion but being a member of a Christian church headed by a fiery preacher. Yet, hardly a Sunday Mr. Obama is not observed attending church with his family. Clearly then, he is religious and as such, god-fearing! Therefore, how can he declare war on God! As such, some people shamelessly exploit God's name for political gain but astute observers see them really as charlatans and opportunists misusing the name of God!

OBAMA - MASTER AND COMMANDER

Obama - Master and Commander 517. John Ericsson Memorial.

55. Not 1979
By
Dr. Fred Monderson

A number of important developments resulted from the events of the 1979 taking of the American Embassy staff hostage and holding these diplomats for 444 days. Naturally, President Carter's failed military rescue taught military planners some valuable lessons in conducting this type of mission that proved so successful decades later in the assault on Osama bin-Laden's compound. The award winning ABC news broadcast **Nightline** grew out of the earlier version "America Held Hostage" under the leadership of news-broadcaster Ted Koppel. While the ongoing hostage debacle aided by Kennedy's attacks enabled Ronald Reagan, the Hollywood icon, to become President, the long-lasting dastard-deed and Reagan's persona instilled a fear that he would do the unthinkable and this forced the Iranians to give up their captives the instant he assumed the reins of power.

FREDERICK MONDERSON

However, while the Iranians continued to spew anti-American venom on their domestic platform, in the eyes of the international community, the nation had crossed the line!

At the world leaders gathering for the 2012 annual United Nations meeting, the current Iranian leader Mahmoud Ahmadinejad ranted anti-American and anti-Israeli flourishes while trying to extol the ancient nature of Iran's culture, etc. Interesting that, prior to the hostage taking, the modern world respected Iran as the earliest nation to respect and provide protection for diplomats and diplomatic missions in ancient times. The hostage taking and seizure of the American Embassy contravened that powerful and historical ideal the Iranian nation had given birth to. Nevertheless, all these events notwithstanding, for Governor Romney and his campaign personnel, in attacking President Obama in wake of the Libya assault and killing of the Ambassador and three other Americans, as they tried to equate events of the two time periods is somewhat disingenuous, for a number of reasons. First, while one event was sustained for more than a year and that President Carter exhausted all reasonable options to not endanger the lives of the numerous hostages; the other was of very short duration and lost of 4 lives, the events that precipitated the outburst were completely different.

Second, the world had changed tremendously between 1979/1980 and 2012; technologically, the shrinking of the globe and the manifestation of a revolution in people's thinking and thought equally recognizes there is a war on terror and the notion of the embassy remains inviolate.

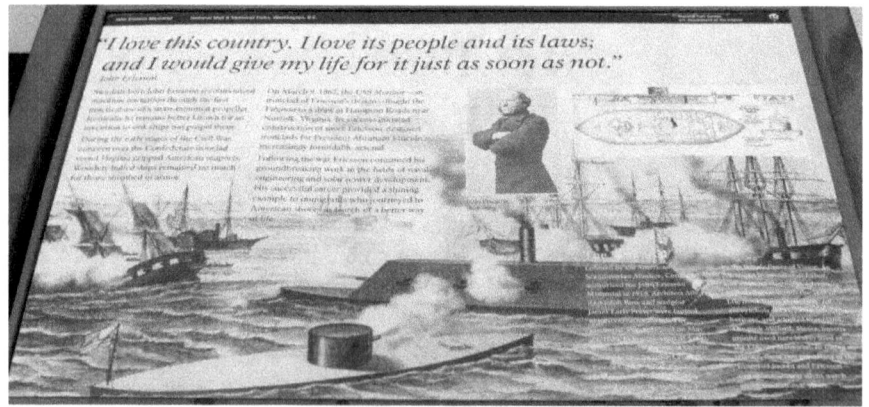

Obama - Master and Commander 518. John Ericsson. (1803-1889). The man who said: "I love this country. I love its people and its laws; and I would give my life for it just as soon as not."

OBAMA - MASTER AND COMMANDER

Obama - Master and Commander 519. Government building with Doric columns.

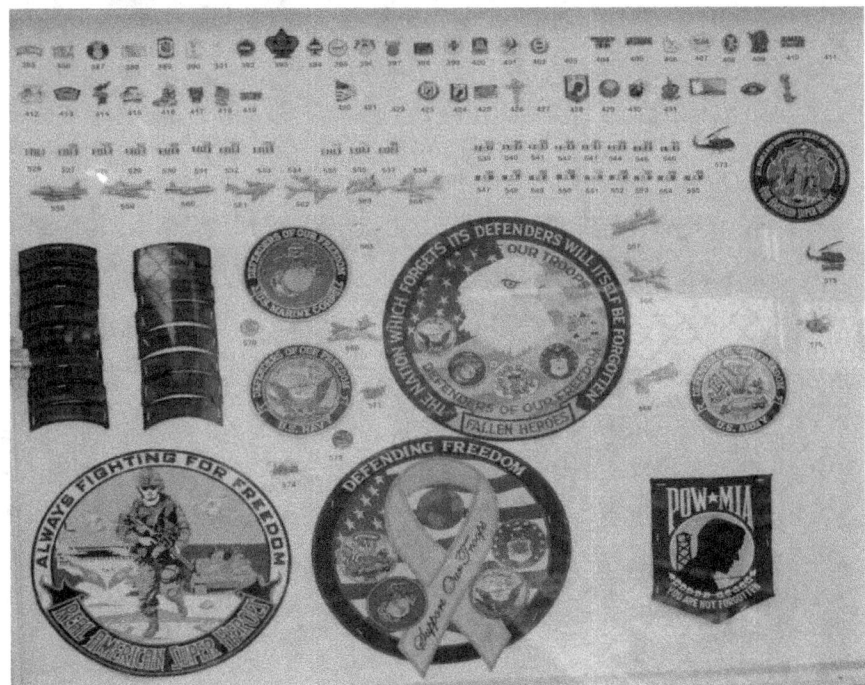

Obama - Master and Commander 520. Insignias of the forces the Commander readily have at his disposal.

FREDERICK MONDERSON

Obama - Master and Commander 521. Insignias of the forces the Commander readily have at his disposal.

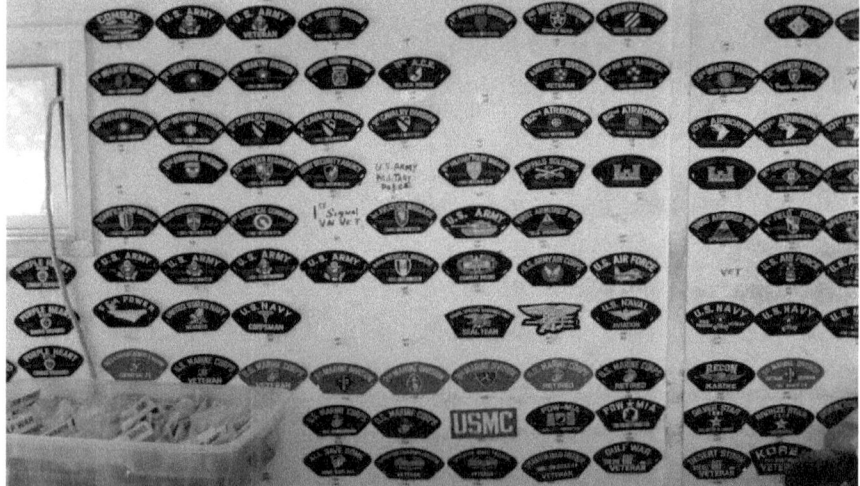

Obama - Master and Commander 522. More of the insignias the forces at the service of the Commander-In-Chief.

OBAMA - MASTER AND COMMANDER

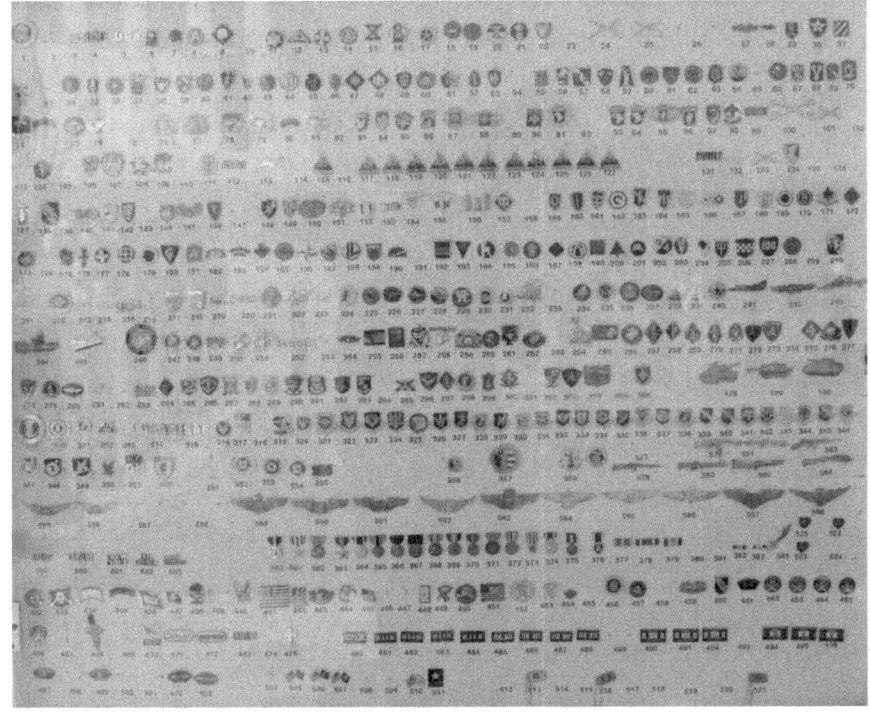

Obama - Master and Commander 523. Dress insignias of the Commander's forces.

Third, while there was a principal, albeit religious, figure coordinating events in Ayatollah Khomeini who solidified the revolution and opposition to American support for the Shaw Riza Pahlevi, there was no such unifying figure in Libya. At play were a hodgepodge of militant groups, militias, held-over from the revolution who had coalesced in opposition to the Khadafy regime. Thus, though they were in the process of consolidating the government, the revolution was far from solidifying leadership and security having armed hotheads crisscrossing the country establishing rules of law to their liking.

Fourth, while in Iran anti-Americanism gave vent to the revolution before a captive audience and Americans could only watch from a distance; the deceased Ambassador and his team had been instrumental in guiding the success of the rebels; and after their victory, in helping to formulate policy, cementing foreign relations and helping to shape Libya's future.

FREDERICK MONDERSON

Fifth, in Iran the revolution and seizure of the hostages was championed and directed by a domestic movement with participation from the national military apparatus, many of whom changed allegiance from the Shaw to the Ayatollah. They stood in alliance with some disaffected soldiers, students and mullahs of the Ayatollah's brigade. This was not so in Libya! While the Iranian revolution was a single and isolated incident in a vast region, the revolt in Libya was part of an international rebellious movement dubbed the "Arab Spring" where success in one country emboldened other participants in another. Equally, while the thrust of the Iranian rebellion was a domestic revolt against the status quo, the United States and NATO forces in an international effort aided the Libyan rebels and this contributed to their success. Again, the Libyan revolt involved foreign fighters of which elements of Al Qaeda were participants. Thus, once victory was assured, the drawn out process of creating a national military force with accountability as part of the nation's goals and responsibilities had not been accomplished and purportedly armed militants with ties abroad may have been instructed to launch the assault because of recent American gains against the war on terror, particularly around the time of the anniversary of "September 11th." Like a cop investigating a crime, no nation's intelligence can predict every course of action by opponents nor "friendly fire" developments before they happen. One of the reasons why the perpetrators of 9/11 were successful, America always guarded against foreign attacks and similarly the insidious filmmaker blind-sided the nation with his smut. The lurking "dark forces" took advantage of this, the legitimate protests and launched their assault. There is reason to believe Al Qaeda wanted to make a splash on the 9/11 anniversary.

Sixth, America was not at war in the throes of the Iranian revolution but during the "Arab Spring," with forces deployed in Iraq, Afghanistan, elsewhere in Africa and challenging Somali Pirates, albeit successfully, in all theaters of operation, it is sophistry to claim a lack of leadership at this time.

Seventh, while the Iranian nation stagnated in their anti-Americanism rancor during the hostage crisis, so much so, in three decades they were suppressing their own people seeking change through the ballot box. However, in Libya, the people stood up, challenged and chased the militant perpetrators of the crime. Unlike Iran, the Libyans became enlightened, perhaps they were moved by the great loss of the American Ambassador's efforts and remembering how the world aided their cause. Thus, they chose a more rational and constructive approach rather than be constrained by the archaic albatross of militant beliefs the civilized world frowns upon.

Eighth, while President Jimmy Carter didn't have to face the military challenges posed to Barack Obama and so had no such success in this respect; Mr. Obama could boast of his efforts to contend and end the Iraq and Afghanistan conflicts,

OBAMA - MASTER AND COMMANDER

decimation of Al Qaeda and killing of Osama bin-Laden and curtailing Somali Pirates' activities. Certainly, this is demonstrated leadership!

Obama - Master and Commander 524 Civil War Memorial.

Obama - Master and Commander 525. Civil War Memorial. Important battles of the conflict.

Obama - Master and Commander 526. Civil War Memorial. Important battles of the conflict.

FREDERICK MONDERSON

Obama - Master and Commander 527. Civil War Memorial. Important battles of the conflict.

Obama - Master and Commander 528. Civil War Memorial. Important battles of the conflict.

Ninth, while President Carter could not boast of any equally world challenging activities on his watch, Mr. Obama's realization of the role Islam plays in the modern world, his outreach for better relations and calls for justice therein in Turkey and Cairo speeches must get him some credit for encouraging a climate that changed gthe world's view of America and spawned the "Arab Spring" which disengaged dictators in Tunisia, Libya, Egypt, forced changes in Yemen and encouraged, though not successfully so far, the aspirations of the people of Syria. Certainly, therefore, Mr. Obama's stature gets some credit. In the movie **Ten Commandments**, despite its falsity and misguided representation, Joshua told Moses, "Stand on the high ground and extend your arms so the people will see your silhouette and have hope;" the story of Mr. Obama's influence in these developments has hardly been told, though many have not lost hope in his leadership. It was leadership that changed the world's perception of America after the Republican tenure. It was leadership that rescued the nation's economy from its downhill plunge in bank failure, Wall Street contraction, escalating housing industry hemorrhaging, the rising numbers in job losses, runaway credit card interest rates, troublesome numbers in student loans, etc. Despite what has been

OBAMA - MASTER AND COMMANDER

said, stimulus dollars saved the day and Wall Street bailout enabled the Dow to rebound to double what it was when Mr. Obama first took office. It was the same leadership that has allowed Vice President Joe Biden to boast, "General Motors is alive and Osama bin-Laden is dead!"

Tenth, it is amazing leadership that Mr. Obama could conceive of and campaign for and pass affordable Health Care Reform that Republicans facetiously and maliciously call "Obama Care" as well as the equally significant Lilly Ledbetter law giving women equal pay for equal work despite the work of headhunters as McConnell, DeMint, Santorum and Gingrich. Thus, when Governor Romney seeks to equate events of 1979 with development of 2012, perhaps he should read this piece, otherwise he needs better advisers or he should stick to the things he knows well such as "saving the Olympics," out-sourcing under Bain Capital, banking overseas and maintaining accounts in the Bahamas and Switzerland as well as changing his position on issues as a chameleon changes his colors.

Obama - Master and Commander 529. Civil War Memorial. Important battles of the conflict.

Obama - Master and Commander 530. Civil War Memorial. Important battles of the conflict.

FREDERICK MONDERSON

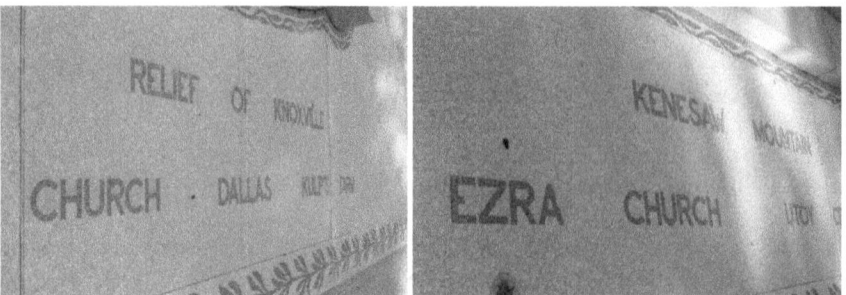

Obama - Master and Commander 531. Civil War Memorial. Important battles of the conflict.

56. Here as "Eye Candy!" by Dr. Fred Monderson

After making his address to world leaders at the United Nations, President Obama, accompanied by his wife Michelle, came to ABC TV, Chanel 7, New York, as a guest of "**The View**" as he said, as "Eye Candy!" This is because **The View**, hosted by four ladies, is thought to be "a ladies show" and Mr. Obama has consistently advocated on behalf of women, particularly so in the Lilly Ledbetter Equal Pay for Equal Work legislation; the appointment of two women to the Supreme Court; his insistence on employer supplied birth control prescriptions; passed the Health Care Reform Law that substantially affects women, particularly as mothers; plus the fact he is handsome, charming, has a beautiful smile, all buttressed by his glamorous Michelle and daughters Sasha and Malia; and in New York, given these factors, **The View** this is the place to be! However, the President's opponents wanted to make "hash" out of the fact he did not meet with world leaders on a one to one basis after his speech at the U.N. He does this all the time. He just finished addressing the world leaders and his strategists believed meeting with a leader, eight leaders, a dozen leaders, would not have been sufficient. So, don't meet with any leaders individually. However, his "Eye Candy" line did not disturb Michelle for like Bess said in her song in *Porgy and Bess*, "I've got my man!"

There is no question the current political campaign is one of chest-like strategy and Mr. Obama has proved an expert at the game given his 2008 winning campaign. He has also managed to keep Republican "wolves at bay" as they seek to effectuate the "McConnell Mandate." Given every move he makes, they counter, not in the interest of the people's business, but rightfully to uphold their philosophic stance as the "Party of No" to "deny Obama a win" and to make him a "one-term president." Since he met with no world leader and they criticized him, if

OBAMA - MASTER AND COMMANDER

he met with any number Republicans would end up insisting he probably meet with every leader present whom he addressed, meet with at the G-8 Summit, practically any day at the White House or on trips abroad. Let us not forget the telephone!

Fact is, Mr. Obama remains cognizant of the multi-million dollar individual donations into his opponents coffer to take his job. However, there is an old saying, "When an opponent is self-destructing, say nothing, just observe!" In this case, young, fit and fashionable Obama decided to play "Eye Candy" games while Romney does his thing! Even more important, however, he wanted to stay in touch with his people, the "grass-lawn roots" by emphasizing how different he is to Governor Romney who will seek, if he becomes President, to eradicate every meaningful piece of legislation the President has enacted, whether Health Care Reform, "Dream Act" legislation, "Don't Ask, Don't Tell," and importantly, equality for all Americans regardless of their sexual orientation. Mr. Obama's position is thus clear, "that all Americans play by the same rules, have equal opportunity on a level playing field," "everybody doing their fair share," relishing in the hope-filled thought that the American Dream is attainable for all who so aspire. Insisting Congress pass his jobs bill, placing great emphasis on educational opportunities, hiring and retraining more teachers as well as first responders - fire and police, encouraging new breakthroughs in clean energy, focusing on environmental controls and global warming. Mr. Obama continues to lay the foundation for a brighter American future. Compare this to Mr. Romney's "Taking America Back" to Pre-Health Care Reform Status; insisting Hispanics "Self deport;" giving more to those like himself who have too much will cause nothing but bitterness in contrast to Mr. Obama's "Candy," "Eye" or otherwise; discarding nearly half of the American electorate in his disrespectful downgrade of their social status with the 47 percent remark, etc. We could add his insult of America's greatest ally, the British, in his Olympics gaffe and his insensitivity to Mr. Obama's delicately but effectively sailing the American ship of state through the changing, challenging and sometimes rough waters of the new reality in the game of nations.

Obama - Master and Commander 532. Civil War Memorial. Important battles of the conflict.

FREDERICK MONDERSON

Obama - Master and Commander 533. Sides of the Civil War Memorial.

57. "OBAMA CARES"
By
Dr. Fred Monderson

Throughout the Republican Campaign, line and staff advocated the Mantra to "Repeal Obama-Care." All along, from Day One, Republicans in and out of Congress had a principal goal to "Deny Obama a Win!" This was part of the many-pronged Grand Strategy to deny Mr. Obama a second term, or as Senator McConnell put it wearing that never-forgotten smirk on his face: "My job is to make sure President Obama does not win re-election, to be a one-term President." To accomplish such they had to obstruct every move the President made, block every legislative action he proposed, not applaud every good idea he presented in the State of the Union Addresses he gave, and then try to portray him in every respect as a weak leader with whom the American people will become disenchanted and he won't be re-elected.

Even blind persons could see there was racial animosity undergirding Republican strategy against Mr. Obama. The surprising thing in all this, the political games notwithstanding, the effete Michael Steel and Allan West shamefacedly hid and

OBAMA - MASTER AND COMMANDER

remained silent as President Barack Obama was verbally assaulted, called the most insidious names, NIGGER, and the like and perhaps, not givemagine if these men had the "Bull's balls" of a Colin Powell, who knows! No wonder these losers lost! Edmund Burke's yardstick, during the backlash of the French Revolution in 1792-93, he wrote: "The only thing necessary for evil to triumph is for good men to say nothing." Thus, using Mr. Burke's operational definition, we ask: "Are Michael Steele and Allan West good men?" But, Obama is bigger than "these two little men," many times over. Brushing aside the flakes of their *ad hominem* attacks he once admonished, "Politics is a contact sport. Let them come" and with that powerfully disarming smile he laughed off the "circus criers" because he knows, he is the reality of power in Washington, DC, this **Master and Commander**!

It was sheer brilliance for Mr. Obama to see the need for Health Care Reform, formulate a strategy to sell it across the American political landscape and once elected, pass it into law. This legislative accomplishment that eluded presidents for some six decades was indeed significant; and there is no need to reiterate Vice President Biden's platitude about the big event; for we can clearly see how Lilliputian Republicans, rather than applaud this significant social edifice; like their assaults on Mr. Obama, they seek to tear it down, despite the fact untold millions of Americans will benefit from its provisions.

This accomplishment troubled Republicans that a black Democrat could achieve this milestone, rescue the millions possessing no health care coverage and show more of an identification with the 99 rather than the 1 percent they represent. Therefore, Republicans doubled down in the fiercest obstructionist strategy as the "Party of No," as they blocked all legislative effort by the President. They unfolded a forked mantra of denying Mr. Obama a second term and propagated falsely about Health Care Reform to win support to gain Congressional advantage and overturn "Obama Care." Alas, noe of this happened in the 2012 election.

Obama - Master and Commander 534. Scene from the Civil War drama.

FREDERICK MONDERSON

Obama - Master and Commander 535. Close-Up of the Civil War Memorial.

Setting faith in the sanctity of the Supreme Court Republicans took their challenge there. With an oftentimes majority on the bench, Republicans were assured Affordable Care Act - Health Care Reform - would be overturned. Picture the

OBAMA - MASTER AND COMMANDER

"losers" Newt and Michele Bachmannn standing in the hollowed space of the Supreme Court gallery as the Chief Justice rendered his verdict!

There is something about Chief Justice Roberts when facing President Obama. Need I say more! Notwithstanding, rather than overturning "Obama Care" the supreme jurist ruled that Health Care Reform was Constitutional, even if it was a tax that even Mr. Obama's team had not envisioned. Nevertheless, at that great disappointment, Republicans in and out of the Court's chamber, viewed Chief Justice Roberts as tantamount to a "traitor" for giving the "Black guy a win!" Thus, losing in the Court of Legal Opinion, they launched a new strategy to persevere in the Court of Public Opinion in the hopes of winning a congressional majority in the upcoming election and then overturning the law, legally.

Dr. Leonard James long believed, "As a black man in a racist society, I expect to be knocked down, but as long as I answer the bell, that is all that matters!" As such, President Obama had made it clear earlier on, "Politics is a contact sport." In the wake of the recent Middle East debacle, the insulting film and widespread backlash, the President made his position clear at the United Nations.

The people who seek to overturn or repeal Obama-Care must not care much for the American people, just as Mr. Romney dismissed the 47 percent. Well, for the some 50 million without health care and the millions more who will benefit from this legislation, I suppose they would honestly say, "Thank God Obama Cares!"

Obama - Master and Commander 536. Civil War Memorial. Generals Ransom and Dodge of the Civil War.

FREDERICK MONDERSON

Obama - Master and Commander 537. Civil War Memorial. Generals Logan and Blair of the Civil War.

Obama - Master and Commander 538. Civil War Memorial. Generals Howard and McPherson of the Civil War.

Obama - Master and Commander 539. Another look at the Civil War Memorial.

58. THREE AMIGOS AND HEALTH CARE
By
Dr. Fred Monderson

Very few men in significant public life have had a champion of substance who made a difference in his quest for the great prize. Barack Hussein Obama was fortunate to have two such stalwarts in his corner.

The argument is plausible that Senator Teddy Kennedy, the "Lion of the Senate," who, in endorsing the young Obama felt he had passed the torch to capable hands and with the wherewithal of his campaign wizardry, the young leader became President of the United States, a significant accomplishment for an African American. Former President Bill Clinton added the icing on the cake to make that first win possible.

The second time around, Bill Clinton has loomed large in his support for President Obama. He understands the issues, has seen Barack's plans and strategies, having

FREDERICK MONDERSON

"been there and done that," he has put his full faith and weight behind the President's re-election. Mr. Clinton has bolstered this by publicly affirming he strongly believes the President will be re-elected! How fortunate Mr. Obama has been to have these two extraordinary stalwarts championing his cause because they discern the Presidential timber in the mountain of a man, Barack Obama. However, this recognition and support did not come easily for Mr. Obama has had to demonstrate the courage, wisdom, foresight and steady nerves that it takes to convince the best to stand by him.

Not only has President Clinton been able to understand Barack's playbook, perhaps it is because some of the advisers of the one supports the other. Even more important, Republican strategy of scorched earth and obstructionism against Barack Obama is a carbon copy of their attacks on Bill. And, just as he weathered that storm and turned back the opposition in fighting the good fight, Barack Obama has trumped his opponents returning their punt for a touchdown.

Obama - Master and Commander 540. Here's another Civil War Memorial.

OBAMA - MASTER AND COMMANDER

Obama - Master and Commander 541. A water-spour with the Capital Police on guard, as always.

Obama - Master and Commander 541a. Coat of Arms and more Coat of Arms on the outer wall of Constitution Hall.

FREDERICK MONDERSON

Obama - Master and Commander 542. The Second Division Memorial to their dead in World War I (1917-1919).

OBAMA - MASTER AND COMMANDER

Obama - Master and Commander 543. The Second Division Memorial to their dead in World War I (1917-1919) and the places where they fought.

FREDERICK MONDERSON

Obama - Master and Commander 544. The Second Division Memorial to their dead in World War I (1917-1919).

Obama - Master and Commander 545. Memorial to the Men of the Library of Congress who died in World War I, 1918.

OBAMA - MASTER AND COMMANDER

59. "SMOKING JOE BIDEN"
By
Dr. Fred Monderson

In the recent Vice-Presidential debate, Joe Biden came to stop the perceived momentum of the Romney/Ryan team, to "Rope a Dope," and that is exactly what he did; taking a page from Mohammed Ali as that champion outlasted George Foreman in their famous fight.

For years, observers have decried the role of the Vice-President as having only one legitimate function, that is, besides "waiting for the President to drop dead!" As President of the Senate, he just sits enjoying the view until the body is dead-locked 50-50 in which case he casts the deciding vote to break the tie! Of course, the Vice-President represents the President at some social functions, in cases of national disaster situations and remains on point when the President leaves the country. Naturally, as successor to the President, if he, the President is incapacitated, the Constitution details the Vice-President succeeds. This latter is interesting!

When President Ronald Reagan was shot by John Hinckley in 1981, it was understood "Daddy Bush," his Vice President should Constitutionally have succeeded his incapacitated boss. Immediately General Haig, the Secretary of State publicly stated, "I'm in charge!" Of course he jumped the gun in attempting to calm the nation, put the Russians on notice our defenses were up and to any potential adversaries, "Don't try anything!"

The good-natured-ness of the act and statement became lost as the Secretary was pilloried and ultimately lost his job because he verbally jumped ahead of the Vice-President in the Succession arrangement.

For example, after the assassination of President John Kennedy, Vice-President Lyndon B. Johnson succeeded him and as the Documentary showed, he took the Oath of Office aboard Air Force One, standing beside Jackie Kennedy to portray continuity in leadership and policy. This one photo proved instrumental in his pushing legislation to create the "Great Society" programs of the president. However, as such, the Vice-President is generally a favorite to succeed the President in the next election. It worked for "Daddy Bush" after Reagan but it did not work for Al Gore after Clinton in 2000. "George Junior" won with assistance from the Supreme Court and thus setting the stage for the calamitous conundrum he left to Barak Obama. However, this time in the Vice Presidential Debate, Joe Biden came to contribute his effort to stem the momentum his opponents had begun to build. As such then, Biden's strategy of questioning, challenging, roping the dope, proved successful in certainly slowing if not stopping Paul Ryan's intellectual express.

Obama - Master and Commander 546. In the World War II Memorial, the emblem of World War II.

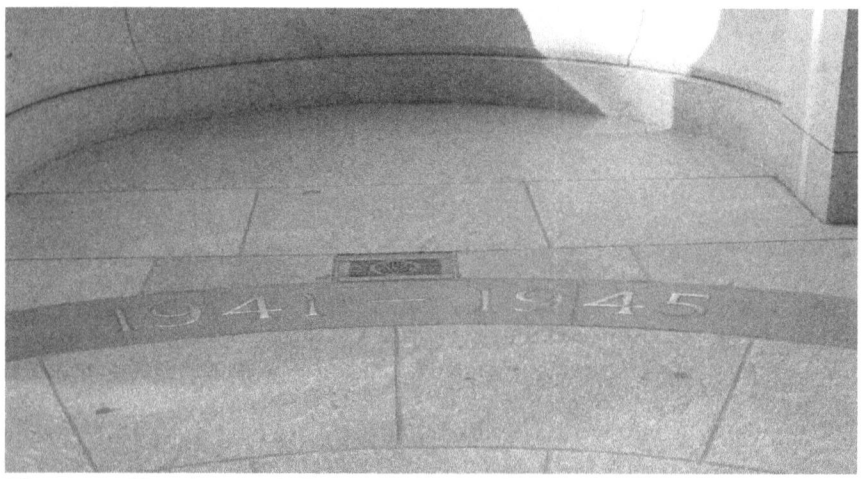

Obama - Master and Commander 547. The duration of World War II from America's involvement beginning on December 7, 1941 to victory in 1945.

OBAMA - MASTER AND COMMANDER

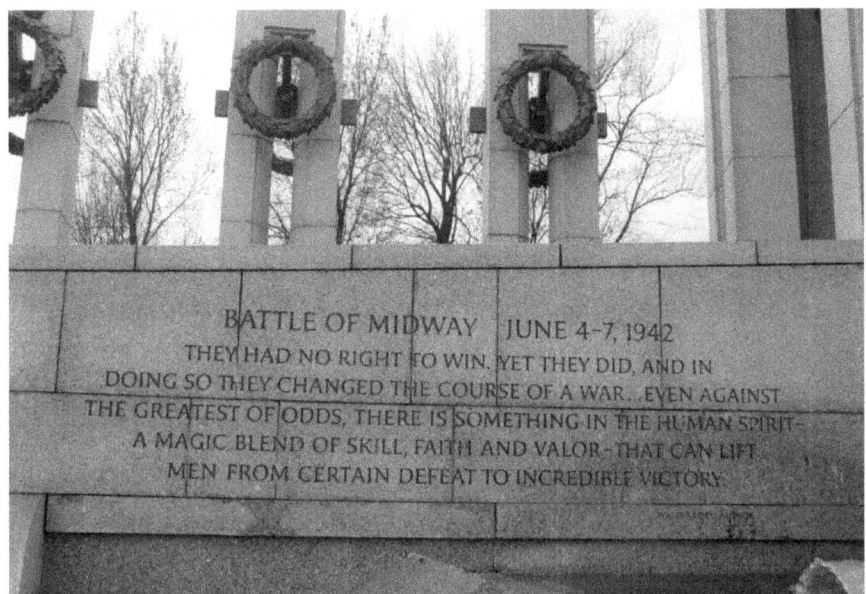

Obama - Master and Commander 548. " **Battle of Midway**" June 4-7, 1942. The Inscription rads: "They had no right to win. yet they did, and in doing so they changed the course of a war. ... Even against the greatest of odds, there is something in the human spirit - a magic blend of skill, faith and valor - That can lift men from certain defeat to incredible victory."

Obama - Master and Commander 549. World War II Memorial to battles fought on the Atlantic and Pacific sides of the nation.

FREDERICK MONDERSON

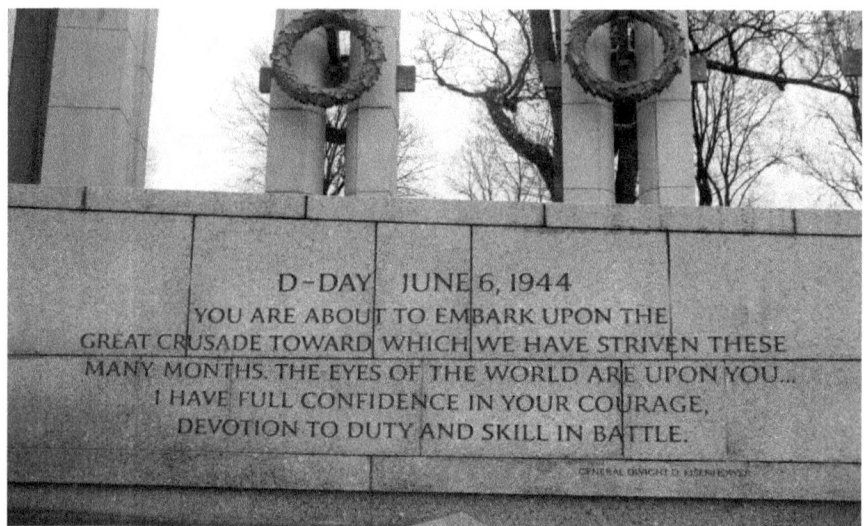

Obama - Master and Commander 550. D-Day June 6, 1944. The Inscription reads: "You are about to embark upon the great crusade toward which we have striven these many months. The eyes of the world are upon you. I have full confidence in your courage, devotion to duty and skill in battle." General Dwight D. Eisenhower

Obama - Master and Commander 551. Wreaths on the "Pacific" side of the Memorial.

OBAMA - MASTER AND COMMANDER

Obama - Master and Commander 552. Looking toward the Pacific Arch through the Antlantic Arch.

Obama - Master and Commander 553. More of the Atlantic wreath with the Pacific wreaths in the rear.

FREDERICK MONDERSON

Obama - Master and Commander 554. Looking through the Atlantic Arch past the Fountain towards the Pacific Arch at the World War II Memorial fought on the Atlantic and Pacific sides of the nation.

OBAMA - MASTER AND COMMANDER

Obama - Master and Commander 555. Looking at the Pacific Arch at the World War II Memorial commemorating the battles fought on that side of the nation.

FREDERICK MONDERSON

Obama - Master and Commander 556. World War II Memorial. The Inscription reads: "Pearl Harbor - December 7, 1941, a date which will live in infamy … No matter how long it may take us to overcome this premeditated invasion, the American people in their righteous might will win through to absolute victory." President Franklin D. Roosevelt

OBAMA - MASTER AND COMMANDER

> THEY HAVE GIVEN THEIR SONS TO THE MILITARY SERVICES. THEY HAVE STOKED THE FURNACES AND HURRIED THE FACTORY WHEELS. THEY HAVE MADE THE PLANES AND WELDED THE TANKS, RIVETED THE SHIPS AND ROLLED THE SHELLS.
>
> PRESIDENT FRANKLIN D. ROOSEVELT

Obama - Master and Commander 557. World War II Memorial. The Dedication to mothers and women in general reads as follows: "They have given their sons to the military services. They have stoked the furnaces and hurried the factory wheels. They have made the planes and welded the tanks, riveted the ships and rolled the shells." President Franklin D. Roosevelt

FREDERICK MONDERSON

> THE HEROISM OF OUR OWN TROOPS... WAS MATCHED BY THAT OF THE ARMED FORCES OF THE NATIONS THAT FOUGHT BY OUR SIDE... THEY ABSORBED THE BLOWS... AND THEY SHARED TO THE FULL IN THE ULTIMATE DESTRUCTION OF THE ENEMY.
>
> PRESIDENT HARRY S TRUMAN

Obama - Master and Commander 558. World War II Memorial. The Inscription reads: "The heroism of our own troops ... was matched by that of the armed forces of the nations that fought by our side. They absorbed the blows and they shared to the full in the ultimate destruction of the enemy." President Harry S. Truman.

OBAMA - MASTER AND COMMANDER

Obama - Master and Commander 559. World War II Memorial. The Inscription reads: "Our debt to the heroic men and valiant women in the service of our country can never be repaid. They have earned our undying gratitude. America will never forget their sacrifices." President Harry S. Truman

FREDERICK MONDERSON

Obama - Master and Commander 560. The Allies fought to obtain "Victory at Sea."

Obama - Master and Commander 561. The Allies fought to obtain "Victory in the Air."

OBAMA - MASTER AND COMMANDER

Obama - Master and Commander 562. The Allies fought to obtain "Victory on Land."

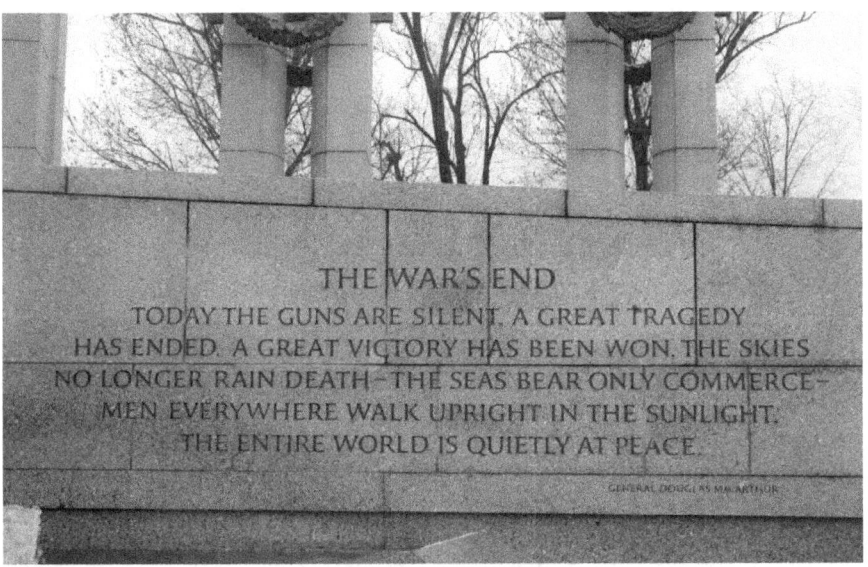

Obama - Master and Commander 563. The Inscription reads: "The War's end. Today the guns are silent. A great tragedy has ended. A great victory has been won. The skies no longer rain death. - The seas bear only commerce. Men everywhere walk upright in the sunlight. The entire world is quietly at peace." General Douglas MacArthur.

FREDERICK MONDERSON

Obama - Master and Commander 564. Mightily the fountain water spout accentuates the segment representing the Pacific portion of the World War II campaign.

60. "TOO CLOSE TO CALL"
By
Dr. Fred Monderson

Too many people hide behind the "Too close to call" obfuscation when asked about the results of the impending 2012 presidential election in which former Massachusetts Governor Mitt Romney, the Republican, is challenging the Democrat President Barack Obama. In contest after contest, in all fields of endeavor, the challenger must always demonstrate a convincing program or message to unseat the incumbent, except when there is a great disaster and the incumbent is directly responsible for the intractable situation the challenger seeks to remedy. Otherwise, the power of incumbency often prevails! For example, observe any Congressional election where it is very difficult to unseat the incumbent. In a House with 435 seats at stake every two years in national elections, a tiny fraction is actually turned over; and in most cases, either the incumbent is retiring, died, or has committed some ethical, moral or even criminal violation of the sacred rules of the institution, then he is re-elected.

OBAMA - MASTER AND COMMANDER

Obama - Master and Commander 565. One of the entrances to the World War II Memorial.

FREDERICK MONDERSON

Fortunately, none of these pathologies can be laid at President Obama's doorstep! The only contestable issue is; he is not satisfactorily addressing one of his fundamental responsibility of being steward of the economy, that is primarily providing jobs. Now, unemployment rates not dropping fast enough to suit the challenger, Mitt Romney's contention that he could do the same job faster and better. However, he may not be aware of it, or he has disregarded fellow Republican Condoleezza Rice's observation, "The view from the Oval Office is different to what most people believe." Nevertheless, to assess the current state of affairs, we should compare conditions facing the nation during the 2008 and 2012 pre-election environment that clearly shows the President more vulnerable in the former than the latter race. Thus, despite the "too close to call" escapist contention, President Obama will be re-elected because people generally go with "The devil they know" rather than "The devil they don't know" particularly when the latter plays it close to the vest raising questions about his leadership and trust, if he is elected. The incumbent, President Obama, as they say, has "a track record." However, despite the Romney/Ryan team's contention, the Obama/Biden team can and has to stand by their record since it has been on public display for four years. As such, let us weigh some facts.

Obama - Master and Commander 566. Spectators sitting around to enjoy the Musical Program at the World War II Memorial.

OBAMA - MASTER AND COMMANDER

Obama - Master and Commander 567. A high ranking female Naval Officer, Rear Admiral, pays attention as the band tunes up.

Obama - Master and Commander 568. "The Price of Freedom." "Freedom Wall holds 4,048 gold stars. Each gold star represents one hundred Amerian service personnel who died or remain missing in the war. The 405,399 American dead and missing from World War II are second only to the loss of more than 620,000 Americans during our Civil War."

FREDERICK MONDERSON

Obama - Master and Commander 569. Another look at the Pacific Arch beyond the Fountain and amidst the states!

Obama - Master and Commander 570. "The Price of Freedom" saluted with wreaths.

OBAMA - MASTER AND COMMANDER

Obama - Master and Commander 571. Naval aides to the Admiral.

Obama - Master and Commander 572. And the Band played on!

First, at the 2008 election timetable with Republicans in the Executive Office, America faced a great many challenges. Unemployment rate was high with the

FREDERICK MONDERSON

nation losing some 500,000-800,000 jobs each month in the last year before the election. The housing industry was in a horrible slump with rising foreclosures, decreasing new housing starts and home values sinking rapidly. Wall Street had descended into unthinkable depths with the DOW at c. 6500; interest rates were rising like the Shuttle ascending into the heavens; the nation's infrastructure of bridges, roads, dams, ports and tunnels were crumbling everywhere. The automobile industry was near bankrupt and banks were rapidly going under. America was engaged in two wars in Iraq and Afghanistan while Osama bin-Laden and his boys were not only wrecking havoc but also gloating at America from their caves and mountainous perches. Given these conditions, the young Senator Barack Obama, an African American, took up the challenge to rescue his beloved nation.

The old aphorism, "Without vision the people perish," was no more appropriate and the mere thought of better times in Mr. Obama's message of hope lifted the people's spirits. In a remarkable campaign, Barack Hussein Obama won the Democratic Primary and the General Election. Electing an African American to lead the nation was not only historically significant, it provided the opportunity to generate new ideas and provided a challenge to the old guard; but it nevertheless gave Mr. Obama, the opportunity to work his fiscal, financial, domestic, foreign and military policy magic to address the mounting problems evident in the tip of the iceberg he inherited. Some four years later, with no one knowing fully the size of the iceberg, and Mr. Obama, working in concert with the private sector, the nation not only stemmed the dive of losing hundreds of thousands of jobs each month but soared in adding several million new jobs; however and understandably, more needs to be done! In addition, the Obama Administration began encouraging outsourced manufacturing industry with jobs to return to America's shores. Emphasizing energy independence, he touted new and revolutionary clean air sources, underwriting some projects but encouraging the genius of American inventiveness in others. He paid more attention to deterioration of the environment and global warming by championing regulation in this and other fields. Folks at the Environmental Protection Agency took their job seriously as stewards of the environment; since, particularly during the Republican Primary debates, practically every candidate, especially Texas Governor Rick Perry, called for the elimination of this vital agency because, through regulation, it checked wanton and unchecked use of the national environment.

While many criticized his actions, the President wisely engineered rescue of the auto and banking industries. Today Detroit is producing more, making better cars, competing more effectively, holding significant market share, and like Vice-President Joe Biden often boasts, "General Motors is alive and Osama bin-Laden is dead!" Banks have not only recouped their losses, paid back most of what they borrowed, are making big profits and handing out big bonuses. The DOW has soared from 6500 to 13,000. President Obama ended the war in Iraq and Afghanistan and is on a course to withdraw from Afghanistan in 2014, bringing

OBAMA - MASTER AND COMMANDER

the boys and girls home! Somali Pirates have been seriously curtailed, Osama bin-Laden is dead, Al Zawihiri is hiding, nearly every top leader in Al Qaeda is dead, their finances are disrupted, "who is not dead is badly wounded" and the rest are on the run! As all these developments unfolded, the "Tea Party" emerged displaying its dirty underwear, Senator Mitch McConnell and his "Mandate" happened, and the "Party of No" launched a consistent obstructionist campaign to "Deny Obama a win!" Notwithstanding, the President passed far-reaching legislation in Lilly Ledbetter fair wages act for women; Health Care Reform that eluded presidents for nearly 6-decades as it is designed to cover untold numbers of Americans who had no coverage; he repealed "Don't Ask, Don't Tell;" issued an Executive Order giving young illegal immigrants an opportunity, considered part of the "Dream Act;" supported the rights of Gay people; insisted women get Birth Control prescriptions from their employers; and has held his own against the McConnells, DeMints, Santorums, Trumps. He also proved to be unmoved by threats to his safety; weathered the racist attacks; watered the "Birther" fire of Donald Trump and his "Circus Criers;" all while not simply changing the world's opinion of America but empanelling policies in a vision which will enable the American eagle to soar to even higher heights. He sought to revolutionize education emphasizing better teaching techniques, equipment and housing infrastructure in a strategy tofacilitate "Race to te Top" designed to "out-educate the world." All this was accomplished without any help from Republicans at a time when America faced its greatest dangers most of which were engineered by the same Republicans whose obstructionism could be considered treasonable. And so, along came the Romney/Ryan team saying "We can do all that better than Obama!" Well, their seeking to reinvent Obama's wheel is certainly questionable and that is why President Obama will be re-elected.

Obama - Master and Commander 573. Emblem of the US Army.

FREDERICK MONDERSON

Obama - Master and Commander 574. Emblem of the US Army Air Forces.

Obama - Master and Commander 575. Emblem of the US Marine Corps.

OBAMA - MASTER AND COMMANDER

Obama - Master and Commander 576. Emblem of the US Navy.

Obama - Master and Commander 577. Emblem of the US Coast Guard.

FREDERICK MONDERSON

Obama - Master and Commander 578. Emblem of the US Merchant Marine.

Despite the fact, Mitt Romney touts his businessman skill as the cure for the economic woes of the country, we all know, for as a great American theorist, James Carvel, recognized, "It's [still] the economy stupid!" Yet, there are other issues that characterize the man who would be President!

Governor Romney banks and saves his money in off-shore accounts in the Bahamas, Cayman Islands and in Switzerland; perhaps he distrusts American financial institutions. Even more important, he has threatened to repeal practically every significant legislative action of President Obama, viz., Health Care Reform, "Don't Ask, Don't Tell," not to mention *Roe v. Wade*, a target of Republicans for many years, that allows a woman to choose whether to carry a pregnancy or not; as well as defund Planned Parenthood; outlaw Birth Control for women, and much more. He, Mr. Romney wants to offer more opportunities for the most wealthy as did President George Bush, who thought the "one percent" his "base." Mr. Romney was against the Detroit Bailout and has offered no concrete Afghanistan policy though he would rush to war with Iran as Bush's "Go it alone" failed policy on Iraq; while President Obama wants to engage the world community against the pariah state. Against the "Dream Act," he wanted illegal immigrants to "self deport." He wants to cut funding for Public Broadcasting and hurt "Big Bird." Meanwhile, according to Robert Reich, former Bill Clinton Secretary of Labor, Mr. Romney wants to give a "huge tax cut mostly for the rich!" in a "supply side economics" strategy that does not work; for its similarity to and particularly as

OBAMA - MASTER AND COMMANDER

"Daddy Bush" described Reagan's economic philosophy of "trickle down" as "Voo Doo economics."

Thus, even though the election "is close," this is what such contests are all about. In the 2012 Olympics in London, during the bicycle race, the two front-runners were nearing the tape when the one in front leaned over his handlebar to look at the competition and the fellow in second place surged ahead to win. In basketball, football, baseball, etc., the final two competing teams are the best in their field signaling a potentially close contest. Yet, the best team wins! As such, while the presidential race is "too close to call," we must remember "Americans are smart!" and though Mr. Romney will have a good showing, the show belongs to Mr. Obama.

Obama will win and be re-elected and this is in the best interest of the nation! As former President Bill Clinton explained, since McConnell and his crew are bent on denying Mr. Obama a second term, once elected and this objective a failure, they must come to the table to co-operate and work in the interest of the American people. Obama will win!!!

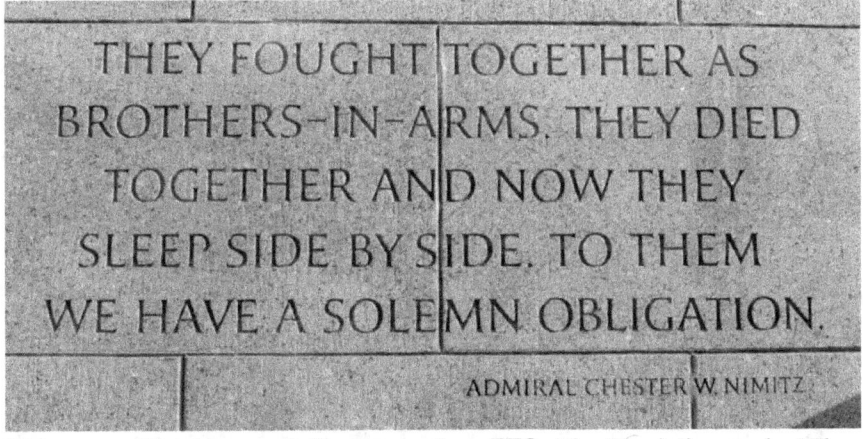

Obama - Master and Commander 579. The Inscription reads: "They fought together as Brothers-in-Arms. They died together and now they sleep side by side. To them we have a solemn obligation." Admiral Chester W. Nimitz

FREDERICK MONDERSON

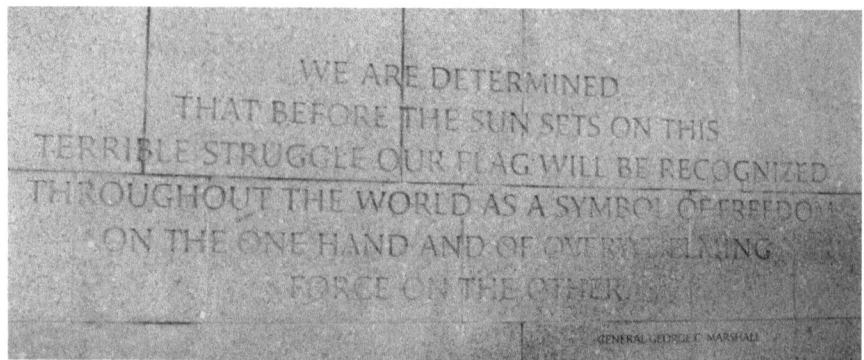

Obama - Master and Commander 580. The Inscription reads: "We are determined that before the sun sets on this terrible struggle our flag will be recognized throughout the world as a symbol of freedom on the one hand and of overwhelming force on the other." General George C. Marshall.

Obama - Master and Commander 581. "Here we mark the price of Freedom!"

OBAMA - MASTER AND COMMANDER

Obama - Master and Commander 582. World War II Memorial copmfort station.

FREDERICK MONDERSON

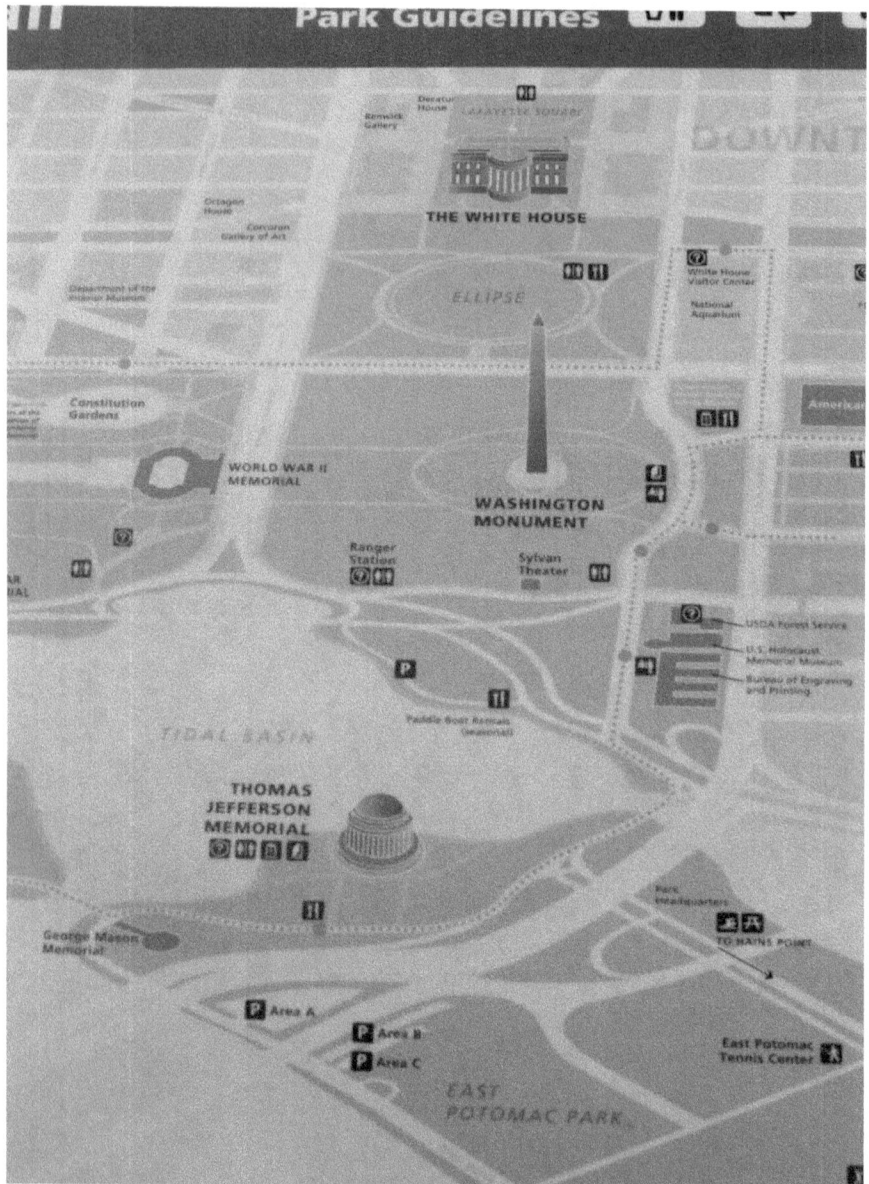

Obama - Master and Commander 583. Word has it that Thomas Jefferson in looking out from his Memorial stares towards that of Washhington as he also keeps tabs on the White House. There is some logic to his line of sight.

OBAMA - MASTER AND COMMANDER

61. ENDORSEMENTS, EDITORIALS AND DEBATES
By
Dr. Fred Monderson

Popular Republican General and former Secretary of State Colin Powell has again endorsed the Obama/Biden ticket, because, as a thinking man, he has weighed the alternative Romney/Ryan ticket. In Mr. Powell's first endorsement of Barack Obama, he identified him as a "transformational figure" with new ideas and being the right man for the job at that time. This time, he mentions compromise as an important tool in moving government along and that Republicans of past significance who were masters of compromise and their craft, are a dying breed. With the intransigence of the "Party of No," this is probably why Mr. Powell endorsed President Obama for re-election. This asks the American people, 'Where are the great contemporary Republicans, theorists, activists, politicians and why can't they see what General Powell does see?" Equally, 'Why are they not making an effort to break the stalemate?'

It is interesting how endorsements and editorials paint a picture of persons running for office that portray true images but also untrue images of people's true character; while debates show the contenders' strengths and weaknesses but observers are sometimes "all over the map" in giving objective assessment of their observations. Even more, newspapers and magazine writers' take describe a person's policies, accomplishments and skills actually reveal the writer's biases instead. First, from a New York perspective aside, some writers of local newspapers have been so anti-Obama, their arrogance and biases are not easily discernible but laughable.

Recently, the *New Yorker* magazine's editorial board endorsed President Obama for re-election. This endorsement was a far-cry from the magazine's Cover article that showed Michelle Obama as a gun-toting revolutionary "watching her husband Barack Obama's back." They dressed him in his paternal ancestor's traditional garb while seemingly trying to convince readers he was secretly a Muslim in order to invoke fears about his presidency. This present endorsement, however, was more an accurate recounting of the President's many accomplishments in light of Republican obstructionism and scorched earth tactics designed "to deny Mr. Obama a win." In this, the magazine compared Mr. Obama to the Republican challenger Mitt Romney in which the Governor appeared somewhat High schoolish to the College graduate President Obama. Thus, this assessment forces onlookers to wonder how can the American people not discern the contrast; or, that, they are driven or indoctrinated to see Mr. Obama from a different

FREDERICK MONDERSON

perspective designed to sully his character. However, because broad segments of the American people are wise, they do not fall for Republican "Hokey Dokey!"

Following the final Presidential debate primarily about Foreign Policy on Monday October 22, 2012, some two weeks before the election, the next day the *Post*, *Daily News* and *Times* commented on the debate as the lead part of their Editorial showed. The first section of each Editorial conveyed the disparate and Rorsarch outlookand different impressions of the same event, but also unmask biases that betray each paper's attitude towards the President and towards the notion of objectivity.

The *New York Post's* Tuesday October 23, 2012, editorial entitled "**MITT'S OPTIMISM**" read as follows:

"President Obama went on the attack against Mitt Romney again last night in their final debate - a tactic usually reserved for the challenger. The president, no doubt, felt the need - given Romney's recent surge in the polls and Obama's disappointing record on foreign-policy issues, the topic of the debate. But Romney more than held his own, proving himself a more-than-credible potential commander-in-chief." Interesting, this "boost" simply says Mr. Romney meets the threshold to be commander-in-chief. Its like saying you need a BA degree to qualify for a job, but this does not put you at the head of the line!

The *Daily News* Tuesday October 23, 2012, P. 26 noted - "The seasoning of four years in the international arena well served President Obama in the third and final presidential debate as he was more sure-footed than Mitt Romney - yet failed to nail the charge that his Republican challenger was 'wrong and reckless.' Many Americans will likely find reassurance in Obama's tempered, knowledgeable presentation on foreign policy, an area in which the President has gotten higher marks from the public than he has on domestic matters." Clearly this endorsement is a "win for Mr. Obama!"

OBAMA - MASTER AND COMMANDER

Obama - Master and Commander 584. Franklin Delano Roosevelt Memorial: **"THE ONLY THING WE HAVE TO FEAR IS FEAR ITSELF!"**

Obama - Master and Commander 585. Franklin Delano Roosevelt, President of the United States 1933-1945.

FREDERICK MONDERSON

Obama - Master and Commander 586. The man behind the name!

Obama - Master and Commander 587. The American Eagle in all its glory as part of Roosevelt's Memorial (1933).

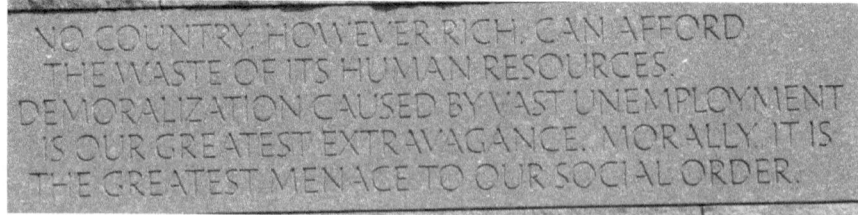

Obama - Master and Commander 588. The Inscription reads: "No country, however rich, can afford the waste of its human resources. Demoralization caused by vast unemployment is our greatest extravagance. Morally, it is the greatest menance to our social order."

OBAMA - MASTER AND COMMANDER

Obama - Master and Commander 589. The Inscription reads: "Men and nature must work hand in hand. The throwing out of balance of the resources of nature throws out of balance also the lives of man."

Obama - Master and Commander 590. The Inscription reads: "We must be the great arsenal of Democracy"

The *New York Times* Tuesday October 23, 2012, P. A22 - **MITT ROMNEY FALTERS ON FOREIGN POLICY, SOUNDING CONFUSED AND INCOHERENT**

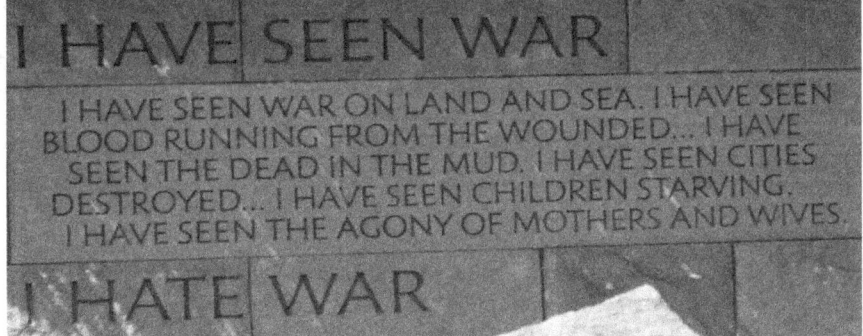

Obama - Master and Commander 591. The Inscription reads: "I HAVE SEEN WAR. I have seen war on land and sea. I have seen blood running from the shoulder of the wounded …. I have seen the dead in the mud. I have seen cities destroYed … I have seen children starving. I have seen the agony of mothers and wives. I HATE WAR"

FREDERICK MONDERSON

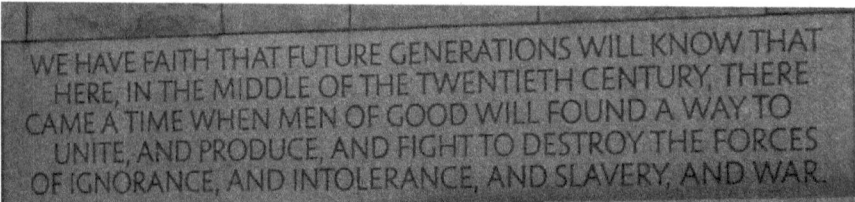

Obama - Master and Commander 592. The Inscription reads: "We have faith that future generations will know that here, in the middle of the Twentieth Century, there came a time when men of good will found a way to unite, and produce and fight to destroy the forces of ignorance, and intolerance, and slavery, and war."

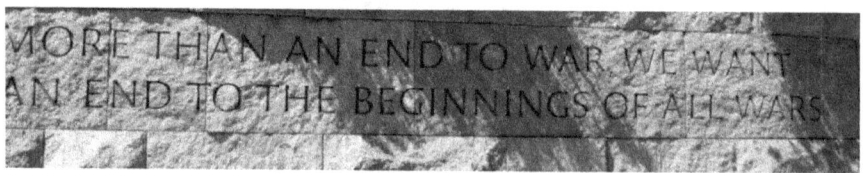

Obama - Master and Commander 593. The Inscription reads: "More than an end to war, we want an end to the beginning of all wars."

"Mitt Romney has nothing really coherent or substantive to say about domestic policy, but at least he can sound energetic and confident about it. On foreign policy, the subject of Monday night's final presidential debate, he had little coherent to say and often sounded completely lost. That's because he has no original ideas of substance on most world issues, including Syria, Iran and Afghanistan. During the debate, on issue after issue, Mr. Romney sounded as if he had read the boldface headings in a briefing book - or a freshman global history textbook – and had not gone much further than that. Twice during the first half-hour, he mentioned that Al-Qaeda-affiliated groups were active in northern Mali, Was that in the morning's briefing book?"

As we continue in this examination, an even closer comparison of two New York newspapers gives an idea of how divided and slanted endorsements are. To begin!

OBAMA - MASTER AND COMMANDER

Obama - Master and Commander 594. Mrs. Eleanor Roosevelt, First United States Delegate to the United Nations and the Inscription reads: "The structure of world peace cannot be the work of one man, one party or one nation … it must be a peace which rests on the cooperative effort of the whole world."

Obama - Master and Commander 595. The "Four Freedoms" touted since the end of World War II: "Freedom of Speech; Freedom of Worship; Freedom from Want; and Freedom from Fear."

FREDERICK MONDERSON

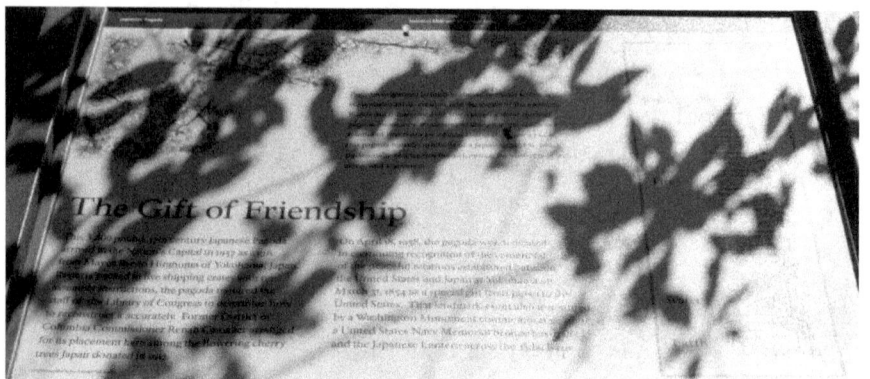

Obama - Master and Commander 596. A gift of friendship of a Japanese Pagoda.

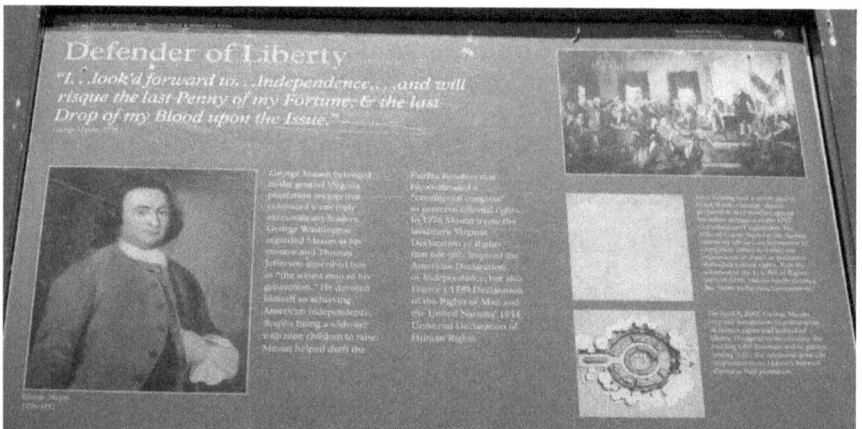

Obama - Master and Commander 597. George Mason: "Defender of Liberty." "I, looked forward to … Independence, … and will risque the last Penny of my Fortune. And the last Drop of my Blood upon the Issue."

OBAMA - MASTER AND COMMANDER

Obama - Master and Commander 598. George Mason relaxing in the wonderful solitude of his Memorial placed between Roosevelt and Jefferson.

The *New York Post's* Editorial on Sunday, October 28, 2012, p. 32 entitled "**A Case Study In Incompetence**" is from a paper that has been Anti-Obama and Pro-Romney for the longest and reads as follows: "Myraid are the failures of the Obama administration, but none is more tragic, or more frightening, or more foreboding of catastrophe than the appalling mishandling of the September 11 terrorist attack on the US Consulate in Benghazi. Details continue to leak, but it'll be hard to top the bombshell from Fox News at week's end reporting that repeated requests for military help during the attack were summarily denied for *hours* .... As does nature, statecraft abhors a vacuum. When one develops, adventurers and advantage-takers appear in short order. Iran continues to build its bomb; Syria burns; Turkey awaits its fate, and Egypt is looking at a Muslim Brotherhood-enforced Sharia state. Think of it as Benghazi writ large. Time to evict the deceiving ameteurs."

FREDERICK MONDERSON

Obama - Master and Commander 599. With boquets, nations pay tribute to the United States for its involvement in the Korean War.

Obama - Master and Commander 600. More of the floral commendation for America's involvement in the Korean Conflict.

OBAMA - MASTER AND COMMANDER

Obama - Master and Commander 601. Still more compliments in honor of America's sacrifice in the Korean conflict.

Obama - Master and Commander 602 Obama - Master and Commander. Even more commendation.

FREDERICK MONDERSON

Contrast this anti-Obama diatribe with another newspaper, the *New York Times* of that same day, Sunday, October 28, 2012, p. 12 which read: "Mr. Obama has earned another term; Mr. Romney offers dangerous ideas, when he offers any."

"The economy is slowly recovering from the 2008 meltdown, and the country could suffer another recession if the wrong policies take hold. The United States is embroiled in unstable regions that could easily explode into full-blown disaster. An ideological assault from the right has started to undermine the vital health reform law passed in 2010. These forces are eroding women's access to health care, and their right to control their lives. Nearly 50 years after passage of the Civil Rights Act, all Americans' rights are cheapened by the right wing's determination to deny marriage benefits to a selected group of us. Astonishingly, even the very right to vote is being challenged. That is the context for the Nov. 6 election, and as stark as it is, the choice is just as clear."

"President Obama has shown a firm commitment to using government to help foster growth. He has formed sensible budget policies that are not dedicated to protecting the powerful, and has worked to save the social safety net to protect the powerless. Mr. Obama has impressive achievements despite the implacable wall of refusal erected by Congressional Republicans so intent on stopping him that they risked pushing the nation into depression, held its credit rating hostage, and hobbled economic recovery."

"Mr. Romney, the former governor of Massachusetts, has gotten this far with a guile that allows him to say whatever he thinks an audience wants to hear. But he has tied himself to the ultraconservative forces that control the Republican Party and embraced their policies, including reckless budget cuts and 30-year-old, discredited trickle-down ideas. Voters may still be confused about Mr. Romney's true identity, but they know the Republican Party, and a Romney administration would reflect its agenda. Mr. Romney's choice of Representative Paul Ryan as his running mate says volumes about that."

"For these and many other reasons, we enthusiastically endorse President Barack Obama for a second term, and express the hope that his victory will be accompanied by a new Congress willing to work for policies that Ameicans need."

Now, if all of America reads these Editorials and votes objectively, Mr. Romney's goose is cooked!

OBAMA - MASTER AND COMMANDER

Obama - Master and Commander 603. Families come to pay tribute to America's fallen, wounded and courage in the Korean War.

Obama - Master and Commander 604. Tail end of a patrol out in the field in Korea.

FREDERICK MONDERSON

Obama - Master and Commander 605. The classic picture of being on point as in Korea during the war.

Obama - Master and Commander 606. The universal cry: **"FREEDOM IS NOT FREE!"**

OBAMA - MASTER AND COMMANDER

Obama - Master and Commander 607. Dead, Missing, Captured and Wounded, t he numbers are staggering for American forces and the UN.

Obama - Master and Commander 608. America paid a price!

FREDERICK MONDERSON

Obama - Master and Commander 609. Even in the other world they help us stay vigilant as a reminder of what a price intolerance demands.

62. HEAVEN HELP AMERICA!
By
Dr. Fred Monderson

There must be some serious praying for America if Mitt Romney is elected President when he lets the likes of John Sununu foul the air with his oral diarrhea. If the buck stops with the man at the top, Mitt Romney, then he is responsible for the big mouth, bigoted John Sununu who called President Obama "stupid." By all standards of decency, this man should be in a lunatic asylum, as he is an embarrassment to Republicans and to the American nation in general. For Mitt Romney to allow the former New Hampshire governor to play such a significant role in his campaign and to espouse such vile comments about Barack Obama, President of the United States either indicate he is not only desperate by employing dreg tactics or is giving warning of how morally deficient his Administration will be. However, the interesting thing about the anti-Obamites that spans the alphabet from Bachmann and the "Black Protester with Guns" and his Pastor praying for the death of Barack Obama to Sununu and Trump; the cool ruler Barack Obama must sit at night and day laughing at these Lilliputian pundits and their circus performance. Equally, when Mr. Obama's opponent goes around the country spreading lies as he has on so many issues, but more important that the President has behaved in such and such a manner, one valid question is, 'Mr. Romney have you chronicled your friends and allies' behaviors towards the office and the man? Nonetheless, one has to be amazed how one individual could attract so much animosity from so wide a phalanx of individuals. The most plausible answer is racist hatred and an avalanche of disrespect for the black man in the White House.

OBAMA - MASTER AND COMMANDER

While we have known of the others' behaviors and attitudes towards Mr. Obama, John Sununu's coming out of the woodwork is somewhat surprising but then again, old men with antiquated ideas do not just arrive bursting with such deep-seated vile hatred. Putting 'Ole John on the psychiatrist bench, we see he probably had aspirations for the presidency himself but could only be Ronald Reagan's Chief of Staff. So, naturally to envision a black man sitting in the chair he so often served made his neck red! But, it's more than that! Mr. Sununu demonstrates an ante-bellum slave-master mentality, a dinosaur's outlook, that preached Black men are genetically inferior in the physical order and thus should be equally inferior in the social order. John Sununu and his kind are the type of persons, the new generation of Americans hope would fade away fast; but, like Michele Bachmann, they sturggle to stay relevant though they are like fishes out of water.

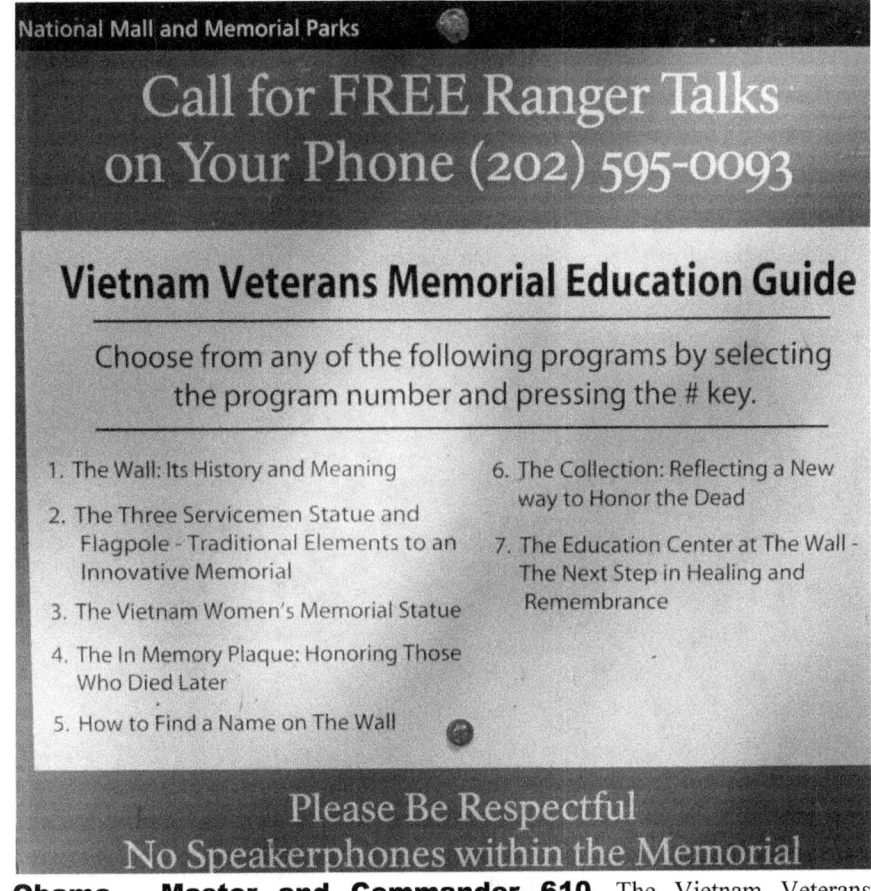

Obama - Master and Commander 610. The Vietnam Veterans Memorial Education Guide instructs what to see.

FREDERICK MONDERSON

Obama - Master and Commander 611. Vietnam Veteran Memorial showing a patrol of three soldiers, the leader, a machine-gunner and rifleman on patrol in the rice paddies.

Obama - Master and Commander 612. The "Wall" that shows the price America paid in that "Conflict!"

OBAMA - MASTER AND COMMANDER

Obama - Master and Commander 613. Looking past the end of h te "Wall" towards the Washington Memorial.

Obama - Master and Commander 614. The role of female Medical Corps cannot be understated for they were with the boys tooth and nail!

FREDERICK MONDERSON

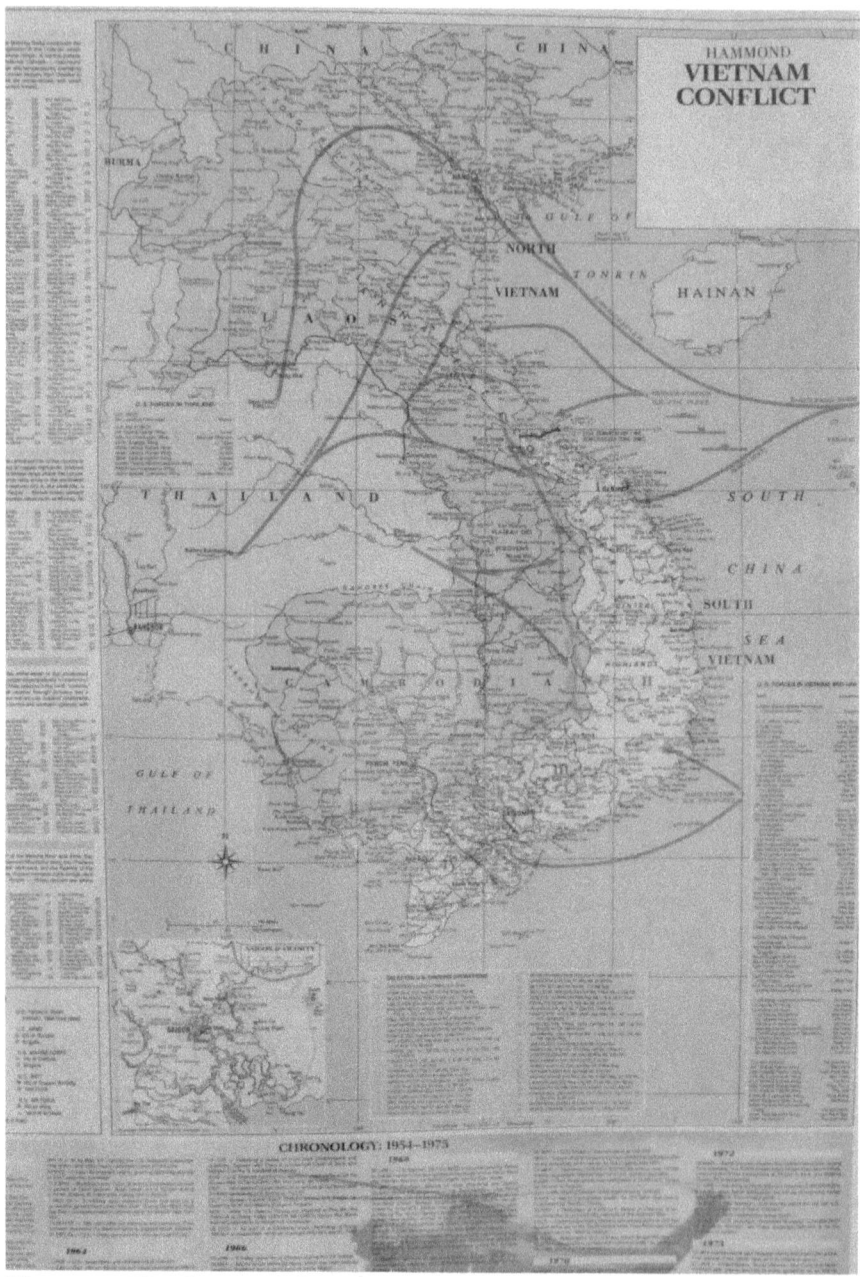

Obama - Master and Commander 615. Vietnam. The Area of Conflict and the Chronology of Events from 1954-1975.

OBAMA - MASTER AND COMMANDER

> To those Missing In Action and Prisoners of War
> Our hearts extend to you and your families.
> To those who have sponsored this structure
> Go our most gracious thanks.
>
> **MidAtlantic Contracting Inc.**
>
> Barrons Lumber
> Design Delmarva
> Dow Building Solutions
> The Roof Center
> Euro Stone Craft
> Laticrete

Obama - Master and Commander 616. A Plaque to families of **MIA**s and **POW**s.

As such, then, the Obama persona is anathema to Sununu's very nature. As a decent man, Governor Romney should have told Governor Sununu, "Tone it down, Johnny!" However, it may very well be Governor Romney will not be able to control loose cannons in his Administration. He also has to figure out how he will repay those who make million dollar donations and will demand untold access for having underwritten his rise to the Presidency. Given the results, pity old Petterffy! After all, it is unreasonable to believe those who gave donations in the millions will not seek access, anything in repayment. Equally, too, if Petterfy single-handedly paid for all those commercials out of his pocket, he has come up a big loser, even more so than Romney!

63. HURRICANE SANDY: ARM OF GOD
By
Dr. Fred Monderson

As the "false patriots" rev-up their insidious activities against the divinely inspired Barack Obama administration, it could be argued, the ancestors chose to intervene by showing Americans how invulnerable they truly are. Never mind, the pronouncements of the rich and powerful, God has a way of making the strong-weak, the high-low and the crooked paths-straight. This nation prides itself in its Christian conviction and practice while also engaging in wickedness in high places, whether this is in state or national legislatures, back rooms and also other secret meeting places of consummation to plot treasonous behaviors against a legitimate government elected to represent the broad masses of the American people.

FREDERICK MONDERSON

If we accept the potency of Jefferson philosophic beliefs then Americans who provided free labor to build America are the legitimate owners of this country. If America had made peace with the British, French, Germans, Italians, Japanese and broad swaths of Arabs, who have killed Americans then it had better be prepared to make peace with African Americans, the most legitimate of all Americans! While the traitorous elements may disrespect Barack Obama and plot the demise of the most powerful man in the world, they better pay attention to Michelle Obama, the great embodiment of the ancestral spiritual heritage in America.

Some time ago recently, the *New Yorker* magazine, in a Cover portrayal, depicted Madam Michelle as a revolutionary with firepower watching "Barack's Back" though they have underestimated this slave daughter's ability to summon the troops. Barack, patriot and gentleman that he is, robably and importantly may have reminded her, "Ok honey, there is no need to call out the troops, yet!"

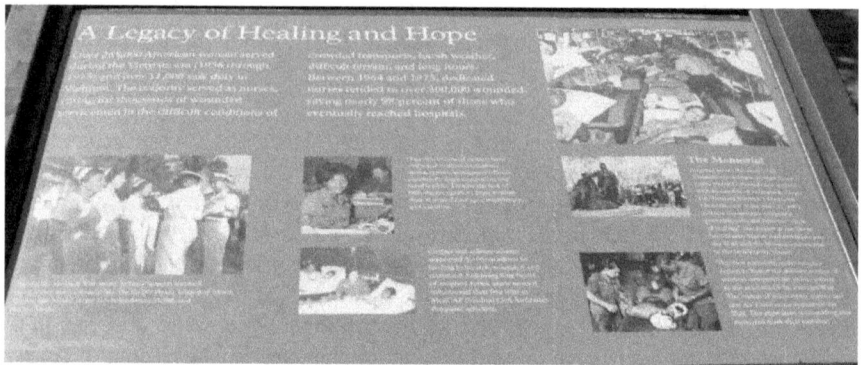

Obama - Master and Commander 617. In "A Legacy of Healing and Hope," the role of female Medical Corps is recounted for their role in Vietnam.

What people have not understood, perhaps the ancestral spirits have coalesced in Hurricane Sandy to remind this nation, that the God they so revere, is angry, has extended his arm to remind the powerful, high and mighty, "I am god, I am mighty and am displeased with the treatment of my divinely inspired son." Sure people may be upset about Barack Obama' relationship to divinity but this was not the way when Michele Bachmann told her "God told me to run" falsity; or even when Ann Romney said God told her husband, Mitt Romney "to run for the presidency" and became so ordained. Perhaps such skeptics are upset because this time it is the Black man with the divine connection.

When it comes to religious matters some of the most knowledgeable scholars confess there are things about divinity, its mystical or magical nature that baffles the greatest of minds. In the case of Hurricane Sandy, the experts speak of three colliding phenomena, the ordinary hurricane, the jet stream and another storm that created the super catastrophe that caused such damages to the American coastline states. What we have not considered is the metaphysical and spiritual reality that African ancestors who have helped to build America may be angry with the behaviors of certain segments of the populace. Either these people's god is false since he seems to pick losers or they are using his name in vain and he is angry. When the real god promises he delivers. When god told abraham to look in the bushes he had made provision for that derective, but not so with Bachmann and Romney! Let us not forget, God is a just god who abhors hypocrisy and deceit.

Obama - Master and Commander 618. The National Mall and Memorial Parks in process of Rehabilitating the Lincoln Memorial Reflecting Pool. Photo by Carol Highsmith.

64. GOVERNOR CHRISTIE!
By
Dr. Fred Monderson

Perhaps there is something to New Jersey Governor Chris Christie after all! He did the unthinkable by praising President Obama on national television in aftermath of his response to the devastating results of Hurricane Sandy. It stands to reason according to disturbed logic, the Governor will receive an avalanche of Republican criticism through the many avenues of telephone and internet communication because he "gave Obama a win!" This, notwithstanding, there seems to be a decency in Governor Christie that is missing among many Republican politicians. Naturally, the question will be asked 'why is this statement being made?'

Sometime during his second administration, perhaps after a shoe was thrown at him, President George Bush was asked, "Can you think of anything you have done wrong as President?" He studied long and hard and finally said no! Imagine this presidentl like other men, never put his socks on the wrong foot, his T-shirt on backwards or made a wrong tie knot. What he could not realize, at the time, he had created a mold that became standard practice for many Republicans seeking the Presidency in this 2012 election.

If memory serves me right, Representative Ron Paul was asked if President Obama had done anything right in his years as the nation's Chief Executive and this Republican "paragon of virtue" studied long and hard and said no! He could not find anything President Obama had done right in four years in office. Either Mr. Paul is a liar or old age is catching up with him. Still, we hope to see him again in 2016. Yet, the Bush mold became a rather useful tool for Republicans, who, not possessing a Hubble Telescope of their own, were unable to be able to find a stitch of a positive accomplishment by the President. This is what makes Governor Christie such a big man, towering over the Lilliputian Neanderthals of his party.

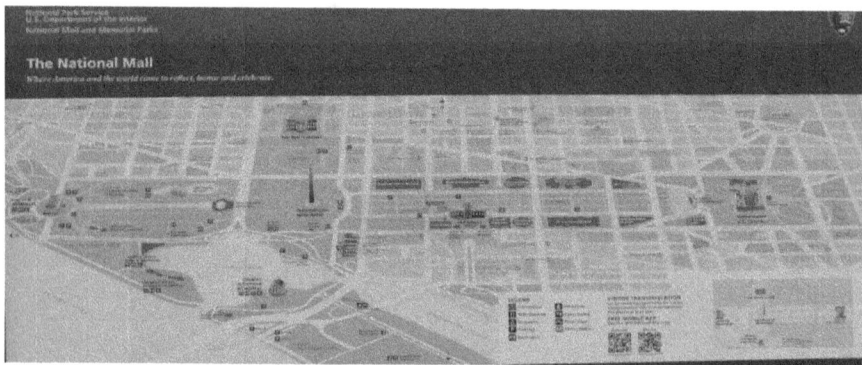

Obama - Master and Commander 619. Instructions on how to read and locate oneself on the National Mall.

Obama - Master and Commander 619a. Department of Justice Building.

OBAMA - MASTER AND COMMANDER

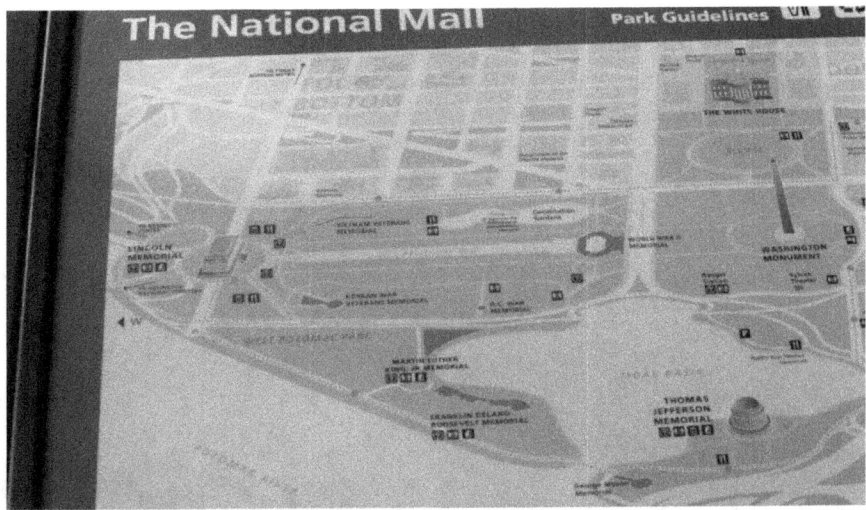

Obama - Master and Commander 620. End of the Mall and Tidal Basin showing the White House, Ellipse and Lincoln, Washington, King, Roosevelt and Jefferson Memorials.

65. VANQUISHING REPUBLICANS
By
Dr. Fred Monderson

Because of the history of African Americans in this country, right wingers with guilt feelings in connection with that history often accuse said people of not being or less patriotic than other Americans. There is one unquestionable fact as to why even cultured ignoramuses can disrespectfully accuse President Obama of being unpatriotic. Whereas, people whose places of origin were at war with America, such as the French, British, Germans, Japanese, etc., their descendants are now in positions of leadership, whether economic or politic in this country. Many of these are very much the "circus criers" who lead the charge in spurious claims against President Obama.

To begin, great western political theorists have long associated the common man with ownership of the land because of their sweat equity especially if done without pay; a sort of Jeffersonian connection. However, because of the trauma African Americans experienced in the institution of slavery and its psychological legacy of social impairment more than a century after outlawing the ghastly experience. This has been a social albatross in many respects. This, nonetheless, has not impaired the African American's desire and intent to serve and defend the American ideal and dreamSuch is evidentce in the history and sacrifice of Crispus Attucks, Salem

FREDERICK MONDERSON

Po and untold millions, who gave their lives, were disabled and in general, served to defend this nation. What the racists may be saying to African Americans, however, is "You may have been enslaved and worked the lnd for free, but we were the one who decimated and killed the Indians (Native Americans). So therefore, we are the owners of the land!

Obama - Master and Commander 621. Not to be outdone by the "Big Boys," the District of Columbia Memorial takes its place in honoring those who serve the nation.

From his defeat of John McCain and Sarah Palin in 2008, Barack Obama has had to perennially combat Republicans who have been un-apologetic in their efforts to make his administration a failure. Only by employing the highest skills, expert leadership, constantly evolving creative administrative strategies, some guile and an avalanche of prayers for his well-being by supporters that Mr. Obama was able to check the unrelenting efforts of Republican lawmakers bent on sabotaging efforts he has made in administering his responsibilities as President of the United States.

OBAMA - MASTER AND COMMANDER

Obama - Master and Commander 622. Martin Luther King, Jr. Memorial.

Obama - Master and Commander 623. "The main entrance to the memorial is the 'Mountain of Despair,' a massive boulder symbolizing the struggle faced in the quest for peace and equality. From within the struggle, a piece has been removed and thrust into the open plaza, the 'Stone of Hope.'"

FREDERICK MONDERSON

Obama - Master and Commander 624. To stand and gaze upon this phenomenon is indeed a moving experience. "Out of the Mountain of Depair, A Stone of Hope!"

Obama - Master and Commander 625. Martin Luther King, Jr., the Man, the Mountain and all that he stood for and more! "The main entrance to the memorial is the 'Mountain of Despair,' a massive boulder symbolizing the struggle faced in the quest for peace and equality. From within the struggle, a piece has been removed and thrust into the open plaza, the 'Stone of Hope.'"

OBAMA - MASTER AND COMMANDER

Obama - Master and Commander 626. "Out of a Mountain of Despair, a Stone of Hope!" This is also a reminder, the man himself stood for justice and equality, for symbolically as a mountain, only such a force of nature could withstand all that was happening in American society prior, then and since!

Obama - Master and Commander 627. One part of the arc of the moral universe that begins the journey in search of truth, justice and equality.

FREDERICK MONDERSON

Obama - Master and Commander 628. The second part of the arc, representative of all that encompasses within the horizontal distance between the two points of the beginning and end.

66. APOLOGIES LOWER STANDARDS
By
Dr. Fred Monderson

Les Payne, the award winning Pulitzer Prize journalist at *Newsday* in New York, has always said, "I say what I want and print it, then duck!" Republicans on the other hand say what they want then apologize! So, why say it if you have to apologize, or is it that they are stupid, ignorant or biased. One has to wonder what Emily Post would say about ethical behaviors in the two situations. For, in the former case the writer speaks "truth to power;" while in the latter case, speaks to shameful embarrassment, yet no one seems to want to hold such miscreants to any shred of accountability. It is as if modern Americans have compromised and acquiesced in the repugnant behavior which calls into question their lowering of standards particularly for public officials and in the apologetic "spin," it is as they seem to have been lulled into acceptance.

OBAMA - MASTER AND COMMANDER

Obama - Master and Commander 629. Conceptually one can see the full duration of the "Arc of the Moral Universe" curing around the mountain of despair as one individual seeks to find his place in the great experience.

Obama - Master and Commander 630. The Inscription reads: "We shall overcome because the Arc of the Moral Universe is long, but it bends towards Justice." District of Columbia, 1968.

FREDERICK MONDERSON

Obama - Master and Commander 631. The Inscription reads: "Darkness cannot drive out Darkness, only Light can do that. Hate cannot drive out Haste, only Love can do that." 1963

Obama - Master and Commander 632. The Inscription reads: "I belive that Unarmed Truth and Unconditional Love will have the Final Word in Reality. This is why Right, Temporarily Defeated is Stronger than Evil Triumphant." Norway 1964

OBAMA - MASTER AND COMMANDER

For those observing this new phenomenon, from the time Senator Barack Obama declared his candidacy for the Presidency of the United States, seems pent-up questionable human behaviors were directed toward this individual in the most disrespectful manner. The "Tea Party" movement was born in the cauldron of racist arrogance directed toward Barack Obama because of his race, African American. It is not surprising that the descendants of the people who enslaved Africans in the horrific institution of slavery, highly and likely traceable to people in positions of political power would maintain the level of disrespect for the man and the office because of his race. It is no wonder, the "hanging, slave states" of the South voted against Mr. Obama rather than for Mr. Romney in the 2012 election.

After the Senator was chosen to be the Democratic Party standard bearer in the national election, torrential outpouring of mis-statements began to inundate political gatherings, in print and on the airwaves. However, the culture of apology had not made their grand entrance as yet. In her classic whipping frenzy at "Tea Party" gatherings, Sarah Palin began talking of "crosshairs;" "Don't retreat, reload;" "Let's take America Back;" and "He is not like us." Ms Palin is also known for her stupid statement: "I can see Russia from my front step." Unfortunately, the Former Governor of Alaska has not as yet evolved as a participant in the culture of apology because she was still caught up in self-adulation, that self-congratulatory and inflated ego resulting from being chosen as Republican Vice Presidential running mate of Senator John McCain and because she is a beautiful woman, speaks fast but is still a "light weight." Unquestionable, she is still a loser to Obama! In that same culture of frenzy, at Republican political gatherings, "Joe the Plumber," himself not licensed, opportunistically emerged for his seven minutes of fame. This is the same Joe whom Allen West endorsed for Congress in 2012 but sadly both Joe and West lost! This is all after Joe had responded to a statement by Mr. Obama saying that it sounded like "Socialism." How much does a plumber know about socialism, that he could "coin a phrase?" Yet, the term stuck and so Mr. Obama became "a socialist" as they sought to define policies he intended to implement if he was elected.

FREDERICK MONDERSON

Obama - Master and Commander 633. The Inscription reads: "Make a career of humanity. Commit yourself to the noble struggle for Equal Rights. You will make a greater person of yoursef, a greater nation of your country, and a finer world to live in." District of Columbia, 1959

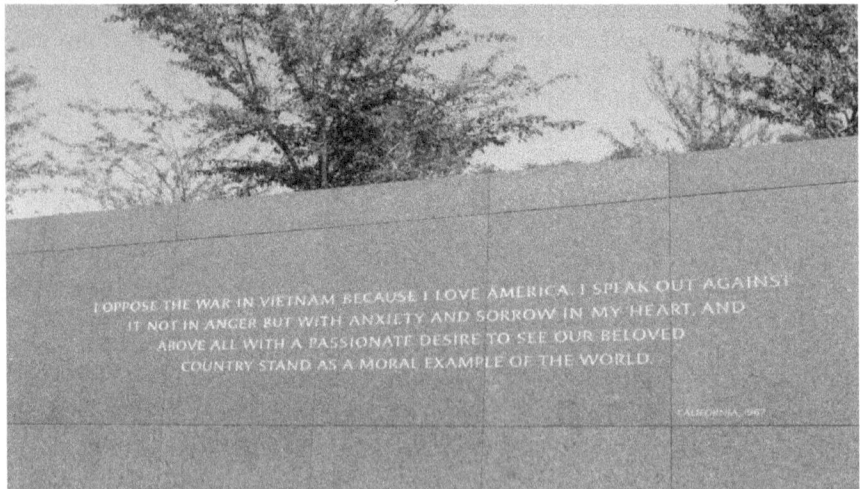

Obama - Master and Commander 634. The Inscription reads: "I Oppose the War in Vietnam Because I Love America. I Speak Out Against it not in Anger but with Anxiety and Sorrow in My Heart. And, Above all with a Passionate Desire to see our Beloved Country Stand as a Moral Example of the World." California 1967

OBAMA - MASTER AND COMMANDER

Obama - Master and Commander 635. The Inscription reads: "If we are to have Peace on Earth, our Loyalties must become Ecumenical rather than Sectional. Our Loyalties must Transcend Our Race, Our Tribe, Our Class, and Our Nation." Georgia 1967

The two cases of Palin and Joe were watersheds that opened the flood-gates of Republican repugnant statements they would come to regret and shame-facedly apologize; for, even if such apologies were shallow they still gave the impression they were contrite. The floodgates soon were awash in torrential invective as Mr. Obama was accused of being a socialist or having socialist intentions; he was charged as being unpatriotic; a Muslim; inexperienced in domestic and foreign affairs; having only a community organizer's experience to his credit and a whole lot more including not being "black enough" or "too black!" As the "Tea Party" began to mobilize at their many political gatherings and they made the most outlandish and derogatory claims about Mr. Obama, still with no apology though they published the most disgusting placard caricatures. As such, one has to wonder how so much pent-up animosity can be generated against a single individual and as the Republican campaign escalated, pent-up arrogance inflated the thought of winning the Presidency. Well, we know the result; Senator Barack Obama became the President-Elect in 2008.

Its generally believed on the day of his Inauguration, a group of high level Republicans, possibly in and out of government met to plan an obstructionist non-cooperation campaign designed to deny the new President any "win" and as Senator Mitch McConnell publicly stated, it was his intention "to make Barack Obama a one-term President." From here the watershed of disrespect and

FREDERICK MONDERSON

apologies began as Republicans felt they could do and say anything and get away with it. They felt they could do and say anything to President Obama and their respective communities would not question their actions nor say or do anything to them. It is as if they were unquestionably speaking for their communities! Not chiding nor firing, but re-electing such means many in their communities feel such reprehensible behavior is acceptable.

The first example of Republican rampaging escapade occurred perhaps days after Inauguration since no Republican members of the House voted for it and only 3 Republican Senators voted in favor, to give the President the opportunity to sign the Stimulus Bill on February 17, 2009. It is interesting how the bill could have so quickly gotten universal Republican opposition in such a short time. Some theorists have postulated the view that on the day of the Inauguration, January 20, or thereabouts, a group of high ranking Republicans met and organized opposition to Mr. Obama. Thus, in just over three weeks the Bill could have generated such universal opposition attests to some gathering to plan the opposition. So much so, by the time of the Stimulus Bill made the rounds, all the actors knew their roles and from here they felt that to disrespect the man in the Office meant nothing because they were all united against the Black guy. The consensus is that these people wanted to have the Black family removed from the White House.

Shortly, thereafter, at the State of the Union Address, South Carolina's Representative Joe Wilson told the President "you lie" in the sacred space of the august House of Representatives. Mr. Wilson wanted to meet with President Obama to apologize but the President advised, "Send it in the mail!" Next it was the events surrounding Health Care Reform debate in which South Carolina Senator DeMint stated on Television, "The President uses bogus numbers" and "We must break him." Further that, "If we can stop Obama" in this his Reform quest, "It will be his Waterloo!" To this course of action, Billy Crystal of the National standard advised, "Go for the kill!" None of these people apologized though it would have assuaged the disgust the American people felt in their insulting our president!

Naturally, this brings us to disrespectful John Sununu. Imagine this former governor as advisor to a president. As a campaign manager and senior advisor to Mitt Romney, this loose cannon startted abusing the President of the United States and Mr. Romney did not care. He had "let his dogs out" because he was about to win the election and take America in another direction. Who knows, with Sununu, Gingrich and Santorum leading his pack, who knows where the nation would end up? Maybe Romney was taking us back to the mentality of the hanging slave states that he won! With t hese states before Mr. Romney's horse , maybe they were taking us back to the dar abes. Maybe Vice President Joe Biden had intellience about his when he said, "They're going to put you all back in chains." Naturally, Mr. Romney did not call Mr. Biden a liar!

OBAMA - MASTER AND COMMANDER

Fate has a way of slapping down losers. Now that General Powell has again endorsed President Obama, Sunnunu, who previously called Mr. Obama "stupid," said the endorsement was because Obama and Powell were of the same race. Naturally, he later ate the whole "crow pie." Perhaps it is because Powell was in the same White House with him as National Security Adviser, and was aware of Sununu's shortcomings that he came at him this way. Its like the President said, Trump's animosity dates to play on the soccer field when they were growing up in Kenya! Now we know, both the President and Mr. Trump played soccer. What we do know, for certain, with the defeat of Mitt Romney, John Sununu will climb back under the rock leading to the unmentionable pit from which he emanated, to spew such vile comments.

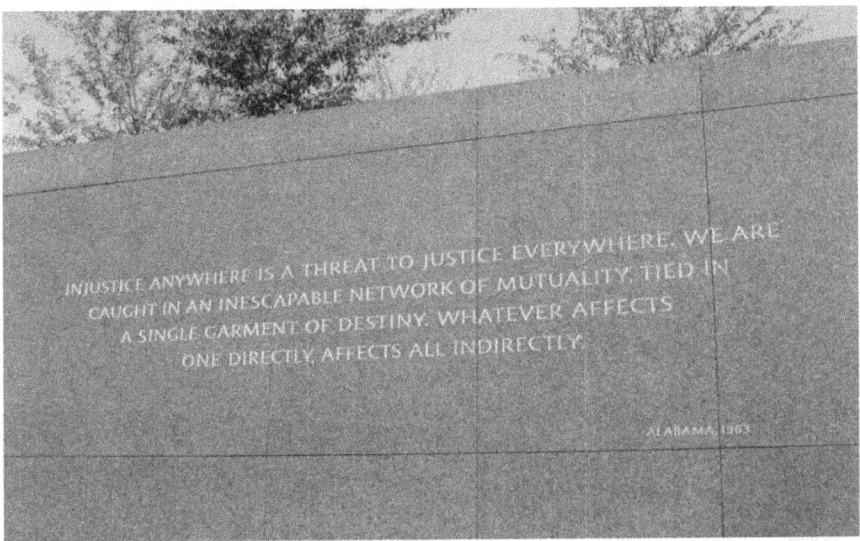

Obama - Master and Commander 636. The Inscription reads: "Injustice Anywhere is a Threat to Justice Everywhere. We are caught up in an Inescapable Network of Mutuality, Tied in a Single Garment of Destiny. Whatever Affects One Directly Affects All Indirectly." Alabama 1963

FREDERICK MONDERSON

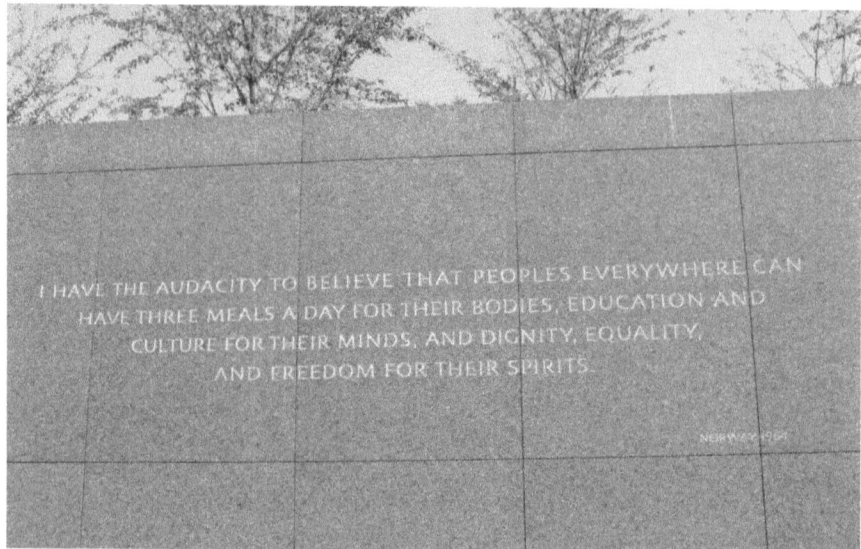

Obama - Master and Commander 638. The Inscription reads: "I have the adacity to believe that peoples everywhere can have three meals a day for their bodies, education and culture for their minds, and dignity, equality, and freedom for their spirits." Norway, 964

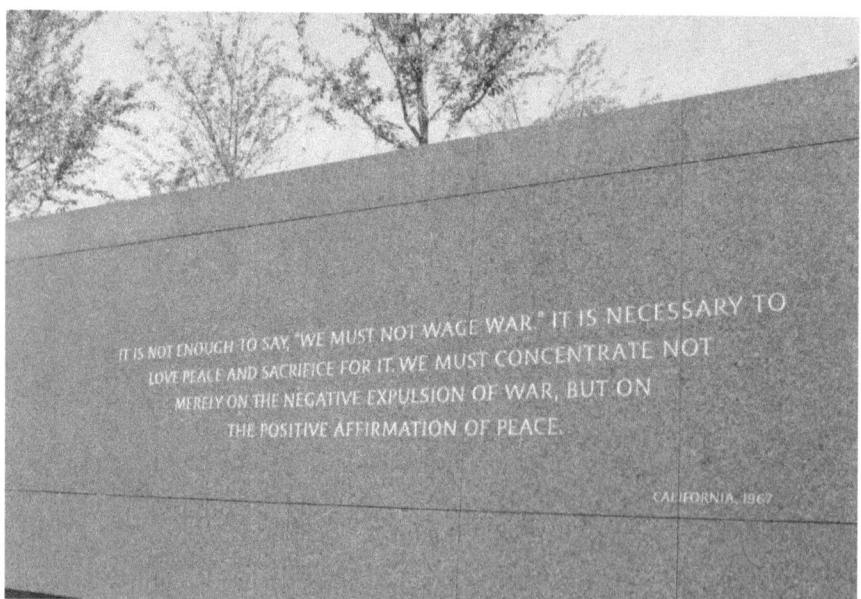

Obama - Master and Commander 639. The Inscription reads: "It is Not Enough to Say, 'We Must Not Wage War.' It is Necessary to Love Peace and Sacrifice for it. We must Concentrate Not Merely on the Negative Expulsion of War, But on the Positive Affirmation of Peace." California, 1967

67. RUDY GIULIANI WINS: "LITTLE MAN AWARD!"
By
Dr. Fred Monderson

We have heard of "Little big man," The Little Man is the Real Man," "Little Women" and even "Little People" but this is probably the first time we are hearing about the "Little Man Award." The first and well-deserved recipient, chosen from a field of out-standing runners-up, is former New York City Mayor Rudy Giuliani, a man of unbridled anger whose disdain for President Obama is visible even within the depths of the blackout in wake of Super-storm Sandy. It can be argued, a principal reason for Mr. Giuliani's animosity towards President Obama stems from his twice failed aspiration to the Office of the Presidency. It is even more stinging to his ego that President Obama accomplished the "unattainable," that Mr. Giuliani would call for his resignation ahead of his second win since the hurt would be twice as bad.

An old folk aphorism reads as follows: "Thief man no like see another thief man with bag!" That is, if one thief sees another thief with a bag, he becomes jealous thinking the other guy got what should be his. However, this play on words in no way implies either Mr. Rudy Giuliani or President Obama is a "Thief man!" It is simply a play on words that implies one individual accomplished what the other was not able to!

Some of the roots of Rudy Giuliani bitterness stems from the events of September 11, 2001, but not as right thinking people would be led to believe. You see, September 11, was the best thing that happened to Rudy Giuliani! But such a statement seems so counter-productive unless properly examined. So a bit of explanation should precede this.

FREDERICK MONDERSON

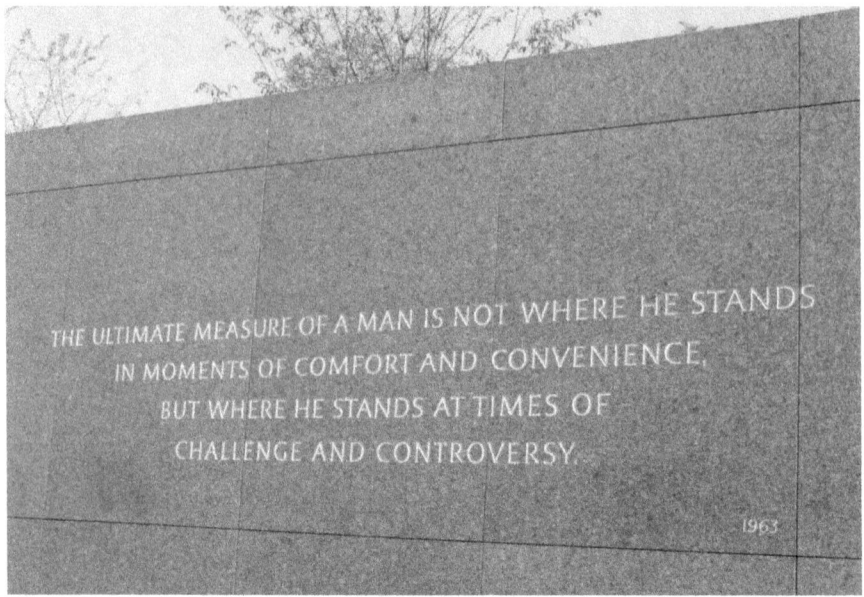

Obama - Master and Commander 640. The Inscription reads: "The Ultimate Measure of a Man is Not Where he Stands in Moments of Comfort and Convenience, But Where he Stands at Times of Challenge and Controversy." 1963

Obama - Master and Commander 641. The Inscription reads: "Every Nation must now Develop an Overriding Loyalty to Mankind as a Whole in Order to Preserve the Best in their individual Societies." New York, 1967

OBAMA - MASTER AND COMMANDER

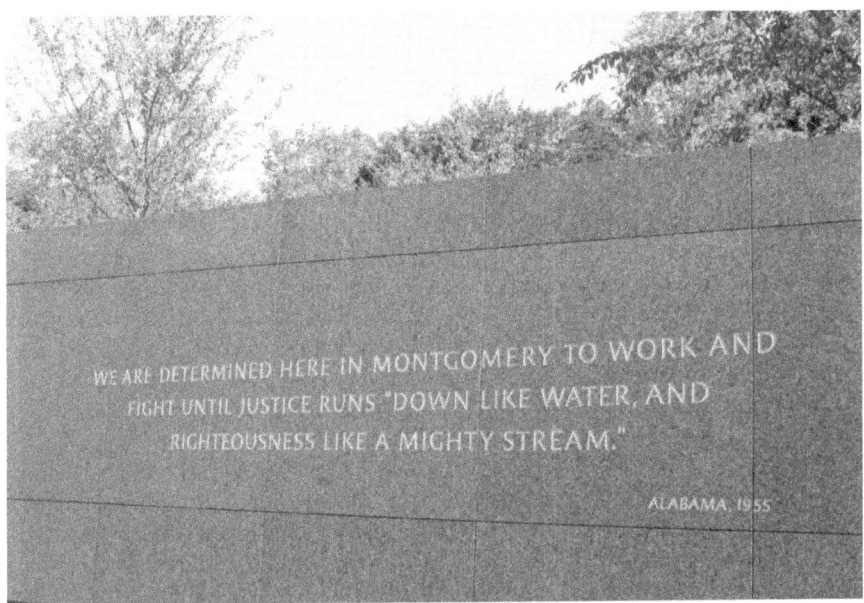

Obama - Master and Commander 642. The Inscription reads: "We are Determined here in Montgomery to Work and Fight Until Justice Runs 'Down Like Water, and Righteousness Like a Mighty Stream.'" Alabama, 1955

Rudy Giuliani was a federal prosecutor in New York City who made his name as a crime-fighter targeting the "Mob." As such, as a lawman many people had a fondness for him. Equally, and especially, employed by the feds, in his "youthful fantasy world" he may have secretly aspired to become the "top fed." Nevertheless, along the way he was ambitious and aspired to be Mayor of New York City; first as a Democrat then as a Republican. He first ran against Edward I. Koch (K-o-c-h, not Coke) in 1985. Unsuccessful, he challenged David Dinkins in 1989 when his racial streak had begun to show but he still was able to garner a miniscule number of Black votes. Crown Heights burst after the unconscionable response to the death of Gavin Cato that saw Mr. Giuliani blame and castigate Mr. Dinkins, cultivate the Jewish vote and locked up the white vote because of his perceived "squeaky clean" image. His campaign attracted some black "soup drinkers," people who drink soup dripping from the table, and the Prosecutor was off to the race in which in 1993, David Dinkins lost his re-election bid.

One of the interesting things about Mr. Giuliani's win as Mayor of New York City on his third try is a little known or remembered sign, especially blazoned in Black neighborhoods that read, "**RUDY G. FIGHTS RACISM**." Turns out he became one of the most racist and polarizing Mayors in New York City's history.

FREDERICK MONDERSON

He blamed Black people; young, old and indifferent; criminal and law-abiding; for the ills the city had begun to experience by the end of Dinkins' term. With a Democrat in the White House, Bill Clinton, and using his federal prosecutor connections as well as people's dislike for crime, the new Mayor unleashed the most draconian strategies to bring crime down. He was successful, to a point. However, Mr. Giuliani earned a new name, BRUTALIANI for his brutal unleashing of efforts against innocent as well as criminal elements in the Black community. Practically everyone stood against him. However, Fernando Ferrer, who ran against him in 1997, was weak and so as the great organization theorist has said, "People sometimes rise to the highest level of their incompetence."

As Mr. Giuliani likes to pin the old President Truman aphorism "The Buck stops here" on President Obama, so it must be pinned on him. His unleashed police tactics allowed cops to spout "We own the night;" leading to utter disregard for black life. As such, two heart rendering episodes unfolded during his tenure as mayor. The first is Abner Louima in whose case a policeman named Volpe rammed a plumber's plunger up a prisoner's rectum in a police station as the culture of indifference permeated the force. No one in the Precinct answered the prisoner's cry as he was left to die. Volpe was later convicted and sentenced to prison. The second is the shooting death of an unarmed West African immigrant Amadou Diallo who was shot at 41 times in a Bronx doorway; 19 of the bullets piercing his mangled body. Officer Weatherspoon found 2 additional bullets though the record only chose to count the original 41. By this time, everyone was against the Mayor. Even Sonny Carson, often called a separatist activist launched his "Million Voter Registration" to unseat the mayor's aspirations to a third term which happened just before term limits. After all, Ed Koch had served three terms. So at his lowest ebb ratings, terrorists attacked the city and the mayor was able to draw upon the resources, conscience and goodwill of all New Yorkers as well as the whole nation in response. He did such a good job, he earned the title "America's mayor." Thus, this is how we arrived at 9/11 being the best thing that happened to Rudy Giuliani. He was so deviously narcisstic he chose a Black man to run New York City's Board of Education simply because his name was Rudy Crew. He was a failure and left, his ideas fruitless.

OBAMA - MASTER AND COMMANDER

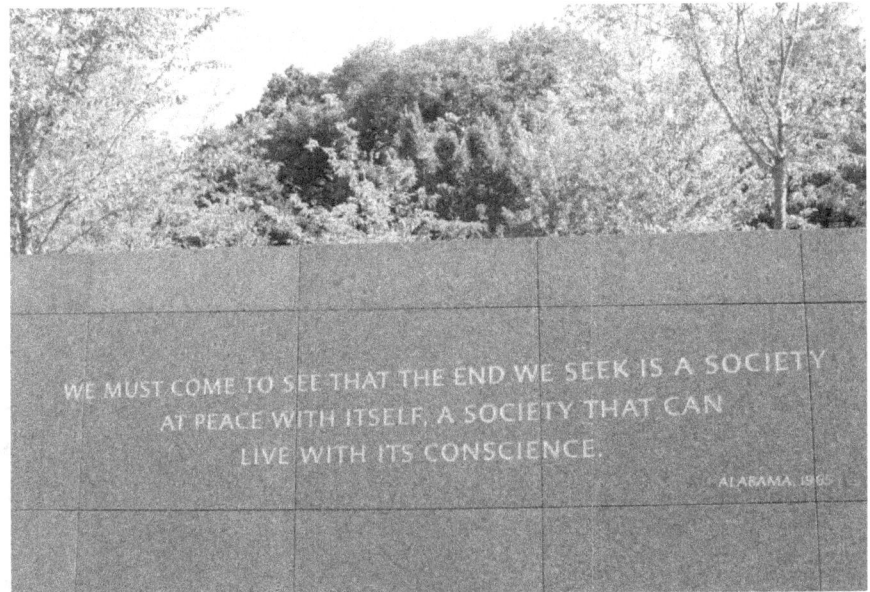

Obama - Master and Commander 643. The Inscription reads: "We Must Come to See that the End We Seek is a Society at Peace with Itself, a Society that can Live with its Conscience." Alabama, 1965

Obama - Master and Commander 644. The Inscription reads: "True Peace is not Merely the Absence of Tension. It is the Presence of Justice." 1958

FREDERICK MONDERSON

Obama - Master and Commander 645. Martin Luther King, Jr. Memorial, *is* Written in Stone!

It should be pointed out, though all New Yorkers supported the total response to the terrorists of 9/11, even activists such as Al Sharpton reminded, any of us, given the dastard deed and the nation's response, would have done as good a job as Mayor Giulinai. His arrogance showed when he refused to leave, or "Get out of Dodge," at the end of his term in 2001, thinking only he could continue the work of repairing the damage of the terrorist attack. Talk about an ego!

Fast forward and Mr. Giuliani chose to parley the fame of being "America's Mayor" into being America's President. Naturally all attempts failed. However, that racial hatred streak that Sonny Carson and so many other Black New Yorkers identified and accused him of, certainly surfaced when he thought of Barack Obama occupying that chair of Presidential responsibility. With his failure in 2008 and again in 2012 when Republicans early rejected his attempts to become the party's nominee, always scheming, the former mayor sought every opportunity to appear vivisble, relevant and to attack the President. This then brings us to Rudy Giuliani calling for the resignation of President Obama; on the eve of his historic victory to a second term.

Naturally the Mayor was incensed, to say the lease, when Governor Christie heaped praise on President Obama for his response to request for federal assistance in the Sandy crisis. Given New Yorkers response of support to his

OBAMA - MASTER AND COMMANDER

efforts after 9/11 claiming the deaths of 3000 people, and the President's equally responsive effort to the Sandy calamity, Rudy could not stomach Christie's fair assessment of Mr. Obama's presidential response.

So fast, fast forward to Friday night's rally in Ohio after the Republican deployed, some say, 100 top level Republicans to save the state from an Obama victory. People such as Guiliani think Black men, especially thinking Black men, are stupid! Imagine a group of people gunning for your job. They are deployed in the field. For sure you do have responsibilities that the office dictate. However, they want you to devote full time to carring out the responsibilities of the office and not devote any time to countering their active efforts to unseat you. The effective leader, administrator, is also the good delegator, for after all, what are subordinates for, particularly those who hold positions of responsibilities for these eventualites. Mr. Giuliani used his time on public televsion to call for the resignation of Mr. Obama because he was campaigning while Mr. Giuliani himself was campaigning against Mr. Obama. He was so callous, when General Clarke appeared on television to lend some clarity to the Benghazi situation, given its classified nature, Mr. Giulinai, thinking he had made his point, reclused himself without responding to the general's comments. One commentator on CNN did point out Mr. Giuliani's criticism was made from a campaign rally! That is to say, while Mr. Giuliani is out in the field fighing the President, he wants Mr. Obama to stand down and pay no attention to the nusiance he is trying to create. These then, are the men, Giuliani, Sununu, Gingrich, Joe Wilson, DeMint, McConnell, who lead or want to lead our nation. These are the men who want to be considered credible leaders of America. Heaven help us for their idea of the future is somewhere around 1000 A.D., perhaps earlier!

There is much more to the little man. Suffice to say, as he and other Republicans were trounced by Mr. Obama's victory, they must now reckon with a more experienced President and all their efforts, scurrilous as they were, are part of the putative record for everyone to see their Lilliputian nature. Hence, Mr. Rudy Giuliani is the recipient of the much deserved "Little Man Award!" Congratulations!

FREDERICK MONDERSON

Obama - Master and Commander 646. Flowers brighten the path through the "Mountain of Despair" entrance.

Obama - Master and Commander 647. The Inscription reads: "With this faith we will be able to hew out of the mountain of despair a stone of hope. With this faith, we will be able to transform the jangling discords of our nation into a beautiful symphony of brotherhood. With this faith we will be able to work together, to pray together, to struggle together, to go to jail together, to stand up for freedom together, knowing that we will be free one day." Martin Luther King, Jr., "**I have a Dream**," August 8, 1963.

The Inscription reads: "The Memorial is strategically place on a direct line between the Lincoln Memorial and the Thomas Jefferson Memorial. The Lincoln Memorial is where Martin Luther King, Jr. gave his 1963 'I have a Dream' speech during the March on Washington for Jobs and Freedom. The statue of Martin Luther King, Jr. gazes across the Tidal Basin towards the Thomas Jefferson Memorial and the promise of freedom found within the Declaration of Independence."

OBAMA - MASTER AND COMMANDER

Obama - Master and Commander 648. This model of the winning design most delightfully utilizes the space alloted for the Memorial.

Obama - Master and Commander 649. The King Memorial Site is strategically and wonderfully situated on the Tidal Basin amongst Washington, Jefferson, Lincoln and Roosevelt Memorials.

FREDERICK MONDERSON

> Martin Luther King, Jr.'s legacy to the world is one of love, justice, democracy and hope. The Washington, D.C. Martin Luther King, Jr. National Memorial Project Foundation, Inc. was established on May 28, 1998 to coordinate the development, funding, and construction of a memorial on the grounds of the National Mall. President William Jefferson Clinton signed a Joint Congressional Resolution authorizing the building of a memorial on July 16, 1998.
>
> - Designer: ROMA Design Group of San Francisco.
> - Architect of Record: McKissack & McKissack.
> - Contractor: McKissack & McKissack / Turner Construction / Tompkins Builders / Gilford Corporation Design-Build Joint Venture.
> - Sculptor of Record: Master Sculptor Lei Yixin.
> - Projected Cost: $120 Million.
> - Projected Completion Date: Late 2011.
>
> For more information, and to view a webcam of construction, please visit...
>
> http://www.mlkmemorial.org/

Obama - Master and Commander 650. The Inscription reads: "Martin Luther King, Jr.'s legacy to the world is one of love, justice, democracy and hope. The Washington, D.C. Martin Luther King, Jr. National Memorial Project Foundation, Inc. was established on May 28, 1998 to coordinate the development, funding, and construction of a memorial on the grounds of the National Mall. President William Jefferson Clinton signed a Joint Congressional Resolution authorizing the building of a memorial on July 16, 1998."

Obama - Master and Commander 651. From the Martin Luther King, Jr. Memorial looking across the Tidal Basin to the Thomas Jefferson Memorial with its colonnade and dome.

OBAMA - MASTER AND COMMANDER

Obama - Master and Commander 652. From across the Tidal Basin, that familiar image of Jefferson between the columns looking out!

68. WOMEN!
By
Dr. Fred Monderson

Much ink has been spilled and debate words uttered about the role of women in politics and as citizens enjoying the social amenities of being about half of the nation population and electorate. Even more important, their role as being significant in the Presidential election has been discussed at length. This has helped to make women and women's issues an important topic in the recently concluded Second Presidential Debate between President Barack Obama and former Governor of Massachusetts Mitt Romney. There it was highlighted they were playing to the all-important and pivotal female vote. So much so, as every such event creates an earmark that becomes a subject of discussion long after, again women issues lingered and got more post-debate publicity. Whereas in the first debate between these two men, observers and commentators gave Mr. Romney a "win" because President Obama seemed lethargic and unprepared. Of course, to this day they never understood his "Rope a Dope" strategy. In the second much anticipated debate, the President "came to play," and by some accounts, trounced Mr. Romney. Many commentators confessed Mr. Obama had come prepared, was more energized, knowledgeable and on point! However, they

FREDERICK MONDERSON

viewed Mr. Romney somewhat opposite, even attributing his "failure" to handling the "woman's issue."

In the debate, when confronted with a women's question, Mr. Romney reflected on his choice of staff upon being elected Governor of Massachusetts. His staff was all male, probably all white but without women. Seeking to correct this, he claims, he contacted women's groups saying "Can you find me qualified women to be part of my staff." In response, he claims, he was supplied with "binders of women." Nonetheless, within minutes, this utterance, "Binders" and "Women" went viral on the Internet when all manner of "Cartoonish" creations flooded the airwaves. Days later, this strange women recruitment description remained a TV and radio talk show topic. Seems this mishandling did not go well with women who had additional "women's issues" with Mr. Romney. Thus, with the election considered, "Too close to call," it became a wait and see situation to determine if this will hurt him.

Conversely, when Mr. Obama assumed the Presidency; in fact, in the Transition Period, he came with his team of qualified women. So much so, at the time Mr. Obama was compared to other presidents who had women in their cabinet. Thus, with women in high profile roles in his cabinet, in support, advisory and decision making roles, Mr. Obama also appointed two women to the United States Supreme Court.

Reflecting on the social challenges his mother faced and the business ceiling that limited his grandmother's aspirations notwithstanding her professional ability to perform functions in her job in a bank; Mr. Obama championed the cause of women by passing the Lilly Ledbetter Fair Pay Act as the first legislative action of his new administration. As stated, recognizing a woman's place is on the Supreme Court, he appointed two to the prestigious judicial body which was in keeping with his inherent belief in the equality of the sexes. However, it could very well be that the President chose the two women, their professional standing notwithstanding, but also their sensitivity to the legal implications of *Roe v. Wade* and the threat that continuously hang over this important legislation that is so significant in terms of giving women a choice!

As a family man with a loving wife, two beautiful daughters and a darling mother-in-law, some of his closest advisers and inner circle people, Mr. Obama could be considered a "women's man," if you will pardon the pun!

OBAMA - MASTER AND COMMANDER

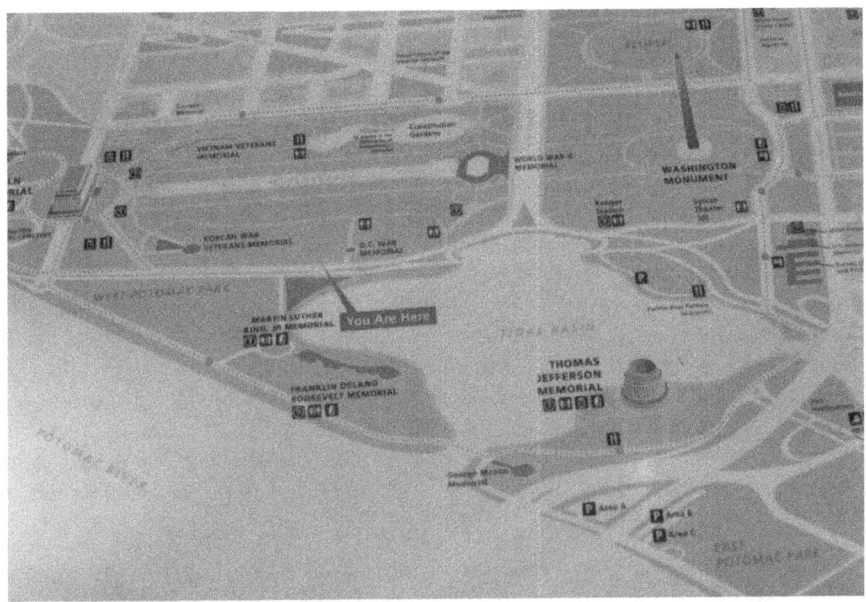

Obama - Master and Commander 653. Panoramic view of historic monuments that characterize Washington, DC as a city of exemplary memorial, viz., Lincoln, Vietnam Veterans, World War II, Washington, DC War, Martin Luther King, Jr., Franklin Delano Roosevelt, George Mason and Thomas Jefferson, all enjoying the cool breeze of the Tidal Basin fed by the Potomac River.

"With a combined length of approximately 500 feet, the granite 'Inscription Wall' arcs on either side of the Mountain of Despair, engraved with Dr. King's speeches and writings which embody the universal themes of love, justice, democracy and hope." Master Sculptor Lei Yixin's masterpiece, the 'Stone of Hope,' includes a 28 foot tall statue of Martin Luther King, Jr., emerging from the granite."

Within the "Don't Ask, Don't Tell" conundrum women were also an issue since Lesbians and transgender individuals were also counted in this group. The President believed women should get contraception medication from their bosses and he spoke to this effect. In such situations as his insistence on hiring of teachers; his proposing that women go back to college to further their education; certainly recognizing their important roles in family health when he passed Health Care Reform; and their roles as head of families when he extended the nation's safety net through the support of food stamps; Mr. Obama has always been conscious of the significant role women play in the society and he has supported them without question. However, because of Republican predisposition to oppose the President, every issue he proposed, especially women's issues, they had to and

FREDERICK MONDERSON

did oppose. Nevertheless, he can certainly claim to have stood up for women in his administration because of their importance and to expect large chunks of their vote is not unreasonable!

Old folks always said, "If you want to know about 'eight' ask 'seven' and 'nine' because they live next door!" Despite the glossy picture Mitt Romney paints of himself as Governor of Massachusetts, we must give credence to the thoughts of Senator John Kerry a lifelong resident of the state and Governor Deval Patrick because he moved into the office Governor Romney vacated. Mr. Kerry lived through the Governor's term and Mr. Patrick was forced to clean up after Mr. Romney. Sadly, he often explained what a mess he inherited but the Romney machinery seemed to blunt this important message from "nine" and "seven" about "eight."

Obama - Master and Commander 654. The Ulysses S. Grant Memorial stands before the U.S. Capital Building.

OBAMA - MASTER AND COMMANDER

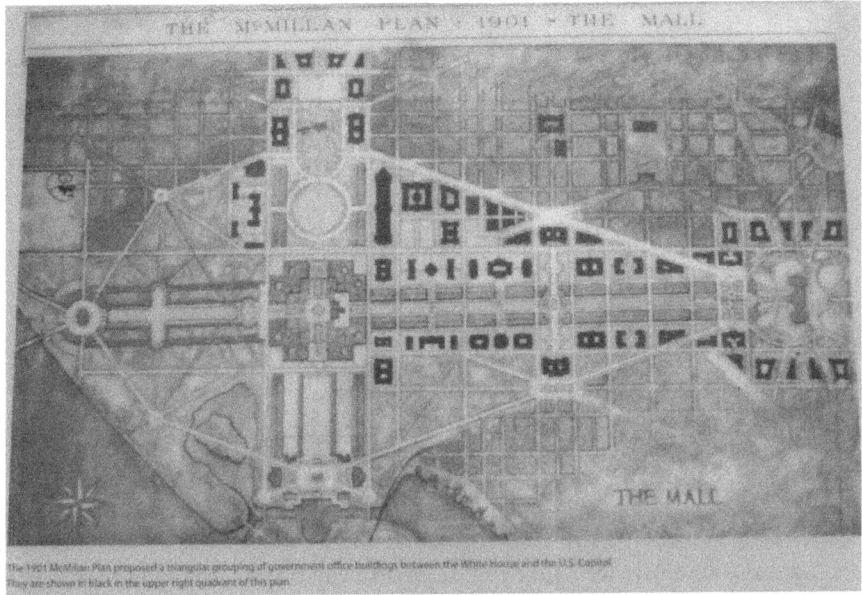

Obama - Master and Commander 655. The 1901 McMillan Plan proposed a triangular grouping of government office buildings between the White House and the U.S. Capital. They are shown in black in the upper right quadrant of this plan.

Obama - Master and Commander 656. The U.S. Navy Memorial was dedicated in 1987, the Navy's 212th Anniversary. President Roosevelt at his desk in the White House, 1935.

FREDERICK MONDERSON

Obama - Master and Commander 657. Corinthian colonnades front the Capital Building at the House (left) section, central entrance (middle) and stairs to the Senate section.

Obama - Master and Commander 658. The International Brotherhood of Teamsters Headquarters.

OBAMA - MASTER AND COMMANDER

Obama - Master and Commander 659. The Federal Triangle Heritage Trail showing government buildings between the Capital Building and the White House.

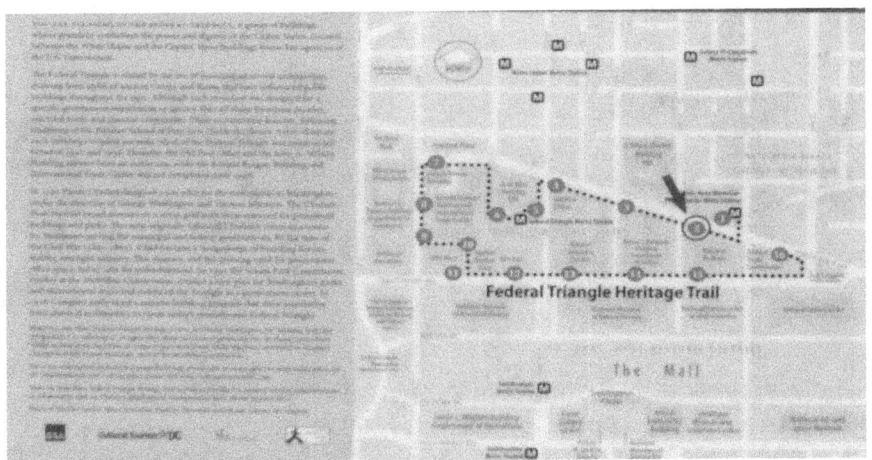

Obama - Master and Commander 660. More detailed placement of the government buildings within the Federal Triange Heritage Trail.

FREDERICK MONDERSON

Obama - Master and Commander 661. A great admonition at the base of a statue at the National Archives that instructs, and insists people "Study the Past" for therein lies the record of the whole pastime!

Obama - Master and Commander 662. The sculptured frieze of the decorated Pediment of the National Archives atop an architrave supported by Corinthian capital columns.

OBAMA - MASTER AND COMMANDER

Obama - Master and Commander 663. Seated in contemplation before the National Archives Building.

Obama - Master and Commander 664. Instruments of human and scientific development that have moved humanity along the pageantry of history.

FREDERICK MONDERSON

Obama - Master and Commander 665. Seated in contemplation with reading material, this base reminds, "Study the Past!"

Obama - Master and Commander 666. Close-up view of the base of the above statue, accoutrements that have advanced the pageantry of human development.

OBAMA - MASTER AND COMMANDER

Obama - Master and Commander 667. "The Heritage of the Past is the Seed that Brings Forth the Harvest of the Future."

Obama - Master and Commander 668. *Ars Boni* decorative feature of a Pediment atop an architrave buttressed by Ionic pillars adorning the National Archive.

FREDERICK MONDERSON

Obama - Master and Commander 669. *Ars Aequi* decorative feature of a pediment atop an architrave buttressed by Ionic pillars adorning the National Archive.

69. SOME PERSPECTIVES ON THE OBAMA AGE
By
Dr. Fred Monderson

President Obama has been villainized by so many persons who lay claim to being "analysts" one has to wonder how we could trust such persons assessmentsince they who have now shown their biased, even bigoted, underbelly. One thing that can be said for Mr. Obama, he takes these insults and shallow assessments in stride allowing others to see how ridiculously insulting, to the President of the United States, the most powerful man in the world, these individuals could be in demonstrating their ingorant behaviors.

In aftermath of the Navy Seals' raid on Osama bin-Laden's compound, at the height of his "birther charade," in the *New York Post* a political cartoon appeared showing President Obama instructing his forces "the next compound you will raid will be Trump Towers." Unfortunately, this never materialized for Donald Trump soon self-destruct and reclused himself as a Presidential contender. Yet he lingers in the media airwaves like that disgusting mosquito nuisance that keeps buzzing your ear with no bite! Conversely, the brilliance of Obama is seen in his brushing

OBAMA - MASTER AND COMMANDER

the nuisance from his shoulder and allowing such disrespectful clients to bake and eat their own "crow pie."

It is interesting how Republicans, unable to tarnish Obama's brilliance in their never ending critique of his social policies constantly revert to their last line of armament, *ad hominem*. So much like that ridiculous blonde woman who accused President Obama of being "an inadequate black man" they cannot touch his moral fiber, his family values! See how President Obama ascends and descends Air Force One, he runs! In the Second Debate, when the president said Mitt Romney was playing loose with the facts, or as some said, "Lying," his son later said he felt he could go up there and slap the President of the United States. Never mind the Secret Service, fit as Mr. Obama seems, he certainly could handle that fellow.

Obama - Master and Commander 670. The Ulyses S. Grant Memorial stands at the head of the National Mall and before the Marble Terrace of the Capital Building at his rear, with the Madison Building and the Jefferson Building of the Library of Congress and the Supreme Court nearby at the rear.

FREDERICK MONDERSON

Obama - Master and Commander 671. From behind the Grant Memorial, a semblance of his view towards the Washington Memorial and beyond.

Obama - Master and Commander 672. Another view of Grant from a different angle with the Botanic Gardens off to the left.

OBAMA - MASTER AND COMMANDER

Obama - Master and Commander 673. This view of President Ulysses S. Grant is from his front with the Dome of the Capital Building in the rear.

Obama - Master and Commander 674. Men at war in defense of **Liberty**!

FREDERICK MONDERSON

Obama - Master and Commander 675. More men at war in defense of **Liberty**!

Obama - Master and Commander 676. Even more men at war in defense of **Liberty**!

OBAMA - MASTER AND COMMANDER

Nevertheless, one has to wonder at Republican "big guns" McCain, Palin, McConnell, Boehner, DeMint, etc., after a "busy day at the office," when they get home, flop down on the couch, unfold the newspaper or turn on the TV, only to be greeted by the fallout of "One of our guys," "our allies" has called President Obama a "dick" or as Rep. Wilson did in the Chamber of the House, tell the President "you lie," or even "Bye, Bye!" Joe Walsh who said the President was a "tyrant" because he stood up for the American people against special interests, etc. Do these guys high-five themselves, get on the phone to congratulate each other for another notch of insult in their belt or squirm in the seats or hide under the sofa, having unlocked Pandora's, I mean, the Republican's "box" of disrespectful and odious negativite behavior.

Obama - Master and Commander 677. View of the Capital Building's Marble Terrace and dome from the Plaza Green.

FREDERICK MONDERSON

Obama - Master and Commander 678. View of the Capital Building from beside the Navy and Marine Marble Monument.

Obama - Master and Commander 679. Statue of E. Barrett Prettyman and a group standing before the United States Court House named in his honor.

The newest "shoot from the lip" attack on the character of the President was made by Congresswoman Michelle Bachmann who accused Mr. Obama of "running a

OBAMA - MASTER AND COMMANDER

gangster government in Washington!" Naturally, Ms. Bachmann did not like the Introductory song as she appeared on a "Late-Night" show. In the litany of Republican *ad hominem* insults we cannot forget Mark Halperin, a commentator on MSNBC who thought he was on "delayed feed," called Mr. Obama a "Dick" while on the air because of his perceived view of a presidential action. The CNN ticker then reported "MSNBC panelist suspended after Obama insult." In this case, while Republicans may be able to claim Mr. Halperin is not a "card carrying member" of their club, independent critics opposed to Mr. Obama are on their side of the line and therefore are unwilling and as such, perhaps, unintentional allies.

Another example of shameless anti-Obamite "foot-in-mouth" misstatements occurred on the now defunct CNN's "In the Arena" with Elliot Spitzer, former Governor of New York, where a commentator Abrams seemed one of the first and honest voices, in commenting on MSNBC's action in response to the President's press conference and Mr. Halperin's remarks. He said "This is not something you say about the President of the United States."

What this may teach us, even "nice looking" "normal" people can drop "bombs" and one has to wonder what is it about President Obama that really motivates people to speak so loosely and disrespectfully about this man. Here we recently have a Republican Senator say on the floor "The President should be ashamed ...." For what? He did not reach to grab some person's ankle in a public restroom! He has never been "hiking the Appalachian Trail." Imagine that guy, seeking hermit silitude, out there alone hikig the trail when he s hould be in his lover's arems in Brazil. Say it loud, President Obama has not fathered any illegitimate children and been unfaithful to his wife! He has certainly not sent lewd photos of himself in the mail.

FREDERICK MONDERSON

Obama - Master and Commander 680. President Garfield's statue stands in the quintessential street entrance to the house of power!

Obama - Master and Commander 681. United States Botanical Gardens.

OBAMA - MASTER AND COMMANDER

Obama - Master and Commander 682. From the street, view of the fence and green lawn that esplanades the Capital Building.

Obama - Master and Commander 683. Tablenacles atop floral decorated stone jambs adorning the southern entrance to the Capital Building signalling this is the place were "all the power" resides and emanates from.

FREDERICK MONDERSON

How comical it seems, in the smoke and mirrors euphoria that clouded the actor "Arnold's" rise to become Governor of California. In that malaise, Republicans began championing the notion of changing the constitutional requirement that a presidential candidate not necessarily be native born so Arnold Schwarzenegger could run for and become president! This was also the instant these people were denying the citizenship of the President of the United States. How beautiful the music of that Pied Piper tune sounded! Unfortunately and unknown to many, Mr. Schwarzenegger had social and moral skeletons in his closet. Meanwhile, and again, other elements of the Republican Party were incessantly, vehemently and inclandestinely denying Barack Obama's citizenship designed to challenge his right to be President. As betting men, these Republicans, in their tunnel vision, chose the potential long shot as a safe bet, while relegating the safe bet to a long shot! In other words, they were willing to choose a man who cheated on his wife, sleep with the help, fathered an illegitimate child over a respectable married man with a beautiful wife and two lovely children who are ideals of what even Republicans themselves want in a family and leader. These are shades of why Republicans ran the country into the ground.

However, for argument sake, let us suppose the covered farce was successful, the constitutional requirement changed so that a foreign born could run for the office and Mr. Schwarzenegger elected President of the United States. So here we have him attending a G-8 meeting abroad and there he is on the platform with leaders of the other great nations waiting for the photo opportunity with the customary anarchists outside picketing. Then, Wikileaks leader Assange releases the ethically damaging information about his philandering, embarrassing the nation through another childish Republican behavior.

An even more embarrassing Republican episode on Spitzer's program occurred when a Republican Congressman boasted and took credit for saying the President should be ashamed, for whatever. Now, here we have an intelligent, professionally and academically qualified Mr. Obama, whose stamina and strategies and tactics awarded him the US Presidency. Most people, whether in government or not, who have disparaged Mr. Obama constantly, do not have the intellectual fortitude or academic accreditation of a man genuinely committed to improving the condition of his nation from these changing times. Word has it, in the academic age of the 1970s, when young Adjuncts and Professors applied for teaching positions, particularly in the Community Colleges, the people in control of P and B (Personnel and Budget) would demand some of the highest qualifications from these new people. They, on the other hand, had "slipped in" with degrees in "Basket-making" and "Pottery" and sustaining their jobs were now in those powerful committees controlling the college.

OBAMA - MASTER AND COMMANDER

Obama - Master and Commander 684. View of the Dome from the manicured lawn.

Obama - Master and Commander 685. View of the back colonnade of the House side of the Capital Building from the manicured lawn.

FREDERICK MONDERSON

Solomon G. Brown

Solomon G. Brown (1829-1906), the Smithsonian's first African-American employee, retired in 1906 after 54 years of service. Brown, well-known for his lectures on natural history, was also an avid poet and Anacostia community leader.

Wisdom from these minds would flow
Increasing knowledge more and more;
Now younger men can easily learn
Just how these great men were concerned
In diffusing usefull knowledge. . . .

By Solomon Brown, 1902, in honor of his 50th year at the Smithsonian Institution

Obama - Master and Commander 686. Solomon G. Brown, the Smithsonian's first african-American employee, retired in 1906 after 54 years of service.

Perhaps if these people had the educational qualifications of Mr. Obama then they would not be so outlandish. With a sound educational background, you see the world and people differently.

OBAMA - MASTER AND COMMANDER

Again, that Congressman added, the president launched his re-election campaign nearly two years before election date. What he did not include, President Obama has been attacked before he became President, while he is president, on his way to re-election, and will be even after he is re-elected and perhaps after he leaves office in 2017. The Congressman had amnesia for he did not remember he was in the initial wave who voted atainst Mr. Obama's Stimulus Bill, on February 17, 2009 and remained intransigently opposed until this election. They exhibit "Group think!"

Among the recent crop of Republican Presidential candidates, many commentators highlight Newt Gingrich is the most intellectual among the lot. In choosing leaders and sound leadership, those who choose should realize, intellectuality and arrogance are incompatible. Witness his arrogant "I will be the nominee" boast and his lead-weight drop in the polls. Contrast this with the academic achievements of Mr. Obama and his suave and sophisticated demeanor whether on the campaign trail, attending to the people's business, informing the nation of the fate of Osama bin Laden or even representing the nation abroad. Couple this with the question that Mr. Obama has pursued a policy of appeasement. His honest, cool and straightforward answer has been, "Ask Osama bin-Laden, Awlaki, the Somali Pirates and some 22 of 30 top Al Qaeda operatives if I appease them!" What Mr. Obama's critics want is for him to publicly state what are his plans for the "bad boys." This he cannot do.

Well, let the American people "do the math!" However, that is why they chose Mr. Obama as the most admired man of 2011 and will re-elect him in 2012!

Obama - Master and Commander 687. Though the grounds are being repaired, an opening in the fence is permitted to allow visitors to take that important picture with the resplendence of the Capital Building as a background.

FREDERICK MONDERSON

Obama - Master and Commander 688. Peace and tranquility on the Capital Building Grounds. As a gifted author once said, "You have no idea of what Heaven looks like until you get there!" Fred Monderson

Obama - Master and Commander 689. Another view of that wonderful scene of green and marble against a blue sky!

OBAMA - MASTER AND COMMANDER

70. ASSESSING THE OBAMA PRESIDENCY
By
Dr. Fred Monderson

As the Republican candidates battle to be chosen as their party's standard bearer to oppose President Obama in the 2012 national elections, besides beating up on each other, they yet stand unalterably opposed to the man whose job they are seeking. That is, if the President favors an issue the Republicans oppose it in a manner that all Republicans are so disposed. In this respect, the President's every action has fallen short of Republican expectations, no matter how such policy or practice benefits the nation, more than 9 1/2 out of 10 times it falls below Republican expectation and as they generally play to their base. Something seems wrong with that math wherein a culture of division is fostered. Many have interpreted all the flack directed towards President Barack Obama as racial hatred; while others, however, even Mr. Obama, chose to see it as Republicans "playing hard." Nevertheless and perhaps, if an adversary executed some vile act against the nation, Republicans will demonstrate solidarity in support of a response but even then they would criticize the manner in which the President handled the matter.

On rare occasions as when Mr. Obama extended the millionaires tax cut, despite Republican insistence on fiscal austerity and this measure added to the deficit, Republicans were pleased in what seemed a hypocritical stance. Or, in the Debt Ceiling debacle, in what was tantamount to an old adage, "I robbed Obama blind;" Speaker John Boehner boasted "We got 98 percent of what we wanted," as some wanted to believe Mr. Obama had capitulated to his opponents. But as a realist he executed the best possible strategy at the time in a strategic compromise in the nation's interest while some observers considered Republicans at the trough in lipstick were still pigs no matter the squeal. Realistically, if one side could boast of getting such a high percentage of what they sought in a bargaining trade off, then something is wrong with that math!

Now, despite this negativist view, Barack Obama achieved a great deal as President. Or, as a current political commercial reminds. "The Presidency is a management position" and Mr. Obama has exemplified the highest form of management, that is, Republican criticism, playing to its base, notwithstanding, when we consider the depths to which the American state had succumbed, internationally and domestically; the rescue, recovery and revamping or resuscitation of the nation's economics; moral fiber; foreign policy transformation; its insistence on and recultivation of America's creative spirit of giving, imbuing the nation with a greater force to slingshot into a brighter and even more successful future. We see Obama leadership. Thus, when all things are considered, the current round of Republican contenders pales in insignificance when compared with President Barack Obama. Whereas, in the 2008 election the significant

FREDERICK MONDERSON

attraction was the election of the first African American President. This election of 2012 is a referendum on a man of tremendous moral stature, possessing and employing a work ethic not only unparalleled but he strives to advance the cause of all Americans in many facets of their social and legal existence. All this is buttressed by some of the most capable advisers, viz., military, economic, family, political and moral and spiritual. Thus, Mr. Obama continues to dumfound his critics in practically every conceivable way, so much so, the *Newsweek* magazine ran a cover feature entitled "Why are Mr. Obama's critics so Dumb!" Well, let's take a look at the Obama record as President because in answer to "What has President Obama accomplished in the last three years?" the following will show he has done a great deal and having sailed the ship of state out of the perilous waters of international scorn, two active wars, terrorist confrontation, Somali Pirates, an economy tremendously hemorrhaging jobs and a depressing housing market, and much more. Under the President's continued leadership with the policies he has instituted America will be able to boast its greatest days lie yonder in the calm waters, under the blue skies and among even greener pastures of the future.

Obama - Master and Commander 690. Two statues adorn the entrance to the Rayburn House Office Building.

OBAMA - MASTER AND COMMANDER

Obama - Master and Commander 691. Entrance to the Cannon House Office Building.

FREDERICK MONDERSON

Obama - Master and Commander 692. The Cannon House Office Building boasts its own distinct style with elevated Doric columns.

Obama - Master and Commander 693. James Madison Memorial as part of the Library of Congress.

OBAMA - MASTER AND COMMANDER

Obama - Master and Commander 694. James Madison sits majestically in a hall on the first floor of his Library in the Library of Congress tripartie.

One of the first significant acts of the Obama Presidency was the passage into law of the Lilly Ledbetter Fair Pay Act designed to ensure women get paid the same as men for doing the same type of work. Beginning this year, new health insurance plans will be required to cover women's preventative services such as mammograms, domestic violence screenings and contraception without charge. As Republicans tried to roll back a woman's right to choose and defund Planned Parenthood, the President showed some grit by standing up to them and even reversed the Global Gag Rule which banned government from providing aid to international family planning groups.

Everyone should be familiar with the contentious nature of the environment surrounding discussion and passage of the landmark Affordable Care Act designed to restore health care as a basic cornerstone of middle class security in America. This Health Care Reform Act as its also called, was not only historic because many previous administrations had tried to get it passed and Mr. Obama was the first to get as far and succeed; but it also brought out the worst in Republicans. Let us not forget "Waterloo DeMint," "Go for the Kill" Billy Krystal, and the coalescing of the "Tea Party" who had some vicious things to say about Mr. Obama and demonstrated the most vile and disrespectful caricature of the man.

FREDERICK MONDERSON

Yet still, he prevailed because the Democrats were in the majority in Congress and that new reality emboldened them to be part of this historic legislation. Some of the provisions of the Health Care Reform Act designed to help the nearly fifty million Americans who have no health insurance have so aggravated Republicans, repeal of the measure has been a hallmark platform issue for them ever since going into the election.

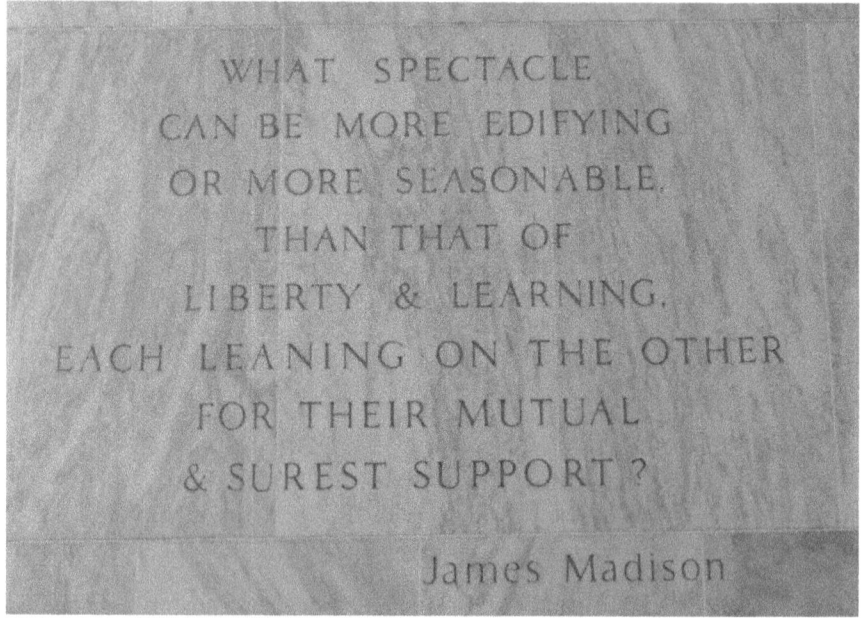

Obama - Master and Commander 695. The Inscription reads: "What spectacle can be more edifying or more seasonable than that of liberty and learning. Each leaning on the other for their mutural and surest support?" James Madison.

In this Affordable Care Act Mr. Obama's strategy has been to end insurance company abuses by prohibiting insurers from denying coverage to people with pre-existing conditions and cancelling coverage when someone gets sick. As an effort to keep premiums low, the act has insisted insurance companies must justify rate hikes; provide rebates if they don't spend at least 80% of consumers' premiums on care instead of overhead, marketing and profits. This issue is so significant, it boasts of providing first time affordable insurance to more than 32 million Americans and that nearly all Americans - 95 % of those under the age of 65 will have health insurance. In closing the Medicare Prescription Drug "Donut Hole" more than 2.6 million seniors have saved an average of over $550.00 each annually on their prescription drugs and by 2020 the Medicare "Donut hole" will be completely closed.

OBAMA - MASTER AND COMMANDER

In the election year of 2008 the nation's job loss was somewhere around 800,000 per month and by February of 2009 when Mr. Obama took office the nation had lost some 5.1 million jobs. The president thus took immediate action to address the crisis particularly as it affected the middle class, hurting not simply from job loss but also from home foreclosures and declining home value. Initiating an economic recovery program that supported as many as 3.6 million jobs by cutting taxes, investing in clean energy, repairing roads and bridges, keeping teachers in the classrooms and protecting unemployment benefits. Bailing out the auto industry prevented the loss of more than 1.4 million jobs. In response, these auto industry people printed shirts for the 2012 election that read: "He saved our jobs. Now we must save his!"In fighting for passage of the American Jobs Act and encouraging private sector job creation, some 3.5 million jobs were created between February 2010 and February 2012. In fact, as of today March 10, 2012, the latest labor report shows job growth for the third month in a row.

From day one of his administration the President has concentrated on strengthening the economy so that Americans will be able to raise a family, send their kids to school, own a home and put enough away to retire. In order to do this, he emphasized Education reform through restructuring to "out-educate the world." In this, he emphasized strengthening Community Colleges and making college education accessible to hundreds of thousands more students by ending billions of dollars in subsides to banks and using savings to double funding for Pell Grant recipients. Mr. Obama made substantial investments in clean energy manufacturing to create jobs of the future in America and reduce the nation's dependence on foreign oil. Addressing the Wall Street mess he insisted on reform to protect American families from unfair lending practices, rein in excesses on Wall Street and prevent future financial crises. Today the DOW stands at double whenhe took office. He also called for closing tax loopholes to ensure millionaires and billionaires don't pay less in taxes than the middle class.

FREDERICK MONDERSON

Obama - Master and Commander 696. The Thomas Jefferson Building of the Library of Congress.

OBAMA - MASTER AND COMMANDER

Obama - Master and Commander 697. The "Blashfield Wheel" and the "Wise Owl" of the Library of Congress.

In his campaign for the Presidency Mr. Obama pledged to end the war in Iraq in a responsible manner and he kept his word by bringing the troops home. However, in transitioning full responsibility to the Iraqi people, the US remains committed to Iraq's long-term security and will continue to develop a strong and enduring partnership with that nation. During this current presidential campaign Republican contenders, in playing to their base, accused Mr. Obama of appeasement to terrorists and other "bad boys." His response in the White House Briefing Room was simply "Ask Osama bin-Laden and the 22 of 30 top Al Qaeda leadership removed from the battlefield if I'm an appeaser!" In this, he remains committed to dismantling and defeating Al-Qaeda and its affiliates. To honor his commitment to the great warriors of Iraq, Afghanistan and those who captured Osama bin-Laden and all servicemen, the President proposed tax credits to encourage businesses to hire unemployed and disabled veterans. Michelle Obama and Jill Biden have been working with and in support of military families. In addition to seekign jobs, veterans are encouraged to use the GI Bill to go to college or get technical training.

FREDERICK MONDERSON

Obama - Master and Commander 698. Benjamin Franklin's statue outside of the Federal Building.

OBAMA - MASTER AND COMMANDER

Obama - Master and Commander 699. A masterpirece of Washington D.C. and American building practices appropriately featuring American Craft.

Obama - Master and Commander 700. The pinnacle of the Washington Monument, "Old Glory" and the MIA remembrance.

FREDERICK MONDERSON

Obama - Master and Commander 701. John Paul Jones of "I have not begun to fight" fame and "Raise the Colors!"

Obama - Master and Commander 702. "The Gift of Trees."

Obama - Master and Commander 703. Colonades in the center and left and right of the principal entrance to the Capital Building with its wonderfully decorated cornice that depicts a scene from the time of the Declaration of Independence.

71. BROADSIDE AGAINST OBAMA:
Unfair
By
Dr. Fred Monderson

In "Not the man America voted for" as a **Sunday Opinion** in *New York Daily News*, Sunday November 13, 2011, pp. 38-39, guest columnist historian John Steele Gordon stated, "The 2008 Barack Obama went on to squander voters' goodwill." How wrong could he be! In fact, David Hanna of Madison Wisconsin, New Jersey, in expressing the **Voice of the People**, Sunday November 13, 2011, p. 40 replied: "I think John Steele Gordon is wrong. President Obama's supporters have been disappointed, but not because he's been too partisan. Rather, its because he hasn't been partisan enough! If he's smart [and he is], he will keep hammering home a repeal of the Bush tax cuts on those making more than $250,000 per year. He'll be accused of waging class warfare - but, then again, so were Theodore Roosevelt and his cousin Franklin in their time. I'd say that's pretty good company." Equally, Kevin Beers of Brooklyn said: "It seems inappropriate to refer to John Steele Gordon as a historian when he seems more interested in rewriting history. He refers to President Obama as 'a hyper-partisan liberal ideologue with arrogance and rigidity.' I'm afraid that such epithets, except for the liberal tag, are more appropriately ascribed to Republicans like Mitch McConnell and John Boehner, who have been absolutely uncooperative."

FREDERICK MONDERSON

While many people would tend to agree with these two voices, there's much more to Mr. Gordon's position. He states the President "has only two major legislative accomplishments to his credit: the Stimulus Bill and Obama Care." He forgets to count the "Lilly Ledbetter Law" giving women equal pay for equal work. Considering that nearly half the workforce is female; they certainly are significantly in the voting pool; thus, to make their wages comparative to males, would certainly be considered major to this constituency.

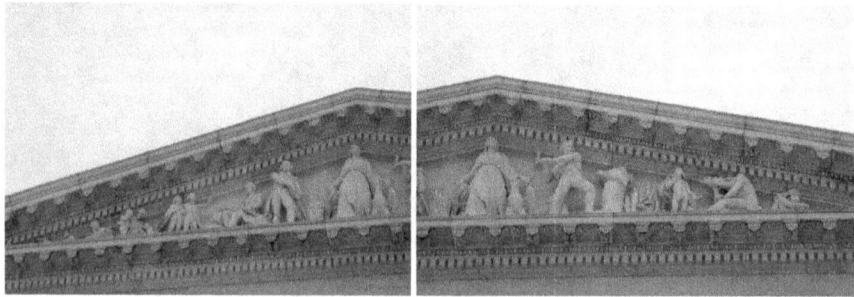

Obama - Master and Commander 704. The two halves of the same cornice atop the Capital Building.

Obama - Master and Commander 705. Iconic image of America's July Fourth Declaration, the Constitution and the Liberty it stands for!

72. WEST AND RUSHMORE
By
Dr. Fred Monderson

There goes Cornell West again, criticizing President Obama for "being concerned about his legacy," being concerned about getting his name on "Mount Rushmore." If this is so, Mr. Obama truly deserves the honor of being on the iconic Mount Rushmore, but not for the reasons Mr. West would assign when viewed from his

OBAMA - MASTER AND COMMANDER

narrow, anti-Obama stance. After all, Cornell West has consistently criticized the President for his performance, for "not doing enough for Black people," and now being concerned about his legacy. Purportedly, this has to do with his re-election, for the status of Mount Rushmore erection is only accorded to great presidents who, for one thing, were elected to two terms. Even if the President has the tenacity and vision to look to change on Mount Rushmore, he has had to rescue the nation, fight to defuse the "Party of No" minefield he has had to function in, chart a vision for the future and fight back the significant re-election challenge of Super PACs such as Carl Rove's running $25m of negative Ads and Ricketts $10m proposal to use Rev. Wright as a negative tool.

Two things quickly. First, while we're told Mitt Romney repudiated the Ad featuring Rev. Wright as an anti-Obama strategy, we must not be mislead into believing he was being civil, humane and considerate towards the President. Then again, the Media spin is that this was just an idea that was dismissed. Quite the contrary! According to Jeff Zeleny, this idea got "pretty far in the discussion phase." Fact is, since Rev. Wright is a religious figure, religion would become an issue and this introduces Mr. Romney's Mormon faith as a subject of discussion. Equally, the Mormon's exclusion of Blacks is a Pandora Box issue Romney does not want to open. Thus, self-interest guided his decision to not go Wright!

Second, one has to wonder if Mr. West knows the origin of the Mount Rushmore idea which, thus far, has to do with the desire to honor the American Presidents George Washington, Thomas Jefferson, Teddy Roosevelt and Abraham Lincoln, whose images adorn the mountainside near Keystone, in South Dakota.

Obama - Master and Commander 706. Close-up of the columns with Corinth Capitals below the decorated ceiling and also showing column shaft, capital, architrave, the simple pediment to the windows and the decorated zenith of the engaged pillared walls.

Zahi Hawass, the Egyptian Egyptologist, once remarked Mr. Obama looks like King Tut, so it is not inconceivable the President knows more than Cornell West and wants to identify with this little known aspect of his roots. In Frederick Monderson's *Hatshepsut's Temple at Deir el Bahari* (Amazon) he quotes N. de Garis Davies "The Tomb of Senmen, Brother of Senmut" from the *Society of*

FREDERICK MONDERSON

Biblical Archaeology 75 (December 10, 1913) whose description of this site is quite interesting for Davies states: "'Higher upon, on the same hill-side is a feature unique in the Necropolis, a group of man, woman and child, carved out of a great boulder, the back of which is still left in the rough.' Three thousand years later, American Presidents would be glorified in this Mount Rushmore phenomenon, an African replica." However, consistent with the "age of distortion" Davies never let on about this African origin of the American phenomenon!

Obama - Master and Commander 707. The "Ark of the Covenant" that has been so instrumental in American religion and politics.

While Mr. Cornell West is asking what is the President doing for Blacks or that the President is not doing enough for Blacks, the question should be, 'What is Mr. West doing for Blacks?' other than trying to tear down the President who has made black people proud of him, his family and his service! One good question for Mr. West, as an academic, "How many Black Ph.D candidates have Mr. West successfully advanced in his elevated academic leadership position." However, despite left, right and center criticisms, Mr. Obama can still boast he stands on his record of sustained job growth, emphasis on education for the young and industrious, health care provision for all Americans, help for the Middle Class, financial and economic regulation, "insourcing" of jobs, and tax assistance for business that hire Veterans, maintaining the social net, and so on. All things being equal, despite beliefs, this election will be close, Mr. Obama will be re-elected and as one politician said recently, "We will download the power of the President's second term." Then, as he fulfils his destiny, Mount Rushmore, and possibly even a monument on the Great Lawn will be a testimonial from a grateful nation to the first great African American President. Then, when school kids are given the Washington Tour and ponder the inspiring figure and personality of Barack

OBAMA - MASTER AND COMMANDER

Obama, Dr. Cornell West will long be a memory, but we will still look for him in the Matrix!

Obama - Master and Commander 708. Union Station has put out the Christmas Mat. Ho. Ho. Ho and on the Cornice at Union Station: **Words of Wisdom I**. The Inscription Reads: "Let all the ends thou aimst at be thy country's, Thy God's, and Truth's; Be Noble and the nobleness that lies in other men, sleeping but never dead, will rise in majest to meet thine own."

73. REPUBLICAN SOPHISTRY
By
Dr. Fred Monderson

The more people listen to Republican false statements or sophistry, the more Herman Cain's gem of "brothers from another mother," of another planet, applies to the pretenders whose arrogance is so revolting one must wonder how can they sleep easily at night. As their "fast and furious playing with the facts" become more evident, right thinking men of substance who see the light are calling them out which on surface seems a contradiction. In fact, as awakened Republicans themselves become more disgusted with their fellow Republicans' statements, advocacies, positions on issues of significance, they are not only distancing themselves but shamelessly crossing the line to endorse, offer support to Democrats who differ greatly from their own "best of a bad lot." The end result, those right thinking Republicans who break ranks are vilified for seeing the true rotten nature of some apples in their own barrel.

The classic example of credible criticism or rejection of Republican sophistry and that of their allies in print and electronic media, was evident in New Jersey Governor Chris Christie's praise of President Barack Obama's response to the devastation needs of his state following the calamity of the super-storm Sandy. The Governor's heaped praise on President Obama was actually a realistic assessment of a truly humanistic response to a widespread tragedy that stunned onlookers and elicited condemnation from fellow Republicans. Their purely partisan criticism of the Governor is simple because, this close to the election, such lucrative praise of the Democratic incumbent by a high profile Republican is like dropping a heavy weight on Mr. Romney's foot while uplifting Mr. Obama.

FREDERICK MONDERSON

But this sore loser tantrum by Republicans is not isolated. Four years ago, General, former Secretary of State, Colin Powell, a Republican, endorsed Mr. Obama when he ran against Senator John McCain. Owing to the problems facing the nation, Mr. Powell thought Barack Obama a unifying and "transformational figure" who would heal the nation and move it forward. As he watched a four year period of Republican machinations, falsity, treasonous behavior, this fountain of wisdom gained from his many years in the penthouse of political decision making easily discerned Mitt Romney's shortcomings. This time his endorsement of President Obama, unexpectedly as it was, generated different responses. Democrats naturally welcomed this elder statesman's experienced assessment of the contenders and relished in his choice. Independents, thinking Powell knew something, began to take a second look at the President, weighing his many accomplishments and assessing his detractors and their intent. Republicans, disappointed by the "treasonous act of one of their own" played the "sour grapes card." Their point man, John Sununu exclaimed, in insulting the former Secretary of State, "he endorsed Barack Obama because they are of the same race." Naturally, "big mouth," even after he had called the President of the United States "stupid" also Sununu later "ate crow," meaning he apologized for his brash, disrespectful comment, because a fellow Republican more accurately assessed the contenders. The significance of General Powel's endorsement is that he is a decent man, more of a patriot than most and his decision was based on the most objective assessment of President Obama's leadership, his efforts and the policies designed to improve the future of the nation. Fact is, General Powell showed he had balls!

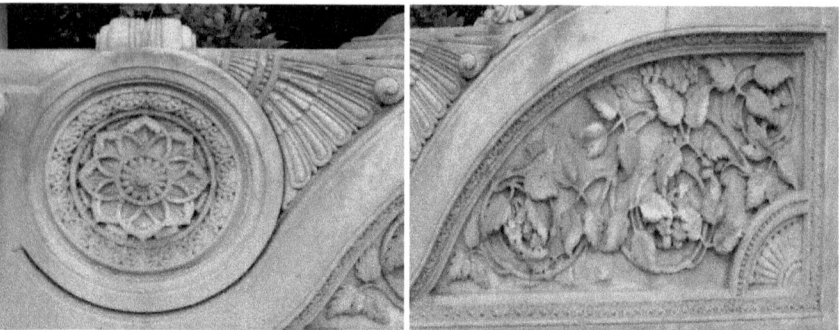

Obama - Master and Commander 709. Decorative features on the Capital Building's fence.

OBAMA - MASTER AND COMMANDER

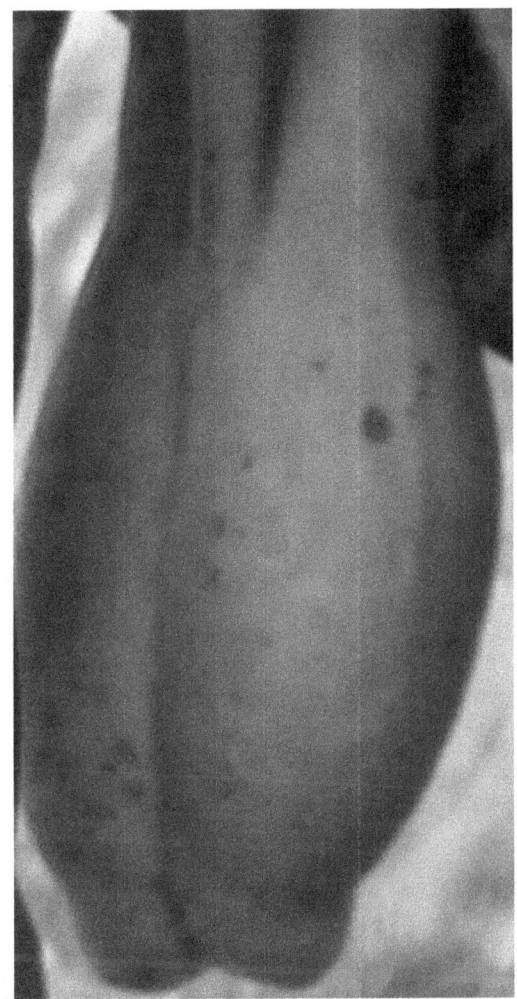

Obama - Master and Commander 710. To go against the grain shows one has balls, big balls!

But, Colin Powell's endorsement was not all-together out of the ordinary. In fact, like so many, Mr. Powell chose not to be associated with the malarkey Republican phalanxes were shoveling. For example, in Florida, the 2010 Primary Republican in opposition to Allen West, endorsed the Democratic opponent of the Congressman, this year, 2012! Fact is, Mr. West's rhetoric was so outlandish, his fellow Republican distanced himself. Perhaps at his party affiliation peril, he recognized West was far out, to say the least! By that standard, Mr. West lost his Congressonal election and is now a former Congressman in the next Congress. But this was a trend of national proportions. In Nebraska, former Republican Senator Hagel supported the Democrat Kerry in Nebraska against his Republican opponent. Even more important, New York City's influential Mayor Michael Bloomberg, himself a businessman who has been a Democrat, Republican and Independent, endorsed President Obama despite his opponent Mitt Romney's claim to fame as a businessman. This was one significant endorsement where the Mayor, while recognizing some shortcomings of the President brought about through Republican "scorched earth" practices, endorsed his role in climate control and by extension the environment. He did, however, emphasize Romney's flip-flopping as so many have pointed out.

Throughout all the scenarios sketched above, every time a Republican broke ranks and supported a Democrat, or say something positive regarding an action or behavior the person demonstrated, Republicans attack or "bad talk" them for their honesty. When Senator Rand Paul was asked on CNN about Mr. Bloomberg's endorsement, he dismissed and trivialized it, referring to Mayor Bloomberg, "You can't even get a 16-oz soda in New York."

Naturally, Republicans welcomed the *New York Post* and even the *Daily News* endorsements in heavily Democratic New York. Equally, they frowned on *The New York Times'* endorsement of Mr. Obama. What this does show, Republicans who have been acrimonious in their criticism of Mr. Obama were more interested in the sophistry of those who relished in the falsity they peddled. Notwithstanding, Americans have the tendency to see beyond smoke-screens and vote their conscience and true interests.

74. Romney's "Bells and Whistles"
By
Dr. Fred Monderson

All the Mitt Romney's "Bells and Whistles" notwithstanding, contrasting the closing remarks of the two presidential contenders, at the final debate forces us to wonder can the governor deceive the American electorate as he had Conservatives. During the Republican presidential primary election, in trying to out-distance his challengers Mitt Romney made a special effort to convince the Republican base how much of an "extreme conservative" he actually is. Later confessing, "All manner of things are said in a campaign," Rick Santorum had blamed Romney for being worse than Obama! Now that Romney has beat back the competition, "Moved to the middle," he made many false claims against the President and in his closing remarks, he not only focused on what the Commander-In-Chief has not done, he himself seems to have offered not one but two pies in the sky. All Mitt's hoopla aside, the President's closing remarks seemed more reasonable, humanistic, future oriented and in humiliation for the opportunity to serve and be concerned about the broad masses of the American people.

OBAMA - MASTER AND COMMANDER

Obama - Master and Commander 711. The President James Garfield Memorial in the Square at the Capital Building's rear entrance.

A few things we must remember!

In his partisan diatribe, Michael Goodwin of the *New York Post* boasted, "Why I'm voting for Romney" and raised the question which candidate was "Presidential;" he favoring Mr. Romney of course. Imagine President Obama not being Presidential!

Representing America abroad, Mr. Obama wowed the British! Romney insulted the British! While Queen Elizabeth II invited the Obamas to tea and promised to visit the White House; as for Mitt and crew, the British hoped they would leave!

FREDERICK MONDERSON

Super-storm Sandy devastated the Eastern Seaboard and the President responded to the calamity in hardest hit New Jersey. The Republican Governor Chris Christie publicly relished great praise on President Obama for his unselfish and Presidential response to the disaster. Interesting, Republicans choose to castigate Mr. Christie who, at their Convention, had spoken boldly against Mr. Obama but now, as they say, Chris Christie "Chose to give Jack," I mean Obama, "his Jacket" by praising his efforts. In an age of party switching, perhaps Mr. Christie will change from Republican to Democrat. Notwithstanding, in response to the catastrophe, Mr. Obama visited the state of New Jersey on the ground, not fly over as President Bush did for Katrina. There the President pledged the federal government's full resources to aid devastated New Jersey much to Mr. Christie's amazement; Mr. Obama proved presidential timber of the most durable mettle, contrasted with Mr. Romney's pitiful showing delivering the case of water to victims of Sandy. The same miserably pitiful manner he seemed pumping his gas days after the election! Mr. Michael Goodwin has failed in his contrast of who is Presidential.

In actually, Mr. Romney got off his economic message and began accusing the President of "blaming, attacking and dividing" the country when he should have united the nation. What Mr. Romney failed to recognize when the President came to power at Inauguration, the country was already divided with much of the country voting against him for Mr. McCain. Even if he did not make an effort to unite the country, one thing is certain. The President was inaugurated January 20, 2009 and by February 17, when the President finally signed the Stimulus Bill, the Republican members of Congress voted overwhelmingly against the bill. This shows, as some have argued, the possibility or actuality of a conspiracy against the President because in such a short time for such solid opposition to materialize to the efforts of a new administration, then there must have had to be division that continued past the last day of the election and, insidiously orchestrated, was easily resusticated lasting for the full four year term of President Obama.

Need I say anymore, Mr. Goodwin. The President's acceptance victory speech is clearly and equivocally a demonstration of his Presidential nature!

Obama - Master and Commander 712. Part of the decoration on the Garfield Memorial.

OBAMA - MASTER AND COMMANDER

75. AN OPEN LETTER TO MICHAEL GOODWIN - Dr. Fred Monderson
mgoodwin@nypost.com

October 31, 2012

Dear Mr. Michael Goodwin,
What a pleasant surprise to now realize you're voting for Mr. Romney. This revelation smacks of hypocrisy; since, for the longest, you have done nothing but pummel President Obama as if acting as a Romney surrogate, the same as your newspaper has done. In fact, all along you seemed like a man with a conclusion looking for a theory which you finally seem to have found! Now, on election eve, in a "spring chicken" awakening you probably moved from "undecided" to telling your readers "Why I'm voting for Romney;" which is your privilege, but your decision sure has an odious smell at this late date! Nonetheless, there are a few issues in your article in the *New York Post* of October 28, 2012, p. 9, entitled "Why I'm voting for Romney," because I'm a bit confused about this and think I should let you know about it.

1. As a "Democrat who votes Independent, now Republican," "You seem all over the place;" I mean election board!

2. At the time of the 2008 election, the nation was "dangerously polarized" you say; yet, four years later people of your persuasion blame President Obama for polarizing the nation. In fact, the nation was so polarized, just below 50 percent of voters voted for Mr. McCain or was it against Mr: Obama! These were essentially Republicans who "had squandered the chance to govern." It is beyond asinine to believe; these persons had put down their swords and picked up plowshares; while dancing to Obama's music. It is interesting that, between the time Mr. Obama was inaugurated on January 20, 2009, and the time he signed the Stimulus Bill on February 17, 2009, some 28 days, spanning the Bill's presentation, debate, passage and signing into law, a wall of Republican opposition had already assembled, organized, so much so, not a single Republican in the House voted for the Bill and only 3 Republican Senators did. If you're unable to make the connection, let me give you a hint. Those people you say "squandered," also fought a losing campaign and harbored their anger. Thus, from day one of Inauguration they probably met and planned to sabotage the administration of the Black man and his family in the White House. Of course, being color blind you cannot see this or even make the connection of a state of affairs that had coalesced with such rapidity as had, during the "Tea Party's" birth and nurturing, sent numerous unmistaken caricatured messages. Therefore, when as you say, Mr. Obama "spoke of uniting the country and I believed he was capable and sincere;" let me also add an old aphorism, "You can take a horse to water, but you can't make him drink!"

FREDERICK MONDERSON

3.   You write Mr. Obama failed as President because he is "incompetent, dishonest and not interested in the work of governing." Who knows, perhaps your vision has become cloudy and you need some rose-colored glasses. In fact, Mr. Obama is brilliant, honest, very much interested in the work of governing which is why, in the first place, he ran for the office to wrest leadership from "squandering" Republicans. Mr. Obama passed significant legislation despite the treasonous efforts of a united and active Republican opposition in government and the mischievous and poisonous pen activities of allies such as yourself and the *New York Post* in private/public service. Equally and important, while the leader of the squandering Republicans, President George Bush received some 3,000 death threats periodically, President Obama was receiving some 12,000 and he still held the reins of government, and accomplished all that he did as Republicans and their allies fought to deny him "a win." Add to this, Senator Mitch McConnell busily continued to work his magic "to make Barack Obama a one term President." Reasonable people could wonder how anyone could succeed against such entrenched and obdurate opposition as the Republicans presented. But, Obama did!

4.   You say, "I don't hate him. But I sure as hell don't trust him." Do you read what you write? Your hate filled poison is so original, readers must wonder if you do write your own material! Does someone hand you a script and say write t his way!

5.   "As for the desperate charge that opposition to Obama makes me a racist, let me note that he was black when I voted for him." The ballot is secret! Anyone can say they voted for someone to seem liberal, likeable and justify their turncoat status. Let's face it; Mr. Obama's time in office was just a meal ticket to so many writers. In your many diatribes of the times, evident from the coalesced opposition, threats, etc. how many articles did you write in the defense of the man you voted for? Whose side did you take when your paper published the "Ape Cartoon" and activists from far and wide wanted to shut down the *New York Post*.

As a man of conscience, when the Arizona pastor, Anderson, began praying for the death of President Obama, did you write in objection or pray the insidious action of this "man of the cloth" never happen. Did you pray for the safety of our President? Fortunately, many people praying for the President's health has offset the false preacher's vocation! Did you raise a voice against the treasonous and racist behavior of Senator Mitch McConnell, Sarah Palin, Joe the Plumber, Joe "You lie" Wilson, Charles "stupid" Grassley; Rick "Poison the well" Santorum; John "stupid" Sununu; "Waterloo" DeMint, "Gangster" Bachmann; Billy "Go for the Kill" Krystal, etc. Did you politely ask that they desist?

6.   This brings us to your lily white Mitt Romney, since, "There is not a hint of scandal in his life or career, and his economic policies could spark real growth in jobs not in food stamps." Captains of industry were always masters of cut throat

OBAMA - MASTER AND COMMANDER

business practices. So, go ahead and vote for Mitt Romney; if there is a sliver of decency left in you and he is elected President, four years from now when he makes the same mistakes as George Bush, you may yet offer a credible assessment of his tenure. Nevertheless, and suffice to say, "food stamps" is part of the nation's safety net. Even more, in his youthful age when the nation was at war, squeaky clean Romney was exempted from military service and went to France to preach the word of God! Today he aspires to be Commander-in-Chief, to send kids to war but with 5 sons, none will go! At least Joe Biden's son Beau, served to defend his country.

What did Mr. Romney have as a credit? He "saved the Winter Olympics," a little affair in which 150 percent of Americans supported him because of the prestige of being host. With no opposition like Mr. Obama has had, people came to have a good time and no one had any intent of sabotaging events. However, when Mr. Romney had a chance to play statesman at the 2012 Summer Olympics, he bombed, insulting the British, our strongest ally. So much so, they began praying for him to leave!

Regarding the growing debt Mr. Romney and you so often speak of, the TARP and Stimulus dollars were spent in this country, not Iraq or Afghanistan, to plug the Republican hole and it hardly made a dent. You go figure!

7. Sure you're right Paul Ryan is smart but he will cut everyone off at the knee and give the wealthy Republican base a pass.

8. Your reference to "Obama's apology tour" is a disputed fact since knowledgeable folks pointed out this is not correct, and like his newest Auto Bailout Ad, Mr. Romney has been accused of "playing fast and loose with the facts." To say Obama lied about the murder of an Ambassador is a stretch since all the evidence is not in and your side needs something negative to pin on the President. That "Obama has made the nation less safe" is a talking point without merit! Other than Pearl Harbor, the biggest and most successful attack on American shores occurred during a Republican Administration and we had to wait upon Mr. Obama's tenacious leadership to remove some two dozen Al Qaeda leaders from the field of battle, including Osama bin-Laden. Important, on 9/11/01 Americans did not play partisan politics but came together as a nation in support of the government as opposed to Mr. Romney fanning flames to exploit the death of the Ambassador and the other 3 in Benghazi, as opposed to the nation's response to the 3,000 American deaths on 9/11/01. So, sophistry in aid of a Republican cause is tantamount to treason! Let us not forget, parents of the Heroes of Benghazi admonished Mr. Romney not to exploit their family name in vain!

You say, "As for being a Mormon, to hold that against Romney is pure bigotry." For the greatest duration, most Americans held Mormonism is a cult, from Rick Perry's "Baptist pastor" to Evangelist Billy Graham who now has become convinced this is not so. What was the revelation? Was it not bigotry that caused Mormons to deny Blacks! Now that it is politically expedient to include them, we ask why in the first place were they excluded. And why now?

10.   "Romney's firm, steady demeanor during Obama's rancid attempts at character assassination demonstrates the presidential character lacking in the incumbent," is a mis-statement of gigantic proportions for Obama is already the President and despite yours and so many others' character assassination, Mr. Obama is still standing and has not embarrassed himself, the Office or nation, at home or abroad! Importantly, Mr. Obama has traveled no place where they prayed for him to leave quickly! Even more, he took the best of the vile low blows leveled against him and family, the threats, obstructionism, treasonous behavior by people in and out of government, even political sabotage as he stood up firmly for the American people. And what did the likes of you do? Throw gasoline on the burning, assaulted President Obama. As he took all this in a gentleman's stride you people condemned him further and when he decided to fight back you further condemn him. Perhaps you and your ilks should read the more enlightened *New York Times* Editorial endorsing President Obama for re-election, as well as the *New Yorker* magazine doing the same, and then perhaps you may learn something and your prejudiced views may get the change it wants and needs!

A question for Mr. Romney, perhaps you could ask him! He promises to add 12 million new jobs in his term. If elected and Mr. Romney is not able to add 12 million jobs to the economy as he states, 'Is he man enough to not seek re-election?'

Yours
Dr. Fred Monderson
fredsegypt.com@fredsegypt.com

76.   CAMPAIGN ROUND-UP

Three men were sitting staring at a glass in the middle of a table top. The first thought the glass empty! The second thought the glass half empty. The third thought the glass half-full. This scenario is reminesence of the observations of three New York City newspapers, the *New York Post*, the *New York Daily News* and *The New York Times*. This is the image they sold their customers regarding endorsements in the 2012 presidential election between the Democrat President Barack H. Obama and former Massachusetts Governor Mitt Romney, the Republican. Naturally, as a subscriber to all three newspapers, I was not surprised, surprised and elated about the endorsements of the papers as listed above. As such, then, the newspaper endorsements are included here for those readers who may not have had the opportunity as this writer did in being first hand apprised of the papers' poitions.

OBAMA - MASTER AND COMMANDER

For America's future, The Post endorses Mitt Romney for president.

Four frustratingly long years ago, a war-weary and economically battered America took a flier on a savior.

Obama - Master and Commander 713. Decorative features on the stone fence near the Capital Building.

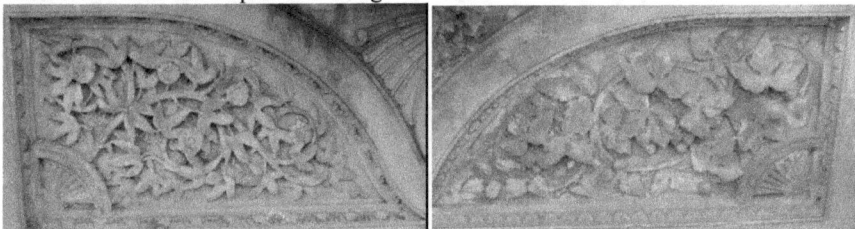

Obama - Master and Commander 714. Decorative features on the stone fence near the Capital Building.

It didn't work out. Now, in 12 days, the nation will return to the polls - to reject, or to ratify, the results of the great Barack Obama experiment. That is, to reject or to ratify the notion that hoping for change is a sound footing for productive national policy. But, by the evidence, it is not. It cannot create jobs. It cannot reduce deficits. It cannot restore foreign confidence in America - or Americans' confidence in their own great nation.

America needs more than hope. It needs leadership. That is why *The Post* today endorses the candidacy of Mitt Romney for president of the United States.

FREDERICK MONDERSON

Obama - Master and Commander 715. Decorative features on the stone fence near the Capital Building.

Obama - Master and Commander 716. Decorative features on the stone fence near the Capital Building.

Scrape it down to bedrock, and Mitt Romney knows that there is but one issue in this campaign: America's woeful economy, and the demonstrated inability of President Obama to cope with it.

Obama says he inherited the mess, but he's done nothing to fix it. Borrow, spend, regulate and redistribute is not a prescription for sustainable growth, yet that has been the totality of his program.

He says things will get better - soon. But there's no evidence for that.

Obamanomics has produced:

* A sky-high national debt, now at a stupefying $16 trillion and growing.

* Intractable unemployment and a workforce hemorrhaging discouraged workers.

* No perceptible economic growth.

OBAMA - MASTER AND COMMANDER

* Historic expansion in welfare programs - especially food stamps.

Obama proposes massive tax increases aimed not so much at the rich, as he claims, but squarely at the middle class and small business, which is insane: Small business - the real engine of American job creation - needs to be nurtured, not squeezed dry.

Obama - Master and Commander 717. Decorative features and Tabernacle on the stone fence near the Capital Building.

Obama - Master and Commander 718. Decorative features on the stone fence near the Capital Building.

Americans need jobs - jobs for those trying to raise family, jobs for those who are leaving school, jobs *period!*

FREDERICK MONDERSON

Instead, they are about to be saddled with an unworkable health-care boondoggle that will suck hundreds of billions from a private-sector economy that could better use the cash to create - yes - *more jobs*!

Can Mitt Romney really turn all this around? Yes, he can.

In the debates, Americans saw a leader.

They saw a man with the experience, the temperament, the principles and the knowledge to address America's economic woes instead of just blaming others.

After all, as governor of deep-blue Massachusetts, he worked with a Democratic legislature to close a $3 billion deficit without raising taxes or borrowing.

There is one other significant issue.

Four years ago, Obama vowed "to restore America's standing in the world." But he has sown rancor and confusion instead.

Our friends don't know if they're still our friends; our enemies wonder whether we have the courage to stand up to them.

The result has been a cataclysmic breakdown of US leadership in the Middle East. Israel - and not *just* Israel - questions whether Obama is committed to curbing Iran's nuclear threat.

Syria is in open civil war, while Egypt and Libya teeter on the brink. Osama bin Laden may be dead, but al Qaeda has hardly been contained - as Benghazi tragically proved.

In contrast, the smoke now hanging over the Middle East testifies to Obama's inability to get the job done.

Any job.

Because, in the end, the fundamental problem is the president's core philosophy.

He believes in equality of outcome, not equality of opportunity and that is not - how America is supposed to work.

America is *not* working right now.

Forward?

OBAMA - MASTER AND COMMANDER

For four *more* years?

We think not.

Mitt Romney for president.

Obama - Master and Commander 719. Decorative features on the stone fence near the Capital Building.

Obama - Master and Commander 720. Ark and Tabernacle, the foundation for Judeo-Christian religious and political belief and practice as emanating from this center of power.

FREDERICK MONDERSON

Obama - Master and Commander 721. The White House with its immaculate and manicured grounds.

OBAMA - MASTER AND COMMANDER

Obama - Master and Commander 722. The Oval Office where those significant decisions are made.

FREDERICK MONDERSON

Obama - Master and Commander 723. A young American aspiring to sit in that important seat!

So here's the other Hometown Newspaper stating "Our choice for America's future," wherein, *The Daily News* endorses Mitt Romney for president.

America's heart, soul, brains and muscle - the middle - and working-class people who make this nation great - have been beset for too long by sapping economic decline.

So, too, New York breadwinners and families.

Paychecks are shrunken after more than a decade in which the workplace has asked more of wage earners and rewarded them less. The decline has knocked someone at the midpoint of the salary scale back to where he or she would have been in 1996.

Then, the subway fare, still paid by token, was $1.50, gasoline was $1.23 a gallon and the median rent for a stabilized apartment was $600 a month. Today, the base Metro Card subway fare is $2.25, gasoline is in the $3.90 range and the median stabilized rent is $1,050, with all the increases outpacing wage growth.

OBAMA - MASTER AND COMMANDER

Obama - Master and Commander 724. The White House and its lawn from a different direction.

FREDERICK MONDERSON

Obama - Master and Commander 725. Home of the President's Commission on White House Fellowships and the Harry S. Truman Scholarship Foundation.

Obama - Master and Commander 726. At the above address, is located the White House Council on Environmental Quality and the White House Historical Association.

OBAMA - MASTER AND COMMANDER

Obama - Master and Commander 727. The above address is home to the Council on Environmental Quality.

A crisis of long duration, the gap between purchasing power and the necessities of life widened after the 2008 meltdown revealed that the U.S. economy was built on toothpicks - and they snapped.

Nine million jobs evaporated. The typical American family saw $50,000 vanish from its net worth, and its median household income dropped by more than $87 a week. New Yorkers got off with a $54 weekly hit.

Our leaders owed us better than lower standards of living, and we must have better if the U.S. is to remain a beacon of prosperity where mothers and fathers can be confident of providing for their children and seeing them climb higher on the ladder.

Revival of the U.S. as a land of opportunity and upward mobility is the central challenge facing the next President. The question for Americans: Who is more likely to accomplish the mission - Barack Obama or Mitt Romney?

Four years ago, the *Daily News* endorsed Obama, seeing a historic figure whose intelligence, political skills and empathy with common folk positioned him to build on the small practical experience he would bring to the world's toughest job.

We valued Obama's pledge to govern with bold pragmatism and bipartisanship. The hopes of those days went unfulfilled.

Achingly slow job creation has left the U.S. with 4.3 million fewer positions than provided incomes to Americans in 2007. Half the new jobs have been part-time, lower-wage slots, a trend that has ruinously sped a hollowing of the middle class.

The official unemployment rate stands at 7.9%, marking only the second month below 8% after 43 months above that level. Worse, add people who are working part-time because they have no better choice and the rate leaps to almost 15%. Still worse, add 8 million people who have given up looking for employment and the number who are out of jobs or who are cobbling together hours to scrape by hits some 23 million people.

Only America's social safety net, record deficits and the Federal Reserve's unprecedented low-interest policies have kept the label Great Depression II on the shelf.

Obama - Master and Commander 728. Advocating for more Jobs, Jobs, Jobs and the Eisenhower Building fronted by the First Infantry Division Memorial.

Obama - Master and Commander 729. American Federation of Labor - Council of Industrial Organizations (AFL-CIO) and Laborers' International Union of North America buildings.

New Yorkers have fared no better. The state is alone among the 50 in suffering significantly rising unemployment over the last 12 months, with the rate now at 8.9%. The city's pain index is 8.8%, and the five boroughs have been trading down in salaries.

The trend over the Obama years: Goodbye to middle - and high-income jobs in New York City; hello to positions that pay less than $45,000 a year.

Recovery from the disaster that Obama inherited was going to take time. But four years is a long, long slog. Had the President guided a typical upswing, America would by now have regained essentially all its lost jobs. At his present pace, Obama would reach that milestone in the third year of a second term.

OBAMA - MASTER AND COMMANDER

The regrettable truth is that Obama built a record of miscalculations and missed opportunities.

First came emergency economic stimulus. Because Obama gave free rein to House and Senate Democrats in deciding how to spend $800 billion, the legislation was heavily designed to satisfy the party's constituencies and hunger for social programs, and inadequately weighted toward job-multiplier projects like building and repairing bridges and railroads - including subways.

After originally projecting that the program would produce 4 million more jobs than the country now has, along with a 5% jobless rate, Obama pleads that he saved Americans from more dire straits.

Obama - Master and Commander 730. National Geographic Society in the Gardiner Green Hubbard Memorial building.

Next came Obamacare. While the country bled jobs, the President battled to establish universal health insurance - without first restraining soaring medical bills. Then he pushed one of the largest social programs in U.S. history through a Democratic-controlled Congress without a single Republican vote.

R.I.P. and never to be resurrected - Obama's promised bipartisanship.

FREDERICK MONDERSON

Obama - Master and Commander 731. The entrance to Constitutional Hall.

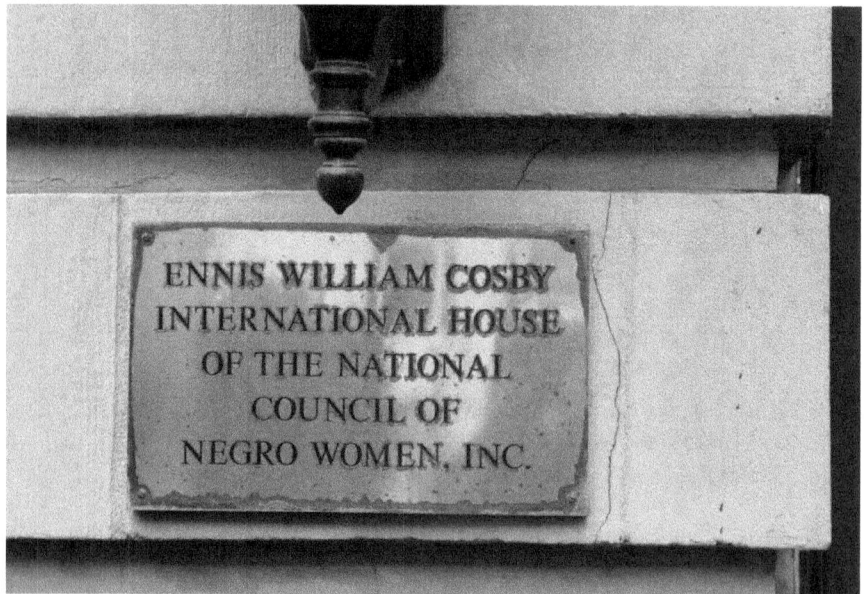

Obama - Master and Commander 732. Ennis William Cosby International House of the National Council of Negro Women, Inc.

OBAMA - MASTER AND COMMANDER

Obama - Master and Commander 733. Institute for the Advancement of Multicultural and Minority Medicine and the building where it is housed.

Obama - Master and Commander 734. The famed Howard University that has educated so many Black professionals.

FREDERICK MONDERSON

Obama - Master and Commander 735. Meridian Hill Park's sign (left) (Malcolm X Park) and four of its Obelisks at one of the entrances (right).

Obama - Master and Commander 736. Meridian Hill (Malcolm X) Park's Waterfall in Summer.

OBAMA - MASTER AND COMMANDER

Obama - Master and Commander 737. Meridian Hill (Malcolm X) Park's Waterfall in Winter.

Obama - Master and Commander 738. Joan of Arc's Memorial in Meridian/Malcolm X Park.

FREDERICK MONDERSON

Obama - Master and Commander 739. Road to Diversity, Malcolm X/Meridian Park poster on Heritage Trail.

OBAMA - MASTER AND COMMANDER

African Liberation Day marchers poured out of the park in 1972.

Obama - Master and Commander 740. Close-Up of this scene, forty years ago, should remind African Americans of "The Art of the Possible" and the meaning and significance of African Liberation Day as well as Black Solidarity Day celebrated in Meridian Hill/Malcolm X Park!

While the legislation has yet to take full effect, the typical family's health insurance premium has risen and many businesses will experience a hike of $70 per week per employee, further restraining wages or producing part-time jobs that lack coverage.

Next came trillion-dollar deficits. Deep in the hole thanks to former President George W. Bush, Obama helped run up a $5 trillion increase in the national debt. Along the way, he appointed a bipartisan commission to devise a plan for restoring America's fiscal health, but he abandoned the panel's menu of spending cuts, entitlement reductions and tax reform. Finally, Obama failed to close a deal with Republican House Speaker John Boehner for budgetary discipline and a path to job creation.

That was 15 months ago. Since then, Obama has presided over paralysis.

There was, of course, more to the President's record than economic stewardship.

FREDERICK MONDERSON

Entries on the plus side of the ledger include Obama's "Race to the Top" school reforms, withdrawal from Iraq and his aggressive drone strikes against Islamist radicals. And then there is, or was, Osama bin Laden. Obama ordered the mass murderer's dispatch in a presidential act of courage for the ages.

In deficit on the balance sheet, he stepped to the front in ratcheting up sanctions against Iran only after the country's regime had moved ominously close to nuclear weapon capability, and he executed a misguided strategy for achieving peace between Israel and the Palestinians that left the parties further from a settlement.

But those pluses and minuses pale in comparison with middle-class prospects in recommending whether to entrust Obama or Romney with the future.

Romney's approach is the stronger.

Obama - Master and Commander 741. Along a pathway, criss-crossing an entrance into Meridian/Malcolm X Park, Obelisks remind of ancient Egypt's influence not only in the Park but throughout the City of Washington, DC.

Critically, he has tailored his policies to create jobs, jobs, jobs.

The centerpieces of Romney's plan call for spending restraint and rewriting the Internal Revenue code to lower rates by 20%. He would make up much of the lost

OBAMA - MASTER AND COMMANDER

revenue by eliminating deductions and loopholes that have made the tax system a thicket of strangling complexities. On its own, paring the personal and corporate rules to the basics would catalyze business and consumer spending.

Obama - Master and Commander 742. Pennsylvania's James Buchannan, President of the United States, 1857-1861, in Meridian Hill/Malcolm X Park, and the Inscription describes the whole story! "The incorruptible statesman whose walk was upon the mountain ranges of the law."

FREDERICK MONDERSON

Obama - Master and Commander 743. Dante in Meridian Hill/Malcolm X Park!

OBAMA - MASTER AND COMMANDER

Romney has pledged that, as a group, the wealthy will bear no less a share of the burden than they do now, while individuals lower down would enjoy breaks. Many contest as mathematically impossible the Republican's ability to cut rates and balance the books through tax reform. He disputes the points but, in an encouraging show of pragmatism, he has made clear that moving the nation toward balance may require sacrificing the size of his rate cut.

Romney's energy plan calls for reemphasizing oil and natural gas production, in a shift away from Obama's tilt toward trying to develop wind and solar into workable alternatives.

His proposal for Medicare would permit future retirees to choose between tried-and-true health care and private insurance to produce savings through competition. It took political bravery even to broach such concepts, and they are well worth exploring.

His immigration strategy entails markedly increasing visas for highly skilled workers, such as engineers and computer scientists, who are in short supply in the United States - and are proven jobs generators. Obama let economic energy go by the boards by declining to up these H1-B work permits.

Obama - Master and Commander 74. National Museum of Women in the Arts.

No, Romney's not perfect. His overall immigration policy falls below comprehensive reform, and he's no friend of gun control. But, under these circumstances, growing the economy takes precedence.

FREDERICK MONDERSON

Offering a rosy vision of a country already on the rise, Obama argues that he would lead a resurgence by staying the course. He posits that spending in areas such as education and clean energy would be beneficial, and he sees raising taxes on high-income earners as key to "balanced" deficit reduction. Each on its own is attractive, but the whole comes up short.

The presidential imperative of the times is to energize the economy and get deficits under control to empower the working and middle classes to again enjoy the fruits of an ascendant America.

So *The News* is compelled to stand with Romney.

Obama - Master and Commander 745. The Smithsonian Museum (left) and the National Museum of African Art on its grounds (right).

By contrast, and this is why *The New York Times* is the "Paper of Record." Here is their take. It's like three guys looking at the same contents of a glass and each sees something differently. Or should I put it this way, a grown up and two children seeing and commenting on the same issue, whether the glass is half empty or half full. Nevertheless:

Editorial
Barack Obama for Re-election, *The New York Times* Sunday, October 28, 2012, p. 12.

Mr. Obama has earned another term; Mr. Romney offers dangerous ideas, when he offers any.

The economy is slowly recovering from the 2008 meltdown, and the country could suffer another recession if the wrong policies take hold. The United States is embroiled in unstable regions that could easily explode into full-blown disaster. An ideological assault from the right has started to undermine the vital health reform law passed in 2010. Those forces are eroding women's access to health

OBAMA - MASTER AND COMMANDER

care, and their right to control their lives. Nearly 50 years after passage of the Civil Rights Act, all Americans' rights are cheapened by the right wing's determination to deny marriage benefits to a selected group of us. Astonishingly, even the very right to vote is being challenged.

That is the context for the Nov. 6 election, and as stark as it is, the choice is just as clear.

Obama - Master and Commander 746. The Garden on the grounds of the Smithsonian Museum.

FREDERICK MONDERSON

Obama - Master and Commander 747. Another section of the Garden with the National Museum of African Art to the top-left and further on the Department of Education Building to the right.

Obama - Master and Commander 748. Still another interesting piece of the Garden at the Smithsonian.

OBAMA - MASTER AND COMMANDER

Obama - Master and Commander 749. The Smithsonian Castle with its superb Garden named in honor of Enid A. Haupt.

President Obama has shown a firm commitment to using government to help foster growth. He has formed sensible budget policies that are not dedicated to protecting the powerful, and has worked to save the social safety net to protect the powerless. Mr. Obama has impressive achievements despite the implacable wall of refusal erected by Congressional Republicans so intent on stopping him that they risked pushing the nation into depression, held its credit rating hostage, and hobbled economic recovery.

Mitt Romney, the former governor of Massachusetts, has gotten this far with a guile that allows him to say whatever he thinks an audience wants to hear. But he has tied himself to the ultraconservative forces that control the Republican Party and embraced their policies, including reckless budget cuts and 30-year-old, discredited trickle-down ideas. Voters may still be confused about Mr. Romney's true identity, but they know the Republican Party, and a Romney administration would reflect its agenda. Mr. Romney's choice of Representative Paul Ryan as his running mate says volumes about that.

We have criticized individual policy choices that Mr. Obama has made over the last four years, and have been impatient with his unwillingness to throw himself into the political fight. But he has shaken off the hesitancy that cost him the first debate, and he approaches the election clearly ready for the partisan battles that would follow his victory.

FREDERICK MONDERSON

We are confident he would challenge the Republicans in the "fiscal cliff" battle even if it meant calling their bluff, letting the Bush tax cuts expire and forcing them to confront the budget sequester they created. Electing Mr. Romney would eliminate any hope of deficit reduction that included increased revenues.

In the poisonous atmosphere of this campaign, it may be easy to overlook Mr. Obama's many important achievements, including carrying out the economic stimulus, saving the auto industry, improving fuel efficiency standards, and making two very fine Supreme Court appointments.

Health Care

Mr. Obama has achieved the most sweeping health care reforms since the passage of Medicare and Medicaid in 1965. The reform law takes a big step toward universal health coverage, a final piece in the social contract.

It was astonishing that Mr. Obama and the Democrats in Congress were able to get a bill past the Republican opposition. But the Republicans' propagandistic distortions of the new law helped them wrest back control of the House, and they are determined now to repeal the law.

That would eliminate the many benefits the reform has already brought: allowing children under 26 to stay on their parents' policies; lower drug costs for people on Medicare who are heavy users of prescription drugs; free immunizations, mammograms and contraceptives; a ban on lifetime limits on insurance payments. Insurance companies cannot deny coverage to children with pre-existing conditions. Starting in 2014, insurers must accept all applicants. Once fully in effect, the new law would start to control health care costs.

Obama - Master and Commander 750. Plaques to Constantine L. Seferlis and Enid A. Haupt at the Smithsonian.

OBAMA - MASTER AND COMMANDER

Mr. Romney has no plan for covering the uninsured beyond his callous assumption that they will use emergency rooms. He wants to use voucher programs to shift more Medicare costs to beneficiaries and block grants to shift more Medicaid costs to the states.

The Economy

Mr. Obama prevented another Great Depression. The economy was cratering when he took office in January 2009. By that June it was growing, and it has been ever since (although at a rate that disappoints everyone), thanks in large part to interventions Mr. Obama championed, like the $840 billion stimulus bill. Republicans say it failed, but it created and preserved 2.5 million jobs and prevented unemployment from reaching 12 percent. Poverty would have been much worse without the billions spent on Medicaid, food stamps and jobless benefits.

Last year, Mr. Obama introduced a jobs plan that included spending on school renovations, repair projects for roads and bridges, aid to states, and more. It was stymied by Republicans. Contrary to Mr. Romney's claims, Mr. Obama has done good things for small businesses - like pushing through more tax write-offs for new equipment and temporary tax cuts for hiring the unemployed.

The Dodd-Frank financial regulation was an important milestone. It is still a work in progress, but it established the Consumer Financial Protection Bureau, initiated reform of the derivatives market, and imposed higher capital requirements for banks. Mr. Romney wants to repeal it.

If re-elected, Mr. Obama would be in position to shape the "grand bargain" that could finally combine stimulus like the jobs bill with long-term deficit reduction that includes letting the high-end Bush-era tax cuts expire. Stimulus should come first, and deficit reduction as the economy strengthens. Mr. Obama has not been as aggressive as we would have liked in addressing the housing crisis, but he has increased efforts in refinancing and loan modifications.

FREDERICK MONDERSON

Obama - Master and Commander 751. Bureau of Engraving and Printing located at www.moneyfactory.gov.

Obama - Master and Commander 752. The National Holocaust Museum to the right (left) and back entrance (right).

OBAMA - MASTER AND COMMANDER

Obama - Master and Commander 753. Department of the Treasury.

Obama - Master and Commander 754. United States Department of Agriculture.

Mr. Romney's economic plan, as much as we know about it, is regressive, relying on big tax cuts and deregulation. That kind of plan was not the answer after the financial crisis, and it will not create broad prosperity.

FREDERICK MONDERSON

Obama - Master and Commander 757. Department of Energy.

Foreign Affairs

Mr. Obama and his administration have been resolute in attacking Al Qaeda's leadership, including the killing of Osama bin Laden. He has ended the war in Iraq. Mr. Romney, however, has said he would have insisted on leaving thousands of American soldiers there. He has surrounded himself with Bush administration neocons who helped to engineer the Iraq war, and adopted their militaristic talk in a way that makes a Romney administration's foreign policies a frightening prospect.

Mr. Obama negotiated a much tougher regime of multilateral economic sanctions on Iran. Mr. Romney likes to say the president was ineffective on Iran, but at the final debate he agreed with Mr. Obama's policies. Mr. Obama deserves credit for his handling of the Arab Spring. The killing goes on in Syria, but the administration is working to identify and support moderate insurgent forces there. At the last debate, Mr. Romney talked about funneling arms through Saudi Arabia and Qatar, which are funneling arms to jihadist groups.

Mr. Obama gathered international backing for airstrikes during the Libyan uprising, and kept American military forces in a background role. It was smart policy. In the broadest terms, he introduced a measure of military restraint after the Bush years and helped repair America's badly damaged reputation in many countries from the low levels to which it had sunk by 2008.

OBAMA - MASTER AND COMMANDER

The Supreme Court

The future of the nation's highest court hangs in the balance in this election - and along with it, reproductive freedom for American women and voting rights for all, to name just two issues. Whoever is president after the election will make at least one appointment to the court, and many more to federal appeals courts and district courts.

Obama - Master and Commander 758. Union Station: **Words of Wisdom II**. The Inscription reads: "Sweetener of hut and of hall; bringer of life out of naught; freedom o Fairest of all; the Daughters of time and thought; Man's imagination has conceived all numbers and letters; All tools, vessels and shelters; Every art and trade; all philosophy and poetry; and all polities. The truth shall make you free!"

Mr. Obama, who appointed the impressive Justices Elena Kagan and Sonia Sotomayor, understands how severely damaging conservative activism has been in areas like campaign spending. He would appoint justices and judges who understand that landmarks of equality like the Voting Rights Act must be defended against the steady attack from the right.

Mr. Romney's campaign Web site says he will "nominate judges in the mold of Chief Justice Roberts and Justices Scalia, Thomas and Alito," among the most conservative justices in the past 75 years. There is no doubt that he would appoint justices who would seek to overturn *Roe v. Wade*.

Civil Rights

The extraordinary fact of Mr. Obama's 2008 election did not usher in a new post-racial era. In fact, the steady undercurrent of racism in national politics is truly disturbing. Mr. Obama, however, has reversed Bush administration policies that

FREDERICK MONDERSON

chipped away at minorities' voting rights and has fought laws, like the ones in Arizona, that seek to turn undocumented immigrants into a class of criminals.

The military's odious "don't ask, don't tell" rule was finally legislated out of existence, under the Obama administration's leadership. There are still big hurdles to equality to be brought down, including the Defense of Marriage Act, the outrageous federal law that undermines the rights of gay men and lesbians, even in states that recognize those rights.

Though it took Mr. Obama some time to do it, he overcame his hesitation about same-sex marriage and declared his support. That support has helped spur marriage-equality movements around the country. His Justice Department has also stopped defending the Defense of Marriage Act against constitutional challenges.

Mr. Romney opposes same-sex marriage and supports the federal act, which not only denies federal benefits and recognition to same-sex couples but allows states to ignore marriages made in other states. His campaign declared that Mr. Romney would not object if states also banned adoption by same-sex couples and restricted their rights to hospital visitation and other privileges.

Mr. Romney has been careful to avoid the efforts of some Republicans to criminalize abortion even in the case of women who had been raped, including by family members. He says he is not opposed to contraception, but he has promised to deny federal money to Planned Parenthood, on which millions of women depend for family planning.

For these and many other reasons, we enthusiastically endorse President Barack Obama for a second term, and express the hope that his victory will be accompanied by a new Congress willing to work for policies that Americans need." Now this is a mature assessment of the facts on a broad scale rather than a narrow view and that is why the other side's guy lost!

OBAMA - MASTER AND COMMANDER

Obama - Master and Commander 759. The Department of Transportation Building.

President Barack Obama's speech in Chicago after his re-election Tuesday night, as transcribed by Roll Call is not simply moving but reflects the equality he hopes to see on the road ahead.

"Tonight, more than 200 years after a former colony won the right to determine its own destiny, the task of perfecting our union moves forward.

"It moves forward because of you. It moves forward because you reaffirmed the spirit that has triumphed over war and depression, the spirit that has lifted this country from the depths of despair to the great heights of hope, the belief that while each of us will pursue our own individual dreams, we are an American family and we rise or fall together as one nation and as one people.

"Tonight, in this election, you, the American people, reminded us that while our road has been hard, while our journey has been long, we have picked ourselves up, we have fought our way back, and we know in our hearts that for the United States of America the best is yet to come.

FREDERICK MONDERSON

"I want to thank every American who participated in this election, whether you voted for the very first time or waited in line for a very long time. By the way, we have to fix that. Whether you pounded the pavement or picked up the phone, whether you held an Obama sign or a Romney sign, you made your voice heard and you made a difference.

"I just spoke with Gov. Romney and I congratulated him and Paul Ryan on a hard-fought campaign. We may have battled fiercely, but it's only because we love this country deeply and we care so strongly about its future. From George to Lenore to their son Mitt, the Romney family has chosen to give back to America through public service and that is the legacy that we honor and applaud tonight. In the weeks ahead, I also look forward to sitting down with Gov. Romney to talk about where we can work together to move this country forward.

"I want to thank my friend and partner of the last four years, America's happy warrior, the best vice president anybody could ever hope for, Joe Biden.

"And I wouldn't be the man I am today without the woman who agreed to marry me 20 years ago. Let me say this publicly: Michelle, I have never loved you more. I have never been prouder to watch the rest of America fall in love with you, too, as our nation's first lady. Sasha and Malia, before our very eyes you're growing up to become two strong, smart beautiful young women, just like your mom. And I'm so proud of you guys. But I will say that for now one dog's probably enough.

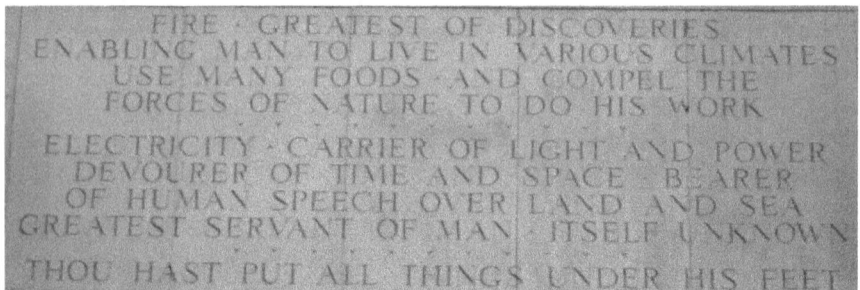

Obama - Master and Commander 760. Union Station: **Words of Wisdom III**. The Inscription reads: "Fire - Greatest of discoveries enabling man to live in various climates, use many foods and compel the forces of nature to do his work.

"Electricity - Carrier of light and power. Devourer of time and space. Bearer of human speech over land and sea. Greatest servant of man - Itself unknown. Thou has put all things under his feet."

"To the best campaign team and volunteers in the history of politics. The best. The best ever. Some of you were new this time around, and some of you have been at my side since the very beginning. But all of you are family. No matter what you do

OBAMA - MASTER AND COMMANDER

or where you go from here, you will carry the memory of the history we made together and you will have the lifelong appreciation of a grateful president. Thank you for believing all the way, through every hill, through every valley. You lifted me up the whole way and I will always be grateful for everything that you've done and all the incredible work that you put in.

"I know that political campaigns can sometimes seem small, even silly. And that provides plenty of fodder for the cynics that tell us that politics is nothing more than a contest of egos or the domain of special interests. But if you ever get the chance to talk to folks who turned out at our rallies and crowded along a rope line in a high school gym, or saw folks working late in a campaign office in some tiny county far away from home, you'll discover something else.

"You'll hear the determination in the voice of a young field organizer who's working his way through college and wants to make sure every child has that same opportunity. You'll hear the pride in the voice of a volunteer who's going door to door because her brother was finally hired when the local auto plant added another shift. You'll hear the deep patriotism in the voice of a military spouse who's working the phones late at night to make sure that no one who fights for this country ever has to fight for a job or a roof over their head when they come home.

"That's why we do this. That's what politics can be. That's why elections matter. It's not small, it's big. It's important. Democracy in a nation of 300 million can be noisy and messy and complicated. We have our own opinions. Each of us has deeply held beliefs. And when we go through tough times, when we make big decisions as a country, it necessarily stirs passions, stirs up controversy.

"That won't change after tonight, and it shouldn't. These arguments we have are a mark of our liberty. We can never forget that as we speak people in distant nations are risking their lives right now just for a chance to argue about the issues that matter, the chance to cast their ballots like we did today.

"But despite all our differences, most of us share certain hopes for America's future. We want our kids to grow up in a country where they have access to the best schools and the best teachers. A country that lives up to its legacy as the global leader in technology and discovery and innovation, with all the good jobs and new businesses that follow.

"We want our children to live in an America that isn't burdened by debt, that isn't weakened by inequality, that isn't threatened by the destructive power of a warming planet. We want to pass on a country that's safe and respected and admired around the world, a nation that is defended by the strongest military on earth and the best troops this - this world has ever known. But also a country that moves with confidence beyond this time of war, to shape a peace that is built on the promise of freedom and dignity for every human being.

FREDERICK MONDERSON

"We believe in a generous America, in a compassionate America, in a tolerant America, open to the dreams of an immigrant's daughter who studies in our schools and pledges to our flag. To the young boy on the south side of Chicago who sees a life beyond the nearest street corner. To the furniture worker's child in North Carolina who wants to become a doctor or a scientist, an engineer or an entrepreneur, a diplomat or even a president - that's the future we hope for. That's the vision we share. That's where we need to go - forward. That's where we need to go.

"Now, we will disagree, sometimes fiercely, about how to get there. As it has for more than two centuries, progress will come in fits and starts. It's not always a straight line. It's not always a smooth path. By itself, the recognition that we have common hopes and dreams won't end all the gridlock or solve all our problems or substitute for the painstaking work of building consensus and making the difficult compromises needed to move this country forward. But that common bond is where we must begin.

"Our economy is recovering. A decade of war is ending. A long campaign is now over. And whether I earned your vote or not, I have listened to you, I have learned from you, and you've made me a better president. And with your stories and your struggles, I return to the White House more determined and more inspired than ever about the work there is to do and the future that lies ahead.

"Tonight you voted for action, not politics as usual. You elected us to focus on your jobs, not ours. And in the coming weeks and months, I am looking forward to reaching out and working with leaders of both parties to meet the challenges we can only solve together. Reducing our deficit. Reforming our tax code. Fixing our immigration system. Freeing ourselves from foreign oil. We've got more work to do.

"But that doesn't mean your work is done. The role of citizen in our democracy does not end with your vote. America's never been about what can be done for us. It's about what can be done by us together through the hard and frustrating, but necessary work of self-government. That's the principle we were founded on.

"This country has more wealth than any nation, but that's not what makes us rich. We have the most powerful military in history, but that's not what makes us strong. Our university, our culture are all the envy of the world, but that's not what keeps the world coming to our shores.

"What makes America exceptional are the bonds that hold together the most diverse nation on earth. The belief that our destiny is shared; that this country only works when we accept certain obligations to one another and to future generations. The freedom which so many Americans have fought for and died for come with

OBAMA - MASTER AND COMMANDER

responsibilities as well as rights. And among those are love and charity and duty and patriotism. That's what makes America great.

"I am hopeful tonight because I've seen the spirit at work in America. I've seen it in the family business whose owners would rather cut their own pay than lay off their neighbors, and in the workers who would rather cut back their hours than see a friend lose a job. I've seen it in the soldiers who reenlist after losing a limb and in those SEALs who charged up the stairs into darkness and danger because they knew there was a buddy behind them watching their back.

Obama - Master and Commander 761. The Lyndon Baines Johnson Department of Education Building.

"I've seen it on the shores of New Jersey and New York, where leaders from every party and level of government have swept aside their differences to help a community rebuild from the wreckage of a terrible storm. And I saw just the other day, in Mentor, Ohio, where a father told the story of his 8-year-old daughter, whose long battle with leukemia nearly cost their family everything had it not been for health care reform passing just a few months before the insurance company was about to stop paying for her care.

"I had an opportunity to not just talk to the father, but meet this incredible daughter of his. And when he spoke to the crowd listening to that father's story,

FREDERICK MONDERSON

every parent in that room had tears in their eyes, because we knew that little girl could be our own. And I know that every American wants her future to be just as bright. That's who we are. That's the country I'm so proud to lead as your president.

"And tonight, despite all the hardship we've been through, despite all the frustrations of Washington, I've never been more hopeful about our future. I have never been more hopeful about America. And I ask you to sustain that hope. I'm not talking about blind optimism, the kind of hope that just ignores the enormity of the tasks ahead or the roadblocks that stand in our path. I'm not talking about the wishful idealism that allows us to just sit on the sidelines or shirk from a fight.

"I have always believed that hope is that stubborn thing inside us that insists, despite all the evidence to the contrary, that something better awaits us so long as we have the courage to keep reaching, to keep working, to keep fighting.

"America, I believe we can build on the progress we've made and continue to fight for new jobs and new opportunity and new security for the middle class. I believe we can keep the promise of our founders, the idea that if you're willing to work hard, it doesn't matter who you are or where you come from or what you look like or where you love. It doesn't matter whether you're black or white or Hispanic or Asian or Native American or young or old or rich or poor, able, disabled, gay or straight, you can make it here in America if you're willing to try.

Obama - Master and Commander 762. Union Station: **Words of Wisdom IV**. The Inscription reads: "The farm - best home of the family; Main source of national wealth; foundation of civilized society; the natural providence."

"The old mechanic arts controlling new forces; build new highways for goods and men; override the ocean and make the very ether carry human thought. The desert shall rejoice and blossom as the rose."

"I believe we can seize this future together because we are not as divided as our politics suggests. We're not as cynical as the pundits believe. We are greater than

OBAMA - MASTER AND COMMANDER

the sum of our individual ambitions, and we remain more than a collection of red states and blue states. We are and forever will be the United States of America.

Obama - Master and Commander 763. The National Education Association Building, "Fired Up" for 2012.

"And together with your help and God's grace we will continue our journey forward and remind the world just why it is that we live in the greatest nation on Earth.

"Thank you, America. God bless you. God bless these United States."

"In Hope and Change: Part II" Thomas L. Friedman wrote in the *New York Times* OP-ED Wednesday, November 7, 2012, p. A27:

"In October 2012, Senator Mitch McConnell, the Republican leader, famously told The National Journal, "The single most important thing we want to achieve is for President Obama to be a one-term president." And that's how he and his party acted.

Well, Mitch, how's that workin' out for ya?

No one can know for sure what complex emotional chemistry tipped this election Obama's way, but here's my guess: In the end, it came down to a majority of Americans believing that whatever faults, Obama was trying his hardest to fix what ails the country and that he had to do it with a Republican Party that, in its guts, did not want to meet him halfway but wanted him to fail - so that it could

FREDERICK MONDERSON

swoop in and pick up the pieces. To this day, I find McConnell's declaration appalling. Consider all the problems we faced in this country over the last four years - from debt to adapting to globalization to unemployment to the challenges of climate change to terrorist - and then roll over that statement: 'The single most important thing we want to achieve is for President Obama to be a one-term president.'

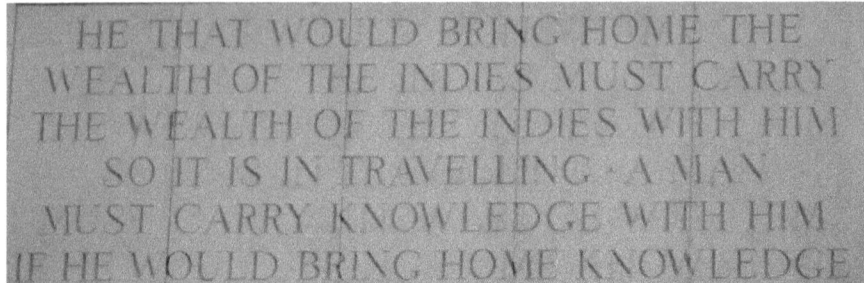

Obama - Master and Commander 764. Union Station: **Words of Wisdom V**. The Inscription reads: "He that would bring home the wealth of the Indies must carry the wealth of the Indies with him; So it is in traveling; A man must carry knowledge with him if he would bring home knowledge!"

That, in my view, is what made the difference. The G.O.P. lost an election that, given the state of the economy, it should have won because of an excess of McConnell-like cynicism, a shortage of new ideas and an abundance of really bad ideas - about immigration, about climate, about how jobs are created and about abortion and other social issues."

In "**Now a Chance to Catch Up to His Epochal Vision**" Jodi Kantor writes in *The New York Times* Wednesday, November 7, 2012, P. P 1:

"From the first time Barack Obama summoned the country's leading presidential historians to dinner, they saw that the type of discussion he wanted would be different from their talks with previous Oval Office occupants."

"There was almost no small talk, for this was no idle exercise. Though Mr. Obama knew many of his predecessors' stories cold, he was no history buff; he showed little curiosity about their personalities and almost no interest in the founding fathers. His goal, the historians realized, was more strategic. He wanted to apply lessons of past presidential triumphs and failures to his own urgent project of setting the country on a new path."

"All three private annual gatherings during his first years in office, he asked pointed questions: How did Ronald Reagan engineer his 1984 re-election despite a poor economy? Where did the Tea Party fit in the tradition of American protest

OBAMA - MASTER AND COMMANDER

movements? Theodore Roosevelt by-passed Congress to launch progressive programs; could Mr. Obama do the same?"

Explaining that Mr. Obama was writing the book on his place in history, Jodi Kantor continued, "On Tuesday, Mr. Obama successfully wrote his next chapter, joining the club of presidents who have secured second terms. Yet the man who once envisioned himself in the pantheon of transcendent presidents enters his next term as a far more conventional, partisan leader than he intended to be. He defeated a mistake-prone challenger of unsteady popularity within his own party in an election in which he never quite explained how he would deliver on his unmet promises."

"Now Mr. Obama, a specialist in long shots, faces what may be the climatic challenge of his political career: a second chance to deliver the renewal he still promises, but without a clear mandate, a healthy economy or willing Republican partners."

"scholars could see the urgency and seriousness that he brought to his role,"... "his fraustrations" ... "a leader ... who preferred to think in terms of the sweeps of years rather than of the tick of hours or days ...."

"At the first dinner, in 2009, he exuded optimism, repeating his desire for a presidency that would transform the nation, and asked for a tutorial on timing a first-year agenda - almost, some of the historians thought, as if learning more about the past could compensate for his Washington inexperience." Mr. Obama advised a youngster "Dream big dreams!"

"He was struggling to understand the Tea Party and a levlel of opposition he said was 'not normal' by historical standards. Several of the scholars told him that the Tea Party members were like the 19th century Populists, less motivated by economic self-intereest than by nativism and a fear of modernity."

"There is something subterranean about what these folks are saying."

"Like Mr. Obama, Roosevelt often expressed disdain for legislators, praised universal health care and rammed a progressive agenda past a hostile Congress."

The author speaks of "the intellecutal foundation of his second term" and so forth.

The *New York Times* EDITORIAL Wednesday, November 7, 2012, P. A26 stated:

"President Obama's dramatic re-election victory was not a sign that a fractured nation had finally come together on Election Day. But it was a strong endorsement of economic policies that stress job growth, health care reform, tax increases and balanced deficit reduction - and of moderate policies on immigration, abortion and same-sex marriage. It was a repudiation of Reagan-era bromides about tax-cutting and trickle-down economics, and of the politics of fear, intolerance and disinformation.

Obama - Master and Commander 765. Tree planted in honor of Dr. Martin Luther King, Jr.

The president's victory depended heavily on Mid-western Rust Belt states like Ohio, where the bailout of the auto industry - which Mr. Obama engineered and Mr. Romney opposed - proved widely popular for the simple reason that it worked. More broadly, Midwestern voters seemed to endorse the president's argument that the government has a significant role in creating private-sector jobs and boosting the economy. They rejected Mr. Romney's position that Washington should simply stay out of such matters and let the free market work its will.

The Republicans' last-ditch attempt to steal away Pennsylvania by stressing unemployment was a failure there and elsewhere. Voters who said unemployment was a major issue voted mainly for Mr. Obama.

Mr. Romney, it turns out, made a fatal decision during the primaries to endorse a hard line on immigration, which earned him a resounding rejection by Latinos. By adopting a callous position that illegal immigrants could be coerced to 'self-deportation' and by praising Arizona's cruel immigration law, Mr. Romney made his road in Florida and several crucial states much harder. Only one-third of voters said illegal immigrants should all be deported, while two-thirds endorsed some

OBAMA - MASTER AND COMMANDER

path to legal residency and citizenship. The Republican approach, if unchanged, will cost them dearly in the future."

Contrast the actual women vote to an article written by Rich Lowry entitled **"WOMEN AREN'T DUMB, O**" in the *New York Post*, Wednesday, October 31, 2012, P. 27, that, inter alia states:

"It's a mercy that the suffragettes aren't around to see President Obama's campaign for the women's vote. It would make them weep in dismay.

Almost a hundred years after passage of the 19th Amendment, the president is making perhaps the most superficial, misleading and insulting appeal for the support of women in American presidential politics ever. It's a wonder that his target audience doesn't rise up as one and say, "Please stop condescending to us."

If David Axelrod is right, what women care about most is making other people, even religious employers, pay for their birth control. They love abortion with a single minded passion. They are so easily manipulated that they can be motivated to oppose Mitt Romney because he said innocently in a debate that his aides brought him "binders of women" to consider for his cabinet as Massachusetts governor.

They can be convinced that they are the victims of a "war on women" as long as the slogan is repeated over and over again. They can be made to believe that the Lilly Ledbetter Act merely tilts the playing field against employers and toward trial lawyers by allowing lawsuits years after alleged acts of pay discrimination ....

Not that the Romney campaign hasn't engaged in its own embarrassingly single-minded courtship of female voters. Its convention was devoted to it, and - reassuringly enough - got Romney nothing. He made his strides among women with a performance in the first debate that was substantive, future oriented and designed to speak to the entire country rather than to narrow slivers of the electorate.

The president is increasingly incapable of the latter. The former uniter is now a divider hoping enough women buy his insipid pitch."

Rich, whose name is probably Richard, also insipidly and condescendingly crows "Obama is the great Provider for the women in his coalition. He gives them material and emotional support. He helps them not have children, protects them from the depredations of their male employers and scorns any suggestion that anyone ever has to fall back on self-reliance."

When readers assess how, as Malcolm X used to say, "These things have written into them," one gets the impression these writers' office is in the sewer. Their stuff

FREDERICK MONDERSON

is so insipidly original, one has to also wonder if they write their own material. It's as if, down there, someone pushes, as Romney would say, "Division, anger and hate" in front of them and says "write this way!"

Here's another piece from the *Post* espousing the same mindset. This one is entitled, "**Why the President's Losing the Youth Vote**" by Ron Meyer and Celia Bigelow in the *New York Post*, Wednesday, October 31, 2012, P. 27, which states:

"Katy Perry concerts and MTV appearances won't help President Obama with young voters this time around.

On Friday, Obama appeared on MTV for "**ASK OBAMA LIVE: An MTV Interview with the President**" for one last push to win over the hearts of the generation that secured his victory in 2008.

"The president had no fresh material, but it was clear he knows his campaign is hemorrhaging support from the more than 20 million 18 - to 29-year-olds who'll vote this year - votes he can't afford to lose.

Obama beat John McCain by 34 points in this group, but Mitt Romney has chopped that deficit in half and is in striking distance of closing the gap entirely.

The president will milk every ounce of celebrity status he can, because he sure can't run on his economic youth record or his broken promises."

Ron and Celia go on to spew statistics then speak of "The lack of job prospects..."

"President Obama's lofty rhetoric..."

Obama also said he'd "cut the deficit we inherited in half by the end of my first term" ....

"In one term, Obama has morphed from the 'purple president' into a candidate whose ads have been 73 percent negative, compared to 36 percent for Romney. The optimism from 2008 has vanished." What these writers miss is the four years of negativity. This 36 percent is the tail end of that four years of mischief.

"Young Americans couldn't be more disappointed, ..."

"He promised to unify the country and give everyone a fair shot. Four years later, the president has failed to keep his promises, and young Americans have lost faith in the political system."

OBAMA - MASTER AND COMMANDER

"No matter how many times Katy Perry and Bruce Springsteen beg them, young Americans won't (to steal a phrase from Obama) get 'Obamnesia' and forget the last four miserable years. We haven't gone 'forward,' we haven't seen positive 'change' and we've lost 'hope.' Slogans and celebrities won't fool young voters again." You two have lost hope!

They go on to list that Ron Meyer is the press secretary and Celia Bigelow is the campus director for American Majority Action.

This organization is one of the many that have spewed anti-Obama rhetoric ante-Day-One. You ask them how many times they have come to the president's rescue by writing something positive in support of the man and see what type of response you get.

> ON FEBRUARY 19, 1942, 73 DAYS AFTER THE UNITED STATES ENTERED WORLD WAR II, PRESIDENT FRANKLIN D. ROOSEVELT ISSUED EXECUTIVE ORDER 9066 WHICH RESULTED IN THE REMOVAL OF 120,000 JAPANESE AMERICAN MEN, WOMEN AND CHILDREN FROM THEIR HOMES IN THE WESTERN STATES AND HAWAII.
>
> ALLOWED ONLY WHAT THEY COULD CARRY, FAMILIES WERE FORCED TO ABANDON HOMES, FRIENDS, FARMS AND BUSINESSES TO LIVE IN TEN REMOTE RELOCATION CENTERS GUARDED BY ARMED TROOPS AND SURROUNDED BY BARBED WIRE FENCES. SOME REMAINED IN THE RELOCATION CENTERS UNTIL MARCH 1946.
>
> IN ADDITION, 4,500 WERE ARRESTED BY THE JUSTICE DEPARTMENT AND HELD IN INTERNMENT CAMPS, SUCH AS AT SANTA FE, NEW MEXICO. 2,500 WERE ALSO HELD AT THE FAMILY CAMP IN CRYSTAL CITY, TEXAS.
>
> ANSWERING THE CALL TO DUTY, YOUNG JAPANESE AMERICANS ENTERED INTO MILITARY SERVICE, JOINING MANY PRE-WAR DRAFTEES. THE 100TH INFANTRY BATTALION AND 442ND REGIMENTAL COMBAT TEAM, FIGHTING IN EUROPE, BECAME THE MOST HIGHLY DECORATED ARMY UNIT FOR ITS SIZE AND LENGTH OF SERVICE IN AMERICAN MILITARY HISTORY. JAPANESE AMERICANS IN THE MILITARY INTELLIGENCE SERVICE USED THEIR BILINGUAL SKILLS TO HELP SHORTEN THE WAR IN THE PACIFIC AND THUS SAVED COUNTLESS AMERICAN LIVES. THE 1399TH ENGINEER CONSTRUCTION BATTALION HELPED FORTIFY THE INFRASTRUCTURE ESSENTIAL FOR VICTORY.
>
> IN 1983, ALMOST FORTY YEARS AFTER THE WAR ENDED, THE FEDERAL COMMISSION ON WARTIME RELOCATION AND INTERNMENT OF CIVILIANS FOUND THAT THERE HAD BEEN NO MILITARY NECESSITY FOR THE MASS IMPRISONMENT OF JAPANESE AMERICANS AND THAT A GRAVE INJUSTICE HAD BEEN DONE.
>
> IN 1988 PRESIDENT RONALD W. REAGAN SIGNED THE CIVIL LIBERTIES ACT WHICH MADE AN APOLOGY FOR THE INJUSTICE, PROVIDED MINIMAL COMPENSATION AND REAFFIRMED THE NATION'S COMMITMENT TO EQUAL JUSTICE UNDER THE LAW FOR ALL AMERICANS.

Obama - Master and Commander 766. Memorial Commemorating the Internment of Japanese Americans during World War II.

FREDERICK MONDERSON

Optimism on part of these people has vanished. When the Germans were pounding the British during the Battle of Britain in World War II, the British never lost one iota of optimism. We must come back to the racism of this nation. Let us not forget, at his Inauguration in January of 2005, President Bush spoke out against insipid racism in this country. While those same young people Ron and Celia speak about, sought change, the dinosaurs these writers represent (to steal a phrase from Santorum) poured more "poison in the well!" That is why the likes of these Neanderthals went down in defeat. It is what Van Jones called, "The backlash against the backlash!"

Obama - Master and Commander 767. The House of the Temple on 16th Street.

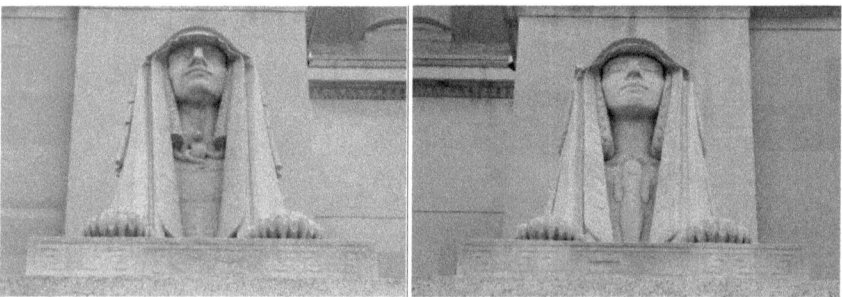

Obama - Master and Commander 768. Images at the foot of the stairway to the House of the Temple on 16th Street.

OBAMA - MASTER AND COMMANDER

Obama - Master and Commander 769. The Scottish Rite Temple also on 16th Street.

It is because the Coalition of 2008 thought Obama a better choice than Romney in 2012 that they voted for him. Sure captains of industry have been successful but at a price of the working man and their competition. People did not fall for Romney's pie in the sky promises to provide 12 million jobs in 4 years. They must have considered how many victims he would have left on the field of business. Obama, on the other hand, whose efforts have stemmed the tide of fiscal and economic collapse, put in place policies and practices that have begun to bear fruit, despite the entrenched opposition and obstructionism to make his term in office a failure, could still boast of Lilly Ledbetter, contraception, marriage equality, the appeal to women, be buttressed by African Americans, still attract the youth, especially first time voters, who wanted to experience the joy of the first vote that those of 2008 enjoyed. Then again, let us not forget how Obama masterfully played the "Latino card." However, let us all forget the negativity and as they say on TV, "stay tuned" for there was an election and Obama won despite the falsity of the pessimists as some quoted here. It is people like Ron and Celia who have lost hope, who can't see that two women on the Supreme Court and Lilly Ledbetter is change, so too the Auto Bailout is change. The Affordable Care Act is change, so too is decimation of Al Qaeda and the death of bin Laden. The end of American involvement in Iraq is change and change is bringing home the troops from Afghanistan, sent there by a Republican administration. Yes there must still be change! Africans Americans must get the respect they deserve in this nation and not be victims of institutional and social racism and religious bigotry. They must get their share of jobs, slots in school, and Boardrooms, university teaching and administrative positions, and general prootions in the military, while not becoming victims of racial profiling especially when "Driving while Black," or "Shopping while Black."

FREDERICK MONDERSON

In a Letter to the Editor, Re: "**Obama's Night**" (nytimes.com, Nov. 7), *The New York Times* Wednesday, November 7, 2012, P. A26, Alfred Waddell of West Dennis, Mass., Nov 7, 2012, wrote:

"The 2012 election result should serve as wake-up call to many in the Republican Party that the future is about real inclusiveness. The America that once was, reflected in the crowds that Mitt Romney drew on the campaign trail, is a fading America that is holding onto outdated notions.

With President Obama's victory, the world has witnessed an America leading the way toward a tent where all ideas are heard and all talents are considered. That America was seen in the crowds that President Obama drew on the campaign trail. That America will lead the world in tolerance."

In *Post* Opinion entitled "**A Brilliant Victory**," *New York Post*, Wednesday, November 7, 2012, p. 37, John Podhoretz writes:

"Barack Obama is one of the greatest politicians in American history. After a historic national election in 2008 based on a vague message of hope and change, he has just shifted gears and won a second term with a tough-minded, hard-grinding state-by-state get-out-the-vote effort that overcame this fundamental fact: He shouldn't have won at all.

Obama - Master and Commander 770. The Executive Office, Eisenhower Building.

"I said several times over the course of this year in this column that he would lose, because the condition of the country under the years of his stewardship would make it impossible for him to survive the electorate's judgment. There was ample

OBAMA - MASTER AND COMMANDER

recent precedent for this: Gerald Ford hadn't survived it in 1976; Jimmy Carter hadn't survived it in 1980; George H.W. Bush hadn't survived it in 1992.

"But even as he made this rather modest case for himself, he was in effect aiming a billion-dollar howitzer at a single target: Romney.

"And here was where his campaign genius came into play. Its leaders spent the summer 'defining' Romney in effectively harsh terms, while Romney mostly raised money to compete in the fall. And they did so only where they needed to do it most - in the states that provided Romney a path to the White House ....

"Still, one must stand in awe of Barack Obama, who really pulled a rabbit out of the hat and magicked himself up four more years. Bravo.

"I fear very much what he is going to do to the country, but you have to admire this political master and his amazing handicraft."

77. ELECTION DAY COMMENTARY

In viewing some of the commentary a number of comments were expressed about problems in the voting process. One such "mistake" had President Obama listed as a Republican. There was a voting machine in Pennsylvania that changed votes for President Obama into votes for Mitt Romney. Some say the machines were programmed by Republicans and they should be blamed for any problems!

James Carville, the wizard instrumental in Bill Clinton's 1992 win and famous for the equally famous saying, "It's the economy stupid!" in expressing his thoughts on a CNN panel simply summed up the election this way: "If President Obama wins Virginia, I'm calling the race!" He said further, "Obama should get more of what he wants because we had an election" and that "Obama has to respect the views of the voters!"

The Republican strategist Alex Castellanos thought President Obama, after his victory acceptance speech, was as "gracious as he was passionate." He rightly characterized the results as a "beating that was so severe" Republicans "need to move forward not sideways!"

Gloria Borger expressed the view "The President has to lead" even though she thought this a "negative, nasty campaign that did not rise" above partisanship.

Margaret Hoover, pointing to contemporary voting trends noted, especially since young people voted for Al Gore and Barack Obama twice, offered the view, "This generation is lost to the Republican Party" and that "Republicans will descend into Warlordism."

FREDERICK MONDERSON

Anna Navarro, a Republican strategist, believed Mitt Romney "Self deported from the White House." Further she explained, Latinos were "Disillusioned by Obama but terrified by Romney." Even further, she offered, "The Republican Party will have to reassess itself. The Tea Party has cost them dearly."

David Gergen, one of the most senior commentators who served as advisor to several President offered the view, President Obama must "close the chapter on his first term and open a new chapter." He said further, "Many of the President's efforts were rebuffed" and "Given that an African American can win once, twice, means there is need for more moderation in our politics."

The Democratic strategist, Van Jones pointed out, Mr. Obama was "Demonized, mistreated" but still "vindicated." More importantly he asked, "If Barack Obama is not acceptable, Who is?" Even more, Mr. Jones said he was "Proud of America" and "Proud of the coalition." Finally, he argued, since Mr. Obama campaigned on it and he won, "This is a mandate. There will be taxes."

Obama - Master and Commander 771. The Washington Center for Internships and Academic Seminars.

Obama - Master and Commander 772. "Dedicated to Art."

OBAMA - MASTER AND COMMANDER

78. CONCLUSIONS I
By
Dr. Fred Monderson

In retrospect, when we analyze events of the 2012 election, a number of questions seem apparent principal of which is "How could the Media get it so wrong?" Perhaps unintentionally they did the President a favor by calling the contest "too close to call" and this emboldened Mr. Romney! It also helped galvanize Mr. Obama's base, particularly African Americans. Thus, the "young whippersnapper" Romney was poised to dethrone the old champ, Obama! They say, "A new broom sweeps clean, but the old broom knows the corners." They also say, "Young and impetuous" challengers always have a problem or gets it wrong. Pardon the pun!

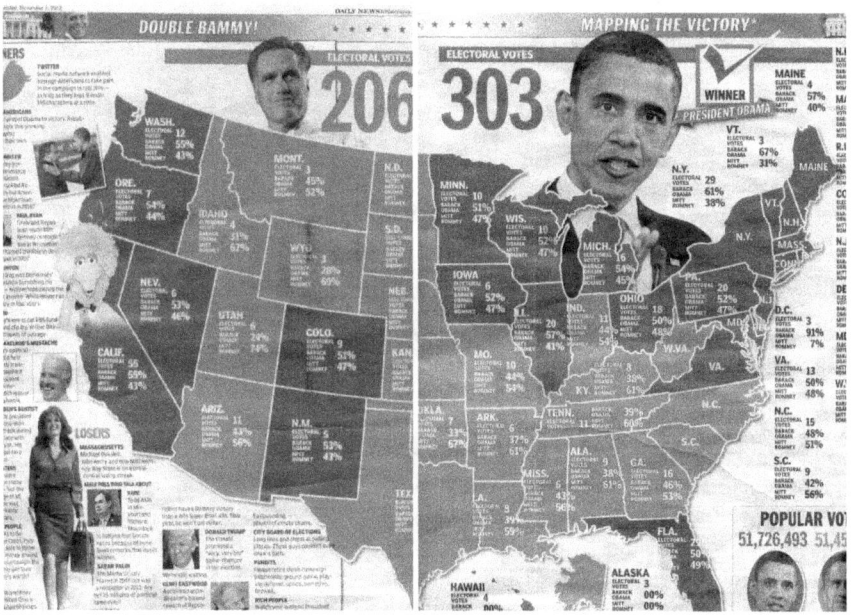

Obama - Master and Commander 773. *Daily News* of November 7, 2012, showing results of the election of 2012 and identifying winners and losers and the candidates popular votes.

FREDERICK MONDERSON

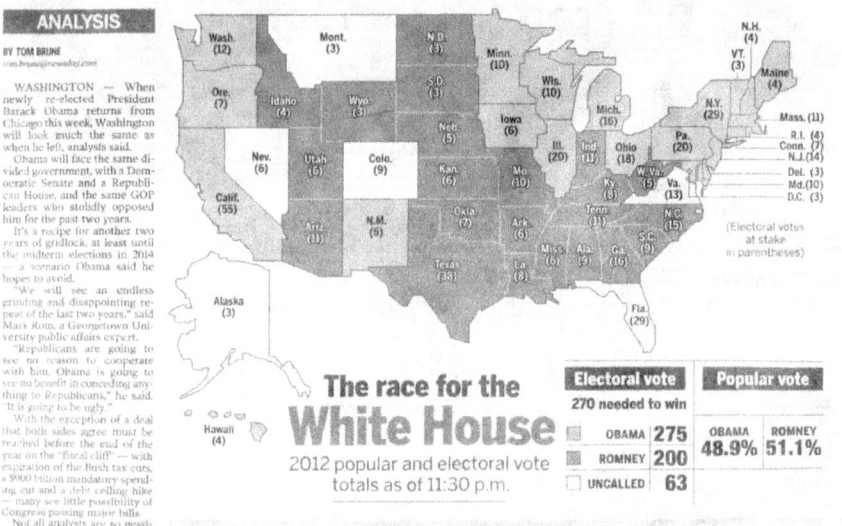

Obama - Master and Commander 774. Early projection of outcome of the election of 2012, naturally the Media, *Newsday*, was wrong.

Two bulls stood on a hill overlooking a pasture of grazing heifer cows. The young bull turned and said to the oldster, "Let's run over and do a few!" The old bull, full of experience and tricks simply responded, "Let's walk over and do them all!" In the race between the hare and the tortoise, hard as the hare ran, the tortoise always seemed ahead of him. All these aphorisms point to one inescapable fact; that is, Barack Obama allowed Mitt Romney to outspend his political capital in the vein of Republican strategy of attacking him through *ad hominem* arguments. His frontal attack against Obama was conceived under the umbrella strategy of the "McConnell Mandate" and so he could not keep his eyes on the prize. His accusations against Mr. Obama of "division, anger and hate" is actually the mold of Republican treasonous obstructionism against Mr. Obama's efforts to govern effectively. When people of Mr. Romney's hue accuse Mr. Obama of dividing the nation, they betray ignorance of Republican opposition against the president, and the psychological imbalance created in threats against him. Who could forget the frenzy created at the beginning of his term when militias stocked up on armaments because in their twisted minds, Mr. Obama was going to change the Constitution and equally, they were getting ready for a "race war." Perhaps a downside of that

OBAMA - MASTER AND COMMANDER

unchecked stockpiling of armaments probably allowed the theater massacre perpetrator to acquire the arsenal that killed all those innocent people in the crowded movie house!

What the public spewers of hate such as Rush Limbaugh, Ann Coulter, John Sununu, etc., as well as many of the established media could not comprehend the meaning of Condoleezza Rice's insightful statement that: "The view from the Oval Office is different to what we believe!"

Single and simple minded commentators such as Rudy Giuliani and Mitt Romney, among others, who harp on President Obama's broken promises of uniting the nation, also dwell on his supposed partisanship and choose to disregard Ms. Rice's observation. Now, for argument sake, let us place the President in the Oval Office looking out the window toward Lafayette Park with elements of the Tea Party in full battle gear characterizing him. So, there "Joe the Plumber" carrying his "socialism" banner; Sarah Palin is half-way whipping up the crowd to fever pitch, then she says, "He's not like us! So, let's take our country back!" Pausing for breath she repeats that stupid line, "I can see Russia from my front steps." Then "Mama Grizzly" reiterates, "Don't retreat, Reload!"

Observing these development from his front row seat, Mr. Obama views these "Good ole boys at play!" One of his advisers says, "Mr. President, it is your responsibility to protect these people's right to condemn you." He responds, "Yes I agree!" Then he calls in the head of security and instructs him, "Make sure these people protesting are protected. Make sure they walk good, in the corner. Don't let motor car mash them!"

Thus, the anti-Obamites are in glee. The President is soft. He is an appeaser. Meanwhile, the Commander-in-Chief has retired to the War Room and is targeting Osama bin-Laden, the Somali Pirates, Al-Awlaki and other terrorists at war with America. Meanwhile, on the road to the 2012 election, as we encounter Mitch and Johnny busily at work, lubricating the apparatus of treason, we finally enter the unfolding Republican Presidential Primary.

FREDERICK MONDERSON

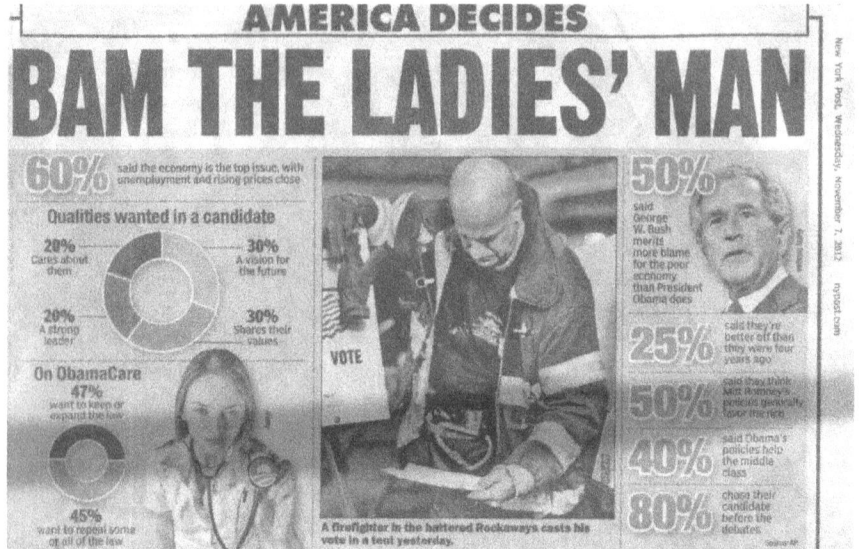

Obama - Master and Commander 775. The *New York Post* of Wednesday, November 7, 2012, showing some results of the election of 2012.

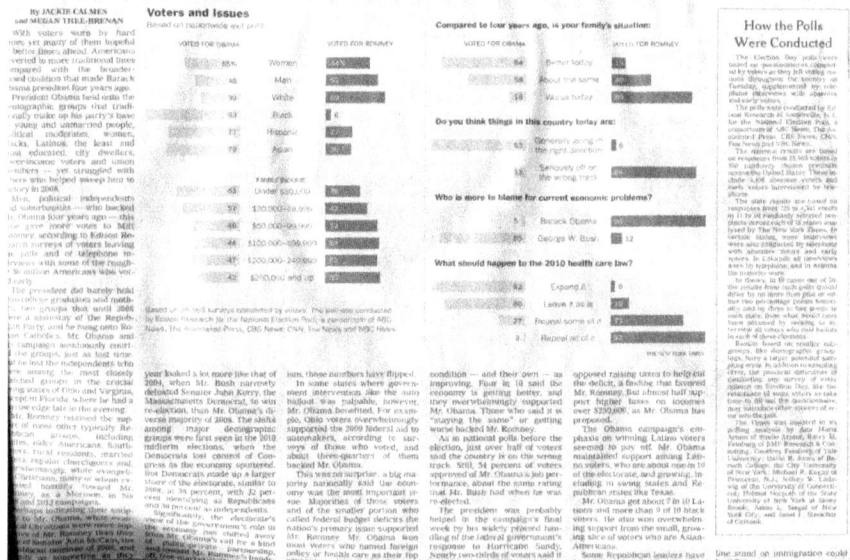

Obama - Master and Commander 776. The *New York Times* of November 7, 2012, showing results of the election of 2012.

OBAMA - MASTER AND COMMANDER

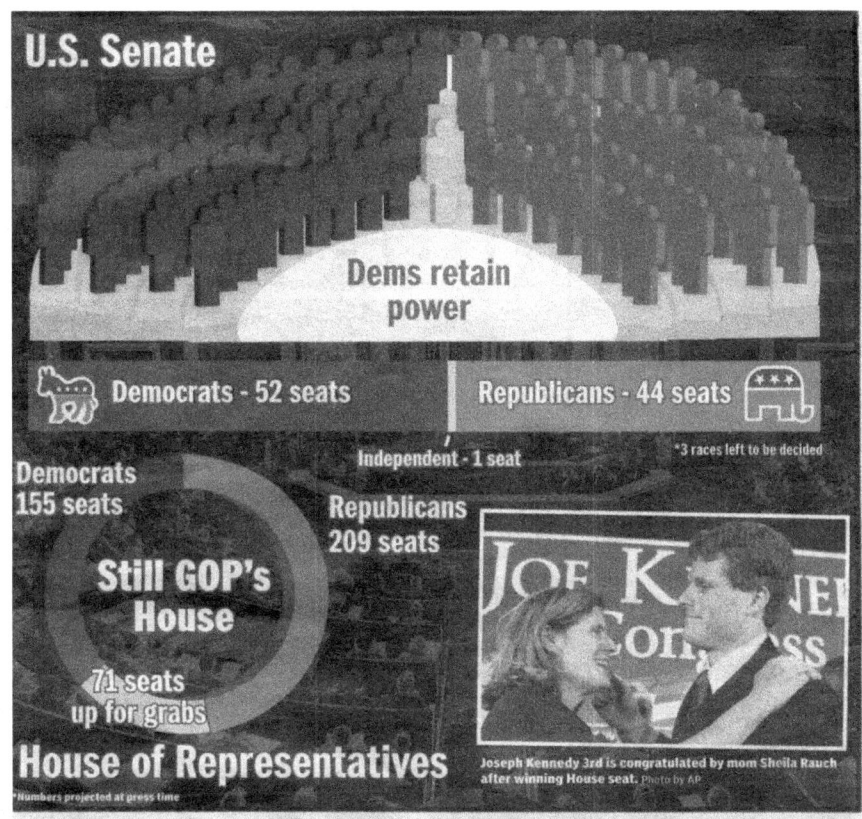

Obama - Master and Commander 777. The *Daily News* of November 7, 2012, showing results of the election of 2012.

FREDERICK MONDERSON

At the tape of this race stand Rick "Oops" Perry; Michele "Gangster Government" Bachmann; Herbert "Blacks are brainwashed for voting Democrat" Cain; Ron perhaps "Convered on the road to the White House" Paul; Mitt "12 million jobs Bain Capital" Romney; Newt "I'm going to be the nominee" Gingrich; and others who can be considered "losers!" Meanwhile, President Obama conspicuously dismissed those who would become losers focusing on Romney and his business experience as the potential last Republican left standing and the one the Republican National Convention will crown for the fall campaign against him, whom, for the longest, they have been trying to make a one-term president.

Therefore, Romney is the man Obama had to surprise. As his strategy incubated, before, during and after the Democratic National Convention, the seeds of Mr. Obama's carefully planted economic program began to shoot. Unemployment numbers began to get better; businesses began to continuously add jobs; Mr. Romney went to the Olympics in London and insulted the British. So much so, while the British prayed he would soon depart, bookmakers began to take bets on the pending fight between Donkey and Elephant. Many began wondering if Jackass would outlast elephant and the Media played on!

Obama - Master and Commander 778. Well, there you have it, Donkey up front by a nose and smiling!

The story is recounted of a pugilistic encounter in times past where a blind white man went to "See a fight" between a black guy and a white guy. At ringside, his armrest companion, called the fight blow by blow. As the contest waged on, the blind man finally asked of his partner, "What's happening now?" He responded,

OBAMA - MASTER AND COMMANDER

"The white guy has the black guy down." In turn the blind man responded, "The black man down? Keep him down, for when the black man raise hell raises!"

Throughout his campaigning Mitt Romney made fatal mistake after mistake, perhaps because he read newspapers like the *New York Post*, listened to his ill-informed advisers, surrogates, associates and allies, especially the biased and dunce Media. They convinced themselves and the candidate they were closing in on the White House. In fact, so assured, Mr. Romney told Barack Obama to "start packing!" Writing their own material and falling for the falsity they were shoveling, they underestimated the intellectual strategic nature of the President's mindset and the power of incumbency. So much so, their "Plan B" was really "Plan A." As skewed polls began to show Mitt "closing the gap" and the race became "too close to call," the Governor's arrogance ballooned, accusing the President of sowing "division, anger, hate," though as a classic chess player Obama was setting them up. Then the first debate happened! Romney won! The press and his entourage gloated. They began writing Obama's epitaph. No one considered Obama was playing possum in a trap set for Romney. The arrogance of gloaters is evident. They blow their horn! Some have argued, the President allowed Mr. Romney to win the first debate to show all his cards as he prepared for the second and third debates.

Strategically closing the ranks of his trap, he sent in "Smoking Joe Biden" to rope the dope in the Vice Presidential Debate. In response to a question about his strategy, and stealing a line from Mohammed Ali, Joe confessed, "I'm here to rope a dope!"

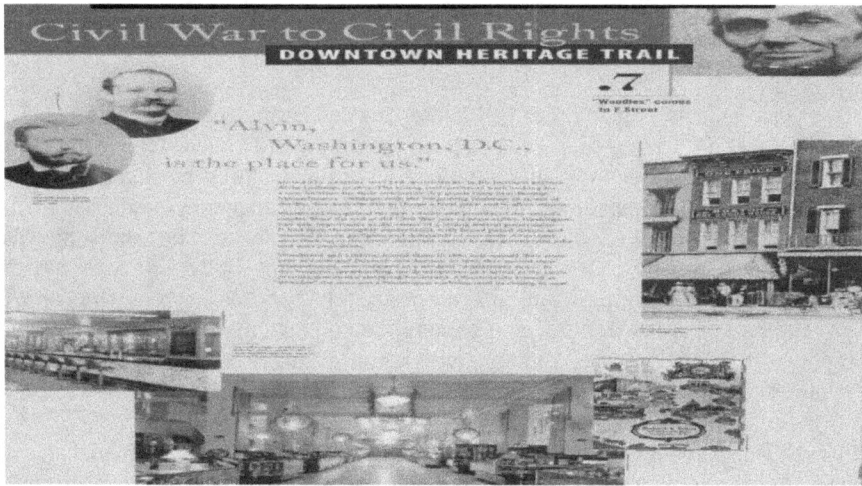

Obama - Master and Commander 779. "Civil War to Civil Rights" on the Downtown Heritage Trail.

FREDERICK MONDERSON

The New York Times breakdown of exit poles in various states show:

Electorate Reverts to a Partisan Divide as Obama's Support Narrows

OBAMA – MASTER AND COMMANDER 780. Exit polls. NYT 11-7-2012.

Everyone and his grandmother had heard of Paul Ryan's brilliance. Remember, Joe Biden is no "spring chicken" either. In the movie El Dorado, John Wayne was a fast gun who came up against a real fast gunslinger hired by a cattle boss in battle against his competition. Previously they had exchanged pleasantries in the slogan, "Professional Courtesy!" In a scene, John Wayne was shot and somewhat incapacitated, yet he chose to confront the gun-slinging bully who was sure he could take on the cripple. Yet, Wayne bested him, and as he lay dying on the ground, he asked, "How did I let a cripple like you take me?" To this Mr. Wayne replied, "You're too good. I can't give you an even break!" This was a sort of rehashed version of "Never give a sucker an even break!"

Joe Biden, known for his flourishes, bested Paul Ryan in their debate by interrupting him with facts; by challenging his falsity; by laughing; by consistently speaking over him; as they say, "Never give a sucker an even break!"

OBAMA - MASTER AND COMMANDER

Frederick, the journey ahead is going to be long. And it is going to be hard. But know that is how change always happens in this country. And if we keep showing up, if we keep fighting the good fight, then eventually we get there. We always do. — Michelle Obama

Obama - Master and Commander 781. Staying the course with Barack Obama and Michelle.

To Frederick,
Our success is due to your dedication, friendship, and support. We thank you from the bottom of our hearts. — Barack Obama, Joe Biden

Obama - Master and Commander 782. Staying the course with Obama and Biden!

Biased media praised Mitt Romney's first debate win and blasted Joe Biden's "unprofessional tactics." yet, the old scrapper did his job! He derailed the Ryan Express and in doing so, stopped the Romney/Ryan momentum. However, in

FREDERICK MONDERSON

extolling Romney's first debate, Republicans began winding up their "fat lady" rehearsing in the back room but she turned out to simply be a cardboard cut-out.

On November 6th, let's keep moving America forward
Obama - Master and Commander 783. This is leadership. Looking out and knowing the people are with you! Go Obama!

All of a sudden Mr. Obama put a "Tyson rush" on Mr. Romney. Some have argued in the first debate the moderator seemed more Pro-Romney. Now, in the second debate as Mr. Romney, in an unpatriotic manner tried to exploit the Benghazi travesty, the moderator corrected him saying, "No Mr. Romney, Mr. Obama did describe the incident as a terrorist act." Mr. Vibert Gibson thought Mitt Romney's "blood got hot and so he became confused and couldn't keep his eyes on the prize!" Now discombobulated, the straw man stood there clueless and only visionaries could see this was the beginning of the end. So much so, by the third debate on foreign policy, Mr. Romney, seemingly punch drunk, began agreeing with everything President Obama said. He seemed to act like Mike Tyson after Lennox Lewis put a whipping on him. Tyson approached Lewis' mother, telling her what a good boy her son was. That is after promising to eat his family.

The reason why the media got it wrong was simply because they could not see Obama's rope a dope strategy, as part of his overall intellectual brilliance. Remember Newt's brilliance and Ryan's brilliance, but Obama is in the White House for a second term! Yet, the Media kept regurgitating Romney's first debate win over and over even though Mr. Obama had said his piece, folded his arms and allowed Romney to show his everything, or to "punch himself out." The most some comentators could say about Mr. Obama is that he fought dirty in the debates. Imagine these "people gunning to skin you alive," in a profound struggle

OBAMA - MASTER AND COMMANDER

of good over evil and they wanted Mr. Obama to play nice guy where they had faulted him earlier for being a nice guy!

Strange that these commentators who live in America and are bombarded with sports playoffs scenarios never accepted he who wins the first contest does not necessarily win the title prize. That is, except this year when San Francisco Giant swept the Detroit Tigers to win the Baseball World Series Championship in four games. However, the sport lost untold revenue because there was no seventh game!

Obama - Master and Commander 784. How it must pain the *New York Post* to print this lead!

FREDERICK MONDERSON

Obama - Master and Commander 785. First Lady Michelle Obama's gown used for the First Inaugural Ball and now in the Smithsonian Museum and her second inaugual Ball's dress as she stands beside her husband, even showing the first gown.

Obama - Master and Commander 786. The Capital Building and Dome at night!

OBAMA - MASTER AND COMMANDER

Obama - Master and Commander 787. There's that quintessential American family in their most gleeful moment!

Obama - Master and Commander 788. There's that quintessential American family again!

FREDERICK MONDERSON

Obama - Master and Commander 789. The people have spoken! This is a preliminary showing of how the electorate expressed the choice between Mitt Romney (Red) and Barack Obama (blue).

OBAMA - MASTER AND COMMANDER

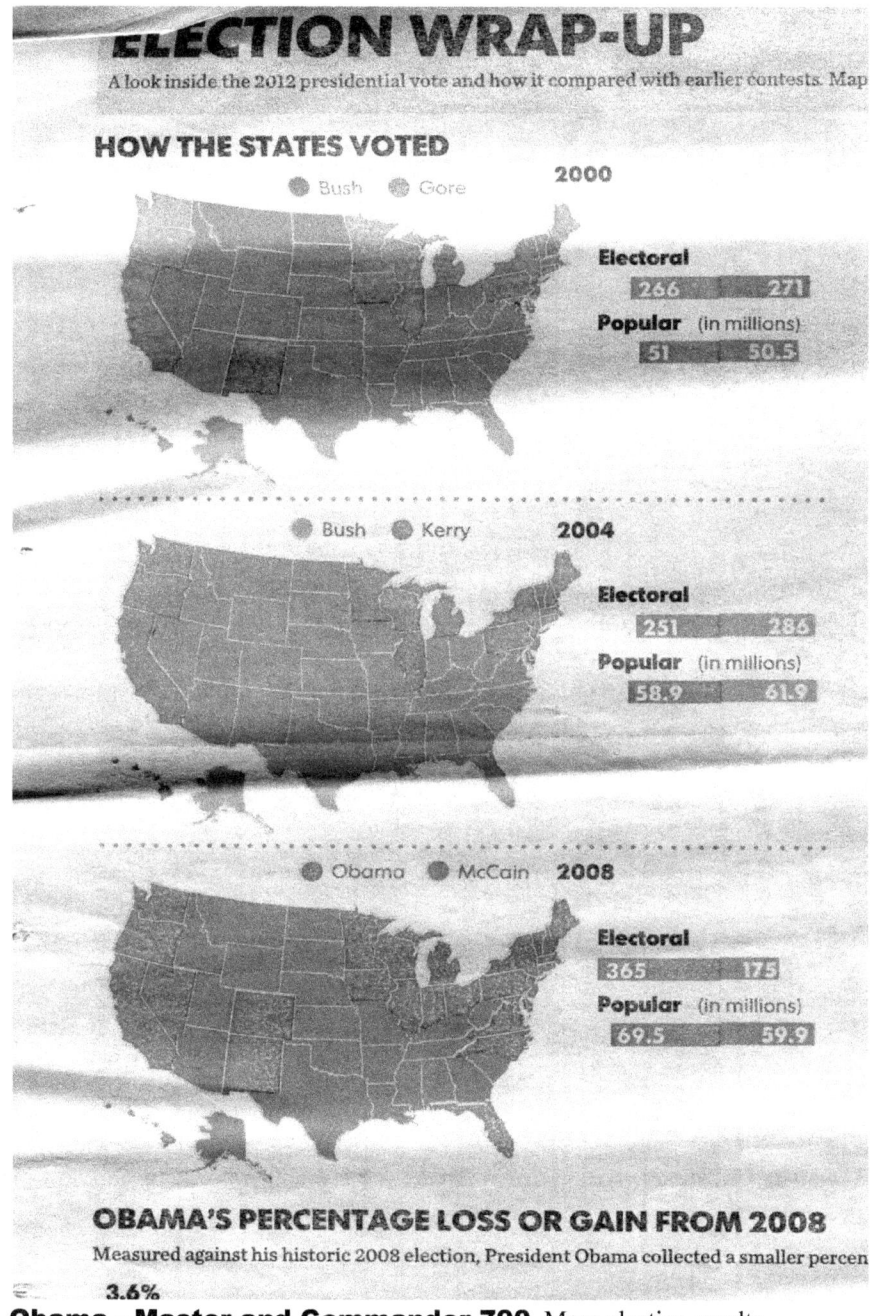

Obama - Master and Commander 790. More election results.

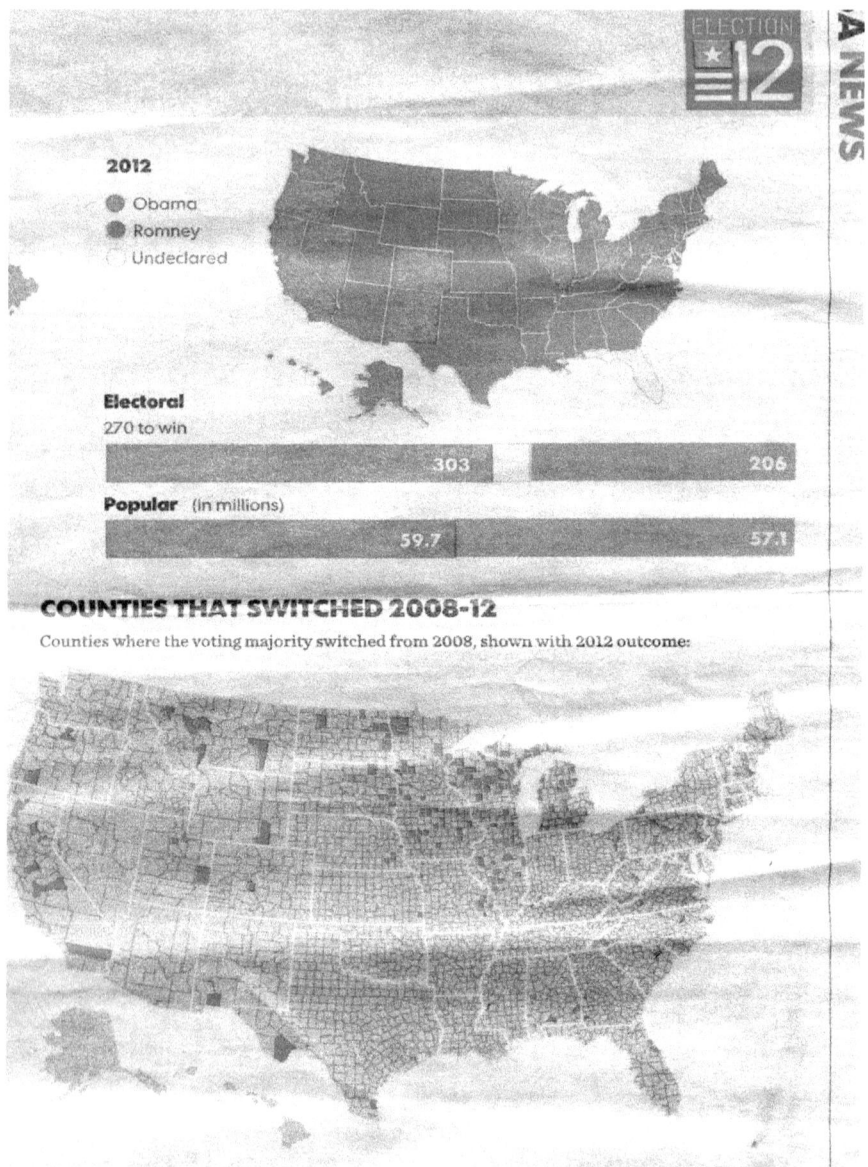

Obama - Master and Commander 791. Another breakdown of how the people voted.

OBAMA - MASTER AND COMMANDER

79. CONCLUSIONS II

Now that the election is over, the numbers counted, pundits recognized the errors of their ways, candidates conceded and people either won or lost, there is one unmistaken fact, there was an election and President Obama was re-elected. That is, Mr. Obama won and Republicans, who pursued obstructionist and treasonous behavior from day one, lost! In as much as Democrats retained the White House and Senate and Republicans remained in control of the House of Representatives, the question has again surfaced as to whether Mr. Obama can govern effectively given Congress' behavior for the last four years of his first term and Republicans in control of the House over the last two years. Still, many people blame President Bush for the calamitous economic state Mr. Obama inherited and despite Obama's every and unrelenting efforts, Congressional Republicans have been as un-co-operative as possible, pledging to an individual, an ideal and disregarding the wishes of the American people whose lot Mr. Obama has genuinely been trying to improve. However, though the power of incumbency generally improves chances of retaining certain elected positions, the American electorate has nevertheless retained a negative view of that branch of Congress controlled by Republicans heavily influenced by "Tea Party" members. Yet, as a counterweight to the President still voted for Republicans to remain in control of the House.

Finally, some Republicans have realized the destructive nature of their party's folly in following "Tea Party" leadership. That being so, not only did some members endorse Democrats, others have renounced the "No Tax Cut" pledge given to Grover Norquist. Imagine this man, as President Obama battles the economic maladies of the nation, Norquist presided over a conundrum of "No" men and women, and his stance loomed larger than the President of the United States at a time when the nation faced some of its most difficult challenges. Now, imagine timid Joe Walsh who had the gall to call Mr. Obama a "tyrant" but not the balls and so "can't touch" Grover. Pit Joe with his "men of big affairs" friends, colleagues, allies in opposition whose treasonous actions against the President of the United States not simply held the nation hostage but allowed thinking people the world over to wonder whether American mentality has slithered back into its 19th Century past!

Grover for his part, while recognizing his "Ducks are no longer lining up" as Republicans break with the "No Tax Pledge" because they, finally like "Plato's escaped prisoner," realize "The world is not flat" and unlike President Obama will face the heat of the electorate in two years time; Mr.Norquist now threatens to "go after them." As someone pointed out, that "Pledge" was for the "prior Congress" and should not hold to a new one. The question then is, "Where does this leave poor Grover and the remaining ducks?"

FREDERICK MONDERSON

Obama - Master and Commander 792. Very few times in American history have African Americans been shown in such massive and positive display of an example of America's exceptionalism, *Daily News* 11-7-2012.

Obama - Master and Commander 793. *The New York Times* captured the excitement of this moment as Obama's supporters celebrated, NYT 11-7-2012.

OBAMA - MASTER AND COMMANDER

Obama – Master and Commander 799. *The New York Times* Page One says it all NYT 11-7, 9- 2012!

FREDERICK MONDERSON

Obama - Master and Commander 800. Yes! The T-Shirts are out there!

Meanwhile, Republicans are slowly beginning to realize there was an election and the President was re-elected. Therefore, when the record is tallied on the one hand, Mr. Obama will boast we accomplished this, this and that; Republicans, on the other hand, will only be able to say we accomplished "No," "Yes." I mean "No!" That is, nothing substantive; and yes, in their monumental quest to effectuate the "McConnell Mandate" of "making Barack Obama a one term President" did they succeed, the answer is a resounding No! Then, as Bill Clinton so eloquently pointed out, they must now come to the table to work with the President to pass his Jobs Bill, help encourage development of clean, renewable energy, assist in improving and excelling in education challenges, caring for the environment and even helping to maintain the safety net and fix Health Care Reform by removing all the glitches that weigh heavily on the idea that seeks to care for all Americans irrespective of their ability to pay for health care.

We must keep in mind, the American ideal and empire is expansive and the pool of recruits from which its military defenders are drawn is equally vast. How comfortably can a young man or woman serve in defense of America thinking a mother, father, young brother or sister back home is denied health care for whatever ailment. All this while Wall Street thrives and Main and Back Streets falter! As Americans we must come together to make this nation work effectively in a world tremendously competitive where the sum of its parts may be much more than a single entity, regardless of how exceptional some think we are. Let us not forget, Sandy and the tornadoes have reminded us of how vulnerable we truly are!

OBAMA - MASTER AND COMMANDER

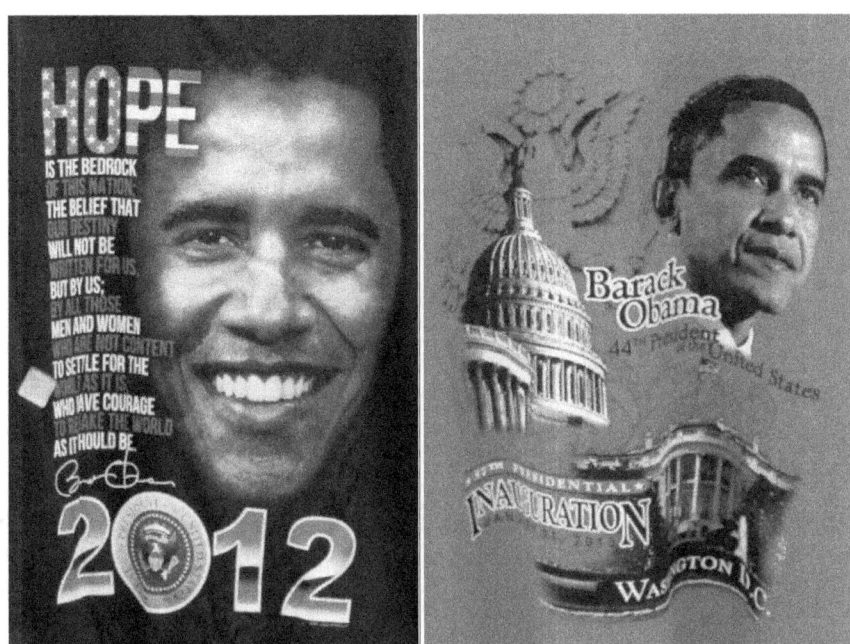

Obama - Master and Commander 801. Even more colorful images of the newly elected 44th President Barack Obama.

Many commentators have expressed the view Republicans need to be more inclusive of the diversity that now encompasses America, but they must also shed that invidious negativity that characterized the party in 2012. "Neanderthals" as Allen West, Joe Walsh, Joe Wilson and so many others should be winnowed out and even the likes of Rick Santorum should get no sanctuary in the Republican Party. In fact, they should "Self Deport" from Politics. Let's face it. Democrats will be extremely happy if Republicans choose narrow-minded Rick Santorum as their standard bearer in 2016! Equally, Allen West, who sees Americans as "the enemy" should receive a serious wake up call! Even Mitch McConnell needs to realize the imprint of his anti-Obama tirade stamps him as a bigoted, treasonous big man who is really little, for he blatantly championed a vile effort that was a losing strategy and tremendously anti-American. As such, he became a principal guest at the losers ball where the main course is roasted crow! And as he sits to dine, crying in his hot beer, he need be reminded, his monumental task of defeating the President must equal his effort in cooperation to minimize his going out from politics as a "loser." After all, this is one time when a loser will be remmembered more so than a winner since the "McConnell Mandate" will become a significant "black mark" asterisk in American history!

FREDERICK MONDERSON

Obama - Master and Commander 802. The results or Break-down of the combatitive critical states Mr. Obama carried overwhelmingly *Daily News* and *The New York Times* front page of Thursday, November 8, 2012, shows some of the break-down of the election results.

Obama - Master and Commander 803. Musical icons Jay-Z and his wife Beyonce make the front page of the *New York Post*, 1-23-2013, and then some.

OBAMA - MASTER AND COMMANDER

80. POST SCRIPT:

"Don't boo, Vote!"

"You didn't build that!"

"Forty-seven percent will vote for Obama, no matter what!"

"I intend to make Obama a one term president."

"We are brothers of another mother."

"I may be the only one but I'm more optimistic about the President now."

"Osama bin Laden is dead and General Motors is alive!"

"He saved our jobs. Now we must save his!"

81. EPILOGUE

The unmistaken fact is, there was a Presidential Election in 2012 and Senator Mitchell was unable to bring his mandate, "To make Barack Obama a one-term President," into fruition. Therefore, in the great divide, Mr. Obama is considered a winner and Mr. McConnell a loser! In this respect, each individual heads a list of their respective followers, given as follows: In the winner column headed by President Barack Obama and Vice-President Joe Biden, First Lady Michelle Obama and Mrs. Jill Biden, can also be mentioned among the winners the American people, Health Care Reform advocates and beneficiaries, Obama's Volunteers, *The New York Times*, *The Steve Harvey Morning Show* for giving the masses access to the President and Mrs. Obama, David Axelrod's Moustache, former President Bill Clinton, Veterans and the Armed Forces, and importantly the 47 Percent. Behind the losing candidate Mitt Romney, comes the Media, Mitch McConnell, Jim DeMint, the charlatan Reverend Anderson "praying for the death of Barack Obama" and his misguided desciple "Black protester with guns," Michael Goodwin of the *New York Post*, Fox News, Professor Roberto Unger, Hannity, the *New York Post*, John Steele Gordon, Allen West, Herman Cain, Rick Santorum, Newt Gingrich, Michele Bachmann, Carl Rove, the owner of TD Bank, Joe Walsh, Joe Wilson, "Joe the Plumber," Grand Pappy, and the Republicans with their "Tea Party" members, their allies and more!

FREDERICK MONDERSON

82. INAUGURATION SPEECH

Vice President Biden, Mr. Chief Justice, Members of the United States Congress, distinguished guests, and fellow citizens:

Each time we gather to inaugurate a president, we bear witness to the enduring strength of our Constitution. We affirm the promise of our democracy. We recall that what binds this nation together is not the colors of our skin or the tenets of our faith or the origins of our names. What makes us exceptional - what makes us American - is our allegiance to an idea, articulated in a declaration made more than two centuries ago:

"We hold these truths to be self-evident, that all men are created equal, that they are endowed by their Creator with certain unalienable rights, that among these are Life, Liberty, and the pursuit of Happiness."

Today we continue a never-ending journey, to bridge the meaning of those words with the realities of our time. For history tells us that while these truths may be self-evident, they have never been self-executing; that while freedom is a gift from God, it must be secured by His people here on Earth. The patriots of 1776 did not fight to replace the tyranny of a king with the privileges of a few or the rule of a mob. They gave to us a Republic, a government of, and by, and for the people, entrusting each generation to keep safe our founding creed.

For more than two hundred years, we have.

Through blood drawn by lash and blood drawn by sword, we learned that no union founded on the principles of liberty and equality could survive half-slave and half-free. We made ourselves anew, and vowed to move forward together.

Together, we determined that a modern economy requires railroads and highways to speed travel and commerce; schools and colleges to train our workers.

Together, we discovered that a free market only thrives when there are rules to ensure competition and fair play.

Together, we resolved that a great nation must care for the vulnerable, and protect its people from life's worst hazards and misfortune.

Through it all, we have never relinquished our skepticism of central authority, nor have we succumbed to the fiction that all society's ills can be cured through government alone. Our celebration of initiative and enterprise; our insistence on hard work and personal responsibility, are constants in our character.

OBAMA - MASTER AND COMMANDER

Obama - Master and Commander 804. The President waves to the crowd from the podium (above) and blows the crowd a kiss on Pennsylvania Avenue as he and Mrs. Obama left "the Beast" to greeet throngs lining the way (below) NYP 1-22-2013.

But we have always understood that when times change, so must we; that fidelity to our founding principles requires new responses to new challenges; that preserving our individual freedoms ultimately requires collective action. For the American people can no more meet the demands of today's world by acting alone

FREDERICK MONDERSON

than American soldiers could have met the forces of fascism or communism with muskets and militias. No single person can train all the math and science teachers we'll need to equip our children for the future, or build the roads and networks and research labs that will bring new jobs and businesses to our shores. Now, more than ever, we must do these things together, as one nation, and one people.

This generation of Americans has been tested by crises that steeled our resolve and proved our resilience. A decade of war is now ending. An economic recovery has begun. America's possibilities are limitless, for we possess all the qualities that this world without boundaries demands: youth and drive; diversity and openness; an endless capacity for risk and a gift for reinvention. My fellow Americans, we are made for this moment, and we will seize it - so long as we seize it together.

Obama - Master and Commander 805. Inaugural happenings and omparison of dresses of Michelle Obama and Beyonce Carer.

For we, the people, understand that our country cannot succeed when a shrinking few do very well and a growing many barely make it. We believe that America's prosperity must rest upon the broad shoulders of a rising middle class. We know that America thrives when every person can find independence and pride in their work; when the wages of honest labor liberate families from the brink of hardship. We are true to our creed when a little girl born into the bleakest poverty knows that she has the same chance to succeed as anybody else, because she is an America

n, she is free, and she is equal, not just in the eyes of God but also in our own.

OBAMA - MASTER AND COMMANDER

We understand that outworn programs are inadequate to the needs of our time. We must harness new ideas and technology to remake our government, revamp our tax code, reform our schools, and empower our citizens with the skills they need to work harder, learn more, and reach higher. But while the means will change, our purpose endures: a nation that rewards the effort and determination of every single American. That is what this moment requires. That is what will give real meaning to our creed.

We, the people, still believe that every citizen deserves a basic measure of security and dignity. We must make the hard choices to reduce the cost of health care and the size of our deficit. But we reject the belief that America must choose between caring for the generation that built this country and investing in the generation that will build its future. For we remember the lessons of our past, when twilight years were spent in poverty, and parents of a child with a disability had nowhere to turn. We do not believe that in this country, freedom is reserved for the lucky, or happiness for the few. We recognize that no matter how responsibly we live our lives, any one of us, at any time, may face a job loss, or a sudden illness, or a home swept away in a terrible storm. The commitments we make to each other - through Medicare, and Medicaid, and Social Security - these things do not sap our initiative; they strengthen us. They do not make us a nation of takers; they free us to take the risks that make this country great.

Obama - Master and Commander 806. Bill and Hillary; Mrs. Obama at dinner near Speaker John Boehner; crowds savoring the moment; and Senator Charles Schumer of *New York Daily News* 1-22-2013.

FREDERICK MONDERSON

We, the people, still believe that our obligations as Americans are not just to ourselves, but to all posterity. We will respond to the threat of climate change, knowing that the failure to do so would betray our children and future generations. Some may still deny the overwhelming judgment of science, but none can avoid the devastating impact of raging fires, and crippling drought, and more powerful storms. The path towards sustainable energy sources will be long and sometimes difficult. But America cannot resist this transition; we must lead it. We cannot cede to other nations the technology that will power new jobs and new industries - we must claim its promise. That is how we will maintain our economic vitality and our national treasure - our forests and waterways; our croplands and snowcapped peaks. That is how we will preserve our planet, commanded to our care by God. That's what will lend meaning to the creed our fathers once declared.

We, the people, still believe that enduring security and lasting peace do not require perpetual war. Our brave men and women in uniform, tempered by the flames of battle, are unmatched in skill and courage. Our citizens, seared by the memory of those we have lost, know too well the price that is paid for liberty. The knowledge of their sacrifice will keep us forever vigilant against those who would do us harm. But we are also heirs to those who won the peace and not just the war, who turned sworn enemies into the surest of friends, and we must carry those lessons into this time as well.

Obama - Master and Commander 807. Sasha and Malia (left) and Alicia Keys being escorted by the President, while Jennifer Hudson sings her heart out and Vice President Joe Biden and Mrs. Jill Biden dance the night away.

OBAMA - MASTER AND COMMANDER

We will defend our people and uphold our values through strength of arms and rule of law. We will show the courage to try and resolve our differences with other nations peacefully - not because we are naïve about the dangers we face, but because engagement can more durably lift suspicion and fear. America will remain the anchor of strong alliances in every corner of the globe; and we will renew those institutions that extend our capacity to manage crisis abroad, for no one has a greater stake in a peaceful world than its most powerful nation. We will support democracy from Asia to Africa; from the Americas to the Middle East, because our interests and our conscience compel us to act on behalf of those who long for freedom. And we must be a source of hope to the poor, the sick, the marginalized, the victims of prejudice - not out of mere charity, but because peace in our time requires the constant advance of those principles that our common creed describes: tolerance and opportunity; human dignity and justice.

We, the people, declare today that the most evident of truths - that all of us are created equal - is the star that guides us still; just as it guided our forebears through Seneca Falls, and Selma, and Stonewall; just as it guided all those men and women, sung and unsung, who left footprints along this great Mall, to hear a preacher say that we cannot walk alone; to hear a King proclaim that our individual freedom is inextricably bound to the freedom of every soul on Earth.

It is now our generation's task to carry on what those pioneers began. For our journey is not complete until our wives, our mothers, and daughters can earn a living equal to their efforts. Our journey is not complete until our gay brothers and sisters are treated like anyone else under the law - for if we are truly created equal, then surely the love we commit to one another must be equal as well. Our journey is not complete until no citizen is forced to wait for hours to exercise the right to vote. Our journey is not complete until we find a better way to welcome the striving, hopeful immigrants who still see America as a land of opportunity; until bright young students and engineers are enlisted in our workforce rather than expelled from our country. Our journey is not complete until all our children, from the streets of Detroit to the hills of Appalachia to the quiet lanes of Newtown, know that they are cared for, and cherished, and always safe from harm.

That is our generation's task to make these words, these rights, these values - of Life, and Liberty, and the Pursuit of Happiness - real for every American. Being true to our founding documents does not require us to agree on every contour of life; it does not mean we will all define liberty in exactly the same way, or follow the same precise path to happiness. Progress does not compel us to settle centuries-long debates about the role of government for all time - but it does require us to act in our time.

For now decisions are upon us, and we cannot afford delay. We cannot mistake absolutism for principle, or substitute spectacle for politics, or treat name-calling as reasoned debate. We must act, knowing that our work will be imperfect. We

FREDERICK MONDERSON

must act, knowing that today's victories will be only partial, and that it will be up to those who stand here in four years, and forty years, and four hundred years hence to advance the timeless spirit once conferred to us in a spare Philadelphia hall.

My fellow Americans, the oath I have sworn before you today, like the one recited by others who serve in this Capitol, was an oath to God and country, not party or faction – and we must faithfully execute that pledge during the duration of our service. But the words I spoke today are not so different from the oath that is taken each time a soldier signs up for duty, or an immigrant realizes her dream. My oath is not so different from the pledge we all make to the flag that waves above and that fills our hearts with pride.

They are the words of citizens, and they represent our greatest hope.

You and I, as citizens, have the power to set this country's course.

You and I, as citizens, have the obligation to shape the debates of our time – not only with the votes we cast, but with the voices we lift in defense of our most ancient values and enduring ideals.

Let each of us now embrace, with solemn duty and awesome joy, what is our lasting birthright. With common effort and common purpose, with passion and dedication, let us answer the call of history, and carry into an uncertain future that precious light of freedom.

OBAMA - MASTER AND COMMANDER

Obama - Master and Commander 808. The gathering on the West Front, the Grand Marble Terrace, of the Capital Building where all the celebreties came to pay witness to the dynamics of American democracy.

FREDERICK MONDERSON

CHANG W. LEE/THE NEW YORK TIMES

"I'm not going to see this again," President Obama remarked, scanning the crowd.

Obama - Master and Commander 809. The moment when the President called on Aemricans to pursue a policy of equality and when the chose to take a second look at the crowd that had gathered to pay tribute to his Inauguration.

Obama - Master and Commander 810. Mrs. Obama mugs for the camera.

750

OBAMA - MASTER AND COMMANDER

Obama - Master and Commander 811. The Obamas "walking the walk" on Pennsylvania Avenue, he walking towards his seat on the West Front Marble Terrace for the Ceremony, and then saluting the Sanitation workers who will clean-up after the parade.

Obama - Master and Commander 812. Part of the mixed crowd enjoying the historic moment.

FREDERICK MONDERSON

Obama - Master and Commander 813. "Dancing the Night Away" and raising his cup to salute and toast those gathered after the ceremony.

Obama - Master and Commander 814. An accounting of the persons seated at the Inauguration.

Thank you, God Bless you, and may He forever bless these United States of America.

www.ingramcontent.com/pod-product-compliance
Lightning Source LLC
Chambersburg PA
CBHW061947300426
44117CB00010B/1247